TRANSNATIONAL TERRORISM AND STATE ACCOUNTABILITY

Every State has an obligation to prevent terrorist attacks emanating from its territory. This proposition stems from various multilateral agreements and UN Security Council resolutions. This study exhaustively addresses the scope of this obligation of prevention and the legal consequences flowing from its violation, so as to provide greater clarity on governments' counterterrorism duties and to enhance State accountability for preventable wrongs. It defines the contents and contours of the obligation while placing critical emphasis on the mechanics of State responsibility. Whether obscured by new technologies like the Internet, the sophisticated cellular structure of some terrorist organisations or convoluted political realities, the level of governmental involvement in terrorist activities is no longer readily discernible in every instance. Furthermore, the prospect of governments waging surrogate warfare through proxies also poses intractable challenges to the mechanism of attribution in the context of State responsibility.

This monograph sets out the shortcomings of the extant scheme of State responsibility while identifying a paradigm shift towards more indirect modes of accountability under international law, a trend corroborated by recent State and institutional practice. Drawing on varied legal and theoretical influences, the study devises and prescriptively argues for the implementation of a strict liability-inspired model grounded in the logic of indirect responsibility with a view to enhancing State compliance with counterterrorism obligations. This shifts the policy focus squarely to prevention, while promoting multilateralism and transnational cooperation. Ultimately, the legal and policy sensibilities underlying the book converge into a new theory of prevention in counterterrorism contexts.

Volume 9 in the series Hart Monographs in Transnational and International Law

Hart Monographs in Transnational and International Law

Series Editor: Craig Scott, Professor of Law, Osgoode Hall Law School of York University, Toronto

The objective of this series is to publish high-quality scholarship in public international law and private international law, as well as work that adopts 'transnational law' as its thematic, theoretical or doctrinal focus. The series strives to be a leading venue for work of the following sort:

* critical reappraisals of foundational concepts and core doctrinal principles of both public and private international law, and their operation in practice, including insights drawn from general legal theory;
* analysis and development of conceptions of 'transnational law', including in relation to the role of unofficial law and informal processes in transnational regulation and in relation to theories and studies of 'governance' in transnational spheres; and
* empirical studies of the emergence, evolution and transformation of international and/or transnational legal orders, including accounts and explanations of how law is constructed within different communities of interpretation and practice.

The series will also be home to monographs that explore the interactions between the ever-integrating fields of public and private international law. Of special interest are explorations of the extent to which these interactions are structured by higher-order principles and policies, on the one hand, and by politics and the exercise of various forms of power, on the other hand.

The series is open to work not only by law scholars but also by scholars from cognate disciplines.

Recent titles in this series

Volume 4 Between Governing and Governance: On the Emergence, Function and Form of Europe's Post-National Constellation
Poul Kjaer

Volume 5 Rough Consensus and Running Code: A Theory of Transnational Private Law
Gralf-Peter Calliess and Peer Zumbansen

Volume 6 The Payment Order of Antiquity and the Middle Ages: A Legal History
Benjamin Geva

Volume 7 The Concept of Unity in Public International Law
Mario Prost

Volume 8: Interlocking Constitutions: Towards an Interordinal Theory of National, European and UN Law
Luis I Gordillo

Transnational Terrorism and State Accountability

A New Theory of Prevention

Vincent-Joël Proulx

with a Foreword by Bruno Simma

·HART·
PUBLISHING

OXFORD AND PORTLAND OREGON
2012

Hart Publishing
An imprint of Bloomsbury Publishing Plc

Hart Publishing Ltd
Kemp House
Chawley Park
Cumnor Hill
Oxford OX2 9PH
UK

Bloomsbury Publishing Plc
50 Bedford Square
London
WC1B 3DP
UK

www.hartpub.co.uk
www.bloomsbury.com

Published in North America (US and Canada) by
Hart Publishing
c/o International Specialized Book Services
920 NE 58th Avenue, Suite 300
Portland, OR 97213-3786
USA

www.isbs.com

British Library Cataloguing-in-Publication Data
A catalogue record for this book is available from the British Library.

ISBN: 978-1-84946-285-3

Typeset by Hope Services, Abingdon
Printed and bound in Great Britain by
Lightning Source UK Ltd

A mes parents

Foreword

International terrorism is one of the pressing contemporary challenges facing international lawyers. In this ambitious work, Vincent-Joël Proulx seeks to grapple with the notion of terrorism within the ambit of State responsibility, and in particular, of indirect State responsibility for terrorist acts.

The work presents a two-tiered, strict liability-inspired model using a State's failure to prevent terrorist acts as the legal foundation for attributing responsibility. Even if one might disagree with the bases on which the author constructs his argument, the execution of the argument is solid and thorough. The coverage of the major policy arguments and the available legal source materials is equally impressive. Moreover, the author's positions are genuinely progressive and present a fairly innovative solution, in the form of a strict liability mechanism. Although some might regard this approach as somewhat ahead of its time, the present work may well come to be used by policy-makers seeking an appropriate legal tool to prevent terrorism and to hold those responsible for terrorist acts accountable. It behoves all scholars and practitioners of international law with an interest in combating international terrorism to consider the proposals outlined in this book.

Judge Bruno Simma
International Court of Justice

Acknowledgements

This book is partially based on a doctoral dissertation that was written and defended at McGill University's Faculty of Law. First and foremost, I express my deepest gratitude to René Provost for his unending support and impeccable supervision throughout my doctoral journey. Words can not do justice to both the quality and assiduity of his presence and mentorship. He faithfully provided guidance and input of the highest quality and challenged my thinking on this topic, whilst respecting my own vision and the various directions in which I wanted to take the project. His current and future graduate students are extremely fortunate to benefit from his counsel and supervision.

Stephen Toope also acted as a superb supervisor during the first two years of the project. Together with Professor Provost, he provided, and continues to provide, a wonderful template of academic pursuit for any aspiring pedagogue. I am also deeply indebted to Jaye Ellis and Frédéric Mégret for their unwavering support and guidance. I warmly acknowledge the other members of my viva committee for engaging in a spirited dialogue with me during my doctoral defence: Alain Breuleux, Suzanne Lalonde, Payam Akhavan and Angela Campbell.

An incalculable debt of gratitude is owed to His Excellency Judge Bruno Simma for graciously agreeing to act as external examiner for my PhD and for kindly contributing the foreword to this monograph. I am honoured not only to have received his invaluable feedback, but also to see his name associated with this work. I am equally grateful for the remarkable support and guidance received from His Excellency President Peter Tomka. Over the years, I have been extremely fortunate to benefit from the inspiring mentorship and support of HE Judge Mohamed Bennouna, The Honourable Robert J Sharpe and The Honourable Eleanore A Cronk. My exchanges with other Members of the International Court of Justice, especially HE Judges Keith, Cançado Trindade and Greenwood were also particularly illuminating. The library staff at the ICJ, especially Corinne Fumé, was extremely helpful and diligent in accommodating my many requests.

I acknowledge with deep gratitude the financial support provided during my doctoral studies by the Canadian Council on International Law, the Social Sciences and Humanities Research Council of Canada, the Department of National Defence/Association of Universities and Colleges of Canada, McGill University's Graduate and Postdoctoral Studies Office, McGill University's Faculty of Law and the Canada Institute at the Wilson Center.

My exchanges at NYU with Joseph HH Weiler, Eyal Benvenisti, Richard Pildes, Benedict Kingsbury and Stephen Holmes served as an invaluable sounding board for the formulation of some of the ideas expressed in this book. My thinking in this area was also greatly enhanced during my tenure as Quebec Scholar at the Woodrow Wilson International Center for Scholars in Washington, DC. I extend warm gratitude to the Canada Institute and the Division of International Security Studies for providing a welcoming intellectual home and to the staff at the Wilson Center library for its assistance. I am also very grateful for the input and feedback I received from colleagues and students at various conferences and guest lectures over the years.

During the course of writing this book, I benefited immensely from the counsel of friends and colleagues at different stages of the project. I am deeply privileged to have sought guidance from people so conversant in various fields and disciplines. Special thanks are owed to Aaron Dhir, Gérardine Goh, Maurizio Ragazzi, Florence Zaoui, Pascal Chenivesse, Catherine Quinn, Dominika Švarc, Miriam Cohen, Jutta Brunnée, Ruby Gropas, Mihail Neamtu, Tom McMorrow, Rosalie Jukier, Shauna Van Praagh, Carlos Iván Fuentes, Karen Crawley, Patrick Delaney, David Glenn and the Chronicle of Higher Education, Gertie Burgers, Mario Prost, Jan Räker, Alireza Falsafi, Benoit Pelletier, Wouter Werner, Michael Labib, Sadler Clersaint, Eric Paradis, Shane Sweet, Andrea Arce Rojas, Robbie Cherry, Maribel Arce Rojas, Nandini Ramanujam, Jean-Ray Arsenau, Michael Fakhri, Mercedes Perez, Lisa Romano, Gleider Hernández, Fedelma Smith, Cristina Hoss, Michael Becker, Yukiko Takashiba, Chad Farrell, Faisal Bhabha, Suzanne Arseneault, Robert Arseneault, Rafaele Tahan, Bart Szewczyk, Daniel Sheppard, Justin Safayeni and Ted Kill. I am very grateful for the support of my family and friends who, unfortunately, I cannot exhaustively acknowledge here. Thank you for fueling my life and my mind. I am also very grateful to Elsa for her love and support.

I extend warm gratitude to the staff at Hart Publishing, especially Richard Hart, Rachel Turner and Mel Hamill for their patience, professionalism and diligence in editing and preparing the book. They provided top-flight assistance and guidance throughout the publication process.

Lastly, I could not have pursued graduate studies without the love, support and enormous generosity of my parents, Denise and Pascal. They were unflinching emotional and spiritual pillars throughout that journey. I am deeply indebted for everything they have taught me and continue to teach me, including the very notion of responsibility. I hope that they will see from what I have written, or perhaps from what I have left out, how deeply I value their guidance. This work is dedicated to them.

Table of Contents

Table of Cases

Canada

Eritrea-Ethiopia Claims Commission

European Court of Human Rights

European Court of Justice

France

Germany

Inter-American Court of Human Rights (IACHR)

International Arbitral Awards

International Centre for Settlement of Investment Disputes (ICSID)

International Court of Justice

International Criminal Tribunal for the former Yugoslavia

Iran-US Claims Tribunal

League of Nations

Permanent Court of International Justice (PCIJ)

UN Human Rights Committee

United Kingdom

United States of America

US-Columbia Claims Tribunal

World Trade Organization

Table of Legislation

Canada

United States of America

Table of Conventions, Treaties etc

Disclaimer

This monograph was written by the author solely in his personal capacity. All views expressed herein, errors and omissions remain those of the author and are not in any way attributable to the International Court of Justice, the United Nations or to any other institutions or individuals.

Introduction

I. INTRODUCTORY REMARKS

TRANSNATIONAL TERRORISM POSES increasingly difficult challenges for international law, along with the enforcement and elaboration of international legal norms. Several studies have attempted to elucidate the relationship between international law and terrorism, while drawing on the benefits that can be derived from the former to combat the latter.[1] However, contrary to terrorists of the 1960s, 70s, and 80s, modern terrorists wield a considerably expanded scope of reach and influence.[2] Modern technology not only provides them unparalleled access to new and devastating weaponry, but also allows them to broadcast their messages of intimidation and intolerance in unprecedented fashion, on a truly global stage. Indeed, it is with horror that the world watched the events of the Mumbai terrorist attacks unfold on television and over the Internet in real-time. These types of private actors egregiously subvert legal rules and obfuscate the requisite nexuses between States and individuals upon which the traditional application of international legal norms is painstakingly dependent. Oftentimes remaining indistinguishable from the civilian populations in which they seek solace, private terrorist entities may operate in State-like fashion and inflict broad-reaching transnational violence across borders and cultures, whilst eluding State-like responsibility.[3] As a corollary, the more diffused and highly de-hierarchised model of terrorism engendering massive and large-scale attacks is of relatively recent vintage.[4]

[1] See, eg: A Bianchi (ed), *Enforcing International Law Norms against Terrorism* (Oxford, Hart Publishing, 2004); J-C Martin, *Les Règles internationales relatives à la lutte contre le terrorisme* (Brussels, Bruylant, 2006); P Klein, 'Le Droit international à l'épreuve du terrorisme' (2006) 321 *Recueil des Cours* 203; PA Fernández-Sánchez (ed), *International Legal Dimension of Terrorism* (Leiden, Nihjoff, 2009). The emergence of transnational terrorism also generated international legal scholarship prior to 9/11: see R Higgins and M Flory (eds), *Terrorism and International Law* (London, Routledge, 1997).

[2] For instance, the 'war' on terror has arguably enhanced the status of transnational terrorists on the international plane. See M-E O'Connell, 'Enhancing the Status of Non-State Actors through a Global War on Terror?' (2005) 43 *Columbia Journal of Transnational Law* 435.

[3] See, eg: T Becker, *Terrorism and the State: Rethinking the Rules of State Responsibility* (Oxford, Hart Publishing, 2006) 1. See also generally: K Mulaj (ed), *Violent Non-State Actors in World Politics* (New York, Columbia University Press, 2010).

[4] See, eg: R Gunaratna, *Inside Al Qaeda: Global Network of Terror* (London, Hurst, 2002).

Decidedly, transnational terrorism poses a new and singular problem for international law. Emerging from the vestiges of the antiquated 'foreign office' model of public international law, and borne out from the now-prevalent phenomenon of the disaggregated State, the repression of privately inflicted transnational violence falls outside of the ambit of traditional international legal protection, at least at the State level. Historically, international law was far more concerned with potential usurpation of sovereign powers and privileges, breaches of territorial integrity and inter-State violence than with internationally wrongful acts carried out by non-State actors. In addition, norms governing the use of force consistently responded to a unitary typology, whilst the recourses offered rested on predominantly bilateral conceptions of legal relationships. Human rights protections sought to extend to populations suffering under domination and mistreatment carried out by their own governments. In such scenarios, international law had a clear frame of reference in assigning blame and striving towards deterrence and reciprocity: such exercise invariably pointed to the nation-State.[5] However, from a *lex ferenda* perspective, the debate surrounding State responsibility increasingly takes stock of contemporary developments pertaining to the involvement of private actors and individuals on the international scene. Eminent scholars lament the fact that the International Law Commission (ILC) has excised the role of non-State actors from the purview of State responsibility by focusing exceedingly on 'bilateral', 'individualistic' and 'privatistic' conceptions of that body of law.[6] Granted, in some sectors private actors seek to elude regulation by self-regulating, through the adoption of corporate codes of conduct for example, or by reference to soft law regimes.[7] As certain facets of international law shift away from a State-centric paradigm to an increasingly transnational reality, non-State actors now challenge the rules of State responsibility, at least by their actions. They also propel to the fore the need to revisit legal frameworks so as to bolster and identify potential deterrence models in order to prevent and suppress terrorism.[8] Responding after the

[5] See, eg: Becker, above n 3 at 1.

[6] See generally: RP Mazzeschi, 'The Marginal Role of the Individual in the ILC's Articles on State Responsibility' (2004) 15 *Italian Yearbook of International Law* 39.

[7] For instance, the Montreux Document is predicated on a transnational impetus towards self-regulation by the private military and security companies industry. See The Montreux Document on Pertinent International Legal Obligations and Good Practices for States Related to Operations of Private Military and Security Companies during Armed Conflict (17 September 2008), UN Doc A/63/467-S/2008/636. Conversely, States cannot hide behind private military firms to elude official involvement in conflict settings: 'if the acts of PMFs are attributed to States, the States will lose their claim to neutrality and non-involvement'. See OR Jones, 'Implausible Deniability: State Responsibility for the Actions of Private Military Firms' (2009) 24 *Connecticut Journal of International Law* 239, 258. Soft law is typically perceived as embodying imprecise legal norms or non-legally binding obligations. See, eg: KW Abbott and D Snidal, 'Hard and Soft Law in International Governance' (2000) 54 *International Organization* 421, 422; K Raustiala, 'Form and Substance in International Agreements' (2005) 99 *AJIL* 581 (2005).

[8] This concern shifts the focus of the inquiry squarely on the relationship between State responsibility and terrorism. See, eg: KN Trapp, *State Responsibility for International Terrorism* (Oxford, OUP, 2011); RP Barnidge, Jr, *Non-State Actors and Terrorism: Applying the Law of State Responsibility and the Due Diligence Principle* (The Hague, TMC Asser Press, 2008).

fact is important in terms of allocating blame, but a sharp focus should nonetheless be placed on prevention; international legal rules should be harnessed with an equal view to allocating risk *and* to stamping out the roots of transnational terrorism.[9]

Transnational terrorism is a polymorphic threat – its very practice in various permutations, whether translating in large-scale attacks, more subtle, isolated strikes or Internet-based intimidation, obfuscates traditional law enforcement. Preventing terrorism has become a pressing social phenomenon: its authors often do not possess a fixed address; they often blend indiscriminately within the civilian populations that host them; they may operate autonomously and without much State support; and, in most cases, they flout international law, the principle of reciprocity and the punishment/deterrence dichotomy.[10] International criminal law has a role to play in repressing terrorism and it partially attains this objective through the channel of *ad hoc* international criminal tribunals, namely under the Statute of the International Criminal Tribunal for Rwanda, which subsumes the crime of 'terrorism' under the Tribunal's expertise. Other international instruments similarly focus on holding the perpetrators of terrorism legally accountable. Yet, international criminal law is, by no means, the default regime for repressing and preventing terrorism. The implementation of the Guantánamo Bay detention centre, the Annex to the Rome Statute of the International Criminal Court (ICC) and the criminalisation under domestic law of behaviours that, historically, solely amounted to evidentiary elements in criminal cases (eg: registration in private pilot schools, procurement of sources on explosive-making, dissemination of certain types of speech, membership in certain groups etc), clearly point in the direction of domestic criminal law as the preferred regime for holding individuals accountable. The international criminal model, therefore, is an interesting exception to the default regime that is undoubtedly acquiring traction, but that remains nonetheless limited and constrained by jurisdictional, conceptual and political impediments.

Whilst international initiatives aiming to bolster individual accountability are laudable, they fall short in ensuring the accountability of those States that harbour terrorists or in better circumscribing the role(s) that States play in supporting or in failing to prevent terrorism. Of vital importance are the conclusions formulated by the United Nations-mandated High-level Panel on Threats, Challenges and Change in its report, titled *A More Secure World*. The Panel proclaimed that 'States are still the front-line responders to today's threats' and that fruitful international actions to 'reduce terrorism and halt the spread of dangerous materials all require capable, responsible States as partners. It

9 See, eg: M Bennouna, 'Réflexions sur la régulation internationale du risque à propos du concept de prévention' in R Hostiou et al (eds), *Terres du droit: Mélanges en l'honneur d'Yves Jégouzo* (Paris, Dalloz, 2009) 371 at 382.

10 On the non-applicability of reciprocity to terrorists, see R Provost, 'Asymmetrical Reciprocity and Compliance with the Laws of War', Unpublished Manuscript (14 January 2010), available at http://ssrn.com/abstract=1427437 at 3 n13; MJ Osiel, *The End of Reciprocity: Terror, Torture, and the Law of War* (New York, CUP, 2009).

follows that greater effort must be made to enhance the capacity of States to exercise their sovereignty responsibly'.[11]

States have a duty to protect their own citizens against terrorist attacks in light of international counterterrorism obligations and other relevant developments in international law, such as the Responsibility to Protect Doctrine (R2P). For example, the conceptual tenets of the R2P Doctrine have been brandished in order to substantiate more acute government intervention into the affairs of the Liberation Tigers of Tamil Eelam (LTTE) secessionist organisation in Sri Lanka.[12] Whilst international terrorism is at times becoming a highly de-territorialised and decentralised phenomenon, prompting policy-makers to focus their energies on ungoverned spaces and safe havens for terrorists, this study will demonstrate that terrorists are nonetheless highly dependent on sanctuary or toleration within State borders in order to plan and carry out their actions.[13] Surely, States may not wield as much control or influence over private terrorist activities taking place on their territory in all cases, thereby inheriting a more passive role in the violation of primary international legal rules.[14] Yet, States still have an important – sometimes determinant – place in the chain of events leading up to the perpetration of transnational terrorist attacks, as their authors often rely on governmental inaction, toleration, acquiescence, wilful blindness or ineffective counterterrorism infrastructures as propitious incubators for their agendas.[15] Consequently, 'When terrorists attack, their victims may not know where to find them, but there is an address for their grievances and their fears. It is the State'.[16]

The major challenges for international law reside not at the semantic level, but rather in the efforts to better circumscribe *legal* definitions and frameworks. A particularly challenging objective is that of integrating all relevant actors under a normative framework with a view to bolstering prevention and promoting State compliance with counterterrorism obligations. In that regard, this study strives to subscribe to what Judge Mohamed Bennouna has described as the ethos of contemporary international law, 'dont la signification ultime réside dans son apport à l'amélioration du sort des personnes humaines, quelles qu'elles soient, dans tous les secteurs d'activités, et par delà l'écran étatique'.[17] But how, exactly, can international law, a discipline traditionally

[11] Report of the High-level Panel on Threats, Challenges and Change, 'A More Secure World: Our Shared Responsibility', UN Doc A/59/565 (2004), 2 December 2004 at 18. See also: ibid at 1, 9.

[12] See, eg: P Gunewardene, 'There's No Unwinnable War: Only a Mission to Crush Terrorism', *Daily News*, 24 March 2008, available at www.dailynews.lk/2008/03/24/fea02.asp.

[13] See, eg: below ch 2, section IV.A). See also: R Värk, 'State Responsibility for Private Armed Groups in the Context of Terrorism' (2006) 11 *Juridica International* 184, 184.

[14] The duty to prevent terrorism incontrovertibly constitutes a primary obligation under international law. Correspondingly, its violation sets in motion the application of the secondary rules of State responsibility. See, eg: Bennouna, above n 9 at 373; J Barboza, *Liability: Can We Put Humpty-Dumpty Together Again?* (2002) 1 *Chinese Journal of International Law* 499, 500.

[15] See Becker, above n 3 at 2.

[16] ibid.

[17] M Bennouna, 'La Protection diplomatique: du standard minimum de traitement des étrangers aux droits de l'Homme' in A Constantinides and N Zaïkos (eds), *The Diversity of International Law: Essays in Honour of Professor Kalliopi K. Koufa* (Leiden, Nijhoff, 2009) 481 at 486.

concerned with focusing on State action, regulate the acts of private entities and non-State actors? How can it engage Iran's international responsibility for funding and training Hezbollah factions carrying out attacks against civilians? Possible scenarios are as endless as relevant interlocutors are diverse.

Legal scholars are increasingly grappling with these questions and seeking ways to regulate the problem of domestic violence and to crack down on internationally wrongful acts carried out by non-State actors. This question was a central concern in the *Velásquez Rodríguez Case*, with the Inter-American Court of Human Rights (IACHR) investigating the potential application of State responsibility principles to private acts.[18] We are seeing similar efforts across a broad range of situations where privately inflicted harm is tackled through the screen of the State, be they aimed at ascertaining the legal consequences of the actions of rebel groups in armed conflict settings, delineating State responsibility for the actions of private military contractors,[19] or regulating the activities of transnational corporations.[20] After all, if host-States could abdicate their obligation to prevent terrorist attacks emanating from their territory on the basis that the perpetrators are non-State actors, wouldn't that assumption effectively eviscerate the State's sovereign privileges of any significance for the schemes of human security and human rights?[21] States act as the sole regulators of private conduct within their own borders, as the warrantors of human security in the same setting, and retain an unmatched monopoly over recourse to force in international relations: they should not be able to dissociate those prerogatives from the responsibilities that inherently flow from them and compel State compliance with international obligations, such as counterterrorism undertakings. Those powers should be harnessed with a view to vindicating specific policy goals and fulfilling common interests on a global scale.

Preventing and suppressing transnational terrorism decidedly qualifies as one of those objectives and constitutes the linchpin of the intellectual inquiry espoused in this project. With this in mind, this volume proposes to weigh different arguments in order to determine whether the law of State responsibility can play a role in the prevention and suppression of terrorism, without casting this body of rules as a cure-all or holistic solution to that problem. After all, State responsibility law has always entertained the possibility of holding States

[18] *Velásquez Rodríguez Case*, Inter-Am Ct HR Decisions and Judgments 91 (ser C) No 4 (1988), especially at paras 161–85.

[19] See, eg: H Tonkin, *State Control over Private Military and Security Companies in Armed Conflict* (Cambridge, CUP, 2011); C Hoppe, 'Passing the Buck: State Responsibility for Private Military Companies' (2008) 19 *EJIL* 989; M-L Tougas, 'La responsabilité internationale d'État pour le fait d'entreprises militaires privées' (2007) 45 *Canadian Yearbook of International Law* 97.

[20] See, eg: R McCorquodale and PC Simons, 'Responsibility Beyond Borders: State Responsibility for Extraterritorial Violations by Corporations of International Human Rights Law' (2007) 70 *Modern Law Review* 598; J Kuusi, *The Host State and the Transnational Corporation: An Analysis of Legal Relationships* (Farnborough, Saxon House, 1979); SBO Gutto, 'Violation of Human Rights in the Third World: Responsibility of States and TNCs' (1983) 23 *Indian Journal of International Law* 56.

[21] See Becker, above n 3 at 2.

accountable for failing to regulate internationally wrongful private conduct. When seeking legal solutions to bolster prevention and enhance multilateral cooperation and compliance with counterterrorism obligations, the importance of State responsibility cannot be sidestepped: its affinity with the global struggle against terror seems almost indisputable given its centrality in public international law. As one commentator remarks, 'State responsibility is, after all, the sacred cow of international law, and terrorism its *bête noire*'.[22] Therefore, the rules of State responsibility must be thoroughly and critically explored in order to ascertain whether they can play a role in this quest, or whether they should be revisited in light of contemporary events and in the face of considerably enhanced terrorist capacity. That is the objective of the present study.

The study will advance an argument to the effect that international law can countenance a shift towards a law of indirect State responsibility for failures to prevent terrorism. Whilst some important aspects of direct responsibility will be canvassed, the thrust of the argument will hinge on the fact that States have a primary duty to control their national territory under international law, which also entails a need to control terrorist factions and activities percolating therein.[23] As a result, we are witnessing a shift in both legal and policy inclinations towards indirect modes of accountability that are concomitantly i) contingent on governmental failures to act or intervene in preventing transnational terrorism and ii) consonant with recent Security Council practice, which almost invariably conflates the obligation to prevent terrorism with the duty of all States to refrain from supporting or harbouring terrorists on their soil. Unlike Tal Becker's study, which centres on the role of causation in elucidating the role of State responsibility in responding to terrorism,[24] this book will rather examine the benefits that may be derived from infusing the law of State responsibility with strict liability logic both from mechanical and substantive perspectives. The present study subscribes to a portion of Becker's analytical framework in that it does not purport to address the straightforward question of State terrorism, but rather concerns itself with elucidating the role of State responsibility in suppressing and preventing acts of private terrorism, namely where State sponsorship and/or support tends to be far more subtle.[25]

At the outset, it should be emphasised that endeavouring to define the term 'terrorism' extends beyond the scope of this project, a task better left to sea-

[22] A Nissel, 'Tal Becker, Terrorism and the State: Rethinking the Rules of State Responsibility (Oxford: Hart Publishing, 2006)' (2007) 5 *Journal of International Criminal Justice* 245, 245.

[23] Subject to the context-sensitive policy analysis developed below in Part II, this signals that, once a terrorist strike is orchestrated on, or carried out from, a State's territory, a presumption of indirect responsibility automatically flows to that State which, in turn, must refute that presumption by reference to due diligence principles and other policy factors, as applied against the specific facts at hand. But see: OD Frouville, 'Attribution of Conduct to the State: Private Individuals' in JR Crawford et al (eds), *The Law of International Responsibility* (Oxford, OUP, 2010) 257 at 261–62.

[24] See Becker, above n 3. See also: M Straus, 'Causation as an Element of State Responsibility' (1984) 16 *Law and Policy in International Business* 893.

[25] A more exhaustive discussion of the rapprochements and dissimilarities between Becker's study and the present account is deployed below in ch 3, section II.

soned legal scholars and policy-makers. Exceedingly relevant is Rosalyn Higgins' assertion that 'terrorism' amounts to a term 'without legal significance', aiming to create a separate category or infraction to condemn widely-decried acts of a public or private nature that employ illegal tactics and/or strike at protected targets.[26] Whilst Higgins also equated 'terrorism' with a 'term of convenience' elsewhere,[27] her analysis becomes particularly compelling when she explores the wisdom of developing a separate 'international law of terrorism'. Ultimately, she ponders whether international law has created a distinct subset of substantive principles under the rubric of 'counterterrorism', or whether scholars are simply extending or applying international legal concepts to a present-day concern.[28]

This project operates on the second proposition and, therefore, does not purport to deliver any expert-level account on terrorist practices or terrorism, more generally. It starts from the assumption that varying degrees of terrorism exist and casts itself, first and foremost, as a study in the law of State responsibility. In so doing, it aims to apply and reformulate some of the underlying tenets of State responsibility in the context of counterterrorism. Bringing Higgins' argument full circle, it follows that the law of State responsibility is sufficiently delineated to encompass acts of terrorism under the rubric of 'internationally wrongful acts', without the need to resort to supplementary definitional contortions.[29] At any rate, the definitional debate is inconsequential for the purposes of reforming the law of State responsibility: as one commentator underscores, the lack of consensus on a universally-accepted definition of 'terrorism' 'does not necessarily raise a major issue for identifying the rules of international law applicable for combating terrorism, this including the pertinent secondary rules of State Responsibility'.[30]

II. OVERVIEW OF RESEARCH

In advocating a model of indirect State responsibility for failing to prevent transnational terrorism, this project is divided into two parts. Part I sets out the impact of the events surrounding 9/11 on international law and State responsibility. In opening up the discussion, chapter one explores the emergence of the

[26] See R Higgins, 'The General International Law of Terrorism' in Higgins and Flory, above n 1 at 28. Echoing Higgins' remarks, Richard Baxter similarly declared that 'We have cause to regret that a legal concept of 'terrorism' was ever inflicted upon us. The term is imprecise; it is ambiguous; and above all, it serves no operative legal purpose'. See RR Baxter, 'A Skeptical Look at the Concept of Terrorism' (1974) 7 *Akron Law Review* 380, 380.

[27] See Higgins, above n 26 at 27. Ben Saul also invokes the term 'political expediency' when discussing Higgins' writings on the matter. See *Defining Terrorism in International Law* (Oxford, OUP, 2006) 177.

[28] See Higgins, above n 26 at 13.

[29] See, eg: ibid at 26. See also: Saul, above n 27 at 177.

[30] P-M Dupuy, 'State Sponsors of Terrorism: Issues of International Responsibility' in Bianchi, above n 1 at 5.

obligation of prevention under international law and acts as a general introduction to the topic by framing the major stakes and problems to be addressed in the inquiry, along with the shortcomings of State responsibility in responding to transnational terrorism. Chapter two maps out these implications more explicitly and delves into the emerging dichotomy of direct and indirect responsibility. The chapter further attempts to elucidate the consecration of indirect State responsibility by examining the emergence of the 'harbouring' and 'supporting' rule, canvassing specific historical precedents involving the application of that rule and, ultimately, situating the Security Council's posture in the debate both before and after 9/11.

Part II moves towards a more substantial and ambitious proposal for legal reform, arguing that the concept of attribution should be excised altogether from the equation of State responsibility in the context of transnational terrorism. Chapter three begins by critically exploring the possible importation of causal models in the area under study before investigating the difficulties associated both with generalising terrorism and developing abstract rules of responsibility in the field. Canvassing inadequate scholarly and policy treatments of the topic and surrounding issues, the chapter then undertakes the task of rethinking secondary rules of responsibility from a critical standpoint. It casts State responsibility as a partial politico-legal solution to transnational terrorism, whilst investigating the difficulties associated with self-judging, autoqualification and the quantitative and qualitative exercise of devising legal consequences following the violation of the obligation to prevent terrorism.

Chapter four proceeds to revisit certain secondary norms, particularly attribution, with a view to developing a more efficient model of international responsibility. In so doing, the study draws heavily on domestic legal analogies, with particular emphasis on tort law and strict liability regimes. Alternatively, it takes stock of other potential legal and policy reforms of State responsibility, such as the implementation of automatic attribution mechanisms. Chapter five ultimately proposes the implementation of a two-tiered strict liability-inspired model in assessing the responsibility of sanctuary States. The discussion, which is pervaded by several rationalist accounts, considerations pertaining to the developing world, and a tension between upholding sovereignty and combating terrorism efficiently, ultimately leads to the exploration – and consequent reformulation – of the obligation of prevention.

Part I

The International Response to 9/11 and Its Impact on the Law of State Responsibility

1

State Responsibility, Terrorism and International Law

I. GENERAL REMARKS: STATE RESPONSIBILITY AS A COMPLEMENTARY SOLUTION

THE HORRIFIC ATTACKS of 9/11 and the responses thereto have generated a considerable amount of legal academic writing. In fact, those events have radically challenged certain tenets of the legal and political zeitgeist. Both internationally and domestically, several issues of legal, political and sociological relevance have been propelled to the forefront of academic debate. Recurrent scholarly themes in the 'war' on terror include the parameters of *jus ad bellum*,[1] issues of international jurisdiction over suspected terrorists,[2] constricting the flow of terrorist funding,[3] immigration policy,[4] violation of human rights and due process[5] and pre-emptive self-defence.[6] Through

[1] See, eg: M Byers, 'Terrorism, the Use of Force, and International Law After 11 September' (2001) 51 *ICLQ* 401; JI Charney, 'The Use of Force against Terrorism and International Law' (2001) 95 *AJIL* 835.

[2] See, eg: CC Joyner, 'International Extradition and Global Terrorism: Bringing International Criminal to Justice' (2003) 25 *Loyola of Los Angeles International and Comparative Law Review* 493; L Martinez, 'Prosecuting Terrorists at the International Criminal Court: Possibilities and Problems' (2002) 34 *Rutgers Law Journal* 1; V-J Proulx, 'Rethinking the Jurisdiction of the International Criminal Court in the Post-September 11th Era: Should Acts of Terrorism Qualify As Crimes against Humanity?' (2004) 19 *American University International Law Review* 1009.

[3] See, eg: NJ Crimm, 'High Alert: The Government's War on the Financing of Terrorism and its Implications for Donors, Domestic Charitable Organizations, and Global Philanthropy' (2004) 45 *William and Mary Law Review* 1341; ME Engel, 'Donating "Blood Money": Fundraising for International Terrorism by United States and the Government's Efforts to Constrict the Flow' (2004) 12 *Cardozo Journal of International and Comparative Law* 251; B Zagaris, 'The Merging of the Anti-Money Laundering and Counter-Terrorism Financial Enforcement Regimes After September 11, 2001' (2004) 22 *Berkeley Journal of International Law* 123.

[4] See, eg: L Lebowitz and I Podheiser, 'A Summary of the Changes in Immigration Policies and Practices after the Terrorist Attacks of September 11, 2001: The USA Patriot Act and Other Measures' (2002) 63 *University of Pittsburgh Law Review* 873; KC Tumlin, 'Suspect First: How Terrorism Policy Is Reshaping Immigration Policy' (2004) 92 *California Law Review* 1173.

[5] See, eg: E Gross, 'The Influence of Terrorist Attacks on Human Rights in the United States: The Aftermath of September 11, 2001' (2002) 28 *North Carolina Journal of International Law and Commercial Regulation* 1; HH Koh, 'On American Exceptionalism' (2003) 55 *Stanford Law Review* 1479.

[6] See, eg: MJ Glennon, 'The Fog of Law: Self-Defense, Inherence, and Incoherence in Article 51 of the United Nations Charter' (2002) 25 *Harvard Journal of Law and Public Policy* 539, 546–49;

a vast hit-and-miss range of means, the international community is seeking ways to prevent and suppress transnational terrorism. In their response to the 9/11 attacks, the US and its allies elected forcible self-defence as an extreme course of action to redress the initial harm and to repel or contain further threats.[7] Whilst some commentators rallied behind the military campaign in Afghanistan or inferred that it could be countenanced under existing self-defence precepts,[8] others called it into question.[9] This military response cast further doubt as to the appropriate level of retaliation and, more precisely, as to the categorisation of available legal responses following 9/11, given that both terrorism and counterterrorism policy do not fit neatly within the 'crime' or 'war' paradigms.[10] In stark contrast with the armed conflict angle, others analysed the response to 9/11 through a law enforcement paradigm.[11]

Aside from the extreme scenario of invading Afghanistan, there exists a multiplicity of complementary, sometimes overlapping, legal regimes that may be harnessed with a view to counteracting transnational terrorism. Among these, international criminal law is becoming an increasingly attractive option, especially since the advent of the ICC, with scholars calling for the categorisation of acts of terrorism as both crimes against humanity[12] and war crimes.[13] Whilst

C Greenwood, 'International Law and the Pre-emptive Use of Force: Afghanistan, Al-Qaida, and Iraq' (2003) 4 *San Diego International Law Journal* 7; MN Schmitt, 'Preemptive Strategies in International Law' (2003) 24 *Michigan Journal of International Law* 513.

[7] See D Balz, 'U.S., Britain Launch Airstrikes against Targets in Afghanistan', *The Washington Post*, 8 October 8 2001 at A1 (detailing the military campaign in Afghanistan aiming to root out Al-Qaeda).

[8] See, eg: ME O'Connell, 'Lawful Self-Defense to Terrorism' (2002) 63 *University of Pittsburgh Law Review* 889; G Walker, 'The Lawfulness of Operation Enduring Freedom's Self-Defense Responses' (2003) 37 *Valparaiso University Law Review* 489.

[9] See, eg: TM Franck, 'Terrorism and the Right of Self-Defense' (2001) 95 *AJIL* 839; J Quigley, 'The Afghanistan War and Self-Defense' (2003) 37 *Valparaiso University Law Review* 541; ME O'Connell, 'American Exceptionalism and the International Law of Self-Defense' (2002) 31 *Denver Journal of International Law and Policy* 43; JJ Paust, 'Use of Armed Force against Terrorists in Afghanistan, Iraq, and Beyond' (2002) 35 *Cornell International Law Journal* 533, 533–41.

[10] See, eg: N Feldman, 'Choices of Law, Choices of War' (2002) 25 *Harvard Journal of Law and Public Policy* 457; MA Drumbl, 'Terrorist Crime, Taliban Guilt, Western Victims, and International Law' (2002) 31 *Denver Journal of International Law & Policy* 69.

[11] For various considerations on the law enforcement paradigm and related issues, see RM Chesney, 'Civil Liberties and the Terrorism Prevention Paradigm: The Guilt by Association Critique' (2003) 101 *Michigan Law Review* 1408 (reviewing D Cole and JX Dempsey, *Terrorism and the Constitution: Sacrificing Civil Liberties in the Name of National Security*, 2nd edn (New York, New Press, 2002); D Cole, *Enemy Aliens: Double Standard and Constitutional Freedoms in the War on Terror* (New York, New Press, 2003)); ME O'Connell, 'To Kill or Capture Suspects in the Global War on Terror' (2003) 35 *Case Western Reserve Journal of International Law* 325.

[12] See, eg: R Arnold, *The ICC As a New Instrument for Repressing Terrorism* (Ardsley, Transnational Publishers, 2004) 202–72; Martinez, above n 2 at 52; A Mahiou, 'Le Projet de Code des crimes contre la paix et la sécurité de l'humanité' (1997) 3 *L'Observateur des Nations Unies* 177, 182.

[13] See, eg: S Jodoin, 'Terrorism as a War Crime' (2007) 7 *International Criminal Law Review* 77. Others opine that terrorism amounts to a customary law crime. See, eg: A Cassese, *International Criminal Law* (Oxford, OUP, 2003) 139; JJ Paust, 'Addendum: Prosecution of Mr. Bin Laden et al. for Violations of International Law and Civil Lawsuits by Various Victims' (2001) 77 *American Society of International Law Insights*, available at www.asil.org/insigh77.cfm#addendum5.

absolutely fundamental under international law, State responsibility is often overshadowed in the policy debates and the present project starts from the premise that its corpus of rules can be brought to bear on the post-9/11 world. Hence, this book concerns itself with studying the ways in which State responsibility can contribute to the global struggle against terrorism, without aiming to replace or supplant the aforementioned regimes which, it must be stressed, remain complementary.

For instance, the features State responsibility can contribute to the ongoing counterterrorism campaign will remain complementary to international criminal legal mechanisms. That said, one has to be cautious not to overextend the analysis in the opposite direction by disproportionately grounding accountability mechanisms on an individualised level. Whilst there has been a marked tendency to individualise the discipline in the wake of post-Cold War internal armed conflicts, this by no means absolves governments from potential accountability when breaching their international legal obligations.[14] State responsibility can apply coextensively with, or in parallel fashion to, liability schemes targeting individuals for authoring violations of international law;[15] the instruments and mechanisms invoked to enforce responsibility will obviously differ whether faced with individual responsibility versus State responsibility. As a corollary, States undoubtedly risk the prospect of incurring responsibility should they choose to support or harbour terrorists on their territory.[16] Whilst the possibility of criminalising State responsibility extends beyond the scope of this study, it should nonetheless be recalled that General Assembly resolution 40/61 on *Measures to Prevent International Terrorism* explicitly proclaimed that criminal liability automatically flows from the perpetration of terrorist acts, irrespective of their author's or authors' identity and structure, be they State-based, State-condoned, State-sponsored or purely individualised.[17]

State responsibility's strength ostensibly lies in its potential *preventive* character, if infused with adequate mechanisms and underlying philosophy. Because we are dealing, under that rubric, with governments that have to withstand international scrutiny, as opposed to highly motivated individuals pursuing their own politico-ideological goals, the mere threat of triggering responsibility might compel States to combat terrorism more efficiently within their borders and shift the focus on prevention. For instance, States have increasingly begun to criminalise what used to constitute mere evidentiary elements – ie restricting access to certain literature, cracking down on bomb making-related activities, monitoring flight/pilot school enrolments, prohibiting membership in certain

[14] See A-M Slaughter and W Burke-White, 'An International Constitutional Moment' (2002) 43 *Harvard International Law Journal* 1, 19.

[15] See, eg: GT Yates, 'State Responsibility for Nonwealth Injuries to Aliens in the Postwar Era' in RB Lillich (ed), *International Law of State Responsibility for Injuries to Aliens* (Charlottesville, University Press of Virginia, 1983) 213.

[16] See, eg: JA Cohan, 'Formulation of a State's Response to Terrorism and State-Sponsored Terrorism' (2002) 14 *Pace International Law Review* 77, 95.

[17] GA Res 40/61, UN GAOR, 40th Sess, Supp No 53, UN Doc A/RES/40/61 (1985) 301.

organisations, freezing the assets of individuals associated with certain organisations and blocking certain charitable donations – as one of the ways to comply with primary counterterrorism obligations (eg the prescriptions stemming from Security Council resolution 1373).[18] As a result, we are witnessing a series of shifts towards modes of indirect responsibility as bases for engaging accountability both at the national and international levels, and both at the individual and State levels.[19] For one thing, these shifts probably reflect the significant difficulty in securing evidence to support a conviction for terrorism, per se. More importantly, in applying a healthy dose of diligence in meeting international obligations through the adoption of more stringent domestic criminal standards, States are signalling that they consider their potential responsibility on the international scene as one of the factors governing and shaping the allocation of their (sometimes scarce) resources in combating terrorism. By shifting their domestic policy infrastructures in light of indirect rationales for accountability, those States might not only be able to actually prevent specific terrorist excursions, but also to pre-empt the application of State responsibility altogether by successfully fulfilling their primary international obligations.

Thus, the prospect of incurring responsibility, coupled with the apprehension of destabilised reciprocal behaviour patterns in international relations, may actually shift incentives onto governments and induce them to comply with their obligations, provided the content of those duties is sufficiently defined. As Brunnée and Toope underscore, 'For some, reciprocity or reciprocal advantage, quintessentially rationalist concepts, lie at the root of legal obligation'.[20] Along similar lines, when dealing with State responsibility's decentralised rationale and its repertoire of countermeasures, some authors equate the unilateral enforcement of international law with a 'function of power'. In other words, States' compliance with legal obligations is conditioned or shaped, first and foremost, by political and economic concerns and, only secondly (sometimes distantly), by considerations of law and justice.[21] Whilst such a view undoubtedly fuels the subsequent analysis, the notion of 'reciprocity' – whether sys-

[18] The scope of resolution 1373 will be explored below, especially in ch 4, section V.A).

[19] For an exploration of these issues, see M Lehto, *Indirect Responsibility for Terrorist Acts: Redefinition of the Concept of Terrorism beyond Violent Acts* (Leiden, Nijhoff, 2010).

[20] J Brunnée and SJ Toope, 'Persuasion and Enforcement: Explaining Compliance with International Law' (2002) 13 *Finnish Yearbook of International Law* 273, 279. See also: R Higgins, *Problems & Process: International Law and How We Use It* (Oxford, OUP, 1994) 16. For classical explorations of the basis of international legal obligation, see H Lauterpacht and CHM Waldock (eds), *The Basis of Obligation in International Law and Other Papers by the Late James Leslie Brierly* (Oxford, Clarendon Press, 1958); M McDougal et al, 'Theories About International Law: Prologue to a Configurative Jurisprudence' (1968) 8 *Virginia Journal of International Law* 188, 188–94.

[21] See, eg: K Zemanek, 'Does the Prospect of Incurring Responsibility Improve the Observance of International Law?' in M Ragazzi (ed), *International Responsibility Today: Essays in Memory of Oscar Schachter* (Leiden, Brill, 2005) 125 at 128; K Zemanek, 'The Unilateral Enforcement of International Obligations' (1987) 47 *Zeitschrift für ausländisches öffentliches Recht und Völkerrecht (ZaöRV)* 32, 43.

tematised or bilateral – also remains a vital driving force for the purposes of better explaining norm compliance.

To invoke constructivist parlance, the prospect of incurring responsibility might promote a 'shared understanding' among nations that transnational cooperation should be increased, and vigilant law enforcement heightened and refined in the face of increasing global threats.[22] A poignant brand of reciprocity correspondingly animates the law of State responsibility – thereby permeating diplomatic relations with a view to enticing States' self-interested compliance with counterterrorism obligations – and will be a running theme throughout this volume. As Robert Keohane posits, reciprocity 'seems to be the most effective strategy for maintaining cooperation among egoists'.[23] But reciprocity can also cut the other way, that is to say that States can refrain from carrying out specific conduct because they believe they can derive self-interested benefits from that behaviour. As a corollary, consensus-based constructions of international law similarly entail that 'consensus comes about because states perceive a reciprocal advantage in cautioning self-restraint'.[24] Thus, the central argument will rely, heavily at times, upon rationalist accounts in order to better understand and shape a working model of State responsibility for failing to prevent terrorism.[25]

The purpose of this project lies in articulating potential deterrence models and contributions to counterterrorism within the formal body of rules constituting the law of State responsibility, as incremental as those advances may be. Yet, those contributions may in fact become more significant than they appear upon first glance. Indeed, whilst the US initially focused its rhetoric on holding individual terrorists accountable after 9/11,[26] another objective emerged in the 'war' on terror – working in tandem with the first priority and labelled a

[22] See the following works by Jutta Brunnée and Stephen J Toope: 'Persuasion', above n 20 at 274–75; 'International Law and Constructivism: Elements of an Interactional Theory of International Law' (2000) 39 *Columbia Journal of Transnational Law* 19; 'Interactional International Law' (2001) 3 *International Law Forum de droit international* 186; 'The Changing Nile Basin Regime: Does Law Matter?' (2002) 43 *Harvard International Law Journal* 105 (applying the above conclusions to a case study).

[23] RO Keohane, *After Hegemony: Cooperation and Discord in the World Political Economy* (Princeton, Princeton University Press, 1984) 214.

[24] Higgins, above n 20 at 16. See also: M Koskenniemi, *From Apology to Utopia: The Structure of International Legal Argument* (Helsinki, Finnish Lawyers', 1989) 74.

[25] See below, particularly ch 4, section V.B); ch 5, section III.A).

[26] See, eg: GW Bush, 'Address Before a Joint Session of the Congress on the United States Response to the Terrorist Attacks of September 11' in 'America's Ordeal: "'Our Grief Has Turned to Anger"', *Newsday*, 21 September 2001 at A2; T Blair, 'Why Saddam Is Still a Threat to Britain', *Daily Express*, 6 March 2002 at 12; J Sullivan, 'Why War against Terrorism Is Justified', *Financial Gazette*, 1 November 2001. The US government's belief is that the Al-Qaeda network, along with other extremist Islamic terrorist organisations, embodies one of the most serious threats to national security. See Statement of James Caruso, Deputy Executive Assistant Director for Counterterrorism, Federal Bureau of Investigation in *Combating Terrorism: Protecting the United States, Parts 1 and II: Hearings before the House Subcommittee on National Security, Veterans Affairs and International Relations of the Committee on Government Reform, House of Representatives, One Hundred Seventh Congress, Second Session, March 12 and 21, 2002* (Washington, DC, US GPO, 2002) 155–56.

'secondary goal' by some[27] – thereby shifting the focus squarely onto holding States responsible for providing assistance to terrorist groups.[28] The American posture in this regard, also mirrored in the policies of other States and organisations, clearly targeted State sponsors of terrorism, even those merely providing sanctuary to terrorist organisations, and purported to hold those States responsible for their involvement in terrorism.[29] In this context, the law of State responsibility does not supersede national or criminal legal systems, nor does it operate in disharmony with other concurrent legal regimes such as the respective schemes of international humanitarian law (IHL) and human rights. In fact, those regimes work complementarily and, by the same token, superimpose complementary sources of obligations and specific, often-compatible duties as well.[30] The primary objective in invoking State responsibility in this setting resides in that system's proclivity to render governments accountable vis-à-vis their counterterrorism obligations and to induce them to take preventive action regarding those undertakings, whilst also favouring transnational cooperation in adopting possible solutions to stamp out terrorism.

The interplay between State responsibility and terrorism becomes particularly relevant and compelling when one considers that Iran provided missiles and other types of weaponry to Hezbollah factions in their attacks against Israel, or that Afghanistan afforded Al Qaeda members the opportunity to seek refuge on its territory prior to 9/11. In such factual scenarios – where criminal justice is often eschewed or short-circuited because of the inability to capture or produce suspected terrorists – the international community must seek ways to buttress the application of State accountability mechanisms, so as to fight impunity, complicity and prevent further terrorism. These specific accounts will be amply discussed throughout this project.

Before reviewing potential levels of governmental involvement in terrorism, a healthy dose of political realism seems apposite here. Any study attempting to recast the rules of State responsibility with certain policy objectives in mind will

[27] See, eg: SE Smith, 'International Law: Blaming Big Brother: Holding States Accountable for the Devastation of Terrorism' (2003) 56 *Oklahoma Law Review* 735, 736.

[28] See, eg: J Diamond, 'Powell Sets Terms for a New Regime', *Chicago Tribune*, 25 October 2001, at 6; US National Security Council, *The National Security Strategy of the United States of America* (17 September 2002), available at http://merln.ndu.edu/whitepapers/USnss2002.pdf at 6, 13–16; JM Vogelson, 'Multinational Approaches to Eradicating International Terrorism' (2002) 36 *International Lawyer* 67, 70. But see: M Levitt, 'Patterns of Terrorism 2002: Terror, Counterterror, and State Sponsorship' (30 April 2003) *Washington Institute for Near East Policy*, available at www.thewashingtoninstitute.org/templateC05.php?CID= 1631.

[29] See US National Security Council, *National Strategy for Combating Terrorism* (February 2003), available at https://www.cia.gov/news-information/cia-the-war-on-terrorism/Counter_Terrorism_Strategy.pdf at 15, 17–19.

[30] See, eg: F Azzam, 'The Duty of Third States to Implement and Enforce International Humanitarian Law' (1997) 66 *Nordic Journal of International Law* 55, 56, 69; R Dufresne, 'Reflections and Extrapolation on the ICJ's Approach to Illegal Resource Exploitation in the Armed Activities Case' (2008) 40 *NYU Journal of International Law and Politics* 171, 182. The law of international State responsibility also operates complementarily with other domestic regimes, such as civil liability. See, eg: AE Boyle, 'Globalising Environmental Liability: The Interplay of National and International Law' (2005) 17 *Journal of Environmental Law* 3, 23–24.

inexorably have to grapple with the idea that the uncertainty surrounding potential legal responses to terrorism will be exacerbated by the margin of appreciation wielded by States (particularly aggrieved ones) as to what constitutes 'terrorism'.[31] More importantly, the compliance pull of primary counterterrorism obligations will unquestionably remain informed and shaped by the resources at the disposal of States in combating terrorism. For instance, it may well be that a State possessing scarce resources decides that it would not be justified in diverting them towards counterterrorism programmes. To counteract this eventuality, arguments are increasingly put forth that such States have a positive duty under international law to acquire the requisite counterterrorism capacity and, as a corollary, to harness it with a view to stamping out terrorism percolating within their borders.[32]

Nevertheless, because the topic at hand primarily deals with State negligence at the preventive level, the crux of relevant policy considerations will hinge, to a large extent, on the host-State's degree of autonomy in making policy choices and in prioritising counterterrorism initiatives. Unsurprisingly, certain factual scenarios will elicit very little contestation as a matter of principle. For instance, the magnitude of the 9/11 attacks makes those excursions hardly contestable in terms of Afghanistan's failure to fulfil its international obligations. Indeed, there is virtually no opposition to the fact that the Afghan government supported and harboured members of Al-Qaeda on its territory, offered them logistical support and repeatedly ignored calls from the Security Council to cease and desist in this behaviour. Yet, not all factual scenarios will be as straightforward or as clear-cut for the purposes of international responsibility; one can envisage marginal cases involving transnational terrorism and carrying peripheral implications for the relevant host-States. For instance, what are a host-State's obligations with respect to individuals maintaining a website for the purposes of recruiting terrorists when the relevant Internet service provider is physically located within its borders, such as is the case of Belgium vis-à-vis the activities of Malika El Aroud?[33] Similarly, the reality prevalent in Canada, where there is strict control over both national territory and terrorist activities occurring therein, but where terrorist cells may nonetheless propagate, is far removed from other situations. In that regard, vigilant law enforcement paired with strict judicial involvement have, thus far, achieved significant gains in thwarting potential terrorist plots and dismantling cells on Canadian soil. A case in point undoubtedly resides in the warehouse arrest of 18 individuals in Toronto involved in lining cardboard boxes with plastic in order to store

[31] This will have significant implications for the interrelationship between autoqualification and State responsibility: see below, ch 3, section III.A).

[32] See, eg: T Becker, *Terrorism and the State: Rethinking the Rules of State Responsibility* (Oxford, Hart Publishing, 2006) 143–44, 146. See also: R Pisillo-Mazzeschi, 'The Due Diligence Rule and the Nature of the International Responsibility of States' (1992) 35 *German Yearbook of International Law* 9, 25–26.

[33] This case will be further explored below in ch 5, section IV.B).

fertiliser, unloading considerable quantities of ammonium nitrate, and carrying out other preparative activities in a foiled plot that would have entailed, inter alia, detonating bombs outside the Toronto Stock Exchange and the Canadian Security Intelligence Service headquarters. This law enforcement blitz has led to the conviction and imprisonment of Saad Khalid, to admissions of guilt by both Saad Gaya and Mohamed Ali Dirie, and to an admission of guilt by Zakaria Amara, one of the operation's ringleaders.[34] Consequently, no successful transnational terrorist strike has been launched from Canada. Conversely, counterterrorism structures in other States generate a far less fruitful record of compliance with international obligations. Such is the case of Lebanon, which fails to effectively control a large portion of its territory and which has been frequently used to launch terrorist attacks against civilians, most notably located in Israel. As a result, a complex factual interface arises and militates in favour of a context-sensitive, policy-informed approach in tackling these difficult legal and political questions, which shall be developed further in Part II. In the interim, it is important to briefly discuss the emergence of the obligation of prevention on the international plane.

II. EMERGENCE OF THE OBLIGATION OF PREVENTION

A salient observation may be gleaned from contemporary international developments: States are expected to forestall terrorist activities emanating from their territory and causing harm. This idea has long been ingrained in international law, albeit in other branches of the discipline such as in environmental law's treatment of transboundary pollution, most notably in Principle 21 of the Stockholm Declaration.[35] This rule was reaffirmed in Principle 2 of the 1992 Rio Declaration and again reiterated in the 2002 World Summit on Sustainable Development. It has also been transposed into UN declarations, such as the Charter of Economic Rights and Duties of States and the World Charter for

[34] See 'Alleged Toronto 18 Ringleader Pleads Guilty', *CBC News*, 8 October 2009, available at www.cbc.ca/canada/toronto/story/2009/10/08/toronto-18-plot-guilty-plea.html; 'Another 'Toronto 18' Member Pleads Guilty', *CBC News*, 29 September 2009, available at www.cbc.ca/canada/toronto/story/2009/09/28/toronto-18-terrorism-guilty482.html; 'Toronto Bomb Plotter Khalid Gets 14 Years', *CBC News*, 4 September 2009, available at www.cbc.ca/canada/story/2009/09/03/terror-trial-sentence090309.html; 'Saad Khalid Jailed Over Foiled Plot to Bomb Canadian Military Base', *Herald Sun*, 4 September 4, available at www.heraldsun.com.au/news/world/saad-khalid-jailed-over-foiled-plot-to-bomb-canadian-military-base/story-e6frf7lf-1225769367333. The Court of Appeal for Ontario also contributed to Canada's counterterrorism crackdown by increasing the sentence of Mohammad Momin Khawaja, the first individual charged and convicted under Canada's *Anti-Terrorism Act*, from 10.5 years in prison to life imprisonment. The charged offences revolved around Khawaja's involvement in a plot to plant fertiliser bombs in the United Kingdom and his connections and contact with British Islamists preparing the attack. See *R v Khawaja* [2010] 103 OR (3d) 321, permission to appeal to the SCC granted on 30 June 2011.

[35] See, eg: UN Conference on the Human Environment, Stockholm Declaration, 16 June 1972, UN Doc A/CONF.48/14, Principle 21 reprinted in (1972) 11 ILM 1416 at 1420.

Nature, and has been formally adopted by other international organisations and conferences.[36]

Therefore, a State will be responsible for 'noxious fumes' emanating from its territory when caused by a terrorist organisation.[37] That imagery is rooted in the famous *Trail Smelter* arbitration where the Tribunal was faced with transboundary pollution originating from Canada and hindering American interests.[38] Similarly, the responsibility of States to ensure that activities carried out within their jurisdiction do not spill over and adversely affect the environment of third States was consecrated by the ICJ as a well-established principle of international law in both the *Nuclear Weapons Advisory Opinion* and the *Gabčíkovo-Nagymaros* Case.[39] However, as will be explored in greater detail momentarily, some scholars call into question the relevance and 'precedential' value of *Trail Smelter*, particularly as an incubator for a rule compelling States to prevent *any* harm emanating from their territory. Nevertheless, whilst disputed in some circles, the importance of this case cannot be overlooked in any serious treatment of State responsibility. In its famous *Corfu Channel* decision, the ICJ similarly ruled that States may not allow their territory to become launch pads for harmful conduct.[40] Such conclusion must also be considered in

[36] See, eg: Preliminary Declaration of a Programme of Action of the European Communities in respect to the Environment (1973) OJC 112/1 (20 December); Final Act, Conference on Security and Cooperation in Europe, Helsinki, 1 August 1975, available at www.osce.org/mc/39501; Art 20 of the ASEAN Agreement on the Conservation of Nature and Natural Resources (Kuala Lumpur, 9 July 1985), available at www.asean.org/1490.htm; Art 194(2) of the UN Convention on the Law of the Sea, 10 December, UN Doc A/Conf.62/122 (1982) reprinted in (1982) 21 ILM 1261 (in force, 28 July 1996) at 1308; Convention on Long-Range Transboundary Air Pollution, 13 November, UN Doc ECE/HLM.1/R.1 (1979) reprinted in (1979) 18 ILM 1442 (in force, 16 March 1983); Preamble of the United Nations Framework Convention on Climate Change, 9 May (1992) reprinted in (1992) 31 ILM 849 (in force, 21 March 1994) especially at 851; Art 3 of the UN Convention on Biological Diversity, 5 June (1992) reprinted in (1992) 31 ILM 818 (in force, 29 December 1993) at 824. See also: R Lefeber, *Transboundary Environmental Interference and the Origin of State Liability* (The Hague, Kluwer, 1996) 19–47.

[37] Referring to the widely used *Trail Smelter* metaphor: see *Trail Smelter Case* (*US v Canada*) (1941) 3 *Reports of International Arbitral Awards* 1905. See also: JR Crawford, *International Law Commission's Articles on State Responsibility: Introduction, Text and Commentaries* (Cambridge, CUP, 2002) 140.

[38] For a variety of contributions discussing this seminal decision, see RM Bratspies and RA Miller (eds), *Transboundary Harm in International Law: Lessons from the Trail Smelter Arbitration* (New York, CUP, 2006) (for the purposes of State responsibility and terrorism, specifically, see the contributions of MA Drumbl, 'Trail Smelter and the International Law Commission's Work on State Responsibility for Internationally Wrongful Acts and State Liability' in ibid, at 85–98; C Hoss and P-M Dupuy, 'Trail Smelter and Terrorism: International Mechanisms to Combat Transboundary Harm' in ibid, at 225–39).

[39] *Legality of the Threat or Use of Nuclear Weapons*, Advisory Opinion of 8 July, *ICJ Reports* (1996) 226 at 241–42, at para 29; *Gabčíkovo-Nagymaros Project (Hungary/Slovakia)*, Judgment of 25 September, *ICJ Reports* (1997) 7 at 77–78, para 140.

[40] See generally: *Corfu Channel* Case *(United Kingdom of Great Britain and Northern Ireland v Albania)*, Merits, Judgment of 9 April, *ICJ Reports* (1949) 4 at 22. See also: M García-Mora, *International Responsibility for Hostile Acts of Private Persons against Foreign States* (The Hague, Nijhoff, 1962) 109–12, 130; H Duffy, *The 'War on Terror' and the Framework of International Law* (Cambridge, CUP, 2005) 42; J-C Martin, *Les règles internationales relatives à la lutte contre le terrorisme* (Brussels, Bruylant, 2006) 454. As discussed below, some authors call into question the persuasiveness of this line of cases.

light of the possible eventuality that the Court endorsed a no-knowledge standard of international responsibility therein, a notion explored extensively below.[41] Whilst the norm derived from the ICJ's holding may arguably be construed as rather imprecise or general, the prohibition on States to allow their territories to become bases for harmful activity has nonetheless become a well-established international legal area under the rubric of 'State responsibility', generating 'strong records of influence and compliance'.[42] In the same year *Corfu Channel* was handed down, the UN Survey of International Law inferred that there exists 'general recognition of the rule that a State must not permit the use of its territory for purposes injurious to the interests of other States in a manner contrary to international law'.[43] Forty-seven years after *Corfu Channel*, the ICJ reaffirmed this rule, noting that

> [t]he existence of the general obligation of States to ensure that activities within their jurisdiction and control respect the environment of other States or of areas beyond national control is now part of the corpus of international law relating to the environment.[44]

Here, the violation stems from the State's failure to control its territory and, by implication, irregular units/terrorist factions therein rather than from complicity in terrorist plots or from actual control – effective or comprehensive – over terrorists perpetrating attacks (which could sometimes trigger direct State responsibility).[45] A third decision, the *Lake Lanoux* Case,[46] is also sometimes invoked in support of this proposition.[47] However, some authors call into question the persuasiveness of this line of cases, rather expounding that *Corfu Channel* and *Trail Smelter* fail to ground the existence of an obligation to prevent ultra-hazardous and highly polluting activities.[48]

Jaye Ellis is a particularly vocal proponent of this argument and questions the legitimacy of *Trail Smelter* as a trend-setting precedent, whilst also shedding

[41] See, eg: below section IV.A), especially nn 130–34 and accompanying text; ch 2 nn 81–83, 175–76; ch 4 nn 46–48, 318–20; ch 5 n 242 and accompanying text.

[42] MJ Finnemore and SJ Toope, 'Alternatives to "Legalization": Richer Views of Law and Politics' (2001) 55 *International Organization* 743, 747.

[43] UN Doc A/CN.4/1/Rev.1 at 34 (1949), available at http://untreaty.un.org/ilc/documentation/english/a_cn4_1_rev1.pdf.

[44] *Nuclear Weapons Advisory Opinion*, above n 39 at 241–42, para 29.

[45] See, eg: I Brownlie, *System of the Law of Nations: State Responsibility Part I* (Oxford, Clarendon Press, 1983) 182.

[46] See *Affaire du Lac Lanoux (Spain v France)* (1957) 12 *Reports of International Arbitral Awards* 281.

[47] See, eg: AL Springer, *The International Law of Pollution: Protecting the Global Environment in a World of Sovereign States* (Westport, Quorum Books, 1983) 133–34 (but also acknowledging the ambiguity associated with this line of cases).

[48] See, eg: B Conforti, *International Law and the Role of Domestic Legal Systems* (Dordrecht, Nijhoff, 1993) 170. For a discussion of these three cases, see P Sturma, 'Some Problems of Strict Liability in International Law' in *Thesaurus Acroasium Vol 20: Responsibility of States* (Thessaloniki, Institute of Public International Law and International Relations of Thessaloniki, 1993) 369 at 373–76.

new light on the Tribunal's reliance on, and misquoting of, Clyde Eagleton on State responsibility.[49] As Ellis points out when referring to the cited excerpt, Eagleton essentially reaffirmed the principle of non-attribution of private acts to States,[50] a notion ultimately absent from the Tribunal's ruling:

> [T]he state is never responsible for the act of an individual as such: the act of the individual merely occasions the responsibility of the state by revealing the state in an illegality of its own – an omission to prevent or publish, or positive encouragement of, the act of the individual.[51]

This view presupposes that *Trail Smelter* did not create a duty for States to prevent any harm emanating from their territory resulting from polluting activities. As Eagleton remarked, the focus of the inquiry rather hinges on any positive obligation to prevent certain private conduct incumbent upon States, a notion highly reconcilable with counterterrorism efforts. Thus,

> [t]he state cannot be regarded as an absolute guarantor of the proper conduct of all persons within its bounds. Before its responsibility may be engaged, it is necessary to show an illegality of its own; and this involves simply the question of what duties are laid upon the state with regard to individuals within its boundaries by positive international law.[52]

Whilst *Trail Smelter* undoubtedly sets forth a framework for incorporating responsibility and liability mechanisms within international environmental law, it remains unclear whether it convincingly establishes a strict liability rule that could be transposed integrally to counterterrorism.[53] Nonetheless entertaining this possibility, Kiss and Shelton echo Ellis' concerns about the inherent ambiguity in the Tribunal's reasoning, expounding that the arbitration 'left open the question of whether a State exercising all due diligence would be liable if transfrontier harm results despite the State's best efforts' and adding that 'the tribunal did not clarify whether a State is liable only for intentional, reckless or

[49] JD Ellis, 'Has International Law Outgrown Trail Smelter?' in Bratspies and Miller, above n 38 at 56–65.

[50] The principle of non-attribution can also be traced back to a PCIJ's advisory opinion where it declared that 'States can act only by and through their agents and representatives'. See *German Settlers in Poland* 1923 PCIJ (ser B) No 6 (10 September) at 22. For academic support of this proposition, see R Jennings and A Watts (eds), *Oppenheim's International Law*, 9th edn (London, Longman, 1992–96) 502–03; P Malanczuk, *Akehurst's Modern Introduction to International Law*, 7th rev edn (London, Routledge, 1997) 259; S Talmon, 'Responsibility of International Organizations: Does the European Community Require Special Treatment?' in Ragazzi, above n 21 at 410; R Wolfrum, 'State Responsibility for Private Actors: An Old Problem of Renewed Relevance' in Ragazzi, above n 21 at 424.

[51] Ellis, above n 49 at 56–65 (citing C Eagleton, *The Responsibility of States in International Law* (New York, NYU Press, 1928) 77). But see: R Ago, 'Third Report on State Responsibility' (1971) 2 *Yearbook of the International Law Commission* 199, UN Doc A/CN.4/226 & Add.1-3 at 233.

[52] Eagleton, above n 51 at 77.

[53] Nevertheless, its relevance in general international law should not be underemphasised. See, eg: AP Rubin, 'Pollution by Analogy: The Trail Smelter Arbitration' (1971) 50 *Oregon Law Review* 259.

negligent behavior (fault based conduct) or whether it is strictly liable for all serious or significant transboundary environmental harm'.[54] Conversely, others construe *Trail Smelter* as endorsing the proposition that responsibility should not be based on fault but on standards conceptually adjacent to strict liability.[55] This viewpoint appears congruent with classical doctrines supporting regimes premised on strict liability or absolute liability to better compel financial compensation for ultra-hazardous activities, a policy option principally attributable to economic sensibilities and concerns of 'risk allocation'.[56]

The obligation of States to prevent terrorism emanating from their territory can also be derived from several other sources. With the advent of modern terrorism and transborder insurgency,[57] some publicists extend the scope of this obligation to other international legal spheres. For instance, influential American scholarly voices maintain that States have a collective 'duty to prevent' humanitarian disasters, along with the harbouring, production and deployment of weapons of mass destruction.[58] Similarly, the notion that States are obligated to prevent transnational terrorism, as a stand-alone proposition, has also acquired credence in academic circles.[59] The objective here is not to enumerate all possible sources of this obligation but to acknowledge that it has emerged as an important international legal norm. In fact, the existence of that norm is so widely recognised that it poses no problems and should not fuel a futile or circuitous debate.[60] Pertinent and modern sources of the obligation, such as Security Council resolutions 1368 and 1373, will be engaged in depth below. In the interim, it is helpful to briefly canvass its major sources.

[54] A-C Kiss and DL Shelton, 'Strict Liability in International Environmental Law' in TM Ndiaye and R Wolfrum (eds), *Law of the Sea, Environmental Law and Settlement of Disputes: Liber Amicorum Judge Thomas A. Mensah* (Leiden, Nijhoff, 2007) 1131 at 1131–32.

[55] See, eg: HS Lee, 'Post Trusteeship Environmental Accountability: Case of PCB Contamination on the Marshall Islands' (1998) 26 *Denver Journal of International Law and Policy* 399, 413–14 and authorities cited therein.

[56] See, eg: H Lauterpacht, 'Delictual Relationships between States: State Responsibility' in E Lauterpacht (ed), *International Law: Being the Collected Papers of Hersch Lauterpacht (Vol 1: The General Works)* (Cambridge, CUP, 1970) 251 at 399.

[57] On modern terrorism and international law, see M Lippman, 'The New Terrorism and International Law' (2003) 10 *Tulsa Journal of Comparative and International Law* 297.

[58] See, eg: L Feinstein and A-M Slaughter, 'A Duty to Prevent' (2004) 83 *Foreign Affairs* 136. However, other prominent scholars categorically reject Feinstein and Slaughter's duty to prevent. For instance, Brunnée and Toope take issue with this approach, judging that the duty to prevent unnecessarily merges all justifications for recourse to force into one overriding security threat pre-emption model. See J Brunnée and SJ Toope, 'Slouching towards New "Just" Wars: International Law and the Use of Force after September 11th' (2004) 51 *Netherlands International Law Review* 363, 387–90; J Brunnée and SJ Toope, 'The Use of Force: International Law after Iraq' (2004) 53 *ICLQ* 785, 802–04.

[59] See D Brown, 'Use of Force against Terrorism after September 11th: State Responsibility, Self-Defense and Other Responses' (2003) 11 *Cardozo Journal of International and Comparative Law* 1, 4–5; Lippman, above n 57.

[60] Many commentators recognise this obligation. See, eg: Brown, above n 59 at 4–5, 13–18; Lippman, above n 57; Feinstein and Slaughter, above n 58.

First and foremost, this obligation stems from the basic principle of sovereignty, which entails both rights and obligations.[61] The concept of sovereignty also implies a correlative obligation of *due diligence*, particularly in the field of counterterrorism:

> La diligence est une obligation traditionnelle en droit international général, conçue comme un corollaire de la souveraineté, qui suppose que l'Etat veille, dans la mesure de ses moyens, à ce que ne se développent pas, à partir des territoires soumis à sa juridiction ou à son contrôle, des activités portant atteinte aux intérêts étrangers qui y sont localisés ou aux droits des étrangers.[62]

Significant State practice corroborates the obligation to exercise due diligence[63] and it should be rather uncontroversial to classify it as now immutably ingrained within general international law.[64] Without disregarding potential *erga omnes* implications, under universal neighbouring principles one State's rights end where the territory of another State begins.[65] An obvious source of this obligation further lies in Article 2(4) of the UN Charter, which expressly prohibits Member States from threatening or using force in international relations and

[61] See, eg: L Condorelli, 'The Imputability to States of Acts of International Terrorism' (1989) 19 *Israel Yearbook on Human Rights* 233, 240; AA Cançado Trindade, 'Complementarity between State Responsibility and Individual Responsibility for Grave Violations of Human Rights: The Crime of State Revisited' in Ragazzi, above n 21 at 259. See also: Feinstein and Slaughter, above n 58 at 137 (citing the report of the Evans-Sahnoun Commission on R2P). See generally: SD Krasner, *Sovereignty: Organized Hypocrisy* (Princeton, Princeton University Press, 1999).

[62] 'Due diligence constitutes a classical obligation under general international law and is construed as a corollary of sovereignty. It assumes that States shall, to the best of their ability, ensure that no activities injurious to foreign interests or aliens take root on territories under their jurisdiction or control' (author translation). F Dubuisson, 'Vers un renforcement des obligations de diligence en matière de lutte contre le terrorisme?' in K Bannelier et al (eds), *Le Droit international face au terrorisme: après le 11 septembre 2001* (Paris, Pedone, 2003) 141 at 142.

[63] See, eg: GH Hackworth, *Digest of International Law (Vol V)* (Washington, DC, Department of State Publications, 1940–44) 654–65; MM Whiteman (ed), *Digest of International Law (Vol VIII)* (Washington, DC, Department of State Publications, 1963–73) 815–19, 830–35; E Lauterpacht (ed), *The Contemporary Practice of the United Kingdom in the Field of International Law* (London, British Institute of International and Comparative Law, 1962) 120; A-C Kiss (ed), *Répertoire de la pratique française en matière de droit international public (vol III)* (Paris, Centre national de la recherche scientifique, 1962–72) 590–636; JA Beesley and CB Bourne (eds), 'Canadian Practice in International Law During 1970 As Reflected Mainly in Public Correspondence and Statements of the Department of External Affairs' (1971) 9 *Canadian Yearbook of International Law* 276, 295–97.

[64] See, eg: Brownlie, above n 45 at 162.

[65] See, eg: Declaration on Principles of International Law Concerning Friendly Relations and Co-operation Among States in Accordance with the Charter of the United Nations, GA Res 2625, UN GAOR, 25th Sess, Supp No 28, UN Doc A/RES/25/2625 (1970) 122 [hereinafter Declaration on Friendly Relations]; Declaration on Principles Guiding Relations between Participating States in OSCE Final Act, above n 36 at 3 ff. This proposition can also be traced back to Max Huber's famous arbitral award in the *Island of Palmas Case (US v Netherlands)* (1928) 2 *Reports of International Arbitral Awards* 829. See also: Jennings and Watts, above n 50 § 119 at 385; J Peirano, 'International Responsibility and Cooperation for Development' in Ragazzi, above n 21 at 191. There are also hints of this idea in Hume's seminal works on the theory of politics. See, eg: D Hume, F Watkins (ed), *Theory of Politics* (London, Nelson, 1951) 118 (discussing the law of nations and inferring that 'there arises a new set of duties among the neighbouring states').

reflects customary law.[66] Hence, a host-State that possesses the capability to prevent terrorism but fails to do so will arguably not fulfil its Article 2(4) duty since terrorism almost invariably amounts to recourse to force by definition. This proposition is undoubtedly reinforced when host-States openly support or endorse terrorist attacks on other States' territories.[67] Indeed, we will see that State responsibility for failing to prevent terrorism can be predicated on State authorities' subsequent approval of unlawful behaviour both pursuant to ILC Article 11 and the *Tehran Hostages* Case.[68] This reasoning partly prompted José Alvarez to identify a new rule endorsed by the Security Council following 9/11, thereby correlating States' 'harbouring and supporting' of terrorists with Article 2(4) in the following manner:

> A state's assistance to, harboring of, or post hoc ratification of violent acts undertaken by individuals within its territory, or perhaps even mere negligence in controlling such individuals, may make that state responsible for those acts and justify military action against it. In other words, such state action (or inaction) may constitute a breach of the state's own duty not to violate UN Charter Article 2(4).[69]

In addition to Security Council resolutions 1368 and 1373, several documents adopted under the aegis of the UN,[70] such as other Council resolutions[71] and

[66] See also: Brown, above n 59 at 4. For background discussion on the role of Art 2(4) in international relations, see TM Franck, 'Who Killed Article 2(4)? or: Changing Norms Governing the Use of Force by States' (1970) 64 *AJIL* 809; O Schachter, 'The Right of States to Use Armed Force' (1984) 82 *Michigan Law Review* 1620.

[67] See, eg: MB Baker, 'Terrorism and the Inherent Right of Self-Defense (A Call to Amend Article 51 of the United Nations Charter)' (1987) 10 *Houston Journal of International Law* 25, 42, 48.

[68] *United States Diplomatic and Consular Staff in Tehran* (*United States v Iran*), Judgment of 24 May, *ICJ Reports* (1980) 3 at 33–35.

[69] JE Alvarez, 'Hegemonic International Law Revisited' (2003) 97 *AJIL* 873, 879. But see: A Nolkaemper, 'Attribution of Forcible Acts to States: Connections between the Law on the Use of Force and the Law of State Responsibility' in N Blokker and N Schrijver (eds), *The Security Council and the Use of Force: Theory and Reality – A Need for Change?* (Leiden, Nijhoff, 2005) 133 at 160.

[70] See, eg: Declaration on Friendly Relations, above n 65, which is repeated almost *verbatim* in Declaration on Measures to Eliminate International Terrorism, GA Res 49/60, UN GAOR, 49th Sess, Supp No 49, UN Doc A/RES/49/60 (1994) 303 at Annex Art 5(a). These declarations now reflect customary international law.

[71] Several Security Council resolutions stand for the principle that international terrorism should be eradicated. See, eg: SC Res 883, UN SCOR, 48th Sess, 3312nd Mtg, UN Doc S/RES/883 (1993) 5th preambular ('the suppression of international terrorism . . . is essential for the maintenance of peace and security'); SC Res 1044, UN SCOR, 51st Sess, 3627th Mtg, UN Doc S/RES/1044 (1996) 1st and 2nd preambulars ('Deeply disturbed by the world-wide persistence of acts of international terrorism in all its forms which endanger or take innocent lives, have a deleterious effect on international relations and jeopardize the security of States' and expressing 'deep concern over acts of international terrorism and emphasi[sing] the need for the international community to deal effectively with all such acts'); SC Res 1189, UN SCOR, 53rd Sess, 3915th Mtg, UN Doc S/RES/1189 (1998) 3rd preambular ('reaffirming the determination of the international community to eliminate international terrorism in all its forms and manifestations'); SC Res 1269, UN SCOR, 54th Sess, 4053rd Mtg, UN Doc S/RES/1269 (1999) para 1 ('Call[ing] upon all States to implement fully the international anti-terrorist conventions to which they are parties, encourag[ing] all States to consider as a mater of priority adhering to those to which they are not parties'); SC Res 1267, UN SCOR, 52nd Sess, 4051st Mtg, UN Doc S/RES/1267 (1999) 5th preambular ('reaffirming its conviction that the suppression of international terrorism is essential for the maintenance of international peace and security'); SC Res 1333, UN SCOR, 55th Sess, 4251st Mtg, UN Doc S/RES/1333 (2000) 7th preambular.

multilateral treaties,[72] impose an affirmative duty on States to prevent terrorist acts. The obligation to prevent terrorism has also been emphatically affirmed through international judiciaries.[73] Once a breach of this obligation is established, the mechanism of State responsibility will automatically be triggered, irrespective of whether that obligation was grounded in treaty law,[74] customary law,[75] general rules of international law[76] or *jus cogens*.[77] This obligation is also clearly mirrored under the precepts of IHL.[78]

Moreover, customary law has long established a duty incumbent upon States to diligently suppress and prevent the use of their territory as a launch pad for activities harmful to other States, a norm also encompassing acts carried out by private individuals.[79] Similarly, States are expected to diligently suppress or

[72] Several treaties on combating terrorism are currently in force, thereby strengthening international will in recognising an affirmative obligation of prevention. For a list of treaties and UN resolutions, see A Sambei et al, *Counter-Terrorism Law and Practice: An International Handbook* (Oxford, OUP, 2009) ch 2, ch 6; Proulx, above n 2 at 1031–33 fn 47 and accompanying text. For the text of relevant multilateral conventions, see 'UN Action to Counter Terrorism', available at www.un.org/terrorism/instruments.shtml.

[73] As discussed below in ch 2, the ICJ has recognised it in the *Tehran Hostages* Case, at least by analogy.

[74] See, eg: *North Sea Continental Shelf (Federal Republic of Germany/Netherlands)*, Judgment of 20 February, *ICJ Reports* (1969) 3 at 38–39, para 63; *Military and Paramilitary Activities in and against Nicaragua (Nicaragua v United States of America)*, Merits, Judgment of 27 June, *ICJ Reports* (1986) 14 at 95, para 177. On the relationship between international treaties and State responsibility, see, eg: DW Bowett, 'Treaties and State Responsibility' in M Virally (ed), *Le droit international au service de la paix, de la justice et du développement: mélanges Michel Virally* (Paris, Pedone, 1991) 137–45

[75] *Continental Shelf* Case, above n 74 at 38–39, para 63.

[76] See Crawford, above n 37 at 126.

[77] See Vienna Convention on the Law of Treaties, 23 May 1969, 1155 UNTS 331 (in force, 27 January 1980); Crawford, above n 37 at 127. On this issue, ILC Art 12 establishes that the 'origin and character' of an international obligation is irrelevant in demonstrating a breach of that obligation. See 'State Responsibility: Titles and text of the draft articles on Responsibility of States for internationally wrongful acts adopted by the Drafting Committee on second reading', UN Doc A/CN.4/L.602/Rev.1 (2001). The final draft was adopted by the ILC in 2001, with the UN General Assembly taking note of the Articles and commending them to States. See 'Report of the International Law Commission on the Work of Its Fifty-Third Session', UN GAOR, 56th Sess, Supp No 10, UN Doc A/56/10 (2001) 41 [hereinafter *ILC Articles on State Responsibility*, *Articles on State Responsibility*, or *Articles*].

[78] See, eg: *Nicaragua*, above n 74 at 119, para 255. See also: Martin, above n 40 at 455.

[79] See, eg: *The Alabama Claims (US v Great Britain)* (1871), reprinted in JB Moore, 1 *History and Digest of International Arbitrations to which the United States has been Party* (Washington, DC, Government Printing Office) 495; *Neer Case (US v Mexico)* (1926) 4 *Reports of International Arbitral Awards* 60, 61–62; *Jean-Baptiste Caire Claim (France v Mexico)* (1929) 5 *Reports of International Arbitral Awards* 516; *Texas Cattle Claims* (1944) in MM Whiteman 8 *Digest of International Law* (Washington, DC, Government Printing Office, 1967) 749; *Corfu Channel*, above n 40; *Tehran Hostages* Case, above n 68 at 31–32, paras 63, 67; *Nicaragua*, above n 74. See also: H Lauterpacht, 'Revolutionary Activities by Private Persons against Foreign States' (1928) 22 *AJIL* 105; H Kelsen, RW Tucker, (ed), *Principles of International Law*, 2nd edn (New York, Holt, Rinehart and Winston, 1966) 205–06; I Brownlie, 'International Law and the Activities of Armed Bands' (1958) 7 *ICLQ* 712, 729. This rule can also be derived, inferentially, from *Asian Agricultural Products Ltd v Democratic Socialist Republic of Sri Lanka* (1990) 4 *ICSID Reports* 245 (ICSID Case No ARB/87/3) at 246, 252, 270, 284–85 (stressing that Sri Lanka's obligation to protect foreign nationals and property is not rooted in strict or absolute liability, but rather in due diligence).

prevent harm emanating from private actors and injuring foreign nationals within their own territory.[80] More importantly, both duties have been construed as extending to transnational terrorist acts.[81] On this topic, Brigitte Stern queries 'si n'est pas apparue de façon coutumière *une obligation de diligence renforcée en matière de terrorisme international*'.[82] Drawing on the stringent counterterrorism obligations imposed by the Security Council on the Taliban, she further suggests that 'Cette obligation de diligence peut même apparaître comme *doublement renforcée dans le cas de l'Afghanistan*'.[83] Interestingly, an expression of the judicial genesis of these rules is perhaps embodied in the *Reparation for Injuries* precedent, in which Israel's international responsibility for failing to prevent the assassination of Count Bernadotte – a UN mediator in Palestine – by Jewish extremists in Israel was inferred by the ICJ for the purposes of pursuing its Advisory Opinion.[84]

Hence, it is trite to say that States are responsible for preventing terrorist excursions emanating from their territory.[85] The ILC's *Articles*, which indicate

[80] See, eg: *British Property in the Spanish Zone of Morocco* Case *(UK v Spain)* (1925) 2 *Reports of International Arbitral Awards* 615, 640; *Tehran Hostages* Case, above n 68; *Laura MB Janes (US v Mexico)* (1925) 4 *Reports of International Arbitral Awards* 82, 87; *Gertrude Parker Massey Claim (US v Mexico)* (1927) 4 *Reports of International Arbitral Awards* 155; *Youmans Case (US v Mexico)* (1926) 4 *Reports of International Arbitral Awards* 110; *Solis Case (US v Mexico)* (1928) 4 *Reports of International Arbitral Awards* 358, 361; *Texas Cattle Claims*, above n 79; *Home Missionary Society (US v Great Britain)* (1920) 6 *Reports of International Arbitral Awards* 42; *Walter A Noyes Case (US v Panama)* (1933) 6 *Reports of International Arbitral Awards* 308. See also: Brownlie, above n 45 at 161; RB Lillich and JM Paxman, 'State Responsibility for Injuries to Aliens Occasioned by Terrorist Activities' (1977) 26 *American University Law Review* 217, 222–51, 262–70.

[81] See, eg: Lillich and Paxman, above n 80 at 254–62, 276–307; S Sucharitkul, 'Terrorism as an International Crime: Questions of Responsibility and Complicity' (1989) 19 *Israel Yearbook on Human Rights* 247 (1989); LL Kutner, 'Constructive Notice: A Proposal to End International Terrorism' (1974) 19 *New York Law Forum* 325; TM Franck and D Niedermeyer, 'Accommodating Terrorism: An Offence against the Law of Nations' (1990) 19 *Israel Yearbook on Human Rights* 75, 99–128.

[82] 'Whether a customary international legal obligation of heightened due diligence emerged in the field of international terrorism' (author translation). See B Stern, 'La Responsabilité internationale des Etats: Perspectives récentes' in JC Lloréns (ed), *Cursos euromediterráneos bancaja de derecho internacional (Vol VII)* (Valencia, Tirant lo Blanch, 2003) 659 at 689.

[83] 'The intensity of this heightened due diligence obligation might even appear to be doubled vis-à-vis Afghanistan' (author translation). ibid, at 690. She further adds that 'S'il y a eu violation de ces obligations de *due diligence*, les talibans engagent leur responsabilité internationale, mais la discussion reste ouverte de savoir si la violation de ces obligations permet de leur imputer les actes des terroristes'. But see: ibid, at 692:

> Quoiqu'il en soit, que ce soit du fait d'un acte illicite propre ou de l'imputation de l'acte du particulier, l'Etat est en tout cas responsable des conséquences dommageables de l'acte du particulier, en l'espèce des conséquences dommageables des attentats du 11 septembre.

[84] See *Reparation for Injuries Suffered in the Service of the United Nations,* Advisory Opinion of 11 April, *ICJ Reports* (1949) 174 at 185 ('Here again the Court is authorized to assume that the damage suffered involves the responsibility of a State, and it is not called upon to express an opinion upon the various ways in which that responsibility might be engaged').

[85] See, eg: Y Dinstein, 'The International Legal Response to Terrorism' in R Ago (ed), *International Law at the Time of Its Codification: Essays in Honour of Roberto Ago (Vol II)* (Milan, Giuffrè, 1987) 139 at 145; G Battaglini, 'War against Terrorism Extra Moenia, Self-Defence and Responsibility: A Pure Juridical Approach' in Ragazzi, above n 21 at 143 (framing it as 'international obligations of vigilance'). On the duty of vigilance, as expressed in the *Tehran Hostages*

that internationally wrongful acts can originate from actions or omissions,[86] further support the existence of such obligation when supplemented by the abovementioned sources. Irrespective of possible ontological complexities associated with omissions,[87] the 'crime of omission stands outside the chain of events within which a fact is connected with is consequences' in that 'An ethical duty – moral or legal – required someone to prevent the evil'.[88] A practical illustration of this principle is found in illegal wartime conduct:

> If soldiers are accused of war crimes or if prisoners are tortured, the officers in charge of military discipline had a duty to prevent the perpetration of such wrongful acts and can themselves be punished although they did not materially engage into the conduct.[89]

Although judiciaries have sometimes fumbled over the distinction between omissions and surrounding circumstances,[90] it is uncontroversial to assume that a State's passiveness, complacence or indifference vis-à-vis the concoction of terrorist agendas on its own territory might trigger its international responsibility. This position is further buttressed by ILC Article 14(3), which provides that 'The breach of an international obligation requiring a State to prevent a given event occurs when the event occurs and extends over the entire period during which the event continues and remains not in conformity with that obligation'.[91]

Whilst the *Articles* underscore the distinction between instantaneous and continuing legal breaches,[92] the scope of this project is primarily concerned with the interplay between the obligation to prevent terrorism and the *Articles*, without any emphasis on temporal dimensions surrounding international legal breaches.[93] Once a State fails to fulfil its obligation to prevent terrorism, its

Case, see Y Dinstein, *War, Aggression and Self-Defence*, 4th edn (Cambridge, CUP, 2005) 206; DJ Bederman, 'Contributory Fault and State Responsibility' (1990) 30 *Virginia Journal of International Law* 335, 343; J Lane, 'The Mass Graves at Dasht-e Leili: Assessing U.S. Liability for Human Rights Violations During the War in Afghanistan' (2003) 34 *California Western International Law Journal* 145, 159; J Quigley, 'State Responsibility for Ethnic Cleansing' (1999) 32 *UC Davis Law Review* 341, 355.

86 See Art 2 of the ILC's *Articles*, above n 77. There is no substantial difference between both types of conduct: see Crawford, above n 37 at 82.

87 See, eg: M Bunge, 'The Revival of Causality' in F Guttorm (ed), *Contemporary Philosophy: A New Survey (Vol II: Philosophy of Science)* (The Hague, Nijhoff, 1982) 133 at 136.

88 F Rigaux, 'International Responsibility and the Principle of Causality' in Ragazzi, above n 21 at 82.

89 ibid.

90 See, eg: *Affaire relative à l'acquisition de la nationalité polonaise* (1924) 1 *Reports of International Arbitral Awards* 401; *Corfu Channel*, above n 40 at 22–23; *Tehran Hostages* Case, above n 68 at 63, 67; *Velásquez Rodríguez Case*, Inter-Am Ct HR Decisions and Judgments 91 (ser C) No 4 (1988) at para 170.

91 Art 14(3) of the *ILC Articles*, above n 77.

92 On the distinction between instantaneous and continuing breaches, see below ch 4, section III.A).

93 On the concept of time in the context of State responsibility, see P Tavernier, 'Relevance of the Intertemporal Law' in JR Crawford et al (ed), *The Law of International Responsibility* (Oxford, OUP 2010) 397–403; W Karl, 'The Time Factor in the Law of State Responsibility' in M Spinedi and B Simma (eds), *United Nations Codification of State Responsibility* (New York, Oceana Publications, 1987) 95–114; E Wyler, 'Quelques réflexions sur la réalisation dans le temps du fait internationalement illicite' (1991) 95 *RGDIP* 881. On time and the law, see generally: R Higgins, 'Time and the Law' (1997) 46 *ICLQ* 501.

conduct will attract the application of secondary rules of State responsibility.[94] Catastrophic terrorist strikes, such as those perpetrated on 9/11, may well engender ripple effects and amount to ongoing violations of international law if, for instance: i) host-States are negligent in thwarting post-attack aftershocks, such as further excursions, that could have been prevented with the intelligence now at hand; or ii) further oversight/inaction by the host-States' governments allows individuals to exploit the original attack(s) on their territory for recruitment purposes or political leverage; or iii) host-States knowingly harbour terrorists on their soil and/or disobey binding Security Council resolutions to that effect.[95]

This inquiry certainly holds true regarding the establishment of liability for the purposes of indemnification following terrorist attacks under domestic legal structures. This type of scenario brings about a plethora of additional questions with regard to the State apparatus' diligence:

> Does the loss sustained originate in the measures taken by the police in the field which proved to be insufficient? Or on the contrary, is it the result of the legal preventive orders enacted by the government which proved to be tardy or inadequate? Or again, have inadequacies of the rescue services increased the damage?[96]

Such concerns appear directly transposable to State responsibility and further scrutiny will be accorded to them in subsequent sections. Yet, the argument becomes particularly compelling given intelligence or law enforcement failures – between the CIA and the FBI within the US in terms of domestic liability, for example[97] – or Afghanistan's failure to monitor and thwart Al-Qaeda despite numerous warnings from the Security Council and other political lamentations, in terms of international State responsibility.[98] Keeping the domestic legal indemnification analogy in mind, this rationale carries over to international law and enables the international community to scrutinise the negligence of host-States, especially if a given terrorist attack was foreseeable. Indeed,

[94] On the distinction between primary rules and secondary rules of State responsibility and its underlying philosophy, see Report of the Sub-committee on State Responsibility (1963) 2 *Yearbook of the International Law Commission* 227, UN Doc A/CN.4/152 at 228, para 5; D Alland and J Combacau, '"Primary" and "Secondary" Rules in the Law of State Responsibility: Categorizing International Obligations' (1985) 16 *Netherlands Yearbook of International Law* 81.

[95] See, eg: JA McCredie, 'The Responsibility of States for Private Acts of International Terrorism' (1985) 1 *Temple International and Comparative Law Journal* 69, 86; J Kranz, 'The Use of Armed Force – New Facts and Trends' (2006) 3 *The Polish Quarterly of International Affairs* 68, 80.

[96] TS Renoux and A Roux, 'The Rights of Victims and Liability of the State' in R Higgins and M Flory (eds), *Terrorism and International Law* (London, Routledge, 1997) 251 at 254.

[97] See, eg: SJ Schulhofer, *The Enemy Within: Intelligence Gathering, Law Enforcement, and Civil Liberties in the Wake of September 11* (New York, Century Foundation Press, 2002) 31–33, 63. It should be recalled that 'a State is legally obliged to exercise due diligence to prevent the commission of acts of international terrorism within its jurisdiction'. See *Report of the Sixty-First Conference* (London, International Law Association, 1985) 7. See also: Martin, above n 40 at 459.

[98] On the relationship between the Afghan government and Al-Qaeda, see R Gunaratna, *Inside Al Qaeda: Global Network of Terror* (London, Hurst, 2002) 10–20, 41, 53–60, 66–70, 72, 77–82, 123–24, 128, 131, 134, 142, 146, 151, 154, 159–61, 223, 227–32, 263, 275, 278, 285–86, 289–90, 293, 297–98.

> the administrative judge may find for serious negligence on the part of the police services or a total lack of preventive measures, in so far as the act of terrorism was not absolutely unpredictable with regard to its time and place, and the authorities had failed to take notice of information suggesting the possibility of a terrorist attack.[99]

In tackling these difficult situations, judiciaries emphasise the importance of knowledge possession by States and, perhaps more importantly, the correlation between information gathered and a 'real and immediate' risk to potential victims of attacks.

The European Court of Human Rights was confronted with a relevant fact pattern in the *Osman* Case.[100] Charges were levelled against British police forces for failing to act on death threats directed at particular citizens. In reasoning strangely reminiscent of a widespread reading of *Corfu Channel*, the Court developed the following threshold in assessing the lack of preventive action by the police forces:

> [I]t must be established . . . that the authorities *knew or ought to have known* at the time of the existence of a *real and immediate risk* to the life of an identified individual or individuals from the criminal acts of a third party and that they failed to take measures within the scope of their powers which, judged reasonably, might have been expected to avoid that risk (emphasis added).[101]

Ultimately, it held that the applicants had failed to identify 'any decisive stage' 'in the sequence of the events leading up to the tragic shooting when it could be said that the police knew or ought to have known that the lives of the Osman family were at real and immediate risk'.[102] As will be discussed subsequently, intelligence or law enforcement failures regarding transnational terrorism, or complacency, can be sufficient to crystallise a host-State's international responsibility. Thus, a determinant element will reside in the actual level of risk faced versus the degree of State inaction, all contemplated through the prism of the available information before an attack:

> The fact that a state possessed information as to terrorist threats and failed to act on it could conceivably be sufficient to render the state responsible if the threats are realised, although this would depend on there being clear information indicating a 'real and immediate risk' in circumstances where the state was in a position reasonably to prevent deaths and failed to do so.[103]

Now that an affirmative duty to forestall terrorism encumbering upon all States has been established, the inquiry shifts to counterterrorism contexts and

[99] Renoux and Roux, above n 96 at 254. On the obligation of States to punish the authors of crimes perpetrated against foreigners – framed as an obligation of result – see J Combacau, 'Obligations de résultat et obligations de comportement: quelques questions et pas de réponse' in D Bardonnet et al (eds), *Mélanges offerts à Paul Reuter: le droit international: unité et diversité* (Paris, Pedone, 1981) 181 at 188 (invoking the level of 'diligence requise').

[100] *Osman v United Kingdom* (1998) 29 Eur HR Rep 245.

[101] ibid, at para 116.

[102] ibid, at para 121.

[103] Duffy, above n 40 at 308.

the primary/secondary dichotomy underpinning the relevant normative scheme. It must be emphasised that the rules governing State responsibility are deployed

> in conjunction with other, more particular, rules of international law, which prescribe duties in various precise forms . . . the basic concept of responsibility is a necessary but not a sufficient condition for the imposition of responsibility for breaches of particular legal duties.[104]

In defining the obligation of prevention, the legal community might have to defer to municipal law analogies and insights, as the realm of State responsibility offers a wide margin for cross-sector legal transplantations.[105] The above-mentioned texts form a mere part of the international instruments to combat terrorism; more academic writing is undoubtedly required to tease out the contours of some of the primary obligations contained therein. In that regard, the study now turns to the relationship between counterterrorism objectives and the primary/secondary dichotomy underlying the law of State responsibility.

III. COUNTERTERRORISM OBLIGATIONS AFTER 9/11 AND THE PRIMARY/SECONDARY DIVIDE

The existence of a vital obligation of prevention incumbent upon all States to contain and repel any harmful activity emanating from their territory and injurious to the rights of third States or citizens was discussed in the previous section. While the obligation of prevention is partially grounded in treaty law, very few stringent accountability mechanisms can be derived from specific multilateral or regional conventions.[106] This is most likely attributable to that source of law's overemphasis on extradition[107] and to the fact that modern counterterrorism law is characterised by a piecemeal approach, thereby targeting specific acts or types of terrorism – aeroplane hijacking, high seas excursions, hostage-taking, diplomatic violations etc – without attempting to develop a comprehensive scheme of responsibility for an all-encompassing concept of 'terrorism'.[108] Equally noteworthy in the failure of a more robust and uniform transnational

[104] Brownlie, above n 45 at 40 (also adding that 'The relevance of fault, the relative 'strictness' of the obligation, will be determined by the content of each rule').

[105] But see: R Provost, 'Introduction' in R Provost (ed), *State Responsibility in International Law* (Aldershot, Ashgate/Dartmouth, 2002) xiii (noting the awkwardness of borrowing from municipal tort law or delictual responsibility in the field of State responsibility, and citing H Lauterpacht, *Private Law Sources and Analogies of International Law (With Special Reference to International Arbitration)* (London, Longmans, 1927)).

[106] See, eg: WP Hoye, 'Fighting Fire With . . . Mire? Civil Remedies and the New War on State-Sponsored Terrorism' (2002) 12 *Duke Journal of Comparative & International Law* 105, 108–09.

[107] See WM Reisman, 'International Legal Responses to International Terrorism' (1999) 22 *Houston Journal of International Law* 3, 28.

[108] See, eg: MC Bassiouni, 'Legal Control of International Terrorism: A Policy-Oriented Assessment' (2002) 43 *Harvard International Law Journal* 83, 91; RJ Beck and AC Arend, '"Don't Tread on US": International Law and Forcible State Responses to Terrorism' (1994) 12 *Wisconsin International Law Journal* 153, 169.

law of counterterrorism is the problem of enforcement. For instance, of all relevant regional counterterrorism instruments, the European Convention on Terrorism remains the sole agreement routinely enforced by the contracting parties.[109]

As canvassed above, the obligation of prevention can most persuasively be grounded in the ICJ's holding in the *Corfu Channel* Case,[110] whilst different permutations of the original rule can be traced back to various sources of contemporary public international law.[111] In fact, this obligation cropped up long before 9/11 and historically translated into a due diligence obligation, a veritable corollary of State sovereignty.[112] In counterterrorism, this obligation implies that 'States are required under international law to carry out protection by "due diligence," which means that all reasonable measures under the circumstances must be taken to prevent terrorist acts'.[113]

In the wake of 9/11, the UN Security Council imposed a categorical obligation to prevent terrorism upon all States via resolution 1373.[114] Whilst its contents will be thoroughly engaged throughout this book, it should be immediately stressed that this document likely constitutes the cornerstone of post-9/11 international counterterrorism policy-making. Thus, on 28 September 2001, the Security Council decided that all States shall, inter alia:

– deny safe haven to those who finance, plan, support or commit terrorist acts, or provide safe havens;
– prevent those who finance, plan, facilitate or commit terrorist acts from using their respective territories for those purposes against other States or their citizens; and

[109] See Bassiouni, above n 108 at 92.

[110] *Corfu Channel*, above n 40 at 22. See also: *British Property* Case, above n 80 at 640; *Island of Palmas Case*, above n 65 at 839; *Tehran Hostages* Case, above n 68 at 64; *Janes* Case, above n 80 at 87; *Massey Claim*, above n 80; *Youmans Claim*, above n 80; *Solis* Case, above n 80 at 361; *Texas Cattle Claim*, above n 79 at 749, 753; *Home Missionary Society*, above n 80; *Noyes Case*, above n 80. See also: Lillich and Paxman, above n 80 at 222–51, 262–70.

[111] See, eg: above, section II.

[112] See, eg: *Island of Palmas Case*, above n 65 at 839; Judge Moore's Dissenting Opinion in *SS Lotus (France v Turkey)* 1927 PCIJ (ser A) No 10 (7 September) 65 at 88. See also: P-M Dupuy, 'State Sponsors of Terrorism: Issues of International Responsibility' in A Bianchi (ed), *Enforcing International Law Norms against Terrorism* (Oxford, Hart Publishing, 2004) 3 at 9; Reisman, above n 107 at 51.

[113] McCredie, above n 95 at 86. See also: J-A Romano, 'Combating Terrorism and Weapons of Mass Destruction: Reviving the Doctrine of a State of Necessity' (1999) 87 *Georgetown Law Journal* 1023, 1033; MN Schmitt, 'The Sixteenth Annual Waldemar A. Solf Lecture in International Law: *Bellum Americanum* Revisited: U.S. Security Strategy and the *Jus ad Bellum*' (2003) 176 *Military Law Review* 364, 391.

[114] SC Res 1373, UN SCOR, 56th Sess, 4385th Mtg, UN Doc S/RES/1373 (2001). In subsequent resolutions, the Council also reiterated the obligation to prevent terrorism and/or other corollary duties of all States stemming from resolution 1373. See, eg: Sec Res 1566, UN SCOR, 59th Sess, 5053rd Mtg, UN Doc S/RES/1566 (2004); SC Res 1617, UN SCOR, 59th Sess, 5244th Mtg, UN Doc S/RES/1617 (2005); SC Res 1822, UN SCOR, 62nd Sess, 5928th Mtg, UN Doc S/RES/1822 (2008); SC Res 1963, UN SCOR, 65th Sess, 6459th Mtg, UN Doc S/RES/1963 (2010).

– prevent the movement of terrorists or terrorist groups by effective border controls and controls on issuance of identity papers and travel documents, and through measures for preventing counterfeiting, forgery or fraudulent use of identity papers and travel documents.[115]

In this broad-reaching statement, the Council imposed a wide range of obligations in the most categorical terms. Amongst the most obvious ones is the duty incumbent upon all States to refrain from sponsoring or supporting terrorism on their territory. Implicit in this obligation is the idea that accountability automatically ensues should a State provide such support or sponsorship to terrorists.[116] When coupled with traditional pronouncements on prevention, a more general obligation of prevention can be derived from this resolution in the context of counterterrorism, notwithstanding specific treaty or conventional regimes imposing separate duties.[117] Whilst other ancillary obligations, such as the duties to punish, extradite and prosecute terrorists, will remain important, albeit peripheral to the main discussion, particular emphasis will be placed on the general duty to prevent terrorism. Even prior to 9/11, the primary aim of the international community in this context was to prevent terrorist activity but the events of 9/11, coupled with the legal response thereto, have placed further policy emphasis sharply on prevention.[118]

The obligation of prevention will remain, for all intents and purposes, the 'primary' legal obligation to be scrutinised under the lens of State responsibility. Like any other primary norm under international law, the emergence of such obligation in the post-9/11 legal landscape evokes an important tension. Any study delving into the realm of State responsibility must inexorably come to grips with the distinction between primary and secondary obligations, a dichotomy underpinning the logic of the ILC's *Articles on State Responsibility*,[119] along with modern State responsibility repertoire. Whilst some question the persuasiveness of this distinction,[120] others defend it or, at least, opine that primary and secondary rules cannot, in most cases, be dissociated.[121] Therefore,

[115] PJV Krieken (ed), *Terrorism and the International Legal Order: With Special Reference to the UN, the EU and Cross-Border Aspects* (The Hague, TMC Asser Press, 2002) 5.

[116] See, eg: JM Beard, 'America's New War on Terror: The Case for Self-Defense under International Law' (2002) 25 *Harvard Journal of Law & Public Policy* 559, 582.

[117] See, eg: Dupuy, above n 112 at 11.

[118] On the international objective of prevention in the realm of counterterrorism, see MC Bassiouni, 'Preface' in MC Bassiouni (ed), *International Terrorism and Political Crimes* (Springfield, Charles C Thomas, 1975) xi–xiii; RA Friedlander, *Terrorism: Documents of International and Local Control* (London, Oceana Publications, 1981) 23–25; R Kupperman, 'Facing Tomorrow's Terrorist Incident Today' in EN Lowe and HD Shargel (eds), *Legal and Other Aspects of Terrorism* (New York, Practising Law Institute, 1979) 581–620; McCredie, above n 95 at 71; JF Murphy and AE Evans, 'Introduction' in AE Evans and JF Murphy (eds), *Legal Aspects of International Terrorism* (Lexington, Lexington Books, 1978) xxiii–xxxviii, 3.

[119] *Articles*, above n 77; GA Res 56/83, UN GAOR, 56th Sess, Supp No 49, UN Doc A/RES/56/83 (2001) 499.

[120] See, eg: Alland and Combacau, above n 94; Provost, above n 105 at xii–xiii.

[121] See, eg: M Milanović, 'State Responsibility for Genocide' (2006) 17 *EJIL* 553; T Treves, 'The International Law Commission's Articles on State Responsibility and the Settlement of Disputes' in

the mutual interpenetration of rules at both norm-specific levels of international breaches, along with the emergence of norms concomitantly straddling primary and secondary terrain, signal that both types of obligations remain mutually interdependent and that the overarching distinction prevalent in this area cannot be artificially disabled.[122] Whilst the purpose of this project is not to entertain any particular stance in the broader discussion regarding the validity of the current 'breach-consequence' structure ultimately espoused by the ILC – nor is it to put that polemic to rest – the primary/secondary distinction will nonetheless be invoked rather liberally in subsequent pages.

Hence, the *Articles* dictate that, once a primary obligation has been violated,[123] international law sets in motion the application of secondary rules, which translate into a series of potential legal consequences including restitution and/or compensation for harm done. In sum, the invocation of this now firmly implanted but still controversial distinction will cater to a strict cause-and-effect symbiosis: as soon as a wrongful act is committed, which entails that a State has breached international law, that State's responsibility will be triggered and specific legal consequences will ensue (which may or may not be juxtaposed with further political and/or diplomatic sanctions). As such, careful analysis will be advanced to bolster the idea that selective deconstruction and elucidation of secondary rules of responsibility may, in fact, further illuminate primary rules in the face of normative discrepancies or substantive vacuums, as is the case with certain (poorly defined) counterterrorism obligations.

IV. THE SHORTCOMINGS OF STATE RESPONSIBILITY VIS-À-VIS TERRORISM

At the outset, it is vital to survey how the ILC's current rules operate in harmony with international legal principles. Significant emphasis will be placed on the restrictive, and sometimes short-sighted, nature of the ILC's *Articles* when confronted with novel and challenging transnational activities carried out by private actors. These shortcomings will be brought to the fore by the use of practical scenarios, which concomitantly signal the conceptual weaknesses characterising the scheme of State responsibility and act as a preliminary gloss through which this project should be contemplated. First, however, one must consider the fact that the relationship between counterterrorism and State

Ragazzi, above n 21 at 227; SM Villalpando, *L'émergence de la communauté internationale dans la responsabilité des Etats* (Paris, PUF, 2005) 139–41, 333–34, 384.

[122] See, eg: H Thirlway, 'Injured and Non-Injured States before the International Court of Justice' in Ragazzi, above n 21 at 323. Others opine that the distinction between primary and secondary norms, which was once technical in nature, often relies upon an artificial application. See E David, 'Primary and Secondary Rules' in Crawford et al, above n 93 at 27–33.

[123] The violation of the relevant primary obligation occurs when a State fails to prevent a terrorist attack emanating from its territory and inflicting harm onto the citizens or rights of another State.

responsibility can become permutated in direct correlation with the type and degree of State involvement in terrorist activity.

A) A Gradation of State Involvement

The interplay between the law of State responsibility and counterterrorism is guided by an overarching gradation of State involvement. The idea that a host-State may exert various types of involvement in terrorist activity within its borders is deeply entrenched in international legal consciousness.[124] The UN General Assembly explicitly recognised this eventuality in the 1994 Declaration on Measures to Eliminate International Terrorism, by calling on its Members to 'refrain from organizing, instigating, facilitating, financing, encouraging or tolerating terrorist activit[y]' on their territory.[125] Implicit in this declaration is the idea that 'Like other instruments employing this language, the U.N. indicated that accountability therefore applies to a wide spectrum of State involvement in terrorist activity, from State sponsorship to State acquiescence'.[126]

Whilst large-scale or catastrophic terrorism poses increasingly intractable challenges for the law of State responsibility, this study strives to cast a wide enough net to cover the whole gamut of governmental (in)action in terrorism, be it passive or active.[127] More importantly, chapter two identifies an overarching dichotomy that pervades the new paradigm of State responsibility, dividing possible State involvement in terrorism between two polar opposites, based on a binary continuum.[128] Lying at one extremity of the spectrum, direct State responsibility connotes an active involvement in the planning and execution of terrorist attacks by the State, be it through funding, arming, training, selecting and planning operations or controlling the terrorist factions. On the opposite end of the continuum, indirect State responsibility entails a far more subtle, or passive, involvement ranging from providing logistical support and/or bases of operations to terrorists, to tacit acquiescence to the presence of terrorists on the territory, to mere toleration of terrorists paired with fundraising or lobbying on the territory. Obviously, many other increments coexist on the broad spectrum of possible State involvement and it is the grey areas, really, that raise the most interesting questions for the purposes of the present study. At the 'direct involvement' end of the spectrum, we find States that are flat-out complicit in terrorism

[124] Compare with the respective schematic typologies suggested by the following authors: A Cassese, 'The International Community's "Legal" Responses to Terrorism' (1989) 38 *ICLQ* 589, 597–98; Cohan, above n 16 at 90–92; G Guillaume, 'Terrorisme et droit international' (1989-III) 215 *Recueil des Cours* 287, 396; Martin, above n 40 at 457–58.

[125] Declaration on Measures to Eliminate International Terrorism, above n 70 at Annex Art 5(a).

[126] Smith, above n 27 at 752.

[127] For an interesting discussion of both active and passive sponsorship of terrorist organisations involving States in South Asia and the Middle East, specifically, see DL Byman, *Deadly Connections: States that Sponsor Terrorism* (Cambridge, CUP, 2005).

[128] See also: CM Henderson, 'Michael Byers, War Law: International Law and Armed Conflict' (2007) 12 *Journal of Conflict and Security Law* 150, 152.

or that wage specific military and paramilitary initiatives through surrogate terrorist organisations that they fully control. At the 'indirect involvement' end, we may be faced with simply negligent States that fail to freeze the assets of terrorist groups or merely tolerate the presence of terrorists on their territory without endorsing any of their activities.

More importantly, both of these extreme scenarios could potentially trigger the law of State responsibility, whilst the actual degree of liability might remain contingent on, or commensurate with, the level of harm inflicted through the commission of the internationally wrongful act.[129] In fact, a common but perhaps erroneous reading of the authoritative jurisprudence in this field might postulate that 'Applying the authority provided by the *Corfu Channel Case* to the current international crisis of state-sponsored terrorism, a State cannot *knowingly* acquiesce to terrorist activity within its borders without assuming liability'.[130] However, given a translation discrepancy, one can argue that the 'consent' or 'knowledge' component should be excised altogether from the primary obligation extracted from the *Corfu Channel* Case. More specifically, the French of the original judgment frames the relevant obligation as a duty 'pour tout Etat, de ne pas laisser utiliser son territoire aux fins d'actes contraires aux droits d'autres Etats', whilst the English translation rather invokes an 'obligation not to allow *knowingly* its territory to be used for acts contrary to the rights of other States' (emphasis added).[131] Whilst the issue of knowledge will be engaged later on,[132] one can see at the outset that the English translation carries with it a more onerous burden for establishing responsibility, namely the requirement of knowledge by the host-State that harmful activity is being launched from its territory. In sum, because the French version of the text is authoritative,[133] the obligation of prevention rather entails that States ensure that their territories are not used for activities injurious to third parties and/or States. Put another way, a severe obligation may be extracted from *Corfu Channel* to the effect that States may not allow their territories to be used as launch pads for terrorist excursions, irrespective of whether the involved governments acquiesced to the activities or, arguably, were even cognisant of such operations.[134]

Similarly, the language associated with post-9/11 State responsibility law has been divisive. While some scholars minutely delve into semantics-laden incursions seeking to elucidate the vernacular emerging from years of State support in the Afghanistan-Al Qaeda or Iran-Hezbollah scenarios, for example, others completely discard such endeavours. From a 'qualitative' (to which one could

[129] See below ch 4, section V.

[130] Smith, above n 27 at 754.

[131] *Corfu Channel*, above n 40 at 22.

[132] See below ch 4, sections II.A; IV.B); V.D); ch 5, sections II.C); IV.

[133] *Corfu Channel*, above n 40 at 37.

[134] Whilst the norm elaborated in *Corfu Channel* might appear general or imprecise, Finnemore and Toope, above n 42 at 747, infer that such rule – which they cast as falling under the rubric of 'State responsibility' – has generated strong records of compliance and influence.

add 'quantitative' in some cases) standpoint, commentators assert that the notions of 'State sponsorship' and 'State support' may, in fact, signal two varying types of State participation in terrorism. In a post-9/11 account, one author declares that 'state sponsorship of terrorism is limited to situations where the state planned, directed, and controlled terrorist operations and state support of terrorism includes all other lesser forms of state involvement'.[135] Similarly, in her 2001 Progress Report on Terrorism and Human Rights, Special Rapporteur Kalliopi Koufa noted that – whilst both terms engender considerable confusion when transplanted into the sphere of State practice – they embody distinct legal meanings. The notion of 'State support' inherently encompasses lesser forms of governmental involvement and control over terrorism (eg tacit or logistical support, providing sanctuary, etc).[136]

Governments, the media and other institutions frequently and liberally brandish these terms for a dual purpose: by pure sensationalistic or propagandistic inclination, or to actually cast judgment or pronounce on the legal responsibility of specific host-States vis-à-vis terrorism.[137] However, this particular construction of those notions failed to acquire credence in some academic circles, with several members of the American Society of International Law's Committee on Responses to State-Sponsored Terrorism voicing their 'dissatisfaction with the terms "state sponsorship" and "state support" on the ground that these terms lack precise legal content'.[138] Nevertheless, 'state sponsorship and state support of terrorism are solidly entrenched in the discourse of terrorism and are powerful expressions of state complicity, guilt, and participation in acts of terror'; hence, 'these terms serve an important political and legal function, connecting states, which surreptitiously assist terrorists, to their terrible crimes'.[139] Consequently, specific levels of governmental input and participation in terrorist activities will be canvassed throughout this project. In the interim, it is imperative to briefly survey potential scenarios on the gradation of State failures in preventing terrorism, in order to shed light on the shortcomings of State responsibility.

[135] SM Malzahn, 'State Sponsorship and Support of International Terrorism: Customary Norms of State Responsibility' (2002) 26 *Hastings International and Comparative Law Review* 83, 96. See also: ibid, at 97 (further differentiating State 'sponsorship' and State 'support' of terrorism). See also: M Crenshaw and J Pimlott (eds), *Encyclopedia of World Terrorism, Vol 1* (Armonk, ME Sharpe, 1997) 206–07.

[136] See KK Koufa, 'Terrorism and Human Rights', UN Doc E/CN.4/Sub.2/2001/31 (2001) 15, para 54.

[137] Malzahn, above n 135 at 96.

[138] BH Oxman and JF Murphy (eds), *Nonviolent Responses to Violence-Prone Problems: The Cases of Disputed Maritime Claims and State-Sponsored Terrorism* (Washington, DC, American Society of International Law, 1991) 18–19. See also: AG Hamid, 'Maritime Terrorism, the Straits of Malacca, and the Issue of State Responsibility' (2006) 15 *Tulane Journal of International and Comparative Law* 155, 164.

[139] Malzahn, above n 135 at 97.

B) Scenario 1: Iran-Hezbollah

Let us reconsider the Iran-Hezbollah example invoked above. The publicly available facts reveal that Iran financed, armed, controlled and directed Hezbollah factions in the context of their terrorist attacks against Israel. The government in Tehran unquestionably controlled and directed this terrorist group and the available evidence indicates that their actions qualify as 'terrorism'. In this quintessential case of direct State involvement, Iran's responsibility could be engaged pursuant to a literal reading of ILC Article 8:

> Conduct directed or controlled by a State
>
> The conduct of a person or group of persons shall be considered an act of a State under international law if the person or group of persons is in fact acting on the instructions of, or under the direction or control of, that State in carrying out the conduct.[140]

This type of scenario falls within the purview of what is classified as 'direct State responsibility' throughout the study.[141] It predominantly hinges on the host-State's direct or active support of individuals in their perpetration of internationally wrongful acts. Therefore, the relevant wrongful act can be construed as emanating from the State itself or, at the very least, the State can be seen as complicit in the unlawful act.[142]

Admittedly, the ICJ's holding in the *Genocide Case* would seem to run counter to this construction or, at least, to attenuate its persuasiveness with regard to readily establishing direct responsibility for the acts of non-State actors, even in the presence of clear and compelling evidence of significant links connecting the State apparatus to terrorists. Whilst the ICJ's judgment recognises that collective responsibility for genocide may be acknowledged, the Court did not find Serbia directly responsible for the genocide perpetrated at Srebrenica. Rather, grounding its reasoning in the Genocide Convention, it held that Serbia was only responsible for failing both to prevent the genocide and to cooperate with the ICTY by declining to transfer custody over key actors, including Ratko Mladić.[143] Thus, the Court refused to attribute the acts of General Mladić to the

[140] *Articles*, above n 77.

[141] See particularly: below ch 2, section II.

[142] Some commentators call for the adoption of more stringent State responsibility parameters in light of transnational terrorism, a manifestation of which, they argue, can be contemplated through the prism of a theory of State complicity with terrorism. See, eg: AE Chase, 'Legal Mechanisms of the International Community and the United States Concerning State Sponsorship of Terrorism' (2004) 45 *Virginia Journal of International Law* 41, 133–36.

[143] The Court:

> [N]otes first that no evidence has been presented that either General Mladić or any of the other officers whose affairs were handled by the 30th Personnel Centre were, according to the internal law of the Respondent, officers of the army of the Respondent – a *de jure* organ of the Respondent. Nor has it been conclusively established that General Mladićwas one of those officers; and even on the basis that he might have been, the Court does not consider that he would, for that reason alone, have to be treated as an organ of the [Federal Republic of Yugoslavia] for the purposes of the application of the rules of State responsibility.

Serbian army or to any other official organ of the Serbian governmental apparatus.[144] Although the General seemed to have been 'administered' from Belgrade, even receiving a promotion to the ranks of Colonel General originating from there, the Court nonetheless adduced from the evidence that Mladić's actions could only be attributed to Republika Srpska.[145]

Whilst this puzzling factual interpretation and rigid application of Article 8 has come under trenchant scrutiny, with some calling the Court's decision-making 'an incredible act of myopic legal reasoning',[146] some of the most compelling resistance to the majority's judgment actually emanated from dissenting voices on the bench. In particular, in his Dissenting Opinion Vice-President Al-Khasawneh underscored that Serbia's participation in the genocide could be established by way of 'massive and compelling evidence'.[147] In addition, he lamented the Court's failure to acquire access over Serbia's records from the Supreme Defence Council, an exercise that may have further evinced a direct connection with the Serbian government.[148] Highlighting that the rules of attribution under State responsibility are subject to 'subtle variations' and context-specific considerations, the Vice-President compellingly argued that the threshold of control enshrined in ILC Article 8 operates on a variable scale.[149] In fact, this construction of the notion of 'control' finds credence in both past remarks of ILC members[150] and ICTY jurisprudence, most notably in the *Tadić* and *Čelebići* cases. In the latter case, the Tribunal expounded that 'the "overall control" test could thus be fulfilled even if the armed forces acting on behalf of

Case Concerning the Application of the Convention on the Prevention and Punishment of the Crime of Genocide (Bosnia and Herzegovina v Serbia and Montenegro), Judgment of 26 February, *ICJ Reports* (2007) 43 at 203, para 388.

[144] ibid, at 139, para 387:

> The Applicant has shown that the promotion of Mladić to the rank of Colonel General on 24 June 1994 was handled in Belgrade, but the Respondent emphasizes that this was merely a verification for administrative purposes of a promotion decided by the authorities of the Republika Srpska.

[145] See Dissenting Opinion of Vice-President Al-Khasawneh in ibid, at para 3.

[146] GP Fletcher and JD Ohlin, *Defending Humanity: When Force is Justified and Why* (New York, OUP, 2008) 194–95. On academic reactions and problematic aspects of this case, see below the following notes and accompanying text: 160–61, 169–72; ch 2 nn 66–70; ch 3 nn 26–27, 46–47, 62; ch 4 n 6; ch 5 nn 175–76, 192–93, 330.

[147] Vice-President Al-Khasawneh's Dissenting Opinion in the *Genocide Case*, above n 143 at para 3.

[148] ibid, at para 35.

[149] ibid, at paras 37–39. Compare this Dissenting Opinion with Judge Brower's vocal dissent in *Short v Islamic Republic of Iran* (1987) 16 Iran-US Claims Tribunal Reports 76 at 93–95, 99, 101 (opining that the Tribunal should have instituted a rebuttable presumption that the departure of US citizens from Iran stemmed from that State's wrongful expulsion, and both lamenting and finding that Khomeini's complete failure to 'quell the expulsive fervor . . . should permit attribution to him of responsibility for the consequences. The fire brigade commander who studiously looks the other way while the arsonist is at work in his midst is no less guilty of the wrong').

[150] See, eg: Report of the International Law Commission on the Work of its Fiftieth Session, UN GAOR, 53rd Sess, Supplement No 10, UN Doc A/53/10 and Corr 1, at para 395.

the "controlling State" had autonomous choices of means and tactics although participating in a common strategy along with the "controlling State" '.[151]

Whilst the majority's reasoning is problematic, perhaps even retrogressive from the perspective of international justice,[152] it erects relatively few conceptual barriers to the intellectual inquiry espoused in this project. Surely, classical interpretations of Article 8 appear inordinately onerous and the Court's reasoning in the *Genocide Case* reinforces the commonly held perception that it will remain extremely reluctant to find a State directly responsible for a wrongful act carried out by (putative) private actors. The purpose of invoking this first scenario, therefore, was to demonstrate how the rule *might* work in theory, namely where State support for private terrorist enterprises is so flagrant that the mechanics of responsibility are easily engaged. However, giving effect to the content of this scheme might prove challenging in practice, especially in light of strong judicial resistance to loosening the requirements of Article 8, the lack of clarity surrounding the notion of 'control'[153] and the refusal to inject context-specific sensibilities when applying attribution rules to the acts of non-State actors. Yet, one positive aspect warranting consideration resides in the Court's inclination to hold Serbia responsible for *failing to prevent* genocide, a posture that can be reconciled with the arguments endorsed in this book. The charge levelled in this context, therefore, is international responsibility based on a *failure to act*, which is easily transposable to counterterrorism obligations as governments' direct liability will be difficult to establish pursuant to the classical rules, save in instances of egregious and overt State involvement in terrorism. Thus, the crux of the intellectual inquiry diverts the mechanics of international responsibility towards a model much more compatible with the judicial pronouncements derived from *Corfu Channel* and exemplified in *Tehran Hostages*.

This overture by the ICJ is rather welcome when contrasted with the Iran-US Claims Tribunal's own jurisprudence, which has repeatedly instituted and applied 'an exacting, if not impossible, standard of proof on claimants wishing

[151] Case No IT-96-21-A *Prosecutor v Delalić*, ICTY Appeals Chamber, 20 February 2001, at para 47. See also: Case No IT-94-1-A *Prosecutor v Tadić*, ICTY Judgment, 15 July 1999, reprinted in (1999) 38 ILM 1518 at para 98. The impact of the *Tadić* decision on the law of State responsibility will be thoroughly explored below, particularly in ch 2, section III. At this juncture, however, a healthy dose of pragmatism is apposite. In particular, it is fair to ponder just how much these ICTY cases actually consecrate a variable standard with regard to ILC Art 8, or whether the ICTY simply disagreed with the ICJ's treatment of the proper non-variable standard.

[152] See, eg: K Mohan, 'Terrorism and Asymmetric Warfare: State Responsibility for the Acts of Non-State Entities – Nicaragua, Tadic, and Beyond' (2008) 8 *Journal of the Institute of Justice and International Studies* 211, 219. But see: A Bianchi, 'The Fight for Inclusion: Non-State Actors and International Law' in U Fastenrath et al (eds), *From Bilateralism to Community Interest: Essays in Honour of Judge Bruno Simma* (Oxford, OUP, 2011) 55 (discussing the *Genocide Case* and expounding that 'when opting for the much more stringent criterion of "effective control" [the ICJ] must have had in mind not only the circumstances of the case, but also the potential application of the criterion to other areas, including State responsibility for terrorist acts').

[153] See below ch 4, section II.A).

to establish State responsibility'.[154] Whilst the Tribunal's jurisprudence is not always consistent,[155] some of its seminal pronouncements clearly couched its conceptual inclination within the furrow of agency principles and have had some impact on other decisional bodies, such as the Eritrea-Ethiopia Claims Commission.[156] In a series of widely cited decisions, the Tribunal has insisted upon a crystal clear relationship of agency in order to attribute the acts of non-State actors to Iran, irrespective of its failure to protect foreigners, its influence on the private conduct or its widespread policy condoning the expulsion of non-nationals and anti-American sentiment.[157] Similar rulings have been handed down in disputes involving wrongful expropriation, with all three Chambers of the Tribunal expressly or impliedly consecrating the principles of attribution and agency as now enshrined in the ILC's *Articles*.[158] Equally problematic is the Tribunal's refusal to ascertain Iran's international responsibility on the basis of its failure to exercise due diligence so as to prevent the wrongful private conduct.[159]

Given these evidentiary impracticalities, it will be argued that the preferred course of action for making governments accountable, in situations of support falling short of direct imputability, will no longer hinge on Article 8 but rather focus on the failure of prevention pursuant to a new indirect responsibility paradigm. It follows that Article 8 seems better suited to govern egregious cases of direct and active support of terrorism, a threshold that if one accepts the *Genocide* ruling on its face, coupled with the *Nicaragua* judgment, remains very difficult to establish even where clear and compelling evidence of the host-State's wrongdoing exists. Thus, it is no surprise that eminent publicists have staunchly criticised the ICJ's formalistic application of attribution principles in

[154] Becker, above n 32 at 47. See also: *Rankin v Islamic Republic of Iran* (1987) 17 Iran-US Claims Tribunal Reports 135 (requiring evidence that specific instructions issued to Iranian revolutionary agents caused the departure and property loss under study, irrespective of the systematic and widespread policy of expulsion of non-nationals that was in place at the time); *Arthur Young & Co v Islamic Republic of Iran* (1987) 17 Iran-US Claims Tribunal Reports 154; *Leach v Islamic Republic of Iran* (1989) 17 Iran-US Claims Tribunal Reports 233.

[155] See DD Caron, 'Attribution amidst Revolution: The Experience of the Iran-United States Claims Tribunal' (1991) 84 *ASIL Proceedings* 51, 65.

[156] In a matter related to constructive expulsion, the Eritrea-Ethiopia Claims Commission opined that the impugned expulsion of Ethiopians by Eritrea failed to satisfy the 'high threshold' instituted by the Iran-US Claims Tribunal. See Civilians Claims, Ethiopia's Claim No 5, 17 December 2004, available at www.pca-cpa.org/upload/files/ET%20Partial%20Award%20Dec%2004.pdf.

[157] See, eg: *Short v Iran*, above n 149 at 85; *William Pereira Associates v Islamic Republic of Iran* (1984) 5 Iran-US Claims Tribunal Reports 198; *Computer Sciences Corp v Islamic Republic of Iran* (1986) 10 Iran-US Claims Tribunal Reports 269; *Leonard and Mavis Daley v Islamic Republic of Iran* (1988) 18 Iran-US Claims Tribunal Reports 232; *Robert Schott v Islamic Republic of Iran* (1990) 24 Iran-US Claims Tribunal Reports 203; *Yeager v Islamic Republic of Iran* (1987) 17 Iran-US Claims Tribunal Reports 92 at 105. But see: G Townsend, 'State Responsibility for Acts of De Facto Agents' (1997) 14 *Arizona Journal of International and Comparative Law* 635, 651.

[158] C Brower and JD Brueschke, *The Iran-United States Claims Tribunal* (The Hague, Nijhoff, 1998) 442–71; A Mouri, *The International Law of Expropriation as Reflected in the Work of the Iran-US Claims Tribunal* (Dordrecht, Nijhoff, 1994) 177–91.

[159] See GA Christenson, 'Attributing Acts of Omission to the State' (1991) 12 *Michigan Journal of International Law* 312, 343.

the *Genocide Case*, which was, arguably, carried out without due regard for intricate evolutionary realities involving a multiplicity of non-State actors operating within a multipolar world.[160] However, the *Genocide Case* nonetheless provides an interesting foundation for the further development of the 'violation of an obligation of prevention – reparation' tandem, along with related evidentiary issues.[161]

C) Scenario 2: Iran-Hezbollah

But let us consider a second example whereby Iran solely provides weaponry and other military support to Hezbollah factions without directing or controlling their terrorist operations. Hence, aside from select financial and military assistance, the terrorist organisation is completely independent from the Iranian governmental apparatus and is endowed with its own, distinct chain of command and hierarchy. Whilst carrying out its operations unbeknownst to Iranian authorities, Hezbollah fires rockets into Israeli territory from its bases of operations in Lebanon and kills civilians.

At the outset, it is apparent that the bases for attributing an internationally wrongful act to the State, as prescribed by the ILC *Articles*,[162] begin to blur. Given the facts above, it becomes more difficult to demonstrate that Hezbollah was acting on the instructions of, or under the direction or control of, the Iranian State. Indeed, leaving aside the conceptually problematic notion of 'control' for a moment, it would appear that mere instructions flowing from the host-State to non-State terrorists would satisfy the threshold of direct State responsibility.[163] However, in the present scenario it becomes rather challenging to prove that Iran exerted that kind of direct influence in the preparation or execution of the attacks. Yet, the fact that it provided weapons and funding to the terrorist organisation undoubtedly constitutes an affront to international

[160] See, eg: A Cassese, 'The Nicaragua and Tadić Tests Revisited in Light of the ICJ Judgment on Genocide in Bosnia' (2007) 18 *EJIL* 649; A Cassese, 'On the Use of Criminal Law Notions in Determining State Responsibility for Genocide' (2007) 5 *Journal of International Criminal Justice* 875; M Milanović, 'State Responsibility for Genocide: A Follow-Up' (2007) 18 *EJIL* 669. See also: C Tosh, 'Genocide Acquittal Provokes Legal Debate', *Institute for War & Peace Reporting*, 4 March 2007, available at http://iwpr.net/report-news/genocide-acquittal-provokes-legal-debate (citing Antonio Cassese, Carole Hodge, Andre De Hoogh, Larissa Van den Herik, Robert Cryer and Johannes Houwink ten Cate).

[161] See, eg: A Gattini, 'Breach of the Obligation to Prevent and Reparation Thereof in the ICJ's Genocide Judgment' (2007) 18 *EJIL* 695; A Abass, 'Proving State Responsibility for Genocide: The ICJ in Bosnia v. Serbia and the International Commission of Inquiry for Darfur' (2008) 31 *Fordham International Law Journal* 871.

[162] See, eg: L Condorelli and C Kress, 'The Rules of Attribution: General Considerations' in Crawford et al, above n 93 at 221–36.

[163] See, eg: A Aust, *Handbook of International Law* (Cambridge, CUP, 2005) 412–13 (declaring that 'a State is responsible for the acts of private groups that carry out, say, terrorist attacks on its instructions'). On the provision of instructions or the capability of the sending States to issue orders directly on the ground to organisations, see *Schering Corp* v *Islamic Republic of Iran* (1984) 5 Iran-US Claims Tribunal Reports 361 at 370.

conscience and decency. Pursuant to the classical rules of agency, however, Iran would effectively evade direct responsibility in the above scenario.

Moreover, this application of the traditional rules remains congruent with classical jurisprudential pronouncements, most notably the ICJ's 1986 decision in the *Nicaragua* Case.[164] In that case, the Court was faced with US support of *Contras* rebels in the context of the armed conflict in Nicaragua.[165] Even though the US had provided various forms of assistance to the guerrillas and the rebels were at some point completely dependent on American support to carry out their operations, the Court ultimately refused to declare that the *Contras* constituted a prolongation of the assisting State.[166] In sum, the Court proclaimed that in those types of scenarios, even if 'preponderant or decisive', US participation 'in the financing, organizing, training, supplying and equipping of the *Contras*, the selection of its military or paramilitary targets, and the planning of the whole of its operation, is still insufficient in itself' to trigger direct State responsibility.[167]

In a broad, sweeping judicial precedent, the Court thereby crafted an onerous standard that would become firmly implanted in State responsibility repertoire: the 'effective control' test.[168] According to this construction, a State must exert effective control over individual actors when they perpetrate internationally wrongful acts for direct responsibility to attach. This standard is now embodied in the aforementioned ILC Article 8 and has, most recently, been applied by the ICJ in the *Genocide Case*.[169] Given, inter alia, the possibility that States can wage surrogate warfare via proxies or elude responsibility through other subterfuges, the inadequacy of this normative scheme has prompted certain scholars to challenge the desirability and relevance of this rule and to call for the adoption of new standards, better suited to the changing circumstances of transnational terrorism.[170] Such inference is undoubtedly exacerbated by modern technological advances – more specifically, the Internet – which are ripe for engaging in indirect aggression via proxies so as to eschew State responsibility and further obfuscate evidentiary matters.[171] In fact, this line of thinking is precisely what animated Vice-President Al-Khasawneh's searing indictment of the majority's application of Article 8 in the ICJ's *Genocide Case*. Quite astutely, he

[164] *Nicaragua*, above n 74.

[165] For more background on this precedent, see TM Franck, *Recourse to Force: State Action against Threats and Armed Attacks* (Cambridge, CUP, 2002) 60–63.

[166] *Nicaragua*, above n 74 at paras 110, 115.

[167] ibid, at para 115.

[168] ibid.

[169] *Genocide Case*, above n 143 at 142–49.

[170] For a variety of views touching upon these points both before and after the ICJ rendered the *Nicaragua* decision, see, eg: Slaughter and Burke-White, above n 14 at 20; Condorelli, above n 61; Y Dinstein, *War, Aggression and Self-Defence*, 3rd edn (Cambridge, CUP, 2001) 182–83; Y Dinstein, 'The International Legal Response to Terrorism' in R Ago (ed), *International Law at the Time of Its Codification: Essays in Honour of Roberto Ago (Vol II)* (Milan, Giuffrè, 1987) 139 at 140, 142.

[171] See, eg: SJ Shackelford, 'From Nuclear War to Net War: Analogizing Cyber Attacks in International Law' (2008) 27 *Berkeley Journal of International Law* 191, 232.

voiced a real concern for the fact that 'The inherent danger in such an approach is that it gives States the opportunity to carry out criminal policies through non-state actors or surrogates without incurring direct responsibility therefore'.[172]

This is certainly one possible interpretation of Iran's use of Hezbollah factions in order to fulfil specific missions against Israel, albeit through somewhat veiled structures.[173] When considering that Iran arms, trains and funds such units, whilst also selecting some of their military targets and outlining their missions, it is imperative to ponder whether the *Nicaragua* precedent is adequate to govern the analysis or whether any sort of State assistance to terrorists falling short of the very stringent standard developed in that jurisprudence automatically precludes the application of direct State responsibility. The same line of inquiry undoubtedly extends to past Syrian sponsorship of Palestinian terrorist factions, another arrangement signalling a subsidising State's reliance on covert agents or proxy organisations to carry out excursions with a view to eschewing the consequences of an all-out armed conflict and the application of State responsibility.[174] Lebanon's role in providing a safe haven to Hezbollah factions in the southern portion of its territory in order to better strike Israeli civilians also presents a singularly challenging legal scenario. Allowing Lebanon to elude international responsibility because it does not control the extremist elements found within its borders – yet still provides them with territorial sanctuary – appears to run counter to the fight against impunity and, for all intents and purposes, eviscerates the law of State responsibility of any practical force and utility. In fact, some scholars resoundingly reject the absence of State 'control' of irregular factions as a basis for disabling the application of State responsibility, thereby indicating that new rules are direly required.[175] For present purposes, when transposing the *Nicaragua* precedent to counterterrorism, it 'communicates the message that the I.C.J. will hold few States accountable for supporting or acquiescing to terrorist activity'.[176]

The shortcomings of Article 8 come into sharp relief when considering complex factual patterns – or, perhaps more accurately, factually tenuous scenarios for the purposes of triggering State responsibility – such as the relationship between Lebanon and Hezbollah factions operating in the southern portion of its territory. Whilst discussing the scope of this provision, one commentator underscores that

> Hezbollah's inclusion in the Lebanese government, considered in light of Nasrallah's control over both the organization's political and military wings, is relevant in this

[172] Vice-President Al-Khasawneh's Dissenting Opinion in the *Genocide Case*, above n 143 at para 39.

[173] See, eg: KA Petty, 'Veiled Impunity: Iran's Use of Non-State Armed Groups' (2008) 36 *Denver Journal of International Law and Policy* 191.

[174] See, eg: G Rose and D Nestorovska, 'Towards an ASEAN Counter-Terrorism Treaty' (2005) 9 *Singapore Year Book of International Law* 157, 165.

[175] See, eg: Kranz, above n 95 at 81–82.

[176] AD Sofaer, 'The Sixth Annual Waldemar A. Solf Lecture in International Law: Terrorism, the Law, and the National Defense' (1989) 126 *Military Law Review* 89, 101.

regard. Yet, there is no evidence that the Hezbollah parliamentarians or cabinet members directed or were otherwise involved in the attacks, or that the Lebanese government controlled the organization, either directly or indirectly. Neither could Hezbollah be fairly characterized as 'an organ placed at the disposal of a State by another State' or an entity that 'exercised elements of the governmental authority in the absence or default of the official authorities and in circumstances such as to call for the exercise of those elements of authority' pursuant to Articles 6 and 9, respectively. The organization did not qualify as an 'organ' in the meaning of the former, nor was the situation in southern Lebanon of the nature envisioned by the latter.[177]

D) Scenario 3: Lebanon-Hezbollah (in the Shadows of Iran and Syria's Involvement)

Let us complicate the equation further with a third scenario. In the Iran-Hezbollah situation, it must be recalled that the terrorist organisation was planning and carrying out its attacks from its bases of operations located in the southern portion of Lebanon. Publicly available facts demonstrate that Lebanon at best provided Hezbollah with logistical support, granting it access to bases of operations and training camps on its territory. Upon first glance, this scenario poses considerable challenges to the classical rules formulated under the law of State responsibility. As one commentator notes, 'Controversy and uncertainty arises (heightened post 9/11) as to whether lesser forms of involvement, such as support, "harbouring", encouragement or even passive acquiescence in wrongs is sufficient to render the acts of criminal organizations attributable to the state'.[178] When contemplating both Iran's and Syria's involvement in these operations, the 2006 conflict between Israel and Hezbollah factions situated in southern Lebanon constitutes a salient example of States waging surrogate warfare through a terrorist organisation – a structure presumably aimed at eschewing legal responsibility, inter alia. Although Hezbollah struck civilian and military targets deep inside Israel, clear and compelling evidence indicated that both Syria and Iran were effectively funding, training and arming Hezbollah. On the last day of the war, catalysed by a precarious cease-fire induced by Security Council resolution 1701,[179] 246 rockets were nonetheless launched into Israel.[180]

Manifestly, it would have been impossible for Hezbollah to pursue its military campaign but for such assistance. Therefore, a rather straightforward case of

[177] MN Schmitt, '"Change Direction" 2006: Israeli Operations in Lebanon and the International Law of Self-Defense' (2008) 29 *Michigan Journal of International Law* 127, 141–42. See also: M Pathak, 'Maritime Violence: Piracy at Sea & Marine Terrorism Today' (2005) 20 *Windsor Review of Legal and Social Issues* 65, 77 (expounding that 'This standard [that Art 8 promulgates that there must be a factual link between the de facto agent and the State] appears to have steadily eroded by the *Tadic* Case and the global war on terrorism').

[178] Duffy, above n 40 at 49.

[179] SC Res 1701 of 11 August, UN Doc S/RES/1701 (2006).

[180] See 'Nasrallah Wins the War', *The Economist*, 19–25 August 2006 at 9.

direct State responsibility can arguably be ventured against Syria and Iran for past and future Hezbollah attacks, subject to the caveats usually associated with *Nicaragua*'s onerous burden of attribution (and the related thresholds of 'control' and interdependency that must be met when analysing the relationship between supporting States and terrorists). Indeed, since the end of the Cold War both Iran and Syria have been active and direct sponsors of terrorist enterprises.[181] Such claim of direct involvement would be predicated on aforementioned Article 8 and, potentially, on Article 4, which provides:

> *Conduct of organs of a State*
>
> 1. The conduct of any State organ shall be considered an act of that State under international law, whether the organ exercises legislative, executive, judicial or any other functions, whatever position it holds in the organization of the State, and whatever its character as an organ of the central Government or of a territorial unit of the State.
> 2. An organ includes any person or entity which has that status in accordance with the internal law of the State.[182]

Conversely, a claim of indirect responsibility can be levelled against Lebanon for allowing terrorist factions to operate within its territory (a more direct accusation could be alleged against it, should one accept the argument that Hezbollah has been subsumed under Lebanon's official State apparatus).[183] In fact, this latter argument has acquired credence in some academic circles, with some commentators opining that 'under the rules of international state responsibility Hezbollah's acts can be attributed to the state of Lebanon'.[184] However, establishing a relationship of 'effective control' between the Lebanese State and Hezbollah factions would prove rather challenging if contemplated through the prism of the traditional legal rules governing attribution. Such linkage between the host-State and non-State actors in allocating blame for an internationally wrongful act – in this case embodied in Lebanon's failure to prevent transnational terrorism – is best determined as a result of that State's tacit or passive acquiescence to terrorists on its territory (ie the 'harbouring and supporting' rule) or, alternatively, of its unwillingness or inability to thwart terrorist

[181] See, eg: AK Cronin, 'The Role of Modern States in the Decline and Demise of Terrorism' in A Bianchi and A Keller (eds), *Counterterrorism: Democracy's Challenge* (Oxford, Hart Publishing, 2008) 93 at 96–97.

[182] *Articles*, above n 77.

[183] For an application of this reasoning, along with a review of the history of Hezbollah and of the 2006 conflict, see S Kirchner, 'Third Party Liability for Hezbollah Attacks against Israel' (2006) 7 *German Law Journal* 777, 783.

[184] A Skordas, 'Hegemonic Intervention as Legitimate Use of Force' (2007) 16 *Minnesota Journal of International Law* 407, 442. For accounts confirming that Hezbollah was subsumed under the State apparatus, along with the influence it wields on Lebanon, see D Byman, 'Should Hezbollah Be Next?' (2003) 82 *Foreign Affairs* 54; D Byman, 'Hezbollah's Dilemma', *Foreign Affairs*, 13 April 2005 (author's update), available at www.foreignaffairs.com/articles/64234/daniel-byman/hezbollahs-dilemma; J Slomich, 'The Ta'if Accord: Legalizing the Syrian Occupation of Lebanon' (1998–99) 22 *Suffolk Transnational Law Review* 619, 633.

threats.[185] Thus, with the responsibility of both Iran and Syria being difficult to establish under classical rules of attribution, especially in light of the ICJ's decision in the *Genocide Case*, the study's principal focal point will be to elucidate State responsibility in cases analogous to that of Lebanon. With particular emphasis on *Corfu Channel*, the main argument herein operates on the premise that States have a primary obligation to control their national territory. Indirect modes of State responsibility are thus required to respond to vaguer types of governmental inaction that stray away from the Afghanistan-Al Qaeda model; indeed, more challenging cases arise when governments perpetrate due diligence failures falling short of 'supporting and harbouring' (eg Canada fails to prevent LTTE from raising funds on its territory), which, in turn, intertwine with other legal norms such as freedom of expression (ie what are the legal limits of LTTE's freedom of speech activities in Canada?). The best way to deploy models of indirect responsibility, therefore, is to acknowledge that the territorial dimension underpinning the relationship between terrorists and their host-States not only significantly affects the equation, but remains a catalyst in engaging that very responsibility (ie terrorists almost invariably operate out of a given territorial State).[186] Simply put, Lebanon was in an altogether different position when compared to Syria and Iran: not only was it better situated to comply with counterterrorism obligations – just like Albania was in a better position to control its national territory in *Corfu Channel* – but it also had to uphold IHL in this specific context.

However, some measure of political realism seems apposite here, as this type of scenario should ineluctably prompt the question whether Lebanon is actually in a position to *effectively* thwart the threat. The Lebanese model is far removed from the reality prevalent in Canada, for instance, where there is strict control over both the territory and terrorist activities taking root therein. As a result, government action against home-grown terrorism – fuelled by more significant resources – is far more effective under this latter structure. Conversely, in Lebanon the situations involving terrorism fall within what could be considered a greyer area. Indeed, much of southern Lebanon still eludes effective governmental control, thereby serving as an incubator for terrorist factions to exploit what are essentially, from a pragmatic standpoint, ungoverned spaces.[187] Consequently,

[185] For a preliminary discussion of these issues, see MJB Bottoms, 'When Close Doesn't Count: An Analysis of Israel's Jus Ad Bellum and Jus in Bello in the 2006 Israel-Lebanon War' (2009) *April Army Lawyer* 23, 48–50.

[186] See, eg: MC Waxman, 'The Structure of Terrorism Threats and the Laws of War' (2010) 20 *Duke Journal of Comparative & International Law* 101, 112. For a recent study on the role of territory in triggering State responsibility, see PD Szigeti, 'Territorial Bias in International Law: Attribution in State and Corporate Responsibility' (2010) 19 *Journal of Transnational Law and Policy* 311.

[187] See, eg: H Rishikof, 'Long Wars of Political Order – Sovereignty and Choice: The Fourth Amendment and the Modern Trilemma' (2006) 15 *Cornell Journal of Law and Public Policy* 587, 618 (underscoring that 'ungoverned spaces . . . provide succor for international terrorism'). See also: JG Dalton, 'The United States National Security Strategy: Yesterday, Today, and Tomorrow' (2005) 52 *Naval Law Review* 60, 62.

this type of structure adds an extra layer of complexity to the project of elucidating State responsibility for failing to prevent transborder terrorist excursions. In short, when no effective governmental control over both territory and/or terrorists can materialise, the host-State's lack of capacity to intervene will obfuscate the analysis. As a corollary, the very notion of counterterrorism capacity will also significantly affect the deployment of secondary rules of international responsibility, most notably when ineffective or 'failed' States are implicated.[188] Ultimately, it is difficult to categorically pronounce on such situations in the abstract given the factually dense nature of determining governmental involvement in terrorism and, from a more indirect perspective, of establishing State failures in preventing wrongful private conduct that they *could/should* have thwarted. In the hopes of somewhat mitigating those analytical pitfalls, a context-sensitive and factually-based policy inquiry will be espoused.[189]

Coming back to the above fact pattern, in the very unlikely and tenuous scenario that Lebanon was found to be complicit with Iran and/or Syria in waging aggression against Israel through Hezbollah factions, Lebanese responsibility could also be triggered through the doctrine of complicity, pursuant to Article 16 of the *ILC Articles on State Responsibility*.[190] That provision reads as follows:

> *Aid or assistance in the commission of an internationally wrongful act*
>
> A State which aids or assists another State in the commission of an internationally wrongful act by the latter is internationally responsible for doing so if:
>
> (a) that State does so with knowledge of the circumstances of the internationally wrongful act; and
>
> (b) the act would be internationally wrongful if committed by that State.[191]

[188] See, eg: below ch 5, section II.B).

[189] See below ch 5, section IV.

[190] See, eg: N Ronzitti, 'Italy's Non-Belligerency during the Iraqi War' in Ragazzi, above n 21 at 197, 205.

[191] *Articles*, above n 77. The notion of complicity, as embodied in ILC Art 16, was addressed by the German Federal Constitutional Court in a decision granting extradition of a Yemeni national to the US. German officials had arrested the individual pursuant to a warrant issued by the US District Court for the Eastern District of New York, after American authorities charged the individual with having provided financial assistance to, and having recruited members for, terrorist groups (particularly Al Qaeada and Hamas). The complainant travelled to Germany on the basis of discussions with a Yemeni citizen who was part of a covert operation led by US authorities aiming to extradite him. Since unlawful behaviour by the US would trigger its international responsibility vis-à-vis Yemen, 'there would be the risk that by extraditing the complainant, Germany would support a United States' action that is possibly contrary to international law, which would make Germany itself responsible under international law *vis-à-vis* Yemen'. See Al-M, Individual Constitutional Complaint Procedure, Bundesverfassungsgericht, 2 BvR 1506/03, Federal Constitutional Court, 5 November 2003, 109 *Entscheidungen des Bundesverfassungsgerichts* 13, at para 47, *International Law in Domestic Courts* 10 (DE 2003); 'Report of the Secretary-General on Responsibility of States for Internationally Wrongful Acts', 62nd Sess, 9 March, UN Doc A/62/63 (2007) at 12, paras 23–26. Whilst the Court ultimately allowed the extradition, it made explicit reference to ILC Art 16. For further discussion of the case, see also: A Nollkaemper, 'Internationally Wrongful Acts in Domestic Courts' (2007) 101 *AJIL* 760, 762, 779–80; T Schweisfurth, 'The International Law Commission's Articles on State Responsibility and the German Federal Constitutional Court' in Fastenrath et al, above n 152 at 1300–01.

Ultimately, it remains improbable that these scenarios could be governed by the long-established rules on attribution. In order to engage the responsibility of both Lebanon and Iran, one would have to either accept a relaxation of attribution standards or entertain the possibility that a new rule of State responsibility has emerged since the *Nicaragua* Case. A case will be made on both grounds throughout this study. On one hand, contemporary events have significantly challenged, if not loosened, the rules of attribution and, on the other, a new paradigm shift can be identified towards a more expansive rule of indirect responsibility, better suited to tackle non-traditional State sponsorship or toleration of terrorism. At the outset, the facts underlying the *Nicaragua* Case can be analogised to terrorism, even though it technically dealt with State-sponsored guerrilla warfare. Whilst those rapprochements are inevitably possible and instructive for the purposes of the present volume, it is likely that new legal standards are also being shaped by modern events so as to better adapt to the threats of transnational terrorist activity. Building on this inference, commentators argue that *Nicaragua*'s 'effective control' test has been overridden by those recent events.[192] Not to mention that in *Nicaragua*, the *Contras*' insurgency was not itself an international crime, thereby making some parallels with the Iran/Syria/Lebanon-Hezbollah relationships challenging. This is not to say, however, that *Nicaragua* does not apply to terrorism, but rather that its rationale might be tempered in certain circumstances. With this in mind, the present project will place more emphasis on the *Corfu Channel* decision when engaging potential legal responses to transnational terrorism, as territorial sovereignty radically alters the nature of the debate and further distances it from the facts of *Nicaragua*. As a corollary, the crux of the arguments to follow will be premised on the existence of a primary obligation of States to control their national territory. This last scenario thus brings us squarely to those relevant events that have significantly challenged the law of State responsibility.

E) Scenario 4: Afghanistan-Al Qaeda

Similarly to the Lebanon-Hezbollah scenario invoked above, the Afghanistan-Al Qaeda precedent arguably legitimises the emergence of a new rule of State responsibility. More specifically, it appears that the international response to 9/11 has, for all intents and purposes, disabled the effective control test and the

[192] eg, Travalio and Altenburg expound that 'the rules regarding the imputation of state responsibility for terrorist attacks have evolved since the Nicaragua and Iran Hostages Cases'. See G Travalio and J Altenburg, 'Terrorism, State Responsibility, and the Use of Military Force' (2003) 4 *Chicago Journal of International Law* 97, 110 (arguing that 'these two cases should be confined to their facts and are not applicable to transnational terrorist groups who threaten previously unimagined destruction'). ibid, at 105. See also: Slaughter and Burke-White, above n 14 at 20; P Margulies, 'When to Push the Envelope: Legal Ethics, the Rule of Law, and National Security Strategy' (2007) 30 *Fordham International Law Journal* 642, 647 fn 21 (suggesting that a 'broader standard is appropriate to encourage State diligence').

Nicaragua precedent, at least in cases of State-supported or State-tolerated terrorism.[193]

Prior to 9/11, Afghanistan volunteered no direct support to the Al-Qaeda network, rather providing it with limited logistical support, such as access to training camps and bases of operation on its territory. As discussed in chapter two, we are no longer confronted with the classical paradigm of direct State involvement in terrorism, whereby the analysis hinged on the internationally wrongful act itself (namely the terrorist attack), perpetrated by non-State actors but nonetheless attributable to the host-State because of its complicity or participation in the chain of events. This last scenario rather falls under the rubric of indirect State involvement in terrorism and centres on the sanctuary State's actual wrongful conduct, be it synonymous with negligence vis-à-vis prevention or with a failure to comply with its due diligence obligations.

This study argues that this evolution towards indirect State responsibility for terrorism remains consonant with recent Security Council practice, which almost invariably conflates the obligation of prevention with the duty of all States to refrain from supporting or harbouring terrorists on their territory. More importantly, this formula appears to better reflect modern reality with respect to State support of terrorism, except in clear-cut cases of direct involvement (eg Iran, Libya and Syria). When applying this rationale to Afghanistan before 9/11, a model of indirect State responsibility corresponds: publicly available facts reveal that the government of Afghanistan, at best, provided logistical support to Al-Qaeda without directly participating in the planning or execution of the 9/11 attacks. Quite to the contrary, the public record demonstrates that Al-Qaeda acted autonomously within Afghan territory.[194]

In the future, whenever a terrorist strike is launched from, or organised on, a State's territory, the international community might very well examine what means that State could have employed to prevent the excursion. Thus, the focus of the inquiry now shifts to questions of governmental inaction when there was a positive duty to intervene, be it motivated by complacency, negligence or wilful blindness. In advocating possible models of responsibility to counteract terrorism, significant emphasis will be placed on the assertion, now apparent from the foregoing, that the ILC's *Articles* were drafted with a more traditional direct State involvement nexus with non-State actors in mind, particularly given their insistence on the notions of control and interdependency.[195]

[193] See, eg: C Stahn, 'Terrorist Acts As "Armed Attack": The Right to Self-Defense, Article 51 (1/2) of the UN Charter, and International Terrorism' (2003) 27 *Fletcher Forum of World Affairs* 35, 37. See also: C Stahn, '"Nicaragua is Dead, Long Live Nicaragua": The Right to Self-Defense under Art. 51 UN Charter and International Terrorism' in C Walter et al (eds), *Terrorism as a Challenge for National and International Law: Security Versus Liberty?* (Berlin, Springer, 2004) 827; R Wolfrum, 'The Attack of September 11, 2001, the Wars against the Taliban and Iraq: Is There a Need to Reconsider International Law on the Recourse to Force and the Rules in Armed Conflict?' (2003) 7 *Max Planck Yearbook of United Nations Law* 1.

[194] See, eg: Brown, above n 59 at 11.

[195] In all likelihood, this model could fit within what Tal Becker has labelled the traditional 'agency paradigm'. See, generally: Becker, above n 32.

V. ADAPTING THE LAW OF STATE RESPONSIBILITY TO COUNTERTERRORISM

In light of the foregoing, compelling academic and non-academic calls have been issued to overhaul certain rules of international responsibility. This project strives to answer those calls and help remedy the conceptual dearth. One possible solution is to envisage the ILC's *Articles* as a contextual tool – part codified customary law, part evolutionary vehicle – capable of adapting to modern and contemporaneous realities. Even if critical observations or revisions to the *Articles* are put forth, one hopes that their current structure can provide for some level of integration of those criticisms without resorting to new codification. As a result, their application and development should reflect those challenges that are ultimately espoused.[196] This project seeks to advance such challenges, especially with regard to the rules of attribution and Article 8.[197]

In this regard, Dupuy's prophetic words should be taken into account as a quintessential preface to this work. Specifically referring to Article 8, he notes:

> This formulation leaves much room for interpretation. In particular, it is not quite clear whether 'acting on the instructions' of a State is considered by the ILC as being exactly on the same level as being 'under the direction or control' of the State. This ambiguity was most probably left purposely in order to maintain some flexibility for different possible interpretations.[198]

Subsequent pages will heed that invitation and attempt to shed greater light on politically desirable and more efficient rules of State responsibility, so as to better contribute to making the 'war' on terror a preventive rather than curative effort.[199] Not only is this legal exploration welcome from the perspective of international law, it also carries with it significant policy implications, both from domestic and international standpoints.

VI. POLICY RELEVANCE

Vital to the project at hand is the objective of promoting transnational cooperation on counterterrorism policy, which ineluctably entails a strong focus on intelligence-gathering and intelligence-sharing.[200] Vigilant law enforcement and intelligence-sharing are both crucial to an effective counterterrorism campaign not only on a national level (ie between sub-national agencies) but also on a

[196] See, eg: C Yamada, 'Revisiting the International Law Commission's Draft Articles on State Responsibility' in Ragazzi, above n 21 at 118.

[197] For the text of ILC Art 8, see above n 140 and accompanying text.

[198] Dupuy, above n 112 at 10.

[199] But see: MMD Banks, 'Addressing State (Ir-)Responsibility: The Use of Military Force as Self-Defense in International Counter-Terrorism Operations' (2009) 200 *Military Law Review* 54, 57.

[200] See generally: P Romaniuk, *Multilateral Counter-terrorism: The Global Politics of Cooperation and Contestation* (London, Routledge, 2010).

transnational level. For instance, intelligence-sharing networks and exchanges between Canada and the US after 9/11 offer a rich and oftentimes divergent record, a topic that has featured prominently in certain policy communities' research dialogue.[201] As noted in those communities' programme of research, those States' respective perceptions of the risks and threats involved in fighting terrorism have also been, at times, divergent.[202] More importantly, there is no doubt that States' perception and reaction to the perceived risk of domestic and transnational terrorism will have a considerable impact not only on the formulation of their own policies, but also on their observance of international counterterrorism obligations and adherence to Security Council resolutions. This type of inquiry foreshadows both the notion of risk assessment – which pervades the present project – and the utility of the environmental sector when drawing policy-based analogies with the State responsibility/terrorism research agenda.[203]

In short, States' compliance with international legal undertakings hinges, to a large extent, on the ways in which domestic policies and reactions mirror some degree of commitment to those international obligations. A case in point, illustrating the practical and policy effects of Security Council engagement in counterterrorism issues, resides in the Council's handing down of economic sanctions targeting individuals suspected of entertaining links with Al Qaeda and the Taliban.[204] On one hand, concerned States must certainly take stock of these important legal prescriptions in order to ensure that they meet their international obligations. At the same time, however, States implementing those international policies must also ensure that they do not conflict with other equally important human rights undertakings.[205] This policy quest undoubtedly starts with a healthy horizontal dialogue at a sub-national level (eg law enforcement cooperation between Montreal and Toronto), at a bilateral level (eg Canada-US),

[201] See, eg: RD Henderson and F Hitz, 'One Issue, Two Voices: Intelligence Sharing between Canada and the United States: A Matter of National Survival', The Canada Institute, *Woodrow Wilson International Center for Scholars* (2007), available at www.wilsoncenter.org/sites/default/files/Canada_6.pdf.

[202] See, eg: K Bowman and F Graves, 'One Issue, Two Voices: Threat Perceptions in the United States and Canada: Assessing the Public's Attitudes toward Security and Risk in North America', The Canada Institute, *Woodrow Wilson International Center for Scholars* (2005), available at www.wilsoncenter.org/topics/pubs/threats.pdf.

[203] See, eg: J Barboza, *The Environment, Risk and Liability in International Law* (Leiden, Nijhoff, 2011).

[204] See the following Security Council resolutions: 1267 of 15 October 1999; 1333 of 19 December 2000; 1363 of 30 July 2001; 1388 of 15 January 2002; 1390 of 16 January 2002; 1452 of 20 December 2002; 1455 of 17 January 2003; 1456 of 20 January 2003; 1526 of 30 January 2004; 1617 of 29 July 2005; 1699 of 8 August 2006; 1730 of 19 December 2006; 1732 of 21 December 2006; 1735 of 22 December 2006.

[205] See, eg: Joined Cases C-402/05P and C-415/05P *Yassin Abdullah Kadi and Al Barakaat International Foundation v Council and Commission*, European Court of Justice, 3 September 2008, [2008] ECR I-6341, (2008) 47 ILM 923 (invalidating a regulation promulgated by the Council of the EU targeting specific individuals by virtue of UN Security Council resolutions and, therefore, arrogating power to review and control such powers and the resolutions of the Security Council, albeit indirectly).

at a regional level (eg European Union) and, finally, at a truly transnational level.

In that regard, the Canadian government recently took the lead by adopting rhetorically cautious but legally superfluous legislation dealing with holding States accountable for harbouring terrorists. The newly-enacted Justice for Victims of Terrorism Act proposes removing State immunity for those States that the Canadian government deems 'supporters of terrorism', thereby amending the State Immunity Act and effectively creating a mechanism to sue both terrorist organisations and foreign States for acts of terrorism.[206] Whilst the introduction of this legislation may legitimately be construed as a 'political ploy' – as it could cogently be argued that similar mechanisms are already at the disposal of victims of transnational terror – this legislative scheme nonetheless propels the issue of State responsibility to the forefront of post-9/11 legal and political debate.[207] Indeed, it strikes at the core of the primary inquiry of the present study: holding States responsible for failing to prevent terrorism. Under this legislative scheme, State funding of terrorism and more passive types of State involvement might be sufficient to trigger the application of the Act and justify litigation against responsible States.[208] This development will have significant implications for the paradigm shift towards indirect responsibility advocated in chapter two, along with the modulated content of the obligation of prevention explored in chapter five.

More importantly, these foregoing policy concerns should always be contemplated as a preliminary gloss through which the present account should be read.

[206] See *Justice for Victims of Terrorism Act*, SC 2012, c 1. For more background on this legislation prior to its enactment, see, eg, J Stoyles, 'State Immunity and Canadian Law, in Light of Proposed Amendments for Torture and Terrorism' (2011) *Journal of Parliamentary and Political Law* 227, 233–34; G Galloway, 'Van Loan Details Terror-victim Bill', *The Globe and Mail*, 2 June 2009. Similarly, there is ongoing litigation in the US involving civilians attempting to recoup damages against the PLO for terrorist attacks carried out in Israel. See, eg: D Wise, 'Effort to Collect $116 Million from PLO May Go to Trial', *New York Law Journal*, 15 May 2008.

[207] For trenchant criticism of this legislation voiced before its adoption, see René Provost's commentary in G Galloway, 'Terror-victim Law Would Only Apply to Listed Countries', *The Globe and Mail*, 8 June 2009; G Galloway, 'Canada Hurt by Anti-Terror 'Diversion' Law', *The Star Phoenix*, 4 June 2009. Absolutely crucial to the discussion found in subsequent pages is Provost's assertion that one of the major problems associated with this legislation 'would be to attribute an act of terror to a foreign government'. In fact, attribution of internationally wrongful acts to host-States will remain a central point of analysis throughout the present project, and will be thoroughly explored below in Part II. See also: D Quayat et al, 'Victims of Terrorism: Compensation Legislation Likely Ineffective', *The Lawyers Weekly*, 21 October 2011 at 10–11.

[208] This type of rationale has failed to acquire traction in other judicial jurisdictions, particularly in France. On 9 March 2011, the *première chambre civile* of the Court of Cassation granted jurisdictional immunity to Libya given that it could not attribute a specific terrorist attack to the Libyan State. Libya was not accused of having directly sponsored or orchestrated the terrorist attack on a UTA DC-10 aeroplane, which exploded on 19 September 1989 over the Ténéré desert in Niger, thereby killing its passengers. Rather, Libya was accused of having failed to prosecute the culprits, to disavow the impugned terrorist acts and to refrain from supporting the unlawful behaviour. See Case of Cour de cassation, 9 March 2011 (case Cour de cassation, Chambre civile 1, 9 March 2011, 09-14.743, publié au *Bulletin*), available at www.legifrance.gouv.fr/affichJuriJudi.do?oldAction=rechExpJuriJudi&idTexte=JURITEXT000023694014&fastReqId=1867849044&fastPos=1.

With this initial direction now conveyed, the study now turns to the precise and central objective of determining what role State responsibility can play in the prevention and suppression of transnational terrorism. In so doing, the next chapter explores the post-9/11 paradigm shift towards a law of indirect State responsibility.

2

The Impact of 9/11 on International Law and Beyond[1]

If you harbor terrorists, you are terrorists. If you train or arm a terrorist, you are a terrorist. If you feed a terrorist or fund a terrorist, you're a terrorist, and you will be held accountable by the United States and our friends.

– President George W Bush[2]

I. GENERAL REMARKS

OF ALL THE challenges facing the international community, the role of State responsibility is certainly a source for concern. It has been described as the 'most ambitious and most difficult topic of the codification work of the International Law Commission'.[3] This problem is further compounded when secondary norms are applied in order to hold governments accountable for failing to prevent terrorist acts. Even if one assumes that relevant primary counterterrorism obligations are adequately circumscribed, the task of triggering and deploying State responsibility in practice remains 'hotly contested' and subject to political whims, factual idiosyncrasy and, often,

[1] Some of the premises of what follows considerably expand on the remarks found in V-J Proulx, 'Babysitting Terrorists: Should States Be Strictly Liable for Failing to Prevent Transborder Attacks?' (2005) 23 *Berkeley Journal of International Law* 615, reprinted in SR Silverburg (ed), *International Law: Contemporary Issues and Future Developments* (Boulder, Westview Press, 2011) ch 19.

[2] JA Cohan, 'Formulation of a State's Response to Terrorism and State-Sponsored Terrorism' (2002) 14 *Pace International Law Review* 77, 93 (quoting E Bumiller, 'Bush Says War May Go Beyond Afghan Border', *New York Times*, 22 November 2001 at B2).

[3] P Malanczuk, *Akehurst's Modern Introduction to International Law*, 7th rev edn (London, Routledge, 1997) 254. See also: R Higgins, *Problems & Process: International Law and How We Use It* (Oxford, OUP, 1994) 148 (speaking to the inherent difficulty in codification); R Provost, 'Introduction' in R Provost (ed), *State Responsibility in International Law* (Aldershot, Ashgate/Dartmouth, 2002) xii (underscoring the ILC's difficulties in reaching a consensus on the rules to be codified, and stating that 'the diversity of opinions within the Commission mirrors the many real substantial uncertainties which characterize this field of international law'). On private codification initiatives, see L Laithier, 'Private Codification Efforts' in JR Crawford et al (eds), *The Law of International Responsibility* (Oxford, OUP, 2010) 53.

concealment of the relevant constitutive acts from public view.[4] Thus, the true challenge in elucidating the law of State responsibility for fact-specific and transnational phenomena lies in devising appropriate and practicable legal consequences to internationally wrongful acts.[5] In that regard, contemporaneous events shed light on the parameters governing the law of State responsibility, be they the 1968 Beirut raid or the response to Afghanistan's failure to prevent terrorism in 2001. Given the state of modern warfare and ideology-motivated violence,[6] such episodes pose considerable challenges to the law of State responsibility and, more broadly, to the project of better integrating non-State actors within international legal frameworks.

The events surrounding 9/11 significantly challenged existing law, a phrase that is now considered cliché, but nonetheless true with regard to international law and, more specifically, State responsibility.[7] Many factors now extend the debate beyond simply assigning blame to negligent or 'wilfully blind' governments. Whether obscured by intricate information networks, new technologies like the Internet, the sophisticated cellular structure of organisations like Al Qaeda, complex financial systems, convoluted political realities, or other factors, the level of governmental involvement in terrorist activities is no longer readily discernible in many instances.[8] We now live in an era dominated by security concerns with some scholars calling for a revamping or, at least, a reassessment of the parameters of State responsibility vis-à-vis terrorism so as to incentivise governments to comply with counterterrorism obligations and promote transnational cooperation.[9] Furthermore, it is common knowledge that

[4] See, eg: T Becker, *Terrorism and the State: Rethinking the Rules of State Responsibility* (Oxford, Hart Publishing, 2006) 150–51.

[5] Further exploration of this topic is found below in ch 5, section IV.C).

[6] On the fundamentals of new terrorism and modern warfare, generally, see M Lippman, 'The New Terrorism and International Law' (2003) 10 *Tulsa Journal of Comparative and International Law* 297; LP Pojman, 'The Moral Response to Terrorism and Cosmopolitanism' in JP Sterba (ed), *Terrorism and International Justice* (New York, OUP, 2003) 135 at 138–41.

[7] Several commentators generally conclude that US-led military action in Afghanistan fundamentally challenged international law. See, eg: RA Falk, 'Rediscovering International Law after September 11th' (2002) 16 *Temple International & Comparative Law Journal* 359; C Gray, 'A New War for a New Century?: The Use of Force against Terrorism After September 11, 2001' in P Eden and T O'Donnell (eds), *September 11, 2001: A Turning Point in International and Domestic Law* (Ardsley, Transnational Publishers, 2005) 97; LR Helfer, 'Transforming International Law After the September 11 Attacks?: Three Evolving Paradigms for Regulating International Terrorism' in ML Dudziak (ed), *September 11 in History: A Watershed Moment?* (Durham, Duke University Press, 2003) 180; JF Murphy, 'International Law and the War on Terrorism: The Road Ahead' (2003) 32 *Israel Yearbook on Human Rights* 117.

[8] See, eg: RP Barnidge, Jr, *Non-State Actors and Terrorism: Applying the Law of State Responsibility and the Due Diligence Principle* (The Hague, TMC Asser Press, 2008) 153–54, 154 fn 84.

[9] For a discussion of the omnipresence of security concerns in post-9/11 legal policy and more generally, see J Brunnée and SJ Toope, 'Canada and the Use of Force: Reclaiming Human Security' (2004) 59 *International Journal* 247, 248, 249, 258–60; F Mégret, '"War"? Legal Semantics and the Move to Violence' (2002) 13 *EJIL* 361, 367–68. See also generally: R Barnidge, Jr, 'Should National Security Trump Human Rights in the Fight against Terrorism?' (2007) 37 *Israel Yearbook on Human Rights* 85.

certain States are used as frequent launch pads or training grounds for terrorist organisations. However, we must avoid attributing responsibility to those States indiscriminately and rather engage in a serious and methodical analysis of the conduct of the governments involved.

Of particular importance are the jurisprudential developments that have occurred over the last 70+ years. As discussed above, one might invoke the *Nicaragua* decision – a precedent (arguably) subsequently tempered by the *Tadić* judgment – which contributed significantly to the law and the evolution of the academic discussion.[10] More relevantly, the *Corfu Channel* and *Tehran Hostages* cases are also immensely instrumental in this area and, in many ways, respectively mark the starting point and confirmation of the modern concept of indirect State responsibility.[11] Since the 1960s and 1970s, many terrorist attacks punctuated our collective history and stirred the discussion, be they the 1982 Israel-Lebanon conflict or the 1998 bombing of US embassies in Africa. Some of these accounts must be revisited to shed light on the level of responsibility of the States involved, so as to determine whether a shift in accountability mechanisms is acquiring traction in international legal circles.

In 2001, the ILC adopted its *Articles on State Responsibility*, a monumental piece of the legal mosaic on State responsibility.[12] The same year, unprecedented attacks were carried out on US soil by Al Qaeda terrorists, events that are remembered as '9/11'. Following 9/11, the US and its allies staged a military campaign in Afghanistan, which subverted the *Nicaragua* and *Tadić* legacy and, as will be argued, somewhat crystallised the definite move towards the implementation of indirect responsibility in international law.[13] Coupled with today's soaring technological possibilities and far-reaching effects of terrorist structures, these events constitute a larger reality and undoubtedly warrant better integration of non-State actors under international law and the identification of potential deterrence models in the face of enhanced transnational terrorist capacity.

As time passes, international law evolves and, with it, the literature and jurisprudence should follow suit. Many unforeseen elements now shape and inform the equation of State responsibility and, as if confronted with a complex algo-

[10] *Military and Paramilitary Activities in and against Nicaragua (Nicaragua v United States of America)*, Merits, Judgement of 27 June, *ICJ Reports* (1986) 14; Case No IT-94-1-A *Prosecutor v Tadić*, ICTY Judgment, 15 July 1999, reprinted in (1999) 38 ILM 1518.

[11] *Corfu Channel Case (United Kingdom of Great Britain and Northern Ireland v Albania)*, Merits, Judgment of 9 April, *ICJ Reports* (1949) 4; *United States Diplomatic and Consular Staff in Tehran (United States v Iran)*, Judgment of 24 May, *ICJ Reports* (1980) 3.

[12] See, eg: A Pellet, 'The ILC's Articles on State Responsibility for Internationally Wrongful Acts and Related Texts' in Crawford et al, above n 3 at 75–94.

[13] For instance, several commentators agree that the response to the 9/11 has disabled the 'effective control' test. See C Stahn, 'Terrorist Acts As "Armed Attack": The Right to Self-Defense, Article 51 (1/2) of the UN Charter, and International Terrorism' (2003) 27 *Fletcher Forum of World Affairs* 35, 37; J Wouters and F Naert, 'Shockwaves Through International Law After 11 September: Finding the Right Responses to the Challenges of International Terrorism' in C Fijnaut et al (eds), *Legal Instruments in the Fight against International Terrorism: A Transatlantic Dialogue* (Leiden, Nijhoff, 2004) 411.

rithm, we must break down the pieces of this legal puzzle. Since the literature is far from dispositive on the issue, this study proposes to reopen the debate on indirect State responsibility and weigh different arguments in order to illuminate this politically charged area. This chapter will draw a distinction between direct and indirect responsibility before arguing that the international community has, in fact, moved towards a model of indirect responsibility. The ensuing remarks shall, therefore, draw abundantly on past Security Council practice and select ICJ precedents. In developing this argument, the chapter will first delve into the direct/indirect responsibility dichotomy before entertaining a discussion on the foundational concept of attribution under State responsibility. The chapter will then move on to the task of identifying a shift under international law, now mirrored in many domestic criminal and civil liability legal structures, towards more indirect modes of responsibility. In so doing, it will first trace the evolution of indirect responsibility in contemporary international law whilst assessing the emergence of the 'harbouring and supporting' rule in counterterrorism contexts. After underscoring the application of that norm in a sampling of pre-9/11 episodes, the chapter will ultimately culminate in exploring the Security Council's role and scope of influence in this debate.

II. DIRECT VERSUS INDIRECT RESPONSIBILITY

An overarching dichotomy guides the law of State responsibility for internationally wrongful acts.[14] On one hand, a State may be held accountable if it authored a commission or omission leading to a wrongful act.[15] Hence, through its overt and direct involvement in the matter, whether through aiding or abetting a given deed, the State triggers the mechanism of State responsibility.[16] Since the action can be linked directly to the State in question, attribution of the wrongful conduct flows to the State and responsibility attaches. This phenomenon frequently materialises when the act in question is carried out by formal instrumentalities, agents of the State or non-State actors that are deemed synonymous with a prolongation of the State.[17] As seen in chapter one, we may use direct State respon-

[14] For a relevant application of this dichotomy, see AG Hamid, 'Maritime Terrorism, the Straits of Malacca, and the Issue of State Responsibility' (2006) 15 *Tulane Journal of International and Comparative Law* 155, 164 (expounding that 'Terrorist acts are normally committed by private persons. However, a State may directly or indirectly be involved in the terrorist activities').

[15] These terms are also referred to as 'actions' and 'omissions'. For a recent account, see F Latty, 'Actions and Omissions' in Crawford et al, above n 3 at 355–63.

[16] See, eg: MN Schmitt, 'Counter-Terrorism and the Use of Force in International Law', *George C Marshall European Center for Security Studies* (2002) 44–45, available at www.marshallcenter.org/mcpublicweb/MCDocs/files/College/F_Publications/mcPapers/mc-paper_5-en.pdf.

[17] On State responsibility for the unlawful acts of agents of State, see F Przetacznik, 'The International Responsibility of States for the Unauthorized Acts of Their Organs' (1989) 1 *Sri Lanka Journal of International Law* 151. On State responsibility for the acts of non-State actors, see 'State Responsibility: Titles and text of the draft articles on Responsibility of States for internationally wrongful acts adopted by the Drafting Committee on second reading', UN Doc A/CN.4/L.602/Rev.1 (2001); 'Report of the International Law Commission on the Work of Its

sibility to attribute the crimes of a terrorist organisation to a host-State, as though they amounted to the actions of the State itself. Although hardly defensible, this is one possible interpretation of the events surrounding 9/11, as the government of Afghanistan could be deemed to have acted through individuals or a prolongation of the State, namely members of Al Qaeda. Based on the publicly available facts, however, it is not likely that the government of Afghanistan was waging a surrogate war against the US through members of Al Qaeda and this assertion was never explicitly put forth. Although difficult to substantiate, such a claim is not novel. For example, the possibility of a State waging war against the US through a terrorist organisation was raised in the context of the invasion of Iraq.[18]

On the other hand, a more subtle type of responsibility exists, one that hinges on the indirect involvement of a State in a wrongful act. Indirect responsibility usually arises when there is no causal link between the private author of the wrongful act and the State.[19] For instance, if a territory is used as a launch pad for terrorism in which the government in place has no knowledge of such conduct and no ties whatsoever to terrorist operations, it would be difficult to directly impute an attack to that State. At that juncture, the analysis focuses on the State's duty of prevention and whether it failed to thwart a given terrorist strike emanating from its territory. As seen in chapter one, sections IV.C)–E), such scenarios often involve acquiescence or tacit toleration of irregular units on a sanctuary State's territory. Indeed, the State's breach of its obligation can also stem from its failure to regulate the internationally wrongful activity or to provide a remedy for the harm (although this study focuses primarily on the breach of the obligation of prevention, which is nonetheless connected to other ancillary undertakings such as the duties to extradite, prosecute and freeze terrorist assets).[20] This approach certainly finds partial grounding in classical expressions of the 'separate delict theory', formulated in a string of arbitral awards handed down by bilateral decision-making bodies.[21] Keeping in line with the general principle of non-attribution of private conduct, they espoused

Fifty-Third Session', UN GAOR, 56th Sess, Supp No 10, UN Doc A/56/10 (2001) 41 [hereinafter *ILC Articles on State Responsibility*, *Articles on State Responsibility*, or *Articles*] Arts 8 and 11.

[18] See, eg: J Pedigo, 'Rogue States, Weapons of Mass Destruction, and Terrorism: Was Security Council Approval Necessary for the Invasion of Iraq?' (2004) 32 *Georgia Journal of International and Comparative Law* 199, 217.

[19] On this issue, see Becker, above n 4 at 285–360 (advocating the implementation of causation-based State responsibility for terrorist acts). On the issue of causation in State responsibility, see generally: F Rigaux, 'International Responsibility and the Principle of Causality' in M Ragazzi (ed), *International Responsibility Today: Essays in Memory of Oscar Schachter* (Leiden, Brill, 2005) 81–92; below ch 3, section II.

[20] For support of the initial proposition pertaining to 'indirect responsibility', see generally: C Scott, 'Translating Torture into Transnational Tort: Conceptual Divides in the Debate on Corporate Accountability for Human Rights Harms' in C Scott (ed), *Torture as Tort: Comparative Perspectives on the Development of Transnational Human Rights Litigation* (Oxford, Hart Publishing, 2001) 45 at 47–48. On the obligation to prevent terrorism as envisaged in the present study, see above ch 1, section II; below ch 5, section IV.

[21] On the separate delict theory, see Becker, above n 4 at 24–38.

a formal distinction between the original internationally wrongful act carried out by individuals and the State's own wrongdoing (eg failure to punish, extradite or exercise due diligence in repressing the harm). In the *Lovett Case*, the US-Chile Claims Commission of 1892 had to weigh in on the murder of the Governor of the local garrison by guerrillas in Chile. Reaffirming the principle of non-attribution, the Commission declared that 'all the authorities on international law are a unit as regards the principle that injury done by one of the subjects of a nation is not to be considered as done by the nation itself'.[22] Similarly, an umpire in the *Sambiaggo Case* of 1903 reasoned in the same vein, expounding that 'a government, like an individual, is only to be held responsible for the acts of its agents or for acts the responsibility for which is expressly assumed by it. To apply another doctrine . . . would be unnatural and illogical'.[23] Like-minded incarnations of the doctrine were also formulated in early arbitral awards dealing with State responsibility-derived aspects of varied factual scenarios, including the *Underhill Cases* in 1903[24] and the *Home Frontier and Foreign Missionary Society Case* of 1920.[25]

The oft-discussed decision of Max Huber in the *British Property in Spanish Morocco Case* of 1925 also aligned, both conceptually and philosophically, with this construction of indirect State responsibility.[26] Indeed, Huber opined that

> the State is not responsible for the revolutionary events themselves, [but] it may nevertheless be responsible for what the authorities do or do not do to mitigate the consequences as far as possible. Responsibility for the action or inaction of the public authorities is quite different from responsibility for acts that may be imputed to persons outside the control of the authorities or openly hostile to them.[27]

Subsequently, Huber examined issues relating to Spanish responsibility for transboundary thefts in the international zone of Morocco carried out by inhabitants of the Spanish zone. Whilst the arbitrator did not infer responsibility in light of Spain's failure to prevent the thefts, he nonetheless assessed its obligation to prosecute the perpetrators. On that front, Huber held that Spain had 'done nothing to induce the offenders to return the money or to punish them . . . It is justifiable to regard this inaction as a breach of an international obligation'.[28]

[22] *Frederik H Lovett (United States v Chile)* (1892), reprinted in JB Moore, 3 *History and Digest of International Arbitrations to Which the United States Has Been a Party* (1898) 2991.

[23] *Sambiaggo Case (Italy v Venezuela)* (1903) 10 *Reports of International Arbitral Awards* 499, 512.

[24] *Underhill Cases (United Kingdom v Venezuela)* (1903) 9 *Reports of International Arbitral Awards* 155, 159.

[25] *Home Frontier and Foreign Missionary Society of the United Brethren in Christ (United States v United Kingdom)* (1920) 6 *Reports of International Arbitral Awards* 44.

[26] *British Claims in the Spanish Zone of Morocco Case (United Kingdom v Spain)* (1925) 2 *Reports of International Arbitral Awards* 615.

[27] ibid, at 641–42.

[28] ibid, at 709.

However, Huber somewhat tempered this statement by adding that

> [i]t would . . . in no circumstances be justifiable to attribute responsibility for the entire damage to a Government which, although perhaps negligent in that respect, was certainly not responsible for the events which were the immediate cause of the damage . . . Spain's responsibility is based only on the conditions of judicial assistance and not on the circumstances of the actual event which caused the damage.[29]

A notion that State responsibility flowing from failing to prevent or punish does not constitute an exception to the principle of non-attribution can certainly – and persuasively – be extracted from that case. In sum, the thrust of State responsibility in those cases operates by virtue of the State's own wrongdoing and not because of some State-condoned policy or complicity facilitating the act (ie the operation of a primary rather than secondary rule).

A series of additional cases bolster the initial postulate that non-attribution entails that responsibility centres not on grounding accountability on the privately-inflicted wrongful act but rather on the State's failure to comply with its own international obligations. According to classical formulations of the principle of non-attribution, a State's passivity is not sufficient, in and of itself, to trigger the application of responsibility; the State in question must clearly be acting in contravention of an international obligation in relation to the wrongful act carried out by private parties.[30] In addition to garnering academic credence throughout the twentieth century,[31] this posture was perhaps best exemplified through the settlement of international claims. For instance, the *Noyes Case* of 1933 comes to mind and involved an American citizen's injuries inflicted upon him by a drunken mob in Panama. Judging that responsibility did not flow from these private acts, the Commission held that Panama could only be found responsible for its authorities' own 'behaviour in connection with the particular occurrence, or a general failure to comply with their duty to maintain order, to prevent crimes or to prosecute and punish criminals'.[32] Ultimately, the specific circumstances of the case did not warrant a finding of wrongdoing by Panama and, as a corollary, failed to trigger its responsibility. Similar cases following identical reasoning include, inter alia, *Venable*,[33] *Kennedy*,[34]

[29] ibid, at 709–10.

[30] See, eg: H Triepel, *Völkerrecht und Landsrecht* (Leipzig, CL Hirschfeld, 1899) 333–34; C Eagleton, *The Responsibility of States in International Law* (New York, NYU Press, 1928) 77; C Eagleton, 'Measure of Damages in International Law' (1929–30) 39 *Yale Law Journal* 52, 54.

[31] See, eg: D Anzilotti, 'La Responsabilité internationale des États: à raison des dommages soufferts par des étrangers' (1906) 13 *RGDIP* 5, 298–99 (1906); H Arias, 'The Non-Liability of States for Damages Suffered by Foreigners in the Course of a Riot, an Insurrection or a Civil War' (1913) 7 *AJIL* 724, 747; AV Freeman, *The International Responsibility of States for Denial of Justice* (London, Longmans, 1938) 367–69; JG Starke, 'Imputability in International Delinquencies' (1938) 19 *BYIL* 104, 112.

[32] *Walter A Noyes Case (US v Panama)* (1933) 6 *Reports of International Arbitral Awards* 308, 311.

[33] *HG Venable (US v Mexico)* (1927) 4 *Reports of International Arbitral Awards* 219, 229.

[34] *George Adams Kennedy (US v Mexico)* (1927) 4 *Reports of International Arbitral Awards* 194, 199.

Kidd,[35] *Denham*[36] and *Finnish Shipowners*.[37] Needless to say, this conception of State responsibility for private acts is certainly broad enough to encompass a theory of indirect responsibility for failing to prevent transnational terrorism and has, at least in its classical permutations, attracted the endorsement of leading international legal publicists.[38] More relevantly, this construction gained even more traction when Roberto Ago defended it in his fourth report to the ILC in 1972.[39]

Similarly to direct responsibility, the focus here therefore hinges on the State's breach of an international obligation. However, the breach under indirect responsibility will likely translate into an omission related to terrorism,[40] whether deliberate or innocent, rather than into the commission of an act, whether contributory or complicit.[41] When dealing with internationally wrongful acts carried out by individuals that may not be attributed to the relevant sanctuary State, the responsibility 'originates not in the conduct of those individuals, but in the omissions by the State's own organs'.[42] Hence, a State's passiveness or indifference towards the concoction of terrorist agendas on its own territory might trigger its responsibility, possibly on the same scale as though it had actively and directly participated in their planning.[43]

Direct and indirect responsibility may appear conceptually difficult to decipher or distinguish, whilst the delineation between both paradigms has unquestionably blurred on occasion. Although discarded by some scholars, this dichotomy remains a prevalent dimension of State responsibility. In particular, some jurists opine that the direct/indirect dichotomy is erroneous. For instance,

[35] *Annie Bella Graham Kidd (Great Britain v Mexico)* (1931) 5 *Reports of International Arbitral Awards* 142, 144.

[36] *Lettie Charlotte Denham and Frank Parlin Denham (US v Panama)* (1933) 6 *Reports of International Arbitral Awards* 312, 313.

[37] *Claim of Finnish Shipowners against Great Britain in Respect of the Use of Certain Finnish Vessels during the War (Finland v Great Britain)* (1934) 3 *Reports of International Arbitral Awards* 1480, 1501.

[38] See, eg: H Kelsen, *Principles of International Law* (New York, Rinehart & Company, 1952) 121; E Jiménez de Aréchaga, 'International Responsibility' in M Sørensen (ed), *Manual of Public International Law* (London, Macmillan, 1968) 533 at 560; C Rousseau, *Droit international public* (Paris, Recueil Sirey, 1953) 376–77.

[39] See R Ago, 'Fourth Report on State Responsibility' (1978) 2 *Yearbook of the International Law Commission* 71, UN Doc A/CN.4/264 & Add 1 at 99, 124–26.

[40] See K Zemanek, 'Does the Prospect of Incurring Responsibility Improve the Observance of International Law?' in Ragazzi, above n 19 at 131 ('It is a well-known principle of international law that a State which fails in its duty to prevent the use of its territory for acts contrary to the rights of other States is responsible for the omission'). See also: M García-Mora, *International Responsibility for Hostile Acts of Private Persons against Foreign States* (The Hague, Nijhoff, 1962) 109–12, 130. For jurisprudential support of this proposition, see *Corfu Channel* Case, above n 11 at 22.

[41] On complicity in the commission of wrongful acts, see Becker, above n 4 at 280–81; TM Franck and D Niedermeyer, 'Accommodating Terrorism: An Offence against the Law of Nations' (1990) 19 *Israel Yearbook on Human Rights* 75, 79, 99.

[42] J Barboza, 'Invocation of Responsibility' in KK Koufa (ed), *Thesaurus Acroasium Vol 34: State Responsibility and the Individual* (Athens, Sakkoulas, 2006) 7 at 38.

[43] See MMD Banks, 'Addressing State (Ir-)Responsibility: The Use of Military Force as Self-Defense in International Counter-Terrorism Operations' (2009) 200 *Military Law Review* 54, 93 fn 222.

in his Separate Opinion in the *Nicaragua* Case, Judge Ago equated indirect responsibility with the transfer of responsibility flowing from one State to another, when the latter exercises control over the former.[44] In addition, the present project's conception of indirect responsibility has also sometimes been labelled 'vicarious responsibility', much to the dismay of certain leading experts in the field of State responsibility.[45] Nevertheless, the concept of indirect responsibility, as construed in the present monograph, has arguably been invoked by the ICJ in *Nicaragua* and by the Israeli Commission in the context of its investigation surrounding the Beirut Massacre.[46] As a corollary, it follows that the law governing direct responsibility developed considerably faster than indirect responsibility, at least at a conceptual level, given high-profile judicial pronouncements on the matter. However, implementing such judicially-derived conceptual inclinations has proven more challenging. This evolution is not so much imputable to the law's propensity to change, but rather to the intimate relationship between direct responsibility and the concept of attribution. Accordingly, a few preliminary remarks about attribution are apposite here.

III. THE CONCEPT OF ATTRIBUTION

Since the proliferation of Israeli reprisals in the 1960s, which often raised questions pertaining to State responsibility,[47] international judiciaries have formally introduced the concept of attribution.[48] It is also interesting to note that the Definition of Aggression alludes to the question of attribution to States of the acts of their agents. Article 3(g) of the Definition also adds, within the purview of 'aggression', the 'sending by or on behalf of a State of armed bands, groups,

[44] *Nicaragua*, above n 10 at 189–90. In the same spirit, see GA Christenson, 'Attributing Acts of Omission to the State' (1991) 12 *Michigan Journal of International Law* 312, 350, 360–64.

[45] See I Brownlie, *System of the Law of Nations: State Responsibility Part I* (Oxford, Clarendon Press, 1983) 36. On the notion of 'vicarious responsibility' as applicable to individuals, see SR Ratner and JS Abrams, *Accountability for Human Rights Atrocities in International Law: Beyond the Nuremberg Legacy*, 2nd edn (Oxford, OUP, 2001) 129–35.

[46] See 'Final Report of the Commission of Inquiry into the Events of the Refugee Camps in Beirut', reprinted in (1983) 22 ILM 473 at 496, 499; AS Eban, *The Beirut Massacre: The Complete Kahan Commission Report* (Princeton, Karz-Cohl, 1983) 50–63. See also: Becker, above n 4 at 313–14.

[47] See R Provost, *International Human Rights and Humanitarian Law* (Cambridge, CUP, 2002) 188 (highlighting that 'Belligerent reprisals are construed properly as forming part of rules on State responsibility'). However, it is doubtful whether the concept of 'reprisals', which is now enshrined under the rubric of 'countermeasures' in ILC Arts 49–53, forms a component of reciprocity. See, eg: B Simma, 'Reflections on Article 60 of the Vienna Convention on the Law of Treaties and Its Background in General International Law' (1970) 20 *Österreichische Zeitschrift für Öffentliches Recht* 5, 19–22.

[48] For a thoughtful review of the ICJ's treatment of attribution, see R Higgins, 'The International Court of Justice: Selected Issues of State Responsibility' in Ragazzi, above n 19 at 272–75 (reviewing the following cases: *Nicaragua*, *Tehran Hostages*, *Cumaraswamy*, *Avena*, *LaGrand*, *Legality of Use of Force* and *Oil Platforms*). For accounts on the concept, see generally: GA Christenson, 'The Doctrine of Attribution in State Responsibility' in RB Lillich (ed), *International Law of State Responsibility for Injuries to Aliens* (Charlottesville, University Press of Virginia, 1983) 320–60; Starke, above n 31 at 104–17.

irregulars or mercenaries, which carry out acts of armed force of such gravity as to amount to the acts listed [in the preceding paragraphs]'.[49] Speaking to this definition, Thomas Franck points out that 'The prohibition does not specify what "sending" means. Does it include "permitting," or tolerating"?'[50] This carries distinct significance for the study of indirect responsibility for terrorism as it remains unclear, from this definition, whether the mere toleration, the wilful blindness, or the inaction of sanctuary States might corral all necessary requirements to meet the threshold of responsibility. At any rate, it is imperative to review the concept of attribution as it has been constructed and interpreted by international courts, as the obligation to prevent terrorism can decidedly be grounded in other legal schemes.

The ICJ crafted the classical formulation of attribution in the context of its 1986 *Nicaragua* decision, when confronted with US involvement in the funding and training of *Contras* rebels during the Nicaragua armed conflict. Although the US provided various forms of assistance to the rebels and, even when faced with the fact that the guerrillas were completely dependent on US support at some point, and that such aid was 'preponderant or decisive', the Court refused to pronounce the *Contras* rebels de facto US agents.[51] The Court then proceeded to formulate the applicable standard in establishing State responsibility, a postulate that would quickly gain notoriety as the 'effective control test'. In order to hold the US legally responsible for the activities of the *Contras*, it would 'have to be proved that that State had effective control of the military or paramilitary operations in the course of which the alleged violations were committed'.[52] From this decision onwards, it became common practice to analyse the degree of effective control exercised by a State over non-State actors in order to determine its level of involvement and, as a corollary, its level of responsibility. This

[49] Annex to GA Res 3314 (XXIX), UN GAOR, 29th Sess, Supp No 31, UN Doc A/9631 (1974) at 143, Art 3(g).

[50] TM Franck, *Recourse to Force: State Action against Threats and Armed Attacks* (Cambridge, CUP, 2002) 65. Similarly, Pemmaraju Sreenivasa Rao seems to infer that providing safe havens to terrorist organisations does not fall within the 1974 definition of 'aggression'. See PS Rao, 'International Crimes and State Responsibility' in Ragazzi, above n 19 at 68. However, he later adds that 'The conduct enumerated in sub-paragraph 3(g) is not only a crucial element for the definition of aggression but it also constitutes an essential element *for treating intervention and cross-border terrorism as unlawful*' (emphasis added). See ibid, at 74. These considerations will prove extremely relevant in subsequent portions of this study that will discuss the shift towards indirect State responsibility at international law, along with the importance of the 'harbouring and supporting' rule. See also: D Brown, 'Use of Force against Terrorism after September 11th: State Responsibility, Self-Defense and Other Responses' (2003) 11 *Cardozo Journal of International and Comparative Law* 1, 8.

[51] *Nicaragua*, above n 10 at para 115. See also: ibid, at paras 86–93; H Duffy, *The 'War on Terror' and the Framework of International Law* (Cambridge, CUP, 2005) 49. On State responsibility for the acts of de facto State agents, see G Townsend, 'State Responsibility for Acts of De Facto Agents' (1997) 14 *Arizona Journal of International and Comparative Law* 635. On the liability for action of State organs, see: *Difference Relating to Immunity from Legal Process of a Special Rapporteur of the Commission on Human Rights*, Advisory Opinion of 29 April, *ICJ Reports* (1999) 62 at 87, para 62; *Francisco Mallén (Mexico v US)* (1927) 4 *Reports of International Arbitral Awards* 173, 174.

[52] *Nicaragua*, above n 10 at para 115. See also: SA Shah, 'War on Terrorism: Self Defense, Operation Enduring Freedom, and the Legality of U.S. Drone Attacks in Pakistan' (2010) 9 *Washington University Global Studies Law Review* 77, 94.

test proved to be a considerable development since the 60s and 70s, at least in terms of legal semantics and construction. Moreover, as discussed in chapter one, the ICJ reiterated the validity of that approach in its controversial *Genocide* judgment.

Thirteen years after *Nicaragua*, under the aegis of the International Criminal Tribunal for the former Yugoslavia (ICTY), the 'effective control test' was arguably revisited in *Tadić*.[53] The Appeals Chamber found that when private individuals carry out acts contrary to international law, the only way to attribute such acts to the State is to demonstrate that it 'exercises control over the individuals'.[54] The Tribunal also pointed out that the degree of control might vary according to the circumstances; hence, the analysis should be guided by a flexible approach.[55] It then drew a distinction between an individual and an organised group, the latter being usually characterised by a firm command structure, a body of rules, hierarchical authority, and so on. In the latter case – presumably also encompassing non-State terrorist groups – it was now necessary to demonstrate that the State exerted 'overall control' over the group in question, a legal inquiry that marked a significant relaxation of the 'effective control test'.[56] The ICTY pursued its analysis by making a distinction between a group that is militarily organised and a group that is not organised in a military structure.[57] In the former scenario, it would have to be proved that the State 'wields overall control over the group, not only by equipping and financing the group, but also by coordinating or helping in the general planning of its military activity'.[58] Conversely, in the case of groups lacking a military structure, the threshold would be higher, as overall control was deemed insufficient and specific instructions[59] flowing from the State to the group in question were required.[60] Alternatively, the threshold could also be satisfied if the State publicly endorsed or approved the acts ex post facto, a standard now mirrored by Article 11 of the ILC text.[61] Here, it is

[53] See Higgins, above n 48 at 272 (rather inferring that the test of effective control was 'not followed' by the ICTY in *Tadić*).

[54] *Tadić*, above n 10 at para 117.

[55] ibid. The Court also identified various situations where the threshold of control would vary.

[56] ibid, at para 120. For support of the idea that *Tadić* significantly relaxed the *Nicaragua* standard, see, eg: AS Younis, 'Imputing War Crimes in the War on Terrorism: The U.S., Northern Alliance, and "Container Crimes"' (2003) 9 *Washington & Lee Race & Ethnic Ancestry Journal* 109, 114–15.

[57] *Tadić*, above n 10 at para 137.

[58] *Tadić*, above n 10 at paras 131, 137.

[59] The *Tadić* decision essentially did away with the requirement of having specific orders issued from host-States to militarily organised groups. See, eg: Stahn, above n 13 at 47; M Nabati, 'International Law at a Crossroads: Self-Defense, Global Terrorism, and Preemption (a Call to Rethink the Self-Defense Normative Framework)' (2003) 13 *Transnational Law and Contemporary Problems* 771, 781. In this regard, the *Tadić* decision also delivered an important distinction between non-State groups that are organised in a military hierarchy and groups lacking a military structure, a distinction that has often been ignored or misrepresented in recent scholarship

[60] *Tadić*, above n 10 at paras 132, 137.

[61] ibid. On the topic of responsibility by endorsement, see Brown, above n 50 at 10–12. On the possibility of imputing responsibility to the government of Afghanistan for endorsing the 9/11 attacks, Brown further argues, at 11, that 'the publicly available facts are insufficient to impute the

interesting to draw a parallel with the *Tehran Hostages* Case, where the responsibility of Iran for an attack carried out by militants on an American embassy was predicated in part on the State authorities' subsequent approval of the attack. Following Ayatollah Khomeini's endorsement of the attacks, the ICJ equated the continuing occupation of the embassy and the hostage-taking with 'acts of State'. However, it did not attribute the attack and takeover of the embassy to Iran from a purely 'direct' standpoint.[62] In any event, the ICTY arguably advanced the debate on this issue in *Tadić*: if one were to accept that case's central premise on this point, the standard of control exerted by a State over a group would now vary depending on that very group's organisational structure, its relationship to the State, etc. Thus, an argument could cogently be articulated that a network like Al Qaeda resembles a military group given its organisation, training, complex cellular structure, efficient financial structures and the independence between its cells.[63] *Tadić*'s legacy of 'overall control', therefore, governs debates on questions of State involvement in funding and training insurgents or terrorists in the post-*Nicaragua* era, not without some degree of resistance.

An immediate distinguishing factor complicates the equation when attempting to analogise *Tadić*'s reasoning to States for failing to prevent transnational terrorism, such as was the case of Afghanistan on 9/11. Pursuant to the ICTY's analysis, it would follow that, when the terrorist attack or ensuing armed hostilities do not transpire on the controlling State's territory (eg Al Qaeda attacks targets in the US), 'more extensive and compelling evidence is required to show that the state is genuinely in control of the units or groups, not merely by financing and equipping them, but also by generally directing or helping plan their actions'.[64] It should be recalled that *Tadić* dealt primarily with *individual* responsibility, as opposed to *State* responsibility. More specifically, the ICTY was called upon to determine whether the actions of the VRS (Bosnian Serb forces) could be attributed to Yugoslavia (FRY), which required that the Tribunal operate on the premise that an international armed conflict emerged between that State and Bosnia-Herzegovina. As a corollary, the question of attribution remained inextricably linked to the exercise of ascertaining individual responsibility for IHL violations. Therefore, the standards extracted from its ruling reflected the specific rules of IHL considered by the Appeals Chamber. In particular, the Third Geneva Convention of 1949 and the law of organisational structure under humanitarian law commissioned a very specific legal relationship between the relevant actors so as to

September 11th attack to Afghanistan. They do not establish that Al-Qa'ida acted as an agent or instrumentality of the "Afghan state", but rather that Al-Qa'ida acted autonomously within Afghanistan'.

[62] *Tehran Hostages* Case, above n 11 at 33–35.

[63] See, eg: JF Addicott, 'Legal and Policy Implications for a New Era: The "War on Terror"' (2002) 4 *The Scholar: St Mary's Law Review on Minority Issues* 209, 218 (referring to Al Qaeda as a sophisticated 'para-military' terrorist network). See also: R Gunaratna, *Inside Al Qaeda: Global Network of Terror* (London, Hurst, 2002) 93–112.

[64] *Tadić*, above n 10 at para 138.

facilitate the abovementioned determination connecting the VRS and the FRY. Puzzlingly, in what has been widely contemplated through the prism of a judicially driven normative conflict, the ICTY decided to challenge the standard of State responsibility promulgated by the ICJ in *Nicaragua* when seeking to apply adequate legal principles. However, considerable resistance to this jurisprudential inclination was levelled, most interestingly from individual voices on the Tribunal's own bench. In his Separate Opinion, Judge Shahabuddeen called into question the wisdom of contesting the *Nicaragua* precedent when the ICTY's task consisted of pronouncing on the nature of the conflict at play in the factual record before it.[65] Such observations cannot help but cast an aura of legitimate incredulity around the commonly held belief that the *Tadić* court formulated a more nuanced or subtle vision of attribution principles.

Other commentators nonetheless take issue with that characterisation. Antonio Cassese – himself a Judge sitting on that case – reviewed the relevance of the *Tadić* precedent within the framework of the ICJ's *Genocide Case*. In this latter case, the Court applied *Nicaragua*'s 'effective control' standard and ultimately held that the acts of genocide carried out by Bosnian Serb armed forces could not be attributed to the FRY. Moreover, underscoring that the test proposed by the ICTY might be suitable to ascertain whether an armed conflict is international in character, although the Tribunal also cast it as equally applicable to govern State responsibility issues, the ICJ rejected the application of *Tadić*'s line of inquiry, judging that the ICTY's standard would have unduly expanded the scope of State responsibility law.[66] In response, Cassese pointed out that since no rules of IHL were dispositive in determining whether the armed conflict was internal or international in *Tadić*, the ICTY deliberately invoked the rules of State responsibility to fill that void.[67]

In his Dissenting Opinion in the *Genocide Case*, Vice-President Al-Khasawneh echoed similar concerns after lamenting the majority's rejection of the *Tadić* standard, opining that the ILC's Commentary to Article 8 'does little more than note a distinction between the rules of attribution for the purposes of State responsibility on the one hand, and the rules of international humanitarian law for the purposes of individual criminal responsibility on the other'.[68] Tapping somewhat into Cassese's eventual argument, the Vice-President recalled that the

[65] See Separate Opinion of Judge Shahabuddeen in *Tadić*, above n 10 at para 5.

[66] *Case Concerning the Application of the Convention on the Prevention and Punishment of the Crime of Genocide (Bosnia and Herzegovina v Serbia and Montenegro)*, Judgment of 26 February, *ICJ Reports* (2007) 43 at 143–45, paras 402–06. In fact, the ICJ found, particularly at para 403, that the ICTY had essentially overstepped its jurisdiction in *Tadić*. For a critical outlook, see F Zarbiev, 'Les politiques des vérités juridiques en droit international: propos autour d'une controverse juridictionnelle' (2007) 18 *Finnish Yearbook of International Law* (2007) 343.

[67] See A Cassese, 'The Nicaragua and Tadić Tests Revisited in Light of the ICJ Judgment on Genocide in Bosnia' (2007) 18 *EJIL* 649.

[68] Vice-President Al-Khasawneh's Dissenting Opinion in the *Genocide Case*, above n 66 at para 38 (citing JR Crawford, *International Law Commission's Articles on State Responsibility: Introduction, Text and Commentaries* (Cambridge, CUP, 2002) 112).

Tadić court 'had in fact framed the question as one of State responsibility, in particular whether the FRY was responsible for the acts of the VRS and therefore considered itself to be applying the rules of attribution under international law'.[69] In referring to the *Genocide Case*, Cassese ultimately argued that in order to discard the *Tadić* standard, the ICJ

> should have proved that, if applied to state responsibility, 'overall control' was unsupported by state practice and *opinio juris*. It follows that the reader expecting a closely-argued decision will be left instead with the impression that the Court's holdings have a tinge of oracularity (oracles indeed are not required to give reasons).[70]

Consequently, *Tadić*'s contribution to the law governing State responsibility cannot be overlooked and some discussion of the case has been present in virtually all modern accounts addressing that legal field. However, a fairly recent judicial pronouncement on State responsibility emanating from the ICJ expressly rejected the application of *Tadić*, much to the chagrin of some international legal experts.[71] In that light, it follows that the persuasiveness and bindingness of the *Tadić* decision remain highly suspect when applying the rules of State responsibility to counterterrorism. Hence, it is probably safe to assume that only the *Nicaragua* and *Tehran Hostages* cases offered indisputable authority on the issue of attribution for the purposes of State responsibility prior to 9/11. But even this assumption can be left open to challenge, at least with regard to *Nicaragua*. As one commentator underscores, it is

> a fact that the Court in *Nicaragua* set out that [effective control] test without explaining or clarifying the grounds on which it was based. No reference is made by the Court either to state practice or to other authorities. This is in keeping with a regrettable recent tendency of the Court not to corroborate its pronouncements on international customary rules (other than those traditional rules that are largely upheld in case law and the legal literature) with a showing, if only concise, of the relevant practice and *opinio juris*.[72]

Other scholars conversely expound that the ICJ's holding against Iran in the *Tehran Hostages* Case is congruent with the 'effective control' test developed in *Nicaragua*, thereby reasserting its relevance in present-day contexts and across

[69] ibid. Indeed, some commentators infer that both regimes – namely IHL and State responsibility – mutually reinforce each other, thereby signalling that the ICTY was applying an interchangeable standard of attribution. See, eg: R Wolfrum, 'State Responsibility for Private Actors: An Old Problem of Renewed Relevance' in Ragazzi, above n 19 at 429 fn 21; S Kirchner, 'Third Party Liability for Hezbollah Attacks against Israel' (2006) 7 *German Law Journal* 777, 783.

[70] Cassese, above n 67 at 651.

[71] See, eg: C Tosh, 'Genocide Acquittal Provokes Legal Debate', *Institute for War & Peace Reporting*, 4 March 2007, available at http://iwpr.net/report-news/genocide-acquittal-provokes-legal-debate (citing Andre De Hoogh for the proposition that the ICJ should have applied the *Tadić* standard in the case). For the ICJ's rejection of *Tadić*, see *Genocide Case*, above n 66 at 143–45, paras 402–06.

[72] Cassese, above n 67 at 653–54.

a broad range of scenarios linking State involvement with the commission of privately-inflicted harm.[73]

Legal scholarly accounts dealing with State responsibility consistently cast *Tadić* as both an inexorable contestation to the *Nicaragua* holding[74] and, as envisaged above, a potential judicial entry point for the substantial lowering of attribution principles. Yet, alternative constructions of the role of that jurisprudence must also be entertained. First, a careful reading of both cases might reveal more conceptual commonalities than what is usually advertised in the literature. For proponents of this school of thought, sufficient analytical proximity connects both judgments to bolster the conclusion that the seemingly indomitable chasm between both precedents can be dispelled by reference to quantitative considerations, as opposed to more substantive divergences. One author encapsulates this idea: 'the difference between the attitudes of these two courts is one of degree, not of kind'.[75] It follows that by commissioning onerous evidentiary elements by far surpassing financial, logistical or ideological thresholds, the standards of responsibility ultimately endorsed in both decisions fail to provide 'a substantial opportunity to establish direct state responsibility in circumstances of clandestine state support to private actors'.[76]

Secondly, if the conceptual Rubicon dividing both cases cannot ultimately be traversed, it perhaps evinces a normative fragmentation of public international law. The ILC Study Group on Fragmentation of International Law's own view strongly aligns with this second construction and operates on the premise that

> [t]he contrast between *Nicaragua* and *Tadić* is an example of a normative conflict between an earlier and a later interpretation of a rule of international law. *Tadić* does not suggest 'overall control' to exist alongside 'effective control' either as an exception to the general law or as a special (local) regime governing the Yugoslav conflict. It seeks to *replace* that standard altogether.[77]

Finally, some interpretations of *Tadić* cast that decision as enshrining a misreading of the tenets of State responsibility laid down in *Nicaragua*, in which

[73] Duffy, above n 51 at 51 (making this determination on the basis that 'the Iranian State was considered capable of putting a stop to an ongoing situation and instead chose to endorse and to 'perpetuate' it').

[74] See, eg: A Cassese, *International Law*, 2nd edn (Oxford, OUP, 2005) 249. But see: Kirchner, above n 69 at 783 (emphasising that 'the *Tadić*-rule does not replace the *Nicaragua*-formula in the law of state responsibility but is only applicable within the more specialized regime of International Criminal Law').

[75] Becker, above n 4 at 70.

[76] ibid, at 71. See also: ibid, at 266–68.

[77] ILC Study Group on Fragmentation, 'Fragmentation of International Law: Difficulties Arising from the Diversification and Expansion of International Law, Report of the Study Group, finalized by Martti Koskenniemi' (13 April 2006), UN Doc A/6N.4/L.682 at 32, para 50. See also: M Koskenniemi and P Leino, 'Fragmentation of International Law? Postmodern Anxieties' (2002) 15 *Leiden Journal of International Law* 553, 562–67. Along somewhat similar lines, see also: G Guillaume, 'L'unité du droit international public est-elle aujourd'hui en danger?' (2003) 55 *Revue internationale de droit comparé* 23, 29–30; G Guillaume, 'Advantages and Risks of Proliferation: A Blueprint for Action' (2004) 2 *Journal of International Criminal Justice* 300, 301–02.

case no normative conflict would in fact exist between both precedents. A vocal proponent of this decidedly more conciliatory reading of *Tadić* deplores the ICTY's perhaps uncritical treatment of *Nicaragua*, whilst simultaneously highlighting that no due weight was given to the 'alternative of comprehensive control'.[78] As Marko Milanović points out, the *Tadić* judgment painstakingly focuses the crux of its challenge to *Nicaragua* against the standard of 'effective control' as a threshold exclusively commissioning specific instructions. Whilst no inference was ultimately drawn as to whether the circumstances in *Tadić* would have satisfied the 'overall control' threshold, he posits that the more general but exacting standard developed in *Nicaragua* might have, in fact, been better suited to govern the factual record connecting the FRY and the Bosnian Serb Forces.[79]

These competing jurisprudential constructions fail to completely untangle the legal bases militating in favour of a shift towards indirect responsibility. As a result, considerable confusion persists as to one dominant interpretation that may be gleaned from the – supposedly authoritative – precedent laid down in *Nicaragua*.[80] Whilst contemporary scholarly accounts on the intersection of State responsibility and counterterrorism acutely focus on both *Nicaragua* and *Tadić* – and how both judgments mutually inform and/or discredit each other – the potential benefits of placing more analytical emphasis on the *Corfu Channel* decision could yield illuminating results. Indeed, as argued throughout this study,[81] this case sheds a dispositive light on a potential shift towards more indirect forms of responsibility in counterterrorism settings. In particular, a cautious literal interpretation of that judgment enables its reader to draw the inference that the Court essentially engaged Albania's responsibility for failing to prevent transnational harm emanating from its territory. Juxtaposed with more contemporary jurisprudence and scholarship, a general conclusion as to Albania's international liability can be extracted from the ruling on the basis of its failure to take reasonable steps to prevent such harm. What is more, the Court's judgment – which also contained a translation variance in its authoritative French version – arguably opened the door to an enhanced obligation of due diligence incumbent upon States. As a corollary, it presaged an expansive construction of State responsibility should that undertaking become the object of a violation.[82] On the whole, this case at the very least corroborates a shift

[78] See M Lehto, *Indirect Responsibility for Terrorist Acts: Redefinition of the Concept of Terrorism beyond Violent Acts* (Leiden, Nijhoff, 2010) 214.

[79] M Milanović, 'State Responsibility for Genocide' (2006) 17 *EJIL* 553, 579–82. See also: AJJ de Hoogh, 'Articles 4 and 8 of the 2001 ILC Articles on State Responsibility, the Tadić Case and Attribution of Acts of Bosnian Serb Authorities to the Federal Republic of Yugoslavia' (2001) 72 *BYIL* 255, 290.

[80] C Kress, 'L'Organe de facto en droit international public: réflexions sur l'imputation à l'État de l'acte d'un particulier à la lumière des développements récents' (2001) 105 *RGDIP* 93, 106.

[81] See above: ch 1 nn 40–48, 110, 130–34 and accompanying text. See also: below nn 152, 175–76 and accompanying text; ch 4 nn 46–48, 201-02, 206, 318-23 and accompanying text; ch 5 nn 242–43 and accompanying text; Conclusion to Part II.

[82] See above ch 1, section IV.A), nn 130–34 and accompanying text.

towards more indirect modes of State responsibility in the face of enhanced transnational terrorist capacity.[83]

The adoption of the ILC's *Articles* in 2001 deployed another crucial effort for the purposes of the present discussion. This landmark document took on the very sophisticated task of delineating and defining the law of State responsibility via an exercise of codification.[84] Hence, it is now written law that 'Every internationally wrongful act of a State entails the international responsibility of that State'.[85] The *Articles* also set out the elements of a wrongful act, which may consist of an action or omission. However, various judiciaries have struggled in clearly distinguishing between omissions and surrounding circumstances.[86] Thus, it is probably erroneous to contend that, once a terrorist attack is launched from a State's territory, that State will always be held responsible due to an omission.[87] In fact, subsequent sections of this monograph discuss scenarios where States actively attempt to thwart terrorist threats, whether through best efforts or more draconian means, but ultimately fail in containing them. In such instances, can that failure be said to hinge on an omission from a semantic perspective? At the outset, it is thus fair to say that internationally responsible States are not always complacent, inactive or wilfully blind to terrorist activities percolating on their territory.

[83] While some parallels can undoubtedly be drawn with instances of State responsibility for piracy, the nature of that activity – which is often de-territorialised by definition (ie by occurring on the high seas) – can be distinguished from the application of State responsibility to transnational terrorism, in which territoriality plays a central role. That said, and by way of example, some commentators underscore that, while it may not be expected to completely eradicate this criminal practice, Somalia must nonetheless be perceived as taking active steps to prevent and punish the acts of piracy perpetrated by its nationals off its territorial waters. See, eg: R Abeyratne, 'The Responsibility of Somalia for the Acts of the Somali Pirates' (2009) 2 *Journal of Transportation Security* 63. The Security Council has also lamented failures to prosecute pirates. See SC Res 2015, UNSCOR, 65th Sess, 6635th Mtg, UN Doc S/RES 2015 (2011).

[84] On the enormous challenges posed by the codification of the law of State responsibility, see Malanczuk, above n 3 at 254 (citing M Spinedi and B Simma (eds), *United Nations Codification of State Responsibility* (New York, Oceana Publications, 1987)). Moreover, the application of State responsibility to subject-specific areas also poses increasingly intractable problems. For one application, see, eg: I Brownlie, 'The Responsibility of States for the Acts of International Organizations' in Ragazzi, above n 19 at 360.

[85] Art 1, *ILC Articles*, above n 17. As ILC Special Rapporteur James Crawford pointed out, above n 68 at 78, the principle stated in Art 1 – namely that once a wrongful act is committed, supplementary legal obligations are juxtaposed with existing State obligations – had been recognised prior to the Commission's adoption of said provision. On this point, see authorities cited by Crawford in ibid, at 78 fn 49. For instances where the principle contained in Art 1 was recognised after its formulation by the ILC, see also: ibid, at 78 fn 50.

[86] See *Corfu Channel* Case, above n 11 at 22–23. See also: *Tehran Hostages* Case, above n 11 at 63, 67; *Affaire relative à l'acquisition de la nationalité polonaise (Germany v Poland)* (1924) 1 *Reports of International Arbitral Awards* 401, 425; *Velásquez Rodríguez Case*, Inter-Am Ct HR Decisions and Judgments 91 (ser C) No 4 (1988) at para 170 ('under international law a State is responsible for the acts of its agents undertaken in their official capacity and for their omissions').

[87] But consider the following excerpt by Rigaux, above n 19 at 83, which could be transposed integrally to counterterrorism, as States have a positive duty to prevent terrorist attacks emanating from their territory: 'State liability is peculiarly relevant concerning crimes of omission, which imply that someone had the power and the duty to interfere'.

Conversely, it must also be acknowledged – perhaps emphatically – that 'acts of omission often are not simply the result of impotence or lack of awareness of the threats to which a state should respond, but can equally be active forms of policy'.[88] As such, a State may decide to passively adopt a stance of restraint vis-à-vis terrorist activities taking root on its territory, thereby engendering a challenging legal situation for the purposes of State responsibility. In such scenarios, the ensuing legal inquiry rather focalises on issues of toleration or passive acquiescence to terrorist activity, as opposed to overt condonation or active support of private transnational subversion by the governing apparatus. Such considerations lie at the very core of recent debates tackling the integration of international normative frameworks with non-State actors prefaced in the introduction, whilst straddling the conceptual grey areas that the present study seeks to engage. When a government relies on the perpetration of terrorist acts by non-State actors for the furtherance of its own political objectives, by extending undue hospitality to terrorists within its borders so as to derive indirect political benefits from their activities, for example, one can legitimately ponder whether that State's act of omission actually morphs into an act of commission.[89] Compounded by novel and deceptive terroristic structures involving sanctuary governments surreptitiously electing policies of tactical non-involvement or acquiescence, the formal bases of attribution developed under the law of State responsibility to tackle private conduct no longer appear indelible from a *lex ferenda* standpoint.

Under the ILC's *Articles*, one mechanism to trigger responsibility for seemingly private acts hinges on attribution of the wrongful act to the State in question, whilst the act must amount to the breach of an international obligation of the State. This principle, now codified in ILC Article 2, has also received wide jurisprudential support.[90] As a corollary, the obligation incumbent upon the wrongful State to ensure reparation and redress the harm also mirrors a corresponding

[88] A Nolkaemper, 'Attribution of Forcible Acts to States: Connections between the Law on the Use of Force and the Law of State Responsibility' in N Blokker and N Schrijver (eds), *The Security Council and the Use of Force: Theory and Reality – A Need for Change?* (Leiden, Nijhoff, 2005) 133 at 162.

[89] See, eg: Christenson, above n 44 at 369. For a similar argument under self-defence, see MJ Glennon, 'The Fog of Law: Self-Defense, Inherence, and Incoherence in Article 51 of the United Nations Charter' (2002) 25 *Harvard Journal of Law and Public Policy* 539, 550.

[90] Art 2 of the *ILC Articles*, above n 17, reads as follows:

There is an internationally wrongful act of a State when conduct consisting of an action or omission:

(a) Is attributable to the State under international law; and
(b) Constitutes a breach of an international obligation of the State.

This principle is also recognised in jurisprudence, albeit sometimes invoking different jargon. See, eg: *Phosphates in Morocco, Preliminary Objections*, 1938 PCIJ (ser A/B) No 74 (14 June) at 10, 28; *Tehran Hostages* Case, above n 11 at paras 56, 90; *Nicaragua*, above n 10 at para 226; *Gabčíkovo-Nagymaros Project (Hungary/Slovakia)*, Judgment of 25 September, *ICJ Reports* (1997) 7 at para 78; *Dickson Car Wheel Company (USA v Mexico)* (1931) 4 *Reports of International Arbitral Awards* 669, 678.

right, accruing to the aggrieved State, to receive said reparation.[91] These provisions operate on the premise that a primary rule of international law has been violated by a State in order to trigger the application of secondary rules[92] of State responsibility.[93] Hence, we will invariably confront the violation of an international obligation when addressing an internationally wrongful act, irrespective of whether the breach was generated through direct or indirect State involvement. Furthermore, a breach will be established regardless of the origin of the obligation under scrutiny, should it be predicated on treaty law,[94] customary law,[95] general rules of international law,[96] or *jus cogens*.[97]

Whilst these principles are straightforward, their application has not always been limpid with regard to the direct/indirect responsibility dichotomy.[98] By way of example, the Security Council's treatment of attribution vis-à-vis Libya's involvement in the *Lockerbie* incident remains puzzling to this day[99] and can be best explained by reference to a logic of indirect responsibility or, alternatively,

[91] See, eg: Anzilotti, above n 31 at 13; C Calvo, *Le droit international théorique et pratique: Tome premier*, 2nd edn (Paris, Durand et Pedone-Lauriel, 1870–72) 107, 400; C de Visscher, 'Le déni de justice en droit international' (1935-II) 52 *Recueil des Cours* 365, 421, 433; A Verdross, 'Règles générales du droit international de la paix' (1929-V) 30 *Recueil des Cours* 271, 462.

[92] The significance of establishing the parameters of secondary rules of responsibility in the international legal framework cannot be overemphasised. For quintessential appreciations of the ILC's work in this area, see Spinedi and Simma, above n 84.

[93] On the distinction between primary rules and secondary rules of State responsibility and its underlying philosophy, see R Ago, 'Report by Mr. R. Ago, Chairman of the Sub-Committee on State Responsibility' (1963) 2 *Yearbook of the International Law Commission* 227, UN Doc A/CN.4/152 at 228, para 5; D Alland and J Combacau, '"Primary" and "Secondary" Rules in the Law of State Responsibility: Categorizing International Obligations' (1985) 16 *Netherlands Yearbook of International Law* 81.

[94] *North Sea Continental Shelf (Federal Republic of Germany/Netherlands)*, Judgment of 20 February, *ICJ Reports* (1969) 3 at 38–39, para 63; *Nicaragua*, above n 10 at 95.

[95] ibid.

[96] See Crawford, above n 68 at 126.

[97] See Vienna Convention on the Law of Treaties, done at Vienna on 23 May 1969, entered into force 27 January 1980, 1155 UNTS 331, 8 ILM 679, especially Art 53; Crawford, above n 68 at 127. See also: Art 12 of the *ILC Articles*, above n 17 (providing that the 'origin and character' of an international obligation is irrelevant in demonstrating a breach of that duty). For more background on *jus cogens* obligations, see the Dissention Opinion of Judge Kreća in *Case Concerning the Legality of Use of Force (Yugoslavia v US)*, Order of 2 June, *ICJ Reports* (1999) 916 at 965; *Restatement (Third) of Foreign Relations Law of the United States* (St Paul, American Law Institute, 1987) § 102, cmt k. For a recent account canvassing these issues, see Y Nishimura, 'Source of the Obligation' in Crawford et al, above n 3 at 365–69.

[98] This phenomenon is evident in the treatment of attribution by the ICJ. Although not directly on point, the Court's reasoning encapsulates the sometimes conceptually elusive nature of the mechanism of attribution: see *Oil Platforms (Islamic Republic of Iran v USA)*, Merits, Judgment of 6 November, *ICJ Reports* (2003) 161 at paras 48–57. See also: Higgins, above n 48 at 274–75 (discussing attribution through the lens of the burden of proof, and contrasting a crucial distinction between what could be termed a 'whodunit' model of attribution, pursuant to the *Oil Platforms* case, and more substantial bases for attribution).

[99] See, eg: V Gowlland-Debbas, 'Security Council Enforcement Action and Issues of State Responsibility' (1994) 43 *ICLQ* 55, 66 (analysing the Libyan precedent and foreshadowing both a language that would be used recurrently by the Security Council in the field of counterterrorism and a logic that would simultaneously inform that language and, in turn, signal a shift towards a model of indirect responsibility for failing to prevent terrorist attacks).

by concerns of political expediency. A pivotal contemporaneous event, the US-led response to 9/11, also exacerbated the confusion surrounding this legal distinction. Whilst it has evolved over time, the American approach in the 'war' on terror, along with its sometimes conflicting dimensions, has engendered tactical tensions and hardly-reconcilable policy strategies.[100] More importantly, the decision to take action against Afghanistan[101] effectively collapsed both branches of State responsibility – direct and indirect – into one confused framework.[102] Conversely, some scholars construe US involvement in the 'war' on terror as creating a distinct and cognisable objective of holding States accountable for assisting terrorist groups. This priority would, on one hand, unquestionably engage the rules of State responsibility and, on the other, operate in tandem with the primary objective of holding the individual terrorists, themselves, responsible for their attacks.[103]

Although the use of force against Afghanistan obfuscated the legal basis underlying US action,[104] the 9/11 attacks and the reaction thereto, including the international endorsement of the US-led response, clearly engaged the issue of State responsibility.[105] However, it proved difficult to reconcile both of these aspects with existing conceptions of State responsibility for private conduct.[106] This line of argument is certainly not singular when addressing US foreign policy, as commentators also criticise the merging of conceptually distinct legal categories regarding the invasion of Iraq, for instance.[107] Subsequent paragraphs will examine how the international response to 9/11 has potentially created a new precedent under international law, along with a significant shift in the law

[100] See, eg: DH Dunn, 'Bush, 11 September and the Conflicting Strategies of the "War on Terrorism"' (2005) 16 *Irish Studies in International Affairs* 11.

[101] Some of the legal rhetoric following 9/11 was careful in characterising the US-led intervention in Afghanistan. See, eg: J Yoo, Transferring Terrorists (2004) 79 *Notre Dame Law Review* 1183, 1186 (terming it a 'military campaign').

[102] This confusion was exacerbated by the US' initial bellicose rhetoric, which lumped several unrelated factors into one difficult approach. See, eg: GW Bush, 'Address to a Joint Session of Congress and the American People', 20 September 2001, available at http://articles.cnn.com/2001-09-20/us/gen.bush.transcript_1_joint-session-national-anthem-citizens?_s=PM:US. See also: B Stern, 'La Responsabilité internationale des Etats: Perspectives récentes' in JC Lloréns (ed), *Cursos euromediterráneos bancaja de derecho internacional (Vol VII)* (Valencia, Tirant lo Blanch, 2003) 659 at 686 (wondering if this type of 'amalgam' can be envisaged under the law of State responsibility).

[103] See, eg: SE Smith, 'International Law: Blaming Big Brother: Holding States Accountable for the Devastation of Terrorism' (2003) 56 *Oklahoma Law Review* 735, 736.

[104] See, eg: K Zemanek, 'Self-Defence against Terrorism: Reflexions on an Unprecedented Situation' in FMM Menéndez (ed), *El Derecho internacional en los albores del siglo XXI: Homenaje al professor Juan Manuel Castro-Rial Canosa* (Madrid, Ed Trotta, 2002) 695 especially at 702–05. But see: LN Sadat, 'Terrorism and the Rule of Law' (2004) 3 *Washington University Global Studies Law Review* 135, 144.

[105] See, eg: Zemanek, above n 40 at 130.

[106] See, eg: Becker, above n 4 at 216; O Corten and F Dubuisson, 'Opération "Liberté immuable": une extension abusive du concept de légitime défense' (2002) 106 *RGDIP* 51, 66; SR Ratner, 'Jus ad Bellum and Jus in Bello after September 11' (2002) 96 *AJIL* 905, 908.

[107] Brunnée and Toope, above n 9 at 247, 250 (enumerating human rights, refugee protection and threats to international peace and security as all being subsumed into one super-category of 'threat pre-emption').

of State responsibility.[108] In short, this project attempts to re-establish and delineate the boundary between direct and indirect responsibility, whilst devoting careful analysis to the question of indirect State responsibility in preventing terrorism. Let us start from the premise that several scholars acknowledge that 9/11 operated a significant shift in international law or, at least, challenged it and made combating terrorism a priority.[109]

The events of 9/11 incentivised governments, policy-makers and judiciaries around the globe to revisit and revamp their respective legislation, whether dealing with national security issues[110] or immigration policy.[111] In light of notable shortcomings both in jurisprudence[112] and in the international legal order,[113] the international community also initiated significant changes to the law of State responsibility. Clear-cut cases of overt State involvement – whether through planning and overall control of non-State terrorist organisations or encouraging de facto State agents to breach international obligations (ie 'auxiliaries' or 'volunteers' outsourced by State organs to perpetrate unlawful acts)[114] – are governed by the direct responsibility paradigm. Indeed, it is fair to assume that a State that overtly and directly supports,[115] endorses,[116] authorises,[117] and/or con-

[108] This position, which was also defended elsewhere by the present author, has been endorsed by some commentators. See, eg: K Mohan, 'Terrorism and Asymmetric Warfare: State Responsibility for the Acts of Non-State Entities – Nicaragua, Tadic, and Beyond' (2008) 8 *Journal of the Institute of Justice and International Studies* 211, 211.

[109] See, eg: Brunnée and Toope, above n 9 at 247.

[110] See, eg: 'The Uniting and Strengthening America by Providing Appropriate Tools Required to Intercept and Obstruct Terrorism Act of 2001' (USA PATRIOT ACT), Public Law 107-05, 115 Stat 2721.

[111] On the issue of US changes to immigration policies post-9/11, see L Lebowitz and I Podheiser, 'A Summary of the Changes in Immigration Policies and Practices after the Terrorist Attacks of September 11, 2001: The USA Patriot Act and Other Measures' (2002) 63 *University of Pittsburgh Law Review* 873; KC Tumlin, 'Suspect First: How Terrorism Policy Is Reshaping Immigration Policy' (2004) 92 *California Law Review* 1173.

[112] See, eg: A-M Slaughter and W Burke-White, 'An International Constitutional Moment' (2002) 43 *Harvard International Law Journal* 1, 20 ('The traditional 'effective control' test for attributing an act to a state seems insufficient to address the threats posed by global criminals and the states that harbor them').

[113] Some commentators express that international law is inadequate or, at best, inefficiently tailored to address the phenomenon of modern terrorism. See, eg: MC Bassiouni, 'Legal Control of International Terrorism: A Policy-Oriented Assessment' (2002) 43 *Harvard International Law Journal* 83; Y Daudet, 'International Action against State Terrorism' in R Higgins and M Flory (eds), *Terrorism and International Law* (London, Routledge, 1997) 201 (discussing the emergence of State terrorism and noting that 'The solutions invoked by international law have proved both awkward and inadequate').

[114] See Crawford, above n 68 at 110.

[115] Some commentators opine that this type of State support for terrorist activities could be addressed and met with sanctions through the channel of the UN Security Council. See, eg: MB Baker, 'Terrorism and the Inherent Right of Self-Defense (A Call to Amend Article 51 of the United Nations Charter)' (1987) 10 *Houston Journal of International Law* 25, 26–27.

[116] On the question of responsibility by endorsement, see Brown, above n 50 at 12.

[117] Many important international decisions recognise that conduct authorised by a State may be attributed to it. See, eg: *The Zafiro Case (Great Britain v USA)* (1925) 6 *Reports of International Arbitral Awards* 160; *Stephens Brothers Case (US v Mexico)* (1927) 4 *Reports of International Arbitral Awards* 265, 267; *Lehigh Valley Railroad Company and others (USA v Germany) (Sabotage*

dones a terrorist attack against another State will presumably not withstand international scrutiny. However, based on the theory developed by *Nicaragua* and *Tadić*, it is unclear whether a finding of direct responsibility in those instances would require more than fulfilling these elements for that State to attain the 'effective' or 'overall' control thresholds. A salient example of a State engaging in such practices would be that of Iran, which leads the way across the globe in directly/actively sponsoring terrorism[118] through its funding and training of Hezbollah factions, Palestine Islamic Jihad and Hamas.[119] Hence, both from conceptual and theoretical standpoints, direct responsibility does not generate much confusion.[120] However, the issue of indirect responsibility is far more problematic both in terms of policy and legal content, and therefore warrants careful and thorough examination.

It is nonetheless crucial to acknowledge the abovementioned interplay – sometimes bordering on a 'bastardly' conflation of two distinct regimes[121] – between State responsibility and self-defence. Any analytical endeavour seeking to better define the parameters of State responsibility in counterterrorism contexts should always concomitantly consider the potential benefits of reeling in the law of self-defence into the inquiry.[122] The juxtaposition of these two distinct regimes was very much alive in the *Armed Activities* Case, where the ICJ held that Uganda could not invoke a right to self-defence against the Democratic Republic of the Congo because it had harboured an armed militia on its territory.[123] Aside from actually determining responsibility for a State's mere harbouring of terrorists – perhaps coupled with the provision of logistical support and/or weaponry/training – the prospective invocation of self-defence as a response to State failures to prevent terrorism constitutes one of the primary points of friction in terms of legal policy. In particular, once a State's failure to prevent transnational terrorism becomes a predicate for triggering State responsibility, can an aggrieved State redress that harm by adopting a forcible response based on self-defence?

Whilst the purpose of this monograph is not to shed light on the tenets of self-defence – a self-contained and analytically distinct international legal

Cases: Black Tom and Kingsland incidents) (1930) 8 *Reports of International Arbitral Awards* 84 and (1939) 8 *Reports of International Arbitral Awards* 225, 458.

[118] See, eg: US Department of State, 'Patterns of Global Terrorism: 2001' (May 2002) at 64, available at www.state.gov/documents/organization/10319.pdf.

[119] See, eg: ibid; *Anderson v Islamic Republic of Iran* [2000] 90 F Supp 2d 107 (D.D.C.) at 112; WP Hoye, 'Fighting Fire With . . . Mire? Civil Remedies and the New War on State-Sponsored Terrorism' (2002) 12 *Duke Journal of Comparative & International Law* 105, 107–08.

[120] See Baker, above n 115 at 36 ('Of course, where the state itself is directly behind the terrorist attacks, its responsibility is clear').

[121] See, eg: J-C Martin, *Les règles internationales relatives à la lutte contre le terrorisme* (Brussels, Bruylant, 2006) 497.

[122] See generally: J-M Thouvenin, 'Circumstances Precluding Wrongfulness in the ILC Articles on State Responsibility: Self-Defence' in Crawford et al, above 3 at 455–67.

[123] See below ch 3, section III.B).

category[124] – but rather focus on the implications of counterterrorism for the law of State responsibility, it simply cannot dissociate the former regime entirely from the ensuing analysis. First, it is implausible to deny that State responsibility and self-defence have developed considerably since 9/11, both through the vehicle of United Nations and State practice (*lex lata*) and within legal scholarship as well (*lex ferenda*). Secondly, both regimes have evolved in tandem over the last decade. Indeed, several recent accounts dealing with international responsibility mechanisms inexorably delve into the possibility of invoking self-defence as a response to State failures to prevent terrorism, although not unambiguously or uncontroversially in some instances. Put another way, the use of force against terrorism is consistently envisaged through a State responsibility prism. Hence, a study primarily concerned with elucidating the parameters governing the mechanics of State responsibility that failed to acknowledge the self-defence dimension of this legal debate – most relevantly at the stage of devising legal consequences – would not escape some sense of academic paucity. Thirdly, in analysing State practice on holding governments accountable for failing to prevent terrorism, significant emphasis is placed on the deployment of State responsibility as a legal predicate for the invocation of self-defence. Thus, this explains the presence of precedents involving recourse to force in the present chapter's analysis. Yet, the fact that those episodes implicate Article 2(4) and Article 51 considerations does not disqualify them from having some impact on the primary inquiry. Simply put, the mechanics of State responsibility crop up at an earlier stage following a State's breach of international law, but they are not necessarily antithetical to the subsequent deployment of self-defence repertoire. These remarks act as a preliminary gloss through which post-9/11 evolution of indirect responsibility should be contemplated.

IV. A PARADIGM SHIFT: TOWARDS A LAW OF INDIRECT RESPONSIBILITY

A) Evolution of Indirect Responsibility in International Law

As seen above, ILC Article 2 prescribes that the conduct underlying an internationally wrongful act must be attributable to the State in order to trigger responsibility.[125] This conduct may translate into an action or omission; there is no real difference in the application of both types of behaviour.[126] This portion of Article 2 is undeniably founded for cases like *Nicaragua* and *Tadić*, where State actors share an intimate link with the State or when non-State individuals become de facto State actors, through the mechanisms of control and attribution. However,

[124] See, eg: I Brownlie, *International Law and the Use of Force by States* (Oxford, Clarendon Press, 1963) 375 (underscoring that both regimes should not be conflated).

[125] See above n 90.

[126] Crawford, above n 68 at 82.

what these cases did not consider is easily identifiable: modern terrorism.[127] The world is now faced with novel and significant threats, sophisticated terrorist organisations and complex financial structures. There are instances where States wield no control over terrorists operating on their territory. The only causal link between State and wrongdoer is the fact that they share a territorial connection: they coexist in the same geographically and politically delineated area. An additional element is often juxtaposed in this equation, namely State toleration or acquiescence to terrorists electing that territory as a base of operation.

In response to this challenge, a series of arguments advocating the excision of attribution in this context will be put forth in chapter four, with some insistence on hermeneutically focused policy inclinations.[128] It is nonetheless interesting to now raise the possibility that the law of indirect responsibility might be better served by adjusting the content of some key provisions enshrined in the ILC's *Articles*. For instance, it has been shown above that political pragmatism and evidentiary impediments considerably restrict the prospect of establishing direct responsibility against host-States and, as a corollary, that more passive forms of State involvement in terrorism are increasingly attracting attention. The focus of the inquiry, therefore, is increasingly shifting towards indirect modes of liability, as States are expected to comply with their duties to intervene and to prevent terrorism. Thus, the rationale of indirect responsibility explored in the coming pages might be better addressed through a disjunctive – as opposed to conjunctive – reading of ILC Article 2. Consequently, the ensuing policy-based revision of that provision would entail that 'There is an internationally wrongful act of a State when conduct consisting of an action or omission': '(a) is [**unlawful and**] attributable to the State under international law; ~~and~~ [**OR**] (b) constitutes a breach of an international obligation of the State'.[129] In favouring this construction, the second disjunctive component of the Article emphasises unfettered analytical focus on States' obligation to prevent without expending undue attention to meeting the laborious requirements of attribution. This adjustment might better capture the varying roles sanctuary States play in supporting terrorism – ranging from direct control over terrorist agents to passive toleration of irregular units – but which, in the most problematic cases, entail a more hands-off form of involvement.

Whilst particular brands of catastrophic or large-scale terrorism have become increasingly de-territorialised or decentralised phenomena, the prevalent model nonetheless entails that 'Nonstate actors usually establish a base of operations within the boundaries of a sovereign state from which they plan and carry out terrorist actions in other countries'.[130] Given the State's inherent visibility – as

[127] See generally: Lippman, above n 6.
[128] In particular, see the considerations pertaining to Art 12, below ch 4, II.A).
[129] See original version of Art 2, *ILC Articles*, above n 17.
[130] JJ Teurbe-Tolón, 'Questions Concerning the Legality of the Use of Force in Southern Lebanon During the Israel-Hezbollah Conflict of 2006' (2008) 21 *New York International Law Review* 95, 95 fn 3 and accompanying text.

contrasted with the secretive nature of many terrorist cells or groups – it follows that reacting against a host-State can sometimes be more easily achieved than rooting out a terrorist cell within its borders; all subject to usual limitations cautioned vis-à-vis sovereignty-erosive intrusion into the exclusive jurisdiction of States.[131] To invoke popular parlance, such a State-centric model seeks to cut out the 'middle man' and go directly to the source, depending on whom, precisely, the facts of a given scenario reveal as the actual 'enabler' of an impugned terrorist strike. In other words, when and how a State is cast as the 'enabler' depends largely on matters of factual and conceptual interpretation, bearing ultimately little semantic incidence on the broader equation of counterterrorism if one accepts that a shift towards indirect responsibility now pervades international law.

This prompted Luigi Condorelli to underscore that terrorism fermenting on a State's territory – that is to say having cropped up through the usurpation of the 'lawful exercise of sovereignty, or of exclusive rights of jurisdiction, over a certain territory or space' – serves as a 'catalyst' in triggering State responsibility.[132] From the perspective of forcibly stamping out terrorist networks, the (seemingly sacred) principle of territorial integrity underpinning the modern nation-State also impedes available recourses under the rubric of self-defence, given that 'non-state actors do not operate out of the high seas but are based in other states' territories'.[133] Even in situations of repeated transborder insurgency, respecting territorial integrity and political independence remains an important consideration under international law. A case in point is the 1982 Israel-Lebanon conflict, whereby Lebanon lost control of a portion of its territory from which PLO terrorists launched attacks against Israel. During a period of relative calm in the hostilities, the UN General Assembly called for restoration of 'the exclusive authority of the Lebanese State throughout its territory up to the internationally recognized boundaries'.[134]

In sum, it is fair to say that most terrorist organisations 'have some state association, for terrorist actors must act within a system of sovereign states and

[131] On the tensions arising as a result of the intervention in that State's exclusive jurisdiction, see I Brownlie, *Principles of Public International Law*, 4th edn (Oxford, Clarendon Press, 1990) 287, 377. On the clandestine nature of terrorism, see KW Abbott, 'Economic Sanctions and International Terrorism' (1987) 20 *Vanderbilt Journal of Transnational Law* 289, 298–99; Smith, above n 103 at 738 ('the inherently secret nature of terrorism serves to protect terrorists from punishment. Consequently, it is necessary to focus not on deterring the terrorist organizations that actually carry out attacks, but on holding their State sponsors and supporters accountable').

[132] See L Condorelli, 'The Imputability to States of Acts of International Terrorism' (1989) 19 *Israel Yearbook on Human Rights* 233, 240. See also: Ago, above n 39 at 97, para 65 (also invoking the term 'catalyst' in similar circumstances). From the perspective of territorial jurisdiction, it also follows that 'A state may be subject to penalties for a failure to exercise jurisdiction if the offense is committed within its borders'. See JA McCredie, 'The Responsibility of States for Private Acts of International Terrorism' (1985) 1 *Temple International and Comparative Law Journal* 69, 73.

[133] Duffy, above n 51 at 159 (also noting that concerns arise in this setting regarding the invocation of self-defence).

[134] See GA Res 37/123E of 16 December, UN Doc A/RES/37/123 (1982).

virtually always have bases within states',[135] irrespective of the actual degree of governmental involvement in planning or facilitating excursions carried out by those groups. As a general rule, however, it is likely that such involvement will more frequently translate into the mere toleration by a State of terrorists on its territory, as opposed to active or direct sponsorship of terrorist activity.[136] One must avoid falling prey to the temptation of embracing an all-encompassing conception of territorial association between terrorists and sanctuary States, overly inspired by the Afghanistan-Al Qaeda precedent. Given that 'having a base' within a State can become a vague concept under some lights, it is crucial not to espouse an inordinately reductive model of State-terrorist(s) relationships, particularly in cases where host-States are engaged in a struggle against terrorism but are unable to thwart the threat. Doing so would not only militate in favour of instituting an unrealistic and *absolute* territorial counterterrorism obligation – as opposed to a more practicable due diligence standard – but also remove interesting cases from the analytical purview: the Lord Resistance's Army in Uganda, the Shining Path in Peru, the Unified Communist Party (Maoist) in Nepal, the Japanese Red Army in Japan, to list a few.

Conversely, State support of terrorism has historically proven indispensable in enabling some terrorists to carry out their attacks.[137] As former US State Department advisor Abraham Sofaer noted 12 years before 9/11, 'States have the resources to provide [terrorist] groups with the training, equipment, support, and instructions that enable them to inflict far greater damage than would be possible by independent agents'.[138] As a result, the devastation of State-sponsored terrorism arising in the 1980s exponentially surpassed, in scope and magnitude, the terrorist excursions of independent groups.[139] However, the events of 9/11 have also shown that terrorist cells can act autonomously and carry out large-scale attacks without any direct or significant State support. The Al-Qaeda network, which orchestrated a series of transnational terrorist excursions both before and after 9/11, has implemented fundraising mechanisms across the globe through legal and illegal channels and businesses.[140] Whilst this

[135] RJ Beck and AC Arend, '"Don't Tread on US": International Law and Forcible State Responses to Terrorism' (1994) 12 *Wisconsin International Law Journal* 153, 163. See also: Brown, above n 50 at 4; E Gross, 'The Laws of War Waged between Democratic States and Terrorist Organizations: Real or Illusive?' (2003) 15 *Florida Journal of International Law* 389, 444.

[136] See, eg: Smith, above n 103 at 742.

[137] See, eg: MN Schmitt, 'The Sixteenth Annual Waldemar A. Solf Lecture in International Law: Bellum Americanum Revisited: U.S. Security Strategy and the Jus ad Bellum' (2003) 176 *Military Law Review* 364, 377.

[138] AD Sofaer, 'The Sixth Annual Waldemar A. Solf Lecture in International Law: Terrorism, the Law, and the National Defense' (1989) 126 *Military Law Review* 89, 98. See also: B Hoffman, *Inside Terrorism* (New York, Columbia University Press, 1998) 185–86.

[139] See, eg: ibid, at 189; JF Murphy, *State Support of International Terrorism: Legal, Political, and Economic Dimensions* (Boulder, Westview, 1989) 31.

[140] See, eg: US Department of State, 'Patterns of Global Terrorism: 2002' (April 2003) at 119, available at www.state.gov/documents/organization/20177.pdf. As a result, it follows that 'States may no longer serve as the prominent source of life for terrorist cells'. See Smith, above n 103 at 737. On Al-Qaeda's involvement in the majority of terrorist attacks in the five years following 9/11, see

new model warrants further consideration, terrorist organisations will nonetheless continue to rely heavily on territorial support in order to better plan and execute their excursions.[141] It inexorably follows that terrorists 'still require the sanctuary of States to effectively operate' and that 'States remain an important focus in responding effectively to terrorism'.[142] In that regard, the secondary rules of State responsibility must be critically engaged.

Terrorists may also operate independently and unbeknownst to State authorities. Similarly, one can envisage scenarios where terrorist factions carry out internationally wrongful acts – or acts of aggression and/or terrorist activities – from within the borders of a State without its consent.[143] A manifestation of this type of unsanctioned arrangement took root in the 2006 Israel-Hezbollah conflict, during which the armed wing of Hezbollah launched attacks against Israel from the southern portion of the Lebanese territory.[144] Whilst Lebanon's responsibility can arguably be engaged in that account pursuant to general tenets of international law, the precise mechanics and extent of such accountability remain to be clarified.

In that regard, one cannot overemphasise the importance of the *Tehran Hostages* Case in the evolution of legal regimes applicable to host-States. In 1979, a student militant group took over an American embassy and its consulates in Iran, leading to serious vandalism, destruction of property and the capture and detention of 50 American citizens, mostly diplomatic and consular personnel.[145] In light of these facts, the ICJ first had to ascertain whether the takeover, ransacking of the embassy, and hostage-taking – an operation that lasted approximately three hours – was directly attributable to Iran. Whilst its

Statement of James Caruso, Deputy Executive Assistant Director for Counterterrorism, Federal Bureau of Investigation in *Combating Terrorism: Protecting the United States, Parts 1 and II: Hearings before the House Subcommittee on National Security, Veterans Affairs and International Relations of the Committee on Government Reform, House of Representatives, One Hundred Seventh Congress, Second Session, March 12 and 21, 2002* (Washington, DC, US GPO, 2002) 153; M Levitt, 'Patterns of Terrorism 2002: Terror, Counterterror, and State Sponsorship' (30 April 2003) *Washington Institute for Near East Policy*, available at www.thewashingtoninstitute.org/templateC05.php?CID= 1631.

[141] See, eg: US National Security Council, *National Strategy for Combating Terrorism* (February 2003) at 1, 3, 15-17, 19, available at https://www.cia.gov/news-information/cia-the-war-on-terrorism/Counter_Terrorism_Strategy.pdf; ML O'Sullivan, *Shrewd Sanctions: Statecraft and State Sponsors of Terrorism* (Washington, DC, Brookings Institution Press, 2003) 6, 322 fn 9; Schmitt, above n 137 at 377, 379.

[142] Smith, above n 103 at 737.

[143] See, eg: *Tel-Oren v Libya* [1984] 726 F.2d 774 (DC Cir) at 806–08 (distinguishing State responsibility from the accountability of a non-State actor for supporting terrorism). See also: C Tinker, 'Is the United Nations Convention the Most Appropriate Means to Pursue the Goal of Biological Diversity?: Responsibility for Biological Diversity Conservation Under International Law' (1995) 28 *Vanderbilt Journal of Transnational Law* 777, 785 (inferring that State responsibility cannot be triggered solely by the actions of non-State actors).

[144] See, eg: Teurbe-Tolón, above n 130 at 96. For more background on that conflict, see GW Walker, 'The 2006 Conflict in Lebanon, or What Are the Armed Conflict Rules When Legal Principles Collide?' in DK Linnan (ed), *Enemy Combatants, Terrorism, and Armed Conflict Law: A Guide to the Issues* (Westport, Praeger Security International, 2008) 252–79.

[145] See *Tehran Hostages* Case, above n 11.

reasoning somewhat aligned with the underlying philosophy of *Tadić*, the Court formulated the applicable standard in the following terms:

> Their [the militants'] conduct might be considered as itself *directly imputable* to the Iranian State only if it were established that, in fact, on the occasion in question the militants acted on behalf of the State, having been charged by some competent organ of the Iranian State to carry out a specific operation (emphasis added).[146]

Ultimately, the ICJ rejected the rationale of direct State involvement in the attack but recognised that Iran had failed to fulfil its duty to protect foreign diplomatic missions from assault.[147] A finding of direct responsibility in this scenario 'would have required that the attackers act as agents or organs of the Iranian government, but no evidence indicated that to be the case'.[148]

Although Iran was not found *directly* responsible, the Court proceeded on the basis of indirect responsibility, thereby magnifying Iran's obligation to protect the embassy and its personnel, and underlining that its conclusion that:

> [T]he initiation of the attack on the United States Embassy . . . and . . . the attacks on the Consulates at Tabriz and Shiraz the following day, cannot be considered as in itself imputable to the Iranian State does not mean that Iran is, in consequence, free of any responsibility in regard to those attacks; *for its own conduct was in conflict with its international obligations* (emphasis added).[149]

By virtue of several treaty provisions and international legal principles, Iran was deemed to have a duty to protect the victims of the attack, along with the embassy.[150] Furthermore, the Court emphasised the importance of the obligation at hand, labelling it a 'categorical' duty, thereby expecting Iran to 'take appropriate steps' in order to fulfil this undertaking.[151] In an excerpt ostensibly building upon the starting point of modern indirect responsibility formulated in the French text of *Corfu Channel*,[152] the ICJ articulated Iran's failure to protect the embassy in a manner conceptually and philosophically adjacent to the modern obligation to prevent terrorism. The Court emphasised that

> the Iranian Government failed altogether to take any 'appropriate steps' to protect the premises, staff and archives of the United States' mission against attack by the

[146] ibid, at para 58.

[147] See ibid (concluding that, in light of the evidence before it, the Court could not establish the requisite nexus between the State and the militant group).

[148] Brown, above n 50 at 10–11.

[149] *Tehran Hostages* Case, above n 11 at para 61.

[150] ibid, at para 61–62.

[151] ibid, at para 61:

> By a number of provisions of the Vienna Conventions of 1961 and 1963, Iran was placed under the most categorical obligations, as a receiving State, to take appropriate steps to ensure the protection of the United States Embassy and Consulates, their staffs, their archives, their means of communication and the freedom of movement of the members of their staffs.

[152] On the broader reading of State responsibility law in the French version of the *Corfu Channel* decision, see above ch 1, section IV.A), especially nn 130–34 and accompanying text; below nn 175–76 and accompanying text.

militants, and to take any steps either to prevent this attack or to stop it before it reached its completion.[153]

The Court added that 'the failure of the Iranian Government to take such steps was due to more than mere negligence or lack of appropriate means'.[154] Amongst several factors considered by the Court, the question of the State's inaction on that specific day bears special consideration. Indeed, the ICJ reviewed several other similar instances where Iranian authorities reacted pro-actively to thwart hostage situations. In light of previous State involvement in combating insurrectional conduct, the Court found that Iran's passiveness in the *Tehran Hostages* Case was blatantly inconsistent with that line of precedents.[155]

Thus, a more limpid boundary between direct and indirect responsibility was finally drawn in *Tehran Hostages*. It is now clear that, under the direct responsibility paradigm, the initial focus of the inquiry hinges on the conduct of an extraneous person or group and not on the actions of the State itself. The overarching objective, therefore, is to establish whether the wrongful action or omission, engendered by the person or group, is directly attributable to the State. Through the lens of *Nicaragua* and *Tadić*, this primary objective becomes inordinately contingent on questions of control and direction exerted by the State over the person or group that authored the wrongful act. In fact, the question of control exercised by the State has become a sort of touchstone in scholarly attempts to reconcile both judgments.[156] In broader terms, the notion of governmental control over non-official State entities and/or non-State actors often remains inextricably tied to the deployment of State responsibility mechanics. In fact, this idea even became the focal point in situations involving the application of the formal rules of State responsibility within domestic legal repertoire, notably in the *Trendtex Trading* case.[157]

Under the aegis of a strictly traditionalist approach, the analysis culminates into three possible scenarios: the acts of State agents officially emanate from the corresponding State; non-State actors are deemed to be de facto government agents; or the acts of terrorists/insurgents are directly attributable to the State without labelling them formal State instrumentalities or agents per se (ie by way of official State endorsement or adoption of the wrongful conduct).[158] Moreover, in times of war traditional State responsibility encompasses acts of military

[153] *Tehran Hostages* Case, above n 11 at para 63.

[154] ibid.

[155] ibid.

[156] See, eg: D Jinks, 'State Responsibility for the Acts of Private Armed Groups' (2003) 4 *Chicago Journal of International Law* 83, 89.

[157] See *Trendtex Trading Corp v Central Bank of Nigeria* [1977] 1 QB 529 (CA) at 559–60.

[158] Along similar lines, consider P-M Dupuy, 'State Sponsors of Terrorism: Issues of International Responsibility' in A Bianchi (ed), *Enforcing International Law Norms against Terrorism* (Oxford, Hart Publishing, 2004) 3 at 9–11 (distinguishing, on one hand, 'acts of terrorism *directly* perpetrated by a State's organs' from 'acts which were carried out by private persons, but with the support and / or control of a State' and identifying, on the other, similar classifications of State-condoned or ultra vires and non-State actions). See also: P-M Dupuy, 'Quarante ans de codification du droit de la responsabilité internationale des Etats: un bilan' (2003) 107 *RGDIP* 305.

personnel acting both in an official capacity and in an ultra vires fashion, and those perpetrated by individual soldiers in a private capacity.[159] Turning to 9/11, however, it seems improbable that those attacks could be attributed to the Afghan government, even if contemplated through the lens of subsequent endorsement. Indeed, the public record indicates that Al Qaeda benefited from a large margin of autonomy within Afghanistan. Furthermore, there is no evidence that Afghanistan endorsed the attacks. Quite the contrary, it disavowed any involvement in the excursions.[160] Similar reasoning also extends to the lead-up to the 2006 Israel-Lebanon war, as Lebanon never claimed that it 'ordered' Hezbollah to attack Israel or 'provided' any direction on that front.[161] In that regard, Lebanese Prime Minister Siniora rather emphasised that 'The [Lebanese] government . . . was not aware of what was to take place and does not adopt the operation carried out by Hizbullah to capture the two Israeli soldiers'.[162]

Contrary to direct responsibility, which focuses on the wrongful act itself, indirect responsibility is predominantly concerned with the conduct of the State, embodied in its failure to fulfil an international obligation (eg failing to adopt measures to prevent or punish terrorism emanating from its territory) rather than in its commission of some positive act (eg instructing, funding, arming, controlling and sending terrorists to murder civilians in a neighbouring country). This type of responsibility was thoroughly explored in the *Velásquez Rodríguez* Case. Speaking to the interpretation of obligations that could readily be analogised to counterterrorism undertakings, the IACHR voiced its position in the following terms:

> An illegal act which violates human rights and which is initially not directly imputable to a State (for example, because it is the act of a private person or because the person responsible has not been identified) can lead to international responsibility of the State, not because of the act itself, but because of the lack of due diligence to prevent the violation or to respond to it as required by the Convention.[163]

Similarly, whilst the rubric of 'indirect responsibility' should attract a broader categorisation and cannot be reduced to context-specific liability standards (eg *respondeat superior*), it has sometimes been referred to as 'vicarious responsibility', perhaps erroneously.[164] Whilst some international legal accounts dealing with 'vicarious responsibility' make analogies and parallels immensely useful

[159] See, eg: L Condorelli, 'Imputation à l'Etat d'un fait internationalement illicite: solutions classiques et nouvelles tendences' (1984-VI) 189 *Recueil des Cours* 9, 146; Condorelli, above n 132 at 233 ff.

[160] See, eg: Brown, above n 50 at 11.

[161] See 'Statement by Prime Minister Fouad Siniora', *The Daily Star Lebanon*, 16 July 2006, available at www.dailystar.com.lb/article.asp?edition_ID=1&article_ID=74027&categ_id=2#.

[162] ibid.

[163] *Velásquez Rodríguez* Case, above n 86 at para 172.

[164] The concept of indirect responsibility, as construed in the present book, is somewhat compatible with the notion of 'vicarious responsibility' advanced in R Jennings and A Watts (eds), *Oppenheim's International Law*, 9th edn (London, Longman, 1992–96) 502–03. Invoking similar jargon, Brown, above n 50 at 13, also expresses the difference between direct responsibility (labelled 'original responsibility' therein) and indirect responsibility.

on points of detail, this study argues for a stand-alone category of 'indirect responsibility' that may or may not implicate some elements found in context-specific liability standards, depending on the circumstances at hand. Moreover, several municipal legal constructions of the principle of 'vicarious responsibility' predicate the establishment of liability on the absence of any misbehaviour or unlawful act on the part of the party responsible, thereby making a rapprochement with the topic at hand conceptually dubious. Indeed, holding States accountable for failing to prevent terrorism under international law categorically implies wrongdoing by the State, predominantly manifested by its failure to intervene and meet its due diligence threshold when it was compelled to do so by a positive obligation.

In the aftermath of 9/11, a shift towards indirect responsibility has emerged whenever a State's territory is used to launch or prepare a terrorist strike, or when a State harbours terrorists. This evolution now requires meticulous and thoughtful consideration.

B) Impact on Primary Norms: The Emergence of the Harbouring and Supporting Rule

Unlike under the direct responsibility paradigm, indirect responsibility entails a far more subtle type of involvement. As mentioned previously, the focus of the analysis rests on the understanding that, absent any direct/overt involvement of the State in a terrorist attack launched from its territory, that State may still be held accountable for its failure to prevent the excursion.

It is well documented that States will usually not answer for the acts of private or non-State actors or, at the very least, that the unlawful behaviour will not be attributable to them.[165] In other words, only conduct of the State's organs will be imputable to it. However, international law also recognises that the actions of private persons may bind the State, should those actors or groups qualify as 'agents' of the State.[166] Absent any control or instigation by the State so as to elude the considerations extracted from *Nicaragua* and *Tadić*, a terrorist organisation that carries out an attack on a stand-alone basis cannot be tantamount to an 'agent' of the State. The legal regime applicable to those perpetrators' actions, therefore, becomes somewhat intractable or, at least, difficult to circumscribe unless one surmises that the various laws governing international

[165] See, eg: Jennings and Watts, above n 164 at 502–03; Malanczuk, above n 3 at 259. For a thoughtful account on the issue, see Wolfrum, above n 69 at 423–34.

[166] See Brownlie, above n 45 at 132–66; DD Caron, 'The Basis of Responsibility: Attribution and Other Trans-Substantive Rules' in RB Lillich and D Magraw (eds), *The Iran-United States Claims Tribunal: Its Contribution to the Law of State Responsibility* (Irvington-on-Hudson, Transnational Publishers, 1998) 109. On the specific question of Osama bin Laden's status as an agent of the State, see the comments of J Quigley, 'International Law Violations by the United States in the Middle East as a Factor Behind Anti-American Terrorism' (2002) 63 *University of Pittsburgh Law Review* 815, 826.

crimes can fill that void.[167] Significant policy questions crop up: how can we ensure government accountability for failing to diligently suppress terrorism even if the State had no direct involvement in its perpetration? Can State responsibility play a role in suppressing terrorism so as to avoid impunity and shift the focus squarely on prevention, transnational cooperation and vigilant law enforcement?

Historically, the idea that States will usually not be responsible for the actions of private persons was deeply rooted in international legal culture and has been confirmed on a number of occasions, including in the *Tellini* Case of 1923.[168] Following the assassination on Greek territory of several members of an international commission overseeing the delimitation of the Greek-Albanian border, the League of Nations convened a special legal commission.[169] It sought to have that commission address the legal issues raised by the international incident.[170] Although the commission clearly rejected the possible attribution of the assassination to Greece, it opined that a State could be held responsible in like circumstances if it 'has neglected to take all reasonable measures for the prevention of the crime and pursuit, arrest and bringing to justice of the criminal'.[171] This language foreshadowed a move from the more traditional analysis of the connection between State actors and the governing apparatus to a rigorous examination of the conduct of the State itself vis-à-vis the wrongful act authored by private persons. These considerations become even more relevant when contrasted with the *Tehran Hostages* Case.

The parallel between both cases is striking, even though they were decided nearly 60 years apart. In both instances, the inquiry hinged on a rationale of indirect responsibility, with particular emphasis placed on the State's failure to bring its conduct within the purview of its international obligation to prevent the occurrence of a given illicit event. To refute the claim that the acts of private actors may be attributable to the sanctuary State in such circumstances is the best way to understand *Tehran Hostages*:

> For example a receiving State is not responsible, as such, for the acts of private individuals in seizing an embassy, but it will be responsible if it fails to take all necessary steps to protect the embassy from seizure, or to regain control over it.[172]

As mentioned previously, the *Tehran Hostages* decision was instrumental in advancing the law governing indirect responsibility. The ICJ recognised that a

[167] See, eg: Wolfrum, above n 69 at 424 (speaking to the difficulty of conceptualising the law of State responsibility in relation to individuals).

[168] For more background and discussion on this case, see J Barros, *The Corfu Incident of 1923: Mussolini and the League of Nations* (Princeton, Princeton University Press, 1965).

[169] Twenty and twenty-first meetings, League of Nations (1923) 11 *Official Journal*, 4th Year 1338–52 at 1349 (discussing proper jurisdiction for such matters under Art 15 of the *League of Nations Covenant*).

[170] See Crawford, above n 68 at 91.

[171] League of Nations (1924) 4 *Official Journal*, 5th Year at 524. See also: Crawford, above n 68 at 91 fn 99 (citing the *Janes Case (US v Mexico)* (1925) 4 *Reports of International Arbitral Awards* 82).

[172] Crawford, above n 68 at 92.

State can be responsible for the actions of irregulars launched from its territory, especially when the wrongful act could have been avoided or even partially thwarted. ILC Special Rapporteur Crawford acknowledged that 'In the *Diplomatic and Consular Staff* case, the Court concluded that the responsibility of Iran was entailed by the "inaction" of its authorities which "failed to take appropriate steps", in circumstances where such steps were evidently called for'.[173] Bearing in mind that terrorism poses a significant and polymorphic threat, it is apparent that State inaction will be thoroughly scrutinised when a given terrorist strike could have been avoided. At the primary level of the international breach (here, the engagement of State responsibility entails, first and foremost, the violation of a primary norm, eg the obligation to prevent terrorism), the analysis will ineluctably shift towards establishing a duty to forestall attacks as opposed to funding, supporting or directing terrorist activities. As a corollary, this paradigm shift towards indirect responsibility correspondingly signals the imposition of a greater burden of precaution or prevention on States.[174]

These propositions are bolstered by the *Corfu Channel* decision which, in tandem with the fact that its French text is authoritative,[175] provides considerable legal ammunition in advocating the adoption of a responsibility-expansive standard for injurious activities emanating from a State's territory. Indeed, the French version of the judgment excises the notion of 'consent' or 'knowledge' from the equation and creates a stringent obligation upon States to diligently suppress and prevent harmful acts launched from their territory.[176] There is every indication – and certainly strong policy impetus – that this rationale extends to counterterrorism and concomitantly substantiates the adoption of an indirect State responsibility standard for failing to prevent terrorism.

Another undeniable pivotal point of reference in the modern development of indirect responsibility resides in the interpretation of post-9/11 responses. Following the attacks carried out by Al Qaeda against American targets, the US and its allies launched an international response against Afghanistan.[177] Some

[173] ibid, at 82.

[174] An attempt to implement a strict liability-infused approach to facilitate the law of indirect State responsibility is carried out below in ch 4, section V; ch 5. Bearing in mind such domestic law analogies for the moment, it is interesting to note, in passing, that the cost of preventing terrorist acts is particularly acute in the context of landowner liability. See, eg: ML Reynolds, 'Landowner Liability for Terrorist Acts' (1996) 47 *Case Western Law Review* 155, 175. On the question of insurance policies, see TS Renoux and A Roux, 'The Rights of Victims and Liability of the State' in Higgins and Flory, above n 113 at 252 ('As for the insurance companies, they have for a long time excluded terrorist attacks from their risks covered').

[175] See above ch 1 n 133 and accompanying text.

[176] *Corfu Channel* Case, above n 11 at 22.

[177] With regard to the underlying considerations of the US' decision to attack Afghanistan, including self-defence concerns and alternative routes contemplated by the US, see D Abramowitz, 'The President, Congress, and Use of Force: Legal and Political Considerations in Authorizing Use of Force against International Terrorism' (2002) 43 *Harvard International Law Journal* 71.

commentators questioned the legality of such retaliation[178] while others condoned it or, at least, found it justified under existing legal standards.[179] Regardless of one's interpretation of this response, US-led action in Afghanistan has significantly affected international law, especially the field of State responsibility.

One could certainly argue that the classical test of attribution, as formulated in *Nicaragua*, has been subverted by US-led action in Afghanistan. More moderate commentators express that 'aspects of collective response to the September 11 attacks strongly suggest that the threshold for attribution has been lowered substantially'.[180] Others suggest the existence of a varying scale under the *Nicaragua* framework in characterising acts of terrorism as 'armed attacks',[181] by reference to Article 51 of the UN Charter.[182] Regardless of competing legal interpretations of post-9/11 responses – whether framed within the furrow of State responsibility or self-defence – it is difficult to contend that Afghanistan exercised effective or even overall control over Al Qaeda. Publicly available facts tend to demonstrate that this State harboured terrorists and, at best, provided them with limited logistical support.[183] Hence, the attribution argument, as advanced under *Nicaragua*'s and *Tadić*'s line of reasoning, seems to fail at the outset given Al Qaeda's complex structure and large margin of organisational and operational autonomy.[184] In such scenarios, assertions that private conduct

[178] See, eg: J Quigley, 'The Afghanistan War and Self-Defense' (2003) 37 *Valparaiso University Law Review* 541; S Becker, '"Mirror, Mirror on the Wall . . .": Assessing the Aftermath of September 11th' (2003) 37 *Valparaiso University Law Review* 563. For different views on this debate, see also: ME O'Connell, 'Lawful and Unlawful Wars against Terrorism' in VP Nanda (ed), *Law in the War on International Terrorism* (Ardsley, Transnational Publishers, 2005) 79; JJ Paust, 'Use of Armed Force against Terrorists in Afghanistan, Iraq, and Beyond' (2002) 35 *Cornell International Law Journal* 533, 533–57.

[179] See, eg: Brown, above n 50; ME O'Connell, 'Lawful Self-Defense to Terrorism' (2002) 63 *University of Pittsburgh Law Review* 889, 889–909; JJ Paust, 'Post-9/11 Overreaction and Fallacies Regarding War and Defense, Guantanamo, the Status of Persons, Treatment, Judicial Review of Detention, and Due Process in Military Commissions' (2004) 79 *Notre Dame Law Review* 1335, 1344.

[180] Jinks, above n 156 at 89; B Michael, 'Responding to Attacks by Non-State Actors: The Attribution Requirement of Self-Defence' (2009) 16 *Australian International Law Journal* 133, 136.

[181] Similarly, it is widely accepted that international responsibility also entails varying degrees of actual liability. See G Arangio-Ruiz, 'State Fault and the Forms and Degrees of International Responsibility: Questions of Attribution and Relevance' in M Virally (ed), *Le Droit international au service de la paix, de la justice et du développement: mélanges Michel Virally* (Paris, Pedone, 1991) 25; W Riphagen, 'Second Report on the Content, Forms and Degrees of International Responsibility', UN Doc A/CN.4/344 (1981) reprinted in (1981) 2 *Yearbook of International Law Commission* 79, UN Doc A/CN.4/SER.A/1981/Add.1.

[182] See SD Murphy, 'Terrorism and the Concept of "Armed Attack" in Article 51 of the U.N. Charter' (2002) 43 *Harvard International Law Journal* 41.

[183] It appears that Al Qaeda operated independently from the Taliban regime. See, eg: M Mofidi and AE Eckert, '"Unlawful Combatants" or "Prisoners of War": The Law and Politics of Labels' (2003) 36 *Cornell International Law Journal* 59, 75. In justifying self-defence against Afghanistan, the US premised its position according to a two-prong approach. First, it characterised 9/11 as an 'armed attack', pursuant to Art 51 of the UN Charter. Second, it predicated its right to use force on the fact that Afghanistan had 'supported' and 'harboured' members of Al Qaeda. See JI Charney, 'The Use of Force against Terrorism and International Law' (2001) 95 *AJIL* 835; Jinks, above n 156 at 89.

[184] See Brown, above n 50 at 11.

should be attributed to a host-State are generally hard to countenance, given the tenuous connection between the international misfeasor(s) and the official State apparatus.

In retrospect, Afghanistan probably did not have any direct implication in or knowledge of the preparation or planning of the attacks.[185] However, the US could not simply pin responsibility on Al Qaeda alone but 'sought to impute al Qaeda's conduct to Afghanistan simply because the Taliban had harbored and supported the group'.[186] Yet, the US did not initially entertain a claim that Al Qaeda acted on behalf of the Afghan government. It rather favoured a rationale of indirect involvement, stating that Afghanistan had supported members of Al Qaeda.[187] Nevertheless, as the stage was being set for retaliatory strikes against Afghanistan, President Bush pronounced direct accusations against the Afghan government, declaring that its members had committed murder by supporting and harbouring terrorists.[188] Despite this, it is fair to underline that 'the United States and its allies never expressly advanced the argument that the Taliban regime directed or controlled the actions of Al-Qaeda, or adopted Al-Qaeda conduct as its own, thus satisfying standard agency criteria for the attribution of private acts'.[189] The American position was perhaps further buttressed by the fact that the international community had seemingly convicted Afghanistan of harbouring Al Qaeda members on its territory and, additionally, of providing them with logistical support in the preparation of their excursions.[190] This finding, coupled with the quasi-immediate conflation of Al Qaeda and Afghanistan, puzzled certain scholars.[191] This confusion and, perhaps irony, was further exacerbated by the fact that the US Central Intelligence Agency had initially supported the Taliban in their efforts to repel Soviet troops some years earlier.[192]

As the 'war' on terror transitioned into a full-fledged operation, it became clear that the US would not differentiate between host-States and terrorists,[193] and would concomitantly attempt to extirpate 9/11 perpetrators from any territory

[185] See Jinks, above n 156 at 89.

[186] ibid.

[187] See, eg: Letter Dated 9 October 2001 from President Bush to congressional leaders reporting on combat at para 1, available at http://avalon.law.yale.edu/sept11/president_040.asp ('U.S. Armed Forces began combat action in Afghanistan against Al Qaida terrorists and their *Taliban supporters*. This military action is a part of our campaign against terrorism and is designed to disrupt the use of *Afghanistan as a terrorist base of operations'* (emphasis added)).

[188] See, eg: 'A NATION CHALLENGED; Bush's Remarks on U.S. Military Strikes in Afghanistan', New York Times, 8 October 2001 at B6; President Bush's Statement to the UN General Assembly on 10 November 2001, available at www.un.org/webcast/ga/56/statements/011110usaE.htm.

[189] Becker, above n 4 at 216–17. See also: Duffy, above n 51 at 54, 189.

[190] See, eg: M Byers, 'Terrorism, the Use of Force, and International Law After 11 September' (2001) 51 *ICLQ* 401, 403.

[191] See, eg: Dupuy, above n 158 at 9 (characterising this turn of events as 'striking').

[192] See, eg: R Mackenzie, 'The United States and the Taliban' in W Maley (ed), *Fundamentalism Reborn? Afghanistan and the Taliban* (New York, NYU Press, 1998) 90 at 91.

[193] See Jinks, above n 156 at 84–85.

that offered them shelter.[194] As the US shifted its national security posture to a vision of 'strategic unilateralism and tactical multilateralism',[195] it became clear that, with it, its approach in the 'war' on terror also shifted 'from one that targeted terrorists as criminals to one that treats terrorists and supporting States capable of threatening the US and its allies, as threats to national security'.[196] Whilst this inclination prompted scholars to query whether the law of State responsibility would now 'require an even lower standard of control of the "host" state over the terrorists in its midst',[197] it certainly cast a shadow of doubt over the traditional rules governing attribution. Support, even acquiescence, for this position may be found in the global community of States.[198] Nevertheless, the oft-reiterated US belief that there should be no escape clause for States that harbour terrorists triggered a polemic over whether the 'harbouring and supporting' principle created a corresponding primary rule of international law,[199] or whether it solely engendered a change in the secondary rules of attribution. Should the latter interpretation be retained, it might signal that *Nicaragua*'s and *Tehran Hostages*' respective lines of inquiry have been overridden by contemporaneous events.[200]

Through a conceptually nebulous application of international law, the US collapsed direct and indirect responsibility into one unpalatable approach; indeed, the US finding of responsibility against Afghanistan was imbued both with direct and indirect responsibility undertones. From a logical perspective, equating host-States with terrorists is hardly defendable absent clear and compelling evidence of collusion between both entities, including egregious perpetration of terroristic enterprises by State agents or members of the governing apparatus. However, the

[194] In his Statement to the UN General Assembly, above n 188, President Bush also spoke to this point ('The allies of terror are equally guilty of murder and equally accountable to justice. The Taliban are now learning this lesson -- that regime and the terrorists who support it are now virtually indistinguishable').

[195] The language is borrowed from HH Koh, 'Jefferson Memorial Lecture: Transnational Legal Process after September 11th' (2004) 22 *Berkeley Journal of International Law* 337, 350–51.

[196] AA Sofaer, 'On the Necessity of Pre-emption' (2003) 14 *EJIL* 209, 209.

[197] S Wiessner, 'The Articles on State Responsibility and Contemporary International Law' in Koufa, above n 42 at 257–58.

[198] For instance, the European Union General Affairs Council stated the following on 8 October 2001: 'The Al Qaida network and the regime which supports and harbours it are now facing the consequences of their action'. See 'EU Declares Full Solidarity and Wholehearted Support for U.S.', Washington File (EUR515), US Department of State, Washington, DC, 12 October 2001, available at www.european-security.com/index.php?id=525. It should be emphasised that not a single State took issue with the US' posture in the UN General Assembly. Consequently, Travalio and Altenburg infer that 'The world reaction – or more accurately, the lack for a world reaction – to the consistently repeated U.S. position is perhaps the strongest manifestation of evolving customary international law regarding the use of force against terrorism'. See G Travalio and J Altenburg, 'Terrorism, State Responsibility, and the Use of Military Force' (2003) 4 *Chicago Journal of International Law* 97, 109.

[199] See Jinks, above n 156 at 95.

[200] Travalio and Altenburg, above n 198 at 110, expound that 'the rules regarding the imputation of state responsibility for terrorist attacks have evolved since the Nicaragua and Iran Hostages Cases'. They further argue, at 105, that 'these two cases should be confined to their facts and are not applicable to transnational terrorist groups who threaten previously unimagined destruction. See also: Slaughter and Burke-White, above n 112 at 20; P Margulies, 'When to Push the Envelope: Legal Ethics, the Rule of Law, and National Security Strategy' (2007) 30 *Fordham International Law Journal* 642, 647 fn 21 (suggesting that a 'broader standard is appropriate to encourage State diligence').

portion of the 9/11 precedent pertaining to indirect responsibility signals a monumental shift in international law; whilst the US never explicitly set out what, exactly, the notion of 'harbouring' entailed legally, certain scholars nonetheless construe it as the catalyst of a 'revolution in the law of state responsibility'.[201]

Whilst the duty to prevent terrorism can be grounded in general principles of international law and important jurisprudential pronouncements, post-9/11 Security Council practice can nevertheless be construed as a law-shaping endeavour, even accepting the premise that such obligation should be rooted in treaty law, which, incidentally, it also is across a vast spectrum of international instruments. As Professor Franck highlights, 'practice cannot by itself amend a treaty, but, as the Court has also pointed out [in the *Namibia Advisory Opinion*], the practice of a UN organ may be seen to interpret the text and thereby to shape our understanding of it'.[202] On another occasion dealing solely with State practice in the *Nicaragua* decision, the ICJ delivered similar reasoning:

> The significance for the Court of cases of State conduct prima facie inconsistent with the principle of non-intervention lies in the nature of the ground offered as justification. Reliance by a State on a novel right or an unprecedented exception to the principle might, if shared in principle by other States, tend towards modification of customary international law.[203]

Scholars have put forth like-minded advances regarding the *ILC Articles on State Responsibility*, most notably to the effect that their future development and application should take certain suggested revisions and criticisms into account.[204] In the aggregate, therefore, it is fair to interpret US action in Afghanistan as motivated by the Afghan State's failure to prevent terrorist attacks emanating from its territory and its refusal to stop harbouring Al Qaeda members.[205] As a corollary, the impact of the US-led invasion of Afghanistan on the law of State responsibility needs to be ascertained more clearly; it appears,

[201] See, eg: S Shahshahani, 'Politics Under the Cover of Law: Can International Law Help Resolve the Iran Nuclear Crisis?' (2007) 25 *Boston University International Law Journal* 369, 399–400.

[202] Franck, above n 50 at 174 (citing *Legal Consequences for States of the Continued Presence of South Africa in Namibia (South West Africa) Notwithstanding Security Council Resolution 276 (1970)*, Advisory Opinion of 21 June, *ICJ Reports* (1971) 16 at 22, para 22). See also: *Nicaragua*, above n 10 at 109, para 207.

[203] *Nicaragua*, above n 10 at 109, para 207.

[204] See, eg: C Yamada, 'Revisiting the International Law Commission's Draft Articles on State Responsibility' in Ragazzi, above n 19 at 118.

[205] There are hints of this reasoning in Letter dated 7 October 2001 from the Permanent Representative of the United States of America to the United Nations addressed to the President of the Security Council, UN Doc S/2001/946 (2001):

> [M]y Government has obtained clear and compelling information that the Al-Qaeda organization, which is supported by the Taliban regime in Afghanistan, had a central role in the attacks . . . The attacks . . . and the ongoing threat to the United States . . . posed by the Al-Qaeda organization have been made possible by the decision of the Taliban regime to allow the parts of Afghanistan that it controls to be used by this organization as a base of operation.

See also: ibid ('From the territory of Afghanistan, the Al-Qaeda organization continues to train and support agents of terror who attack innocent people'); CS Wren, 'US Advises UN Council More Strikes Could Come', *New York Times*, 9 October 2001 at B5.

at least prima facie, that this precedent has considerably relaxed some standards of State responsibility and consecrated a shift towards a law of indirect responsibility when dealing with counterterrorism obligations.

This type of legal reasoning is not entirely novel. The terms of the 1970 UN Declaration on Friendly Relations were also precursory to the modern law of indirect responsibility, as they prescribed that

> [e]very State has the duty to refrain from organizing, instigating, assisting or participating in acts of civil strife or terrorist acts in another State *or acquiescing in organized activities within its territory* directed towards the commission of such acts, when the acts referred to in the present paragraph involve a threat or use of force (emphasis added).[206]

It becomes apparent that the UN General Assembly might have been concerned not only with host-States directly orchestrating attacks against other nations, but also with the possibility of passive, wilfully blind or negligent governments not exercising a sufficient degree of control or diligence over irregular units. Prior to 9/11, it was still unclear whether the mere tolerance or passive support of terrorist organisations on its territory was sufficient to trigger a State's responsibility for failing to prevent or monitor their activities.[207] State terrorism was, and should be, perceived as particularly serious for it constitutes a fundamental breach of international law. Yet, the practice of State terrorism may arguably take on different forms – from direct action to mere tolerance – thereby obfuscating the search for clear legal postulates governing the direct/indirect dichotomy (eg when does mere toleration fulfil the criteria of State terrorism and trigger the mechanics of direct responsibility, and when does the same conduct trigger the application of indirect responsibility?).

Although somewhat relevant prior to 9/11, the concept of 'harbouring' and 'supporting' terrorists now seems to have achieved international precedence over more traditional, agency-based applications of attribution. This change is particularly significant when considering that both *Nicaragua*[208] and *Tadić*[209] rejected financial and military assistance as the sole basis for imputing direct

[206] Declaration on Principles of International Law Concerning Friendly Relations and Co-operation Among States in Accordance with the Charter of the United Nations, GA Res 2625, UN GAOR, 25th Sess, Supp No 28, UN Doc A/RES/25/2625 (1970) 122; Baker, above n 115 at 38. See also: J Peirano, 'International Responsibility and Cooperation for Development' in Ragazzi, above n 19 at 191.

[207] See, eg: Daudet, above n 113 at 202.

[208] The ICJ also added, in *Nicaragua*, above n 10 at para 115, that the participation by the State,

> even if preponderant or decisive, in the financing, organizing, training, supplying and equipping of the *contras*, the selection of its military or paramilitary targets, and the planning of the whole of its operation, is still insufficient in itself . . . for the purpose of attributing to the United States the acts committed by the *contras*.

See also: ibid, at para 110.

[209] *Tadić*, above n 10 at para 130 ('it is not sufficient for the group to be financially or even militarily assisted by a State').

responsibility to a State,[210] even if such aid proved 'preponderant or decisive'. Taking this finding as one of the only consistent and uncontroversial points between these two decisions, coupled with the fact that various actors across the globe are attempting to forestall terrorists' financial autonomy,[211] two conclusions seem apposite.

First, there seems to be an irreconcilable discrepancy between the reasoning underpinning *Nicaragua* and *Tadić*, both of which impose a stringent burden on aggrieved States in order to establish direct responsibility, and the US-Afghanistan precedent, which seems to alleviate an injured State's onus on an exponential level when contemplated through a State responsibility prism.[212] The international community is thus shaping a standard that even State-sponsored, State-organised or State-condoned terrorism cannot obscure or eschew, a standard that would rather simply condemn the opening of national borders to terrorist organisations as a basis for engaging international liability. Based on that logic, the mere provision of logistical support or the sheltering of terrorists on national territory will supplant any inquiry into the level of control a State exerts over a given attack. It follows that the onus of the injured State in establishing indirect responsibility has decreased considerably, whilst the burden of precaution and accountability of the host-State has grown significantly. As a corollary, the notions of risk management, precaution and legal accountability constitute running themes throughout any study of the interplay between State responsibility and transnational terrorism.[213] As ILC Special Rapporteur Sreenivasa Rao concluded in his Third Report on international liability for injurious consequences arising out of acts not prohibited by international law, 'prevention . . . is concerned with the management of risk'.[214]

[210] For a discussion of these aspects, see Wolfrum, above n 69 at 428–29. For a recent application of this idea by the ICJ, see *Genocide Case*, above n 66 at 139, para 388.

[211] Much has been written on the efforts to freeze terrorist assets and to obstruct fundraising channels of extremist organisations. See, eg: FN Baldwin, 'The Rule of Law, Terrorism and Countermeasures Including the USA Patriot Act of 2001' (2004) 16 *Florida Journal of International Law* 43; NJ Crimm, 'High Alert: The Government's War on the Financing of Terrorism and its Implications for Donors, Domestic Charitable Organizations, and Global Philanthropy' (2004) 45 *William and Mary Law Review* 1341; ME Engel, 'Donating "Blood Money": Fundraising for International Terrorism by United States and the Government's Efforts to Constrict the Flow' (2004) 12 *Cardozo Journal of International and Comparative Law* 251; EJ Gouvin, 'Bringing Out the Big Guns: The USA Patriot Act, Money Laundering, and the War on Terrorism' (2003) 55 *Baylor Law Review* 955.

[212] On the notion of 'injured State(s)' under the law of State responsibility, see G Gaja, 'The Concept of an Injured State' in Crawford et al, above n 3 at 941–47; RH Vinaixa, 'Plurality of Injured States' in ibid, at 949–55.

[213] For thoughtful accounts on the interplay between these concepts and the law of State responsibility, see J Brunnée, 'International Legal Accountability through the Lens of the Law of State Responsibility' (2005) 36 *Netherlands Yearbook of International Law* 21; WG Werner, 'Responding to the Undesired: State Responsibility, Risk Management and Precaution' (2005) 36 *Netherlands Yearbook of International Law* 57.

[214] PS Rao, 'Third Report on International Liability for Injurious Consequences Arising Out of Acts Not Prohibited by International Law (Prevention of Transboundary Damage from Hazardous Activities)', UN Doc A/CN.4/510 (2000) at 13, para 27. See also: PS Rao, 'Prevention of Transboundary Harm from Hazardous Activities: A Sub-topic of International Liability' (2002) 32 *Environmental Policy and Law* 27.

Second, the first conclusion being inextricably tied to this one, there appears to be some resistance from the international community against reverting back to a model of direct State responsibility. Moreover, it is fair to assume that in the future, indirect responsibility will frequently pre-empt most considerations related to a State's level of direct control over a given terrorist enterprise. This shift in international law, which still requires a few adjustments, now completely centres on a State's failure to prevent an excursion led by terrorists from its territory onto another.[215] Some scholars subsume this scenario under the exceptions to the general rule of non-attribution of private conduct, aside from those expressly mentioned in the ILC's *Articles*,[216] but predicate any situation of indirect responsibility on the existence of a primary obligation to intervene.[217] For present purposes, this threshold seems easily met as a primary obligation incumbent upon sanctuary States to repress and prevent terrorism emanating from their territory undeniably exists.

In a broader sense, the true challenge therefore lies in elucidating the relationship between bilateral and multilateral tensions stemming from the mechanics of international responsibility, as they are shaped and transformed by difficult and sometimes fact-specific phenomena such as the proliferation of non-State actors[218] and *erga omnes* obligations.[219] Ultimately, since the ILC's codification is predominantly contingent on State control or endorsement of private conduct, certain tenets of State responsibility must be revisited in light of contemporary involvement of private actors at the transnational level.[220] The bases for attribution under the *Articles* and the de-territorialised nature of certain private activities such as terrorist operations and the outsourcing of State and

[215] Similarly, commentators argue that the US-led response against Afghanistan may have engendered a shift in the law of State responsibility. See Jinks, above n 156 at 83–84; Brown, above n 50 at 2. The present monograph follows a different route by arguing a more radical paradigm shift. On the possible intersection between use of force and State responsibility, generally, see EL Guruli, 'The Terrorism Era: Should the International Community Redefine Its Legal Standards on Use of Force in Self-Defense?' (2004) 12 *Willamette Journal of International Law & Dispute Resolution* 100; L Hannikainen, 'The World after 11 September 2001: Is the Prohibition of the Use of Force Disintegrating?' in J Petman and J Klabbers (eds), *Nordic Cosmopolitanism: Essays in International Law for Martti Koskenniemi* (Leiden, Nijhoff, 2003) 445.

[216] See, eg: Wolfrum, above n 69 at 424–25 (discussing possible scenarios under ILC Arts 8 and 9).

[217] See ibid, at 425 (also citing *Velásquez Rodríguez*, above n 86). In turn, this reality informs Wolfrum's reading of *Yeager v Islamic Republic of Iran* (1987) 17 Iran-US Claims Tribunal Reports 92 at 103–04, and also echoes some of the views already expressed in this chapter, especially with regard to the *Tehran Hostages* Case. It should also be reiterated that his conception of indirect responsibility is contingent on a primary obligation to intervene. See Wolfrum, above n 69 at 430–31.

[218] In discussing non-State actors in relation to State responsibility, Emanuel Roucounas rightly highlights that 'Past efforts to distinguish between direct and indirect responsibility were explained by the need to locate the individual within the system'. See 'Non-State Actors: Areas of International Responsibility in Need of Further Exploration' in Ragazzi, above n 19 at 392.

[219] For instance, SM Villalpando, *L'émergence de la communauté internationale dans la responsabilité des Etats* (Paris, PUF, 2005) 319, underlines that the violation of an obligation *erga omnes* typically engenders different effects for certain States, and applies this reasoning to an armed attack.

[220] See, eg: Roucounas, above n 218 at 392–403.

non-State violence immediately come to mind.[221] This animates Tal Becker's reassessment of the rules of attribution vis-à-vis terrorism:

> Unlike the terrorists of previous decades, many of today's terrorists can operate transnationally without direct State sponsorship. They can function as diffuse networks rather than hierarchical organizations. They can engage in large-scale, indiscriminate and recurring violence with undeterrable conviction. Civilians feel deeply threatened, but they cannot easily identify the source of that threat. It has no fixed address. It offers no easy target for a response.[222]

Furthermore, the very idea of indirect responsibility remains inextricably connected with the need to better circumscribe the role of non-State actors in the scheme of State responsibility. It follows that the ILC's *Articles* remain exceedingly focused on a (perhaps dated) unitary and bilateral conception of inter-State relations.[223] Indeed, certain eminent publicists decry the fact that the *Articles* predominantly focus on inter-State responsibility, operate on a 'bilateral', 'individualistic' and 'privatistic' conception of international law, and ultimately fail in ascribing a better defined role to the individual in establishing the responsibility of States.[224] Consequently, the extant scheme of responsibility should be suited to countenance 'the increasingly significant role of the individual (natural or legal person) and of other non-State entities' in contemporary international relations and, correspondingly, to overcome the '*strictly interstate* character of traditional international law and of the *statist* approach to that law'.[225] Equally evident from this State-centric inclination is that the notion of 'control' underlies much of the logic found in the *Articles*, but fails to provide any concrete solutions in the hard cases involving non-State actors. The present study takes issue with this notion of 'control' in chapter four and consequently argues that the concept of attribution itself is flawed.[226] As certain international legal areas shift away from a State-centric conception towards an increasingly transnational paradigm, the concept of international responsibility must be re-examined in light of modern events and trends. As one commentator observes, 'The fact that today States have to face direct action by individuals so

[221] On this point, see, eg: N Okany, 'State Delegation of Functions to Private or Autonomous Entities: A Basis for Attribution Under the Rules of State Responsibility' in Koufa, above n 42 at 423–34.

[222] Becker, above n 4 at 1.

[223] See generally: G Nolte, 'From Dionisio Anzilotti to Roberto Ago: The Classical International Law of State Responsibility and the Traditional Primacy of a Bilateral Conception of Inter-State Relations' (2002) 13 *EJIL* 1083.

[224] RP Mazzeschi, 'The Marginal Role of the Individual in the ILC's Articles on State Responsibility' (2004) 15 *Italian Yearbook of International Law* 39, 39–40. For further discussion on how past efforts to distinguish between direct and indirect responsibility 'were explained by the need to locate the individual within the system', see Roucounas, above n 218 at 392; Crawford, above n 68 at 61–65, 91–122.

[225] Mazzeschi, above n 224 at 39–40.

[226] This line of reasoning is consonant with arguments previously advanced in other accounts. See Proulx, above n 1; V-J Proulx, 'International Responsibility Today: Essays in Memory of Oscar Schachter. L'émergence de la communauté internationale dans la responsabilité des Etats' (2007) 18 *EJIL* 581, 583, 586, 590.

as to put that responsibility into operation is just one other consequence of the evolution of international law'.[227] In light of this quest, the study now turns to the more concrete task of querying whether the 'harbouring and supporting' rule can historically be cast as an analytical stepping stone towards a better understanding of modern State responsibility mechanisms vis-à-vis terrorism.

C) Specific Incidents Involving the Harbouring and Supporting Rule Before 9/11

There is nothing revolutionary in claiming that a State violates its obligations because it harbours or supports terrorists on its territory. In fact, the Security Council has frequently deplored the continuing use of Afghan territory for the 'sheltering' and 'training' of terrorists. Resolution 1267 remains a probative example whereby the Council accused the Afghan government of perpetrating egregious violations of international law by sheltering terrorists, allowing the presence of training camps and providing safe haven to Osama bin Laden and his associates on its territory. The Council urged Afghanistan to 'cease the provision of sanctuary and training for international terrorists and their organizations'.[228] Given the paradigm shift argued above, coupled with the legal response to 9/11, it is fair to assume that indirect responsibility has acquired credence in international law and might constitute the preferred course of action of several injured States in the future. Therefore, considerable weight must be accorded to the implications of 'harbouring and supporting' terrorists for State responsibility.

i) The 1982 Israel-Lebanon Conflict

The 1982 Israel-Lebanon conflict constitutes a salient example of an episode involving the harbouring and supporting rule also stemming from previous friction, namely the 1956 Sinai incident opposing Israel to Egypt. After sending troops across the 1949 cease-fire line into the Sinai, Israel invoked precedents of transborder excursions by Palestinian *fedayeen* as a basis for its own transborder response.[229] This argument was not well received by the Security Council; yet, its ensuing resolution recognised, albeit by implication, a link between the

[227] FO Vicuña, 'The Protection of Shareholders Under International Law: Making State Responsibility More Accessible' in Ragazzi, above n 19 at 169.

[228] Sec Res 1267, UN SCOR, 52nd Sess, 4051st Mtg, UN Doc S/RES/1267 (1999). Similar concerns pertaining to the 'use of Afghan territory' for the 'sheltering and training of terrorists' were expressed in the following resolutions: SC Res 1214, UN SCOR, 52nd Sess, 3952nd Mtg, UN Doc S/RES/1214 (1998); Sec Res 1333, UN SCOR, 55th Sess, 4251st Mtg, UN Doc S/RES/1333 (2000). See also generally: Franck, above n 50 at 95–96. After 9/11, the Security Council repeatedly recognised the responsibility of Afghan authorities to ensure law and order throughout Afghanistan. See, eg: SC Res 1662, UN SCOR, 60th Sess, 5393rd Mtg, UN Doc S/RES/1662 (2006); SC Res 1833, UN SCOR, 63rd Sess, 5977th Mtg, UN Doc S/RES/1833 (2008); SC Res 1868, UN SCOR, 63rd Sess, 6098th Mtg, UN Doc S/RES/1868 (2009); SC Res 1943, UN SCOR, 65th Sess, 6395th Mtg, UN Doc S/RES/1943 (2010); SC Res 2011, UN SCOR, 66th Sess, 6629th Mtg, UN Doc S/RES/2011 (2011).

[229] See UN Doc S/PV.748 (30 October 1956).

Palestinian excursions and Israel's reaction.[230] The draft resolution consequently called upon Israel to withdraw from Egyptian territory. This implicit message was later substantiated by a General Assembly resolution, which allowed the UNEF body to prevent further Palestinian excursions into Israel as part of its peacekeeping mandate. In that document, the Assembly expressly

> [*c*]*onsiders* that, after full withdrawal of Israel from the Sharm el Sheikh and Gaza areas, *the scrupulous maintenance of the Armistice Agreement requires the placing of the United Nations Emergency Force on the Egyptian-Israel demarcation line* and the implementation of other measures (emphasis added).[231]

Following the Sinai incident, it became common practice for Palestinian militants to launch strikes from the Lebanese territory into Israel.[232] After invading a large part of Lebanon, Israel contended that the PLO had effectively turned the southern part of that State into a launch pad for terrorist attacks.[233] Israel further submitted that the PLO had appropriated most of the Lebanese territory[234] and, using language redolent of the paradigm shift towards indirect responsibility, asserted that Lebanon failed to fulfil its 'duty to prevent its territory from being used for terrorist attacks against other States'.[235] In a rebuttal somewhat precursory to both *Nicaragua*'s and *Tadić*'s reasoning, Lebanon refuted responsibility for the incident by alleging that the bases from which the attacks were launched evaded its own control.[236] Subsequently, calling on Israel to withdraw from Lebanon, Ireland spearheaded a resolution that was unanimously endorsed.[237] In the days that followed, Israel put forth several emotive and vivid arguments as to its decision to initiate military action after years of murderous incursions perpetrated by PLO members against Israelis.[238] In its plea, Israel again reiterated that Lebanon had become a launching pad for terrorism, referring to it as a 'logistic centre and refuge for members of the terrorist internationale from all over the world'.[239] The Security Council remained undeterred in its objective to restore peace in the region and a Spanish resolution demanding the cessation of hostilities was ultimately adopted.[240]

[230] See Draft RES S/3710, 748th Mtg (30 October 1956).

[231] GA Res 1125(XI) of 2 February, UN Doc A/RES/1125 (XI) (1957).

[232] S/12598, Letter dated 13 March from Representative of Israel to UN Secretary-General, UN Doc A/33/64 (1978).

[233] See Franck, above n 50 at 57.

[234] ibid. See also: D McForan, *The World Held Hostage: The War Waged by International Terrorism* (New York, St Martin's Press, 1987) 46–47 (stating that the PLO operated as a 'state within a state').

[235] Letter dated 27 May 1982 from the representative of Israel to the UN Secretary-General, UN SCOR, 37th Year, UN Doc S/15132 (1982) at 119.

[236] Franck, above n 50 at 57.

[237] SC Res 509, UN SCOR, 2375th Mtg, UN Doc S/RES 509 (1982).

[238] See, eg: Statement by the Representative of Israel during the SC debate on Operation *Peace for Galilee* in Lebanon, UN SCOR, 37th Year, 2375th Mtg (1982) at 4, para 38.

[239] Ibid, at 5, para 47. See also: McForan, above n 234 at 45–46 (stating that the 'Lebanese Government's inability to rectify the situation, resulted in Lebanon sacrificing its sovereignty to the Palestinian terrorists').

[240] See SC Res 508, UN SCOR, 2375th Mtg, UN Doc S/RES/508 (1982); resolution 509, above n 237.

Both the Sinai and the 1982 incidents can be convincingly analogised to the US-Afghanistan situation, as the excursions were instigated by irregular forces, namely PLO members, and launched from a third-party State, Egypt and Lebanon respectively.[241] However, the Security Council rejected Israel's plea of self-defence[242] and the PLO irregulars were eventually relocated in Tunis by Lebanon.[243] In the 9/11 scenario, Afghanistan harboured members of the Al Qaeda network without participating in the planning or execution of the attacks. However, in contrast with the 1982 incident, the Council permitted US-led action in Afghanistan.[244] This discrepancy in the application of international law is difficult to rationalise and is premised on a two-fold conclusion.

First, the 9/11 experience plausibly illustrates the shift towards indirect responsibility as the superseding model, now fully endorsed by the international community. In other words, the arguments presented by Israel in 1982 did not resonate with the international community. Almost 20 years later, the Afghan State having provided safe haven to Al Qaeda members, a similar factual situation engendered an unprecedented international response along with the breeding of a 'war' that is both novel and indeterminate in character.[245] Whilst it is true that the Council might have allotted more weight to questions of sovereignty in the Lebanese incident, a legally emphatic affirmation of the indirect responsibility paradigm seems equally indicative of what transpired after 9/11.

Secondly, an interesting tension between respecting the sovereignty/territorial integrity/dignity of States and combating terrorism efficiently pervades these precedents.[246] As a result, two vital interests come into conflict. On one hand, the international community must protect its fundamental values, especially

[241] In the context of the 1982 incident, Franck, above n 50 at 59, explores the responsibility of the third-party sanctuary State through the lens of self-defence: 'In that light, Israel's claim to be acting in self-defense precisely poses the question whether such a right arises *against a state which harbors infiltrators and permits transborder subversion, yet has not itself participated in these armed attacks*' (emphasis added)). Based on 9/11, the answer to this question seems to be affirmative.

[242] Some scholars also opine that Israel's claim to self-defence is barred by the illegal occupation of certain territories. See, eg: C Gray, *International Law and the Use of Force* (Oxford, OUP, 2000) 102. At the outset, this proposition seems to bring about a distinguishing factor with the US-Afghan example given that before attacking Afghanistan in 2001, the US did not occupy the Afghan territory illegally.

[243] Franck, above n 50 at 59.

[244] SC Res 1368, UN SCOR, 56th Sess, 4370th Mtg, UN Doc S/RES/1368 (2001).

[245] On the topic of the duration of the 'war' on terror, some commentators opine that the military conflict will be 'measured by the persistence of fear that the enemy retains the capacity to fight'. See J Fitzpatrick, 'Speaking Law to Power: The War against Terrorism and Human Rights' (2003) 14 *EJIL* 241, 251. As a corollary, 'there is a real risk of a perception of 'permanent emergency' whereby the exception becomes the norm'. Duffy, above n 51 at 346. See also: UN Human Rights Committee, CCPR General Comment No 29: Derogations during a State of Emergency (Article 4), 31 August 2001, UN Doc CCPR/C/21/Rev.1/Add.11 especially at para 2.

[246] It is helpful to recall that, in the context of the 1982 incident, a few days after Israel declared a cease-fire, the UN General Assembly sought to consecrate Lebanon's 'sovereignty, territorial integrity, unity and political independence'. See GA Res ES-7/5 of 26 June, UN Doc A/RES/ES-7/5 (1982). On the question of Israel's unilateral cease-fire, see (1982) *United Nations Yearbook* 440.

when dealing with serious violations of community norms.[247] This might entail adopting more stringent and sovereignty-corrosive standards of State responsibility. On the other hand, the Westphalian system of nation-States places particular emphasis on the respect of every State's sovereignty.[248] The argument becomes particularly compelling when transferring this tension to counterterrorism as human lives are often at stake, sometimes on a large scale. In a chapter on State responsibility and diplomacy, after reviewing the USS Pueblo case of 1968 opposing the US and North Korea, Kazuhiro Nakatani suggests that this tension be resolved in favour of human security (for present purposes, by combating terrorism efficiently): 'For modern democratic States, what is paramount is to protect their nationals' lives rather than uphold in the abstract the dignity of the State. Therefore, similar responses will continue to occur in future cases, when human lives are at peril'.[249] From a broader pragmatic perspective, this line of thought must always be tempered by or balanced against egregious political self-interest, a veritable driving force and catalyst in dictating compliance or disregard for international legal rules. One must not lose sight of the fact that many States may be more concerned with sheltering themselves from direct responsibility than with the ability to pin such responsibility on other States, even if their own nationals are victims of the internationally wrongful act in question.[250] As discussed in chapter five, section III.B), the international legal mechanisms governing responsibility cast the State in a considerably stigmatic light. Therefore, devising effective counterterrorism policies will ineluctably entail a reconsideration of the virtues and limits of State sovereignty.

The ensuing dilemma can be summarised as follows: if a State cannot efficiently thwart terrorism emanating from its territory, or has lost control over the region where bases of operation are located, should we expect it to require extraneous forces or law enforcement units to enter its territory and repress the

[247] See generally: A-L Vaurs-Chaumette, 'The International Community as a Whole' in Crawford et al, above n 3 at 1023–28. For seminal accounts on international law's shift from consent-based bilateral legal rapports to a broader international community safeguarding both community interests and the specific interests of States, see: B Simma, 'From Bilateralism to Community Interest in International Law' (1994–VI) 250 *Recueil des Cours* 217; B Simma, 'Universality of International Law from the Perspective of a Practitioner' (2009) 20 *EJIL* 265, 268; B Kingsbury and M Donaldson, 'From Bilateralism to Publicness in International Law' in U Fastenrath et al (eds), *From Bilateralism to Community Interest: Essays in Honour of Judge Bruno Simma* (Oxford, OUP, 2011) 79; B Simma and A Paulus, '"The International Community": Facing the Challenge of Globalization' (1998) 9 *EJIL* 266, 268.

[248] Villalpando, above n 219 at 119, speaks to this point, albeit through the lens of international criminal responsibility.

[249] See K Nakatani, 'Diplomacy and State Responsibility' in Ragazzi, above n 19 at 40–41. It should be stressed that the 'State responsibility component' of Nakatani's account deals primarily with a diplomatic impasse, albeit predicated on a devastating human tragedy. Yet, it remains quite illuminating for present purposes. Similarly, the relationship between terrorism, diplomacy and State responsibility is certainly in need of further exploration. See, eg: E Marks, 'Diplomacy and Terrorism: Conflicting Systems' in HH Han (ed), *Terrorism & Political Violence: Limits & Possibilities of Legal Control* (New York, Oceana Publications, 1993) 41. For more background on the USS Pueblo incident, see 'Release at Panmunjom of Crew of U.S.S. Pueblo' (1969) 63 *AJIL* 682.

[250] See, eg: Becker, above n 4 at 35.

threat? Should this type of reaction be framed within the ambit of countermeasures under State responsibility, it brings the concern of the proportionality of those countermeasures to the fore.[251] It follows that disproportionate countermeasures may also trigger the responsibility of the State that instituted them. Expanding on these considerations, one author identifies a viable solution:

> On peut au contraire considérer que l'incursion limitée de forces de police, pour capturer un terroriste que l'État sur le territoire duquel il évolue refuse de poursuivre ou d'extrader en contradiction d'une obligation internationale, conventionnelle par exemple, peut être une contre-mesure proportionnée.[252]

The tension between upholding State sovereignty and combating terrorism efficiently also came to life in the context of the 1995 Turkey-Iraq crisis. Turkish forces invaded the north-western portion of the Iraqi territory, as it was used as a frequent launch pad for attacks against Turkey by Kurdish irregulars. Iraq brandished the recurrent claim as to the violation of its territorial integrity and sovereignty.[253] Although Iraq persisted in levelling allegations against the Turkish invasion, the Security Council remained unmoved by the Iraqi plea.[254] This type of inaction by the Council foreshadowed the new indirect responsibility paradigm: a State could now attempt to repress transborder subversion in a neighbouring country where terrorist launch pads and bases of operation are located. The guiding principle, however, still seemed to hinge on the proportionality of the response to the cross-border insurgency.[255]

When writing about lawful countermeasures in *Nicaragua*, the ICJ hinted at the fact that proportionate, forcible countermeasures might be available to a victim-State in responding to an internationally wrongful act involving the use of force, but falling short of an 'armed attack'. This has implications for this study insofar as an internationally wrongful act involving force carried out by terrorists could technically be attributed to the host-State without fulfilling the requirements of an 'armed attack' and, therefore, be assessed through the lens

[251] See generally: *Gabčíkovo-Nagymaros*, above n 90 at 56, para 85; *Case Concerning the Air Services Agreement of 27 March 1946 (US v France)* (1978) 54 International Law Reports 303 at 337. See also: C Antonopoulos, *The Unilateral Use of Force by States in International Law* (Athens, Sakkoulas, 1997) 319–20; R O'Keefe, 'Proportionality' in Crawford et al, above n 3 at 1157–68.

[252] 'For instance, a limited incursion by police forces to capture a terrorist onto the territory of a State that refuses to prosecute or extradite such individual – in contravention of an international obligation (eg prescribed by a treaty) – may amount to a proportionate countermeasure' (author translation). Martin, above n 121 at 493.

[253] See (1995) *United Nations Yearbook* at 494; UN Doc S/1995/272 of 7 April 1995.

[254] See UN Doc S/1996/401; UN Doc S/1996/762; UN Doc S/1996/860; UN Doc S/1996/1018; (1996) *United Nations Yearbook* at 236-37. Turkey also has a history of pursuing irregulars across the border into Iraq's territory, particularly members of the Kurdistan Workers Party (PKK). See KN Trapp, *State Responsibility for International Terrorism* (Oxford, OUP, 2011) 56–57.

[255] For an application of this principle post-9/11 and other guidelines regularising recourse to force against terrorism, see MC Bonafede, 'Here, There, and Everywhere: Assessing the Proportionality Doctrine and U.S. Uses of Force in Response to Terrorism after the September 11 Attacks' (2002) 88 *Cornell Law Review* 155; SR Knauft, 'Proposed Guidelines for Measuring the Propriety of Armed State Responses to Terrorist Attacks' (1996) 19 *Hastings International and Comparative Law Review* 763. On the Turkey-Iraq situation, see Franck, above n 50 at 63–64.

of State responsibility. Hence, counteracting mechanisms would reside in whatever proportionate countermeasures are ultimately endorsed and adopted by the victim-State (which could, presumably, include some incremental or limited incursions involving reduced types of force, such as local law enforcement arrangements or, more controversially, modest military action), a proposition that does not run counter to conventional wisdom (especially after 9/11 and 7/7). Whilst the ILC's *Articles* preclude the adoption of forcible countermeasures,[256] legal scholarship sometimes frames such reactions, either explicitly or implicitly, within the corpus of State responsibility norms and gives credence to the idea that some limited forcible reaction to terrorism could fit within the broader framework of countermeasures under general international law (which, incidentally, constitutes a *renvoi* to the customary rules of State responsibility).[257]

In exposing its reasoning in *Nicaragua*, the Court first drew a distinction between the degrees of forcible wrongful acts, thereby concluding that 'it will be necessary to distinguish the most grave forms of the use of force (those constituting an armed attack) from other less grave forms'.[258] In further exploring the adoption of lawful countermeasures, the Court expounded that 'a use of force of a lesser degree of gravity cannot . . . produce any entitlement to take collective counter-measures involving the use of force' but left the door open to the unilateral adoption of such countermeasures – albeit proportionate – by the aggrieved States (eg El Salvador, Honduras or Costa Rica).[259] Whilst this tension clearly has some incidence on the territorial integrity of sovereign nations,[260] it is also interesting to note that prior to 9/11, commentators opined that the harbouring of terrorists by a State should in fact pre-empt any claim to sovereignty.[261]

Furthermore, the very notion of 'sovereignty' in this setting is not only shaped by the above tension, but is also ultimately transformed by the juxtaposition of other competing legal regimes in the ensuing legal inquiry, such as the R2P Doctrine. As such, certain scholars – most notably Anne-Marie Slaughter – correspondingly underscore a 'tectonic shift' in the etymology of the concept of 'sovereignty'.[262] Similarly, the R2P Report produced by the International

[256] See *Articles*, above n 17, Art 50(1)a); Crawford, above n 68 at 281, 283.

[257] See, eg: Y Arai-Takahashi, 'Shifting Boundaries of the Right of Self-Defence – Appraising the Impact of the September 11 Attacks on Jus Ad Bellum' (2002) 36 *International Lawyer* 1081, 1085–86.

[258] *Nicaragua*, above n 10 at 96–97, para 191.

[259] ibid, at 127, para 249. See also: ibid, at 110–11, paras 210–11.

[260] This tension will be further explored below in section V; ch 5, sections II.B); III.B). See also: WM Reisman, 'International Legal Responses to International Terrorism' (1999) 22 *Houston Journal of International Law* 3, 50–51.

[261] See Baker, above n 115 at 40. In the same vein, see I Brownlie, 'International Law and the Activities of Armed Bands' (1958) 7 *ICLQ* 712, 718 (inferring that the support or toleration of terrorist activities by a host-State amounts to aggression); Condorelli, above n 132 at 233–46; Y Dinstein, *War, Aggression and Self-Defence*, 3rd edn (Cambridge, CUP, 2001) 182–83; Rao, above n 50 at 66; Reisman, above n 260 at 39; N Ronzitti, 'Italy's Non-Belligerency during the Iraqi War' in Ragazzi, above n 19 at 205.

[262] A-M Slaughter, 'Security, Solidarity, and Sovereignty: The Grand Themes of UN Reform' (2005) 99 *AJIL* 619, 627.

Commission on Intervention and State Sovereignty recognises the emergence of a terminological change in public international law from a 'right to intervene' to a 'responsibility to protect'. This inexorably entails a recasting and a re-conceptualisation of the very notion of State sovereignty, a vision that would presumably steer the present discussion into a responsibility-expansive direction.[263] In fact, it would appear that the law of State responsibility could become coextensive with the R2P Doctrine for the purposes of ascertaining violations of international obligations. Taking the case of the Sudan, for instance, this would entail not only an obligation on that State to protect its own people, but it would also subject it to international scrutiny in light of the mechanisms of State responsibility. As a corollary, it would also open it up to unilateral and/or collective responses by virtue of R2P for failing to thwart massive human rights abuse, a situation that might be analogised to some failures to prevent terrorism as discussed throughout this study.[264] Coming back to the historical treatment of the 'harbouring and supporting' rule, it should be briefly highlighted that the events surrounding the Beirut Raid are also instructive.

ii) The Beirut Raid

Bowett rightly asserted, especially in light of the Beirut raid, that the Security Council usually discards the notion of 'collective guilt' in situations lying at the periphery of traditional State responsibility, where civilians aid or harbour terrorists.[265] Following the attack on the El Al Boeing 707 at Athens airport by two possible members of the Popular Front of the Liberation of Palestine, Israel failed in its attempt to establish the responsibility of Lebanon.[266] In fact, a flight from Beirut to Athens constituted the only territorial link connecting the two perpetrators and Lebanon.[267] In language premonitory of the new paradigm of indirect responsibility, Israel accused Lebanon of 'assisting and abetting acts of warfare, violence, and terror by irregular forces and organizations'.[268]

[263] International Commission on Intervention and State Sovereignty, *The Responsibility to Protect: Report of the International Commission on Intervention and State Sovereignty* (Ottawa, International Development Research Centre, 2001) 11–12. The Commission added that, 'while it [the shift in language] can remove a barrier to effective action, [it] does not, of course, change the substantive issues which have to be addressed'. See ibid, at 12. This reality also connotes a shift from collective security to a responsibility to protect. See, eg: RC Thakur, *The United Nations Peace and Security: From Collective Security to the Responsibility to Protect* (Cambridge, CUP, 2006).

[264] See J Brunnée and SJ Toope, Norms, 'Institutions and UN Reform: The Responsibility to Protect' (2005) 2 *Journal of International Law & International Relations* 121, 128.

[265] DW Bowett, 'Reprisals Involving Recourse to Armed Force' (1972) 66 *AJIL* 1, 13. On the notion of collective guilt, generally, see GP Fletcher, 'The Storrs Lecture: Liberals and Romantics at War: The Problem of Collective Guilt' (2002) 111 *Yale Law Journal* 1499.

[266] For details of the account, see Bowett, above n 265 at 13 fn 53 and authorities cited.

[267] For a detailed account on the Beirut raid, see Baker, above n 115 at 34–35.

[268] Letter dated 29 December 1968 from Israel to the President of the Security Council, UN Doc S/8946 (1968).

However, the argument did not convince the Council and was rejected accordingly.[269]

The decision by the Council not to endorse Israel's reprisal was met with great disapproval by that State, declaring that the Council was one-sided in its finding of international responsibility and emphasising the fact that Lebanon's role had not been thoroughly scrutinised.[270] Most importantly, the reasoning behind the refusal to condone the Israeli reprisal in 1968 signals another important difference when contrasted with the modern posture vis-à-vis indirect responsibility. In the Beirut raid days, the commission of a previous wrongful act by the State predicated recourse to a reprisal against it as a target:

> Clearly, even under traditional law, the target of any reprisal had to be shown to have committed a prior delict so that, without proof of delictual conduct *by the Lebanon*, the Council was disinclined to accept Israel's plea of justification, quite apart from the issue of proportionality.[271]

Although the threshold of 'prior delict' might be fulfilled through a State's failure to prevent terrorist excursions emanating from its territory,[272] the US-Afghanistan precedent has substantially lowered this standard.

Indeed, Afghanistan did not participate in the planning or execution of the 9/11 attacks. The 'prior delict' it committed was harbouring and offering logistical support to Al Qaeda members, which still amounted to a violation of its obligation of prevention; virtually no evidence corroborating governmental direction or control over the terrorist network can be corralled from the public record.[273] This reality must always be contrasted with *Nicaragua* and *Tadić*, which both expounded that financial and military assistance to terrorists is insufficient to attribute direct responsibility to the subsidising State(s). Departure from this important notion foreshadows a quasi-definite shift from direct responsibility to indirect modes of international responsibility. The above review of relevant incidents deliberately excluded the US-Nicaragua situation, as the US took *direct* part in the activities by sending and training irregular forces. That fact pattern can be distinguished from situations where States harbour completely autonomous terrorists, whilst having no direct implication or knowledge of the activities being planned on their territory. Should a similar

[269] UN Doc S/PV. 1460, 1460th Mtg, 29 December 1968 at 28–30. The Beirut raid is not the only course of action of its kind, as other States have used force to retaliate against terrorism. Israel's raid of Entebbe in 1976 and the US bombing of Libyan camps in 1986 come to mind. For a detailed account of the facts surrounding both incidents, see Baker, above n 115 at 39 fns 76, 94 and accompanying text. For a discussion on the raid of Entebbe from the perspective of international responsibility, see G Battaglini, 'War against Terrorism *Extra Moenia*, Self-Defence and Responsibility: A Pure Juridical Approach' in Ragazzi, above n 19 at 146.

[270] See RA Falk, 'The Beirut Raid and the International Law of Retaliation' in MA Kaplan (ed), *Great Issues of International Politics: The International System and National Policy* (Chicago, Aldine Publication Company, 1970) 38–39. See also: RA Falk, 'The Beirut Raid and the International Law of Retaliation' (1970) 63 *AJIL* 415.

[271] Bowett, above n 265 at 14.

[272] The obligation to prevent transnational terrorism will be explored in detail below in ch 5.

[273] See, eg: Becker, above n 4 at 217.

situation to that of *Nicaragua* arise, it would likely be covered by the new indirect responsibility paradigm with less conceptual difficulty than cases merely involving tacit or passive acquiescence/toleration of terrorists. For example, if an aggrieved State cannot establish direct responsibility, it could alternatively focus on the host-State's obligation to prevent terrorist attacks emanating from its territory. This study contends that this second mechanism should not merely be reduced to an alternative route and could, arguably, supplant the direct responsibility paradigm altogether in many cases. For one thing, that posture would partly do away with the legal and political pitfalls associated with branding States 'directly' responsible, a prospect that the ICJ is extremely reticent to facilitate. The work of the Security Council following 9/11 also weighs heavily in the balance.

V. THE SECURITY COUNCIL'S POSTURE BEFORE AND AFTER 9/11

Of particular significance to the discussion of indirect responsibility is Security Council resolution 1373,[274] which moved towards a general and severe prohibition against supporting and harbouring terrorists.[275] The Council proclaimed that 'all States shall . . . Refrain from providing any form of support, *active or passive*, to entities or persons involved in terrorists act . . . *Deny safe haven* to those who finance, plan, support, or commit terrorist acts, or provide safe havens' (emphasis added).[276] Much in the same vein, whilst perceived as a 'root cause' of terrorism,[277] the notion of denying safe havens to terrorist organisations was very much alive in the ILC's work in attaining a definition of the crime of 'terrorism' in the context of the *Draft Code of Offences against Peace and Security of Mankind*.[278] Although *Nicaragua* and *Tadić* recognised that the provision of military and financial support to terrorists would not suffice, in itself, to establish direct State accountability, the move initiated by resolution 1373 has completely overshadowed the debate over direct responsibility.[279] In fact, it may have completely supplanted it: a State that provides any kind of tangible support to terrorism will inevitably be caught under the discipline of resolution 1373. A corresponding shift has been observed in the literature to the effect that

[274] SC Res 1373, UN SCOR, 56th Sess, 4385th Mtg, UN Doc S/RES/1373 (2001).

[275] For a general discussion on Security Council posture and resolutions in dealing with terrorism, see Battaglini, above n 269 at 141.

[276] Resolution 1373, above n 274.

[277] This language is loosely based on Rao's own words, above n 50 at 69.

[278] See, eg: Formulation of the Nürnberg Principles, GA Res 488(V), 320th Plenary Meeting, 12 December 1950 in DJ Djonovich (ed), *United Nations Resolutions (Series 1, Vol 1)* (Dobbs Ferry, Oceana Publications, 1973–88) 151; *The Work of the International Law Commission (Vol 1)*, 6th edn (New York, United Nations, 2004) 76. See also: Rao, above n 50 at 69.

[279] See, eg: ET Jensen, 'The ICJ's "Uganda Wall": A Barrier to the Principle of Distinction and an Entry Point for Lawfare' (2007) 35 *Denver Journal of International Law and Policy* 241, 267 (noting that 'the international community is moving to a system where states are held indirectly liable for the actions of entities within their borders').

the international community has moved towards of model of indirect responsibility: it 'appears that violation of 1373 *itself* is increasingly being characterized as constituting a threat to international peace and security'.[280] Conversely, certain publicists call into question the widely perceived lucidity underlying resolutions 1368 and 1373.[281]

Up until 9/11, the establishment of State responsibility for the excursions of irregular groups focused on the degree or level of control exercised by the originating State. For example, several years prior to the formulation of the 'effective' and 'overall' control standards, writing about the Israeli strike of 24 February 1969 against guerrilla camps located in Damascus, one scholar expressed that

> [i]t may be doubted whether this notion of 'collective responsibility' will commend itself to the Security Council so as to avoid condemnation. Nor, indeed, is it clear why it should, unless and until Israel can demonstrate that the various 'liberation movements' *fall under common planning and control*, and so far the evidence is very much to the contrary (emphasis added).[282]

As this study has shown, the Security Council often rejected the idea of collective guilt, along with a finding of responsibility solely based on harbouring terrorists. In cases where it found States responsible on that basis, the Council often condemned the reaction of the aggrieved States as disproportionate.[283] Given the potential harm to innocent civilians posed by terrorism, coupled with the far-reaching effects of resolution 1373,[284] the international community appears to have crystallised the shift towards indirect responsibility. From now on, the analysis will be far more concerned with a State's responsibility to *prevent* terrorism rather than with the question of attribution. As a corollary, the rationale underpinning resolution 1373 renders the discussion of 'control' somewhat futile. The global community acknowledges that terrorism is a phenomenon that must be combated seriously and methodically. Thus, the degree of control exerted by a State over a terrorist organisation does not hold the rel-

[280] CM Bailliet, 'The "Unrule" of Law: Unintended Consequences of Applying the Responsibility to Prevent to Counterterrorism, A Case Study of Columbias's Raid in Ecuador' in CM Bailliet (ed), *Security: A Multidisciplinary Normative Approach* (Leiden, Nijhoff, 2009) 175 at 176.

[281] Mégret, above n 9 at 375, is particularly critical of the Security Council or, alternatively, of the general perception of its post-9/11 counterterrorism efforts, also remarking that 'the picture that emerges is more that of a Council stumbling in the dark than of it signing a blank cheque to the anti-terrorism coalition'. See also: Hannikainen, above n 215 at 446–48. But see: Sadat, above n 104 at 145 (noting that, 'although notably silent on the use of force', resolutions 1368 and 1373 'recognize "the inherent right of self defense"'). For more discussion on the content of resolutions 1368 and 1373, see B Saul, *Defining Terrorism in International Law* (Oxford, OUP, 2006) 233–38.

[282] Bowett, above n 265 at 15, fn 61.

[283] This was the case with regard to Israel's invasion of Lebanon in 1982. In that regard, see Martin, above n 121 at 493.

[284] For detailed discussion of resolution 1373 and its implications for counterterrorism, see E Rosand, 'Security Council Resolution 1373, the Counter-Terrorism Committee, and the Fight against Terrorism' (2003) 97 *AJIL* 333; E Rosand, 'Security Council Resolution 1373 and the Counter-Terrorism Committee: The Cornerstone of the United Nations Contribution to the Fight against Terrorism' in Fijnaut et al, above n 13 at 603–32.

evance it once did. In mounting its international response, at no time did the US focus on Afghanistan's control over Al Qaeda. In fact, the evidence clearly suggests that Al Qaeda acted independently, without any outside interference or input into its complex cellular structure.[285] These developments evince that the international community is imposing a heavier burden of precaution on States, and rightly so.[286]

Before 9/11, the Council's attitude towards the repression of transborder subversion had been, at best, confused or fact-specific.[287] In some instances, the Council remained unmoved by a State's plea of territorial infringement when a neighbouring State invaded its territory in pursuit of cross-border insurgents. Whilst the object of the injured nation was to eliminate terrorist bases within the sanctuary State, the international community condoned a right to use force in certain circumstances. The events of 1995–96, when Turkish forces set foot on Iraqi soil in pursuit of Kurdish irregulars, serve as one example.[288] Iran shortly followed suit, resorting to aerial attacks on Kurdish bases from which insurgent troops launched excursions.[289]

This evolution becomes even more striking when contrasted with certain analogous episodes in the Arab-Israeli experience. For example, on 24 February 1969, Israel proceeded with aerial assaults on terrorist camps belonging to the Popular Front for the Liberation of Palestine.[290] It was suspected that these acts were provoked by two previous attacks, namely 'the attack on El Al aircraft at Zurich on February 18 and the bombing of a Jerusalem supermarket'.[291] However, a rival terrorist organisation known as Al Fatah claimed responsibility for the incidents. As emphasised by some, the Council would likely not be convinced by the legitimacy of such retaliation and the crux of the legal analysis would hinge on whether the guerrilla bands actually fell under 'a unified command'.[292] Once again, the legal discussion ineluctably reverted back to the question of 'control' over terrorist organisations rather than that of establishing the responsibility of the territorial State for harbouring terrorists (ie the State's control *over national territory*).

Interestingly, Bowett called into question the 'assumption . . . that the territorial state assumed responsibility because it had the power to prevent these activities'.[293] He claimed that it is probably unrealistic, based on arguments of size and capacity of host-States,[294] to expect countries like Jordan and Lebanon to

[285] See Gunaratna, above n 63 at 72-112.

[286] See, eg: R Wedgwood, 'The ICJ Advisory Opinion on the Israeli Security Fence and the Limits of Self-Defense' (2005) 99 *AJIL* 52, 58.

[287] On the incongruities found in such practice, see Franck, above n 50 at 64–68.

[288] See the previous comments on this account, above nn 253–54 and accompanying text.

[289] See UN Doc S/25843 (1993); UN Doc S/1996/602 (1996). See also: (1996) *United Nations Yearbook* at 268–69.

[290] Bowett, above n 265 at 14.

[291] ibid.

[292] ibid, at 15.

[293] ibid, at 20.

[294] These concerns will be addressed below in ch 5.

efficiently thwart all terrorist operations on their territory.[295] These concerns evidence the complexity of such scenarios and evoke the abovementioned tension between respecting territorial sovereignty and combating terrorism efficiently. In fact, this tension has been very much alive in post-9/11 transnational attempts to thwart terrorism. The perhaps legally untenable – and politically questionable – flipside to this argument is that, once a State reveals itself to be incapable of preventing terrorist strikes emanating from its territory, aggrieved States may be inclined to circumvent habitual politico-legal avenues (ie UN procedure, diplomacy) and adopt unilateral responses. In turn, such responses may arguably be undertaken in violation of relevant human rights standards or other international legal norms. The US' missile strike on Al Qaeda targets in Yemen in November 2002 arguably falls under that category.[296] In substantiating its action, the US heavily relied upon 'Yemen's apparent inability to exert much control over its remote and largely lawless border region with Saudi Arabia, which the Americans say serves as the country's main sanctuary for Al Qaeda'.[297] From a policy perspective, therefore, if we accept that Lebanon cannot efficiently thwart terrorist activities on its own territory because of widespread guerrilla activities, what exactly do we expect it to do? Based on resolution 1373, we should probably require it to allow extraneous forces or law enforcement units on its territory to suppress the threats, although such a response would erode the concept of sovereignty (but, in that case, Lebanon would be incapacitated and therefore unable to exercise its sovereignty in the first place, or at least incompatibly with the obligation of non-intervention in the affairs of other States).[298] Indeed, the concept of governmental inefficiency will become

[295] Bowett, above n 265 at 14.

[296] Some reported that the Yemeni government pre-authorised the US-led attack. See, eg: W Pincus, 'U.S. Strike Kills Six in Al Qaeda; Missile Fired by Predator Drone; Key Figure in Yemen Among Dead', *Washington Post*, 5 November 2002 at A1. In response, some authors conclude that, whether truthful or not, Yemen's approval 'hardly matters for the sake of maintaining the formalities of international law', as 'the appearance of sovereignty and sovereign equality of states is maintained' when States agree to cooperate with the US on international efforts in repressing terrorism. See ML Cook, 'Ethical and Legal Dimensions of the Bush "Preemption" Strategy' (2004) 27 *Harvard Journal of Law and Public Policy* 797, 809.

[297] J Risen and J Miller, 'C.I.A. Is Reported to Kill a Leader of Qaeda in Yemen', *New York Times*, 5 November 2002 at A14; Pincus, above n 296 at A1. Similarly, in the years following 9/11, the US engaged in various military operations in the Philippines, Georgia and Pakistan. See, eg: S Mydans, 'Threats and Responses: Asian Front: Filipinos Awaiting U.S. Troops with Skepticism', *New York Times*, 28 February 2003 at A11.

[298] Ironically, Hersch Lauterpacht believed that 'the traditional respect for State sovereignty refrained the development of the law of international responsibility, particularly regarding the consequences of responsibility'. It followed that

> the traditional theory limited responsibility only to the reparation for damage (material and moral), without it being possible for States, as a result of their sovereignty, to be punished. This vision, however, in exempting the State from the consequences of its own violations of the law, appeared entirely arbitrary, limiting the action of justice at the international level.

See AA Cançado Trindade, 'Complementarity between State Responsibility and Individual Responsibility and Individual Responsibility for Grave Violations of Human Rights: The Crime of State Revisited' in Ragazzi, above n 19 at 261. See also: H Lauterpacht, 'Règles générales du droit de la paix' (1937-IV) 62 *Recueil des Cours* 95, 339, 349–50, especially at 350–52.

pivotal in the second tier of the strict liability-infused approach advocated in chapter four and was very much alive in the 2006 Israel-Hezbollah conflict. Following allegations of Lebanon's inefficiency in constricting the flow of Hezbollah weapons and ammunition originating from Syria and Iran,[299] a UN-mandated team of experts assessed the situation prevalent along the Lebanese border. Amongst its conclusions was the fact that Lebanese border guards demonstrated a 'worrying lack of performance' and, in addition to accusations of corruption by the guards, the experts determined that whilst the Lebanese army had deployed more than 8000 troops to secure the 250-kilometre frontier with Syria in the autumn of 2006, 'Lebanese security forces lacked adequate resources to accomplish their objective'.[300]

These considerations illustrate the inherent difficulty in analogising a collective history of terrorism and reprisals such as the Arab-Israeli record to single events or to an uninterrupted chain of events, such as the 9/11 attacks or the train bombing in Madrid. Conversely, an argument can be advanced that the US-Afghanistan scenario might fit, albeit difficultly, under what could be termed an 'overall relationship' theory, especially given the series of terrorist excursions perpetrated against American targets.[301] These considerations become even more relevant in light of ILC Article 14(3), which expressly governs the extended breach of an obligation premised on a duty to prevent (ie the obligation to prevent terrorism). That provision specifies that 'The breach of an international obligation requiring a State *to prevent a given event* occurs when the event occurs and extends over the entire period during which the event continues and remains not in conformity with that obligation' (emphasis added).[302]

Whilst the obligation of prevention and its implications will be discussed subsequently, a few preliminary remarks are warranted. A relatively straightforward case can be made that Afghanistan repeatedly failed to fulfil its obligation to prevent terrorism when considering the aforementioned series of Al Qaeda-led excursions linked with the Afghan territory and previous Security Council condemnations. Hence, there was a continuing international breach by

[299] On Iran's and Syria's support of Hezbollah factions, see N Bakri, 'Backers of Hezbollah and Government Clash As Strike Disrupts Lebanon', *New York Times*, 8 May 2008 at A6; N Bakri and G Bowley, 'Confrontation in Lebanon Appears to Escalate', *New York Times*, 8 May 2008 at A6; N Bakri, 'Clashes in General Strike in Lebanon', *New York Times*, 8 May 2008 at A6; RF Worth and N Bakri, 'Hezbollah Threatens Attacks on Israeli Targets', *New York Times*, 15 February 2008 at A6.

[300] CI Bosley, 'Iran Allegedly Skirts Hezbollah Arms Ban' (September 2007) *Arms Control Today/ Arms Control Association*, available at www.armscontrol.org/act/2007_09/IranSkirts.

[301] In sum, the US continuously maintained an adversarial posture vis-à-vis Afghanistan following the perpetration of several terrorist attacks substantially linked with the Al Qaeda network, a significant contingent of which was sheltered on Afghan territory (ie thereby signalling a violation of that State's obligation of prevention). However, not all these attacks were similarly linked to the Afghan territory and, in apportioning State responsibility, serious consideration should also be given to the potential involvement, direct or indirect, of Iran, Saudi Arabia and Sudan in those attacks. Those terrorist strikes include the bombing of the Khobar Towers, the US embassy bombings in Africa, the bombing of the USS Cole and the events of 9/11.

[302] *Articles*, above n 17. See also: below ch 4, section III.A).

Afghanistan, as evidenced by its repeated failures to thwart terrorist threats percolating on its territory. Thus, Afghanistan would be indirectly responsible for an internationally wrongful act. ILC Article 14 and *Corfu Channel*, coupled with *Tehran Hostages* which alludes to 'successive and still continuing breaches by Iran of its obligations to the United States under the Vienna Conventions of 1961 and 1963',[303] all support a finding of indirect responsibility in the US-Afghanistan scenario. In the context of counterterrorism, therefore, the rationale underpinning Article 14 is probably better tailored to govern lasting relationships – albeit punctuated by attacks and reprisals – between two or more States.[304]

The law of indirect responsibility must be clearly ascertained in conformity with the will of the international community to combat terrorism efficiently, using 'all necessary steps'.[305] True enforcement of this objective will either occur through a substantial strengthening of the regime of responsibility, thereby enhancing prevention, or via a significant loosening or decimation of State sovereignty. The latter option probably proves temporarily adequate to appease concerns pertaining to ineffective or 'failed' States,[306] as harbouring terrorists has sometimes been equated with relinquishing sovereignty or, at best, with the exercise of a State function that is deeply incompatible with the cardinal principles of sovereignty.[307] However, the former scenario seems better suited to the current state of international law and is, arguably, the most effective way to empower a global counterterrorism campaign while upholding fundamental values of the international legal order, such as the sovereign equality between States. The protection of human life also comes to mind, especially when considering that terrorism claims the lives and limbs of innocent civilians and remains a particularly repugnant offence.[308]

[303] *Tehran Hostages* Case, above n 11 at paras 78, 80.

[304] On the distinction between instantaneous and continuing breaches, see *Rainbow Warrior (New Zealand v France)* (1999) 10 *Reports of International Arbitral Awards* 217, 264, para 101. On the question of continuing breaches, generally, see J Pauwelyn, 'The Concept of a "Continuing Violation" of an International Obligation: Selected Problems' (1995) 66 *BYIL* 415.

[305] Resolution 1368, above n 264.

[306] For a thoughtful discussion of this issue from the perspective of failed States, see Zemanek, above n 40 at 131. See also: A Cassese, 'Terrorism Is Also Disrupting Some Crucial Legal Categories of International Law' (2001) 12 *EJIL* 993, 997; R Geiss, 'Civil Aircraft As Weapons of Large-Scale Destruction: Countermeasures, Article 3Bis of the Chicago Convention, and the Newly Adopted German "Luftsicherheitsgesetz"' (2005) 27 *Michigan Journal of International Law* 227, 247; Mégret, above n 9 at 383–84.

[307] See, eg: B Netanyahu, 'Terrorism: How the West Can Win' in B Netanyahu (ed), *Terrorism: How the West Can Win* (New York, Farrar, Straus, Giroux, 1986) 220; JJ Paust, 'Federal Jurisdiction Over Extraterritorial Acts of Terrorism and Non-immunity for Foreign Violators Under the FSIA and the Act of State Doctrine' (1983) 23 *Virginia Journal of International Law* 191, 221–25.

[308] See, eg: International Commission of the Red Cross, *Basic Rules of the Geneva Conventions and Their Additional Protocols*, 2nd edn (Geneva, International Committee of the Red Cross, 1983); EK Kwakwa, *The International Law of Armed Conflict: Personal and Material Fields of Application* (Dordrecht, Kluwer, 1992) 39. The ICJ also pronounced on the importance of protecting civilian life. See, eg: *Legality of the Threat or Use of Nuclear Weapons*, Advisory Opinion of 8 July, *ICJ Reports* (1996) 226 at 257, para 78 (categorising the non-targeting of civilians as one of the 'cardinal principles' of humanitarian law).

Contemporary Security Council posture on indirect State responsibility has not always been consistent. For instance, 'in September 2000, the Security Council specifically rejected the Rwandan authorities' claim to a right to attack Hutu insurgents operating out of neighboring territory'.[309] Reviving the aforementioned tension between sovereignty and preventing transborder subversion, the Council invoked the violation of territorial integrity as one of the bases for condemning the Rwandan excursion.[310] Irrespective of the discrepancies found in recent Council resolutions, the US-led response to 9/11 seems to have crystallised the modern shift towards indirect responsibility.[311]

Moreover, this response marked a clear but potentially exceptional departure from the uncertainty of previous practice. This evolution is attributable, first and foremost, to the unprecedented level of support generated by the US in mounting its response to 9/11.[312] On 12 September 2001, the UN General Assembly adopted a resolution, which '*Urgently call[ed]* for international cooperation to prevent and eradicate acts of terrorism, and stresse[d] that those responsible for *aiding, supporting or harbouring* the perpetrators, organizers and sponsors of such acts *will be held accountable*' (emphasis added).[313] On the same day, the Council categorically condemned the attacks and, invoking language redolent of the paradigm shift, emphatically prompted all States 'to work together urgently to bring to justice the perpetrators, organizers and sponsors of these terrorist attacks . . . that those responsible for *aiding, supporting or harbouring* the perpetrators, organizers and sponsors *will be held accountable*' (emphasis added).[314] Resolution 1368 was followed 16 days later by resolution 1373,[315] the landmark document in modern counterterrorism initiatives. Although resolution 1368 recognised the inherent right to invoke individual or collective self-defence, resolution 1373 reiterated that right but reaffirmed 'the need to combat *by all means*, in accordance with the Charter, threats to international peace and security caused by terrorist acts' (emphasis added).[316] This set of legal prescriptions signalled a departure from previous Security Council

[309] Franck, above n 50 at 66.

[310] See SC Res 1304, UN SCOR, 55th Sess, 4159th Mtg, UN Doc S/RES/1304 (2000) at 2, which speaks of the 'violation of the sovereignty and territorial integrity of the Democratic Republic of Congo'.

[311] Consider Franck, above n 50 at 54, 66–67.

[312] See Proulx, above n 1 at 640 (discussing support from the North Atlantic Treaty Organization, the Organization of American States and other prominent intergovernmental bodies).

[313] GA Res 56/1, UN GAOR, 56th Sess, UN Doc A/RES/56/1 (2001).

[314] Resolution 1368, above n 244.

[315] Resolution 1373, above n 274.

[316] ibid. These two documents have also paved the way for other Security Council resolutions on the US-Afghanistan relationship. See, eg: SC Res 1383, UN SCOR, 56th Sess, 4434th Mtg, UN Doc S/RES/1383 (2001); SC Res 1386, UN SCOR, 56th Sess, 4443rd Mtg, UN Doc S/RES/1386 (2001). Most importantly, the Security Council adopted SC Res 1378, UN SCOR, 56th Sess, 4415th Mtg, UN Doc S/RES/1378 (2001), which expressly embraced the new indirect responsibility paradigm by condemning 'the Taliban for *allowing Afghanistan to be used as a base for the export of terrorism* by the Al-Qaida network and other terrorist groups and for *providing safe haven* to Usama Bin Laden, Al-Qaida and others associated with them' (emphasis added).

practice[317] and consecrated the international community's newfound obdurate will in combating terrorism.[318]

The question now becomes whether this one precedent instituted a viable and enduring rule of international law, or whether it simply amounted to a one-time distortion of the rules governing State responsibility in order to cater to a (seemingly incontestable) response to a horrific and unprecedented series of attacks. As discussed subsequently, other incidents corroborate the notion that the rules governing State responsibility are evolving, and rightly so from a *lex ferenda* perspective, so as to better address transnational violence and enhance governmental accountability. Since terrorists have themselves subverted international legal norms by their actions, certain commentators expound that 'Where the rules of the game are indeed changing appears to be in the jettisoning of the rules pertaining to international legal responsibilities'.[319] Similarly, the application of State responsibility norms is literally being challenged and ultimately tempered in real-time. For instance, Pakistan's and India's potential involvement in the (failed) prevention of the terrorist attacks in Mumbai may further inform the evolution of these norms through the vehicle of State practice.[320] Indeed, it seems that Lashkar-e-Taiba, the terrorist network behind the devastating Mumbai attacks of November 2008, has only intensified since those episodes and is once again determined to strike India.[321] Not only do these events suggest that efforts should be stepped up to dismantle this organisation and other similar networks, but they also evince the pressing need to devise effective and enhanced deterrence/prevention models to address the scourge of transnational terrorism. As argued in the present study, this objective can be partly achieved through the paradigm shift towards indirect responsibility.

[317] For instance, the Security Council did not recognise a right to self-defence in favour of the US following the 1998 bombing of the embassies in Tanzania and Kenya. On this point, see Jinks, above n 156 at 85–86. In response to 9/11, Jinks, above n 156 at 86, further argues that 'the Security Council impliedly endorsed, without expressly authorizing, the use of force against Afghanistan'. See also: N Rostow, 'Before and After: The Changed UN Response to Terrorism Since September 11th' (2002) 35 *Cornell International Law Journal* 475. On the Security Council's role in combating international terrorism, see CA Ward, 'Building Capacity to Combat International Terrorism: The Role of the United Nations Security Council' (2003) 8 *Journal of Conflict and Security Law* 289.

[318] Resolution 1368, above n 244 at para 5, also evinced the Council's 'readiness to take all necessary steps to respond to the terrorist attacks of 11 September 2001, and to combat all forms of terrorism'. See also: Battaglini, above n 269 at 140; RA Caplen, 'The 'Charlie Brown Rain Cloud Effect' in International Law: An Empirical Case Study' (2008) 36 *Capital University Law Review* 693, 741. See also generally: O Corten, 'Vers un renforcement des pouvoirs du Conseil de sécurité dans la lutte contre le terrorisme?' in K Bannelier et al (eds), *Le Droit international face au terrorisme: après le 11 septembre 2001* (Paris, Pedone, 2003) 259.

[319] E Hughes, 'Entrenched Emergencies and the "War on Terror": Time to Reform the Derogation Procedure in International Law?' (2007) 20 *New York International Law Review* 1, 58.

[320] See, eg: R Abeyratne, 'Terror in Mumbai – A Legal Perspective', *Daily News*, 29 November 2008, available at www.dailynews.lk/2008/11/29/fea01.asp (discussing several bases for assessing State responsibility vis-à-vis the terrorist attacks in Mumbai).

[321] See, eg: L Polgreen and S Mekhennet, 'Militant Network Is Intact Long after Mumbai Siege', *New York Times*, 30 September 2009 at A1.

Conclusion to Part I

IT IS HIGHLY probable that the response to 9/11 crystallised the modern shift toward indirect State responsibility, irrespective of the overwhelming or exceptional support it received from the international community. Two conclusions may be drawn from the accounts described above, which collectively fostered this new paradigm. First, whilst the 'harbouring and supporting' principle was somewhat ingrained in international legal culture during the 1970s, there has been a significant recrudescence of claims against transborder subversion in non Arab-Israeli contexts. It is now accepted practice for an injured nation to accuse a sanctuary State of not preventing excursions launched into the former's territory. As a direct consequence of establishing State responsibility, the aggrieved State may be permitted to use force to restore peace and security in some cases. As one commentator expounds, 'Although traditionally addressed as a law enforcement problem, it is now clear that international terrorism will often necessitate some sort of military response'.[1]

Secondly, the question of 'control' is now overshadowed by other considerations. It seems that the 'effective-overall control' dichotomy has eroded and, with it, the direct responsibility paradigm has started to fade considerably. It is fair to consider obliterating the legal tests formulated in *Nicaragua* and *Tadić* from the equation, save in clear and wanton cases of direct State involvement in terrorism. As the events of 9/11 have shown, terrorist organisations often operate independently and autonomously, making their connection to governments blurred or virtually untraceable. In addition, the prospect of governments waging surrogate warfare through private individuals or proxies also poses a significant challenge to the mechanism of attribution. Indeed,

> [t]he tendency for those in power to achieve their ends through private or non-State actors, thereby avoiding attribution, engenders a wide range of conduct by inaction where both deniability and non-attribution serve to enhance the power of those in control of a State, if they in fact have control.[2]

[1] D Jinks, 'State Responsibility for the Acts of Private Armed Groups' (2003) 4 *Chicago Journal of International Law* 83, 91; RO Keohane, 'The Globalization of Informal Violence, Theories of World Politics, and the "Liberalism of Fear"' (2002) *Dialogue I-O* 29.

[2] GA Christenson, 'Attributing Acts of Omission to the State' (1991) 12 *Michigan Journal of International Law* 312, 313.

Commentators similarly hint at the idea that the level of State accountability for terrorism could be commensurate with the degree of governmental sponsorship of such activity; the actual connection between a host-State and a terrorist cell might concomitantly affect this computation and pose further evidentiary challenges.[3] After all, in many instances 'A State's involvement in terrorism is inevitably clandestine and exceedingly difficult to prove'.[4] These considerations serve as reliable building blocks for discussing the inadequacy of the notion of 'control' as a principal basis for establishing State responsibility under the ILC's *Articles*.[5]

In many instances, no principal-agent nexus can be demonstrated between a terrorist organisation and the State apparatus, another militating factor favouring a regime of indirect responsibility. In such scenarios, the central preoccupation rather hinges on i) whether the State harboured terrorists and ii) whether it fulfilled its obligation to prevent terrorism emanating from its territory. In sum, the response to 9/11 likely initiated a significant shift toward indirect responsibility but the journey does not end there: the efficiency, or lack thereof, of the current scheme of State responsibility vis-à-vis transnational terrorism must be re-examined.[6] Such an endeavour should inevitably call into question the raison d'être of the concept of attribution, a hypothesis that drives the premises underpinning Part II of the present volume.

[3] See, eg: SN Schiedeman, 'Standards of Proof in Forcible Responses to Terrorism' (2000) 50 *Syracuse Law Review* 249, 261; SE Smith, 'International Law: Blaming Big Brother: Holding States Accountable for the Devastation of Terrorism' (2003) 56 *Oklahoma Law Review* 735, 746 ('State accountability becomes less clear as the relationship between the State and the terrorist cell weakens, and the evidence to prove the existence of such a relationship disappears').

[4] T Becker, *Terrorism and the State: Rethinking the Rules of State Responsibility* (Oxford, Hart Publishing, 2006) 150.

[5] See below ch 4, section II.A).

[6] WM Reisman, 'International Legal Responses to International Terrorism' (1999) 22 *Houston Journal of International Law* 3, 42, delivers a quintessential formulation of the problem at hand in the following terms: 'We are concerned here with the policies that have been prescribed in contemporary international law with respect to a state in whose territory terrorist acts are planned when the state has the capacity to prohibit such action'.

Part II

Rethinking State Responsibility After 9/11: Defining the Scope of States' Counterterrorism Obligations and Implementing a Model to Ensure Compliance with Those Obligations

Introduction

The first part of the book shed some light on the modern development of State responsibility in counterterrorism contexts. It framed some of the potential contributions of international law to counterterrorism policy within the formal rules of State responsibility. The latter portion of the first part identified a paradigm shift towards indirect State responsibility, a trend supported both by recent State and Security Council practice. That analysis will act as a preliminary gloss through which Part II of the study should be read, as the project now moves on to the more sophisticated task of revisiting State responsibility law from a *lex ferenda* perspective. Equally important to the discussion to follow are institutional sensibilities, which should always guide the analysis, and Security Council practice, specifically, which should act as somewhat of a benchmark in developing policy-based revisions to State responsibility.

Whilst there are clear divisions within the literature about the proper legal interpretation of the relevant facts, the 2001 response against Afghanistan certainly propelled the issue of State responsibility to the forefront of academic debate. Since 9/11, much has been written on the legality of US-led action in Afghanistan, with particular emphasis on the parameters of use of force and the corresponding shift in the law of *jus ad bellum*. Unfortunately, the question of indirect State responsibility for failing to prevent terrorism remains somewhat elusive to this day. Building on the legal trends and relevant concepts canvassed in the first part of the volume, this second part purports to prescriptively delineate the parameters of the regime of indirect responsibility, given that the literature and jurisprudence are far from dispositive on the matter.

Although little consensus has been achieved on this issue, it is widely recognised that States must prevent terrorist attacks emanating from their territory and injurious to other States. However, the contours of this obligation of prevention are far more problematic, both in terms of legal content and policy. Therefore, in order to better define the application of secondary norms of State responsibility, one must first consider better circumscribing primary counterterrorism duties. Indeed, there has been acute confusion in identifying how, exactly, the rules of State responsibility would apply to the violation of obligations related to transnational activity, such as global warming and transnational pollution.[1]

[1] See, eg: R Verheyen, *Climate Change Damage and International Law: Prevention Duties and State Responsibility* (Leiden, Nijhoff, 2005) 225–32; P Cullet, 'Liability and Redress for Human-

Whilst this uncertainty is undoubtedly exacerbated by a 'multiplicity of actors, different types of damages and non-linear causation', the existence of 'vague primary rules' also further complicates the post-breach equation.[2] Alternatively, as explored below, those primary obligations might in fact acquire better traction and clarity through a revamping of secondary norms and trans-substantive rules of State responsibility. This approach might facilitate circumventing difficult policy debates and definitional impasses or political deadlocks – exemplified by the lack of international consensus in defining the concept of 'terrorism', for example – typically associated with the further elaboration of contentious primary obligations. In fact, this type of reasoning is precisely what animated Roberto Ago's decision to shift the focus of the ILC away from the development of substantive rules related to the protection of aliens, a seemingly intractable exercise initially triggered by Special Rapporteur García-Amador, to the adoption of general rules of State responsibility formulated at a high level of abstraction.[3] As such, 'Ago created a politically safe space within which the ILC could work and largely avoid the contentious debates of the day about expropriation and valuation of property'.[4] This section of the project espouses this vision and perhaps refines it with a view to further delineating those secondary obligations, so as to generate effective accountability mechanisms and deterrence models vis-à-vis governmental failures to prevent terrorism.

The analysis expands upon the brief overview of the direct/indirect responsibility dichotomy presented above, while bearing in mind ways to integrate and, ultimately, resolve the reservations associated with the concept of attribution that have cropped up in Part I. Similarly, whilst a significant shift in international law towards indirect responsibility, evidenced by recent Security Council and State practice, has been demonstrated, important interrogations remain: what policy and legal standards do we apply to actuate this regime of indirect responsibility and how, exactly, is this responsibility triggered between sovereign States?

Along with *Corfu Channel*, three significant developments are instrumental in ascertaining this evolution: international jurisprudence, which includes the *Nicaragua*, *Tehran Hostages* and *Tadić* decisions, the adoption of the ILC's *Articles* in 2001, and the US-led international response against Afghanistan. Yet, additional discussion is needed to determine how these elements interact

Induced Global Warming: Towards an International Regime' (2007) 43A *Stanford Journal of International Law* 99, 107; R Pisillo-Mazzeschi, 'Forms of International Responsibility for Environmental Harm' in F Francioni and T Scovazzi (eds), *International Responsibility for Environmental Harm* (London, Graham & Trotman) 15.

[2] See C Voigt, 'State Responsibility for Climate Change Damages' (2008) 77 *Nordic Journal of International Law* 1.

[3] See, eg: Y Matsui, 'The Transformation of the Law of State Responsibility' (1993) 20 *Thesaurus Acroasium* 1, 55. See also generally: D Müller, 'The Work of García Amador on State Responsibility for Injury Caused to Aliens' in JR Crawford et al (eds), *The Law of International Responsibility* (Oxford, OUP, 2010) 69.

[4] D Bodansky and JR Crook, 'Introduction and Overview (Symposium: The ILC's State Responsibility Articles)' (2002) 96 *AJIL* 773, 780.

and inform an effective and preventive model of State responsibility. In so doing, Part II considers difficult but related questions such as the involvement, or lack thereof, of 'failed' States in preventing terrorism, the overemphasis on the notions of control and interdependence between host-States and non-State actors under the ILC's *Articles*, evidentiary impediments engendered by extant international responsibility repertoire, and so on. Ultimately, Part II gravitates towards the proposal that the concept of attribution should be excised altogether from the equation of State responsibility in counterterrorism contexts or, alternatively, replaced by a model of automatic attribution. Drawing on the discussion of previous chapters, this second part of the project proposes the implementation of a two-tiered strict liability-infused model in assessing the responsibility of sanctuary States. The discussion, which is pervaded by a tension between upholding sovereignty and combating terrorism efficiently, ultimately leads to a critical exploration of the obligation of prevention with a view to bolstering prevention and promoting multilateralism and transnational cooperation on counterterrorism policy. The ensuing analysis is replete with policy sensibilities, which considerably inform and shape the *lex ferenda* approach contained therein. Part II strives to better integrate non-State actors within the purview of international liability mechanisms; it does so whilst concomitantly striking a balance between devising effective deterrence models rooted in the logic of State responsibility, especially in the face of enhanced transnational terrorist capacity, and developing a legal narrative that is sensible to the realities facing the developing world while also promoting the sovereign equality of States, to the extent possible.

Before turning to the potential benefits that may be derived from a strict liability-infused approach, chapter three first takes stock of other advances made in identifying models for engaging the international responsibility of States that tolerate terrorists on their territory. In particular, one hypothesis put forth promotes a model of responsibility based on causality, a proposal that, for reasons explored immediately at the beginning of the chapter, poses some problems. The next section thus attempts to situate and assess the proposal advocated in the present project against this model of causation and, after canvassing other scholarly incursions into the debate at hand, sets the stage for an exploration of strict liability and other relevant policy considerations.

3

Unity Through Vagueness: The Challenges of Devising General Rules of Responsibility

I. INTRODUCTION

IN IDENTIFYING WAYS to harness legal norms with a view to preventing and suppressing transnational terrorism, this study has elected the realm of State responsibility as an incubator for potential deterrence models. It will weigh the possibility of implementing a mechanism inspired by strict liability that is nonetheless balanced out by principles of due diligence and consideration for the obligation of result/conduct dichotomy (themselves often shaped by political considerations and moral imperatives). In short, the project's overarching philosophy is guided by the idea that revisiting secondary rules of State responsibility – especially attribution – is a desirable process when attempting to balance out the principle of non-intervention into State affairs against the need to root out transnational terrorist networks.

This approach is by no means the sole possible interpretation or recasting of the rules of responsibility. Indeed, a multiplicity of theoretical insights can be brought to bear upon the objectives of enhancing transnational cooperation on counterterrorism and reducing governmental involvement in terrorism, be they envisaged through the New Haven School's emphasis on a global perspective, a leading French vision of State responsibility or more theoretical insights, for example.[1] Whether inspired by causation, strict liability or complicity theories, these rich theoretical explorations pave the way for fruitful discussion on accountability mechanisms and appear united by their disdain for the onerous attribution standards developed in *Nicaragua*.[2]

[1] Compare the approaches advanced in WM Reisman, 'International Legal Responses to International Terrorism' (1999) 22 *Houston Journal of International Law* 3, 56–57; P-M Dupuy, 'State Sponsors of Terrorism: Issues of International Responsibility' in A Bianchi (ed), *Enforcing International Law Norms against Terrorism* (Oxford, Hart Publishing, 2004) 3–16; T Becker, *Terrorism and the State: Rethinking the Rules of State Responsibility* (Oxford, Hart Publishing, 2006) 332.

[2] See, eg: RL Johnstone, 'State Responsibility: A Concerto for Court, Council and Committee' (2008) 37 *Denver Journal of International Law and Policy* 63, 90 (citing works by Tal Becker, José Alvarez, Vincent-Joël Proulx and Eduardo Savarese).

II. ALTERNATIVE RESPONSE: CAUSATION

Of particular interest is the model advocated by Tal Becker in a monograph, a work often referenced throughout the present study.[3] Whilst the purpose here is not to exhaustively review all of Becker's contributions, it is nonetheless useful to briefly canvass the major points of rapprochement with the present study. Particularly relevant to a critical exploration of State responsibility is that author's reliance on causation and causally-inspired models from municipal law in crafting his proposal for legal reform. After all, attribution can sometimes be construed as a 'surrogate for causation'.[4]

The thrust of Becker's argument is that the traditional application of State responsibility for seemingly private conduct remains unnecessarily grounded in principles of agency, a relatively uncontroversial proposition if one subscribes to the principal tenets of this study.[5] Similarly to this project, Becker calls for a revamping of the rules of State responsibility so as to adapt that body of law to the polymorphic and transnational nature of terrorism. Ostensibly seeking inspiration from a tortfeasor's duty of care under domestic law, he advocates the implementation of a causation-based model of responsibility, a structure ripe, he argues, for better connecting privately-inflicted internationally wrongful acts to States. Delving into both international and comparative jurisprudence, Becker proposes a four-tiered methodological inquiry in applying State responsibility, which operates as follows: i) on a factual basis, was the wrongful act caused by the State (thereby encompassing previously unattributable State conduct within the scope of that category)?; ii) from a legal perspective, did the State behaviour constitute a breach of the State's international obligation(s)?; iii) from a causal standpoint, what is the ensuing damage that may be included within the purview of State responsibility?; and iv) from a policy standpoint, do non-causal factors militate in favour of attenuating or increasing responsibility?[6]

As amply discussed above, the ILC's *Articles* predominantly rest on notions of control and interdependence between the State apparatus and private actors when triggering the mechanics of State responsibility.[7] Modern-day terrorism largely differs from transborder excursions carried out in the 60s, 70s and 80s. In that context, where hijacking undeniably constituted the dominant terroristic model, 'the concern may have been that States would control private terrorist groups, transforming them into a threat of international dimension'.[8] By

[3] Becker, above n 1.

[4] DJ Bederman, 'Contributory Fault and State Responsibility' (1990) 30 *Virginia Journal of International Law* 335, 347.

[5] But see: E De Brabandere, 'Non-State Actors, State-Centrism and Human Rights Obligations' (2009) 22 *Leiden Journal of International Law* 191, 203.

[6] For the theoretical framework of this inquiry, see Becker, above n 1 at 285–330. For an application of the proposed model to terrorism, see ibid, at 331–60.

[7] See, eg: below ch 4, section II.A).

[8] Becker, above n 1 at 252.

contrast, the dynamic has drastically changed today, undoubtedly exacerbated by the advent of modern technology, the multiplication of integrated and transnational networks, the development of new, broad-reaching weaponry and the possibilities offered by the Internet.[9] Consequently, the concern is that terrorist 'groups operate outside State control: that they endanger human security on a global scale, but offer no fixed global address towards which principles of legal accountability, reciprocity or deterrence can be directed'.[10]

Becker's argument becomes more compelling when considering the extent to which post-9/11 State practice has been constitutive of a shift in international law. In fact, if there was ever a moment to recognise the crystallisation of State practice or perhaps even the formulation of instant custom,[11] the international response to 9/11 might be as good a contender as any other. Indeed, in the *North Sea Continental Shelf* Cases the ICJ declared that 'the passage of only a short period of time is not . . . a bar to the formation' of a customary rule of international law.[12] Whether the response to 9/11 was, in fact, constitutive of instant custom will depend, to a large extent, on how much weight will ultimately be accorded to the 'State practice' component of customary law.[13] Whilst State practice on this front is rather heterogeneous, select States and commentators have nonetheless openly endorsed a general rule permitting the invocation of self-defence against States harbouring or supporting terrorists.[14] For instance, Christine Gray suggested that State support for the US-led campaign in

[9] Internet and the broad-reaching options it offers terrorists pose significant challenges to international law. See U Draetta, 'The Internet and Terrorist Activities' in Bianchi, above n 1 at 453–64; R Garnett and P Clarke, 'Cyberterrorism: A New Challenge for International Law' in ibid, at 465–90.

[10] Becker, above n 1 at 252.

[11] See, eg: B Langille, 'It's "Instant Custom": How the Bush Doctrine Became Law after the Terrorist Attacks of September 11, 2001' (2003) 26 *Boston College International and Comparative Law Review* 145. See also generally: A Székely, 'Compliance with International Environmental Treaties' (1997) 91 *ASIL Proceedings* 234, 236 (emphasising that as 'a purported new source of international law', the notion of instant custom 'has remained a hotly debated issue').

[12] *North Sea Continental Shelf (Federal Republic of Germany/Netherlands)*, Judgment of 20 February, *ICJ Reports* (1969) 3 at 44, para 74. For a variety of views on the formation process and source materials of instant custom, see TM Franck and MJ Glennon, *Foreign Relations and National Security Law: Cases, Materials and Simulations*, 2nd edn (St Paul, West Publishing, 1993) 283; ME Villiger, *Customary International Law and Treaties: A Study of their Interactions and Interrelations with Special Consideration of the 1969 Vienna Convention on the Law of Treaties* (Dordrecht, Nijhoff, 1985) 28–29; A D'Amato, 'The Concept of Human Rights in International Law' (1982) 82 *Columbia Law Review* 1110, 1129.

[13] See AT Guzman, 'Saving Customary International Law' (2005) 27 *Michigan Journal of International Law* (2005) 115, 157–59. It follows that the creation of instantaneous custom would hinge on a variety of 'policies, principles, precedents, analogies and considerations of fairness'. See MS McDougal, 'Editorial Comment: The Hydrogen Bomb Tests and the International Law of the Sea' (1955) 49 *AJIL* 356, 359 fn 10. But see: G Guillaume, 'Terrorism and International Law' (2004) 53 *ICLQ* 537, 546–47. For a general critique of the creation of instant custom, see GJH Van Hoof, *Rethinking the Sources of International Law* (Deventer, Kluwer, 1983) 86.

[14] See, eg: A Nolkaemper, 'Attribution of Forcible Acts to States: Connections between the Law on the Use of Force and the Law of State Responsibility' in N Blokker and N Schrijver (eds), *The Security Council and the Use of Force: Theory and Reality – A Need for Change?* (Leiden, Nijhoff, 2005) 133 at 136–37 and authorities cited therein.

Afghanistan could be tantamount to instant custom and, correspondingly, signals a revolutionary interpretative reframing of the UN Charter.[15] However, even if the response to 9/11 is construed as an isolated precedent violating international law, it does not necessarily follow that it necessarily prompted a change in the relevant primary rules.[16] Even if that precedent is heeded and repeated by a varied number of States – thereby signalling that the pertinent rule is consistently violated – a corresponding shift in the law can only be crystallised by a genuine belief by the relevant objectors and by third States that the bindingness of the norm has begun to wane. For example, in *Nicaragua* the fact that the prohibition of the use of force and the intervention in the internal affairs of States was frequently violated did not sway the ICJ to discredit the customary character of the rule under study.[17]

Given State and Security Council practice canvassed above, it can be cogently argued that the initial American-led posture clearly supported the paradigm shift identified in chapter two:

> In the wake of those attacks, not only did the United States regard the Taliban as equally responsible for the Al-Qaeda attacks on the basis that it had harbored the organization, but it seemed to receive the endorsement of most of the international community in doing so. In this case, the absence of any agency relationship did not prevent treating the Taliban as itself responsible, not just for its own counter-terrorism violations, but also for the act of terrorism perpetrated by Al-Qaeda.[18]

The international reaction to the US position certainly provided a strong indication of State practice on the application of State responsibility. Even prior to 9/11, American political rhetoric clearly forewarned Afghanistan and Sudan that they would be held directly responsible for Al Qaeda attacks emanating from their territory.[19] Moreover, the response to 9/11 was unprecedented in scope, both legally and politically, with the Security Council, the Organization of American States, the EU, NATO and various national actors and communities all mounting a constituency of conscience leading to the condemnation of Afghanistan's harbouring of Al-Qaeda. This reaction signalled, for the first time, the international community's conviction that 'It was the act of

[15] C Gray, 'The Use of Force and the International Legal Order' in MD Evans (ed), *International Law* (Oxford, OUP, 2003) 589 at 604. See also: M Byers, 'Terrorism, the Use of Force, and International Law After 11 September' (2001) 51 *ICLQ* 401, 409–10; MN Schmitt, 'Preemptive Strategies in International Law' (2003) 24 *Michigan Journal of International Law* 513, 538; HH Koh, 'The Spirit of the Laws' (2002) 43 *Harvard International Law Journal* 23, 28; R Wedgwood, 'Responding to Terrorism: The Strikes against Bin Laden' (1999) 24 *Yale Journal of International Law* 559, 564.

[16] See, eg: H Duffy, *The 'War on Terror' and the Framework of International Law* (Cambridge, CUP, 2005) 8; J Charney, 'Universal International Law' (1993) 87 *AJIL* 529, 543–45.

[17] See *Military and Paramilitary Activities in and against Nicaragua (Nicaragua v United States of America)*, Merits, Judgement of 27 June, *ICJ Reports* (1986) 14 at para 186.

[18] Becker, above n 1 at 208.

[19] See A Nissel, 'Tal Becker, Terrorism and the State: Rethinking the Rules of State Responsibility (Oxford: Hart Publishing, 2006)' (2007) 5 *Journal of International Criminal Justice* 245, 247.

"allowing" Al-Qaeda to operate in its territory that rendered the Taliban directly accountable'.[20] This posture was also endorsed in post-9/11 legal literature.[21]

In many ways, therefore, Becker's analysis aligns with the arguments espoused in this volume. For instance, some of the factual mitigating or attenuating components of the second tier inquiry explored below in chapter five evoke some connection with the principle of causation. Yet, many considerations invoked at that analytical stage do not solely rest on causal principles but also find grounding in various policy dimensions, whilst attempting to: i) strike a balance between respecting sovereignty and combating terrorism efficiently while upholding the sovereign equality between States in the face of disparate power dynamics; ii) protect developing States from the imposition of unrealistic or disproportionate legal standards that would indiscriminately subject them to attack or outside interference; iii) enhance and promote transnational cooperation and multilateralism; and iv) recognise the role of non-State actors not only in norm-creation but also in norm-enforcement.[22] Interestingly, this last policy ground has been brandished in scholarly enterprises vindicating acutely sceptical appraisals of the benefits of State responsibility in repressing international crimes. Frédéric Mégret's treatment of the question – redolent of critiques advancing that State responsibility responds to seemingly immutable bilateral typology – levels an important charge against the ILC's *Articles*. Mégret's contention is that, in light of State responsibility's entrenched inter-State inclination, such body of law fails to provide an apt incubator for the deployment of purely *erga omnes* reactions to international crimes, a scheme of recourses presumably encompassing a role for individuals in that author's view.[23] Ultimately, he resolves this conceptual disparity by transposing the impugned bilateralism under the lens of State responsibility to an individualised setting, expounding that 'Perhaps a better ground is the idea that, if crimes are committed by individuals, then other individuals should also be allowed to stop their

[20] Becker, above n 1 at 218.

[21] SR Ratner, 'Jus ad Bellum and Jus in Bello after September 11' (2002) 96 *AJIL* 905, 905; M Milanović, 'State Responsibility for Genocide' (2006) 17 *EJIL* 553, 583 ff.

[22] Compare with Becker, above n 1, especially at 281 (essentially arguing that responsibility should be synonymous with capacity and emphasising that a legal analysis assessing State responsibility for terrorism should acknowledge that 'because of the causal link between the State's wrongdoing and the private terrorist activity that it makes sense to treat the State, in certain circumstances, as responsible for the private act even though it is not its immediate perpetrator'). Becker's approach nonetheless leaves some questions up for debate, prompting scholars to query: 'When can it be shown incontrovertibly that the victim state has satisfied its burden of putting forward a "necessary link between the terrorist attack and the host State"'. RP Barnidge, Jr, 'Tal Becker, Terrorism and the State: Rethinking the Rules of State Responsibility' (2007) 12 *Journal of Conflict & Security Law* 331, 331–32 (citing Becker, above n 1 at 343). On non-State norm enforcement/creation, see, eg: E Dannenmaier, 'The Role of Non-State Actors in Climate Compliance' in J Brunnée et al (eds), *Promoting Compliance in an Evolving Climate Regime* (Cambridge, CUP, Forthcoming 2012) ch 7; A Peters et al (eds), *Non-State Actors as Standard Setters* (Cambridge, CUP, 2009).

[23] F Mégret, 'Beyond "Freedom Fighters" and "Terrorists": When, if Ever, Is Non-State Violence Legitimate in International Law?' Unpublished Manuscript (6 April 2009) at 10 fn 45, available at http://ssrn.com/abstract=1373590.

perpetration'.[24] These observations bring the recurrent theme of adapting State-centric legal schemes to meet the challenges of counterterrorism back into sharp relief. As seen throughout this volume, States have some role to play in deterring terrorism but they do not bear the sole burden of enforcing international law. A legally pluralistic structure seeking to integrate a multiplicity of actors against a multipolar political backdrop must be emphasised.

Vital to justifying the policy crux of both studies is the notion that the world is now different and that State responsibility must be envisaged in a different light to ensure any kind of effective enforcement of counterterrorism obligations. It follows that 'the State still enjoys many of the benefits of sovereignty and still carries its burdens. But it is also a world in which private actors can wield State-like power'.[25] The law of State responsibility should accommodate modern realities – either by loosening its standards on attribution or through a more ambitious regime overhaul – an eventuality eschewed by the ICJ when handing down its *Genocide* judgment in 2007, much to the chagrin of the proponents of a responsibility-expanding scheme of liability.[26] Interestingly, after arguing that the ICJ could not have gone as far as to revisit its test on attribution therein, others rather expound that 'it is precisely the Court's silence on the matter than can allow state practice to develop unimpeded, and perhaps eventually produce new tests of attribution'.[27]

Becker's searing indictment of the ILC's *Articles* comes into sharp focus when contemplating the rigid dichotomy between the private and public sphere underpinning State responsibility.[28] Despite warnings issued by feminist scholars such as Chinkin, Mackinnon and Olsen against this (perhaps antiquated) distinction when exposing the Victorian roots of Anglo-American public law,[29] it nonetheless found its way – in a very central fashion – in the ILC's finalised project. As Becker points out, the ILC's agency standard remains ill-suited to adequately tackle and depict the *real* interrelationships connecting terrorists and the States that harbour them. In short, agency miscasts most prevalent

[24] ibid.

[25] Becker, above n 1 at 361.

[26] J Griebel and M Plücken lament the Court's failure to take stock of the 9/11 precedent when assessing the rules governing State responsibility in the *Genocide Case*. See 'New Developments Regarding the Rules of Attribution? The International Court of Justice's Decision in Bosnia v. Serbia' (2008) 21 *Leiden Journal of International Law* 601, 618. Conversely, other scholars resisted the need to alter the extant scheme of public international law, even prior to the *Genocide Case*. See, eg: G Abi-Saab, 'There Is No Need to Reinvent the Law', *A Defining Moment – International Law Since September 11: The Magazine* (September 2002), available at www.crimesofwar.org.

[27] M Milanović, 'State Responsibility for Acts of Non-State Actors: A Comment on Griebel and Pluecken' (2009) 22 *Leiden Journal of International Law* 307, 321. Interestingly, Becker, above n 1 at 324, rather frames the issue of imputability in a different light, expounding that 'The principles of attribution are better understood as a mechanism for defining an act of State only, without limiting the *scope* of responsibility that that act may generate'.

[28] This distinction is also tackled below in section IV.D) (through the lens of the primary/secondary obligations dichotomy) and ch 5, section II.A) (through the lens of limiting governmental interference in the private sphere whilst combating terrorism).

[29] See Nissel, above n 19 at 247. For a sampling of the feminist approach vis-à-vis this rigid dichotomy, see, eg: C Chinkin, 'A Critique of the Public/Private Dimension' (1999) 10 *EJIL* 387.

arrangements between host-States and terrorists save in clear-cut cases of direct State involvement in such activity.[30] As such,

> agency suggests a joint endeavour knowingly initiated by the principal and faithfully executed with the consent of the obedient agent. Responsibility is engaged because of an express or implied agreement between the principal and the agent, creating a direct relationship between the agent's actions and the principal's direction and control.[31]

Yet, recent events and increasingly prevalent de-territorialised and decentralised models of terrorism evince that State involvement is often 'more about acquiescence than direction and control'.[32] These concerns also fit neatly within the framework advanced in this monograph, especially in the spirit of the paradigm shift towards indirect responsibility identified in chapter two, further bolstering the impetus for devising new or more flexible rules of responsibility.

Ultimately, the present project shares several points of rapprochement with Becker's own recasting of secondary norms, a crucial one being that both studies allow for the consideration of policy factors in increasing or decreasing the responsibility of States. Whilst inextricably intertwined with evidentiary issues and compatible with the attenuating elements explored below in chapter five, Becker acknowledges that 'Relevant factors in this regard could include the gravity of the terrorist attack, the nature of the State's wrongdoing, the particular response pursued by the victim, and the political standing and credibility of the accuser and the accused respectively'.[33]

One of the main points of contention between both accounts resides in the fact that Becker's analysis further extends what was conceived, in the earlier stages of this study, as 'direct responsibility' to States.[34] Correspondingly, his argument operates on the possibility of imputing hitherto unattributable private conduct to States; contrary to the analysis advocated throughout this study, however, his inquiry does not entirely focus on the distinct obligation to prevent terrorism, but rather expounds that, in certain scenarios of mere toleration and acquiescence, a State can be found directly responsible for the wrongful act itself (ie the terrorist attack), via causation. In short, the host-State can be seen

[30] Whilst certain scholars, led by Antonio Cassese, argue for the adoption of *Tadić*'s overall control standard, it is not even certain that Afghanistan would have been found responsible for the 9/11 attacks on the basis of that rule. Given the relevant facts, we must ponder whether the less exacting standard of 'harbouring and supporting' could produce that legal result. On the agency standard's miscasting of real host-State/terrorists relationships in the context of Becker's treatment of the topic, see J Rosenthal, 'Book Annotations' (2006) 39 *NYU Journal of International Law and Politics* 141, 147:

> By misunderstanding the nature of public involvement in the private sphere of terrorism, the agency paradigm mistakenly absolves states of responsibility when the true nature of their support, often in the form of a persistent failure to prevent private wrongs, allows terrorist activity to succeed.

[31] Becker, above n 1 at 258.

[32] ibid.

[33] ibid, at 150.

[34] See particularly: above ch 2, section II.

as having *caused* terrorism and is, therefore, responsible. Admittedly, whilst the underlying objectives of Becker's model oscillate between promoting deterrence and ensuring that States take their counterterrorism duties seriously, similar policy goals are vindicated through the prima facie presumption of indirect responsibility and corresponding shift in onus suggested below. However, after attempting to somewhat neutralise asymmetric power dynamics and produce a levelled playing field, the proposed model triggers the assessment of various policy and factual considerations. That is not to say that Becker's approach fails to incorporate policy and 'non-causal' factors in the fourth tier of his inquiry to determine whether responsibility should be increased or decreased. Nevertheless, the thrust of this study consistently couches its proposed legal reform at the level of prevention and within the purview of international responsibility. In so doing, it sometimes analytically merges elements of the relevant jurisprudential tests with the 'harbouring and supporting' standard and/or promotes automatic attribution or circumventing attribution in certain cases, or perhaps ultimately challenges the rigid private/public sphere dichotomy underpinning the ILC's *Articles*. But it never seeks to effectively conflate terrorists and their host-States on the basis of causation, save in flagrant cases of direct State involvement in terrorism.[35] When confronted with egregious and direct State involvement in terrorism or, alternatively, ex post facto endorsement by the governing apparatus of the wrongful act, responsibility may be established by way of normative operation under the *Articles*, that is to say by virtue of attribution and not through the concept of causation. For every situation in between, new rules of international responsibility are direly needed.

Interestingly, some feminist legal scholars inexorably pit Becker's own vision of a fructuous State responsibility reform against what constituted the initial theoretical articulations of the present study. The ensuing analysis, therefore, is cast at the level of indirect versus direct, as a theory working within the classical paradigm versus a re-conceptualisation of relevant rules involving a radical overhaul of the public/private dichotomy. This is not to say that the present study, or previous accounts relating to it, eschews a critique of the public/private dimension of State responsibility. In fact, this line of contestation invariably amounts to the recurrent unifying thread amongst recent progressive scholarly endeavours advocating a reformulation of State responsibility

[35] This position stands in sharp contrast with the model of indirect State responsibility advocated in the present study. Put another way, Becker's approach allows – through the mechanism of causation – for the attribution of conduct that would not ordinarily trigger direct State responsibility under the classical rules to nonetheless (and perhaps 'artificially') meet that threshold. See Becker, above n 1 at 335:

> The principal benefit of the causality based approach is that it avoids the automatic rejection of direct State responsibility merely because of the absence of an agency relationship. As a result, it potentially exposes the wrongdoing State to a greater range and intensity of remedies, as well as a higher degree of international attention and opprobrium for its contribution to the private terrorist activity.

rules.[36] Indeed, the adoption of truly innovative legal mechanisms in this field entails challenging the rigid conceptual and analytical barrier that flows from the agency paradigm underpinning the mechanics of the ILC's *Articles*. One feminist reading of the policy reforms put forth identifies two distinct shifts in perspectives along the following lines: whilst the central argument advanced herein likely 'works within the classical framework with a greater focus on the positive obligations of states to prevent terrorism and a higher degree of due diligence', Becker's own treatment of the topic 'questions the entire basis of the public/private dichotomy, insists that terrorists cannot be distinguished from the states in which they are permitted to operate, and that state responsibility for terrorist activities should be direct'.[37]

Conversely, the present study focuses squarely on shifts towards more indirect modes of responsibility, an approach predicated on governmental failures to intervene, which, in turn, translate into failures to prevent terrorism. As seen in chapter two, the US-led response against Afghanistan seems to have effectively collapsed the conceptual barrier once erected between direct and indirect responsibility, perhaps better exemplified by responsibility for actions versus omissions. Whilst Travalio and Altenberg view this reality as necessarily reflecting the state of contemporary international law, the crux of the policy argument advanced herein is rather one 'where there remains a distinction between direct responsibility (for organs and agents who fail to respect international law) and indirect responsibility (for the failure of due diligence to prevent non-state violations of international law)'.[38] Thus, the contentions advanced in this book are redolent of the arguments espoused within the pragmatic feminist scholarly canon, perhaps best spearheaded by Rebecca Cook. It stresses focus on enlarging the scope of international responsibility for omissions whilst simultaneously casting policy recommendations within a framework that can be reconciled with the ethos of public international law.[39] Under both approaches, therefore, the notion of indirect responsibility becomes paramount in the analysis, thereby dictating a call for greater protection of women's human rights within Cook's own scholarship, and for renewed analytical emphasis on governmental failures to prevent terrorism herein (ie omissions under State

[36] See RL Johnstone, 'Unlikely Bedfellows: Feminist Theory and the War on Terror' (2009) 9 *Chicago-Kent Journal of International and Comparative Law* 1, 28 (invoking the works of Greg Travalio and John Altenberg, Vincent-Joël Proulx and Tal Becker).

[37] ibid, at 18 (contrasting the works of Vincent-Joël Proulx and Derek Jinks with those of Tal Becker and Greg Travalio and John Altenberg).

[38] ibid, at 29.

[39] See, eg: RJ Cook, 'State Accountability Under the Convention on the Elimination of All Forms of Discrimination against Women' in RJ Cook (ed), *Human Rights of Women: National and International Perspectives* (Philadelphia, University of Pennsylvania Press, 1994) 228; RJ Cook, 'Accountability in International Law for Violations of Women's Rights by Non-State Actors' in DG Dallmeyer (ed), *Reconceiving Reality: Women and International Law* (Washington, DC, American Society of International Law, 1993) 93. Along similar lines, see also: K Roth, 'Domestic Violence as an International Human Rights Issue' in RJ Cook (ed), *Human Rights of Women: National and International Perspectives* (Philadelphia, University of Pennsylvania Press, 1994) 326.

responsibility).[40] Both visions likely strive towards a more egalitarian and legitimate application of legal norms, thereby signalling the limitations of adopting a purely causal model under the aegis of the framework proposed in this study.

Another more significant problem with Becker's thesis is his assertion that State responsibility is only contingent on the eventuality that the host-State *could have* thwarted a terrorist excursion, had it fulfilled the due diligence standard.[41] In other words, only where an attack can be averted via diligent conduct will the host-State be held to its obligation to prevent terrorism on the basis of direct responsibility. Becker frames the thrust of his argument in causal terms; everything hinges on the State having somehow contributed to the triggering of a chain of events leading to the wrongful act, a prospect seemingly far removed from the rationale of indirect responsibility, which acknowledges that governments will sometimes be held responsible irrespective of any clear, contributory cause-and-effect participation in transnational terrorism. His analysis becomes one of causal apportionment and blame allocation, which can in turn obfuscate the establishment of clear legal postulates governing accountability mechanisms: is mere toleration of terrorists sufficient to legally *cause* an attack or can it just contribute incrementally to the perpetration of the wrongful act – let's arbitrarily say 20 per cent? Or are there other relevant non-governmental *causes* that may facilitate the commission of the wrongful act? For instance, can we assimilate the breakdowns in US intelligence with contributory negligence vis-à-vis the 9/11 attacks?[42] How do we decipher which cause contributed to what percentage of the wrongful act? etc. This debate inexorably steers us back to the problematic – and sometimes circuitous – fact-finding mission embodied in ILC Article 47(1).[43] It is doubtful whether this model would be sustainable in cases where several preparatory terrorist acts span over different territories: how would one apportion liability for the 9/11 attacks based on a causal model (eg: 60 per cent for Afghanistan, 10 per cent for Saudi Arabia and 20 per cent for Germany, etc)? Similarly, how would we determine the level of participation and, consequently, of liability of both Yemen and the Netherlands in failing to foil the actions of Umar Farouk Abdulmutallab (aka the 'Underwear Bomber')? Similar concerns apply to the *Lockerbie* attack, which entailed at least the passive involvement of several States such as Cyprus and Germany. In all of these scenarios, there is some due diligence failure at every step but it is unclear how a causation-based model of responsibility would address such omissions.

Becker illustrates his conception of this norm by way of example:

> Suppose that a State that has the capacity to prevent terrorist activity neglects this responsibility and fails to deploy its security forces effectively for this purpose. In

[40] For further analysis on this point, see Johnstone, above n 36 at 29–30.

[41] Becker, above n 1 at 334.

[42] Consider *The 9/11 Commission Report*: *Final Report of the National Commission on Terrorist Attacks Upon the United States* (New York, WW Norton, 2004) 339–53; TE Copeland, *Fool Me Twice*: *Intelligence Failure and Mass Casualty Terrorism* (Leiden, Nijhoff, 2007).

[43] On Art 47(1), see below ch 5 nn 205, 280–88, 314 and accompanying text.

> principle, this may be a violation of the general duty to exercise due diligence in preventing terrorist action. It is a wrongful omission for which State responsibility may be engaged. But it does not necessarily follow that this omission is the cause of a specific terrorist attack.[44]

Here, Becker is seeking to extend the discipline of State responsibility to the act *itself*, so as to cast the host-State as 'directly' responsible for terrorism (ie as though it had itself perpetrated the attack). More importantly, Becker's posture comes into sharper focus through his treatment of the question of capacity, which he views as depending

> on the particular factual circumstances. In each case, it will be necessary to establish that the fulfillment of the State's due diligence obligations would have prevented the terrorist activity. Without such a showing, the unlawful omission is not a condition *sine qua non* of the subsequent terrorist attack and cannot, therefore, generate responsibility for it on causal grounds.[45]

This line of argument seems to misfire on two counts. Equating due diligence solely with the fact that failure of its exercise would have caused the attack is not only extremely difficult to prove, it also misses the mark. Revamping State responsibility towards more efficient methods of ensuring governmental accountability and, as a corollary, bolstering deterrence models is not just about ascertaining that States are somehow involved in terrorism. It also expresses the acknowledgement that those actors should take their counterterrorism obligations seriously, while promoting transnational cooperation and multilateralism. This might entail adopting more stringent mechanisms of responsibility – which the prima facie presumption of indirect responsibility and corresponding shift in onus advocated below heed, at least partially – to increase accountability and shift the focus squarely on prevention. Indeed, this might constitute an effective way to uphold the content and integrity of primary rules, no matter how vaguely they may be formulated. Without enforcement or the threat of incurring responsibility, broad and sweeping obligations are essentially eviscerated of any real binding power. We must instil some traction into resolution 1373 and similar instruments; otherwise, primary counterterrorism obligations will be relegated to pure form. In order to promote substance over form, the present study, along with Becker's own analysis, attempts to achieve this objective via rethinking State responsibility.

Furthermore, by equating due diligence solely with the fact that failure of its exercise would have caused the attack, Becker's proposal seems to conflict with the ICJ's *Genocide* Judgment. In that case, the Court focused its inquiry on the obligation to prevent under the Convention on the Prevention and Punishment of the Crime of Genocide. It opined that responsibility is not solely contingent on States failing to exercise due diligence in preventing genocide if doing so would have averted the wrongful act. In short, the Court rejected the creation of

[44] Becker, above n 1 at 334.
[45] ibid.

an escape clause enabling States to claim that full compliance with due diligence would have fallen short in preventing the unlawful act, moving towards a multilateral expectation that several States – 'each complying with its obligation to prevent' where the efforts of a single nation might have failed – can perhaps bring about the desired result.[46] While the ICJ's reasoning was framed exclusively within the furrow of the Genocide Convention,[47] this logic easily carries over to counterterrorism duties, especially the obligation to prevent terrorism explored herein.[48] Consequently, additional writing on the application of the due diligence standard to transnational terrorism is undoubtedly required.[49]

Even if State responsibility can play some role in the prevention and suppression of terrorism, considerable obstacles impede the full deployment of consistently effective enforcement or coercive measures pursuant to that normative scheme. The book now turns to some of those intractable obstacles before advocating a perhaps more radical policy shift towards a strict liability-infused model.

III. DEVELOPING GUIDELINES AND GENERAL PRINCIPLES FOR FACT-INTENSIVE, FACT-SPECIFIC PHENOMENA

A major challenge affecting this project stems from the fact-specific nature of terrorism, which complicates the elaboration of general rules and guidelines applicable to all breaches of counterterrorism obligations. This difficulty is exacerbated by the processes of self-judging and autoqualification which inevitably crop up in many areas of international law and remain central features in the law of State responsibility. As a result, victim-States often sit as final arbiters of wrongful acts and must, correspondingly, devise countermeasures in order to redress those international breaches. The present section seeks to tease out the political and policy implications of such arrangements in counterterrorism settings.

A) Partial Solutions: State Centrism and Other Limits of State Responsibility

Whilst certain aspects of international law are decidedly shifting towards an increasingly transnational paradigm, the global order arising out of the

[46] *Case Concerning the Application of the Convention on the Prevention and Punishment of the Crime of Genocide (Bosnia and Herzegovina v Serbia and Montenegro)*, Judgment of 26 February, *ICJ Reports* (2007) 43 at para 430.

[47] ibid, at para 429.

[48] See also: Barnidge, Jr, above n 22 at 332. See also generally: A Zimmermann, 'The Obligation to Prevent Genocide: Towards a General Responsibility to Protect?' in U Fastenrath et al (eds), *From Bilateralism to Community Interest: Essays in Honour of Judge Bruno Simma* (Oxford, OUP, 2011) 629–45 (applying similar reasoning to treaty-based obligations to prevent, in particular genocide and war crimes).

[49] Certain scholars have delved into this difficult topic. See generally: RP Barnidge, Jr, *Non-State Actors and Terrorism: Applying the Law of State Responsibility and the Due Diligence Principle* (The Hague, TMC Asser Press, 2008). See also: below ch 5, section IV.

post-Westphalia landscape devolved all sovereign powers and prerogatives into the hands of States. As a result, recourse to force standards and international law, generally, rested predominantly upon bilateral conceptions of legal relationships. This state of affairs was perpetuated during the Cold War era, where inter-State (re)action provoked by original private wrongdoing would undoubtedly have been perceived as highly destabilising and detrimental in the grander scheme of nuclear *rapports de force*.[50] In short, international law was traditionally envisaged as a State-centric endeavour, a characteristic that some ineluctably call into question or, alternatively, construe as symptomatic of the modern international legal order.[51]

Yet, State responsibility has long sought to adapt to private wrongdoing with a view to determining whether such conduct could be regulated, or neutralised, through the screen of the State. Challenges should be levelled, where relevant, against the wisdom of maintaining liability norms 'based on the separation of the state from the individuals and associations of which it is composed'.[52] Theoretical advances based on complicity, collective responsibility or condonation, each at times more raw and unsophisticated than the other, were articulated around one organising principle: a connection between private behaviour and the control wielded by a State over the territory in which such conduct takes place. After all, 'throughout the 19th and early 20th century, private insults could still propel nations towards war. The act of the State and the acts of its subjects remained interlinked'.[53]

Modern events and the advent of the disaggregated State have dramatically challenged this international legal order. States no longer detain an unrivalled monopoly over power and wealth. Quite to the contrary, they must coexist with highly influential non-State actors; as a result, States and non-State actors now share power and influence on an unprecedented level.[54] As seen above, they are partners not only in norm enforcement but also in norm creation.[55] Two of their most important shareholders are undoubtedly the international community, which vests the viability of many of its interests in State compliance with obligations protecting those interests, and the human security scheme[56] – sometimes

[50] See, eg: Becker, above n 1 at 361.

[51] See, eg: M Kaplan, 'Using Collective Interests to Ensure Human Rights: An Analysis of the Articles on State Responsibility' (2004) 79 *NYU Law Review* 1902, 1902–03.

[52] W Friedmann, 'The Growth of State Control Over the Individual and its Effect upon the Rules of International State Responsibility' (1938) 19 *BYIL* 118, 144.

[53] Becker, above n 1 at 361.

[54] For an exploration of similar ideas, see R McCorquodale, 'Beyond State Sovereignty: The International Legal System and Non-State Participants' (2006) 8 *Revista Colombiana de Derecho Internacional* 103.

[55] See, eg: Frédéric Mégret's thought-provoking work on the role of non-State actors in implementing international law in the context of international resistance: 'Can International Law Be a Law of Resistance? Ten Steps for a Renewal of International Normative Ambition', Unpublished Manuscript (8 August 2007), available at http://ssrn.com/abstract=1212542; 'On the Legitimacy of 'Insurgency': Rise and Fall of the Idea of Resistance to Occupation', Unpublished Manuscript (5 November 2008), available at http://ssrn.com/abstract=1296060.

[56] See H Owada, 'Human Security and International Law' in Fastenrath et al, above n 48 at 505–20.

dependent not only on loose coordination between governmental networks and non-State actors but also challenged and shaped by non-State actors. Transnational terrorist networks such as Al Qaeda have challenged and, to some extent, changed the rules of the game or, at the very least, prompted the international community and local governments to revisit certain policies. After all, 'globalization can be an incredible force-multiplier' thereby evincing both a rich interplay/power sharing and power struggle between States and non-State actors.[57] The resulting interplay between law and terror translates into two colliding networks, namely the emergence of transnational terrorist networks (eg Al Qaeda) and the network of law (which comprises transborder regulatory regimes, transnational litigation, the structures of public international law, etc).[58] Ensuring that an effective transnational counterterrorism campaign acquires traction requires not only a rethinking of certain components within the network of law, but also the harmonisation and bolstering of both international and domestic aspects of that very network.[59]

In this new reality, private actors can arrogate State-like power and influence with either positive or potentially devastating circumstances.[60] In seeking ways to regulate this behaviour and to prevent catastrophic terrorism, it is imperative to further analyse the role of States in tolerating and supporting terrorism. Delineating accountability levels of involved governments, along with the elaboration of general precepts governing all breaches of counterterrorism obligations, not only acknowledges the broad-reaching capacities of non-State actors but can also help identify deterrence models and shift the focus squarely on prevention through the screen of the State.

This study heeds this trend and argues for a substantive rethinking – or, at least, a different interpretation – of the rules of State responsibility.[61] In many ways, it strives to join, and casts itself as philosophically adjacent to, scholarly contributions calling for a reassessment of the rules governing attribution in light, inter alia, of the ICJ's *Genocide Case*.[62] This inquiry, however, inexorably runs against one obstacle. Whilst traditional conceptions of public international

[57] TL Friedman, *Longitudes and Attitudes: Exploring the World after September 11* (New York, Farrar, Straus, Giroux, 2002) 5.

[58] See generally: CJ Borgen, 'A Tale of Two Networks: Terrorism, Transnational Law, and Network Theory' (2009) 33 *Oklahoma City University Law Review* 409.

[59] See, eg: ibid, at 410.

[60] See, eg: JT Matthews, 'Power Shift' in RJ Lieber (ed), *Foreign Policy* (Aldershot, Ashgate, 2008) 219; JT Matthews, 'Power Shift' in D Held and A McGrew (eds), *The Global Transformations Reader: An Introduction to the Globalization Debate* (Cambridge, Polity, 2003) 204; JT Matthews, 'Power Shift' (1997) 76 *Foreign Affairs* 50.

[61] See also: JA Hessbruegge, 'The Historical Development of the Doctrines of Attribution and Due Diligence in International Law' (2004) 36 *NYU Journal of International Law and Politics* 265, 280–81.

[62] See, eg: Griebel and Plücken, above n 26; A Cassese, 'The Nicaragua and Tadić Tests Revisited in Light of the ICJ Judgment on Genocide in Bosnia' (2007) 18 *EJIL* 649. For similar reasoning, albeit from the perspective of fragmentation, see R Goldstone and R Hamilton, 'Bosnia v. Serbia: Lesson from the Encounter of the International Court of Justice with the International Criminal Tribunal for the Former Yugoslavia' (2008) 21 *Leiden Journal of International Law* 95.

law might have been initially State-centric both in scope and philosophy, contemporary events evince that non-State actors can now subvert this vision and challenge the rules that result from it, thereby shifting the focus away from an overemphasis on statehood in the search for solutions to truly transnational problems. For example, human rights-based discourse is shifting increasingly towards a cogent and coherent challenge against the dominance of State-centrism in tackling violations of fundamental international legal norms.[63] The academic dialogue is 'therefore moving away from the traditional view that under human rights law the individuals hold the rights while only states bear the obligations'.[64] Arguing that such contestation is predicated both on normative and descriptive components, certain scholars argue that the State's centrality in international law is by no means indelible and that it no longer enjoys the benefits of being the predominant actor in the discipline, or even its central stakeholder.[65]

Yet, in a seemingly paradoxical stance vis-à-vis the rise of the disaggregated State, the present study tackles the problem of transnational terrorism through the State-centric regime *par excellence*: the law of State responsibility. However, it does so – and any project analysing the interplay between State responsibility and terrorism should follow suit – whilst acknowledging the role of non-State actors in shaping and advancing international law. More importantly, the rules governing State responsibility are probably far more adaptable to contemporary realities than would appear upon first glance, subject of course to the different interpretations and adjustments advocated herein. As Brownlie rightly underscored, 'The continuing relevance of the principles of state responsibility is not to be underestimated. In any event, these principles are more versatile than specialist writers are prepared to recognize'.[66] Whilst non-State actors wield an unprecedented level of power and influence on the global scale, there is no reason to preclude the potential contributions of State responsibility in tackling privately-inflicted harm through the screen of statehood, be it authored by rebel groups or transnational corporations.[67] State responsibility remains a dominant player in international relations and, at the very least, warrants consideration whenever the commission of an internationally wrongful act is ascertained, irrespective of the enforcement deliverables it can or cannot ultimately produce.

[63] See, eg: P Alston, *Non-State Actors and Human Rights* (Oxford, OUP, 2005); A Clapham, *Human Rights Obligations of Non-State Actors* (Oxford, OUP, 2006); O De Schutter (ed), *Transnational Corporations and Human Rights* (Oxford, Hart Publishing, 2006).

[64] De Brabandere, above n 5 at 192.

[65] SD Marks, 'State-Centrism, International Law, and the Anxieties of Influence' (2006) 19 *Leiden Journal of International Law* 339, 340. But see: JE Alvarez, 'The Return of the State' (2011) 20 *Minnesota Journal of International Law* 223.

[66] I Brownlie, *Principles of International Law*, 6th edn (Oxford, OUP, 2003) 190.

[67] State responsibility for non-State actions has generated considerable writing. See, eg: R McCorquodale and PC Simons, 'Responsibility Beyond Borders: State Responsibility for Extraterritorial Violations by Corporations of International Human Rights Law' (2007) 70 *Modern Law Review* 598; J Kuusi, *The Host State and the Transnational Corporation: An Analysis of Legal Relationships* (Farnborough, Saxon House, 1979); SBO Gutto, 'Violation of Human Rights in the Third World: Responsibility of States and TNCs' (1983) 23 *Indian Journal of International Law* 56.

Conversely, applying the law of State responsibility to terrorism cannot make any credible claim to exhaustion of all remedies or legal regimes that can be harnessed with a view to combating transnational crime. Nor does it strive to do so. This reality can be framed in rather reductive terms. If one were to conceive of an international society comprised of geo-politically delimited, separate entities – let's call them nation-States – entitled to certain rights and inheriting certain obligations pursuant to a set of organising principles – let's call that backdrop the international community – that arrangement would invariably be prone to occasional power struggles and conflict. It is further exacerbated by the fact that this society is at times populated by egoists solely guided by the pursuit of self-interest, and predominantly characterised by disparate economic relations and asymmetrical power dynamics.[68] However, there still needs to be some modicum of law and order, even when faced with the most tempestuous and asymmetrical dynamics. Accordingly, a sort of conceptual and legal safety net is devised to regulate and, ultimately, punish violations by States of a core group of agreed-upon rules and principles in this international order. That is the exclusive dominion of State responsibility. The principal difficulty lies in the absence of a centralised enforcement monopoly, as opposed to those found in domestic constitutional orders; States are, therefore, left to their own devices in applying and implementing the consequences of State responsibility. As explored above, the notion of *reciprocity* often remains the only engine of survival in this setting.[69] Whilst counterterrorism issues are generally not suited for the application of reciprocity in some fields, such as humanitarian law,[70] the law of State responsibility eludes this categorisation and, rather, largely depends on reciprocity for successful deployment. The scope of analysis of that body of law coincidentally happens to straddle counterterrorism in the present project and correspondingly explores the extension of this traditional corpus of norms to the subversive activities of non-State actors. Yet, reciprocal mechanics are operationalised and achieved on a State-to-State basis, thereby disabling problematic applications of reciprocity to asymmetric situations involving private actors at sub-State levels.

Consequently, States will exert a broad margin of appreciation not only on the applicability and – once that applicability is ascertained – on the modalities

[68] See the discussion on rationalist considerations below ch 4, section V.B) and, to a lesser extent, above ch 1, section I.

[69] See, eg: below ch 5, section III.A). See also generally: above ch 1, section I. On the vitality of reciprocity in the application and development of international law, see Separate Opinion of Judge Simma in *Application of the Interim Accord of 13 September 1995 (the former Yugoslav Republic of Macedonia v Greece)*, Judgment of 5 December, *ICJ* (2011) 3–4, para 10, available at www.icj-cij.org/docket/files/142/16829.pdf.

[70] See R Provost, 'Asymmetrical Reciprocity and Compliance with the Laws of War', Unpublished Manuscript (14 January 2010) at 3 fn 13, available at http://ssrn.com/abstract=1427437 (expounding that 'it is unwarranted to develop an analysis on the place of reciprocity in the laws of war around issues connected to anti-terrorism'). For a cynical treatment of reciprocity, see MJ Osiel, *The End of Reciprocity: Terror, Torture, and the Law of War* (New York, CUP, 2009). But see: S Watts, 'Reciprocity and the law of War' (2009) 50 *Harvard International Law Journal* 365, 431.

of State responsibility repertoire vis-à-vis State failures to prevent terrorism, but also on what constitutes 'terrorism' in any given case. This brings the question of governmental autoqualification into sharp relief and steers the purview of legal analysis towards 'Kelsen's proposition that only state parties to a controversy could autoqualify it'.[71] As a result, when a State breaches the obligation to prevent terrorism, competing interpretations and constructions of State responsibility law – especially regarding appropriate countermeasures – and of what, exactly, constitutes 'terrorism' will ineluctably arise.[72] The ensuing margin of appreciation is rather broad and often divisive. As a corollary, potential conflicting qualifications also stem from the process of self-judging, itself also a central feature of the default system of State responsibility.

Interestingly, ILC Special Rapporteur Arangio-Ruiz lobbied the Commission in 1992–93 to adopt a mechanism of mandatory dispute settlement that would obligate States to exhaust all available dispute resolution options prior to adopting unilateral countermeasures.[73] As part of his revolutionary proposal, he envisaged a third-party objective body mandated with monitoring and reviewing the adoption of countermeasures to ensure that their application remained just and equitable.[74] It is no surprise, therefore, that Arangio-Ruiz construed the prior settlement of disputes before resorting to countermeasures as an integral component of States' obligation to favour the peaceful resolution of their disputes.[75] The Special Rapporteur's vision even included a draft article, which was incorporated into one of the Commission's drafts:

> In cases, however, where the dispute arises between State Parties to the present articles, one of which has taken countermeasures against the other, the State against which they are taken is entitled at any time unilaterally to submit the dispute to an arbitral tribunal to be constituted in conformity with Annex II to the present articles.[76]

[71] R Provost, *International Human Rights and Humanitarian Law* (Cambridge, CUP, 2002) 338 fn 2. See also: H Kelsen, *Peace Through Law* (Chapel Hill, University of North Carolina Press, 1944) 13–14; L Gross, 'States as Organs of International Law and the Problem of Autointerpretation' in G Lipsky (ed), *Law and Politics in the World Community* (Berkeley, University of California Press, 1953) 59 at 72–73. See also generally: L Gross, 'States as Organs of International Law and the Problem of Autointerpretation' in L Gross (ed), *Selected Essays on International Law and Organization* (Irvington-on-Hudson, Transnational Publishers, 1993) 167.

[72] For instance, in *Nicaragua* the Nicaraguan government classified the *Contras* rebels as 'terrorists'. See *Nicaragua*, above n 17 at 63–64, para 113 and at 68, para 121. Similarly, Michael J Glennon and Donald T Fox carried out a fact-finding mission on the operations and tactics employed by the *Contras* before testifying before the ICJ that the rebels had engaged in terrorism. See TD Gill, *Litigation Strategy at the International Court: A Case Study of the Nicaragua v. United States Dispute* (Dordrecht, Nijhoff, 1989) 193–94.

[73] G Arangio-Ruiz, 'Counter-Measures and Amicable Dispute Settlement Means in the Implementation of State Responsibility: A Crucial Issue before the International Law Commission' (1994) 5 *EJIL* 20.

[74] See 'Report of the International Law Commission on the Work of its Forty-Fifth Session', UN GAOR, 48th Sess, Supp No 10, UN Doc A/48/10 (1993) at 38, para 228.

[75] See G Arangio-Ruiz, 'Fourth Report on State Responsibility' (1992) 2(1) *Yearbook of the International Law Commission* 1, UN Doc A/CN.4/444/Add 1-3 at 19–21, paras 41–51.

[76] Draft Art 5(2) in (1995) 2(2) *Yearbook of the International Law Commission* 78.

If adopted, such provision would have instituted a mandatory dispute resolution exigency and correspondingly signalled a monumental shift in the law of State responsibility.[77] Unsurprisingly, the proposal gained some traction in certain academic circles – most notably spearheaded by Schachter[78] – but ultimately failed to generate consensus. More importantly, Arangio-Ruiz's suggested amendments

> would have eliminated in one move the right of an injured party to judge for itself the use of a sanction. They would have eliminated self-judging in the enforcement of international law in all cases except the immediate, emergency decision to use armed force in self-defence.[79]

Ultimately, the finalised ILC *Articles* excised, from the codified rules governing State responsibility, the notion of predicating the adoption of unilateral countermeasures on prior mandatory dispute settlement.

In sum, absent any mandatory adjudicatory phase in the implementation of responsibility – or barring any institutional intercession in the process – a victim-State has seemingly unfettered discretion in determining that another State has violated its counterterrorism obligations and can, in turn, adopt unilateral countermeasures against it. Such notions, paired with the ability of States to ascertain whether there has been an 'armed attack' before invoking their right to self-defence, have acquired credence in legal literature.[80] Speaking to the question of indeterminacy and international law's 'modulated response' to that challenge in the 'context of application and the nature of norms in human rights and humanitarian law', René Provost underscores that there will be a '"dialogue" on international norms between these two or more actors holding possibly divergent views on the nature of the situation'.[81] Based on the foregoing, this conclusion certainly holds true for the application of State responsibility to breaches of counterterrorism duties, provided the wrongful State is not completely inimical to the idea of diplomatic engagement.

[77] See ME O'Connell, 'Report of the Economic Sanctions Committee: The Impact of Sanctions on the Development of New International Law' (2001–02) *Proceedings of the American Branch of the International Law Association* 86, 93–94.

[78] O Schachter, 'Dispute Settlement and Countermeasures in the International Law Commission' (1994) 88 *AJIL* 471, 476. For a critical comment, see B Simma, 'Counter-measures and Dispute Settlement: A Plea for a Different Balance' (1994) 5 *EJIL* 102.

[79] ME O'Connell, 'Controlling Countermeasures' in M Ragazzi (ed), *International Responsibility Today: Essays in Memory of Oscar Schachter* (Leiden, Brill, 2005) 49 at 56.

[80] See, eg: D Alland, *Justice privée et ordre juridique international: étude théorique des contre-mesures en droit international public* (Paris, Pedone, 1994) 107–20; Gross, 'States As Organs' in Lipsky, above n 71 at 80–81; Provost, above n 71 at 338. See also: I Brownlie, *Principles of Public International Law*, 7th edn (Oxford, OUP, 2008) 745–46 (inferring that an aggrieved State may invoke self-defence if a terrorist attack involves the responsibility of a host-State, and illustrating this rationale with the US-led attacks on Afghanistan and Sudan after both the 1998 bombings of American embassies in Africa and the 9/11 excursions).

[81] Provost, above n 71 at 338. Here, Provost writes about this 'dialogue' as pertaining to an internal armed conflict, whereby insurgents are afforded a 'measure of functional sovereignty' in order to make a 'valid legal characterization of the conflict', which, in turn, might run against competing qualifications of the conflict formulated by other involved actors.

Therein lies the response to the principal obstacle identified above: attempting to adapt a traditionally State-centric legal regime (State responsibility) to an increasingly transnational paradigm (terrorism). Whilst it has been demonstrated that certain aspects of State responsibility can adapt to the evolution of terrorism, that this normative scheme is so central in international law that it cannot be overlooked, and that terrorism often remains dependent on States for its successful execution,[82] a simpler conclusion warrants consideration. To envisage State responsibility as a cure-all legal solution – or even as a consistently effective regime to thwart or punish State involvement in terrorism – is illusory. In the highly decentralised and unregulated (or self-regulated) setting described above, where unilateral mechanisms for determining illegality and enforcing sanctions are predominantly vested in sovereign States, many recourses to State responsibility remain subject to political considerations, score-settling and overreaction. Conversely, State responsibility can decidedly play some role in shifting incentives onto governments, enhancing transnational cooperation and stabilising international relations.[83] For instance, the international responsibility of Libya following the *Lockerbie* incident: i) bolsters the idea that liability schemes can offer some degree of closure vis-à-vis terrorism, via the mechanisms of satisfaction and reparation; and ii) supports Security Council intercession in this process.[84] But State responsibility – whether implemented via institutionalised structures or through more traditional inter-State vehicles – cannot completely or exhaustively address all challenges posed by transnational terrorism or even offer any broad array of prospective solutions. Yet, it remains a central feature of international law, a sort of default regime that can only be set aside conventionally or by *lex specialis*.[85] And this ties into a second obstacle with which any project of this type will invariably grapple.

When confronted with any scholarly treatment of the legal accountability of States for private transnational activity, detractors of the relevance of State responsibility in the terrorism debate borrow a page from the sceptics' handbook: what is the point? What can State responsibility really bring to the table? This impression might even sporadically creep into the reader's mind while absorbing this study, which is perfectly understandable. State responsibility remains an elusive and challenging topic; its potential contributions, whilst sometimes severely limited, cannot always be accepted on faith. But they can certainly be envisaged short of acting on a leap of faith. Sceptics query how the formal rules of public international law can be brought to bear upon an undefined concept, namely that of 'terrorism'. However, the notion of 'terrorism' is sufficiently circumscribed – either through State practice or via the elaboration of international criminal law – to warrant in-depth legal analysis leading to the

[82] See, eg: above ch 2, section IV.A).
[83] See above ch 1, section I; below ch 5, section III.A).
[84] See, eg: below ch 4, section V.D).
[85] See, eg: H Thirlway, 'Injured and Non-injured States before the International Court of Justice' in Ragazzi, above n 79 at 324.

identification of potential models for its prevention and suppression.[86] Alternatively, compelling arguments have been put forth to the effect that 'terrorism' amounts to a mere term of convenience, thereby disabling the need to devise a separate 'international law of terrorism'; the fact that it is subsumed under existing international legal structures therefore provides argumentative ammunition for sidestepping the whole definitional polemic.[87]

Furthermore, detractors of the main argument espoused in this study most consistently voice their disapproval in terms of the limits of international law from the perspective of enforcement. Put another way, this line of reasoning implies that State responsibility is a toothless tiger: since there is no way of ensuring enforcement of the legal consequences of an international breach, why should we even bother invoking the secondary rules of responsibility, especially given that terrorism is an increasingly transnational phenomenon? There is certainly some validity to this line of argument stemming from the tension between State responsibility's centrality in international law and its absence from the legal assessment of – or from the dialogue surrounding – certain major incidents facilitated by State wrongdoing or failures in preventing harmful activity. State responsibility aspires to act as the default regime, a sort of safety net encompassing all breaches of international obligations. But it does not purport to achieve perfect symmetry or to generate an infallible track record – in fact, it cannot do so by its very nature and makeup, which meld politics, law, self-judging and unilateralism. Quite the contrary, its failures have been at times spectacular, especially in the environmental field. Indeed, whilst State responsibility arguably constitutes a fundamental tenet of international environmental law, its application was eschewed following the disastrous nuclear accident in Chernobyl and in the aftermath of the deleterious pollution of the river Rhine by the pharmaceutical company Sandoz.[88] Moreover, States often prefer to exclude the application of State responsibility for environmental degradation via the adoption of other conventional or liability regimes, in order to avoid

[86] See, eg: above Introduction nn 26–30; below nn 169–74; ch 4, section II.B).

[87] But see: H El Amine, 'Pourquoi la Cour pénale internationale n'est-elle pas compétente en matière de terrorisme international' in MJ Glennon and S Sur (eds), *Terrorism and International Law* (Leiden, Nijhoff, 2008) 247 at 267. On the difficulty of defining 'terrorism', see also: GP Fletcher, 'The Indefinable Concept of Terrorism' (2006) 4 *Journal of International Criminal Justice* 894.

[88] No EU countries affected by the Chernobyl incident ever instituted claims against the Soviet Union. See D McClatchey, 'Chernobyl and Sandoz One Decade Later: The Evolution of State Responsibility for International Disasters, 1986-1996' (1996) 25 *Georgia Journal of International and Comparative Law* 659. See also: A-C Kiss, 'L'accident de Tchernobyl et ses conséquences au point de vue du droit international' (1987) 32 *AFDI* 139. Alexandre-Charles Kiss has also written extensively on the Rhine River incident and related issues. See, eg: '"Tchernobale" ou la pollution accidentelle du Rhin par les produits chimiques' (1988) 33 *AFDI* 719; 'The Protection of the Rhine against Pollution' in AE Utton and LA Teclaff (eds), *Transboundary Resources Law* (Boulder, Westview Press, 1987) 51; 'La Pollution du Rhin et le droit international public' in R Hueting et al (eds), *Rhine Pollution: Legal, Economic and Technical Aspects* (Zwolle, Tjeenk Willink, 1978) 59.

diplomatic complications associated with the application of that normative scheme and State-versus-State adjudication.[89]

In response to sceptics, it should be stressed that framing the issue over-emphatically as one of 'enforcement' is not particularly helpful and, in many ways, misses the whole purpose of State responsibility. State responsibility operates on the prospect of triggering responsibility for the wrongdoing *of the State* in failing to prevent subversive activity, provided its ambit has not been excluded conventionally or via *lex specialis*.[90] It acknowledges that governments are expected to fulfil their obligations to protect their populations from harm and prevent injurious activities affecting the rights of third States and individuals – terrorism incontestably falls under that rubric – be they rooted in customary law, the R2P Doctrine or general principles of international law. As one commentator highlights, 'The language and conceptions of State responsibility define the boundaries of a sovereign's accountability in its relations with other States . . . they set the limits of what citizens can expect and demand from the countries in which they live'.[91] In juxtaposition with State responsibility's potential curative character, typically actuated through the 'wrongful act–attribution–legal consequences/reparation' syllogism, secondary norms can also produce a preventive effect and correspondingly shift incentives onto governments to comply with counterterrorism obligations. As explored earlier, the prospect of incurring responsibility can generate desirable policy initiatives, stabilise international relations and palliate the enforcement gap that is symptomatic of the international society's anarchical structure (in this case, perhaps even before the perpetration of a wrongful act given that the overarching principle is prevention).[92]

But applying State responsibility to terrorism is by no means aimed at assigning blame for the *whole* terrorist excursion. It acknowledges that States play some role in the chain of events leading to the execution of terrorist strikes and strives to establish some degree of responsibility, commensurate with actual State involvement in any given case. In attaining this policy objective, as argued below in chapter five, it becomes clear that a variable threshold or standard – coupled with a context-sensitive legal approach – is warranted. Inexorably, some level of causal sensibility is also called for in the analysis, as one publicist suggests 'that the state is responsible for acts of international terrorism that it

[89] See, eg: A-C Kiss and D Shelton, *International Environmental Law*, 3rd edn (Ardsley, Transnational, 2004) 320; HW McGee, Jr, 'Litigating Global Warming: Substantive Law in Search of a Forum' (2005) 16 *Fordham Environmental Law Review* 371, 391.

[90] See, eg: B Simma and D Pulkowski, 'Of Planets and the Universe: Self-Contained Regimes in International Law' (2006) 17 *EJIL* 483, 490 (noting that 'a strong form of *lex specialis* could exclude the application of the general regime of state responsibility altogether, either by explicit provision or by implication, that is, by virtue of a regime's particular structure or its object and purpose'). See also generally: B Simma and D Pulkowski, '*Leges Speciales* and Self-Contained Regimes' in JR Crawford et al (eds), *The Law of International Responsibility* (Oxford, OUP, 2010) 139–63.

[91] Becker, above n 1 at 155.

[92] See, eg: K Zemanek, 'Does the Prospect of Incurring Responsibility Improve the Observance of International Law?' in Ragazzi, above n 79 at 125–34.

supports along a sliding scale of state responsibility that takes into account the state's misconduct and the causative nexus between the state's misconduct and the harm'.[93] Whether similar determinations spill over to other facets of international law depends on the facts of the case but does not, in any way, impinge on the application of any concurring or overlapping regimes. In other words, the application of State responsibility provides only partial redress – a partial politico-legal solution – amidst a multiplicity of available recourses and policy avenues to stamp out terrorism, be they criminal, financial, reputational,[94] domestic, international, law enforcement, etc. A striking parallel emanates from international criminal law, a structure under which justice can seldom be achieved and exhausted in favour of all victims and mourners: only a handful of beneficiaries are directly affected by the outcomes of specific cases. Yet, this normative corpus is still widely perceived as a worthwhile enterprise that contributes to international justice and deterrence. As a corollary, it offers some level of cathartic release, even to those not specifically targeted by the outcome of criminal proceedings but nonetheless invested in fighting impunity for the crimes under scrutiny.

Oftentimes, international criminal justice is a largely symbolic remedy because it cannot truly redress every stakeholder's rights or interests in the grander scheme of things. The administration and operation of international criminal tribunals, which are partially shaped by budgetary constraints and political impediments, translate into a highly selective endeavour: only a few, sometimes 'high-profile', trials may be pursued, without providing solace in the way of 'individualised' justice to all relevant stakeholders.[95] Yet, the deployment of international criminal law nonetheless sends a powerful message whilst promoting deterrence and enhancing reconciliation. Similar objectives can sometimes be attained through the mechanisms of State responsibility; it provides some degree of cathartic release by ascertaining every entity's role within the chain of wrongdoers and within the broader chain of events leading to a wrongful act – host-States and non-State actors being conceptualised distinctly within that normative framework. Hence, like international criminal justice, State responsibility remains a sometimes symbolic and partial response to a

[93] SM Malzahn, 'State Sponsorship and Support of International Terrorism: Customary Norms of State Responsibility' (2002) 26 *Hastings International and Comparative Law Review* 83, 96.

[94] Certain aspects of State responsibility can also offer some redress via reputational avenues. See, eg: the discussion on the social stigma argument pertaining to State responsibility, below ch 5, section III.B). According to some international relations theorists, a State's international reputation is often construed as the most important generator of its compliance with international law. See generally: AT Guzman, *How International Law Works: A Rational Choice Theory* (Oxford, OUP, 2008). For a critique of Guzman's treatment of the subject, see R Brewster, 'The Limits of Reputation on Compliance', Unpublished Manuscript (1 July 2009), available at http://ssrn.com/abstract=1337826. For a broader discussion on reputational costs, see R Brewster, 'Unpacking the State's Reputation' (2009) 50 *Harvard International Law Journal* 231.

[95] See, eg: JE Alvarez, 'Crimes of States/Crimes of Hate: Lessons from Rwanda' (1999) 24 *Yale Journal of International Law* 413 (applying similar reasoning to the ICTR).

problematic phenomenon: transnational terrorism.[96] The idea of symbolic redress is, itself, firmly entrenched in State responsibility repertoire, exemplified by the notions of satisfaction and guarantees/assurances of non-repetition. Moreover, these facets of symbolic justice are themselves mirrored in international criminal law and increasingly attracting scholarly attention.[97] Picking up on the above thread, a more apt analogy is to accept that the law of State responsibility can become a toothless tiger under some lights, but that it can nonetheless register some normative and remedial impact by using its paws and claws. Put another way, the fact that State responsibility sometimes falls short in providing an exhaustive set of remedies does not correspondingly signal its failure in contributing to the fight against impunity, nor should it be discarded as irrelevant because it offers partial or inconsistent results. When State responsibility's role is diminished, the dominant tension is not one of bark versus bite, but rather one of scratch versus bite.

Therefore, whilst central in international law, we must avoid casting the role of State responsibility too broadly with regard to transnational terrorism. To envisage that regime as a holistic solution, or even as a consistently effective recourse against terrorism, erroneously frames its legal features and runs the risk of overemphasising or inflating its potential contributions. Conversely, for reasons advocated herein, its importance cannot be understated either. After all, for commentators who do not entirely subscribe to Kelsen's vision of a necessarily coercive international legal order, State responsibility for the commission of wrongful acts amounts to a sanction in and of itself.[98] It is sometimes sufficient for a State to be branded as a violator of international law for some degree of justice to be fulfilled. Moreover, even if one accepts that this normative

[96] The ILC's commentary on Art 49 speaks to this point in the following terms:

> In normal situations, satisfaction will be symbolic or supplementary and it would be highly unlikely that a State which had ceased the wrongful act and tendered compensation to the injured State could properly be made the target of countermeasures for failing to provide satisfaction as well.

See JR Crawford, *International Law Commission's Articles on State Responsibility: Introduction, Text and Commentaries* (Cambridge, CUP, 2002) 358, para 8.

[97] See, eg: F Mégret, 'The International Criminal Court and the Failure to Mention Symbolic Reparations', Unpublished Manuscript (13 August 2008), available at http://ssrn.com/ abstract= 1275087. In the context of repressing terrorism, one scholar queries whether

> the goal of punishment [is] something more communicative and pedagogical – namely, what I call *expressivism* – to augment the moral value of law, stigmatize those who break it, and establish an authoritative public, and transnational, narrative regarding the heinousness of terrorist violence.

See MA Drumbl, 'The Expressive Value of Prosecuting and Punishing Terrorists: Hamdan, the Geneva Conventions, and International Criminal Law' (2007) 75 *George Washington Law Review* 1165, 1170.

[98] See, eg : B Bollecker-Stern, *Le préjudice dans la théorie de la responsabilité internationale* (Paris, Pedone, 1973) 20–21; C Leben, *Les sanctions privatives de droits ou de qualité dans les organisations internationals spécialisées: recherches sur les sanctions internationales et l'évolution du droit des gens* (Brussels, Bruylant, 1979) 49–52; P Reuter, 'Principes de droit international public' (1961-II) 103 *Recueil des Cours* 425, 590, 595; M Virally, *La pensée juridique* (Paris, LGDJ, 1960) 108 (framing the question in general theory of law).

scheme plays a role in the prevention and suppression of terrorism, developing general rules of responsibility applicable to all breaches of the obligation to prevent terrorism is no small task. This challenge is further compounded by the difficulty of generalising terrorism.

B) Generalising Terrorism and State Responsibility

'Terrorism' constitutes a particularly intractable case study for any project aiming to revisit the formal rules of international law. Not only does 'terrorism', on its face, remain an acutely polymorphic phenomenon, but the sheer volume of precedents of terrorist activity involving some transnational dimension impedes any attempt to streamline and coordinate legal responses thereto. As a result, any project exploring the realm of State responsibility in this context cannot escape some sense of methodological arbitrariness, despite invoking many instances of terrorism as examples. After all, according to the Popperian approach to scientific justification, what is at stake here is not so much the infallibility of the methodology, but rather any potential falsification of the study's hypothesis. However, this argument must be appreciated with caution, as every hypothesis is prone to some degree of falsification and one would be hard-pressed to conjure up a perfect, airtight hypothesis.[99] That is the nature of the beast: so many precedents of terrorism exist and can be distinguished on a factual basis, thereby making the identification of any one dominant model of transnational violence rather elusive. The policy and deterrence models put forth in this book attempt to internalise this by advocating a fact-sensitive, context-specific approach – particularly epitomised in the second tier of the strict liability-infused inquiry – so as to better gauge the level of State involvement in terrorism and determine corresponding levels of international responsibility.[100]

In addition to their politically volatile nature, the legal uncertainty surrounding the notions of 'terrorism' and its support likely drove the ICJ to eschew those issues altogether in both the *Nicaragua* and *Tehran Hostages* cases.[101] Furthermore, this approach prevented the Court from elaborating the rules of responsibility governing transnational violence carried out by non-State actors. In fact, that stance aligns with the Court's reluctance to distance itself from

[99] See generally: KR Popper, *The Logic of Scientific Discovery* (London, Hutchinson & Co, 1959). The contributions of Popper's methodological approach in the context of moral argument are also explored in RM Hare, *Freedom and Reason* (Oxford, Clarendon Press, 1963) 87–93. See also: J Waldron, 'Community and Property – For Those Who Have Neither' (2009) 10 *Theoretical Inquiries in Law* 161, 170.

[100] See below ch 5.

[101] For a discussion of that aspect of those cases, see J-M Sorel, 'Existe-t'il une définition universelle du terrorisme' in K Bannelier et al (eds), *Le Droit international face au terrorisme: après le 11 septembre 2001* (Paris, Pedone, 2003) 35 at 44; G Guillaume, 'Terrorisme et droit international' (1989-III) 215 *Recueil des Cours* 287, 306; B Hoffman, *La mécanique terroriste* (Paris, Calmann-Lévy, 1999) 230; H Labayle, 'Droit international et lutte contre le terrorisme' (1986) 32 *AFDI* 105, 126.

very onerous attribution principles when confronted with non-State actors, especially in the post-9/11 legal landscape. In the *Armed Activities* Case, the ICJ was called upon to ascertain whether the actions of an armed band operating out of the territory of the Democratic Republic of Congo (DRC), the Allied Democratic Forces (ADF), could be attributed to that State.[102] On this point, the Court held that Uganda could not invoke a right to self-defence against the DRC because it had harboured the armed militia on its territory.[103] This posture seems at odds with post-9/11 State practice – spearheaded by US-led action in Afghanistan and further bolstered by the quasi-unanimous support it received – and runs counter to the paradigm shift identified above in chapter two.[104]

Judge Kooijmans reiterated the position he initially endorsed in the *Wall Advisory Opinion* and lamented the majority's approach to this question in the *Armed Activities* Case, rather expounding that recent Security Council resolutions ground a right of self-defence against an armed attack carried out by private actors 'without any reference to an armed attack by a State'.[105] Whilst relevant for present purposes because dealing with transborder terrorism, the *Wall Advisory Opinion* ultimately fell short in advancing the intellectual discourse on this issue. In the General Assembly on 20 October 2003, Israel defended the construction of the wall by declaring that Security Council resolutions 'have clearly recognized the right of States to use force in self-defence against terrorist attacks' and further stated that it must 'therefore surely recognize the right to use non-forcible measures to that end'.[106] Higgins highlights that 'This opened the door to counsel appearing in the Advisory Opinion case . . . *to fashion their arguments on self-defence within the parameters of the law of State responsibility generally and of countermeasures specifically*' (emphasis added).[107] The Court ultimately ruled that the scope of Article 51 and self-defence found in the UN Charter was confined to cases of armed attacks by one

[102] *Armed Activities on the Territory of the Congo (Democratic Republic of Congo v Uganda)*, Judgment of 19 December, *ICJ Reports* (2005) 116.

[103] ibid, at paras 131–35, 146. For discussion of the case, see JT Gathii, 'Case Concerning Armed Activities on the Territory of the Congo (Democratic Republic of the Congo v. Uganda) (International Decision)' (2007) 101 *AJIL* 142.

[104] See also: SA Barbour and ZA Salzman, '"The Tangled Web": The Right of Self-Defense against Non-State Actors in the Armed Activities Case' (2008) 40 *NYU Journal of International Law and Politics* 53, 74–75; K Mohan, 'Terrorism and Asymmetric Warfare: State Responsibility for the Acts of Non-State Entities – Nicaragua, Tadic, and Beyond' (2008) 8 *Journal of the Institute of Justice and International Studies* 211, 218–19.

[105] See Separate Opinion of Judge Kooijmans in the *Armed Activities* Case, above n 102 at 28. Compare with Separate Opinion of Judge Simma in ibid, at 335–38, and Separate Opinion of Judge Simma in *Oil Platforms (Islamic Republic of Iran v USA)*, Merits, Judgment of 6 November, *ICJ Reports* (2003) 161. See also: JT Gathii, 'Irregular Forces and Self-Defense under the UN Charter' in ME O'Connell (ed), *What Is War? An Investigation in the Wake of 9/11* (Leiden, Nijhoff, Forthcoming 2012) 91.

[106] See UN GA Emergency Special Session, UN GAOR, 58th Sess, 21st Mtg, 20 October, UN Doc A/ES-10/PV.21 (2003) at 6.

[107] R Higgins, 'The International Court of Justice: Selected Issues of State Responsibility' in Ragazzi, above n 79 at 271–86.

State against another.[108] Betraying some degree of sympathy for a more pluralistically inclined international community, unfettered by overzealous State-centrism, Judge Higgins took issue with this finding in her Separate Opinion,[109] whilst the Court offered the following clarification: 'However, Israel does not claim that the attacks against it are imputable to a foreign State'.[110] Once again, Higgins 'doubted the pertinence – or the realism – of this observation, observing that "The question is surely where responsibility lies for the sending of groups and persons who act against Israeli civilians"'.[111] The Court's recalcitrance to address the issue of a potential right to respond with force is indicative of a broader trend within its jurisprudence, evincing inflexibility in adapting the rules governing recourse to force between States to scenarios involving non-State actors. In many ways, similar logic animates the critiques of State responsibility's seemingly limited potential in responding to transnational phenomena. Whilst this charge has been levelled vociferously on issues lying at the intersection of war and commerce, there is every indication that more liberal interpretations of the relevant rules now underpin proposals for policy reform in the area of counterterrorism.[112]

It also paves the way for the need to rethink extant State responsibility rules away from the *Nicaragua* model towards a flexible and contextual regime, far better suited to the intricate nature of contemporary State-terrorist dynamics. Two commentators rightly underscore that

> [t]he effective control test is an 'all-or-nothing' approach to State responsibility that leaves no room for the more complex forms of State involvement illustrated by the DRC case. In Military and Paramilitary Activities, the absence of sufficient proof to demonstrate that the Contras were the de facto agents of the U.S. government meant that the United States escaped any responsibility for the Contras' actions.[113]

[108] *Legal Consequences of the Construction of a Wall in the Occupied Palestinian Territory*, Advisory Opinion of 9 July, *ICJ Reports* (2004) 136 at para 139.

[109] Separate Opinion of Judge Higgins in ibid, at para 33.

[110] *Wall Advisory Opinion*, above n 108 at para 139.

[111] Higgins, above n 107 at 276–77. See also: the Separate Opinion of Judge Higgins in the *Wall Advisory Opinion*, above n 108 at para 34.

[112] For instance, James Thuo Gathii underscores that

> although on the public side international law has a standard of especially higher normativity prohibiting the use of force between States, on the private side there is no equivalent norm prohibiting to the same extent the use of violence at the intersection of war and commerce.

See *War, Commerce, and International Law* (Oxford, OUP, 2010) 221. He also acknowledges that different considerations likely govern the debate surrounding the adaptation of those international rules to counterterrorism policy. In that regard, he adds that his

> claim is limited to cases at the intersection of war and commerce where there is generalized state collapse or ineffective control by a State such as in the Democratic Republic of Congo. There are instances in which the conduct of irregular forces or non-State actors can be much more readily attributable to an effective State.

ibid, at 221–22 fn 112 and authorities cited therein.

[113] Barbour and Salzman, above n 104 at 74 (footnotes omitted). See also: JN Maogoto, *Battling Terrorism: Legal Perspectives on the Use of Force and the War on Terror* (Aldershot, Ashgate, 2005) 158. In *Nicaragua*, above n 17 at 86, for instance, the Court held that Nicaragua could not be deemed responsible for the importation of arms into El Salvador and originating from its territory.

In his Dissenting Opinion in the *Armed Activities* Case, Judge *ad hoc* Kateka opined that the Court's persistent reliance on a legal threshold embedded with the notion of 'substantial involvement' actually promotes impunity.[114] Similarly, critics of seemingly-too-onerous responsibility standards, especially the 'effective control' test, expound that such criteria allow States assisting or tolerating terrorists and other armed militia to elude liability.[115] This jurisprudential trend was maintained by the ICJ in its *Genocide* Judgment and has been a central incubator for discussion throughout this project.[116]

The difficulty in devising general guidelines for the application of State responsibility to counterterrorism is further exacerbated by the very form of the most authoritative instrument on the matter: the ILC's *Articles*. Although the General Assembly intends on converting this partial codification of existing international customary rules into a multilateral convention, the *Articles* in their current form exert diffused influence on the development of State responsibility, even regarding subject-matter-specific areas.[117] However, as Provost highlights, this arrangement also cuts the other way: 'codification can provoke doctrinal sclerosis, dissuading creative and critical analysis by imposing a set of basic assumptions as the necessary starting point of any study on state responsibility'.[118] This study attempts to push those boundaries whilst reconceptualising certain tenets of State responsibility within that regime's existing boxes, so to speak.

Admittedly, an additional layer of complexity pervades the gradual development of State responsibility. The ILC's *Articles* resulted from almost 50 years of intense debates, extensive revisions, a succession of differing and ideologically-driven Special Rapporteurs, and conflicting views – all with an end product conceived within a political safe place so the ILC could sidestep the elaboration of issue-specific standards of responsibility (in the areas of terrorism, environmental law, etc).[119] This can also be partially explained by States' 'unwillingness to foster the development of legal principles that might one day be applied against them', thereby evidencing why nations routinely exclude State responsibility for environmental degradation, for example, via the adoption of alternate settlement regimes (diplomatic means, negotiation and specific agreements).[120] A

[114] See Dissenting Opinion of Judge *ad hoc* Kateka in the *Armed Activities* Case, above n 102 at para 34 (also expounding that such standard will be invoked 'by culprits to avoid responsibility for wrongful acts').

[115] See, eg: Maogoto, above n 113 at 157 (citing works by Abraham D Sofaer and Yoram Dinstein).

[116] See particularly: above ch 1, sections IV.B) and C).

[117] See the discussion and sources cited below in ch 5 nn 160–63 and accompanying text.

[118] R Provost, 'Introduction' in R Provost (ed), *State Responsibility in International Law* (Aldershot, Ashgate/Dartmouth, 2002) xx.

[119] See, eg: P Cullet, 'Liability and Redress for Human-Induced Global Warming: Towards an International Regime' (2007) 43A *Stanford Journal of International Law* 99, 107; P Cullet, 'Liability and Redress for Human-Induced Global Warming: Towards an International Regime' (2007) 26A *Stanford Environmental Law Journal* 99, 107.

[120] ibid (noting that States 'have usually preferred to use other mechanisms to solve their disputes. In the case of the environment, states seem to have been even more reluctant to use the mechanism of state responsibility to address the consequences of environmental damage').

further explanation for both the overarching generality of State responsibility rules and States' preference for alternate regimes in the environmental sector stems from potential tensions arising between the application of secondary norms and State sovereignty over natural resources.[121] These factors impede the development and interpretation of those secondary rules that could be transposed to the struggle against terror to enhance prevention.

Moreover, the intellectually incestuous relationship characterising the ILC-ICJ institutional dialogue – a dynamic appearing sometimes far too insular – has also affected, perhaps adversely, the further development of State responsibility. The *Gabčíkovo-Nagymaros Project* and *LaGrand* cases constitute striking examples of a problematic or, at least, stagnating practice whereby the ILC unstintingly invokes ICJ precedents in substantiating its legal constructions, whilst the ICJ in turn cites the ILC's *Articles* to bolster its findings.[122] Aside from perhaps granting the ICJ a questionable monopoly over the development of State responsibility in an age of legal pluralism and fragmentation, this relationship prompts Reisman and his co-authors to ponder whether this practice is tantamount to a 'citation carousel', an apt characterisation indeed.[123] This incestuous dynamic is further reinforced by what scholars term the 'ILC-ICJ feedback loop', whereby a common career trajectory dictates that ILC members – initially involved in the development and codification of State responsibility rules – are ultimately appointed by their home States and elected to the ICJ, where they engage in the judicial interpretation of those same norms.[124] For some interlocutors and publicists, this institutional practice sometimes breeds intractable decision-making patterns or colours judicial interpretation of secondary norms, as exemplified by the restrictive construction of the proportionality requirement for the application of countermeasures in the *Gabč íkovo-Nagymaros Project* Case and Article 51.[125]

Whilst there is some scholarly support for the further elaboration of general and specific principles applicable to State breaches of international obligations (ie if the rules are too generalised or abstracted, they lead to interpretative paralysis),[126] it is impossible to fit all terrorist strikes or all obligations of

[121] See, eg: D Mayer, 'Deforestation and Global Warming: The Conflict between State Responsibility and Sovereignty over Natural Resources' (1990) 9 *Midwest Law Review* 4.

[122] One author summarises this incestuous relationship perfectly with reference to the *LaGrand* Judgment. See S Sullivan, 'Changing the Premise of International Legal Remedies: The Unfounded Adoption of Assurances and Guarantees of Non-Repetition' (2002–03) 7 *UCLA Journal of International Law and Foreign Affairs* 265, 300–01. The work of the Institute of International Law could also be categorised as falling within this insular dynamic.

[123] WM Reisman et al, *International Law in Contemporary Perspective*, 2nd edn (New York, Foundation Press, 2004) 899–900.

[124] See ibid, at 900.

[125] For instance, Bederman's critique is redolent of the previous group of authors' own reservations on the topic. See DJ Bederman, 'Counterintuiting Countermeasures' (2002) 96 *AJIL* 817, 819.

[126] See, eg: RR Baxter, 'Reflections on Codification in Light of the International Law of State Responsibility for Injuries to Aliens' (1964–65) 16 *Syracuse Law Review* 745, 747–48; RB Lillich, 'The Current Status of the Law of State Responsibility for Injuries to Aliens' in RB Lillich (ed), *International Law of State Responsibility for Injuries to Aliens* (Charlottesville, University Press of

prevention, for that matter, within a single legal matrix. It is precisely this delicate balance between developing general rules and guidelines applicable to all breaches of the obligation of prevention, ie a State's failure to prevent terrorism triggers a prima facie presumption of indirect responsibility, and the acknowledgement that certain policy considerations will govern the ex post facto analysis of a terrorist attack, ie through variable constructions of the obligation of prevention, that this monograph seeks to achieve.[127] Therefore, the intellectual inquiry exploring the interplay between State responsibility and the prevention/suppression of terrorism requires some modulated response: a case-by-case approach nonetheless articulated around certain key organising principles. Consequently, the second portion of the two-tiered strict liability-infused approach advocated in chapter five specifically purports to accommodate a fact-intensive and policy-informed analysis of terrorism, so as to ensure that a host-State's responsibility remains commensurate with its wrongdoing. In striking a balance between devising general rules applicable to all breaches and recognising the complex nature of transnational terrorism, careful attention should be paid to whatever benefits may be derived from drawing legal analogies, be they domestically-driven or internationally-based.

IV. DOING AWAY WITH ATTRIBUTION: TOWARDS A MODEL OF STRICT LIABILITY?[128]

Given the international community's will to eradicate terrorism, coupled with the Security Council's emphatic condemnation of terrorist acts and its resolve to eliminate threats to peace and security 'by all necessary means',[129] it is imperative to rethink the underlying tenets of indirect responsibility. Whilst the substantiality of States' obligation to prevent terrorism should be addressed, the trans-substantive rules of responsibility must also be revisited in light of the paradigm shift described earlier. The thrust of the policy argument advanced herein, therefore, is that the counterterrorism interests and priorities of the

Virgina, 1983) 21; MS McDougal et al, *Human Rights and World Public Order: The Basic Policies of an International Law of Human Dignity* (New Haven, Yale University Press, 1980) 762 fn 92.

[127] See the two-tiered strict liability model developed below in ch 5.

[128] Some of the premises of what follows significantly expand on the remarks found in V-J Proulx, 'Babysitting Terrorists: Should States Be Strictly Liable for Failing to Prevent Transborder Attacks?' (2005) 23 *Berkeley Journal of International Law* 615.

[129] Similarly, in the context of Iraq's invasion of Kuwait, Security Council resolution 678 authorised 'Member States . . . co-operating with the government of Kuwait . . . to use all *necessary means* to uphold and implement Resolution 660 [a prior resolution ordering Iraq to comply with its international obligations]' (emphasis added). See SC Res 678, UN SCOR, 45th Sess, 2963rd Mtg, UN Doc S/RES/678 (1990). In addition, the '"*all necessary means*" language, while a euphemism, is universally understood in the diplomatic context as synonymous with the authorization of necessary force'. See Duffy, above n 16 at 175. However, see ibid, at 175 fn 142 ('By contrast . . . the absence of such language in the post-September 11 resolutions was critical to their being broadly considered not to authorize the use of force in Afghanistan').

international community would be better achieved by circumventing certain trans-substantive rules, particularly attribution. This line of reasoning seems reminiscent of certain precursory scholarly statements articulated before 9/11 emphasising the need to rethink some of the underlying tenets of State responsibility. In a somewhat premonitory statement for present purposes, Gordon Christenson raised the possibility of rethinking attribution in order to better reflect modern reality. He noted that

> [t]he tradition of civil society with intermediate institutions that are neither market nor State offers a form of pluralism to rethink the international legal order's attention to attribution theory. Allocating supervisory responsibility and control to conduct of modern States in relation to non-State actors in an exclusive system of territorial States will revise attribution theory to reflect the new realities of power.[130]

As demonstrated in chapter one, the extant scheme of State responsibility remains marred by several limitations when traditional attribution rules are applied uncritically. The defect, therefore, is that of the adaptability of a State-centric legal system to transnational phenomena such as terrorism, so as to best integrate a multiplicity of actors within a multipolar political reality. Having now identified these conceptual and legal shortcomings, along with a paradigm shift in both State and institutional practice towards more indirect modes of international responsibility,[131] the study now turns to more tangible policy recommendations. In so doing, it remains challenged by the hard cases canvassed above, namely where the State's involvement is sufficiently divorced from the private perpetration of terrorism to eschew the classical rules of attribution. For instance, the above scenario whereby Lebanon fails to control the southern portion of its territory, which is used as a launch pad for attacks carried out by Hezbollah factions, remains a quintessential encapsulation of the legal 'grey area' that this project seeks to elucidate.[132] Accordingly, some commentators rightly call for a rethinking of attribution rules so as to better address the modern challenges of terrorism.[133] Yet, too little scholarly emphasis has been placed – or, conversely, has sometimes been misplaced – on critically appraising and reconceptualising the rules governing State responsibility. This next section will therefore canvass key points of contention triggered by post-9/11 scholarly shortcomings warranting further consideration before setting out a proposal for policy reform. As a corollary, this exploration of doctrinal shortcomings will also pave the way for an attempt to redress the literary dearth dealing with State responsibility and terrorism. Subsequent portions will move towards the precise task of revisiting trans-substantive rules, especially attribution, and propose the implementation of a strict liability-inspired responsibility model.

[130] GA Christenson, 'Attributing Acts of Omission to the State' (1991) 12 *Michigan Journal of International Law* 312, 369.

[131] A paradigm shift towards a law of indirect State responsibility for failing to prevent transnational terrorism was explored above in ch 2.

[132] See above ch 1, section IV.D).

[133] See, eg: Becker, above n 1.

A) Limited Scholarly Advances in Devising Potential Deterrence Models

Both before and after 9/11, commentators highlighted the inadequacy of State responsibility in addressing terrorism while placing significant emphasis on shortcomings associated with *Nicaragua* and *Tadić*'s respective formulations of attribution, especially in light of States waging surrogate warfare via subterfuges or wilful blindness.[134] Similarly, after canvassing conceptual problems surrounding the response to 9/11, some argue that the current State-to-State responsibility scheme is 'inadequate to assure the observance of international law'.[135] Others flat-out question the authority of *Nicaragua*, *Tehran Hostages* and *Tadić*.[136] Conversely, following 9/11 some of the criticism pertaining to a possible shift in the law of State responsibility deplored the revision of trans-substantive rules over primary legal norms. In other words, critics believed that revisiting secondary norms of responsibility, such as attribution, was ineffective and that the policy objectives of the international community would be better vindicated through the reaffirmation of States' primary obligations.[137] The present study casts part of its proposal for reform at the level of secondary norms and, as prefaced above, now briefly canvasses the shortcomings of post-9/11 literature so as to identify specific areas in need of further consideration.

B) Rethinking Trans-substantive Rules

For various policy reasons explored below, the utility of the principle of attribution in the context of counterterrorism will be thoroughly revisited. Whilst the interplay between transnational terrorism and State responsibility has generated some academic writing, the validity of attribution as a concept altogether does not seem to have seriously been called into question. This is not to say that, historically, the ILC's treatment of attribution did not generate its share of controversy. For instance, before 2001 there had been significant concern over the distinction between the mechanism of attribution and whether fault on part of a State was required to trigger its responsibility regarding a wrongful act.[138]

[134] See, eg: Y Dinstein, *War, Aggression and Self-Defence*, 3rd edn (Cambridge, CUP, 2001) 182–83; Reisman, above n 1 at 39. See also: I Brownlie, 'International Law and the Activities of Armed Bands' (1958) 7 *ICLQ* 712, 718; Y Dinstein, 'The International Legal Response to Terrorism' in R Ago (ed), *International Law at the Time of Its Codification: Essays in Honour of Roberto Ago (Vol II)* (Milan, Giuffrè, 1987) 139 at 140, 142.

[135] Zemanek, above n 92 at 132.

[136] Becker, above n 1 at 268.

[137] See, eg: D Jinks, 'State Responsibility for the Acts of Private Armed Groups' (2003) 4 *Chicago Journal of International Law* 83, 83; Milanović, above n 27 at 323–24; E Nielsen, 'State Responsibility for Terrorist Groups' (2010) 17 *UC Davis Journal of International Law and Policy* 151. For a more nuanced argument dealing with the flexibility of secondary norms, see R Värk, 'State Responsibility for Private Armed Groups in the Context of Terrorism' (2006) 11 *Juridica International* 184, 186.

[138] See, eg: M Bedjaoui, 'Responsibility of States, Fault and Strict Liability' (1987) 10 *Encyclopedia of Public International Law* 358–62; A Gattini, 'La notion de faute à la lumière du projet de conven-

Whilst the possible inclusion of fault and strict liability is not an original idea in State responsibility scholarship, and conventional wisdom does not preclude the implementation of such features, a proposal aiming at excising the concept of attribution altogether from the equation seems novel and forms part of the politico-legal impetus underpinning this study. This is also not to say that attribution has not generated some scholarly attention after 9/11, with some authors calling for substantial rethinking of State responsibility rules.[139] However, considerable shortcomings exist in the literature and significantly impede the prospect of advancing new proposals for reform via scholarly output.

Whilst this review of those legal opportunity areas is not exhaustive, it nonetheless strives to evince the symptomatic lack of critical thinking surrounding the treatment of attribution in this new era of terrorism. More importantly, it attempts to direct the reader to contentious conceptual areas within State responsibility scholarship that will, in turn, become fertile breeding grounds for policy reforms that integrate non-State actors and States within a liability framework aimed at combating impunity and surrogate warfare. The most recurrent areas warranting further clarification hinge on a combination of factors surrounding, on one hand, the importation of domestic legal analogies within State responsibility repertoire and the notion of 'control' as promulgated under the ILC's *Articles* and, on the other, the better definition of both primary and secondary legal obligations. These two strands of scholarship are analysed sequentially below before moving on to an exploration of the need to develop general guidelines in this area, an exercise conceptually hampered by the primary/secondary dichotomy under the *Articles*.

i) Shortcomings on Domestic Legal Analogies and the Notion of 'Control'

Under the first general strand of scholarship, commentators run through the motions of linking State responsibility with counterterrorism without offering much in the way of critique or legal reform regarding State accountability for terrorism perpetrated by private individuals.[140] For instance, the first portion of Helen Duffy's book, which explores the framework of international legal rules vis-à-vis terrorism, concludes by discussing the responsibility of States for terrorist activities emanating from their soil whilst acknowledging the viability of

tion de la Commission du droit international sur la responsabilité internationale' (1992) 3 *EJIL* 253; P Sturma, 'Some Problems of Strict Liability in International Law' in *Thesaurus Acroasium Vol 20: Responsibility of States* (Thessaloniki, Institute of Public International Law and International Relations of Thessaloniki, 1993) 369 at 373–76.

[139] See, eg: Becker, above n 1.

[140] This principle was also very much alive at the Hague Codification Conference of 1930. See, eg: (1975) 2 *Yearbook of the International Law Commission* 76, paras 19–21, UN Doc A/CN.4/Ser.A/1975/Add.1. On the lack of critical analysis regarding the concept of attribution and State responsibility for terrorism, see generally: V-J Proulx, 'The "War on Terror" and the Framework of International Law' (2007) 40 *Canadian Journal of Political Science* 278.

individual responsibility mechanisms.[141] Although Duffy does not completely dispel the lack of analytical nuance that has plagued recent State responsibility scholarship, especially with respect to the fading legal bases of attribution vis-à-vis unconventional actors, she delivers a thoughtful account of what could be termed the agency paradigm or a control-based application of State responsibility. Ultimately, her contribution rests on the premise that in order to engage that body of law in counterterrorism settings, any legal assessment should solely seek to determine whether attribution standards developed in international jurisprudence and mirrored in the ILC's *Articles* have been satisfied.[142] Implicit in this approach, and in contrast to the arguments advanced in chapter two, is the fact that no substantive change or challenge to the law of State responsibility derives from the response to 9/11.

Initial concerns that come to mind also include Duffy's failure to unequivocally recognise the direct/indirect responsibility dichotomy, which underlies many of the difficulties related to holding States accountable for failing to prevent terrorism.[143] The author does make reference to 'vicarious liability' only to highlight that that term has engendered controversy, a reality endorsed below in the ensuing analysis. Yet, this stands in sharp contrast with the categorical views expressed by other influential scholars who reserve a very central role for vicarious liability in correlating the law of State responsibility with counterterrorism efforts. For example, writing about the 9/11 attacks, Harold Koh argues that 'Within the U.N. Charter framework, forceful actions against states within whose territory such actors may be found can only be justified on the grounds of vicarious state responsibility'.[144] Similarly, the mere harbouring of known terrorists, perhaps coupled with the failure to extradite or punish them once they have launched an attack, could also catalyse responsibility through the channels of this conception of 'vicarious liability'.

Whilst domestic law analogies may be drawn from vicarious liability schemes by seeking inspiration from the Canadian experience, for example, the transplantation of that strand of liability remains severely limited when applying State responsibility to counterterrorism.[145] This is not to say that such analogies are not helpful; in many ways, they allow the inquiry to test out the limits of agency – by reference to informal employer/employee relations being transposed to host-State/terrorist dynamics for instance – a worthwhile exercise lying at the periphery of agency/State negligence with the ensuing analysis being interstitially situated between direct/indirect responsibility. By way of example, consider Article 1463 of the *Civil Code of Québec*, which provides that 'The

[141] See Duffy, above n 16 at 47–70.

[142] ibid, at 48.

[143] But see her thoughtful discussion of what could be termed 'direct' and 'indirect' international criminal responsibility in ibid, at 94–95.

[144] Koh, above n 15 at 28.

[145] See the Supreme Court of Canada's analysis in two important decisions: *Bazley v Curry* [1999] 2 SCR 534; *EB v Order of the Oblates of Mary Immaculate in the Province of British Columbia* [2005] 3 SCR 45.

principal is liable to reparation for injury caused by the fault of his agents and servants in the performance of their duties; nevertheless, he retains his recourses against them'.[146] Transposing this line of thinking to State responsibility would be limited to flagrant, clear-cut cases of direct responsibility, namely where a sanctuary State clearly controls a terrorist organisation or when this faction is subsumed under, or subject to, the official State's hierarchy of commands. In light of a fictionalised scenario proposed by one scholar nonetheless drawing inspiration from real individuals and past terrorism, such would have been the case of the 2004 Islamic Movement of Uzbekistan-Taliban operations in Central Asia orchestrated by Tahir Yuldashev. According to this fictional account, as part of a vast, Islamist expansionist military campaign relying heavily on ties with Al Qaeda, Yuldashev's regime proceeded to institute a profoundly oppressive Wahabbist State and proclaimed the Islamic Emirate of Uzbekistan.

The imagined offensive culminated in 2004 when a group of Yuldashev-backed irregulars convened in Tashkent to devise a strategy to extirpate American presence from the 'Muslim land', and carried out a series of terrorist attacks against American and international targets based in Central Asia. American embassies in Tashkent, Astana, Kazakhstan and Turkmenistan as well as the offices of the Amoco Oil Company in Astana and Dushanbe, Tajikistan, the offices of the World Bank and the UN Development Program in Fergana City and the headquarters of the 10th Mountain Division at its base in Khanabad, Afghanistan were all attacked and 5000 people killed, including high-ranking CIA and FBI directors. In response, the US government requested that 'the Yuldashev regime either extradite a list of suspects, including Usama bin Laden, or else accept responsibility for their actions on the theory of vicarious state responsibility'.[147]

Another application – this time to real facts – of this type of rationale in clear-cut and relatively uncontroversial cases of direct responsibility is that of Iranian support of Hezbollah in its 2006 conflict with Israel. Consequently, State responsibility mechanics operate smoothly and liability flows organically, as

> Iran is thought to continue to exercise such a degree of control over Hezbollah that the country is considered to have been calling the shots in this conflict – in the most literal sense: it is thought that the use of longer-range missiles by Hezbollah would have required . . . approval by Teheran . . . the troops on the ground are likely to have needed 'direct Iranian help in the field to fire' the rockets.[148]

[146] *Civil Code of Québec*, RSQ ch 64, Art 1463.

[147] W Bradford, 'Barbarians at the Gates: A Post-September 11th Proposal to Rationalize the Laws of War' (2004) 73 *Mississippi Law Journal* 639, 790 (footnotes omitted). See also: M Lacey, 'Self-Defense or Self-Denial: The Proliferation of Weapons of Mass Destruction' (2004) 10 *Indiana International and Comparative Law Review* 293, 305 (arguing that 'vicarious state responsibility' governs situations where host-States allow terrorists to operate within their borders).

[148] S Kirchner, 'Third Party Liability for Hezbollah Attacks against Israel' (2006) 7 *German Law Journal* 777, 778–79. See also: ibid, at 783–84 (noting the high degree of control exerted by Tehran over virtually all significant activities carried out by Hezbollah factions and inferring attribution of those acts to both Iran and Syria). See also: H Dakroub, 'Hezbollah Says It Fired New Rocket in Strike on Israeli City South of Haifa', *Associated Press Worldstream*, 28 July 2006 (cited in ibid, at 778).

Perhaps difficult to substantiate conceptually because falling more convincingly under the indirect responsibility paradigm, similar reasoning could arguably also extend to Lebanon's failure to prevent Hezbollah-led attacks emanating from its territory, with commentators remarking that 'Israel held Lebanon *directly* responsible' (emphasis added).[149] If one subscribes to the propositions espoused in this book, it would seem that this last scenario rather falls under the indirect responsibility paradigm. Nevertheless, the traditional instructions-based, agency-derived direct responsibility model poses relatively few conceptual problems in straightforward situations, at least in theory.[150] But this standard cannot be integrally transferred to challenging cases – such as that of Afghanistan vis-à-vis the 9/11 attacks – especially given that the notion of 'control' under the ILC's *Articles* 'requires a degree of dependency and a lack of autonomy on the part of the private actor being controlled, in particular regarding the damaging activity'.[151] This description remained foreign to the situation prevalent on Afghan soil prior to 9/11. Quite the contrary, publicly available facts indicate that the relationship between Al-Qaeda and Afghanistan was anything but one of interdependency.[152] In fact, the record convincingly evinces that Al-Qaeda enjoyed a high level of autonomy within the Afghan State, that its membership comprised mostly non-Afghani nationals,[153] and that the government of Afghanistan only provided logistical support to the organisation. As discussed below, the limits of 'vicarious liability' and other direct modes of responsibility also come into sharp relief when confronted with more mixed models of compliance and toleration, such as the situations prevalent in Yemen and Pakistan.

This type of situation seems hardly reconcilable with straightforward and direct support of terrorists – ie arming, training and funding irregular factions – as embodied in Iran-Hezbollah relationships. Indeed,

> it turns out that the state's responsibility in the case of infringement on an international legal norm may result not only from controlling irregular units, but also from the lack of sufficient control over them, or failure to act, or negligence, including the failure to comply with legally binding resolutions of the Council.[154]

Consequently, the occasional merging of State responsibility and recourse to force repertoire, a trend characterising some post-9/11 literature, shifts the focus

[149] AJ Colangelo, 'Constitutional Limits on Extraterritorial Jurisdiction: Terrorism and the Intersection of National and International Law' (2007) 48 *Harvard International Law Journal* 121, 145 fn 153. See also: G Myre and S Erlanger, 'Clashes Spread to Lebanon as Hezbollah Raids Israel', *New York Times*, 13 July 2006 at A1.

[150] See, eg: Zemanek, above n 92 at 131.

[151] Kirchner, above n 148 at 783.

[152] Yet, some commentators still call into question the nature of this relationship. See, eg: A-M Slaughter and W Burke-White, 'An International Constitutional Moment' (2002) 43 *Harvard International Law Journal* 1, 20.

[153] See, eg: M Mofidi and AE Eckert, '"Unlawful Combatants" or "Prisoners of War": The Law and Politics of Labels' (2003) 36 *Cornell International Law Journal* 59, 75.

[154] J Kranz, 'The Use of Armed Force – New Facts and Trends' (2006) 3 *The Polish Quarterly of International Affairs* 68, 80.

of inquiry from full control to relative control, to the duty to maintain due diligence and, ultimately, to the presumption of absolute responsibility.[155]

At the other end of the spectrum, detractors reject the notion of indirect responsibility, which has sometimes been construed as vicarious responsibility, perhaps erroneously.[156] A famous passage discarding the concept of indirect responsibility, as construed in the modern paradigm, emanated from Justice Ago's Separate Opinion in *Nicaragua*, which essentially equated indirect responsibility with the transfer of responsibility flowing from one State to another when the latter exercises control over the former.[157] Regardless, ILC Article 4 will govern de jure relationships in straightforward cases, namely where a terrorist organisation can be clearly construed as forming part of the State's structure.[158] If it cannot be formally linked to the State apparatus, it may nevertheless become a de facto agent of the State pursuant to the 'complete dependence' standard consecrated in *Nicaragua* and applied by the ICJ in the *Genocide Case*.[159] In such cases, we are faced with de facto State officials, construed as employees, 'agents or servants' to invoke *Civil Code of Québec* parlance: this construction can in turn facilitate analogies with Canadian common law and Québec civil law, or with other cognate jurisdictions. At the other end of the continuum, however, when dealing with cases of indirect responsibility whereby a State merely allows terrorists to seek refuge on its territory (eg Pakistan, Yemen), the vicarious liability connection becomes more tenuous. Aside from the terrorists' use of that territory, no evident relationship of interdependence can be ascertained and the bases of liability, as enshrined in Article 1463 of the *Civil Code of Québec*, start to wane. More importantly, vicarious liability is typically not predicated on any wrongdoing by the responsible party in domestic settings, thereby making a rapprochement challenging in cases of indirect responsibility. At any rate, host-States are nonetheless legally responsi-

155 See ibid.

156 See, eg: D Brown, 'Use of Force against Terrorism after September 11th: State Responsibility, Self-Defense and Other Responses' (2003) 11 *Cardozo Journal of International and Comparative Law* 1, 13. See also: H Lauterpacht (ed), *International Law: A Treatise by Lassa Oppenheim (Vol 2: Disputes, War and Neutrality)*, 7th edn (London, Longmans, 1952) § 145 at 502, para 145.

157 See Judge Ago's Separate Opinion in *Nicaragua*, above n 17 at 189–90. See also: Christenson, above n 130 at 350, 364; KA Bove, 'Attribution Issues in State Responsibility' (1990) 84 *ASIL Proceedings* 51, 56 (citing remarks by Gordon A Christenson).

158 Art 4 provides:

1. The conduct of any State organ shall be considered an act of that State under international law, whether the organ exercises legislative, executive, judicial or any other functions, whatever position it holds in the organization of the State, and whatever its character as an organ of the central Government or of a territorial unit of the State.
2. An organ includes any person or entity which has that status in accordance with the internal law of the State.

'State Responsibility: Titles and text of the draft articles on Responsibility of States for internationally wrongful acts adopted by the Drafting Committee on second reading', UN Doc A/CN.4/L.602/Rev.1 (2001); 'Report of the International Law Commission on the Work of Its Fifty-Third Session', UN GAOR, 56th Sess, Supp No 10, UN Doc A/56/10 (2001) 41.

159 *Genocide Case*, above n 46 at 140–41.

ble for some level of wrongdoing: failing to prevent terrorism and/or to exercise due diligence.

In a broader sense, Duffy's chapter on international responsibility offers a quintessential illustration of the rhetorical and conceptual problems associated with the notion of 'control', which anchors the ILC's *Articles*, unnecessarily breaking down and obfuscating international counterterrorism obligations.[160]

Within this first strand of scholarship, Jean-Christophe Martin's book also partly explores legal responses to terrorism by relying on State responsibility repertoire. Whilst his contribution delves slightly deeper into the conceptual and legal impediments related to linking State responsibility and terrorism, it ultimately fails in advancing any proposal for legal reform in the targeted area, rather concluding that reactions grounded in State responsibility are generally erratic.[161] Although true in some instances, this finding steers the reader away from any concrete suggestion regarding the elaboration of general guidelines or organising principles when exploring State-based accountability issues.

ii) Shortcomings on Defining the Content of Primary and Secondary Obligations

Under the second general strand of scholarship, commentators investigate whether attribution can adapt to modern realities with a specific focus, or lack thereof, on the content of pertinent rules. This line of thinking must be framed within the prism of Schacter's visionary remarks prior to the adoption of the ILC's *Articles*. Indeed, he rightly opined that the ILC's codification of responsibility would be subject to necessary evolution, whilst remaining vulnerable to modification or to a complete overhaul as dictated by practice and custom: 'the articles and commentary will acquire added authority through their practical application and the accompanying accretion of *opinio juris* even if in some cases they might be modified (or overridden) as a consequence of practice'.[162]

In a collection of essays in honour of Schachter, several high-profile jurists provide a solid foundation for revisiting attribution or give credence to the idea that attribution is by no means immutable and should be approached with some degree of flexibility when dealing with unconventional actors. Varying dicta on attribution animate the discussion and ultimately fuel an enriching horizontal dialogue. For instance, Amerasinghe queries, from the standpoint of semantics, whether attribution should be translated into a general principle, while Caron suggests it should be revisited so that it would vary depending upon whether ordinary or criminal State responsibility was engaged.[163] Addressing international

[160] For a discussion of Duffy's chapter, see Becker, above n 1 at 219 (terming the account a 'classical expression' of the agency paradigm).

[161] See J-C Martin, *Les règles internationales relatives à la lutte contre le terrorisme* (Brussels, Bruylant, 2006) 451–98.

[162] Schachter, above n 78 at 477.

[163] See CF Amerasinghe, 'The Essence of the Structure of International Responsibility' in Ragazzi, above n 79 at 5, querying

organisations, Yamada argues that attribution should be fragmented into two distinct branches, one dealing with conduct and the other with responsibility.[164] Similarly, Higgins discusses attribution through the lens of the burden of proof whilst distinguishing between what could be termed a 'whodunit' model of imputation, pursuant to *Oil Platforms*, and more substantial bases for attribution.[165] Finally, Talmon invokes Annex IX of the *United Nations Convention on the Law of the Sea* as embodying attribution of responsibility rather than attribution of conduct, and explores whether its provisions turn on *allocation* of responsibility as opposed to *attribution* of responsibility.[166] Before further tackling attribution, however, attention must be paid to the actual juridical obligations that trigger the mechanics of attribution.

Aside from specific illuminating passages,[167] too little emphasis is placed on the actual role of the content of primary obligations across all canvassed fields in actuating liability schemes, thereby signalling a need to better define State responsibility for private actors. Indeed, 'considerable doubt remains as to the content of customary rules defining the obligations of states in the fight against international terrorism' and this situation 'is compounded by relative uncertainty surrounding the meaning to be attributed, for instance, to the concept of "harbouring and supporting" terrorism'.[168] This is particularly relevant vis-à-vis

> why should a general principle be made of 'attribution' of the act or omission to the State. It is sufficient to point out that the act or omission must be *by* a State. All that is necessary then is that what is meant by this be explained in the section which is now Chapter II of the Commission's articles.

He further asks, at n 6, *in fine*, 'Why has the term been jettisoned in the International Law Commission's draft?' See also: DD Caron, 'State Crimes: Looking at Municipal Experience with Organizational Crime' in ibid, at 30.

[164] C Yamada, 'Revisiting the International Law Commission's Draft Articles on State Responsibility' in Ragazzi, above n 79 at 121–22 (also providing the example of UN peace-enforcement initiatives and the attribution of responsibility to its members in support of his position).

[165] Higgins, above n 107 at 272–75.

[166] S Talmon, 'Responsibility of International Organizations: Does the European Community Require Special Treatment?' in Ragazzi, above n 79 at 410–14. 'Allocation' of responsibility refers to the actual mathematical apportionment of liability under the treaty regime, which, in this case, is based on a division of obligations under the *United Nations Convention on the Law of the Sea*. 'Attribution' of responsibility refers to the normative operation that seeks to link the actions of non-State actors or of official agents to the governing apparatus for the purposes of establishing international responsibility. The latter does not necessarily follow from the former. In short, even within a party's 'allocated' area of responsibility, Talmon points out that State responsibility would only ensue if a wrongful act can be attributed to that Member State.

[167] See, eg: T Scovazzi, 'Some Remarks on International Responsibility in the Field of Environmental Protection' in Ragazzi, above n 79 at 210–12 (discussing the character of obligations pertaining to the prevention of transboundary environmental damage and drawing a distinction between prohibited conduct and prohibited result); E Roucounas, 'Non-State Actors: Areas of International Responsibility in Need of Further Exploration' in ibid, at 401–02 (discussing the idea of strict liability in environmental law and underlining that there are 'unresolved questions on primary rules expressing concepts such as the precautionary principle, sustainable development, common but differentiated responsibilities').

[168] Duffy, above n 16 at 57–58. She further adds, at 58, that the 'concept appears to import a degree of intentionality, but it is unclear, for example, whether weak states would also be deemed to harbour terrorist groups if they prove unable to control their activity within its territory'.

the abovementioned counterterrorism obligations. Granted, the Security Council has imposed several obligations upon States, ranging from the criminalisation of terrorism and of its support or endorsement to the freezing of terrorist assets. However, little focus has been directed to the actual role of the content of these obligations in triggering international responsibility; the ensuing confusion is further exacerbated by the lack of consensus on the definition of 'terrorism'.[169]

Perhaps the best way to sidestep this political impediment is to align with Higgins' view of 'terrorism' and acknowledge that it 'is a term without legal significance . . . merely a convenient way of alluding to activities, whether of states or individuals, widely disapproved of and in which the methods used are either unlawful, or the targets protected, or both'.[170] Conversely, other influential scholarly voices opine that the concept of 'terrorism' is sufficiently circumscribed to find grounding in international criminal law. In particular, Article 4 of the ICTR Statute includes 'terrorism' as a crime under the Tribunal's jurisdiction, thereby acknowledging that the term has acquired the requisite legal and conceptual significance to qualify as an international crime and to substantiate prosecutions.[171] Similar arguments are advanced with regard to the International Criminal Court, albeit advocating a constructive application or extension of 'terrorism' under the Rome Statute.[172]

Reiterating her original posture and writing about the 1954 Draft Code of Offences against the Peace and Security of Mankind, Higgins again asserts that the inclusion of 'terrorism' under the rubric of State aggression was tantamount to a 'term of convenience'.[173] This inference leads her to further conclude that State responsibility is sufficiently circumscribed to cover acts of terrorism, both through direct and indirect channels, without the need to superfluously reference the (undefined) language of 'terrorism'.[174] As Higgins previously wrote,

[169] Ibid, at 37–38, 70.

[170] R Higgins, 'The General International Law of Terrorism' in R Higgins and M Flory (eds), *Terrorism and International Law* (London, Routledge, 1997) 13 at 28.

[171] See A Cassese, *International Criminal Law* (Oxford, OUP, 2003) 120–21. See also: Duffy, above n 16 at 39 (discussing Art 4 of the Statute of the ICTR). Others opine that terrorism amounts to a customary law crime. See, eg: Cassese, above n 171 at 139; JJ Paust, 'Addendum: Prosecution of Mr. Bin Laden et al. for Violations of International Law and Civil Lawsuits by Various Victims' (2001) 77 *American Society of International Law Insights*, available at www.asil.org/insigh77.cfm#addendum5.

[172] See, eg: R Arnold, *The ICC As a New Instrument for Repressing Terrorism* (Ardsley, Transnational Publishers, 2004) 202–72; V-J Proulx, 'Rethinking the Jurisdiction of the International Criminal Court in the Post-September 11th Era: Should Acts of Terrorism Qualify As Crimes against Humanity?' (2004) 19 *American University International Law Review* 1009. But see: Duffy, above n 16 at 39 (but see also at 95, 100, 118, arguing that there should be little controversy in stating that the acts of 9/11 qualify as crimes against humanity); C Damgaard, *Individual Criminal Responsibility for Core International Crimes: Selected Pertinent Issues* (Berlin, Springer, 2008) 393.

[173] Higgins, above n 170 at 27. Ben Saul rather invokes the term 'political expediency' when discussing Higgins' work. See *Defining Terrorism in International Law* (Oxford, OUP, 2006) 177.

[174] Higgins, above n 170 at 26. See also: Saul, above n 173 at 177, discussing this position and observing that

> Higgins' analysis is accurate to the extent that there is no normative void in international law in relation to responsibility for the acts of States envisaged by Article 2(6). The law of State respon-

less attention should be paid to the content of international obligations when looking at State liability scenarios, along with their connection with the general corpus of State responsibility.[175] Rather, the analytical focus should simply hinge on the application of State responsibility mechanisms (attribution, reparation, countermeasures, etc) once a breach has been determined.

One reading of Higgins' work even more categorically suggests that the exploration of these concepts (eg detailing reparation, countermeasures, etc) should be curtailed in favour of breach-attributability-duty-to-make-reparation mechanics. Hence, State responsibility is not interchangeable with, nor constitutes an incubator for, the further delineation of international obligations.[176] Similarly, Brownlie underscored that 'too much attention is focused upon uninformative or superficial categories such as 'mob violence'. The focus should be upon the incidence of the particular rules and standards of the law'.[177] This reasoning is conceptually analogous to his subsequent claim against unduly partitioning State responsibility. Indeed, he levelled staunch criticism against the creation of analytically distinct categories of responsibility for private acts, environmental damage or judicial transgressions. Rather, he believed that all these scenarios remain united under the umbrella of State responsibility, which should be applied accordingly to factual scenarios, as situations warrant, and be informed by the specific primary obligation dictated by international law.[178] Therefore, this canon of scholarship generates traction towards greater unity in the application of secondary norms as opposed to focusing on primary norms, whilst arguably lobbying for the elaboration of general guidelines in order to provide greater clarity in the area. Ironically, this line of argument lends some credence to the idea of achieving unity through vagueness.

C) Need for the Development of General Rules or Guidelines

In light of the two major strands of scholarship explored above, there is certainly a need to establish general parameters/principles applicable to all international breaches and, more importantly, vis-à-vis unconventional actors. After all, it is no secret that 'the law of State responsibility is applied inconsistently'.[179] Whilst some partly defend the ILC's decision not to cover new actors and the novel/complex situations they engender in its finalised text, 'The result is,

sibility and law on the use of force undoubtedly already apply to unlawful acts committed in these circumstances.

175 See R Higgins, *Problems & Process: International Law and How We Use It* (Oxford, OUP, 1994) 159–65.

176 See ibid, at 161–63. See also: P Allott, 'State Responsibility and the Unmaking of International Law' (1988) 29 *Harvard International Law Journal* 3, 13.

177 I Brownlie, *System of the Law of Nations: State Responsibility Part I* (Oxford, Clarendon Press, 1983) 160.

178 ibid, at 163.

179 K Nakatani, 'Diplomacy and State Responsibility' in Ragazzi, above n 79 at 37.

nevertheless, that the respective conduct is not guided by firm legal rules but left to political *ad hoc* decisions with an uncertain and varying outcome, in the hope that one day custom might fill the gap'.[180] This concern echoes Cassese's remarks, made 12 years before 9/11, whereby he cautioned that analysing modest governmental involvement in terrorism 'is clearly an area where it is difficult to formulate generalized rules'.[181] Equating this field of unsettled law with a 'grey' area, he further opined that governmental input may take on various forms, including 'the entire training, moving lodging and equipping of an insurgent army, assistance which should engage the State's responsibility for attacks by the troops'.[182] At the opposite end of the spectrum, governmental participation 'may involve merely permitting insurgents to sleep in disused huts in remote border areas, assistance which should not of itself engage the State's responsibility for an armed attack'.[183] The fact that no general principles can be convincingly or uniformly applied to the latter cases at present further reinforces the need to better explore potential deterrence models grounded in international responsibility.

Conversely, a liberal dose of scepticism can be applied the other way: even if generalised rules can be developed in the field of secondary obligations, the phenomenon of transnational terrorism is difficultly generalised for the purposes of establishing a dominant model across the board. Whilst this reality was explored above,[184] the present inquiry remains focused on opportunity areas arising specifically in the field of State responsibility. Whilst there is some acknowledgement of a need to elaborate general guidelines, the widespread deficiency in State responsibility literature is also compounded by the primary/secondary dichotomy, which received the ILC's imprimatur.

D) Complicating the Equation under the ILC *Articles*: The Primary/ Secondary Dichotomy

The distinction between primary and secondary rules, which has been persuasively defended,[185] permeates State responsibility dialogue and remains widely

180 Zemanek, above n 92 at 134.

181 A Cassese, 'The International Community's "Legal" Responses to Terrorism' (1989) 38 *ICLQ* 589, 599. But see: ibid, at 600, arguing that in cases of indirect or 'passive' governmental involvement

> the rules are far from clear and States still have plenty of room for manoeuvre. While this element of flexibility may be seen as an advantage, it can ever yield only short-term gains. In the long run clear, rigorous legal restraints on the use of force are needed, for, without them, we can all too easily descend into a whirlpool of spiralling violence.

182 ibid.

183 ibid. On the various levels of State involvement in terrorism, see above ch 1, sections IV.A)–E).

184 Section III.B).

185 See, eg: Milanović, above n 21. Villalpando's treatment of the primary/secondary dichotomy remains persuasive, as he advances a series of arguments for upholding extant state responsibility structures. See SM Villalpando, *L'émergence de la communauté internationale dans la responsabilité des Etats* (Paris, PUF, 2005) 139–41, 333–34, 384.

discussed, including in contemporary scholarly accounts.[186] It is unsurprising, therefore, that this dichotomy occupies a central place in the discussion and will continue to drive the analysis.[187] Although this distinction has generated its share of controversy in scholarship,[188] it becomes clear that the interplay between primary and secondary norms hinges, to a large extent, on the level of governmental involvement in international breaches. As evidenced by chapter two, the assertion that indirect responsibility for private acts is contingent on the State's primary obligation to intervene brings the relationship between direct and indirect responsibility into sharp relief.[189]

Contemporary studies fall short in elucidating the consequences and implications of this distinction in the hard cases, where governmental input is virtually indecipherable or where non-State actors subvert and challenge traditional rules of responsibility, at least through their actions.[190] As a corollary, since unconventional actors can potentially obfuscate the prescriptions laid down in the ILC's *Articles* by their behaviour, there is a pressing need to rethink, or better adapt, existing State responsibility rules.[191] In the wake of the adoption of the *Articles*, two commentators were directly on point: 'The degree to which states should be held responsible for conduct involving private actors is an increasingly significant contemporary issue, as nonstate actors such as Al Qaeda, Somali warlords, multinational corporations, and nongovernmental organizations play greater international roles'.[192] Transnational terrorism is without doubt a case in point; recent academic contributions supplement existing post-9/11 commentary exploring its link with State responsibility.[193] Whilst there has been some scholarly output on State responsibility and terrorism after 9/11, aside from Tal Becker's book, however, contributions remain in large part uncritical, too superficial or cursory.[194]

[186] See, eg: T Treves, 'The International Law Commission's Articles on State Responsibility and the Settlement of Disputes' in Ragazzi, above n 79 at 227; Thirlway, above n 85 at 323. See also: LANM Barnhoorn and KC Wellens (eds), *Diversity in Secondary Rules and the Unity of International Law* (The Hague, Nijhoff, 1995); JR Crawford, 'First Report on State Responsibility', UN Doc A/CN.4/490/Add.4 (1998) at 4–6; International Law Commission, 'Report of the International Law Commission on the Work of Its Fifty-Second Session', (2000) 2(2) *Yearbook of the International Law Commission* 18, UN Doc A/55/10.

[187] See, eg: above ch 1, section III; ch 2, section IV.B).

[188] See, eg: D Bodansky and JR Crook, 'Introduction and Overview (Symposium: The ILC's State Responsibility Articles)' (2002) 96 *AJIL* 773, 781.

[189] See, eg: R Wolfrum, 'State Responsibility for Private Actors: An Old Problem of Renewed Relevance' in Ragazzi, above n 79 at 425, 430–31, 434.

[190] See, eg: G Battaglini, 'War against Terrorism *Extra Moenia*, Self-Defence and Responsibility: A Pure Juridical Approach' in Ragazzi, above n 79 at 138–39.

[191] See, eg: Zemanek, above n 92 at 132–33.

[192] Bodansky and Crook, above n 188 at 782. See also: Wolfrum, above n 189 at 424.

[193] See Battaglini, above n 190 at 137–49; Zemanek, above n 92 at 130–32, 134.

[194] See Becker, above n 1. But see: KN Trapp, *State Responsibility for International Terrorism* (Oxford, OUP, 2011). Before 9/11, very little scholarship existed on the interplay between terrorism and State responsibility. One noteworthy account resided in JA McCredie, 'The Responsibility of States for Private Acts of International Terrorism' (1985) 1 *Temple International and Comparative Law Journal* 69. Although not directly on point, consider also: D Shelton, 'Private Violence, Public Wrongs, and the Responsibility of States' (1989–90) 13 *Fordham International Law Journal* 1.

Because of the sometimes convoluted legal interface deriving from overlapping obligations and juxtaposed sources of law (eg concurrent treaty law and custom), coupled with the potential *erga omnes* implications of counterterrorism norms, new rules on attribution and responsibility could significantly enhance efficiency. Mindful of the sometimes-elusive primary/secondary normative distinction and critical of the private/public sphere dichotomy that underlies State responsibility, Chinkin queries whether ILC-codified attribution is unnecessarily reductive in its treatment of private conduct. Underscoring that State responsibility is a 'legal construct that allocates risk' for wrongful acts 'to the artificial entity of the state', she further posits that the 'human link is provided by the doctrine of attributability, but this maintains the fiction of public and private actions'. This prompts her to call into question the rationale behind non-attribution of private conduct and ponder whether such rule seeks to protect 'the state, individual freedom of action, or the most powerful who are able to remain outside the scope of international regulation'. Chinkin ultimately delivers an immensely pertinent hypothesis in light of States' primary obligation to control their territory advocated in Part I, expounding that 'it might therefore be appropriate to assert responsibility for all wrongful acts emanating from it, or from nationals subject to its jurisdiction'.[195]

This line of reasoning is easily transposable to counterterrorism, as the focus of inquiry now shifts to prevention – irrespective of whether the governmental apparatus is involved – which also signals a marked departure from overemphasis on the distinction between public and private conduct. Counterterrorism efforts are not so concerned with labelling terrorist acts with regard to their institutional (private or public) origins or affiliations,[196] but rather with actually forestalling them, an objective that will turn to a large extent on the formulation of deterrence models. Consequently, the articulation of such schemes should operate a corresponding increase in State accountability which, for present purposes, would translate into a more fluid or flexible application of attribution, regardless of the authorship of the wrongful acts impugned. Bearing in mind that the international community should attempt to prevent rather than cure, it might be useful to resort to the artificial screen of statehood as a sort of legal common denominator, so as to apply a primary counterterrorism obligation of prevention across the board, to a wide array of types of conduct, be they private or public.[197]

However, ILC Special Rapporteur Crawford discarded this line of argument, rather emphasising that accountability mechanisms vis-à-vis primary rules could accommodate a much wider panoply of wrongful private conduct.[198] This

[195] Chinkin, above n 29 at 395 (also noting that 'Such questions require nuanced and contextual responses that are little assisted by too much emphasis on a distinction between public and private spheres of action').

[196] For a thoughtful discussion of the private/public dichotomy with regard to terrorism and State responsibility, specifically, see Becker, above n 1 at 272–76.

[197] But see: Zemanek, above n 92 at 133.

[198] JR Crawford, 'Revising the Draft Articles on State Responsibility' (1999) 10 *EJIL* 435, 439.

position could undoubtedly find support in the *Tehran Hostages* Case[199] and in the implementation of 'environmental agreements that require states to limit national emissions of pollutants, including those by private entities'.[200] It also steers international law towards the realisation that

> the rules of attribution set forth in the articles represent only the tip of the iceberg as to when private acts can create state responsibility. Most such responsibility arises as a result of primary rules – for example, to prevent or limit particular types of private conduct.[201]

Accordingly, some authors fall short in their attempts to further delineate the elusive mechanics of international responsibility. For example, Villalpando's treatment of the topic ultimately fails in adapting to the abovementioned reality and is symptomatic of the conceptual and practical challenges associated with breaking down the structure of secondary norms. Although he recognises the newly formed legal relationship resulting from the breach of an obligation as a pervasive component of State responsibility,[202] his construction of the actual contents and contours of this relationship is challenged by the widely held view within the ILC, to which the present study subscribes, that secondary rules empower and determine which States may protect collective interests vis-à-vis a breach.[203] This clash of positions entails significant implications for the application of counterterrorism duties and, in turn, for the responses to breaches of such obligations. Villalpando ultimately resists this theory, opting for a more homogenous application of State responsibility, and infers that whatever situation is prevalent at the primary normative level necessarily carries over to the relationship generated by the secondary level of the breach.[204] Implying a potential overlap of norm partners at all stages, he posits that the major actors involved in the newly formed, secondary legal relationship must correspond to those who may claim an interest in having the primary obligation upheld.[205] This construction inexorably reverts back to the involvement of the international community as a whole at both the primary and secondary levels of breaches, remaining predicated on Villalpando's assertion that the cohesion characterising that community rests upon the solidarity of its members in safe-

[199] *United States Diplomatic and Consular Staff in Tehran* (*United States v Iran*), Judgment of 24 May, *ICJ Reports* (1980) 3.

[200] Bodansky and Crook, above n 188 at 781.

[201] ibid, at 783. See also generally: Christenson, above n 130. It logically follows that the observance of primary international obligations such as counterterrorism duties or environmental obligations will also depend on the actions of private parties. See, eg: Bodansky and Crook, above n 188 at 783.

[202] See Villalpando, above n 185 at 132.

[203] For thoughtful accounts on collective rights and interests, see, eg: DG Newman, 'Collective Interests and Collective Rights' (2004) 49 *American Journal of Jurisprudence* 127; DG Newman, *Community and Collective Rights: A Theoretical Framework for Rights Held by Groups* (Oxford, Hart Publishing, 2011).

[204] Villalpando, above n 185 at 313–14.

[205] ibid, at 247.

guarding collective interests.[206] Thus, his approach conceptualises State responsibility in terms of a binary continuum involving individual interests and collective interests at opposite poles, whilst also identifying a common regime and a community regime of responsibility.[207] The latter is also subdivided into a common regime (covering all violations of obligations *erga omnes*) and an aggravated regime (applicable to the most serious violations).[208]

V. CONCLUSION

Against the criticism purporting to disable the primary/secondary distinction,[209] it is submitted that further defining secondary norms would actually shed a new light and, perhaps, better circumscribe primary obligations. This argument becomes particularly compelling when faced with terrorism and the corresponding lack of consensus on both its definition and on what States are actually expected to do to repel it (ie the primary obligation).[210] These impediments, which are partially caused by unclear legal language and largely driven by politics, could be addressed by revisiting certain aspects of the current law, thereby making the case for a responsibility-expanding regime more attractive. Equally questionable is whether attribution is adequately suited to address these volatile situations and whether the notion of 'control', which remains inextricably connected to attribution in the ILC's *Articles*, should be excised altogether in certain circumstances involving non-State actors. Although met with some resistance, this exercise remains a valid one. The academic pronouncements canvassed in this chapter evidence the need for more scholarly writing on the concept of attribution and its relevance to present-day concerns, along with the formulation of general principles to govern State violations in this field.[211] Indeed, this project strives to expand upon previous scholarly accounts attempting to elucidate the thorny interplay between non-State actors and State responsibility.[212] With this in mind, the next chapter calls into question the validity of attribution with a view to devising specific policy proposals and deterrence models.

[206] ibid, at 25–29.

[207] ibid, at 224, 242, 246, 251, 254.

[208] ibid, at 246–59. For an equally relevant discussion on these matters, see generally: B Simma, 'From Bilateralism to Community Interest in International Law' (1994-VI) 250 *Recueil des Cours* 217.

[209] For a discussion of this distinction and the new legal relationship formed by the application of secondary rules, see Roucounas, above n 167 at 398–99.

[210] This confusion has also been acute in other areas of transnational activity, such as global warming and climate change. See generally: C Voigt, 'State Responsibility for Climate Change Damages' (2008) 77 *Nordic Journal of International Law* 1.

[211] See generally: V-J Proulx, 'International Responsibility Today: Essays in Memory of Oscar Schachter. L'émergence de la communauté internationale dans la responsabilité des Etats' (2007) 18 *EJIL* 581.

[212] See, eg: M García-Mora, *International Responsibility for Hostile Acts of Private Persons against Foreign States* (The Hague, Nijhoff, 1962).

4

Rethinking the Rationale Underlying State Responsibility for Terrorism: Trans-substantive Rules, Domestic Analogies and the Rationalist Agenda

I. INTRODUCTION

THE PRESENT STUDY takes issue with the claim that revising trans-substantive rules, especially attribution, would not yield effective results. Global counterterrorism efforts constitute an exercise in risk assessment.[1] Indeed, the philosophical questions raised by the 'war' on terror definitely have Kantian roots and lend themselves to several ethical, social and philosophical considerations.[2] Kant's theory that a human being should not be used as a means towards the collective well-being comes to mind, bolstering the proposition that we should not balance human lives in the name of collective security.[3] As a corollary to this categorical imperative, it follows that this legal reform exercise inexorably touches upon the struggle between collective and individual rights,[4] and

[1] See generally: V-J Proulx, 'If the Hat Fits Wear It, If the Turban Fits Run for Your Life: Reflections on the Indefinite Detention and Targeted Killing of Suspected Terrorists' (2005) 56 *Hastings Law Journal* 800, 804–05.

[2] See also: M Koskenniemi, 'Constitutionalism as Mindset: Reflections on Kantian Themes about International Law and Globalization' (2007) 8 *Theoretical Inquiries in Law* 9, 14–15.

[3] See I Kant, RP Wolff, (ed), LW Beck, (tr), *Foundations of the Metaphysics of Morals with Critical Essays* (Indianapolis, Bobbs-Merrill, 1969) (1785) 52, 54. See also: I Kant, HJ Paton, (tr), *Groundwork of the Metaphysic of Morals* (New York, Harper & Row, 1964) (1785) 36–37. On Kantian elements under State responsibility, see GA Christenson, 'Attributing Acts of Omission to the State' (1991) 12 *Michigan Journal of International Law* 312, 319–20 and authorities cited therein. This phenomenon has carried over to other areas of the 'war' on terrorism, especially in national jurisdictions where various decision-makers are called upon to balance security and civil liberties. Hints of Kant's theory are present in A Gewirth, 'Are There Any Absolute Rights?' (1981) 31 *Philosophical Quarterly* 1, 8–16; R Dworkin, 'Terror & the Attack on Civil Liberties' *New York Review of Books*, 6 November 2003 at 37.

[4] See, eg: M Koskenniemi, *The Gentle Civilizer of Nations: The Rise and Fall of International Law 1870-1960* (Cambridge, CUP, 2002) 99 (discussing this in the context of sovereignty, civilization, international lawyers and imperialism from 1870–1914). For an application of this principle to the 'war' on terror, see, eg: TT Gonzales, 'Individual Rights Versus Collective Security: Assessing the Constitutionality of the USA Patriot Act' (2003) 11 *University of Miami International and Comparative Law Review* 75 (2003).

further reinforces the need to rethink State responsibility in that light. Furthermore, 'The increase in individuals' human rights is inevitably accompanied by an increase in their responsibility for human wrongs, even when committed under the color of state authority'.[5] Hence, there are no ideal scenarios or perfect solutions: mitigation of the disparity in political and economic power between States, coupled with the goals of protecting civilians and the sovereign equality between States, all remain noble objectives.

This chapter explores the possibility of revisiting trans-substantive rules of State responsibility, whilst critically assessing the notion of 'control' in that normative scheme. Canvassing the temporal dimensions of international legal breaches, rationalist sensibilities and apposite domestic law analogies, it ultimately sets the stage for the importation of a strict liability-infused regime of responsibility.

II. REVISITING TRANS-SUBSTANTIVE RULES

Revisiting trans-substantive rules of State responsibility operates on a challenge to the assumptions underlying that corpus of norms, ultimately purporting to enhance the efficiency of accountability mechanisms in counterterrorism contexts. An apt starting point is without question the notion of 'control', a central component of the ILC's *Articles* in triggering responsibility. Following the scholarly outcry in response to the ICJ's *Genocide Case*, there has been renewed emphasis on ascertaining what standard of 'control' (ie 'effective' versus 'overall') is required to attribute private conduct to States.[6] Yet, few have called into question the actual notion of 'control' as an overarching or organising principle in attributing behaviour that ostensibly obfuscates traditional intra-State hierarchies or command structures. Terrorism constitutes a case in point, at least when the inquiry shifts from State terrorism to the greyer areas of modest or passive State support, leading some scholars to advocate alternate legal bases for attribution, such as causation.[7] Subsequent sections proceed with a view to vindicating similar policy considerations, albeit via a perhaps more radical route.

A) The Notion of 'Control' Under the ILC *Articles*

As seen in chapter two, indirect responsibility is now the rule of thumb in counterterrorism and will often supplant a finding of direct responsibility, given the

[5] TM Franck, *Fairness in International Law and Institutions* (Oxford, Clarendon Press, 1995) 264. On the emergence of public responsibility and enforceable accountability in international law, see, eg: P Allott, 'The True Function of Law in the International Community' (1997–98) 5 *Indiana Journal of Global Legal Studies* 391, 412.

[6] See the discussion above in ch 2, section III.

[7] See generally: T Becker, *Terrorism and the State: Rethinking the Rules of State Responsibility* (Oxford, Hart Publishing, 2006).

inherent difficulty in substantiating the latter. Indeed, 'a transparent relationship between terrorist actors and the state is predictably uncommon'.[8] The response to 9/11 has empowered aggrieved States to elect indirect responsibility over direct responsibility as the preferred mechanism in establishing the liability of host-States. Even in the context of the Armistice Agreements in Arab-Israeli relations, the parties expressed the wish to implement a mechanism of indirect responsibility by making the territorial State accountable for the excursions of irregular forces outside its territory.[9] However, ILC Article 2 now requires that a breach of an international obligation be attributable to the wrongful State for responsibility to attach.[10] However, given the paradigm shift towards indirect responsibility, Article 2 seems superfluous in the context of counterterrorism.[11] Alternatively, an argument was advanced earlier to bridge the divide between increasingly prevalent modes of indirect responsibility under international law and the prescriptions enshrined in the ILC's *Articles*. It was suggested that a disjunctive reading of Article 2 might cater to this objective by emphasising analytical focus on a host-State's *failure to prevent* terrorism rather than on the intricacies of attribution.[12] Furthermore, in light of contemporary State and Security Council practice, maintaining a rationale of attribution vis-à-vis indirect responsibility relies predominantly on poor semantics. The *Nicaragua* precedent confirms that the notions of control and attribution should be, in most circumstances, excised altogether from the equation of indirect State responsibility. Indeed, the fashion in which the ICJ framed the central question incontrovertibly associates the concept of attribution with *direct* State involvement:

> What the Court has to investigate is not the complaints relating to alleged violations of humanitarian law by the *contras*, regarded by Nicaragua as imputable to the United States, but rather unlawful acts for which the United States *may be responsible directly in connection with the activities of the contras* (emphasis added).[13]

[8] SN Schiedeman, 'Standards of Proof in Forcible Responses to Terrorism' (2000) 50 *Syracuse Law Review* 249, 262.

[9] See V-J Proulx, 'Babysitting Terrorists: Should States Be Strictly Liable for Failing to Prevent Transborder Attacks?' (2005) 23 *Berkeley Journal of International Law* 615, 631 fn 83.

[10] This principle has also been consecrated in jurisprudence. See, eg: *Phosphates in Morocco, Preliminary Objections*, 1938 PCIJ (ser A/B) No 74 (14 June) at 10, 28; *United States Diplomatic and Consular Staff in Tehran (United States v Iran)*, Judgment of 24 May, *ICJ Reports* (1980) 3 at paras 56, 90; *Military and Paramilitary Activities in and against Nicaragua (Nicaragua v United States of America)*, Merits, Judgment of 27 June, *ICJ Reports* (1986) 14 at para 226; *Gabčíkovo-Nagymaros Project (Hungary/Slovakia)*, Judgment of 25 September, *ICJ Reports* (1997) 7 at para 78; *Dickson Car Wheel Company (USA v Mexico)* (1931) 4 *Reports of International Arbitral Awards* 669, 678.

[11] For a brief discussion of Art 2, see V Pechota, 'The Limits of International Responsibility in the Protection of Foreign Investments' in M Ragazzi (ed), *International Responsibility Today: Essays in Memory of Oscar Schachter* (Leiden, Brill, 2005) 170 at 176.

[12] See above ch 2, section IV.A).

[13] *Nicaragua*, above n 10 at para 116. See also: JR Crawford, *International Law Commission's Articles on State Responsibility: Introduction, Text and Commentaries* (Cambridge, CUP, 2002) 110–11, confirming that this question 'was analyzed by the Court in terms of the notion of "control"'.

If the objective is truly, as the Council declared it, to eradicate terrorism using 'all necessary steps', international mechanisms should remain unfettered by secondary rules and the case for a responsibility-expanding regime should be more radical. In that vein, commentators rightly argue that the 'war' on terror should attract new rules.[14] Consequently, recent trends in State responsibility for failing to prevent terrorism should be governed solely by ILC Article 12, as a matter of hermeneutics alone: 'There is a breach of an international obligation by a State when an act of that State is not in conformity with what is required of it by that obligation, regardless of its origin or character'.[15] It follows that the 'essence of an international wrongful act lies in the non-conformity of the State's actual conduct with the conduct it ought to have adopted in order to comply with a particular international obligation'.[16] Although the traditional approach has been to attribute wrongful acts to States, even when involving failures in prevention in some instances, this method should be revisited. Contrary to what certain commentators might anticipate, circumventing attribution altogether may prove efficient in the 'war' on terror and eschew the main criticisms levelled at revising trans-substantive rules.

At first glance, this posture seems paradoxical when contemplated through the prism of the ILC *Articles* – almost anti-State responsibility perhaps – because it shifts much of the focus away from secondary rules, which make up the bulk of the actual law on State responsibility. In many ways, this argument advocates a return to the substantiality of primary rules, without placing so much emphasis on sometimes-burdensome secondary norms. As Prosper Weil proclaimed, 'La fonction ultime de la responsabilité internationale est d'assurer le respect des règles primaires'.[17] This is not to say that secondary norms are always superfluous in and of themselves, but rather that they can flow more organically from international breaches: their application logically derives from the breach of primary obligations and, correspondingly, they strive to achieve some level of coherence in the international legal order in the post-breach calculus. In most cases, primary and secondary rules are, for all intents and purposes, inseparable.[18] Moreover, it is fair to query whether some provisions contained in

[14] See, eg: A-M Slaughter and W Burke-White, 'An International Constitutional Moment' (2002) 43 *Harvard International Law Journal* 1, 2.

[15] 'State Responsibility: Titles and text of the draft articles on Responsibility of States for internationally wrongful acts adopted by the Drafting Committee on second reading', UN Doc A/CN.4/L.602/Rev.1 (2001); 'Report of the International Law Commission on the Work of Its Fifty-Third Session', UN GAOR, 56th Sess, Supp No 10, UN Doc A/56/10 (2001) 41 [hereinafter *ILC Articles on State Responsibility*, *Articles on State Responsibility*, or *Articles*].

[16] Pechota, above n 11 at 176.

[17] P Weil, *Ecrits de droit international* (Paris, PUF, 2000), cited in A Miron, 'La responsabilité de l'Etat pour violations des droits de l'homme par des acteurs non-étatiques' in KK Koufa (ed), *Thesaurus Acroasium Vol 34*: *State Responsibility and the Individual* (Athens, Sakkoulas, 2006) 415 at 434 fn 61.

[18] See, eg: T Treves, 'The International Law Commission's Articles on State Responsibility and the Settlement of Disputes' in Ragazzi, above n 11 at 227. He further adds that 'The consequences of a breach – the main subject of the articles – cannot in most concrete disputes be determined without ascertaining whether there has been a breach, namely without considering the primary

the ILC's *Articles* dissimulate primary rules themselves, or whether the application of secondary norms can sometimes straddle 'primary rule' terrain.[19] By excising or adapting unnecessarily cumbersome secondary and trans-substantive rules, we may achieve greater clarity in the elaboration of primary rules and bridge the divide between primary and secondary stages of international breaches in a more coherent fashion.

The traditional rule is that States are not responsible for the actions of private persons or groups.[20] In that light, the language surrounding attribution appears somewhat dissonant with the new paradigm shift towards indirect responsibility. For example, ILC Article 8 characterises private conduct as an 'act of State' as long as their authors are acting 'on the instructions' or 'under the direction or control' of the State.[21] Hence, prior to 9/11, the debate ineluctably reverted back to the question of control in a circuitous fashion, inspired by both *Nicaragua* and *Tadić*.[22] Implicit in this reality was the fact that States had to wield influence over the relevant irregular factions and activities, a notion that carried over predominantly to the formulation of the *Articles* as a catalyst for responsibility running through the screen of statehood.[23] Moreover, States had to be capable of issuing orders or instructions directly to the actors on the field.[24] Prior to 9/11, influential scholarly voices expressed this idea, albeit through a dichotomy of eventualities susceptible of triggering State responsibility for failing to prevent harm emanating from private actors. Whilst a State would not usually be held responsible for such privately caused harm unless attributable to it, it could become accountable for a due diligence failure in preventing the activ-

rule'. See also generally: J Combacau, 'Obligations de résultat et obligations de comportement: quelques questions et pas de réponse' in D Bardonnet et al (eds), *Mélanges offerts à Paul Reuter: le droit international: unité et diversité* (Paris, Pedone, 1981) 181 at 192.

[19] See, eg: A Nissel, 'The ILC Articles on State Responsibility: Between Self-Help and Solidarity' (2005–06) 38 *NYU Journal of International Law and Politics* 355, 361. See also: JR Crawford, 'Counter-Measures as Interim Measures' (1994) 5 *EJIL* 65, 66.

[20] See Crawford, above n 13 at 110, para 1.

[21] See Art 8, *ILC Articles*, above n 15. For a discussion of this provision, see R Wolfrum, 'State Responsibility for Private Actors: An Old Problem of Renewed Relevance' in Ragazzi, above n 11 at 427–33 (amply discussing the notion of 'control' under the ILC's *Articles*). See also: R Higgins, *Problems & Process: International Law and How We Use It* (Oxford, OUP, 1994) 150. But see: I Brownlie, *System of the Law of Nations: State Responsibility Part I* (Oxford, Clarendon Press, 1983) 164 (labelling the classification of 'acts of State' as 'esoteric' and as a 'theoretical question of 'essence' without any practical significance').

[22] As mentioned above, the Armistice Agreements in Arab-Israeli relations reflected the parties' intention to implement a mechanism of indirect responsibility. However, in a subsequent resolution dealing with the truce, the Security Council unequivocally brought back the terms of the agreements within the ambit of the 'effective/overall' control scheme. See the language in S/RES/983 of 19 August 1948. For a quintessential control-based application of State responsibility, see H Duffy, *The 'War on Terror' and the Framework of International Law* (Cambridge, CUP, 2005) 50–51.

[23] See, eg: *Schering Corp v Islamic Republic of Iran* (1984) 5 Iran-US Claims Tribunal Reports 361 at 370; E Roucounas, 'Non-State Actors: Areas of International Responsibility in Need of Further Exploration' in Ragazzi, above n 11 at 392.

[24] ibid. On the required issuing of orders, see, eg: *Flexi-Van Leasing Inc v Islamic Republic of Iran* (1986) 12 Iran-US Claims Tribunal Reports 335 at 349.

ity[25] or, alternatively, if it exerted a certain degree of *control* over the non-State actors.[26]

An interesting case in point logically flows from the potential responsibility of Lebanon for allowing Hezbollah factions to operate within parts of its territory and launch strikes into Israel. As discussed previously,[27] such determination would evidently stem from Lebanon's 'lack of sufficient control' over the irregular factions and could potentially engage its international responsibility. Analogous claims as to Lebanon's responsibility for the role it played leading up to the 2006 war involving Israel may be cast simultaneously as a violation of its obligation not to harbour or support terrorists, and as an unwillingness or inability to perform its due diligence duties.[28] Concomitantly, this legal categorisation also derives from Lebanon's failure to comply with Security Council resolutions urging it to stamp out Hezbollah factions operating within its borders.[29] The failure by a State to comply with binding Council resolutions and, by the same token, to repel terrorist threats within its territory could be perceived as tantamount to the adoption, by that State, of the terrorists' conduct (eg pursuant to ILC Article 11 on responsibility via endorsement).[30] Moreover, this proposition appears to align with certain eminent jurists' view that the failure to prevent a wrongful act might, in fact, be equivalent to having caused the harmful activity itself.[31] This essentially signals that, barring any clear and compelling evidence that the State either attempted to repress the terrorist activity or, alternatively, that it lacked the sufficient means to do so, its failure to thwart an excursion will be perceived as having been engendered by it. As one commentator observes,

> [w]hat generates the responsibility of a given State and exposes it to the remedies permitted by international law, including when applicable the exercise of self-defence, is the conduct that conclusively reveals its unwillingness to stop the terrorist activities from being carried out within its territory, and a fortiori its support for them. A formal endorsement of the acts of the terrorist is not necessary.[32]

[25] See, eg: *Velásquez Rodríguez Case*, Inter-Am Ct HR Decisions and Judgments 91 (ser C) No 4 (1988) at paras 171–72.

[26] See, eg: I Brownlie, *International Law and the Use of Force by States* (Oxford, Clarendon Press, 1963) 371–72. See also: B Saul, *Defining Terrorism in International Law* (Oxford, OUP, 2006) 197.

[27] See above ch 1, sections IV.B)–D). For a concrete application of State responsibility mechanics vis-à-vis the Lebanon scenario within the broader deterrence model advanced in this book, see below ch 5 nn 247–52.

[28] See, eg: MJB Bottoms, 'When Close Doesn't Count: An Analysis of Israel's Jus Ad Bellum and Jus in Bello in the 2006 Israel-Lebanon War' (2009) *April Army Lawyer* 23, 48–50.

[29] See, eg: SC Res 1559, UN SCOR, 59th Sess, 5028th Mtg, UN Doc S/RES/1559 (2004).

[30] T Gazzini, 'The Rules on the Use of Force at the Beginning of the XXI Century' (2006) 11 *Journal of Conflict & Security Law* 319, 333–34.

[31] See, eg: R Ago, 'Le délit international' (1939-II) 68 *Recueil des Cours* 415, 502; Q Wright, 'The Prevention of Aggression' (1956) 50 *AJIL* 514, 527. This might also disable a large part of Becker's thesis on causation-based State responsibility for terrorism, above n 7. See also: above ch 3, section II.

[32] Gazzini, above n 30 at 334.

Reverting back to the 9/11 precedent, this is not to say that the notion of 'control' was completely irrelevant in that scenario. Establishing a claim of responsibility against Afghanistan would most likely be predicated on the fact that its government wielded quasi-exclusive control over the Afghan *territory*. Implicit in this proposition is the idea that government control over a territory remains intimately tied to a sanctuary State's failure in preventing terrorism. As discussed later on, eminent publicists connect the idea of due diligence with the control a State is *supposed* to exert over its territory in order to prevent it from becoming a launch pad for injurious activities.[33] Actual territorial control, not sovereignty or legitimacy of the ruling authority, constitutes the determinant factor in establishing State responsibility. The ICJ's holding in the seminal *Namibia Advisory Opinion* is instructive in this regard. After confirming South Africa's responsibility for creating an unlawful situation, the Court held that the liable State was obligated to withdraw its administration from Namibia and that 'By maintaining the present illegal situation, and occupying the Territory without title, South Africa incurs international responsibilities arising from a continuing violation of an international obligation'.

The Court went on to declare that

> [t]he fact that South Africa no longer has any title to administer the Territory does not release it from its obligations and responsibilities under international law towards other States in respect of the exercise of its powers in relation to this Territory. *Physical control of a territory, and not sovereignty or legitimacy of title, is the basis of State liability for acts affecting other States* (emphasis added).[34]

Whilst some aspects of the *Namibia* ruling can be distinguished in the face of modern terrorist activity,[35] this swift judicial stroke of the pen seems to lay all debates pertaining to the Taliban's status as a de facto governmental authority to rest. This holding undoubtedly prompted Condorelli to infer that 'according to international law, the State concerned has the same duties of territorial control in the protection of other States' interests, notwithstanding the persistent illegal character of its presence on the territory in question'.[36]

[33] See, eg: M Bennouna, 'Réflexions sur la régulation internationale du risque à propos du concept de prévention' in R Hostiou et al (eds), *Terres du droit: Mélanges en l'honneur d'Yves Jégouzo* (Paris, Dalloz, 2009) 371 at 373.

[34] *Legal Consequences for States of the Continued Presence of South Africa in Namibia (South West Africa) Notwithstanding Security Council Resolution 276 (1970)*, Advisory Opinion of 21 June, *ICJ Reports* (1971) 16 at 54. See also: JHW Verzijl, *International Law in Historical Perspective: Part 6: Juridical Facts as Sources of International Rights and Obligations* (Leiden, Sijthoff, 1973) 712–15.

[35] See, eg: Brownlie, above n 21 at 181.

[36] L Condorelli, 'The Imputability to States of Acts of International Terrorism' (1989) 19 *Israel Yearbook on Human Rights* 233, 241. This reality was also very much alive in the ICJ's *Armed Activities* Case, albeit in the context of belligerent occupation. The Court concluded that Uganda had been an occupying power in the Congolese province of Ituri and was thus under an obligation to undertake all measures to restore and ensure public order and safety in the occupied zone, whilst also upholding the laws in force in the Democratic Republic of the Congo. In light of the facts, it found that Uganda's responsibility was engaged both for the acts of its military that violated international undertakings and for its lack of diligence in preventing IHL and human rights violations.

It appears unquestionable that the Taliban government indeed constituted the 'controlling socio-political entity throughout most of Afghanistan' during the relevant periods.[37] In determining its potential responsibility, the sole fact that it controlled the territory on which Al-Qaeda's bases of operations and training camps were located, coupled with its failure to exercise due diligence, would suffice in establishing the requisite nexus between the 9/11 excursions and the State machinery. Of course, this argument is only palatable if one accepts the emergence of the recent paradigm shift towards indirect responsibility for transnational terrorism. At the other end of the spectrum, it is relatively uncontroversial to declare that a State that openly supports,[38] endorses[39] or authorises[40] transborder excursions – by providing direct or active support to a terrorist group – will be held accountable under the same model.

Through its delivery of the *Articles*, the ILC seems to have narrowed the language of attribution to more traditional models of State-condoned or State-sponsored insurgency, thereby eschewing isolated attacks or massive one-time strikes such as 9/11, especially when premised on failures to act. The commentary on Article 8 constitutes a salient example of the narrow application of attribution before 9/11. Underscoring that circumstances may arise where seemingly private conduct may be attributable 'because there exists a specific factual relationship' between its author and the State, ILC Special Rapporteur Crawford solely identified two examples: that of 'persons acting on the [State's] instructions' and where 'private persons act under the State's direction or control'.[41] Transposed to the 'war' on terror, the ILC commentary makes attribution dependent on some level of control exerted by the State over a terrorist organisation, or on a patent factual nexus between both. This provision does not extend to situations where terrorist organisations act independently or

See *Armed Activities on the Territory of the Congo (Democratic Republic of Congo v Uganda)*, Judgment of 19 December, *ICJ Reports* (2005) 116 at paras 166–80.

[37] A Gruber, 'Who's Afraid of Geneva Law' (2007) 39 *Arizona State Law Journal* 1017, 1026 fn 54.

[38] This reality was recognised long before 9/11. See, eg: MB Baker, 'Terrorism and the Inherent Right of Self-Defense (A Call to Amend Article 51 of the United Nations Charter)' (1987) 10 *Houston Journal of International Law* 25, 36; AR Coll, 'The Legal and Moral Adequacy of Military Responses to Terrorism' (1987) 81 *ASIL Proceedings* 297, 305; JF Murphy, *State Support of International Terrorism: Legal, Political, and Economic Dimensions* (Boulder, Westview, 1989) 99–109; Higgins, above n 21 at 146–68.

[39] See D Brown, 'Use of Force against Terrorism after September 11th: State Responsibility, Self-Defense and Other Responses' (2003) 11 *Cardozo Journal of International and Comparative Law* 1, 10–12. Part of the responsibility imputed to Iran in the *Tehran Hostages* Case was predicated on the fact that State organs subsequently endorsed the attack and ransacking of the American embassy. See *Tehran Hostages* Case, above n 10 at 33–35.

[40] International jurisprudence has long recognised that wrongful conduct may be attributed to a State if it authorised such conduct. See, eg: *The Zafiro Case (Great Britain v USA)* (1925) 6 *Reports of International Arbitral Awards* 160; *Stephens Brothers Case (US v Mexico)* (1927) 4 *Reports of International Arbitral Awards* 265, 267; *Lehigh Valley Railroad Company and others (USA v Germany) (Sabotage Cases: Black Tom and Kingsland incidents)* (1930) 8 *Reports of International Arbitral Awards* 84 and (1939) 8 *Reports of International Arbitral Awards* 225, 458.

[41] Crawford, above n 13 at 110.

autonomously from State organs, as was the case in Afghanistan.[42] Expressing a minority view, some scholars puzzlingly contend that Al Qaeda members constituted agents controlled by the Afghan State, also amounting to an armed band determined to attack the US pursuant to the pronouncements developed in *Nicaragua*.[43] Irrespective of the validity of this tenuous argument, the threshold of 'control' seems ill-suited to respond to factually intractable scenarios, whereby States wield little or no actual control over terrorists operating within their borders. Steven Ratner rightly underscores that the 'orthodox view of state responsibility has effectively vanished, a victim, in part, of its origins in customary law and its seeming inability to address the current challenges of transnational terrorist networks'.[44] In fact, coupled with the vital question of *knowledge* investigated in *Corfu Channel*, evidence of State control is in many instances impossible to demonstrate following terrorist strikes. This problem is further compounded when a host-State's structure or makeup is antithetical to Westphalian democratic ideals, or simply hostile to openness, thereby making any inquiry into the factual link between its apparatus and terrorists much more complex or unfeasible owing to political/military impediments. Consequently, 'the assertion of State responsibility for violations by non-State actors rests upon assumptions of knowledge and control that in many cases States simply do not possess'.[45]

This is not to say, however, that the notion of 'control' should be excised altogether from the range of considerations governing the establishment of indirect responsibility for terrorism. Rather, the determinant factor should turn on the State's *failure to control* its territory and harmful terrorist activities emanating from its soil. In line with *Corfu Channel*, the question of knowledge might become pivotal in establishing the State's responsibility:

> [W]here the loss complained of results from acts of individuals not employed by the state, or from activities of licensees or trespassers on the territory of the state, the responsibility of the state will depend on a *failure to control*. In this type of case questions of knowledge may be relevant in establishing the omission or, more properly, responsibility for failure to act.[46]

[42] In a very rare stroke of the pen, some commentators ponder whether Al Qaeda members could be considered de facto State agents of Afghanistan. See, eg: G Gaja, 'In What Sense Was there an "Armed Attack"?' (2001) *EJIL Discussion Forum*, cited in P Kovács, 'Beaucoup de questions et peu de réponses: autour de l'imputabilité d'un acte terroriste à un État' (2001) 17 *Anuario de derecho internacional* 39, 47, fn 14.

[43] See, eg: P-M Eisemann, 'Attaques du 11 septembre et exercice d'un droit naturel de légitime défense' in K Bannelier et al (eds), *Le Droit international face au terrorisme: après le 11 septembre 2001* (Paris, Pedone, 2003) 243–44. On Osama bin Laden's status as a State agent, see J Quigley, 'International Law Violations by the United States in the Middle East as a Factor Behind Anti-American Terrorism' (2002) 63 *University of Pittsburgh Law Review* 815, 826.

[44] See SR Ratner, 'Jus ad Bellum and Jus in Bello after September 11' (2002) 96 *AJIL* 905, 920.

[45] C Chinkin, 'Human Rights and the Politics of Representation: Is There a Role for International Law?' in M Byers (ed), *The Role of Law in International Politics: Essays on International Relations and International Law* (Oxford, OUP, 2000) 131 at 146.

[46] Brownlie, above n 21 at 45.

In *Corfu Channel*, the Court predicated Albania's knowledge of the presence of the minefield in its territorial waters on the fact that the government closely and routinely monitored the area where the mines were laid.[47] Again, this viewpoint must be carefully balanced out by the translation error found in the *Corfu Channel* Judgment, which may have opened the door to a rationale of indirect, no-knowledge State responsibility.[48]

Thus, attribution will likely be an appropriate mechanism 'only if the non-state actor was "in fact acting on the instructions of, or under the direction or control of, that State in carrying out the [wrongful] conduct"'.[49] Furthermore, based on the reasoning developed in *Tehran Hostages*, attribution can also be triggered by subsequent acknowledgement and adoption of the wrongful conduct by the State as its own. This legal device was expressly incorporated into ILC Article 11, which states that non-attributable conduct 'shall nevertheless be considered an act of that State under international law if and to the extent that the State acknowledges and adopts the conduct in question as its own'.[50] However, this aspect of the *Tehran Hostages* decision, which is premised on direct responsibility, is not particularly helpful for the further development of indirect modes of responsibility.[51] Consequently, attribution is to be understood primarily in conjunction with the notion of 'control' and as semantically adjacent to direct State participation in terrorism in some way, shape or form. The ILC's work prior to 9/11 expounded that State control constitutes the linchpin – or catalytic device – of the mechanism of attribution (at least with regard to the dominant approach to State responsibility for private acts, namely the 'agency paradigm').[52] But now that contemporaneous realities challenge that normative scheme, we must ponder whether the threshold of 'control' remains adequately suited to govern situations involving terrorism. As evidenced by the situations prevalent in Afghanistan and Yemen, terrorist organisations sometimes operate with a large degree of autonomy within State territories, making the issuing of instructions and/or State control over terrorists unviable mechanisms for engaging classical responsibility frameworks.

[47] *Corfu Channel Case (United Kingdom of Great Britain and Northern Ireland v Albania)*, Merits, Judgment of 9 April, *ICJ Reports* (1949) 4 at 19.

[48] See, eg: above ch 1 nn 130–34 and accompanying text.

[49] D Jinks, 'State Responsibility for the Acts of Private Armed Groups' (2003) 4 *Chicago Journal of International Law* 83, 88. There are also hints of this idea in 'Report of the International Law Commission', above n 15 at 121, para 5.

[50] Art 11 of the *Articles*, above n 15. On responsibility by endorsement, see above ch 2 nn 61–62 and accompanying text; Brown, above n 39 at 10–13. On the specific endorsement of the 9/11 attacks, see ibid, at 11 (rejecting a rationale of endorsement with regard to Afghanistan's role in the 9/11 attacks). But see: P-M Dupuy, 'State Sponsors of Terrorism: Issues of International Responsibility' in A Bianchi (ed), *Enforcing International Law Norms against Terrorism* (Oxford, Hart Publishing, 2004) 3 at 11. See also generally: Baker, above n 38 at 36.

[51] Not to mention that a more general application of the *Tehran Hostages* Case to terrorism appears limited by the fact that the obligation at play in that case was conventional, as opposed to broad-reaching like the one emanating from Security Council resolution 1373.

[52] Crawford, above n 13 at 110.

Writing about the 9/11 attacks and the 2004 Madrid bombings, Karl Zemanek called into question the relevance of the concept of 'control' over irregular groups, thereby echoing the above views. He queried whether a State knowing about a terrorist organisation part of a broader network using its territory as a base incurs liability if it fails to share the information with potentially affected States.[53] The planning or carrying out of terrorist agendas on the soil of 'failed' or ineffective States further compounds this scenario, an argument addressed at length below. In the interim, attention must be paid to how such queries affect the deployment of primary obligations.

B) Defining Primary Counterterrorism Obligations

The main argument against revisiting attribution is that the international community should instead focus on better delineating and defining international legal primary rules. As discussed above, all States have an obligation to prevent attacks emanating from their territory and injurious to other States.[54] To challenge this principle is futile and unnecessarily circuitous for reasons of legal language or characterisation.

In terms of legal language, there is still no consensus within the international community as to an accepted universal definition of 'terrorism'.[55] Particular resistance emanates from several Arab States, which do not agree on what actually constitutes an act of terrorism. Yet, the concept is sufficiently circumscribed to entail international responsibility especially coupled with the well-established principle that States have to answer for attacks emanating from their territory. This legal scheme clearly illustrates that the international community's shortcomings will not preclude the application of overriding principles of law, such as the prohibition on recourse to force and the obligation to prevent injuries to neighbouring States.

With regard to legal characterisation of terrorism, the question of retaliation against a host-State – whether forcible or legal/diplomatic – has always been a thorny one, especially when attempting to label the original wrongful act. Before 9/11, an aggrieved State would often run into legal and diplomatic problems in characterising the original attack with a view to justifying reprisals against the wrongful State. These concerns arose in the context of Arab-Israeli relations:

[53] K Zemanek, 'Does the Prospect of Incurring Responsibility Improve the Observance of International Law?' in Ragazzi, above n 11 at 131.

[54] See Saul, above n 26 at 213 (speaking about UN General Assembly practice in the law of counterterrorism and grounding the obligation to prevent terrorism in customary law).

[55] On difficulties in adopting a definition of 'terrorism', see WM Reisman, 'International Legal Responses to International Terrorism' (1999) 22 *Houston Journal of International Law* 3, 9–13. On defining 'terrorism', see Saul, above n 26; B Saul, 'Attempts to Define "Terrorism" in International Law' (2005) 52 *Netherlands International Law Review* 57.

> Even a policy of reprisal which might seek to avoid condemnation because of its 'reasonableness' encounters the initial difficulty of demonstrating the illegality of the activities against which it is directed. This is amply illustrated by the Arab-Israeli situation. Apart from using emotive terms such as 'terrorists', Israel has sought to have the guerilla activities condemned as illegal and has done so on a variety of grounds.[56]

Whilst not directly on point in the context of non-forcible countermeasures, it must be emphasised that Israel often asserted before the Security Council that 'passive' State assistance to terrorists, through providing sanctuary to irregular factions, is sufficient to trigger a right to forcibly respond against the assisting State.[57] Invoking this rationale on numerous occasions, Israel attempted to target Lebanon and other Arab States without swaying the Council in this direction,[58] whilst Israel's posture received the imprimatur of influential publicists.[59] A reading of post-9/11 practice seems to do away with these evidentiary problems: once a terrorist excursion is carried out, one possible approach is to look at it in the abstract, as an attack emanating from a State's territory, and focus on how that State could have limited (or avoided altogether) its international responsibility.

As discussed above, the 'harbouring' and 'supporting' rule seems to have achieved international precedence over the general concept of attribution. This language pervaded much of post-9/11 legal speech, having been invoked in both international politico-legal rhetoric and domestic legislation. Indeed, a significant policy impetus relying on this phenomenon is readily perceptible and can be best explained by the desire to criminalise certain (sometimes otherwise lawful) behaviours under domestic law, pursuant to resolution 1373.[60] Particularly striking is the parallel with domestic criminal law, considering recurrent evidentiary hurdles in national counterterrorism settings relating, inter alia, to the identification of individual suspects and the treatment of evidence, more generally. States have increasingly begun to criminalise what used to merely constitute evidentiary elements – ie restricting access to certain literature, monitoring

[56] DW Bowett, 'Reprisals Involving Recourse to Armed Force' (1972) 66 *AJIL* 1, 17.

[57] But see generally: RJ Erickson, *Legitimate Use of Military Force against State-Sponsored International Terrorism* (Maxwell Air Force Base, Air University Press, 1989).

[58] See the following Security Council resolutions: 228 (1966), 248 (1968), 256 (1968), 262 (1968), 265 (1969), 270 (1969), 316 (1972) and 332 (1973).

[59] See, eg: Y Dinstein, 'The International Legal Response to Terrorism' in R Ago (ed), *International Law at the Time of Its Codification: Essays in Honour of Roberto Ago (Vol II)* (Milan, Giuffrè, 1987) 139 at 146. Implicit in this proposition is the prior establishment of State responsibility for failing to comply with the obligation to refrain from recourse to force in international relations.

[60] On the Canadian context and Bill C-36, see, eg: *Anti-Terrorism Act*, SC 2001, c 41; I Cotler, 'Does the Anti-Terror Bill Go Too Far?' *The Globe and Mail*, 20 November 2001 at A17. Art 83.23 of the *Criminal Code*, RSC 1985, c C-46 (Canada) provides the following:

> Every one who knowingly harbours or conceals any person whom he or she knows to be a person who has carried out or is likely to carry out a terrorist activity, for the purpose of enabling the person to facilitate or carry out any terrorist activity, is guilty of an indictable offence and liable to imprisonment for a term not exceeding ten years.

bomb making-related activities, monitoring flight/pilot school enrolments, prohibiting membership in certain organisations, freezing assets and blocking certain charitable donations – as one of the ways to crack down on home-grown terrorism. For example, US authorities claim to have acquired significant evidence against Najibullah Zazi, a legal immigrant from Afghanistan and Denver airport shuttle driver, regarding one of the most serious terrorist plots since 9/11. Absolutely crucial to mounting this case was the enhanced monitoring of bomb-making activities; his indictment suggested that he purchased chemicals required to build a bomb, including hydrogen peroxide, acetone and hydrochloric acid. Amongst other germane allegations, it was believed that Mr Zazi attended an Al Qaeda training camp in Pakistan, underwent training in explosives and dissimulated in his laptop computer nine pages of bomb-making directions.[61] On 22 February 2010, he pled guilty to conspiring to use weapons of mass destruction, conspiring to commit murder in a foreign country and providing material support to a terrorist organisation.

Whilst such policy inclination bolsters the enforceability of domestic criminal law, it also carries resounding implications for the present study. By criminalising such behaviour, States are accruing due diligence capital for the purposes of mitigating State responsibility engagement and, more importantly, as a way to comply with primary counterterrorism obligations (eg the prescriptions stemming from resolution 1373).[62] Consequently, international law now countenances a series of shifts towards indirect forms of responsibility as bases for engaging accountability both at the national and international levels, and both at the individual and State levels.[63] As discussed earlier,[64] in increasing their diligent efforts to meet counterterrorism obligations by adopting more exacting criminal standards, States might be signalling that they consider their potential liability on the international scene as a factor governing and shaping the allocation of their (sometimes scarce) resources in combating terrorism. By shifting their domestic policy infrastructures towards accommodating indirect rationales for accountability, those States might not only be able to actually thwart specific terrorist excursions, but also pre-empt the application of State responsibility altogether by successfully fulfilling their primary obligations and by diverting the policy focus squarely on prevention.

The widely and domestically criminalised notion of 'harbouring' terrorists or people who are likely to engage in terrorism has manifested itself macrocos-

[61] For more details on the case of Mr Zazi, see D Johnston and S Shane, 'Terror Case Called One of Most Serious in Years', *New York Times*, 25 September 2009 at A1; WR Rashbaum and D Frosch, 'Terrorism Suspect Held Without Bail in Colorado', *New York Times*, 22 September 2009 at A16; D Johnston and WK Rashbaum, 'Terror Suspect Had Bomb Guide, Authorities Say', *New York Times*, 21 September 2009 at A1. See also: WR Rashbaum and L Robbins, 'Terror Suspect Is Transferred to New York for Trial', *New York Times*, 26 September 2009 at A15.

[62] The scope of the Council's pronouncements in this regard is explored below in section V.A).

[63] For an exploration of these issues, see M Lehto, *Indirect Responsibility for Terrorist Acts: Redefinition of the Concept of Terrorism beyond Violent Acts* (Leiden, Nijhoff, 2010).

[64] See above ch 1, section I.

mically, through various permutations striving to elucidate the relationship between Afghanistan and Al-Qaeda. Allegations that the government of Afghanistan 'protected' the Al-Qaeda network come to mind,[65] with others calling for greater accountability of those States 'compromised by terror'[66] or 'allies of terror'.[67] The bulk of the US' claim against Afghanistan hinged on the assertion that the attacks had been 'made possible by the decision of the Taleban regime to allow the parts of Afghanistan that it controls to be used by this organization as a base of operation'.[68] In a thrust that arguably confuses intent and effect, some infer that although the American and British letters to the Council charged Afghanistan with harbouring terrorists, 'they stopped short of alleging that Afghanistan was, as a matter of international law, responsible for the attacks themselves'.[69] Nevertheless, in rhetoric compatible with indirect responsibility, whilst the initial American posture did not attribute the actions of Al Qaeda to Afghanistan,[70] it ultimately accused that State of committing murder by supporting and harbouring terrorists,[71] making it abundantly clear that it would no longer distinguish between terrorists and their sanctuary States.[72] Accordingly, 'President George W. Bush . . . advanced a doctrine of enemy status and state responsibility . . . loosely based on a traditional law concept of "aiding and abetting"' and this posture 'is summarized in President Bush's statement that the United States would consider as enemies "terrorists and those who harbor them"'.[73] Other scholarly voices opine that, whilst

[65] See Statement by NATO Secretary-General, Lord Robertson, 2 October 2001, available at www.nato.int/docu/speech/2001/s011002a.htm.

[66] See, eg: US National Security Council, *The National Security Strategy of the United States of America* (17 September 2002), available at http://merln.ndu.edu/whitepapers/USnss2002.pdf. On this strategy, see AA Sofaer, 'On the Necessity of Pre-emption' (2003) 14 *EJIL* 209, 209. See also: Dupuy, above n 50 at 3. Some authors criticised the US' National Security Strategy as overly 'unilateralist'. See, eg: Duffy, above n 22 at 212.

[67] See President Bush's Statement to the UN General Assembly on 10 November 2001, available at www.un.org/webcast/ga/56/statements/011110usaE.htm; Jinks, above n 49 at 85.

[68] Letter dated 7 October 2001 from the Permanent Representative of the United States of America to the United Nations addressed to the President of the Security Council, UN Doc S/2001/946 (2001) (also highlighting that the US has obtained 'clear and compelling information' to that effect). See also: CS Wren, 'US Advises UN Council More Strikes Could Come', *New York Times*, 9 October 2001 at B5.

[69] C Greenwood, 'International Law and the "War against Terrorism"' (2002) 78 *International Affairs* 301, 311–12. In addition, 'there has been no serious suggestion by States involved in the Afghanistan intervention that that State was legally responsible for the September 11 attacks'. See Duffy, above n 22 at 253.

[70] In establishing its claim against Afghanistan, the US arguably opted for the logic of indirect responsibility. See, eg: Letter Dated 9 October 2001 from President Bush to congressional leaders reporting on combat at para 1, available at http://avalon.law.yale.edu/sept11/president_040.asp.

[71] See, eg: 'A NATION CHALLENGED; Bush's Remarks on U.S. Military Strikes in Afghanistan', *New York Times*, 8 October 2001 at B6; President Bush's Statement, above n 67.

[72] See Jinks, above n 49 at 84–85; President Bush's Statement, above n 67. Hence, use of force against Afghanistan was authorised by Congress. See Authorization for Use of Military Force, Public Law No 107–40, 115 Stat 224 (2001).

[73] MJE Kastenberg, 'The Use of Conventional International Law in Combating Terrorism: A Maginot Line for Modern Civilization Employing the Principles of Anticipatory Self-Defense & Preemption' (2004) 55 *Air Force Law Review* 87, 88.

Afghanistan was 'held directly responsible' for the 9/11 attacks, a response that encountered little or no resistance amongst key actors, this determination is nonetheless difficult to countenance when contemplated through traditional agency standards.[74]

C) The 9/11 Precedent: The Consecration of the 'Harbouring and Supporting' Rule

Similarly, publicists argue that the response to 9/11 crystallised a shift in international law or at least somewhat tempered attribution principles,[75] an approach predicated on the imputation of the 9/11 attacks to Afghanistan via a *renvoi* to the 'harbouring and supporting' rule.[76] Ultimately, we must query 'to what extent the allegations levelled against the Taleban of harbouring and supporting terrorists amount to a legal (as opposed to political) claim at all'.[77] However, the initial American posture following the attacks on the World Trade Centre, the Pentagon, and in Pennsylvania, described by some as 'rhetorically bellicose, but practically cautious' in generating support and legitimacy,[78] ultimately garnered Security Council endorsement. This initial reaction presumably stemmed from the need to build a viable coalition and to enhance and foster multilateral cooperation in combating terrorism.[79] It is also widely thought that the Council authorised recourse to force against Afghanistan following those attacks, thereby effectively reversing decades of restraint in allowing retaliatory force vis-à-vis transborder excursions.[80] Conversely, such shift might also be explained by what amounted to an exceptional reaction to exceptional events.

[74] Becker, above n 7 at 5.

[75] See, eg: J Kranz, 'The Use of Armed Force – New Facts and Trends' (2006) 3 *The Polish Quarterly of International Affairs* 68, 80; Proulx, above n 9. But see: Duffy, above n 22 at 54 fn 44. See also: Jinks, above n 49 at 92.

[76] See, eg: M Sassòli, 'State Responsibility for Violations of International Humanitarian Law' (2002) 84 *International Review of the Red Cross* 401, 409; Jinks, above n 49 at 85–88.

[77] Duffy, above n 22 at 55.

[78] SJ Toope, 'Powerful but Unpersuasive? The role of the United States in the Evolution of Customary International Law' in M Byers and G Nolte (eds), *United States Hegemony and the Foundations of International Law* (Cambridge, CUP, 2003) 287 at 291–92.

[79] See, eg: PE Tyler and J Perlez, 'World Leaders List Conditions on Cooperation', *New York Times*, 19 September 2001 at A1. Similar comments may be applied to the early stages of the Iraq crisis. See, eg: A Paulus, 'The War against Iraq and the Future of International Law: Hegemony or Pluralism?' (2004) 25 *Michigan Journal of International Law* 691, 719.

[80] See Jinks, above n 49 at 85–86. In response to 9/11, Jinks argues that 'the Security Council impliedly endorsed, without expressly authorizing, the use of force against Afghanistan'. ibid, at 86. On this issue, see also: N Rostow, 'Before and After: The Changed UN Response to Terrorism Since September 11th' (2002) 35 *Cornell International Law Journal* 475. On the Council's role in combating international terrorism, see CA Ward, 'Building Capacity to Combat International Terrorism: The Role of the United Nations Security Council' (2003) 8 *Journal of Conflict and Security Law* 289.

The consecration of the 'harbouring and supporting' rule is particularly significant when considering that both *Nicaragua*[81] and *Tadić*[82] rejected financial and military assistance as the sole basis for imputing direct responsibility to a State,[83] even if such aid proved 'preponderant or decisive'.[84] Taking this finding as the only consistent point between those two decisions,[85] coupled with the facts that terrorists need assets to operate and governments are attempting to forestall their financial autonomy,[86] it seems evident that the 9/11 precedent has dug an entirely novel furrow for State responsibility. As Ratner noted,

> it seems clear, on the issue of state responsibility, that none of the tests cited above-those of the ICJ, the ICTY, or the ILC-supports the harboring theory of the United States. That position, stated by President Bush, effectively imputes responsibility based on the toleration of such acts by the government.[87]

It should also be cautioned that, in some instances, armed reprisals or other extreme countermeasures against State toleration of terrorism would have no impact on that host-State's toleration of these activities. In that eventuality, any initiative undertaken by the sanctuary State to eradicate terrorism on its soil would only bring about its own demise via mutiny, insurrection or national unrest.[88] More intriguingly, some commentators persist in asserting that *Tadić* was vindicated by the response to 9/11.[89] Venturing a step further, others suggest

[81] The ICJ also added in *Nicaragua*, above n 10 at para 115, that the participation by the State,

> even if preponderant or decisive, in the financing, organizing, training, supplying and equipping of the *contras*, the selection of its military or paramilitary targets, and the planning of the whole of its operation, is still insufficient in itself . . . for the purpose of attributing to the United States the acts committed by the *contras*.

See also: ibid, at para 110.

[82] Case No IT-94-1-A *Prosecutor v Tadić*, ICTY Judgment, 15 July 1999, reprinted in (1999) 38 ILM 1518 at para 130 ('it is not sufficient for the group to be financially or even militarily assisted by a State').

[83] For a discussion of these aspects, see R Wolfrum, 'State Responsibility for Private Actors: An Old Problem of Renewed Relevance' in Ragazzi, above n 11 at 428–29.

[84] See also: A Cassese, 'The International Community's "Legal" Responses to Terrorism' (1989) 38 *ICLQ* 589, 599.

[85] The *Tadić* Judgment had little to do with State responsibility, rather evoking problems legally adjacent to individual criminal responsibility. Yet, given the circumstances of the case, the Tribunal chose to address the question of State responsibility rather extensively. See above ch 2, section III.

[86] Much has been written on international efforts to freeze terrorist assets and to obstruct fundraising channels of organisations such as Al Qaeda. See, eg: ME Engel, 'Donating "Blood Money": Fundraising for International Terrorism by United States and the Government's Efforts to Constrict the Flow' (2004) 12 *Cardozo Journal of International and Comparative Law* 251; B Zagaris, 'The Merging of the Anti-Money Laundering and Counter-Terrorism Financial Enforcement Regimes After September 11, 2001' (2004) 22 *Berkeley Journal of International Law* 123.

[87] Ratner, above n 44 at 908. This possibility was recognised long before 9/11. See, eg: Baker, above n 38 at 41–42.

[88] On this point, see Bowett, above n 56 at 20. Although not directly on point, consider also: TSR Rao, 'State Terror as a Response to Terrorism and Vice Versa: National and International Dimensions' (1987) 27 *Indian Journal of International Law* 183.

[89] For instance, see JA Hessbruegge, 'The Historical Development of the Doctrines of Attribution and Due Diligence in International Law' (2004) 36 *NYU Journal of International Law and Politics* 265, 305–06.

that Afghanistan wielded 'effective control' over Al Qaeda, thereby framing their investigation upon *Nicaragua*-esque terrain.[90] Whether this legal and factual appraisal of the events surrounding 9/11 is accurate seems highly questionable. Decidedly, the involvement of Afghanistan in the preparation and perpetration of those attacks is aptly characterised as a hard case. As Brigitte Stern underscores, no one claimed that Afghanistan was directly or indirectly involved in the preparation and carrying out of the excursions.[91] Thus, the law governing these difficult situations, along with even more passive types of State involvement in terrorism, 'is not entirely clear'.[92] Or perhaps it *was* not entirely clear before 9/11, the response to those events having now set a new State responsibility precedent.

In contrast, Judges Schwebel's and Jennings' respective Dissenting Opinions in *Nicaragua* militated in favour of a responsibility-expanding analysis of governmental assistance to armed bands.[93] Their views consecrated the principle that 'providing insurgents with logistical support, or at least logistical support coupled with weapons, will generally be sufficient to render the assisting State responsible for an armed attack carried out by the insurgents',[94] a proposition that received subsequent academic approval.[95] Borrowing from this thinking, the objective now focuses on determining to what extent US-led action in Afghanistan has affected the law of State responsibility and, as a corollary, whether alternate liability models can build on this account to enhance the compliance pull and preventive force of counterterrorism obligations.

The response to 9/11 undoubtedly challenged modern international law as we know it.[96] Notable developments have also transpired within the law of recourse

[90] See, eg: MA Drumbl, 'Victimhood in Our Neighborhood: Terrorist Crime, Taliban Guilt, and the Asymmetries of the International Legal Order' (2002) 81 *North Carolina Law Review* 1, 36. For a contrary opinion, ie that Osama bin Laden – not the Taliban – controlled Al Qaeda, see J Bartholet, 'Inside the Mullah's Mind', *Newsweek*, 1 October 2001, p 30 at 32; J Bartholet, 'Method To the Madness', *Newsweek*, 22 October 2001, p 54 at 58; N Lemann, 'What Terrorists Want', *The New Yorker*, 29 October 2001, p 36 at 38. See also: GM Travalio, 'Terrorism, International Law and the Use of Military Force' (2000) 18 *Wisconsin International Law Journal* 145, 153 (extrapolating similar reasoning to the failures of impotent host-States).

[91] B Stern, 'La Responsabilité internationale des Etats: Perspectives récentes' in JC LLoréns (ed), *Cursos euromediterráneos bancaja de derecho internacional (Vol VII)* (Valencia, Tirant lo Blanch, 2003) 659 at 686.

[92] Cassese, above n 84 at 599.

[93] See *Nicaragua*, above n 10 at 346–47 (Judge Schwebel) and 543 (Judge Jennings). See also: Travalio, above n 90 at 152–53, 158–62, 168–69.

[94] Cassese, above n 84 at 599.

[95] See, eg: JN Moore, 'The Nicaragua Case and the Deterioration of World Order' (1987) 81 *AJIL* 151 especially at 154. On the question whether non-State actors can perpetrate an 'armed attack' and surrounding issues, see T Ruys, *'Armed Attack' and Article 51 of the UN Charter: Evolutions in Customary Law and Practice* (Cambridge, CUP, 2010) 419–510.

[96] Several commentators generally conclude that US-led military action in Afghanistan has fundamentally challenged international law. See, eg: A Bâli, 'Stretching the Limits of International Law: The Challenge of Terrorism' (2002) 8 *ILSA Journal of International and Comparative Law* 403; NJ Schrijver, 'Responding to International Terrorism: Moving the Frontiers of International Law for "Enduring Freedom"?' (2001) 48 *Netherlands International Law Review* 271; NJ Schrijver, 'September 11 and Challenges to International Law' in J Boulden and TG Weiss (eds), *Terrorism and the UN: Before and After September 11* (Bloomington, Indiana University Press, 2004) 55–73.

to force, often occurring in tandem with the evolution of State responsibility.[97] However, it is unclear whether this paradigm shift amounts to a loosening of self-defence standards or whether it can be best explained by the emergence of a new rule of State responsibility (or whether those two categories should necessarily be linked). In the latter case, compelling arguments bolster the proposition that State responsibility has been significantly affected and potentially revised by 9/11. Indeed, the 'legal response to the terrorist attacks (and other recent developments) strongly suggest that the scope of state liability for private conduct has expanded . . . the response to the September 11 attacks may signal an important shift in the law of state responsibility'.[98] A caveat should be registered here in deference to scholars who caution against assessing State sponsorship or toleration of guerrillas/terrorists through State responsibility frameworks. This criticism is partly prompted by the ILC's current structure, which only provides for deployment of peaceful or non-forcible countermeasures.[99] These commentators suggest that 'a shift away from this framework may already have taken place, if one evaluates state practice and *opinio juris* since 11 September 2001'.[100] Whilst contemplating State-sponsored terrorism through the lens of self-defence, they discard the agency requirement but fall short of endorsing the 'harbouring and supporting' rule as sole predicate for recourse to force: 'in establishing the necessary link between terrorists and a state for the purposes of self-defence, while proof of agency should no longer be required, one would need to show more than that terrorists are found on the state's territory'.[101] For this argument to become palatable, one must accept that the reaction to 9/11 may be concomitantly framed within State responsibility and recourse to force frameworks.[102] Coming back to international liability

[97] For different views on this debate, see ME O'Connell, 'Lawful and Unlawful Wars against Terrorism' in VP Nanda (ed), *Law in the War on International Terrorism* (Ardsley, Transnational Publishers, 2005) 79-96; JJ Paust, 'Use of Armed Force against Terrorists in Afghanistan, Iraq, and Beyond' (2002) 35 *Cornell International Law Journal* 533, 533–57.

[98] Jinks, above n 49 at 83–84.

[99] See, eg: *Corfu Channel*, above n 47 at 35; *Nicaragua*, above n 10 at 127, para 249; *Guyana v Suriname* (2008) 47 *International Legal Materials* 164 at para 446 (also citing ILC Art 50(1)(a)). See also: B Simma, 'NATO, the UN and the Use of Force: Legal Aspects' (1999) 10 *EJIL* 1, 2; J Brunnée and SJ Toope, 'The Use of Force: International Law After Iraq' (2004) 53 *ICLQ* 785, 794–95 (rejecting the ICJ's requirement of agency in *Nicaragua* 'because it chose to assess the use of force within a framework of State-responsibility'); J Brunnée, 'The Security Council and Self-Defence: Which Way to Global Security?' in N Blokker and N Schrijver (eds), *The Security Council and the Use of Force: Theory and Reality – A Need for Change?* (Leiden, Nijhoff, 2005) 107 at 123; V Gowlland-Debbas, 'The Limits of Unilateral Enforcement of Community Objectives in the Framework of UN Peace Maintenance' (2003) 11 *EJIL* 361, 363.

[100] Brunnée and Toope, above n 99 at 795 (citing Ratner, above n 44 at 908–10).

[101] Brunnée, above n 99 at 123. See also: Schrijver, 'Responding to International Terrorism', above n 96 at 283. Brunnée, above n 99 at 123, further adds that '"Harbouring" terrorists should not be a reason to invoke self-defence unless it amounts to at least tacit approval of terrorist attacks'. On this issue, see also: G Travalio and J Altenburg, 'Terrorism, State Responsibility, and the Use of Military Force' (2003) 4 *Chicago Journal of International Law* 97, 111–13.

[102] For a concise review of the confused relationship between terrorism, use of force and countermeasures through the lens of the ILC's *Articles*, see TM Franck, *Recourse to Force: State Action against Threats and Armed Attacks* (Cambridge, CUP, 2002) 53–55. See also generally: V Gowlland-

exclusively, if one accepts that a shift in the law has taken root after 9/11 and that both *Nicaragua* and *Tadić*, coupled with the ILC's *Articles*, are no longer dispositive of State responsibility in this setting, additional legal anchors and academic writing are presumably required to substantiate this claim.[103]

Drawing from one area propitious for legal reform, it follows that trans-substantive rules of State responsibility could be revamped accordingly: the international community must decide whether to lower imputation standards or to forego attribution altogether in the context of transnational terrorism. Some scholars resolve the discrepancy engendered by melding use of force and State responsibility principles by expounding that the 9/11 precedent substantially relaxed attribution standards under State responsibility repertoire.[104] As evidenced by the foregoing considerations, however, the latter scenario seems better tailored to accommodate current politico-legal realities.[105]

III. THE TEMPORAL ELEMENT OF THE BREACH OF AN INTERNATIONAL OBLIGATION

The relationship between time and State responsibility is of vital importance in reassessing the parameters of indirect responsibility.[106] Central to the inquiry lying ahead is the notion of an ongoing, or continuing, violation of a State's obligation of prevention. The ILC's *Articles* specifically provide for this interrelationship, signalling that transnational terrorism can either be subsumed under a 'single strike' theory or under an 'overall relationship' theory, at least on one level.[107] In the former scenario, a State's responsibility is confined to a one-time failure to prevent an isolated terrorist strike, barring additional attacks or subsequent State endorsement of wrongful acts (eg the 2008 Mumbai terrorist attacks carried out by Pakistani irregulars). In the latter situation, the host-State's history indicates ongoing or repeated transborder subversion originating

Debbas, 'Security Council Enforcement Action and Issues of State Responsibility' (1994) 43 *ICLQ* 55, 56.

[103] See, eg: JE Alvarez, 'Hegemonic International Law Revisited' (2003) 97 *AJIL* 873, 879–80 fn 34.

[104] See, eg: Jinks, above n 49 at 89. Similarly, see also: C Stahn, 'Terrorist Acts As "Armed Attack": The Right to Self-Defense, Article 51 (1/2) of the UN Charter, and International Terrorism' (2003) 27 *Fletcher Forum of World Affairs* 35, 37; R Wolfrum, 'The Attack of September 11, 2001, the Wars against the Taliban and Iraq: Is There a Need to Reconsider International Law on the Recourse to Force and the Rules in Armed Conflict?' (2003) 7 *Max Planck Yearbook of United Nations Law* 1.

[105] But see: L Grosswald, 'Cyberattack Attribution Matters under Article 51 of the U.N. Charter' (2011) 36 *Brooklyn Journal of International Law* 1151, 1153 (querying whether eliminating the concept of attribution in counterterrorism contexts is contradictory to the UN Charter).

[106] See, eg: J Salmon, 'Duration of the Breach' in JR Crawford et al (eds), *The Law of International Responsibility* (Oxford, OUP, 2010) 383–96. Equally important is the nexus between countermeasures and the temporal dimension surrounding their deployment. See, eg: M Kamto, 'The Time Factor in the Application of Countermeasures' in ibid, at 1169–76.

[107] These theories were first explored above in ch 2, section V (see particularly n 301 and accompanying text) and are discussed in further detail below.

from within its borders, a record evincing an ongoing relationship between that State and, typically, a single victim-State (eg Hezbollah-led attacks launched from Lebanon against Israel). The very nature of this transnational subversive activity, coupled with potentially devastating human and economic losses, lends a particularly compelling character to 'prevention' and brings the interplay between 'instantaneous' and 'continuing' violations of international law into sharp relief. On a broader level, the relationship between time and State responsibility warrants further elucidation because a State violates its obligation of prevention as long as it fails to control its national territory or harbours terrorists on its soil. Thus, in theory, there is no need for a terrorist strike to materialise for the obligation of prevention to come into play pursuant to Security Council resolutions; it is an ongoing duty, which may trigger accountability mechanisms. A contrary stance would signal that that obligation is absolute which, in the spirit of prevention, would be counterproductive. Consequently, further consideration must be given to the temporal dimension surrounding the breach of the specific obligation under study.

A) Article 14(3): The Distinction between Instantaneous and Continuing Breaches

The case for circumventing attribution becomes particularly compelling when considering the temporal component of international breaches. The central theme underlying ILC Article 14 concerns the distinction 'between a breach which is continuing and one which has already been completed',[108] a distinction that was explored in the *Rainbow Warrior* arbitration. In that case, the Tribunal was confronted with France's failure to detain two individuals pursuant to an agreement struck with New Zealand. Finding that the breach had a continuous character, the Tribunal delivered an important statement on the nature of the violation:

> [T]his classification is not purely theoretical, but, on the contrary, it has practical consequences, since the seriousness of the breach and its prolongation in time cannot fail to have considerable bearing on the establishment of the reparation which is adequate for a violation presenting these two features.[109]

For instance, the classification of a breach as ongoing may prove helpful in showing that a State has repeatedly failed to prevent terrorism and thereby continues to violate Security Council resolutions. Such protracted failures would thus make the case for expanding State responsibility more palatable. Yet, the distinction between instantaneous and continuing breaches has not, so far, been thoroughly applied to terrorism per se. Rather, it has been central in cases

[108] Crawford, above n 13 at 135.
[109] *Rainbow Warrior (New Zealand v France)* (1999) 10 *Reports of International Arbitral Awards* 217 at 264, para 101.

involving contractual matters,[110] forced or involuntary disappearances,[111] expropriation or wrongful taking of property,[112] treaty obligations,[113] jurisdictional issues[114] and the loss of social status.[115]

The portion of Article 14 dealing with continuing breaches, premised on a State's obligation to prevent a given event, could plausibly extend to situations of repeated cross-border attacks and reprisals.[116] This argument, however, does not suggest that a single terrorist strike, such as the one perpetrated on 9/11, would not engender long-lasting consequences or ripple effects.[117] Nevertheless, such attacks would a priori fall within the realm of instantaneous breaches, as the one-time failure to prevent terrorism indicates a breach by the host-State without having a continuing effect for the purposes of the ILC's text. All surrounding repercussions, whether characterised by collateral damage to civilians and property or ensuing deaths of targeted individuals, fall within the ambit of the consequences of a terrorist attack without confirming, per se, that the failure to prevent the attack has a continuing character.[118]

Conversely, it must be stressed that the *in fine* portion of the same provision is couched in negative terms, which does not preclude the application of the *Articles* to a series of terrorist attacks, such as Al-Qaeda-led strikes when taken in the aggregate, thus including the bombings of the Khobar Towers, the US embassies in Africa, the USS Cole and the 9/11 excursions. When compared to situations involving Hezbollah or the PLO, these accounts might fit within what has been termed the 'overall relationship' theory above. However, setting aside the Arab-Israeli context, a State's duty to prevent terrorism may entail the analysis of an altogether different temporal dimension. Unlike situations of contractual breaches or continued disappearances (where the harm can be redressed in real-time but ex post facto), the primary objective of the duty to prevent terrorist attacks is to actually stop them from occurring. Scenarios involving continuing violations of counterterrorism duties entail a State perpetrating an ongoing violation of international law, a situation that endures as long as it fails to bring its conduct in conformity with its obligation to prevent the given event.

[110] See, eg: ibid and at 265–66, paras 105–06; Dissenting Opinion of Sir Kenneth Keith, at 279–84. See also: *Gabčíkovo-Nagymaros*, above n 10 at 54, para 79.

[111] See, eg: *Blake v Guatemala,* Inter-Am Ct HR Decisions and Judgments (ser C) No 36 (1998) at para 67.

[112] See, eg: *Papamichalopoulos and Others v Greece*, Eur Ct Hr (ser A) No 260-B (1993); *Loizidou v Turkey* (1996-VI) Eur Ct HR 2216.

[113] See, eg: *Tehran Hostages* Case, above n 10 at 145.

[114] See, eg: *Papamichalopoulos*, above n 112; *Loizidou*, above n 112.

[115] See, eg: *Sandra Lovelace v Canada*, UN HR Committee, UN GAOR, 36th Sess, Supp No 40, UN Doc A/36/40 166 at 172, paras 10–11.

[116] See the text of ILC Art 14(3), above n 15 and accompanying text.

[117] See, eg: Reisman, above n 55 at 6–7; 'Report of the ILC', above n 15 reprinted in (2001) 2(2) *Yearbook of the International Law Commission* 31 at 60, para 6 (underscoring that the consequences of an unlawful act may continue after its commission and potentially inform the quantum of compensation without converting the act into a continuing breach).

[118] On the continuing character of international breaches, see Brownlie, above n 21 at 193–98.

In cases of continuing violations vis-à-vis transnational terrorism, the impugned actions have to be continuously linked to the same State or series of States for the logic of Article 14(3) to be cogently engaged. On this front, the 9/11 precedent presents relatively little controversy, as the Security Council had repeatedly deplored the government of Afghanistan's harbouring and protection of Al Qaeda operatives on its territory, along with its toleration of training camps and bases.

Given the international community's obvious resolve in combating terrorism, one could persuasively argue that every State has an interest in preventing terrorist attacks, albeit uneven in scope.[119] Terrorism strikes at the very core of human dignity and security; it might prove illusory to assert that a State has no interest whatsoever in preventing a terrorist attack involving two other States. Based on that logic, the duty to prevent terrorism could arguably qualify as an obligation *erga omnes*.[120] Should this characterisation of the obligation hold, it would entail a significant consequence under the ILC's *Articles*: third States could raise the failure to fulfil that duty in the event that an excursion is launched from one State onto another's territory. This recourse hinges on ILC Article 48(1)(b), which provides that 'Any State other than an injured State is entitled to invoke the responsibility of another State in accordance with paragraph 2 if: . . . (b) the obligation breached is owed to the international community as a whole'.[121] Certain commentators espouse this legal construction, grounding the *erga omnes* character of the obligation of prevention both in widespread State

[119] Indeed, this argument should be appreciated with caution. See J-C Martin, *Les règles internationales relatives à la lutte contre le terrorisme* (Brussels, Bruylant, 2006) 490 ('l'obligation de ne pas soutenir le terrorisme s'inscrit dans un cadre multilatéral, mais tous les États n'ont pas un intérêt égal à son observation' ('whilst the obligation not to support terrorism operates in a multilateral framework, not all States have an equal interest in its observance' – author translation)). For similar reasoning in the context of the ICJ's *Genocide Case*, see above ch 3 nn 46–49 and accompanying text.

[120] On obligations *erga omnes*, see the obiter dictum in *Barcelona Traction, Light and Power Company, Limited, Second Phase*, Judgment of 5 February, *ICJ Reports* (1970) 3 at 32, paras 33–34. See also: *East Timor (Portugal v Australia)*, Judgment of 30 June, *ICJ Reports* (1995) 90 at 102, para 29; *Legal Consequences of the Construction of a Wall in the Occupied Palestinian Territory*, Advisory Opinion of 9 July, *ICJ Reports* (2004) 136 at 199, para 157. For a concise review of obligations *erga omnes*, with particular emphasis on the ICJ's pronouncements on the issue, see A De Hoogh, *Obligations Erga Omnes and International Crimes: A Theoretical Inquiry into the Implementation and Enforcement of the International Responsibility of States* (The Hague, Kluwer, 1996) 49–56; M Ragazzi, *The Concept of International Obligations 'Erga Omnes'* (Oxford, Clarendon Press, 1997) 7–12. On the question of enforcement of obligations *erga omnes*, see CJ Tams, *Enforcing Obligations Erga Omnes in International Law* (Cambridge, CUP, 2005).

[121] Art 48(1)(b) of the ILC *Articles*, above n 15. Should this position be endorsed, the obligation to prevent terrorism would fit within the framework and reasoning of *Barcelona Traction*, above n 120 at 32, para 33. For more background on the interplay between Art 48(1)(b) and obligations *erga omnes*, see G Gaja, 'States Having an Interest in Compliance with the Obligation Breached' in Crawford et al, above n 106 at 957–60; Crawford, above n 13 at 278; L-A Sicilianos, 'The Classification of Obligations and the Multilateral Dimension of the Relations of International Responsibility' (2002) 13 *EJIL* 1127, 1136–38; M Spinedi, 'From One Codification to Another: Bilateralism and Multilateralism in the Genesis of the Codification of the Law of Treaties and the Law of State Responsibility' (2002) 13 *EJIL* 1099, 1113–14.

acquiescence and in Council resolutions 1368 and 1373.[122] Other scholars assert that *jus cogens* obligations also fall within the ambit of ILC Article 48 in that they are 'owed to the international community as a whole', which may or may not encompass the obligation to prevent transnational terrorism.[123] It is unclear, however, if the law of State responsibility would immediately legalise, or legitimise, any countermeasure adopted by third States under the auspices of Article 48 by sole virtue that the recourse in question is implemented in response to a wrongful act with a view to protecting the interests of the international community.[124]

More controversially, the violation of a counterterrorism obligation *erga omnes* could arguably impose new legal duties not only upon the wrongful State, but also upon all other States to cooperate to bring the wrongful act to an end pursuant to ILC Article 41(1).[125] Whether this classification garners adequate traction and practice to become authoritative remains highly debatable; the ILC's own pronouncement on the matter decidedly entertains this eventuality.[126] Conversely, Judge Higgins' Separate Opinion in the *Wall Advisory Opinion* points in the opposite direction, expounding that whilst there are 'certain rights in which, by reason of their importance, "all States have a legal interest in their protection" ', this 'has nothing to do with imposing substantive obligations on third parties to a case'.[127] Ultimately, confirmation of the characterisation of the obligation to prevent terrorism as *erga omnes* will depend largely on the evolution of international law in the upcoming years. In the interim, a single argument remains immutable: to entertain a claim that preventing terrorism does not constitute a concern for the international community as a whole is probably unrealistic.

[122] See, eg: Dupuy, above n 50 at 12.

[123] See, eg: P-M Dupuy, 'A General Stocktaking of the Connections between the Multilateral Dimension of Obligations and Codification of the Law of Responsibility' (2002) 13 *EJIL* 1053, 1061. On the mechanism of ILC Art 48 and the invocation of responsibility, see EB Weiss, 'Invoking State Responsibility in the Twenty-First Century' (2002) 96 *AJIL* 798, 803–06; J Peirano, 'International Responsibility and Cooperation for Development' in Ragazzi, above n 11 at 190; H Thirlway, 'Injured and Non-injured States before the International Court of Justice' in Ragazzi, above n 11 at 311–28.

[124] See, eg: D Alland, 'Les contremesures d'intérêt général' in P-M Dupuy (ed), *Obligations multilatérales, droit impératif et responsabilité internationale des États* (Paris, Pedone, 2003) 167. For a recent study on ILC Art 48, see JR Crawford, 'Responsibility for Breaches of Communitarian Norms: An Appraisal of Article 48 of the ILC Articles on Responsibility of States for Internationally Wrongful Acts' in U Fastenrath et al (eds), *From Bilateralism to Community Interest: Essays in Honour of Judge Bruno Simma* (Oxford, OUP, 2011) 224–40.

[125] See generally: G Gaja, 'Do States Have a Duty to Ensure Compliance with Obligations *Erga Omnes* by Other States?' in Ragazzi, above n 11 at 34–35; NHB Jørgensen, 'The Obligation of Cooperation' in Crawford et al, above n 106 at 695–701. Some scholars describe 'the obligation of States to cooperate with each other' as having attained the status of *jus cogens* norms, without providing further clarification or background on the implications of such designation. See, eg: Peirano, above n 123 at 192–93.

[126] See Crawford, above n 13 at 249.

[127] Separate Opinion of Judge Higgins in the *Wall Advisory Opinion*, above n 120 at 216, para 37.

Coming back to the temporal dimension of breaches, one can argue that an obligation such as the one faced by Afghanistan on 9/11 belonged to the realm of instantaneous breaches. That is not to say, however, that the ILC's *Articles* preclude the breach of an obligation to prevent a given event from having a continuing character; quite the contrary, the failure to comply with the obligation of prevention can constitute a continuing wrongful act.[128] Nevertheless, once an attack is successfully launched from a State, the threat has not been thwarted and the primary object of the obligation is defeated.[129] This context is sometimes very different from non-lethal transboundary environmental damage, for example.[130] Here, the international community is not just concerned with containing the threat if the initial harm is unavoidable. The policy impetus is rather to forestall the initial wrongful act before it can come into existence, thereby pitting the prospect of containment against the reality of prevention. As a result, the failure to prevent the specific event may potentially entail far more serious consequences than the emission of toxic pollutants: human beings are killed and the primary object of the obligation is defeated.[131] Hence, more stringent liability regimes should be imposed, as we are increasingly confronted with situations that signal a departure from the Arab-Israeli record and consequently preclude the application of ILC Article 14(3). If we adopt a consensus that 'one [terrorist] attack is too much', which generally aligns with the laws of war[132] and international law, we must necessarily impose a heavier burden of precaution upon States. Moreover, 'State liability is peculiarly relevant concerning crimes of omission, which imply that someone had the power and the duty to interfere'.[133] This is unquestionably the case with respect to failures to comply with counterterrorism obligations and shifts the focus of the inquiry towards a rationale of strict liability.

[128] See Crawford, above n 13 at 140.

[129] See, eg: B Simma, 'The Work of the International Law Commission at Its Fifty-Third Session (2001)', (2002) 71 *Nordic Journal of International Law* 123, 127 (remarking that ILC Art 14(3) encompasses both continuing breaches of obligations to prevent and cases 'where only the occurrence of a certain event constitutes a breach').

[130] Although it should be stressed that prevention also infuses many of the policy objectives underpinning international environmental law. See, eg: T Scovazzi, 'Some Remarks on International Responsibility in the Field of Environmental Protection' in Ragazzi, above n 11 at 212.

[131] Crawford, above n 13 at 140 (distinguishing between cases where 'the breach may be progressively aggravated by the failure to suppress it' and obligations of prevention 'only concerned to prevent the happening of the event in the first place', in which case 'there will be no continuing wrongful act').

[132] The protection of civilians is paramount in the IHL context. See, eg: International Commission of the Red Cross, *Basic Rules of the Geneva Conventions and Their Additional Protocols*, 2nd edn (Geneva, International Committee of the Red Cross, 1983). The ICJ also pronounced on the importance of protecting civilian life. See, eg: *Legality of the Threat or Use of Nuclear Weapons*, Advisory Opinion of 8 July, *ICJ Reports* (1996) 226 at 257, para 78 (classifying the non-targeting of civilians as a 'cardinal principle' of humanitarian law).

[133] F Rigaux, 'International Responsibility and the Principle of Causality' in Ragazzi, above n 11 at 83.

B) A Rationale of Strict Liability

Once a State fails to fulfil its obligation of prevention, thereby defeating its principal purpose, it should not be able to escape scrutiny for not having acted on the right incentives, save in specific circumstances. For instance, if a primary obligation dictates that specific information not be divulged, 'the whole point of the obligation is defeated' once the information is published, thereby stripping the obligation of a continuing character.[134] For the 'war' on terror to have a preventive rather than curative character, we must tackle the problem at its roots and provide the adequate impetus to States. The law governing State responsibility offers great propensity for prevention, as it can generate serious counterterrorism incentives for governments.[135] Moreover, recent law enforcement initiatives evince a broader international legal trend towards incentivising States to comply with counterterrorism obligations. An apt case in point resides in the UK's prevention of what has been envisaged as the largest transnational terrorist attempt since 9/11. The UK's due diligence led to the conviction of three individuals – Abdulla Ahmed Ali, Assad Sarwar and Tanvir Hussain – who conspired to explode at least seven airliners headed for Canada and the US by using liquid explosives dissimulated in soft drink containers.[136]

In the grander scheme of things, the objective is to efficiently forestall terrorism using, as the Council declares, 'all necessary steps', whilst preventing an abusive application of State responsibility and upholding the sovereign equality of States, to the extent possible. However, the precise content of 'all necessary steps' is far from being determined and hinges, in most circumstances, on questions of fact; it remains to be seen what exact standard is to be ascribed to the Council's prescriptions in its post-9/11 resolution-making.[137] Based on this objective and the paradigm shift towards indirect responsibility, it would seem helpful to forego attribution altogether in the context of transnational terrorism. Besides, the mechanism of indirect responsibility has become a sort of safety net to pin liability on host-States should aggrieved States endeavour to establish direct responsibility but fail to do so for various reasons, ranging from evidentiary obstacles to scrambled factual ties between terrorists and governments.[138] As a proximate inquiry in a different context, scholars ponder whether

[134] See Crawford, above n 13 at 140 fn 270.

[135] See, eg: Stern, above n 91 at 692.

[136] See, eg: '3 U.K. Men Convicted in Airline Bomb Plot', *CBC News*, 7 September 2009, available at www.cbc.ca/world/story/2009/09/07/british-muslims-convicted007.html.

[137] Some puzzlingly infer that 'the duty to take necessary steps does not impose anything more stringent than the requirement of due diligence under customary international law', without further substantiating this claim. See AG Hamid, 'Maritime Terrorism, the Straits of Malacca, and the Issue of State Responsibility' (2006) 15 *Tulane Journal of International and Comparative Law* 155, 172.

[138] Recent scholarly accounts also embody the essence of the terms 'direct responsibility' and 'indirect responsibility', albeit using different language. See, eg: G Battaglini, 'War against Terrorism *Extra Moenia*, Self-Defence and Responsibility: A Pure Juridical Approach' in Ragazzi, above n 11 at 141 (invoking the notions of *active* and *passive* positions of sanctuary States).

'the conduct of those responsible for terrorist atrocities committed in post-occupation Iraq cannot be attributed to Iran as a matter of State responsibility, can it be shown that Iran has violated a due diligence rule through its actions or omissions?'[139]

Thus, it is submitted that counterterrorism policy objectives would be better served by a regime of responsibility inspired by a rationale of strict liability.[140] Whilst much has been written on the notion of fault under State responsibility[141] and traditionally 'states are not strictly responsible for wrongs orchestrated on or emanating from their territory',[142] conventional wisdom does not preclude the implementation of a strict liability mechanism in this legal field.[143] In fact, influential scholarly voices highlight the 'growing contemporary tendency for certain categories of obligations to entail "strict liability"', namely 'responsibility by reference to events, with *culpa* as much an irrelevance as the due-diligence test. This is clearly a growing phenomenon in the international environmental field'.[144]

Andrea Gattini explored the significance of fault in relation to both the law of State responsibility and the ILC's *Articles* before their final adoption.[145] In his

[139] RP Barnidge, Jr, *Non-State Actors and Terrorism: Applying the Law of State Responsibility and the Due Diligence Principle* (The Hague, T.M.C. Asser Press, 2008) 152, 152 fn 77.

[140] But see: Becker, above n 7 at 269–72; A Schwartz, 'The Case against Strict Liability' (1992) 60 *Fordham Law Review* 819 (arguing that the foundational assumptions of strict liability law are false or misguided); S Yee, 'The Responsibility of States Members of an International Organization for its Conduct as a Result of Membership of their Normal Conduct Associated with Membership' in Ragazzi, above n 11 at 441. See also: Duffy, above n 22 at 52, 57 (arguing that counterterrorism obligations do not embody a strict liability character).

[141] Eminent publicists have explored the role of fault in the framework of State responsibility. See, eg: H Lauterpacht, *Private Law Sources and Analogies of International Law (With Special Reference to International Arbitration)* (London, Longmans, 1927) 134–43. Compare with the broader theory of 'outcome responsibility' developed in AM Honoré, *Responsibility and Fault* (Oxford, Hart Publishing, 1999).

[142] Duffy, above n 22 at 49. See also: ibid, at 52. Ultimately, international responsibility regimes are probably not endowed with a system of pure strict liability vis-à-vis terrorism. See, eg: Saul, above n 26 at 94; C Van den Wyngaert, 'The Political Offence Exception to Extradition' (1989) 19 *Israel Yearbook on Human Rights* 297, 302.

[143] Besides, when invoking traditional State responsibility logic, it is clear that 'States are responsible for conduct over which they exercised effective control'. Duffy, above n 22 at 49. See also: R Jennings and A Watts (eds), *Oppenheim's International Law*, 9th edn (London, Longman, 1992–96) 501; H Lauterpacht (ed), *International Law: A Treatise by Lassa Oppenheim (Vol 1: Peace)*, 8th edn (London, Longmans, 1955) 337–38, 341; H Kelsen, RW Tucker, (ed), *Principles of International Law*, 2nd edn (New York, Holt, Rinehart and Winston, 1966) 199–200, all referring to 'vicarious responsibility', although Brownlie called into question this characterisation. See I Brownlie, *Principles of Public International Law*, 6th edn (Oxford, OUP, 2003) 431; Brownlie, above n 21 at 36.

[144] Higgins, above n 21 at 161. See also: N Horbach, *Liability Versus Responsibility Under International Law: Defending Strict State Responsibility for Transboundary Damage* (Boxmeer, NLJT Horback, 1996); LFE Goldie, 'International Principles of Responsibility for Pollution' (1970) 9 *Columbia Journal of Transnational Law* 283, 306–09; VO Okaru, 'The Basel Convention: Controlling the Movement of Hazardous Wastes to Developing Countries' (1993) 4 *Fordham Environmental Law Report* 137, 155.

[145] A Gattini, 'Smoking/No Smoking: Some Remarks on the Current Place of Fault in the ILC Draft Articles on State Responsibility' (1999) 10 *EJIL* 397.

response to Gattini, ILC Special Rapporteur Crawford agreed that 'it is a serious error to think that it is possible to eliminate the significance of fault from the Draft Articles'.[146] However, Crawford opened the door to the transplantation of strict liability therein by contending that it is equally erroneous to adopt a one-size-fits-all approach to the role of fault in this debate, as primary responsibility-generating normative content dictates the formula. He expounded that 'different primary rules of international law impose different standards, ranging from "due diligence" to strict liability'.[147] Given the urgency of combating terrorism, coupled with the objective of actually preventing attacks, the regime of indirect responsibility could transform into a mechanism of strict liability or, at least, a working model drawing inspiration from such standard. As a corollary, ascertaining the breach of an obligation, especially one embodying a duty of prevention, remains largely interdependent with a contextual assessment of the contents of the primary norm under study. Indeed,

> [w]hether a particular obligation is breached forthwith upon a failure to act on the part of the responsible State, or whether some further event must occur depends on the content and interpretation of the primary obligation and cannot be determined in the abstract.[148]

IV. DRAWING ON LEGAL TRADITIONS AND DOMESTIC LAW ANALOGIES TO INFORM THE LAW OF STATE RESPONSIBILITY

Since this project's policy thrust gravitates towards the possible importation of strict liability undertones into State responsibility repertoire, a preliminary discussion on the role and place of domestic legal analogies seems apposite here.

A) The Impenetrability of International Law

Some scholars view the sphere of international law, and State responsibility specifically, as impenetrable, overarching fortresses insulated from domestic law transplantations.[149] Thus, the autonomy characterising international law precludes a State from pleading 'principles of municipal law, including its constitution, in answer to an international claim'.[150] Others caution against being

[146] JR Crawford, 'Revising the Draft Articles on State Responsibility,' (1999) 10 *EJIL* 435, 438.

[147] ibid. See also: CF Amerasinghe, *State Responsibility for Injury to Aliens* (Oxford, Clarendon Press, 1967) 45; Higgins, above n 21 at 160.

[148] 'Report of the International Law Commission', above n 15, Commentary on Draft Article 2, at para 9. See also: J Barboza, 'Legal Injury: The Tip of the Iceberg in the Law of State Responsibility' in Ragazzi, above n 11 at 8.

[149] See, eg: Brownlie, above n 21 at 36 (arguing that the domestic law notion of 'vicarious responsibility' should not be imported into the law of State responsibility).

[150] ibid, at 141. This principle is also grounded in Art 27 of the Vienna Convention on the Law of Treaties, May 23, 1969, UN Doc A/CONF 39/27, reprinted in BE Carter et al (eds), *International Law: Selected Documents*, 4th edn (New York, Aspen, 2003) 49 at 57. This idea somewhat origi-

selective in the transplantation process to avoid importing private law analogies without corresponding procedural safeguards. This reasoning is redolent of Crawford's own scholarly writings calling for the incorporation of the procedural safeguards of democracy into international law, an idea puzzlingly absent from his works as Special Rapporteur on State responsibility.[151] The 'war' on terror constitutes a propitious breeding ground for juridical analogy: legal challenges engendered by novel law enforcement practices, for example, raise concerns for fundamental human rights protection. The practice of targeted killing of suspected terrorists also poses intractable challenges for the human rights project. Unsurprisingly, domestic legal schemes prevalent in most Western nations do not countenance the extrajudicial killing of individuals; there is no intelligible reason why ordinary due process standards afforded all citizens should fail to be mirrored in international law.[152] Others advocate similar caution and adaptation of domestic concepts on the international plane, albeit through more favourable assessments of environmental law.[153]

The practice of domestic law transplantations is ripe for abuse, especially in a field as highly volatile and politically sensitive as counterterrorism. A substantive and procedural overhaul of State responsibility must not translate into another hegemonic outlet for imposing Western-derived ideologies and concepts on a global scale,[154] with little regard for the scarcity of resources available in combating terrorism amongst developing countries and the diversity of worldviews underpinning their relationships with the international legal order. Besides, most States will ultimately reject a State responsibility rule – or a construction of that normative scheme – that would subject them to indiscriminate or unconditional intervention for harbouring terrorists.[155]

nates from the theory of Kelsen, one of the most prominent proponents of the monist conception of international law. See Kelsen, above n 143 at 553–88 (expounding that all rules of international law are supreme over rules of municipal law). See also: P Malanczuk, *Akehurst's Modern Introduction to International Law*, 7th rev edn (London, Routledge, 1997) 63–64, fn 2 (citing H Kelsen, 'Die Einheit von Völkerrecht und staatlichem Recht' (1958) 19 *ZaöRV* 234–48, and discussing Kelsen's notion of a basic rule or *Grundnorm* from which derives all law).

[151] See, eg: JR Crawford, 'Democracy and International Law' (1994) 64 *BYIL* 113; JR Crawford and SD Marks, 'The Global Democracy Deficit: An Essay in International Law and its Limits' in D Archibugi et al (eds), *Re-Imagining Political Community: Studies in Cosmopolitan Democracy* (Stanford, Stanford University Press, 1998) 72. See also: Nissel, above n 19 at 369.

[152] See, eg: P Margulies, 'Making "Regime Change" Multilateral: The War on Terror and Transitions to Democracy' (2004) 32 *Denver Journal of International Law and Policy* 389, 410–11; Proulx, above n 1 at 875–91 and authorities cited therein.

[153] See generally: JB Wiener, 'Something Borrowed from Something Blue: Legal Transplants and the Evolution of Global Environmental Law' (2001) 27 *Ecology Law Quarterly* 1295.

[154] Similar arguments have been made regarding other branches of international law. See, eg: MA Drumbl, 'Toward a Criminology of International Crime' (2003) 19 *Ohio State Journal on Dispute Resolution* 263, 271–72 (applying similar reasoning to the importation of Western criminal law standards into international law); B Kingsbury, '"Indigenous Peoples" in International Law: A Constructivist Approach to the Asian Controversy' (1998) 92 *AJIL* 414, 455; MW Mutua, 'Politics and Human Rights: An Essential Symbiosis' in Byers, above n 45 at 150.

[155] See, eg: M Byers, 'Terrorism, the Use of Force, and International Law After 11 September' (2001) 51 *ICLQ* 401, 408.

The resistance to domestic law transplantations in international law[156] has also carried over to other spheres, such as international organisations[157] and international criminal law (ICL).[158] Granted, in the latter case this resistance has considerably waned and paved the way for ICL to be considerably shaped and influenced by domestic law. Whilst some contend that the horizontal transplantation of judicial precedents between common law and civil law jurisdictions generates viable results,[159] others quarrel with this argument and maintain that transplantation impedes innovation.[160] Regardless, ongoing transnational judicial dialogue and cross-fertilisation actuate the process of legal borrowing: international law, civil law and common law operate as mutually instructive systems, hinging on a reciprocal flow of influences, information and value sharing, a sort of horizontal integration.[161] By analysing possible contributions by certain legal traditions to State responsibility, this study is guided by a simple precept: '[The] borrowing of law is the primary instrument of law's development'.[162] In contrast with the view that the international legal order can only export its components vertically into the civil/common law divide, the law of State responsibility amounts to a mixture of different legal influences, particularly when deploying its fundamental mechanisms. Thus,

> [i]n theory and in practice, the international law of responsibility is applied across the field of international obligations. It comprises areas that – in terms of domestic anal-

[156] Legal transplants from one domestic system to another are usually referred to as 'horizontal integration'. For an assessment of the viability of legal transplantation projects, see, eg: J Mertus, 'From Legal Transplants to Transformative Justice: Human Rights and the Promise of Transnational Civil Society' (1999) 14 *American University International Law Review* 1335, 1377–84.

[157] See, eg: D Sarooshi, 'The Essentially Contested Nature of the Concept of Sovereignty: Implications for the Exercise by International Organizations of Delegated Powers of Government' (2004) 25 *Michigan Journal of International Law* 1107, 1121–22 (citing R Higgins, 'Final Report of the Legal Consequences for Member States of the Non-Fulfilment by International Organizations of their Obligations Towards Third Parties' (1995) 66-I *Annuaire de l'Institut de Droit International* 251, 287); E Raftopoulos, *The Inadequacy of the Contractual Analogy in the Law of Treaties* (Athens, Hellenic Institute of International and Foreign Law, 1990) 201 ff.

[158] See, eg: Drumbl, above n 154 at 268–72.

[159] See RB Ahdieh, 'Between Dialogue and Decree: International Review of National Courts' (2004) 79 *NYU Law Review* 2029, 2067 fn 155 (citing JV Orth, 'The Secret Sources of Judicial Power' (2004) 50 *Loyola Law Review* 529).

[160] For general support of this statement, see, eg: Ahdieh, above n 159 at 2067 fn 155. On the view that horizontal judicial transplantations or 'extrinsic judicial review' constrain innovation, see PB Stephan, 'Redistributive Litigation – Judicial Innovation, Private Expectations and the Shadow of International Law' (2002) 88 *Virginia Law Review* 789, 792.

[161] See, eg: A-M Slaughter, 'A Global Community of Courts' (2003) 44 *Harvard International Law Journal* 191, 193 (citing C L'Heureux-Dubé, 'The Importance of Dialogue: Globalization and the International Impact of the Rehnquist Court' (1998) 34 *Tulsa Law Journal* 15, 16); A-M Slaughter, *A New World Order* (Princeton, Princeton University Press, 2004) 69–79. See also generally: RJ Sharpe and V-J Proulx, 'The Use of Academic Writing in Appellate Judicial Decision-Making' (2011) 50 *Canadian Business Law Journal* 550, 554–58.

[162] HP Glenn, *Legal Traditions of the World*, 2nd edn (Oxford, OUP, 2004) 204 (citing A Watson, *Legal Transplants: An Approach to Comparative Law*, 2nd edn (Athens, University of Georgia Press, 1993)).

ogies – may be seen as like those of contract and tort, and others that might be seen as analogous to public law.[163]

Similarly, vertical integration of international law into domestic systems has been explored in scholarship, be it in ascertaining the former's role in municipal judicial settings[164] or in assessing its place and importance in legal education.[165] However, this project is more concerned with the vertical integration/transplantation of domestic legal concepts into international law, rather than the other way around. Although not directly on point but relevant for enforcement under State responsibility, it could be argued that this line of reasoning is compatible with an inversed interpretation of the doctrine of enmeshment as a theory of compliance.[166] Indeed, enmeshment shares several points of rapprochement with importing domestic legal transplants into international law, thereby suggesting that States might conclude that this area mirrors their owns interests, a notion building on several scholarly works.[167] Under this lens, it is perhaps more accurate to speak about the transplantation of national 'interests' on the international plane, as opposed to the importation of domestic law. Ultimately, importing select municipal analogies into international responsibility frameworks proves helpful in elaborating new interpretive guidelines or theoretical insights when gauging appropriate responses to terrorism, irrespective of the impact of that exercise on State interests.

[163] JR Crawford, 'The ILC's Articles on Responsibility of States for Internationally Wrongful Acts: A Retrospect' (2002) 96 *AJIL* 874, 878.

[164] For varied views under the Canadian experience, see J Brunnée and SJ Toope, 'A Hesitant Embrace: The Application of International Law by Canadian Courts' (2002) 40 *Canadian Yearbook of International Law* 3; R Provost, 'Judging in Splendid Isolation' (2008) 56 *American Journal of Comparative Law* 125; S Beaulac, 'Arrêtons de dire que les tribunaux au Canada sont 'liés' par le droit international' (2004) 38 *Revue juridique Thémis* 359. See more generally: CP Economides, *Les Rapports entre le droit international et le droit interne: Collection Science et technique de la démocratie* (Strasbourg, Conseil de l'Europe, 1993). To a lesser extent and on the American experience, see CA Bradley and JL Goldsmith, 'Customary International Law As Federal Common Law: A Critique of the Modern Position' (1997) 110 *Harvard Law Review* 815.

[165] See, eg: MC Mirow, 'Globalizing Property: Incorporating Comparative and International Law Into First-Year Property Classes' (2004) 54 *Journal of Legal Education* 183; D Otto, 'Handmaidens, Hierarchies and Crossing the Public-Private Divide in the Teaching of International Law' (2000) 1 *Melbourne Journal of International Law* 35; C Valcke, 'Global Law Teaching' (2004) 54 *Journal of Legal Education* 160.

[166] For a thoughtful account on enmeshment, see CR Kelly, 'Enmeshment As a Theory of Compliance' (2005) 37 *NYU Journal of International Law and Politics* 303. For an application of Koh's 'transnational legal process', see WS Dodge, 'The Helms-Burton Act and Transnational Legal Process' (1997) 20 *Hastings International and Comparative Law Review* 713, 723–28. On the mutual interpenetration of domestic law and international law, along with a discussion on competing monist and dualist theories, see Malanczuk, above n 150 at 63–71.

[167] See, eg: A Chayes and AH Chayes, *The New Sovereignty: Compliance with International Regulatory Agreements* (Cambridge, Harvard University Press, 1995); R Goodman and D Jinks, 'Toward an Institutional Theory of Sovereignty' (2003) 55 *Stanford Law Review* 1749; HH Koh, 'The 1998 Frankel Lecture: Bringing International Law Home' (1998) 35 *Houston Law Review* 623, 626–27; HH Koh, 'Why Do Nations Obey International Law?' (1997) 106 *Yale Law Journal* 2599, 2645–58; HH Koh, 'Transnational Legal Process' (1996) 75 *Nebraska Law Review* 181; A Wendt, 'Collective Identity Formation and the International State' (1994) 88 *American Political Science Review* 384, 384–85.

Furthermore, State responsibility repertoire remains endowed with a *sui generis* scheme of enforcement, reciprocity, and countermeasures,[168] a dominant feature absent from domestic systems. Whilst the law governing State responsibility is neither common law nor civil law-derived, but 'purely and simply international' in character,[169] the success of importing concepts derived from those traditions into State responsibility repertoire will remain commensurate with efforts to preserve the integrity of the rules being transplanted. For instance, attempts to import the contractual notion of 'efficient breach' into international law should recognise that common law courts have correspondingly developed the notion of promissory estoppel to shield economically disadvantaged parties; its objectives should also be taken into account and ultimately reflected in the transplantation process.[170] Similarly, before importing the rationale underlying certain domestic tort claims – be it by analogising terrorism to tort law or otherwise – it must be recalled that courts frequently engage in social/public policy analysis when adjudicating alleged violations. Domestic legal systems contain countervailing norms, fictions or practices that ultimately offset the negative aspects engendered by the abusive or misplaced application of legal rules in specific circumstances. This approach should inform any reform of State responsibility after 9/11 and, similarly to sheltering economically disadvantaged parties under municipal law, aligns with the broader objective of protecting weaker States.[171] Whilst it is commonplace for some municipal importations to be transformed throughout the course of transplantation,[172] other transplants can lead to spectacular miscarriages of legal borrowing. A salient transplantation failure undoubtedly resided in the much-decried inver-

[168] See D Alland, 'International Responsibility and Sanctions: Self-Defence and Countermeasures in the ILC Codification of Rules Governing International Responsibility' in M Spinedi and B Simma (eds), *United Nations Codification of State Responsibility* (New York, Oceana Publications, 1987) 143–97.

[169] PS Rao, 'International Crimes and State Responsibility' in Ragazzi, above n 11 at 67 (also citing JR Crawford, 'First Report on State Responsibility', UN Doc A/CN.4/490/Add.1 (1998) at para 60(iv)).

[170] For background discussion on estoppel, also termed 'detrimental reliance', see MB Metzger and MJ Phillips, 'Promissory Estoppel and the Evolution of Contract Law' (1989) 18 *American Business Law Journal* 139. The possible importation of the 'efficient breach' doctrine into State responsibility for failing to prevent terrorism is fully engaged below in section V.B).

[171] This objective is also mirrored in the 'no-harm' principle as articulated by the ILC. See, eg: C Votava, 'The Non-Navigational Uses of International Watercourses' (1990) 84 *ASIL Proceedings* 228, 235–36 (noting that the ILC declared 'that there is such a rule, which is that one state shall not cause harm to another state', expounding that 'it perhaps is not such a bad idea for the no-harm rule to prevail over equitable utilization, in order to protect weaker states and states in vulnerable positions from the exercise of power by larger states', and extending this principle to long-lasting transborder pollution).

[172] See, eg: Crawford, above n 13 at 21. See also: Separate Opinion of Judge Simma in *Application of the Interim Accord of 13 September 1995 (the former Yugoslav Republic of Macedonia v Greece)*, Judgment of 5 December, *ICJ* (2011) at 4, para 13, available at www.icj-cij.org/docket/files/142/16829.pdf. Judge Simma discusses the defence based on the *exceptio non adimpleti contractus* and postulates that

> [t]he question is, of course, the transferability of such a concept developed *in foro domestico* to the international legal plane, respectively the amendments that it will have to undergo in order for such a general principle to be able to play a constructive role also at the international level.

sion of the dichotomy involving obligations of conduct and result into State responsibility repertoire, as originally spearheaded by Roberto Ago and ultimately discarded by the ILC in its finalised text.[173]

Rules should not be selectively displaced and distorted into the international context simply to cater to policy objectives in the 'war' on terror without regard for procedural or substantial safeguards, surrounding legal devices, and inextricable features underlying the norms in question. Accordingly, some commentators highlight the difficulty of importing municipal law analogies into the State responsibility framework, especially those rooted in contract and tort law.[174] This discrepancy is sometimes explained by reference to State responsibility's 'non-jurisdictional' nature, which entails that unlike under domestic legal structures, the application and enforcement of State responsibility rarely engages jurisdictional mechanisms, rather usually occurring within the context of disparate diplomatic relations.[175]

Nevertheless, considering municipal law analogies and importations remains quite illuminating when seeking original solutions to difficult State responsibility issues. In fact, many mechanisms found under State responsibility are mirrored in domestic legal systems. Writing specifically about State responsibility from an international perspective in 1988, Philip Allott recognised this mutual interpenetration. He observed that 'Responsibility is used in municipal law to separate wrongdoing by a person whose mind functions in an abnormal way from the consequences of the wrongdoing', and that 'The concept of responsibility is also used in municipal law to deal with certain problems of attribution or imputation, especially where there is not a direct connection between the wrongdoer and the wrongful act'.[176] Thus, it would probably be much to the dismay of Lauterpacht[177] that contemporary scholarship is replete with discussions on whether municipal law analogies can inform State responsibility,[178] an

[173] See, eg: 'Report of the International Law Commission on the Work of Its Fifty-First Session', UN GAOR, 54th Sess, Supp No 10, UN Doc A/54/10 (1999) at 119–34; B Simma, 'The Work of the International Law Commission at Its Fifty-First Session' (1999) 68 *Nordic Journal of International Law* 293, 301–02; Combacau, above n 18 at 194, 198, 202; R Provost, 'Introduction' in R Provost (ed), *State Responsibility in International Law* (Aldershot, Ashgate/Dartmouth, 2002) xiii. But see: R Pisillo-Mazzeschi, 'The Due Diligence Rule and the Nature of International Responsibility of States' (1992) 35 *German Yearbook of International Law* 9, reprinted in Provost, above n 173 at 129–39 (using the erroneously-imported distinction to invoke 'obligations of diligent conduct' and 'obligations of result').

[174] See Provost, 'Introduction', above n 173 at xiii–xiv. Terrorism has also sometimes been analogised with a 'tort' under the global legal order. See, eg: ER Pollock, 'Terrorism as a Tort in Violation of the Law of Nations' (1982–83) 6 *Fordham International Law Journal* 236.

[175] Provost, 'Introduction', above n 173 at xiv. See also generally: M Waibel, 'The Diplomatic Channel' in Crawford et al, above n 106 at 1085–97.

[176] P Allott, 'State Responsibility and the Unmaking of International Law' (1988) 29 *Harvard International Law Journal* 3, 12–13.

[177] See, eg: Provost, 'Introduction', above n 173 at xiii (noting the awkwardness of borrowing from municipal tort law or delictual responsibility and citing Lauterpacht, above n 141).

[178] See, eg: the sources cited in V-J Proulx, 'International Responsibility Today: Essays in Memory of Oscar Schachter. L'émergence de la communauté internationale dans la responsabilité des Etats' (2007) 18 *EJIL* 581, 589 fn 27.

exercise that seems increasingly attractive with the emergence of non-State transnational actors and the need to better integrate them into international legal frameworks.

Interestingly, some commentators observe that transnational counterterrorism strategies have unnecessarily oscillated between domestic criminal law and international law models. Absent from most post-9/11 legal rhetoric, however, is the possible importation of torts-derived concepts to inform available international legal responses to terrorism.[179] Quite relevantly, one author notes the suspicious absence of the 'civil law of torts' in most discussions surrounding counterterrorism, underscoring that 'Concepts in civil law may be particularly useful in designing effective responses to terrorism, including further development of civil litigation against terrorism'.[180] Others echo similar considerations, opining that 'International responsibility occupies a smaller niche within the realm of the law of tort'.[181] Certain scholars similarly emphasise the inherent compatibility between secondary norms of responsibility and the rules of civil procedure under domestic common law regimes, which 'sets forth a distinctive set of rules that apply across the various substantive areas of law – although the common law still distinguishes civil procedure from criminal and administrative procedure and thus does not treat procedure as a fully homogeneous field'.[182] There is no reason why such reasoning should not extend to both State responsibility and the mechanics for establishing State accountability regarding the acts of non-State actors. In fact, this is already a reality.[183]

The case for working with municipal law analogies, especially those derived from tort law, becomes exceedingly compelling when confronted with significant international practice borrowing from that normative scheme, particularly in the field of State responsibility.[184] Whilst the Iran-US Claims Tribunal itself is

[179] See, eg: Higgins, above n 21 at 155–59 (invoking the tort-inspired notion of 'standard of care' in her chapter dealing with State responsibility). See also: Duffy, above n 22 at 266.

[180] J Kraska, 'Torts and Terror: Rethinking Deterrence Models and Catastrophic Terrorist Attack' (2007) 22 *American University International Law Review* 361, 382–83 (also remarking that 'The application of tort theory to strategic nuclear doctrine offers value in rebuilding deterrence against catastrophic nuclear terrorism'). See also: ibid, at 383 fn 89 *in fine*. Others adopt a more philosophical stance when dealing with the concept of 'responsibility' as more broadly understood in the legal discipline, lamenting lawyers' overemphasis on criminal law at the detriment of civil and public law. See, eg: P Cane, *Responsibility in Law and Morality* (Oxford, Hart Publishing, 2002).

[181] Rigaux, above n 133 at 81.

[182] D Bodansky and JR Crook, 'Introduction and Overview (Symposium: The ILC's State Responsibility Articles)' (2002) 96 *AJIL* 773, 780 fn 51. This position was eventually discarded by the ILC Special Rapporteur. See Crawford, above n 163 at 876 (also citing D Ibbetson, *A Historical Introduction to the Law of Obligations* (Oxford, OUP, 2001)).

[183] As both foundational publicists and contemporary scholars have underscored, municipal legal principles have had a profound influence on State responsibility. See, eg: Lauterpacht, above n 141 at 134–35; DD Caron, 'The Basis of Responsibility: Attribution and Other Trans-Substantive Rules' in RB Lillich and D Magraw (eds), *The Iran-United States Claims Tribunal: Its Contribution to the Law of State Responsibility* (Irvington-on-Hudson, Transnational Publishers, 1998) 109 at 160.

[184] Some describe State responsibility as an international law of tort governing relations between States. See, eg: GT Yates, 'State Responsibility for Nonwealth Injuries to Aliens in the Postwar Era'

barred from settling most disputes arising from torts, related jurisprudence is replete with references to tort law.[185] The UN Compensation Commission, mandated with overseeing reparations flowing from Iraq's responsibility for its unlawful invasion of Kuwait, also evinced international practice drawing heavily on domestic legal influences (including seeking guidance from other international remedial bodies applying those same domestic standards).[186] In fact, the most dominant influences on the implementation of the Compensation Commission derived both from the Iran-US Claims Tribunal and American mass tort claims administration.[187] In devising adequate legal models to process the impressive volume of claims, the architects of the Commission 'looked to U.S. mass tort claims administration which is absolutely applicable', in areas as diverse as environmental damage and liability of manufacturers for defective breast implants and other products.[188] There is every indication that the Commission's legal and operational frameworks were 'using some of the techniques and arts of sampling that were developed in those [asbestos and Dalkon Shield] cases'.[189] The Commission in large part elected the American mass tort claims model as an incubator for international reparation because, at the time of its inception, it was believed that such framework would prove more effective than the arbitral structures espoused by the Iran-US Claims Tribunal.[190] As a

in RB Lillich (ed), *International Law of State Responsibility for Injuries to Aliens* (Charlottesville, University Press of Virgina, 1983) 213. See also: S Sucharitkul, 'State Responsibility and International Liability under International Law' (1996) 18 *Loyola LA International and Comparative Law Journal* 821, 839 (equating 'breaches of all types of international obligations under State responsibility' with 'delicts, torts, or crimes under international law').

[185] By way of example, consider *Roeder v Islamic Republic of Iran* (2002) 195 F Supp 2d 140, 184 (DDC), aff'd 333 F.3d 228 (DC Cir 2003), cert denied, 124 S Ct 2836 (2004) especially at 144. However, it is possible to infer from the Iran-US Claims Tribunal's own jurisprudence that it is habilitated to settle claims involving torts, as long as they relate to property rights in the same manner as an expropriation. See, eg: *Short v Islamic Republic of Iran* (1987) 16 Iran-US Claims Tribunal Reports 76 at 78, para 11; *International Systems and Controls Corp v Industrial Development and Renovation Organization of Iran* (1986) 12 Iran-US Claims Tribunal Reports 239 at paras 94–95; *Yeager v Islamic Republic of Iran* (1987) 17 Iran-US Claims Tribunal Reports 92 at 99.

[186] For more background on the Commission's work, see C Payne and P Sand, *Gulf War Reparations and the UN Compensation Commission* (New York, OUP, 2011); JR Crook, 'The United Nations Compensation Commission: A New Structure to Enforce State Responsibility' (1993) *AJIL* 144.

[187] See, eg: LC Owen, 'Between Iraq and a Hard Place: The U.N. Compensation Commission and Its Treatment of Gulf War Claims' (1998) 31 *Vanderbilt Journal of Transnational Law* 499, 514; K Myers, 'Gulf War Continuing for U.S. Lawyers: Attorneys Battle Iraq in Courtrooms over Billions in Invasion-Related Damages', *National Law Journal*, 20 June 1994 at A1; CM Dombek, 'The Twilight Zone of International Arbitration' (1995) 21 *Litigation* 42.

[188] Myers, above n 187 at A17.

[189] NC Ulmer, 'The Gulf War Claims Institution' (1993) 10 *Journal of International Arbitration* 85, 88. See also: RJ Bettauer, 'The United Nations Compensation Commission –Developments since October 1992' (1995) 89 *AJIL* 416, 418–19; E Schmitt, 'Righting Wrongs of War: Billions in Claims against Iraq', *New York Times*, 18 November 1994 at B9.

[190] See S Mufson, 'The Long Quest for Iraqi Compensation', *Washington Post*, 7 April 1991 at H7. See also: G Townsend, 'The Iraq Claims Process: A Progress Report on the United Nations Compensation Commission & U.S. Remedies' (1995) 17 *Loyola LA International and Comparative Law Journal* 973, 986.

result, the Commission's expedited procedures borrowed directly from US mass tort theory and litigation.[191]

This further lends credence to the idea that domestic law analogies can sometimes play a determinant role in the progressive development of State responsibility.[192] Whilst there is little resistance amongst leading publicists to the idea that 'international responsibility has largely followed a private law model', it is widely perceived as undeveloped from the standpoint of interests private law may need to fulfil in this context (ie the issues to be addressed when tort claims are adjudicated).[193] In addition to the conceptual incongruities associated with private law causation identified in chapter 3, section II, further uncertainty surrounds the questions of extinctive prescription[194] and joint and several liability.[195] Thus, whilst tort law and other domestic legal principles directly informed the implementation of State responsibility and the handling of claims under that regime, such importations were not without problems as seen both in the records of the UN Compensation Commission[196] and the Eritrea-Ethiopia Claims Commission.[197] Further clarity is needed and this monograph strives to lend assistance in remedying the conceptual dearth.

B) Domestic Law Analogies: Moving Towards Strict Liability

The State responsibility regime set forth by the ILC's *Articles* is indeed ripe for analogising or importing domestic law principles. Whilst notions extracted from domestic legal regimes, especially strict liability, might inform the international legal analysis, these notions may themselves become subsequently altered

[191] See D Shelton, 'Righting Wrongs: Reparations in the Articles on State Responsibility' (2002) 96 *AJIL* 833, 856; DJ Bederman, 'The United Nations Compensation Commission and the Tradition of International Claims Settlement' (1994) 27 *NYU Journal of International Law & Politics* 1, 19.

[192] See more generally: W Friedmann, 'The Uses of "General Principles" in the Development of International Law' (1963) 57 *AJIL* 279, 281; Separate Opinion of Judge McNair in *International Status of South West Africa*, Advisory Opinion of 11 July, *ICJ Reports* (1950) 128 at 148 ('International law has recruited and continues to recruit many of its rules and institutions from private systems of law').

[193] A Nollkaemper, 'Constitutionalization and the Unity of the Law of International Responsibility' (2009) 16 *Indiana Journal of Global Legal Studies* 535, 560.

[194] But see: H Hobér, *Extinctive Prescription and Applicable Law in Interstate Arbitration* (Uppsala, Iustus, 2001).

[195] See, eg: JE Noyes and BD Smith, 'State Responsibility and the Principle of Joint and Several Liability' (1988) 13 *Yale Journal of international Law* 225.

[196] See, eg: DD Caron, 'The UNCC and the Search for Practical Justice' in RB Lillich (ed), *The United Nations Compensation Commission* (Irvington, Transnational, 1995) 367 at 377.

[197] See, eg: W Kidane, 'Civil Liability for Violations of International Law: The Jurisprudence of the Eritrea-Ethiopia Claims Commission in The Hague' (2007) 25 *Wisconsin International Law Journal* 23, 37–38. For its part, the ECHR has had to develop its own *lex specialis* on several related matters. See M Pellonpää, 'Individual Reparation Claims under the European Convention on Human Rights' in A Randelzhofer and C Tomuschat (eds), *State Responsibility and the Individual: Reparation in Instances of Grave Violations of Human Rights* (The Hague, Nijhoff, 1999) 109–29.

by the importation process as is often the case with domestic legal transplants.[198] Moreover, in the context of national tort law, it is sometimes more efficient to opt for a rule of strict liability over negligence or fault-based norms.[199] In entertaining the adoption of a positive theory of strict liability in domestic settings, the 'choice between strict liability and negligence depends on the degree to which there is a reciprocal exchange of risk among actors, and the extent to which benefits, in addition to risks, are externalized'.[200] Transposing this line of analysis, host-States are often better positioned to thwart terrorism than civilians or victim-States, thereby militating in favour of a liability rule emphasising the privileged rapport that a host-State entertains with its territory.

In the spirit of *Corfu Channel*, a State's exclusive control over its own territory informs the knowledge it has, or should have, of possible terrorist activities percolating therein. Territorial control then in turn directly affects evidentiary matters, should a claim of indirect responsibility arise. Typically, a wrongful State will be better situated in complying with evidentiary standards than the wronged State following a terrorist attack. Consequently, more latitude will – or should – generally be allotted to the aggrieved State regarding the burden of proof and related issues. *Corfu Channel* is quite instructive:

> [T]he fact of this exclusive territorial control exercised by a State within its frontiers has a bearing upon the methods of proof available to establish the knowledge of that State as to such events. By reason of this exclusive control, the other State, the victim of a breach of international law, is often unable to furnish direct proof of facts giving rise to responsibility. Such a State should be allowed a more liberal recourse to inferences of fact and circumstantial evidence. This indirect evidence is admitted in all systems of law, and its use is recognized by international decisions. It must be regarded as of special weight when it is based on a series of facts linked together and leading logically to a single conclusion.[201]

Building on this holding in the *Oil Platforms* case, the US argued that,

> [p]articularly in light of Iran's exclusive control of the territory in the Faw area from which the missile that hit *Sea Isle City* was fired, this evidence fully satisfies the burden of establishing that Iran is responsible for the attack on the *Sea Isle City*.[202]

However, the ICJ ultimately rejected this view.

[198] See, eg: Crawford, above n 13 at 21; Crawford, above n 163 at 878. Terrorism has also sometimes been construed as a tort under the global legal order. See, eg: Pollock, above n 174 at 236–60. See also generally: Kraska, above n 180.

[199] On this issue, generally, and its application in domestic law, see, eg: S Shavell, 'Strict Liability versus Negligence' (1980) 9 *Journal of Legal Studies* 1.

[200] KN Hylton, 'A Positive Theory of Strict Liability' (2008) 4 *Review of Law and Economics* 153.

[201] *Corfu Channel*, above n 47 at 182. For a discussion of this holding and of surrounding issues, see R Teitelbaum, 'Recent Fact-Finding Developments at the International Court of Justice' (2007) 6 *The Law and Practice of International Courts and Tribunals* 119, 135–39.

[202] Rejoinder of the United States in *Oil Platforms (Islamic Republic of Iran v USA)*, 23 March 2001 at 36, available at www.icj-cij.org/docket/files/90/8634.pdf.

In the 1970s, State responsibility became increasingly akin to the tort concept of negligence or, at least, primarily governed by principles of due diligence and reasonableness.[203] The underlying reasonableness of a response vis-à-vis an original wrongful act guided much of the Security Council's attitude in legitimising reprisals against host-States. This entailed a rigorous evaluation of the host-State's failure to prevent a cross-border attack, along with the significance/ramifications of the terrorist strike itself.[204]

In this respect, commentators raised interesting questions – akin to the tort concept of contributory negligence – regarding the aggrieved State's own conduct: 'Why could not the state have defended itself against these guerilla activities by measures of defense adopted on its own territory?'[205] However, it is unclear whether a victim-State's contributory negligence effectively weighs in the balance for the purposes of establishing responsibility and imposing countermeasures. In *Corfu Channel*, the facts indicated that the UK vessels were cognisant of potential dangers in the channel when they passed through it. Irrespective of this knowledge and the UK's actions, the Court held that Albania's responsibility was not attenuated or mitigated by the sole virtue of the UK's contributory negligence.[206]

Under the new State responsibility paradigm, the Council has distanced itself from its earlier posture of reasonableness and could arguably move towards a more radical conception of indirect responsibility, perhaps embodying strict liability undertones. The objectives enshrined in resolutions 1368 and 1373 might be better served by short-circuiting the concept of attribution altogether in the context of transnational terrorism. Presumably, combating terrorism by all 'necessary steps', to invoke post-9/11 Council parlance, also encompasses 'legal' steps. For various reasons explored subsequently, there is no reason to discard *ipso facto* the prospect of shifting both a rebuttable presumption of indirect responsibility and the onus of refuting that legal inference onto States having failed to prevent transnational terrorism. The proposed strict liability framework is subject to a few caveats and motivated by several policy considerations.

In his seminal doctoral dissertation and other works, Lauterpacht perhaps erroneously correlated the role and place of fault in State responsibility with the notion of absolute responsibility.[207] This nexus is probably better explained by

[203] Hints of this permeate Bowett's seminal work on Israeli reprisals in the 1960s, above n 56 at 20–21, especially regarding the Council's partial acceptance of 'reasonable' reprisals.

[204] On the role of fault in State failures to act in conformity with international obligations, see Christenson, above n 3 at 315–16; P-M Dupuy, 'The International Law of State Responsibility: Revolution or Evolution?' (1989) 11 *Michigan Journal of International Law* 105, 109–12.

[205] Bowett, above n 56 at 20–21. On the question of contributory negligence as it pertains to State responsibility, see generally: DJ Bederman, 'Contributory Fault and State Responsibility' (1990) 30 *Virginia Journal of International Law* 335; A Moutier-Lopet, 'Contribution to the Injury' in Crawford et al, above n 106 at 639–45.

[206] See *Corfu Channel*, above n 47 at 35–36. On the question of due diligence as it pertains to State responsibility, see generally: Pisillo-Mazzeschi, above n 173.

[207] See, eg: Lauterpacht, above n 141 at 134–43; E Lauterpacht (ed), *International Law: Being the Collected Papers of Hersch Lauterpacht (Vol 1: The General Works)* (Cambridge, CUP, 1970) 398–

Lauterpacht's belief that absolute liability stems from the positivists' resistance to importing the domestically-derived concept of fault into State responsibility.[208] Brownlie rightly highlighted Lauterpacht's shortcomings in grasping the common law notion of strict liability, along with the international law-derived idea of objective responsibility. Moreover, it seems that both notions fit neatly within core parameters of State responsibility:

> There's good reason for believing that many publicists, including Lauterpacht, have failed to understand that what in common law terms is called strict liability, and what in the law of nations is denominated objective responsibility, are perfectly compatible with elements of knowledge, advertence, or control.[209]

Of particular relevance is the role of strict liability in civil law systems. Whilst fault unquestionably pervades civilian liability systems, namely by infusing some domestic legal presumptions, certain categories of cases also rely on different manifestations of strict liability.[210]

Under Québec's experience for instance, products liability law offers more of a mixed or complex model. By way of example, Article 1473 of the *Civil Code of Québec* provides that

> [t]he manufacturer, distributor or supplier of a movable property is not liable to reparation for injury caused by a safety defect in the property if he proves that the victim knew or could have known of the defect, or could have foreseen the injury.

The provision further specifies:

> Nor is he liable to reparation if he proves that, according to the state of knowledge at the time that he manufactured, distributed or supplied the property, the existence of the defect could not have been known, and that he was not neglectful of his duty to provide information when he became aware of the defect.[211]

The duty enshrined in the second paragraph of this provision has been affirmed by the Supreme Court of Canada in *Bank of Montreal v Bail Ltée*.[212] Upon first glance, the spirit animating this provision proves difficult to import into State responsibility repertoire or, at least, appears inimical to some tenets of the indirect responsibility paradigm explored above. However, a more focused analysis reveals that the manufacturer, distributor or supplier must demonstrate that the existence of the defect could not have been known in order to seek exoneration.

401; H Lauterpacht, 'Règles générales du droit de la paix' (1937-IV) 62 *Recueil des Cours* 95, 359–64.

208 See, eg: Brownlie, above n 21 at 3.

209 ibid, at 44.

210 See, eg: A Tunc (ed), *International Encyclopaedia of Comparative Law: Vol XI: Torts* (The Hague, Nijhoff, 1983) 48–49, ch 5; FH Lawson, *Negligence in the Civil Law* (Oxford, Clarendon Press, 1950) 43–50; H Mazeaud et al (eds), *Traité théorique et pratique de la responsabilité civile délictuelle et contractuelle (Tomes I and II)*, 6th edn (Paris, Montchrestien, 1965–83) ch 4; FH Lawson and BS Markesinis, *Tortious Liability for Unintentional Harms in the Common Law and the Civil Law (Vol 1)* (Cambridge, CUP, 1982) ch 4.

211 *Civil Code of Québec*, RSQ ch 64.

212 [1992] 2 SCR 554.

Hence, this provision operates on a reversal of the burden of proof which, when transposed to counterterrorism is triggered by strict liability rationale for present purposes, will become the cornerstone of the proposed model advocated below. The policy impetus for advocating a model of strict liability for failing to prevent terrorism purports to avoid transferring an inordinate burden of risk to innocent victims, just as Article 1473 concerns itself with sheltering the consumer from undue risks associated with defective products. Therefore, the burden of precaution in preventing terrorism falls squarely, or predominantly, upon States.[213]

Conversely, in tort law under common law systems, strict liability has sometimes been construed as absolute liability. Following this approach, a manufacturer cannot subtract himself from his obligation to the buyer once harm is done, save in circumstances where causation cannot be established. Generally, defences are not available under a rationale of absolute liability.[214] However, there exists a second influential school of thought on the subject, purporting to demonstrate that several defences exist against a claim of strict liability and that the pivotal device in such litigation resides in the onus shift from plaintiff to defendant.[215] Several parallels may also be drawn from Canadian municipal law, as the Supreme Court's jurisprudence faithfully embodies this second strand of liability by recognising a due diligence defence against an offence of strict liability.[216] Reiterating Lauterpacht's misapplication of absolute liability and underscoring that 'strict liability is only relatively strict, not absolute', Brownlie aptly captured the above argument: 'Strict liability is essentially a *prima facie* responsibility, and various defences or justifications may be available; it is not to be confused with absolute liability for which there can be no mode of exculpation'.[217] However, whilst it has acquired traction in certain theoretical accounts and been invoked across a wide array of fields, sometimes indiscriminately, the notion of strict liability has failed to achieve any sort of consensus or

[213] It is acknowledged that this comparison – not the substance of the ultimate proposal and transplantation – is partially flawed. Analogising products liability to preventing terrorism is misleading as, for one thing, States do not derive profit from terrorist activity (unlike the manufacturer of goods), though they may benefit from tolerating terrorists as a tool of foreign policy.

[214] See, eg: CA Clark, 'Howard v. Allstate Insurance Co. – Louisiana's Attempt at Comparative Causation' (1989) 49 *Louisiana Law Review* 1163, 1166. See also: Brownlie, above n 21 at 44. This argument has also been advanced vis-à-vis strict liability in certain domestic legal fields, such as financial auditing. See, eg: LA Cunningham, 'Choosing Gatekeepers: The Financial Statement Insurance Alternative to Auditor Liability' (2004) 52 *UCLA Law Review* 413, 425; F Partnoy, 'Barbarians at the Gatekeepers?: A Proposal for a Modified Strict Liability Regime' (2001) 79 *Washington University Law Quarterly* 491, 540–46 (both arguing that a strict liability regime would eliminate the due diligence defence in its entirety).

[215] See, eg: ibid; DG Owen, 'Products Liability: User Misconduct Defenses' (2000) 52 *South Carolina Law Review* 1. See also: WL Prosser, *Handbook of the Law of Torts*, 4th edn (St Paul, West Pub Co, 1974) ch 13.

[216] See, eg: *R v Rube* [1992] 3 SCR 159; *Lévis (City) v Tétreault*; *Lévis (City) v 2629-4470 Québec Inc* [2006] 1 SCR 420.

[217] See Brownlie, above n 21 at 44, also underscoring that

> [t]he essence of strict liability in common law is the shift of the burden of proof and, as the dictum of Blackburn J. in *Rylands* v. *Fletcher* indicates with absolute clarity, the defender (defendant) has a good range of defences by way of discharging the burden of exculpation.

uniform application in international law.[218] In fact, it has even engendered practical inconsistencies in domestic legal settings.[219] Ultimately, the model espoused in this study is somewhat influenced by the second conception of strict liability discussed above, although it likely rests in some middle ground between what has sometimes been envisaged as absolute liability under State responsibility, on one hand, and strict liability and vicarious liability under domestic legal structures, on the other.[220]

A dose of political pragmatism seems apposite before moving on to the implementation of the proposed model, as promoting compliance with counterterrorism obligations is predicated on risk assessment and risk management at the domestic level. As seen in chapter one, both these approaches trickle down to States in making budgetary decisions regarding counterterrorism, in establishing domestic law enforcement priorities and, more importantly, in deciding whether or not to divert their resources and policy infrastructures towards the fulfilment of specific international obligations. Obviously, these realities must be balanced against the primary rules regarding prevention developed in *Corfu Channel* and exemplified by the *Tehran Hostages* Case. Moreover, keeping in mind the analogical approach espoused above, such underlying considerations are also mirrored in domestic legal orders. For instance, allocation of resources and manpower in meeting State obligations features prominently in the Supreme Court of Canada's own jurisprudence on the liability of public authorities. In the *Brown* Case, the Court held that the province owed a duty of care to users of its public highways.[221] In that case, Royal Canadian Mounted Police officers failed to respond in a timely fashion to reports of icy highway conditions following road accidents, primarily because the provincial Highways Department was still operating under the summer maintenance schedule. The charge levelled against the relevant public authorities therefore hinged on negligence in a manner reminiscent of the failure to act imputed to Iran in *Tehran Hostages*. Whilst the Court recognised the primary duty owed to the public at large, it absolved the government from liability on the basis that maintaining the summer schedule was truly a decision residing at the governmental level. Its rationale involved classical policy concerns regarding financial and human resources in meeting obligations, along with negotiations with government unions.[222] This representative sampling of a dominant legal trend arising in

[218] See K Zemanek, 'State Responsibility and Liability' in W Lang et al (eds), *Environmental Protection and International Law* (London, Nijhoff/Graham & Trotman, 1991) 187 at 193; TA Berwick, 'Responsibility and Liability for Environmental Damage: A Roadmap for International Environmental Regimes' (1998) 10 *Georgetown International Environmental Law Review* 257, 263.

[219] On the lack of consistency surrounding the notion of strict liability in a specific judicial context, see PM Gerhart, 'The Death of Strict Liability' (2008) 56 *Buffalo Law Review* 245, 304.

[220] See the previous comments on vicarious liability, above ch 2 nn 45, 164; ch 3 nn 144–53, 159–59 and accompanying text.

[221] *Brown v British Columbia (Minister of Transportation and Highways)* [1994] 1 SCR 420.

[222] On these issues in the Canadian context, see, eg: JA Smillie, 'Liability of Public Authorities for Negligence' (1985) 23 *University of Western Ontario Law Review* 213; LN Klar, 'The Supreme Court of Canada: Extending the Tort Liability of Public Authorities' (199) 28 *Alberta Law Review* 648.

domestic common law jurisdictions clearly points in the direction of a context-sensitive, policy-oriented analysis. On one hand, such national judicial pronouncements signal a palpable compatibility with the topic under study in that, in fashion redolent of the *Tehran Hostages* reasoning, the language underpinning this jurisprudence correlates the notion of 'taking reasonable steps' with the fulfilment of the obligation at hand.[223] Put another way, reasonableness remains a cardinal focal point in the factual inquiry. On the other hand, when transposed to the international context, the analysis undoubtedly becomes more complex by virtue of the host-State's capacity – *and* policy inclination – to act and prevent transnational terrorism. With this in mind, the study now turns to the concrete implementation of the strict liability-inspired deterrence model prefaced above.

V. MITIGATING TENSIONS: IMPLEMENTING A MODEL INSPIRED BY STRICT LIABILITY

Risk assessment and management will constitute running themes throughout any theoretically informed inquiry involving the melding of international legal questions and counterterrorism policy. This line of argument becomes particularly evident when considering modern State responsibility, paired with the intricate challenge of devising liability regimes suited to the increasingly sophisticated attacks of non-State actors.[224] Hence, the rationale driving the proposed reform is to provide the *right* incentives to States in combating terrorism. For instance, enforcement measures undertaken under the UN Charter can have deleterious effects on the populations of the targeted States, much in the same fashion that disproportionate countermeasures under State responsibility can engender devastating results for the peoples inhabiting the sanctuary States; all without necessarily inducing the corresponding governments to comply with their international obligations. It follows that 'The objective of enforcement measures is to attempt to provoke a change in the behaviour of the leaders of a country, not to harm innocent people',[225] a policy quest that should be transposed mutatis mutandis to the realm of countermeasures under State responsibility repertoire.

Hence, the objective underpinning a reversal in onus onto the sanctuary State is not only to transfer the burden of proof but also to shift desirable incentives to it. Not surprisingly, generating incentives to ensure State compliance and

[223] See, eg: *Brown* Case, above n 221 at 22 (holding that the State 'is only responsible for taking reasonable steps to prevent injury').

[224] See, eg: SR Ratner, 'Is International Law Impartial?', Unpublished Manuscript, 15 September 2004 at 22, available at http://ssrn.com/abstract=643821 (also citing P Daillier and A Pellet, *Droit international public (Nguyen Quoc Dinh)*, 5th edn (Paris, LGDJ, 1994) 618).

[225] C Dominicé, 'The International Responsibility of the United Nations for Injuries Resulting from Non-Military Enforcement Measures' in Ragazzi, above n 11 at 369.

cooperation under international law pervades rationalist thinking.[226] As mentioned previously, the proposed regime could be tantamount to a compromise between sacrificing a host-State's territorial integrity/sovereignty and upholding its dignity on the international scene. Such model clearly does not suit all areas related to State responsibility, which coexist on a continuum. Certain inter-State conventional breaches likely rest at one end of the spectrum and could never attract a rule of strict liability. At the other end of the continuum, perhaps not as far as the duty to prevent genocide, the obligation to prevent terrorism resides.[227]

Unlike under contract law, when addressing the latter area of State responsibility, the international community often engages in the objective of saving lives and protecting civilians. Moreover, terrorism is a crime so intrinsically repugnant to humanity that it arguably warrants deploying stringent accountability schemes.[228] Understandably, some authors query whether it would have been wiser to include terrorism within the framework of ILC discussions on international crimes, so as to formulate 'increased State responsibility'.[229]

As a corollary, whilst injury is not a constitutive element of responsibility under the ILC's *Articles*, there is undoubtedly a correlation between the nature and magnitude of the harm inflicted by terrorist strikes and the reparation that may be sought under international law. This calculus has a direct incidence on the mechanics of state responsibility: 'Clearly, the amount of reparation will vary according to the quantum of harm'.[230] When dealing with terrorism-induced harm to civilian life and property, appropriate reparation levels owed to the State hosting such individuals and property, or to the State formally espousing their claims,[231] might very well be commensurate with the injury actually sustained.

[226] See, eg: P-H Verdier, 'Cooperative States: International Relations, State Responsibility and the Problem of Custom' (2002) 42 *Virginia Journal of International Law* 839, 843–44, 846, 849, 852–54; JL Dunoff and JP Trachtman, 'Economic Analysis of International Law' (1999) 24 *Yale Law Journal* 1, 32–33.

[227] There were hints of this reasoning in Lauterpacht's remarks in 1955: 'The comprehensive notion of an international delinquency ranges from ordinary breaches of treaty obligations, involving no more than pecuniary compensation, to violations of International Law amounting to a criminal act in the generally accepted meaning of the term'. See Lauterpacht, above n 143 at 339; Lauterpacht, above n 207 at 349–57.

[228] One commentator delivers a vivid testimonial as to the international urgency in combating this crime. See K Kittichaisaree, *International Criminal Law* (Oxford, OUP, 2001) 127. See also: Declaration on Measures to Eliminate International Terrorism, GA Res 49/60, UN GAOR, 49th Sess, Supp No 49, UN Doc A/RES/49/60 (1994) (acknowledging that terrorist attacks violate human rights principles); GA Res 40/61, UN GAOR, 40th Sess, Supp No 53, UN Doc A/Res/40/61 (1985) 301 (recognising that terrorism 'endanger[s] or take[s] innocent human lives, jeopardize[s] fundamental freedoms and seriously impair[s] the dignity of human beings').

[229] Y Daudet, 'International Action against State Terrorism' in R Higgins and M Flory (eds), *Terrorism and International Law* (London, Routledge, 1997) 201 at 202.

[230] Shelton, above n 191 at 846.

[231] See generally: *Case Concerning Ahmadou Sadio Diallo (Republic of Guinea v Democratic Republic of the Congo), Preliminary Objections*, Judgment of 24 May, *ICJ* (2007) at 17, para 39, available at www.icj-cij.org/docket/files/103/13856.pdf (underscoring that 'the scope *ratione materiae* of diplomatic protection, originally limited to alleged violations of the minimum standard of treatment of aliens, has subsequently widened to include, *inter alia*, internationally guaranteed

The original territorial State has to cease harbouring and supporting terrorists on its territory, pursuant to ILC Article 30(a); it may also be called upon to provide assurances/guarantees of non-repetition by virtue of Article 30(b), whilst also effectuating reparation proportionate with the harm inflicted pursuant to Articles 35 and 36 which, incidentally, may involve restitution or compensation.[232] This principle can be traced back to the *Chorzów Factory* Case, which differentiated the rights and interests accruing to individuals following an international breach, on one hand, and the corresponding position of the representing State(s), on the other, which remain(s) the sole rights-bearer(s) for the actuation of State responsibility.[233] It follows that 'The damage suffered by an individual is never therefore identical in kind with that which will be suffered by a State; *it can only afford a convenient scale for the calculation of the reparation due to the State*' (emphasis added).[234] As evidenced by 9/11, once a terrorist strike is carried out and its aftermath resonates long after, the primary objective behind the obligation of prevention has been frustrated. It seems that the objectives underpinning the UN Charter, along with resolutions 1368 and 1373, would be better served by transference of the onus onto host-States. The study now turns to the specific contributions of resolution 1373 in this setting.

A) Security Council Resolution 1373

Resolution 1373, which implements a far-reaching blanket obligation to prevent terrorism, also translates into an almost uncontested rule of customary law.[235] In its recent counterterrorism resolution-making, the Council often used language redolent of a paradigm shift towards indirect responsibility or, at least, prompted the international community to combat terrorism using 'all steps', which presumably includes imposing a heavier burden of precaution on sanctu-

human rights'). On the Canadian experience and the espousal of claims by the State, see J-G Castel, *Legal Services Provided by the Department of External Affairs with Respect to International Judicial Co-operation and Other Matters* (Ottawa, Department of Foreign Affairs, 1987); HM Kindred et al, *International Law: Chiefly as Interpreted and Applied in Canada*, 6th edn (Toronto, Montgomery, 2000) 674–75.

232 *Articles*, above n 15. See also: Dupuy, above n 50 at 11. See generally: O Corten, 'The Obligation of Cessation' in Crawford et al, above n 106 at 545–49; S Barbier, 'Assurances and Guarantees of Non-Repetition' in ibid, at 551–61; B Stern, 'The Obligation to Make Reparation' in ibid, at 563–71; Y Kerbrat, 'Interaction Between the Forms of Reparation' in ibid, at 573–87; C Gray, 'The Different Forms of Reparation: Restitution' in ibid, at 589–97; J Barker, 'The Different Forms of Reparation: Compensation' in ibid, at 599–611.

233 *Case Concerning the Factory at Chorzów (Germany v Poland) (Claim for Indemnity, Merits)* 1928 PCIJ (ser A) No 17 (13 September) at 28. See also: *Mavrommatis Palestine Concessions*, 1924 PCIJ (ser A) No 2 (30 August) at 12.

234 *Chorzów Factory Case*, above n 233 at 28. See also: *Avena and Other Mexican Nationals (Mexico v US)*, Judgment of 31 March, *ICJ Reports* (2004) 12 at 59, para 119.

235 See, eg: P-M Dupuy, 'La communauté internationale et le terrorisme' in Société française pour le Droit international (ed), *Les nouvelles menaces contre la paix et la sécurité internationales* (Paris, Pedone, 2004) 35 at 40.

ary States.[236] Described as the 'most important instrument agreed upon' since 9/11,[237] the reach and effects of the obligations promulgated by resolution 1373 cannot be overstated, applying to both direct/overt and indirect/passive support of terrorism. Indeed, 'UN resolution 1373 might be seen as approval of an expanded theory of state responsibility attributing the behavior of non-state terrorists to a state that knowingly "harbors" terrorists and does not take action to prevent further terrorist attacks'.[238] Undoubtedly, the Council thereby instituted a stand-alone, autonomous obligation to prevent transnational terrorism.[239] It thus declared that all States shall, inter alia: i) deny safe haven to those who finance, plan, support, or commit terrorist acts, or provide safe havens; ii) prevent those who finance, plan, facilitate or commit terrorist acts from using their respective territories for those purposes against other States or their citizens; and iii) prevent the movement of terrorists or terrorist groups by effective border controls and controls on issuance of identity papers and travel documents, and through measures for preventing counterfeiting, forgery or fraudulent use of such documents.[240] Construed as part of a new 'legislative' role for the Council,[241] and 'as one of the most striking examples of both the efficiency and the far reaching bearing of "secondary legislation"',[242] this resolution 'imposes binding obligations on states to take extensive counter-terrorist measures', including 'criminalising "terrorism" and support for it, imposing serious

[236] Landmark UN documents include SC Res 1368, UN SCOR, 56th Sess, 4370th Mtg, UN Doc S/RES/1368 (2001) at 1 (emphatically prompting all States 'to work together urgently to bring to justice the perpetrators, organizers and sponsors of these terrorist attacks . . . that those responsible for *aiding, supporting or harbouring* the perpetrators, organizers and sponsors will be held accountable'); SC Res 1373, UN SCOR, 56th Sess, 4385th Mtg, UN Doc S/RES/1373 (2001) ('all States shall . . . Refrain from providing any form of support, *active or passive*, to entities or persons involved in terrorist acts . . . *Deny safe haven* to those who finance, plan, support, or commit terrorist acts, or provide safe havens' and reaffirming 'the need to combat *by all means*, in accordance with the Charter of the United Nations, threats to international peace and security caused by terrorist acts' (emphasis added)); SC Res 1378, UN SCOR, 56th Sess, 4415th Mtg, UN Doc S/RES/1378 (2001) (condemning 'the Taliban for *allowing Afghanistan to be used as a base for the export of terrorism* by the Al-Qaida network and other terrorist groups and for *providing safe haven* to Usama Bin Laden, Al-Qaida and others associated with them' (emphasis added)); SC Res 1383, UN SCOR, 56th Sess, 4434th Mtg, UN Doc S/RES/1383 (2001); SC Res 1386, UN SCOR, 56th Sess, 4443rd Mtg, UN Doc S/RES/1386 (2001). See also: GA Res 56/1, UN GAOR, 56th Sess, Supp No 49, UN Doc A/56/1 (in which the General Assembly '*Urgently calls* for international cooperation to prevent and eradicate acts of terrorism, and stresses that those responsible for *aiding, supporting or harbouring* the perpetrators, organizers and sponsors of such acts will be held accountable' (emphasis added)).

[237] PJ van Krieken (ed), *Terrorism and the International Legal Order: With Special Reference to the UN, the EU and Cross-Border Aspects* (The Hague, TMC Asser Press, 2002) 5.

[238] JP Kelly, 'The International Law of Force and the Fight against Terrorism' (2003) 21 *Delaware Lawyer* 18, 19.

[239] See, eg: Martin, above n 119 at 457.

[240] See also: above ch 1, section III.

[241] See, eg: S Chesterman, *The UN Security Council and the Rule of Law: The Role of the Security Council in Strengthening a Rules-Based International System: Final Report and Recommendations from the Austrian Initiative, 2004-2008* (Vienna, Federal Ministry of European and International Affairs, 2008) 12. See also generally: PC Szasz, 'The Security Council Starts Legislating' (2002) 96 *AJIL* 901.

[242] Dupuy, above n 135. On this issue, see generally: G Arangio-Ruiz, 'On the Security Council's "Law-Making"' (2000) 83 *Rivista di diritto internazionale* 609.

penalties, freezing assets and excluding "terrorists" from asylum and refugee protection'.[243]

The proposed State responsibility framework constitutes a compromise between two categorical positions. On one hand, some interlocutors might advocate the imposition of an obligation of result upon host-States, indicating that once a terrorist attack is successfully launched, the object of the obligation is frustrated and responsibility automatically follows.[244] Otherwise, host-States may elude responsibility and the purpose of the obligation of prevention will be eviscerated of any enforceability and efficacy. Exploring the interplay between State responsibility and terrorism, one scholar entertains this possibility from a conceptual standpoint: 'L'inaction de l'État peut enfin constituer une violation non d'une obligation de comportement telle l'obligation de diligence, mais d'une obligation de résultat'.[245]

Although not directly on point, Jean Combacau questionably underscored, albeit in the context of injuries to aliens, that States' due diligence obligations to prevent harm to aliens could be fulfilled by repairing the harm after the primary obligation has been breached. This construction ostensibly signifies that the prescribed result could be attained via two possible avenues, an argument that seemingly runs counter to the very essence of obligations of result. Combacau ascribed a binary character to international responsibility frameworks, whereby a wrongful State can dissipate its responsibility by i) either complying with the primary obligation of prevention or, if it fails to do so, by ii) restituting/compensating the wrongful act, which inexorably entails the application of secondary norms under the ILC's *Articles*.[246] This study partially draws from these positions by stating that terrorist strikes should now be looked upon in the abstract, as either completed or prevented, thereby justifying a rationale

[243] Duffy, above n 22 at 45. For discussion of the far-reaching effects of these measures, see E Rosand, 'The Security Council As 'Global Legislator': *Ultra Vires* or Ultra Innovative' (2005) 28 *Fordham International Law Journal* 542, 546–51; I Johnstone, 'Legislation and Adjudication in the UN Security Council: Bringing Down the Deliberative Deficit' (2008) 102 *AJIL* 275. But see: Y Dinstein, 'Terrorism as an International Crime' (1989) 19 *Israel Yearbook on Human Rights* 55, 56–57 (underscoring that the condemnation of terrorism as 'criminal' is hortatory); Saul, above n 26 at 204–05.

[244] On the distinction between obligations of means and result, as applicable to the ILC's *Articles*, see P-M Dupuy, 'Reviewing the Difficulties of Codification: On Ago's Classification of Obligations of Means and Obligations of Result in Relation to State Responsibility' (1999) 10 *EJIL* 371. At 375, he advocates importing this distinction into State responsibility repertoire, especially when considering that States have to deploy best efforts to prevent private harmful activity. See also: P Gautier, 'On the Classification of Obligations in International Law' in HP Hestermeyer et al (eds), *Coexistence, Cooperation and Solidarity: Liber Amicorum Rüdiger Wolfrum (Vol 1)* (Leiden, Nijhoff, 2012) 853 at 854–64; R Wolfrum, 'Obligation of Result versus Obligation of Conduct: Some Thoughts about the Implementation of International Obligations' in M Arsanjani et al (eds), *Looking to the Future: Essays on International Law in Honor of W. Michael Reisman* (Leiden, Nijhoff, 2010) 363.

[245] 'State inaction may ultimately amount to the breach not of an obligation of conduct, such as the duty to maintain due diligence, but rather of an obligation of result' (author translation). Martin, above n 119 at 459–60.

[246] See Combacau, above n 18 at 189.

partly informed by strict liability, at least on a preliminary basis. Invoking again the tension between sovereignty and combating terrorism efficiently, some scholars argue, with particular emphasis on weapons of mass destruction, that a collective duty to prevent legitimises infringing sovereignty should host-States fail to eliminate terrorist threats.[247]

Conversely, others opine that the US effectively lumped analytically distinct categories into one confused framework before invading Afghanistan, thereby eroding or unnecessarily broadening the parameters governing recourse to force in a manner that threatens State sovereignty, non-intervention and political independence.[248] This confusion was perhaps exacerbated by its initial bellicose rhetoric, which conflated several unrelated factors into one legally convoluted approach, making the connection between the 9/11 attacks and State responsibility nebulous, at least upon first glance.[249] At the root of this confusion was

> the fact that Afghan territory and the institutions of the Afghan government were attacked without clarity as to whether the state was considered responsible for the original attack (or for an imminent threat) or only for other wrongs in respect of terrorists on its territory, and what relevance, if any, such responsibility had to the justification of the use of force against it.[250]

This legal uncertainty was further compounded by the US' categorical stance after 9/11, whereby President Bush asserted that in tracking down the culprits, no distinction would be made 'between the terrorists . . . and those who harbor them'.[251] If anything, such posture further obnubilated the above debate concerning the nature of the obligation of prevention for State responsibility purists, potentially obfuscating the grounds upon which – be it means, best efforts, or result – such duty is rooted. Certain publicists rather expound that in

[247] See L Feinstein and A-M Slaughter, 'A Duty to Prevent' (2004) 83 *Foreign Affairs* 136.

[248] See, eg: J Brunnée and SJ Toope, 'Canada and the Use of Force: Reclaiming Human Security' (2004) 59 *International Journal* 247, 248. Toope and Brunnée have also pursued and further elaborated this line of reasoning in a series of thought-provoking accounts. See, eg: 'Slouching towards New 'Just' Wars: International Law and the Use of Force After September 11th' (2004) 51 *Netherlands International Law Review* 363; 'The Use of Force', above n 99 at 785–806. See also: Duffy, above n 22 at 55 (referring to the 'post-9/11 muddying of legal waters' in her chapter on State responsibility).

[249] See, eg: GW Bush, 'Address to a Joint Session of Congress and the American People', 20 September 2001, available at http://articles.cnn.com/2001-09-20/us/gen.bush.transcript_1_joint-session-national-anthem-citizens?_s=PM:US. See also: Stern, above n 91 at 686 (querying if this type of 'amalgam' is desirable).

[250] Duffy, above n 22 at 213. Duffy further ponders whether this precedent will be invoked to justify future recourses to force, 'for example against any of the many other States with terrorist cells operating out of their territory on the basis of unclear standards of responsibility'.

[251] See 'Statement by the President in his Address to the Nation', 11 September 2001, available at www.opm.gov/guidance/09-11-01GWB.htm. See also: 'President Bush's Remarks', *Washington Post*, 12 September 2001 at A2; 'President Shares Thanksgiving Meal With Troops: Remarks by the President to Troops and Families at Fort Campbell', 21 November 2001, available at http://georgewbush-whitehouse.archives.gov/news/releases/2001/11/20011121-3.html; UN Security Council 56th Sess, 4370th Mtg, Verbatim Record, 12 September 2001, UN Doc S/PV.4370 at 7-8 (US); 'President Bush Addresses United Nations General Assembly', 23 September 2003, available at http://georgewbush-whitehouse.archives.gov/news/releases/2003/09/20030923-4.html; President Bush's Statement, above n 67; Saul, above n 26 at 197.

addition to placing emphasis on holding individual terrorists responsible, 'the Bush Administration's War on Terror developed a secondary goal of holding State sponsors of terrorism accountable for their assistance'.[252]

On the other hand, more moderate views might construe the obligation to prevent terrorism as requiring an ex post facto exercise of factual evaluation, to be performed on a case-by-case basis.[253] Regardless of the approach ultimately espoused by the international community, it is clear that an obligation of prevention based on invariably producing a specific outcome is not feasible, let alone reasonable.[254] The IACHR spoke to this point in 1988 and emphasised that obligations of prevention do not necessarily warrant specific results, but should nonetheless be undertaken with the utmost seriousness. Thus, the failure to take the obligation to prevent seriously may, in turn, signal the violation of that legal undertaking, a finding directly transposable to counterterrorism obligations. The Court proclaimed that

> [t]he duty to investigate, like the duty to prevent, is not breached merely because the investigation does not produce a satisfactory result. Nevertheless, it must be undertaken in a serious manner and not as a mere formality preordained to be ineffective… [w]here the acts of private parties that violate the Convention are not seriously investigated, those parties are aided in a sense by the government, thereby making the State responsible on the international plane.[255]

Hence, the most effective way to resolve the tension between opposite views on the nature of the obligation to prevent is perhaps to adopt a framework grounded somewhere in the middle of the two categorical positions. Given the serious nature of terrorism and the objective of protecting civilians, there is more leeway in imposing stricter rules of State responsibility. Indeed, in light of the emergence of harbouring, support and acquiescence to terrorism as dominant bases for invoking responsibility, State practice or, at least, widespread political will supports a corresponding increase in accountability mechanisms. It follows that 'The attitude of states in this area has been evolving towards stricter standards of state responsibility and imposition of clearer obligations'.[256]

[252] SE Smith, 'International Law: Blaming Big Brother: Holding States Accountable for the Devastation of Terrorism' (2003) 56 *Oklahoma Law Review* 735, 736.

[253] Similar reasoning has been extended to the intersection of cyber-warfare and State responsibility. See J Carr, *Inside Cyber Warfare: Mapping the Cyber Underworld*, 2nd edn (Sebastopol, O'Reilly, 2010) 56. Moreover, the implications of applying State responsibility to virtual settings are increasingly being analysed through the lens of the new indirect responsibility paradigm advocated above in ch 2. See, eg: DE Graham, 'Cyber Threats and the Law of War' (2010) 4 *Journal of National Security Law & Policy* 87, 96.

[254] Dupuy characterises obligations of prevention as a sub-category of 'obligations to endeavour' (ie obligations of 'conduct' in the civil law sense). See Dupuy, above n 244 at 380. While not directly on point, see also: AA Cançado Trindade, 'Complementarity between State Responsibility and Individual Responsibility and Individual Responsibility for Grave Violations of Human Rights: The Crime of State Revisited' in Ragazzi, above n 11 at 266.

[255] *Velásquez Rodríguez Case*, above n 25 at para 177.

[256] JM Beard, 'America's New War on Terror: The Case for Self-Defense under International Law' (2002) 25 *Harvard Journal of Law & Public Policy* 559, 579.

B) The Efficient Breach Doctrine and Other Rationalist Considerations

Decidedly, strong law and economics undertones pervade this whole discussion.[257] Although certain noteworthy attempts to extend this theoretical approach to other facets of international legal discourse have been produced, its relationship with State responsibility remains largely underexplored.[258] Conversely, the notion of risk assessment has been applied to international terrorism and yields interesting theoretical insights.[259] As explored in chapter one, a State's decision to comply with counterterrorism obligations will be largely informed by both the resources at its disposal and its capacity to thwart terrorist threats emanating from its territory. As such, that State may well determine that the scarcity of resources does not justify diverting its funds and policy infrastructures towards counterterrorism objectives, an eventuality that is arguably offset by a countervailing obligation to acquire and utilise counterterrorism capacity or, when unable to do so, to seek external assistance in meeting that goal. Irrespective of the angle under which it is tackled, the reform of State responsibility regarding terrorism hinges on different vital considerations from treaty breaches on commercial matters, for instance.

Unlike situations of conventional breaches or other kinds of ongoing harm flowing from initial wrongful acts (ie non-lethal transnational pollution), the rationale underlying the obligation to prevent terrorism will be completely eviscerated if terrorist excursions are not forestalled. In other cases, whilst the harm carried out still contravenes relevant primary obligations, restitutive or compensatory arrangements are available to redress the damage, remaining perhaps even more relevant in dealing with post-breach repercussions than in situations involving transnational terrorism. Granted, ripple effects or ramifications may result from a catastrophic terrorist attack, but the failure to prevent the initial excursion, which translates into the original wrongful act, remains the principal object of the primary rule under study. Contrary to contractual breaches for instance, such scenarios do not solely entail economic loss but also engage the protection of innocent civilians vis-à-vis widespread and systematic annihilation or loss of limb. For example, transferring the contractual notion of 'efficient breach' to the duty to prevent terrorism would yield perverse results, as States could balance human lives in deciding whether or not to breach that obligation. In domestic settings, this proposition entails that a contractual party

[257] For a succinct account of law and economics, see generally: MJ Trebilcock, 'Economic Analysis of Law' in RF Devlin (ed), *Canadian Perspectives on Legal Theory* (Toronto, Montgomery, 1991) 111–21.

[258] See generally: Dunoff and Trachtman, above n 226; JL Dunoff and JP Trachtman, 'The Law and Economics of Humanitarian Law Violations in Internal Conflict' (1999) 93 *AJIL* 394. On economic analysis of the law of State responsibility, specifically, see EA Posner and AO Sykes, 'An Economic Analysis of State and Individual Responsibility under International Law' (2007) 9 *American Law and Economics Review* 72.

[259] See AR Shaikh, 'A Theoretic Approach to Transnational Terrorism' (1992) 80 *Georgetown Law Journal* 2131.

might opt to breach a contract, should unforeseen or more advantageous circumstances arise, thereby offering a more profitable avenue. In the net-gain or cost-benefit scheme of things, therefore, the breach proves more beneficial since the breaching party will only be held to the disbursement of money damages whilst it may recoup its losses, and more, through a second and distinct bargain.[260] Yet, we must recall that the obligation to prevent terrorism partly stems from multilateral conventions. One may not lose sight of the fact that, to a limited extent, 'Treaties have long been analogized to contracts'.[261] Furthermore, since it fails to find persuasive grounding in the civil law tradition, the efficient breach analogy remains exclusively connected with common law repertoire.[262]

Once transposed to State responsibility for failing to prevent terrorism, the efficient breach doctrine would essentially empower States to arbitrarily decide when it is advantageous to breach the corresponding obligation. For example, a State could decide against injecting significant funds into law enforcement or border security measures should its intelligence conclude that potential attacks would only jeopardise a few lives. It would once again be engaging in a delicate exercise of risk assessment, thereby balancing lives and making cost-efficient decisions. However, it would be trading in human capital, as opposed to making cost-benefit determinations solely involving monetary risk or potential property damage. Therefore, in the context of terrorism, the stakes can become inherently greater and justify a stricter regime of State responsibility in order to offset potentially perverse counterterrorism assessments.[263] For reasons of juridical

[260] The contractual doctrine of efficient breach is widely thought to have originated in Oliver Wendell Holmes' statement in 'The Path of the Law' (1897) 10 *Harvard Law Review* 457, 462 ('the duty to keep a contract at common law means a prediction that you must pay damages if you do not keep it – and nothing else'). Since Holmes' statement, many commentators have encapsulated the efficient breach doctrine in various contexts, including under public international law. See, eg: WR Corbett, 'A Somewhat Modest Proposal to Prevent Adultery and Save Families: Two Old Torts Looking for a New Career' (2001) 33 *Arizona State Law Journal* 985, 1031; L Shidlofsky, 'The Changing Face of First-Party Bad Faith Claims in Texas' (1997) 50 *Southern Methodist University Law Review* 867, 893. See also: Dunoff and Trachtman, above n 226 at 31. By comparison, traditional international legal discourse affirmed that 'If one of the parties violates a treaty, such a violation releases the other from its engagements. For every clause has the binding force of a condition'. See H Grotius, *De Iure Belli ac Pacis Libri Tres (Vol 2)* (Paris, apud Nicolavm Bvon, 1625) ch 15, para 15 trans in BP Sinha, *Unilateral Denunciation of Treaty because of Prior Violations of Obligations by Other Party* (The Hague, Nijhoff, 1966) 9. See also: E de Vattel, CG Fenwick, (tr), *The Law of Nations: or The Principles of Natural Law: Applied to the Conduct and Affairs of Nations and Sovereigns: A Work Tending to Display the True Interests of Powers (Vol 2)* (Washington, DC, Carnegie Institution of Washington, 1916) (1758) ch 13, para 200 (underscoring that the State 'which is offended or injured by the failure of the other to carry out the treaty can choose either to force the offender to fulfil its promises or can declare the treaty dissolved because of the violation of its provisions').

[261] Dunoff and Trachtman, above n 226 at 28. On domestic analogies and dissimilarities between treaty and contract law, see ibid, at 29–31.

[262] See RJ Scalise, Jr, 'Why No "Efficient Breach" in the Civil Law?: A Comparative Assessment of the Doctrine of Efficient Breach of Contract' (2007) 55 *American Journal of Comparative Law* 721.

[263] This line of argument is, by no means, aimed at downplaying the economic impact or property damage engendered by transnational terrorism. For more on this topic, see below ch 5 nn 307–08 and accompanying text. For instance, one could easily envisage an economic loss-generating

pragmatism alone, the transplantation of the 'efficient breach' theory to this context also seems ill-advised if only to be contemplated through Macaulay and Macneil's relational theory of contract.[264]

The potential benefits of this transplant are significantly hampered by the fact that in contrast with domestic legal structures, the role and scope of responsibility under international law is simply not as expansive as liability mechanisms found in those municipal settings. This shortcoming is incontrovertibly cast at the level of enforcement, given the existence of competent judicial jurisdictions within domestic legal orders mandated with overseeing the application of contract law, whilst simultaneously promoting commercial transparency and efficacy.[265] Conversely, no corresponding competent international judicial organ can be pointed to as the guardian of the integrity of 'contractual' dealings arising between parties, for lack of a better term. States may voluntarily submit a contentious situation involving the application of State responsibility for resolution by the ICJ or an arbitral tribunal, but this option is by far not the standard avenue pursued by quarrelling nations. Thus, the economic considerations informing a contractual party's decision to breach its obligations at the domestic level simply cannot be framed as narrowly within international legal discourse, especially given the multinational and multi-actor backdrop against which such decision would presumably be contemplated. Nevertheless, importing rationalist-inspired concepts such as the efficient breach doctrine into the present debate raises interesting philosophical questions when analysed through the lens of counterterrorism policy.

As highlighted previously in the context of strict liability, the obligation to prevent terrorism presupposes the existence of a whole range or variants of normativity and enforceability schemes on the international plane. More importantly, prevention of terrorism belongs to the realm of categorical obligations: once a State fails to forestall a terrorist excursion, the principal purpose of the obligation is defeated.[266] This informs theoretical appraisals of the underlying

situation where terrorists target Hydro-Québec facilities in a strike, thereby forcing the organisation to shut down the electricity system in Québec and to revamp some of its infrastructure. See also generally: M Buesa and T Baumert (eds), *The Economic Repercussions of Terrorism* (New York, OUP, 2010).

[264] See generally the following works by Stewart Macaulay: 'Non-Contractual Relations in Business: A Preliminary Study' (1963) 28 *American Sociological Review* 55; 'The Use and Non-Use of Contracts in the Manufacturing Industry' (1963) 9 *Practical Lawyer* 13; 'An Empirical View of Contract' (1985) *Wisconsin Law Review* 465. See also the following works by Ian R Macneil: 'The Many Futures of Contracts' (1974) 47 *Southern California Law Review* 691; 'Contracts: Adjustment of Long-Term Economic Relations under Classical, Neoclassical, and Relational Contract Law' (1979) 72 *Northwestern University Law Review* 854 (1978); *The New Social Contract* (New Haven, Yale University Press, 1980).

[265] See generally the following works by Ian R Macneil: 'Contract Remedies: A Need for a Better Efficiency Analysis' (1988) 144 *Journal of Institutional and Theoretical Economics* 6; 'Efficient Breach: Circles in the Sky' (1982) 68 *Virginia Law Review* 947 especially at 961.

[266] See Crawford, above n 13 at 140 nn 270. That is not to say, however, that a successful terrorist strike is the *sine qua non* predicate for triggering indirect State responsibility. Indeed, States can act in contravention with international law solely by failing to repress terrorists on their territory or

morality and utilitarian considerations pertaining to human beings, whom concomitantly amount to policy end-users and subjects in the reform of State responsibility.[267]

One vision of compliance – be it in national or international contexts[268] – remains inextricably intertwined with price theory. It follows that

> [f]rom this perspective, the key to compliance is the price of breach: where the price of a breach is sufficiently high, compliance will result. The price of breach must be measured both in terms of the measure of damages and of the extent to which institutions exist mandatorily to require the payment of damages.[269]

Aside from possible moral impediments precluding the implementation of efficient breach principles under State responsibility,[270] we must reiterate that domestic contract law is typically operationalised through the mechanism of money damages and ultimately facilitated by effective adjudicatory and enforcement mechanisms and institutions. The availability of monetary awards is central to the law and economics paradigm and, thus, enables stakeholders to engage in cost-benefit analysis.[271] This structure is further supported by vertical enforcement mechanisms within municipal legal systems, a feature absent in international law, which also facilitates the institutionalisation of price theory, along with the quantifiable internalisation of risk. However, extending this line of reasoning to the politically charged area of counterterrorism proves problematic both in legal and philosophical terms: there is no inherent transferabil-

heed Security Council counterterrorism resolutions. For instance, Pakistan violates its counterterrorism obligations if it harbours Al Qaeda members on its territory, irrespective of whether a terrorist strike is ultimately launched from its soil.

267 Jeremy Waldron opines that 'part of the reason why we value [international law] is that it offers to improve the lives of real individuals, billions of them – men, women, and children – in the world'. He further adds that the real purpose of international law and the rule of law 'in the international realm is not the protection of sovereign states but the protection of the populations committed to their charge'. See 'Are Sovereigns Entitled to the Benefit of the International Rule of Law?' (2011) 22 *EJIL* 315, 325.

268 For a range of provocative accounts on compliance under international law, see, eg: J Brunnée and SJ Toope, 'Persuasion and Enforcement: Explaining Compliance with International Law' (2002) 13 *Finnish Yearbook of International Law* 273; GW Downs et al, 'Is the Good News About Compliance Good News About Cooperation?' (1996) 50 *International Organization* 379; BW Kingsbury, 'The Concept of Compliance as a Function of Competing Conceptions of International Law' (1998) 19 *Michigan Journal of International Law* 345; Koh, 'Why Do Nations', above n 167. See also: 'A Symposium on Implementation, Compliance and Effectiveness' (1998) 19 *Michigan Journal of International Law* 303–579.

269 Dunoff and Trachtman, above n 226 at 31 (also pointing out that 'a research program could descriptively evaluate the relative binding nature of international treaties and could normatively suggest changes to treaty structures to enhance their binding nature, where enhanced compliance is in fact desired').

270 This is not to suggest, however, that moral constraints can never be integrated into an economic analysis of law. Indeed, both morality and economic sensibilities can sometimes become mutually reinforcing when exploring potential legal models geared towards the prevention of terrorism. See generally: E Zamir and B Medina, 'Law, Morality, and Economics: Integrating Moral Constraints with Economic Analysis of Law' (2008) 96 *California Law Review* 323.

271 See, eg: Dunoff and Trachtman, above n 226 at 32.

ity of efficient breach principles under State responsibility,[272] at least when contemplated through the lens of counterterrorism and the balancing of lives. Consequently, the stakes can become inherently greater in transnational terrorism contexts and could justify a stricter regime of responsibility. As a corollary, we must ponder whether the objective of instilling some degree of legitimacy and fairness amongst nations through liability mechanisms necessarily entails the rethinking of primary obligations or, alternatively, whether this objective can be vindicated through revisiting trans-substantive rules.[273]

Undoubtedly inspired by the writings of Anne-Marie Slaughter, Pierre-Hugues Verdier once highlighted that 'The most significant recent development in international legal studies has undoubtedly been the collapse of the intellectual barrier between the disciplines of international law and international relations'.[274] Whilst commentators have developed meaningful rationalist-inspired scholarship applying game theory to international and customary law,[275] State responsibility remains largely unexplored in this context, especially given its lack of enforcement mechanisms and inherent generality. This reality also comes into sharp relief through the works of institutionalist scholars:

> [S]ince institutionalist scholars have focused on formal regimes established by multilateral treaties, they have neglected the customary norms and regimes that form the backbone of many fundamental areas of international law. Such is the case of the law of state responsibility, with its customary and only partly codified rules, decentralized (and often non-existent) adjudication and enforcement, and general rather than subject-specific orientation.[276]

This blurring of the frontier between international law and international relations also prompted leading scholars to dig a considerable furrow into international political theory.[277]

[272] See ibid, at 31.

[273] On the question of legitimacy in the global struggle against terrorism, see TM Franck, 'Porfiry's Proposition: The Role of Legitimacy and Exculpation in Combating Terrorism' in Y Dinstein and M Tabory (eds), *International Law at a Time of Perplexity: Essays in Honour of Shabtai Rosenne* (Dordrecht, Nijhoff, 1989) 149–95.

[274] Verdier, above n 226 at 840. For further support, see B Frischmann, 'A Dynamic Institutional Theory of International Law' (2003) 51 *Buffalo Law Review* 689, 680 fn 1. On the role of international law in the discipline of international relations, see F Kratochwil, *Rules, Norms, and Decisions: On the Conditions of Practical and Legal Reasoning in International Relations and Domestic Affairs* (Cambridge, CUP, 1989); Byers, above n 45; A-M Slaughter, 'International Law and International Relations' (2000) 285 *Recueil des Cours* 9. Both neo-realism and neo-liberalism permeate and mould the fusion of international law and international relations theory. See JL Goldstein et al (eds), *Legalization and World Politics* (Cambridge, MIT Press, 2001); PJ Katzenstein et al, 'International Organization and the Study of World Politics' (1998) 52 *International Organization* 645.

[275] See generally: JL Goldsmith and EA Posner, 'A Theory of Customary International Law' (1999) 66 *University of Chicago Law Review* 1113; JL Goldsmith and EA Posner, 'Understanding the Resemblance between Modern and Traditional Customary International Law' (2000) 40 *Virginia Journal of International Law* 639; Dunoff and Trachtman, above n 226 at 33–36.

[276] Verdier, above n 226 at 841.

[277] See, eg: KW Abbott, 'Modern International Relations Theory: A Prospectus for International Lawyers' (1989) 14 *Yale Journal of International Law* 335; A-M Slaughter Burley, 'International

The most interesting argument advanced by Verdier suggested that theoretical debate over State responsibility has largely been cursory, with too little emphasis on the policy underlying actual rules.[278] Verdier lamented that academic discussion surrounding the topic remains far too superficial, simply resorting to the promulgation of abstract liability rules without delving into the policy analysis underpinning the stated rules. It is unsurprising, therefore, that 'this debate has traditionally taken place on an "existential" level, separate from the descriptive task of defining positive rules'.[279] These propositions align with René Provost's own concerns regarding the lack of theoretical insight in this legal realm: 'The law of state responsibility tends to be a complex field in which principles are articulated at a level of abstraction that obfuscates their theoretical underpinning'.[280] In the same spirit, Provost further cautions that relying on these general and abstract rules, a reflex inevitably stemming from any codification exercise, may in fact negatively impede efforts to magnify State responsibility through a more critical or theoretical lens.[281] Indeed, Paul Reuter foreshadowed these considerations years before when writing about the ILC's codification project, terming it a 'political, extensive, abstract and general' endeavour.[282]

Several influential commentators have followed suit and levelled a wide array of criticisms against the progressive codification and development of State responsibility, often invoking the high level of abstraction characterising the ILC's work, or the lack of specificity or pragmatic guidelines in governing concrete scenarios implicating that normative scheme.[283] Implicit in this approach is the notion that State responsibility repertoire cannot seek to achieve greater clarity than the primary rules it strives to serve. As a corollary, the implementation of international liability cannot prove more 'rigorous' and 'effective' than

Law and International Relations Theory: A Dual Agenda' (1993) 87 *AJIL* 205; A-M Slaughter et al, 'International Law and International Relations Theory: A New Generation of Interdisciplinary Scholarship' (1998) 92 *AJIL* 367.

[278] Verdier, above n 226 at 841.

[279] ibid, at 841–42.

[280] Provost, 'Introduction', above n 173 at xix. See also: Bodansky and Crook, above n 182 at 780.

[281] Provost, 'Introduction', above n 173 at xx (expounding that 'codification can provoke doctrinal sclerosis, dissuading creative and critical analysis by imposing a set of basic assumptions as the necessary starting point of any study on state responsibility'). For similar points, see also: I Brownlie, 'The Responsibility of States for the Acts of International Organizations' in Ragazzi, above n 11 at 360; DD Caron, 'The ILC Articles on State Responsibility: The Paradoxical Relationship between Form and Authority' (2002) 96 *AJIL* 857; Treves, above n 18 at 225.

[282] See P Reuter, 'Trois observations sur la codification de la responsabilité internationale des Etats pour fait illicite' in M Virally (ed), *Le droit international au service de la paix, de la justice et du développement: mélanges Michel Virally* (Paris, Pedone, 1991) 389 at 390. See also: Roucounas, above n 23 at 392.

[283] For a sampling of these views, see, eg: RB Baxter, 'Reflections on Codification in Light of the International Law of State Responsibility for Injuries to Aliens' (1964–65) 16 *Syracuse Law Review* 745, 747–48; RB Lillich, 'The Current Status of the Law of State Responsibility for Injuries to Aliens' in Lillich, above n 184 at 21; MS McDougal et al, *Human Rights and World Public Order: The Basic Policies of an International Law of Human Dignity* (New Haven, Yale University Press, 1980) 762 fn 92.

what is prescribed in this regard by the pertinent primary international obligations.[284] The high level of abstraction permeating the ILC's Articles, coupled with the undefined normativity and content of certain primary obligations, further compounds the mechanics of attribution, compliance and return to legality. A case in point undoubtedly resides in certain counterterrorism obligations which leave a large margin of appreciation for implementation and, more importantly, for the ensuing regulation of international breaches of the corresponding primary norms.

C) Confronting Abstraction: The Lack of Specificity in the *Articles*

The broader project of ascertaining existing State responsibility rules is without doubt extremely ambitious and challenging.[285] But devising a specific responsibility regime for transnational terrorism applicable to sanctuary States poses singular challenges. The difficulties associated with mounting such system predominantly reside in the politically sensitive nature of the topic and the inherent interdisciplinary analogies or insights that govern any exhaustive analysis of State responsibility.

The more indomitable problem in implementing positive rules flows from the inherent lack of specificity and political volatility pervading this facet of State responsibility and the field of counterterrorism, more generally. This difficulty is further exacerbated by linguistic and semantic impediments, such as the lack of consensus on a universally accepted definition of 'terrorism'.[286] This lack of consensus necessarily entails that States may be hard-pressed to agree on positive rules given the large margin they possess in characterising what constitutes 'terrorism'. Yet, sanctuary States have a categorical duty to thwart terrorism emanating from their territory. However, international law remains sketchy as to the contents and contours of this obligation, implementation and enforceability mechanisms to ensure its compliance, and its application to context-specific scenarios ranging from historical transborder insurgency (the Israel-Arab record) to the deployment of one-time excursions (9/11 attacks).[287] Similarly to Verdier, some scholars argue that rethinking trans-substantive rules, such as attribution, is ineffective and that desirable policy objectives would be better vindicated through the reaffirmation of States' primary obligations.[288] Yet, nothing in

[284] For an expression of these two ideas prior to the ILC's adoption of its *Articles*, see, eg: Statement by PS Rao, JS (L&T) Ministry of External Affairs, 2 November 1999, Agenda Item 155: Report of the International Law Commission V State Responsibility, available at www.un.int/india/ind93.htm.

[285] See above ch 2 n 3 and accompanying text.

[286] See V-J Proulx, 'Rethinking the Jurisdiction of the International Criminal Court in the Post-September 11th Era: Should Acts of Terrorism Qualify as Crimes against Humanity?' (2004) 19 *American University International Law Review* 1009, 1030 ff.

[287] As discussed above in ch 2, this argument must be appreciated with caution. For further discussion about this caveat, see Proulx, above n 9 at 639 fn 137.

[288] See, eg: Jinks, above n 49 at 83; Brunnée and Toope, above n 99 at 794–95, fn 55.

Verdier's scholarship, or in conventional wisdom for that matter, precludes thorough policy appraisals of the role played by secondary norms of responsibility in preventing and suppressing transnational terrorism.

For reasons highlighted above, this study calls into question the claim that revisiting trans-substantive rules does not yield fruitful results. By circumventing attribution altogether, we are in fact employing an alternate avenue to implement a positive rule on terrorism prevention. By making sanctuary States automatically liable, thereby transferring the onus of refuting the initial finding of responsibility onto them, we are actually imposing a positive duty aiming at eradicating transnational terrorism. In other areas of human activity entailing potential hazardous consequences such as environmental degradation, the focus is now shifting to prevention. Scholars increasingly highlight that 'More interest is now being shown in the creation of legal obligations that would give rise to state responsibility before pollution occurs': State responsibility norms can play a role towards the fulfilment of this objective.[289] It follows that 'no preventive regime can succeed over time without the firm foundation provided by the development of rules of state responsibility that remove existing defenses to state liability and that create significant penalties for the actual violation of pollution thresholds'.[290] Whilst some defences should remain available with liability being nonetheless significantly enhanced, there is no reason why this reasoning could not extend to counterterrorism efforts, although the content of the actual preventive rules may become subject to conflicting constructions. Indeed, this trend has already been observed in the field of international environmental law, where rules governing the prevention of damage are susceptible to conflicting interpretation, even more so than rules of responsibility applicable to situations where damage has already materialised.[291] Implicit in the views of those endorsing this posture is not only a desire to implement efficient preventive measures, but also a quarrel with the perceived inadequacy of secondary rules of responsibility – especially those governing legal consequences of wrongful acts – in remedying environmental harm or forestalling future pollution.[292] Therefore, emphasis on prevention must be that much more pronounced and explicit for the corresponding rules to become effective in thwarting terrorism. One can imagine, without much protest, that the stakes can become inherently greater when dealing with counterterrorism. Contrasted with environmental damage, for instance, the effects of catastrophic terrorism are usually immediate, whilst only sometimes identifiable or even assessable.[293]

[289] AL Springer, *The International Law of Pollution: Protecting the Global Environment in a World of Sovereign States* (Westport, Quorum Books, 1983) 123, 125–26. See also generally: C Nègre, 'Responsibility and International Environmental Law' in Crawford et al, above n 106 at 803–13.

[290] Springer, above n 289 at 124.

[291] ibid, at 144.

[292] ibid, at 124. On the failure of prevention in this context, see also: ibid, at 130.

[293] See, eg: ibid at 142, noting that many of the effects of pollution are 'cumulative, diffused, and subtle' and that

Assessing damage resulting from terrorism is also intimately tied to the notion of legal consequences for internationally wrongful acts pursuant to the ILC's *Articles.*[294] Article 36(2) provides that 'compensation shall cover any financially assessable damage'.[295] This rule has significant and complex implications from a compensatory standpoint in counterterrorism settings: it might become difficult to put a precise dollar figure on terrorism-based damage, be it in human capital or property. A finding of State responsibility usually entails restitution in kind or another type of compensation, but defining restitution or compensation for damage inflicted by transnational terrorism remains problematic, as is the case with environmental damage. Consequently, it might become challenging 'to assess the value of many of the resources and interests, such as unexploited fish and wilderness areas, that are so often the targets of pollution, and equally hard to assign a monetary figure to the degree of damage done'.[296] Identical reasoning is directly transposable: whilst the obvious effects of terrorism may appear immediately cognisable, significant ripple effects and more subtle repercussions might result from an original attack, amongst which the possible degradation of natural ecosystems undoubtedly features.[297]

Confronted with the dilemma of unreliable assessment benchmarks of damage, the International Oil Pollution Compensation Funds take the view that many forms of environmental harm cannot be compensated because the means used to calculate damages in monetary terms are 'abstract' and 'theoretical'.[298] This thinking very much animated the Tribunal's decision in *Trail Smelter* as it refused to compensate the US for damage allegedly sustained by urban businesses and property, arguing that such harmful activity 'even if proved, is too indirect and remote to become the basis, in law, for an award of indemnity'.[299] Moreover, determining the appropriate recipient of compensation can prove difficult, especially when damage engendered by terrorism is caused to resources or persons extending outside of national boundaries or spanning over multiple

scientific knowledge on the linkage of these effects to specific pollution sources is also so limited that 'by the time scientific evidence of the kind that would satisfy the standard of proof of the *Trail Smelter* arbitration is available, irreversible or long-lasting damage may have occurred.

[294] On the legal consequences of internationally wrongful acts, both at domestic and international levels, see FA Mann, 'The Consequences of an International Wrong in International and National Law' (1976–77) 48 *BYIL* 1. See also: Noyes and Smith, above n 195 at 238–42.

[295] *Articles*, above n 15.

[296] Springer, above n 289 at 138.

[297] On the correlation between terrorism and the protection of natural ecosystems, see D Lovitz, 'Animal Lovers and Tree Huggers Are the New Cold-Blooded Criminals?: Examining the Flaws of Ecoterrorism Bills' (2007) 3 *Journal of Animal Law* 79.

[298] The International Oil Pollution Compensation Funds are available to cover damages caused by spills of persistent oil from tankers. Their website is available at www.iopcfund.org. For more background on the Funds, see generally: M Jacobsson, 'The International Oil Pollution Compensation Funds and the International Regime of Compensation for Oil Pollution Damage' in J Basedow and U Magnus (eds), *Pollution of the Sea: Prevention and Compensation* (Berlin, Springer, 2007) 137–50.

[299] *Trail Smelter Case (US v Canada)* (1941) 3 *Reports of International Arbitral Awards* 1905, 1931; Springer, above n 289 at 138.

territories. Whilst not a definite solution, strict liability aims to partly alleviate or, perhaps more appropriately *expedite*, the damage appraisal and assessment process. By accepting that a wrongful act has automatically been committed when States fail to prevent terrorist strikes, the inquiry then shifts to applying secondary rules which entail, inter alia, rigorous examination of damage, cause-and-effect concerns, compensation and other legal consequences flowing from the ILC's *Articles*.

D) Overcoming Evidentiary Hurdles

The most convincing argument for the implementation of strict liability dimensions resides in the evidentiary problems pertaining to the establishment of attribution.[300] The ICJ's holding in *Nicaragua* reveals the intricacies related to gathering evidence with a view to catalysing State responsibility. The Court underscored that the challenge was 'not the legal process of imputing the act to a particular State for the purpose of establishing responsibility, but the prior process of tracing material proof of the identity of the perpetrator'.[301] *Nicaragua* instituted a 'quite unrealistic obligation' upon the party seeking to establish responsibility of marshalling evidence demonstrating the provision of specific instructions or directions flowing from the State to irregulars having perpetrated a transnational attack.[302] Events surrounding post-Cold War internal and international armed conflicts also illustrate the inherent challenges in persuasively establishing State responsibility, particularly regarding genocide, as evidenced by the ICJ's *Genocide Case* or the International Commission of Inquiry for Darfur's holding on the issue.[303]

Whilst no uniform rule can be identified across the board, the standard of proof governing State responsibility proceedings will presumably be different and lower than evidentiary rules applicable to individual responsibility. Whilst the State responsibility standard appears grounded in the 'balance of evidence' submitted by both States to a dispute, scholars debate the content of such rule while nonetheless acknowledging that the ensuing onus is considerably attenu-

[300] For a thoughtful review of evidentiary concerns related to omissions, see D Shelton, 'Judicial Review of State Action by International Courts' (1989) 12 *Fordham International Law Journal* 361.

[301] *Nicaragua*, above n 10 at 39.

[302] R Värk, 'State Responsibility for Private Armed Groups in the Context of Terrorism' (2006) 11 *Juridica International* 184, 189.

[303] See A Abass, 'Proving State Responsibility for Genocide: The ICJ in Bosnia v. Serbia and the International Commission of Inquiry for Darfur' (2008) 31 *Fordham International Law Journal* 871, 871 ff. It is also unclear what legal standards or justifications the Commission relied upon when engaging the issue of international responsibility. Compare Report of the International Commission of Inquiry on Darfur to the Secretary-General, UN Doc S/2005/60 (2005) 38–39 with Report of the Secretary-General Pursuant to Paragraphs 6 and 13 to 16 of Security Council Resolution 1556 (2004), UN Doc S/2004/703 (2004) 5.

ated, as opposed to evidentiary standards associated with ICL.[304] However, the standard of proof governing State responsibility is not necessarily immutable in all instances. In a Dissenting Opinion, Judge Shahabuddeen expressed that 'the standard of proof varies with the character of the particular issue of fact' and that 'a higher than ordinary standard may . . . be required in the case of a charge of "exceptional gravity against a State"'.[305] The ICJ's practice in this field does not operate on any one dominant typology but rather invokes a hierarchy of probative statuses or values when assessing evidence, an approach that varies in light of the facts and circumstances underlying each case.[306] Logically, allegations of State responsibility regarding terrorism should attract more rigorous evidentiary standards before international tribunals in many circumstances.[307]

When faced with the breach of the obligation to prevent terrorism, an aggrieved State is often at a legal impasse in establishing the host-State's responsibility. Undoubtedly, the host-State is often better positioned than the injured State to know what logistical and human means, intelligence, police and military means were at its disposal to eliminate the threat.[308] Speaking to the interplay between corporate social responsibility and international responsibility, David Caron echoed the foregoing considerations:

> [I]t is argued by some that such deterrence is appropriate inasmuch as the corporation after all is in a better position than the State to detect and punish misconduct by its employees. Similarly, it can be argued in the international case that the State is in a better position than the amorphous international community to monitor and punish its agents.[309]

[304] See generally: DV Sandifer, *Evidence before International Tribunals*, rev edn (Charlottesville, University Press of Virginia, 1975) 127. For the ICJ, see S Rosenne, *The Law and Practice of the International Court, 1920-1966*, 3rd edn (The Hague, Nijhoff, 1997) 1089–90. For the Inter-American Court of Human Rights, see T Buergenthal, 'Judicial Fact-Finding: Inter-American Human Rights Court' in RB Lillich (ed), *Fact-Finding Before International Tribunals* (Ardsley-on-Hudson, Transnational Publishers, 1992) 261 at 270–71; Shelton, above n 300 at 384–87. For the Human Rights Committee, see D MacGoldrick, *The Human Rights Committee: Its Role in the Development of the International Covenant of Civil and Political Rights*, 2nd edn (Oxford, Clarendon Press, 1994) 150 (expounding that the applicable standard of proof is the 'balance of probabilities', as opposed to the ordinary 'beyond a reasonable doubt' criminal standard).

[305] See Dissenting Opinion of Judge Shahabuddeen in *Maritime Delimitation and Territorial Questions between Qatar and Bahrain, Jurisdiction and Admissibility,* Judgment of 15 February, *ICJ Reports* (1995) 6 at 63 (citing *Corfu Channel*, above n 47 at 17). For a general study canvassing evidentiary issues before international tribunals, see M Kazazi, *Burden of Proof and Related Issues: A Study on Evidence before International Tribunals* (The Hague, Kluwer, 1996).

[306] See *Case Concerning Ahmadou Sadio Diallo (Republic of Guinea v Democratic Republic of the Congo)*, Judgment of 30 November, *ICJ* (2010) at 21–22, paras 53–57, available at www.icj-cij.org/docket/files/103/16244.pdf; M Kamto, 'Les moyens de preuve devant la Cour internationale de Justice à la lumière de quelques affaires récentes portées devant elle' (2006) 49 *German Yearbook of International Law* 259, 260.

[307] See, eg: A Nollkaemper, 'Potential Consequences of the Rise of Individual Responsibility for the Law of State Responsibility' in Koufa, above n 17 at 74.

[308] See, eg: Barnidge, Jr, above n 139 at 154 fn 87. On the difficulties of proving that a State had the means to prevent terrorism, see Christenson, above n 3 especially at 314 fn 14. See also: Condorelli, above n 36.

[309] DD Caron, 'State Crimes: Looking at Municipal Experience with Organizational Crime' in Ragazzi, above n 11 at 27.

Obtaining a sense of clarity into host-State behaviour regarding impugned terrorist excursions becomes particularly difficult when this State wields exclusive control over the relevant facts.[310] This reality militates in favour of implementing a system obliging the actor controlling such information to tender the relevant evidence so as to counter a claimant State's contention that it failed in preventing transnational terrorism.

As sole sovereigns and legal guardians of their borders, host-States simply enjoy the most reach and insight into terrorist activities conducted on their territory.[311] Establishing attribution based on very limited publicly available facts poses significant obstacles for aggrieved States, especially given that the content of the obligation to prevent is far from being settled law. However, certain scholars reject the implementation of strict or absolute liability in international law, especially in pollution matters, a trend also followed by some regarding terrorism in light of that practice's clandestine nature.[312] Rather, they advocate fault-based State responsibility models, sometimes grounding their assertions on *Corfu Channel* which, in their view, predicated responsibility on Albania's knowledge of the minefield within its territorial sea. Had the Court wanted to circumvent fault and impose strict liability, they argue, it would not have expended considerable time and effort ascertaining the existence of this knowledge, which entails that fault or the lack of due care was required.[313] This line of argument may be reconciled with the writings of eminent publicists endorsing the notion of fault-based State responsibility, although specific legal approaches to fault range from classical subjective 'psychological' fault,[314] to 'normative'

[310] See, eg: Christenson, above n 3 at 315. Similar reasoning extends to human rights litigation where the defence of the State 'cannot lean on the plaintiff's impossibility to gather evidence that, in many cases, cannot be obtained without the cooperation of the State'; moreover, 'the State has control of the means to clarify the facts that took place in its territory'. See, eg: *Caracazo v Venezuela*, Inter-Am Ct HR Decisions and Judgments (ser C) No 95 (2002) at para 56; *Durand and Ugarte Case*, Inter-Am Ct HR Decisions and Judgments (ser C) No 68 (2000) at para 65; *Cantoral Benavides Case*, Inter-Am HR Decisions and Judgments (ser C) No 69 (2000) at para 55; *Neira Alegría et al Case*, Inter-Am HR Decisions and Judgments (ser C) No 21 (1995) at para 65.

[311] Granted, this line of argument must be appreciated with caution and begins to wane when considering host-States which, while rhetorically committed to eradicating terrorism, nonetheless have difficulty in controlling portions of their territory, thereby tolerating extremist elements on their soil. Incidentally, the US and its allies may actually be better situated – or more effective – than Yemen in acquiring insight into terrorist plots and bases of operation in the Abyan, Ma'rib and Shabwa governorates, or than Pakistan in ascertaining the status of Taliban and Al Qaeda fighters in its north-western, semi-autonomous tribal areas.

[312] JA McCredie, 'The Responsibility of States for Private Acts of International Terrorism' (1985) 1 *Temple International and Comparative Law Journal* 69, 94.

[313] See, eg: Springer, above 289 at 131 and authorities cited therein (invoking the works of Louis FE Goldie and Ludwick Teclaff).

[314] Amongst jurists supporting this view, Roberto Ago, above n 31 at 450–98, is often credited as the intellectual founder of the contemporary theory of psychological fault. Those amongst Ago's intellectual progeny include A Ross, *A Textbook of International Law: General Part* (London, Longman, Green and Co, 1947) 241–58; G Schwarzenberger, *International Law (Vol 1: International Law as Applied by International Courts and Tribunals)*, 3rd edn (London, Stevens, 1957) 649 ff.

fault,[315] to 'psychological-normative' fault.[316] Others rather attempt to reconcile fault theory with objective responsibility theory, which is discussed in greater detail below.[317]

Whilst this reading of *Corfu Channel* appears attractive upon first glance, it must always be balanced against the theory rooted in the mistaken translation of the French text discussed elsewhere in the present monograph,[318] which signals that the Court might have endorsed a rationale of strict liability or some similarly-minded standard. This jurisprudential interpretation seems congruent with the Court's factual treatment. In particular, whilst it ostensibly favoured a cautious approach when exploring the relationship between the use of State territory and the issue of knowledge, its ultimate reasoning demonstrated that Albania in fact knew – at least constructively – about the mine-laying and failed to deploy reasonable attempts to prevent the ensuing harm. Nevertheless, the French version of the decision can be construed as imposing some precedent of 'no-knowledge' international responsibility, an analysis easily transposable to State failures in preventing terrorism. What is more, the Court's ruling enlarges States' due diligence activity in meeting international duties, a notion highly compatible with suggestions that post-9/11 counterterrorism obligations constitute 'bolstered' duties ('obligations renforcées' in French scholarship).[319] This development is undoubtedly coextensive with post-9/11 Security Council practice, which also considerably expanded the scope of States' due diligence obligations towards a more exacting standard.[320] Particularly significant are the prescriptions laid down in resolution 1373, which make it

> clear . . . that the . . . Security Council has enhanced the obligations of States to take measures to prevent terrorism. These obligations have effectively changed the low

[315] See, eg: H Accioly, 'Principes généraux de la responsabilité internationale d'après la doctrine et la jurisprudence' (1959-I) 96 *Recueil des Cours* 349, 369–70; B Cheng, *General Principles of Law as Applied by International Courts and Tribunals* (London, Stevens, 1953) 163–240; G Salvioli, 'Les règles générales de la paix' (1933-IV) 46 *Recueil des Cours* 1, 96 ff.

[316] The language is borrowed from Pisillo-Mazzeschi, above n 173 at 99–102. For accounts dealing with 'psychological-normative' fault, see ibid, at 101–02 and authorities cited.

[317] See, eg: Brownlie, above n 21 at 37–49; L Cavaré, *Le Droit international public positif* (Paris, Pedone, 1951) 310–33; P-M Dupuy, 'Le Fait générateur de la responsabilité internationale des Etats' (1984-V) 188 *Recueil des Cours* 9, 21 ff; FV García-Amador, 'State Responsibility – Some New Problems' (1958-II) 94 *Recueil des Cours* 365, 382 ff; C Rousseau, *Droit international public (vol V: les rapports conflictuels)* (Paris, Sirey, 1983) 16 ff; Schwarzenberger, above n 314 at 632–52; K Zemanek, 'La responsabilité des Etats pour faits internationalement illicites: ainsi que pour faits internationalement licites' in K Zemanek and JJA Salmon (eds), *Responsabilité internationale* (Paris, Pedone, 1987) 36 ff.

[318] See above nn 47–48 and accompanying text. See also: above ch 1 nn 40–44, 130–34; ch 2 nn 152, 175–76; below ch 5 nn 242 and accompanying text.

[319] On terrorist funding, see, eg: N Angelet, 'Vers un renforcement de la prévention et la répression du terrorisme par des moyens financiers et économiques?' in Bannelier et al, above n 43 at 219–37.

[320] Compare the wording of SC Res 1373, above n 236, with pre-9/11 scholarly accounts, such as RB Lillich and JM Paxman, 'State Responsibility for Injuries to Aliens Occasioned by Terrorist Activities' (1977) 26 *American University Law Review* 217, 230 ff (recognising that due diligence obligations cannot be cast as absolute, rather requiring States to deploy best possible efforts and to take reasonable steps in light of both their capacity and the relevant circumstances).

threshold due-diligence obligation States had until the U.N. Security Council Resolution 1373 of 2001 to prevent their territory from being used to launch terrorism conduct in other States to requiring States to compulsorily take all measures to prevent terrorism.[321]

Meeting fault-based responsibility standards can prove quite challenging because of the inherent difficulty in proving negligence against wrongful States under international law. This evidentiary impediment is further exacerbated by the fact that the contents of primary counterterrorism obligations are sometimes ill-defined, or expressed in general terms. This reality advocates towards shifting the burden of proof onto wrongful States, so as to alleviate undue pressure placed on victim-States. Indeed, wrongful States are often better situated to have known – or are expected to have known – about terrorist activity on their territory.[322] Taking this reasoning further, some argued that such knowledge – or presumption of knowledge – automatically flows from the exercise of State sovereignty. In his Separate Opinion in *Corfu Channel*, Judge Alvarez wrote:

> [E]very State is considered as having known, or as having a *duty* to have known, of prejudicial acts committed in parts of its territory where local authorities are installed; *that is not a presumption, nor is it a hypothesis, it is the consequence of its sovereignty*. If the State alleges that it was unaware of these acts, particularly if they occurred in circumstances in which vigilance was unavailing – e.g., by the action of submarines, etc. – it must prove that this was the case, for otherwise its responsibility is involved (emphasis added).[323]

Since failing to prevent a given event from occurring is an inherently nebulous concept, the objectives of efficiency and legitimacy might be better vindicated through a shift in onus to host-States,[324] although some call into question the wisdom of this potential shift in environmental matters. Whilst 'a presumption in favor of the pollution victim, if generally accepted, could mitigate some of the negative effects of the fault standard', it 'is likely to be of limited effectiveness on an international level, where states are seldom willing to use formal adjudicative institutions to resolve environmental disputes'.[325] Certainly, States' unwillingness to conform to adjudicative or other compensatory arrangements might significantly impede progress expected from the transference of onus in favour of aggrieved States following catastrophic terrorism. Furthermore, this situation is compounded if sanctuary States refuse to formally accept responsibility for wrongful terrorist acts.

[321] JT Gathii, *War, Commerce, and International Law* (Oxford, OUP, 2010) 235 (footnotes omitted).

[322] Although not directly on point, see Slaughter, *A New World Order*, above n 161 at 170.

[323] Separate Opinion of Judge Alvarez in *Corfu Channel*, above n 47 at 44. Compare with the Separate Opinions of Judge Pasha at 65; Judge Zoricic at 37–38; Judge *ad hoc* Ecer at 127. See also: Schiedeman, above n 8 at 264. But see: McCredie, above n 312 at 86; Lillich and Paxman, above n 320 at 276–79.

[324] Similar reasoning also pervades some facets of IHL. See, eg: Duffy, above n 22 at 262. For a similar discussion on human rights law, see also: ibid, at 305.

[325] Springer, above n 289 at 132.

The *Lockerbie* incident, which was primarily handled by the Security Council, embodies all of these concerns. Whilst Libya continuously refused to bear responsibility for the impugned bombing of Pan Am Flight 103, it accepted to indemnify the families of the victims. However, considerable delays occurred in actually providing compensation, thereby signalling that State responsibility mechanisms can easily become paralysed or ineffectual when falling at the mercy of political whim.[326] Ultimately, Libya officially acknowledged the findings of the Scottish trial and bore the ensuing State responsibility, whilst committing to working in concert with the Security Council to facilitate the ongoing investigation.[327] On 29 April 2003, the Libyan Minister of Foreign Affairs declared: 'Mon pays a accepté de prendre sa responsabilité civile pour les actions de ses fonctionnaires dans l'affaire Lockerbie, conformément au droit civil international et à l'accord survenu en mars à Londres entre les responsables libyens, américains et britanniques'.[328]

Likely prompted by fears of criminalisation of the Libyan State, peculiar language is invoked in this diplomatic statement, with the terms 'responsabilité civile' and 'droit civil international' being ostensibly difficult to substantiate or ground legally.[329] Nevertheless, the tripartite agreement was ultimately ratified by Libyan authorities in a letter to the Security Council, dated 15 August 2003, declaring that Libya 'Has facilitated the bringing to justice of the two suspects charged with the bombing of Pan Am 103 and accepts responsibility for the actions of its officials'.[330] Libya therein formally acknowledged its international responsibility, undertook to refrain from providing any form of support to terrorists and ensured that the proper arrangements were put into place to provide adequate compensation to the concerned individuals.[331] Despite considerable political hurdles and delays, this precedent epitomises a quintessential application of State responsibility mechanics whereby the host-State expressly accepted

[326] On these aspects of the *Lockerbie* incident, see, eg: B Sabahi, 'The ICJ's Authority to Invalidate the Security Council's Decisions under Chapter VII: Legal Romanticism or the Rule of Law?' (2004) 17 *New York International Law Review* 1, 47 fn 226; SD Murphy, 'Libyan Payment to Families of Pan Am Flight 103 Victims' (2003) 97 *AJIL* 987, 989–91; K Sealing, 'Thirty Years Later: Still Playing Catch-Up with the Terrorists' (2003) 30 *Syracuse Journal of International Law and Commerce* 339, 346; M Wooldridge, 'Analysis: Lifting Sanctions on Libya', *BBC News*, 12 September 2003, available at http://news.bbc.co.uk/1/hi/world/africa/3199551.stm.

[327] See, eg: JB Schwartz, 'Dealing with a "Rogue State": The Libya Precedent' (2007) 101 *AJIL* 553, 573.

[328] 'My country has accepted to acknowledge its civil responsibility for the actions carried out by its civil servants in the Lockerbie case, in conformity both with international civil law and the agreement reached in London last March between Libyan, American and British officials' (author translation). 'Attentat de Lockerbie: Tripoli accepte sa responsabilité civile', *Le Monde*, 29 April 2003.

[329] Jean-Marie Sorel writes about 'flou artistique' and 'terme inadapté' when canvassing the Libyan position. See 'L'épilogue des affaires dites de "Lockerbie" devant la C.I.J.: le temps du soulagement et le temps des regrets' (2003) 107 *RGDIP* 933, 943.

[330] UN Doc S/2003/818.

[331] Compensation totalling 2.7 million dollars was disbursed to the Bank for International Settlements on 22 August 2003. On the dispute and ensuing settlement, see Murphy, above n 326 at 987–90.

its accountability in failing to prevent terrorism.[332] Not all cases of tacit or inadvertent assistance to terrorists will compel the involved governments to comply docilely with the prescriptions of international law. In fact, diplomatic resistance or flat-out denial of any complicity/involvement in terrorist plots often goes hand-in-hand with State-condoned policies of surrogate warfare or terrorism via proxy – the whole purpose behind such tactics being, inter alia, to eschew responsibility. Therefore, such reality potentially points to some *lex ferenda* policy inclination towards more stringent liability schemes.

A general conclusion derives from the foregoing considerations: even if we accept the implementation of a positive rule imposing a higher burden of precaution upon States, albeit through rethinking trans-substantive rules, the initial impediments highlighted by Verdier remain pertinent. Extant State responsibility schemes remain characterised by overarching generality, whilst deploying the proposed reform may oscillate towards – often desirable – fact-specific assessments of terrorist strikes or may even foment idiosyncratic reasoning. Thus, this rule can presumably only be operationalised through the mechanism of a variable threshold in order to account for the whole panoply of host-State inaction vis-à-vis terrorism, ranging from passiveness to wilful blindness, to active encouragement. Indeed, modulating the application of international legal standards is not foreign to the discipline of State responsibility or to other international legal fields.[333]

VI. CONCLUSION: CONSOLIDATING RATIONALIST THEORIES AND STATE RESPONSIBILITY

Consequently, it will be helpful to consolidate select rationalist, international relations, and international legal theories through an exploration of the compatibility between State responsibility, terrorism, and legal theory. As explored in this chapter, applying rationalist theories to State responsibility proves particularly illuminating given the inherent struggle between rational choice, compliance, reciprocity, and self-interest which characterises the balancing of competing international policies. We have also seen that this line of argument can be a misleading benchmark, especially in politically charged policy areas

[332] See, eg: Martin, above n 119 at 469. But see: KN Trapp, 'Jean-Christophe Martin, Les règles internationales relatives à la lutte contre le terrorisme, (Brussels, Bruylant, 2006)' (2006) 19 *Revue québécoise de droit international* 399, 403.

[333] See Barboza, above n 148 at 9 (invoking a variable scale metaphor and comparing the structure of Art 1 of the ILC's *Articles* to a set of scales). It is widely accepted that international responsibility also entails varying degrees of actual accountability. See G Arangio-Ruiz, 'State Fault and the Forms and Degrees of International Responsibility: Questions of Attribution and Relevance' in Virally, above n 282 at 25–42; W Riphagen, 'Second Report on the Content, Forms and Degrees of International Responsibility', UN Doc A/CN.4/344 (1981) reprinted in (1981) 2 *Yearbook of International Law Commission* 79, UN Doc A/CN.4/SER.A/1981/Add.1. See also: Battaglini, above n 138 at 147–49 (invoking a geometry-based metaphor to explain certain aspects of international responsibility).

such as counterterrorism. Unlike situations of contractual relationships, against which game theory and efficient breach principles can be applied convincingly, State responsibility can entail intrinsically greater stakes. The delicate balance between security and State sovereignty, which is actuated through the phenomena of risk assessment and risk management, sometimes reveals an altogether different overarching purpose: the protection of civilian life. This scheme entails a wider margin of error and correspondingly shrinks institutional repertoire and enforcement mechanisms on the international scene, which are typically operationalised through monetary compensation or adjudicatory structures in domestic law. Hence, terrorism could require more stringent State responsibility frameworks. Undoubtedly, this challenge is further exacerbated by factual complications engendered by new technological advances (eg Internet), which obfuscate the application of both trans-substantive and secondary norms of State responsibility. For instance, terrorist cyber-attacks significantly hamper the prospect of attributing unlawful conduct to host-States for myriad reasons, including difficulties in determining authorship of the attacks, unreliability of Internet Protocol addresses as a mode of attribution, and the possibility that cyber-terrorist behaviour culminating in a single strike may actually originate in several States from a traditionally 'geographic' standpoint. Therefore, 'To answer these issues of attribution and to pin down those responsible for attacks, it is necessary to institute a standard of state responsibility that recognizes the difficulties inherent in cyber law'.[334]

Moreover, whilst rationalist-inspired approaches to legal compliance might appear desirable from policy standpoints, they remain fraught with an inescapable sense of methodological weakness given that they rely, quite extensively, on a set of basic assumptions that may or may not be present in any given analysis of legal norms. To name but a few, rationalist accounts of international relations invariably rest upon the notion that the maximisation of preferences – presumed to be 'exogenous and constant'[335] – drives the actions of States, which necessarily amount to rationalist actors. In turn, these preferences can run the gamut of State interest, ranging from monetary to moral or aesthetic considerations, and remain characterised by a great margin of heterogeneity on a State-to-State basis.[336] Facilitated by a necessary legal oversimplification in order to countenance the rationalist agenda, these accounts also rest upon the assumption that States constitute unitary actors, a notion appearing at odds with the developments explored above and the objective of developing legal arrangements aimed at better integrating a multiplicity of actors within a multipolar

[334] SJ Shackelford, 'From Nuclear War to Net War: Analogizing Cyber Attacks in International Law' (2008) 27 *Berkeley Journal of International Law* 191, 214. See also: SJ Shackelford and RB Andres, 'State Responsibility for Cyber Attacks: Competing Standards for a Growing Problem' (2001) 42 *Georgetown Journal of International Law* 971.

[335] AT Guzman, *How International Law Works: A Rational Choice Theory* (Oxford, OUP, 2008) 17.

[336] See, eg: JP Trachtman, *The Economic Structure of International Law* (Cambridge, Harvard University Press, 2008) 1.

political framework. In short, methodologically-driven simplifications are required to ensure that rationalist legal models generate verifiable predictions vis-à-vis abstract situations.[337] Arguably, there is no guarantee that such methodologically doctored results would yield similar patterns of State compliance and influence if transposed to the realm of State responsibility in a real-world environment. This fleeting critique is, by no means, meant to act as a complete disavowal of the potential benefits that may be derived from rationalist constructions of international law. Rather, the objective is to put forth an intellectually holistic theoretical approach when considering the possible contributions of various counterterrorism deterrence models within the purview of State responsibility. Indeed, such cautious approach seems on par with scholarly resistance to the rationalist international legal agenda – embodied by the works of Goldsmith and Posner – prompting one commentator to declare that there are limits to *The Limits of International Law*.[338] The solution, therefore, is not to cast all rationalist-driven interpretations of the relevant norms as inherently heretic from an international legal vantage point, but rather to approach them with a critical eye.

This chapter advocated that the proposed reform of State responsibility, via the circumvention of attribution and the implementation of a two-tiered strict liability-infused mechanism, is consonant with several other legal theories. In addition to instilling some degree of legitimacy and promoting fairness amongst nations, it also facilitates the imposition of positive rules in the underlying legal system. Indeed, a recurrent criticism regarding the benefits of State responsibility in post-9/11 commentary is that primary obligations of States are insufficiently circumscribed. By rethinking trans-substantive rules towards enhancing the efficiency of liability models, the proposed reform strives to do away with this impediment so as to clearly affirm the obligation to prevent terrorism. More importantly, as canvassed in the next chapter, this framework fits neatly under an interactional theory of international law, which could mean that formal normativity may be derived from it without reference to the elaboration of new positive rules.

[337] On this point and the considerations explored before it, see generally: N Petersen, 'How Rational Is International Law?' (2010) 20 *EJIL* 1247.

[338] See A van Aaken, 'To Do Away with International Law? Some Limits to 'The Limits of International Law'' (2006) 17 *EJIL* 289 (discussing J Goldsmith and E Posner, *The Limits of International Law* (New York, OUP, 2005)). For a critique articulated from a 'traditionalist' standpoint, see DF Vagts, 'International Relations Looks at Customary International Law: A Traditionalist's Defence' (2004) 15 *EJIL* 1031.

5

Implementing a Two-tiered Strict Liability-infused Model

I. INTRODUCTION

A PRESCRIPTIVE ARGUMENT was put forth in the previous chapter, advocating the adoption of a strict liability-inspired model of State responsibility vis-à-vis State failures to prevent transnational terrorism. The present chapter further explores the rationale behind such proposal and, more importantly, the mechanics of its application. The chapter first delves into the rationales and problems that could become associated with the strict liability model, such as the tension between governmental interference in the private sphere and upholding the sovereign equality between States, the issue of 'failed' States and the desirability of transferring the onus onto host-States. The chapter then sheds light on other advantages deriving from the strict liability-infused model, with particular emphasis on international relations and the potentially stigmatic force of presumptive indirect responsibility. Ultimately, the chapter gravitates towards an in-depth exploration of the content and mechanics of the obligation of prevention, along with the consequences flowing from international wrongful acts in this context, thereby offering a realistic look at the role of State responsibility in our debate.

II. A TWO-TIERED STRICT LIABILITY MECHANISM

The objective in shifting the onus is not only to transfer the burden of proof but also to shift the incentives to host-States.[1] Moreover, it aims at transferring the *right* incentives to concerned governments. This could be achieved, it is argued, through a two-tiered strict liability-inspired mechanism excising attribution from the equation and recognising that, once a terrorist attack has been launched from a State's territory, that State becomes automatically indirectly

[1] One author frames the idea of shifting the onus through the prism of direct responsibility as follows: 'It is necessary to first establish the principles by which direct State responsibility might be engaged, and only then to consider how presumptions and shifting burdens of proof might properly be utilized in making that determination in specific instances'. See T Becker, *Terrorism and the State: Rethinking the Rules of State Responsibility* (Oxford, Hart Publishing, 2006) 271.

responsible for the excursion. In many ways, this reasoning seems congruent with modern conceptions of State responsibility, which strive to engage liability as soon as a wrongful act is committed. Of particular importance is the consecration of the 'wrongful act' as sole trigger of international responsibility and cornerstone of the ILC's construction of liability, along with the eventual deletion of the concept of 'injury' from the ILC's *Articles*. Brigitte Stern highlights that this textual evolution constitutes a departure if 'only semantic, compared with the past approach, displaying the will to bring responsibility into existence as soon as the international legal order is breached, that is to introduce a sort of review of legality through the institution of international responsibility'.[2]

Extending this rationale to counterterrorism, a successful cross-border terrorist strike establishes a prima facie case of responsibility against the host-State. To make this argument palatable, one must accept that, in addition to a sanctuary State's organs having allowed an attack to materialise in a given circumstance, State responsibility 'also might be based on the mere control of the state territory'.[3] Whilst some caution that a norm of customary law is required for State responsibility to be triggered in the latter case, others call into the question the existence of a rule endorsing such broad parameters for State responsibility.[4] Under international law, the emergence of such customary norm should be fuelled not only by pertinent State practice, but also by corresponding *opinio juris*.[5] One could certainly argue that the response to 9/11 generated significant legal capital towards this end, as partially evidenced by the unprecedented international support it garnered.[6]

This reasoning seems to fit neatly within the furrow created by the ILC's *Articles*, which institute a regime reminiscent of 'absolute liability' under some lights. Similarly to when terrorism is carried out and, according to the arguments advanced in this volume, creates a presumption of indirect State responsibility, the *Articles* operate on the premise that once a wrongful act has been committed, responsibility of the wrongful State is triggered through the channel

[2] B Stern, 'A Plea for "Reconstruction" of International Responsibility Based on the Notion of Legal Injury' in M Ragazzi (ed), *International Responsibility Today: Essays in Memory of Oscar Schachter* (Leiden, Brill, 2005) 93 at 94. Furthermore, the *Articles* introduce an 'objective review of legality into the institution of international responsibility'. See B Stern, 'The Elements of an Internationally Wrongful Act' in JR Crawford et al (eds), *The Law of International Responsibility* (Oxford, OUP, 2010) 193 at 194.

[3] S Kirchner, 'Third Party Liability for Hezbollah Attacks against Israel' (2006) 7 *German Law Journal* 777, 781 (applying this rationale to Lebanon's involvement in the 2006 Israel-Hezbollah conflict). Territorial control is central in State responsibility. For a thoughtful discussion of this aspect, see I Brownlie, *System of the Law of Nations: State Responsibility Part I* (Oxford, Clarendon Press, 1983) 180–88.

[4] See Kirchner, above n 3 at 781; J Andrassy, 'Les Relations internationales de voisinage' (1951-II) 79 *Recueil des Cours* 73, 79.

[5] *North Sea Continental Shelf (Federal Republic of Germany/Netherlands)*, Judgment of 20 February, *ICJ Reports* (1969) 3 at 77. Multilateral treaties also exert considerable influence in recording, defining and developing customary rules. See, eg: *Continental Shelf (Libyan Arab Jamahiriya/Malta)*, Judgment of 3 June, *ICJ Reports* (1985) 13 at 29–30, para 27.

[6] Consider H Duffy, *The 'War on Terror' and the Framework of International Law* (Cambridge, CUP, 2005) 49.

of attribution. In this regard, Shabtai Rosenne invoked the term 'absolute responsibility', which may in fact be a misnomer, to describe the ILC's work.[7] He noted that 'The new approach to responsibility adopted by the International Law Commission replaces the traditional notions of fault and damage with a concept of absolute responsibility arising from any breach of an international obligation of the responsible State'.[8] Although Rosenne later mitigated this posture by calling into question the pervasiveness of 'absolute responsibility' under current State responsibility structures,[9] it is nonetheless fair to query whether the ILC's *Articles* implement a regime of strict liability by subtracting fault, intent and injury altogether from the State responsibility calculus. In other words, the rationale underlying the *Articles* is somewhat compatible with the idea of 'absolute liability'.[10] Should this argument fall short, one could certainly rely on the writings of legal scholars arguing that State responsibility doctrine and practice actually support the notion of strict liability.[11] Ultimately, it might prove impracticable to entirely excise the concept of fault from the application of the *Articles*, a notion that may be reconciled with post-9/11 applications of State responsibility and governmental failures to control national territory. For instance, Yemen's potential responsibility in failing to control portions of its territory like the Abyan, Ma'rib and Shabwa governorates, where both Al Qaeda and Aden-Abyan Islamic Army members congregate, must not seek grounding in some absolute construction of international liability, but can rather be substantiated by its consistent failures to comply with Security Council prescriptions to stamp out terrorist networks within its borders and by reference to general international law.[12]

Therefore, a more proper term to describe ILC codification might actually be 'objective responsibility',[13] although the *Articles* arguably rely on both *objective* (ie a wrongful act consisting of an act or omission constitutes a breach of an international obligation) and *subjective* (ie the wrongful act is attributable to the State under international law, which depends on a subjective application of

[7] Brownlie, above n 3 at 3, similarly pointed out Lauterpacht's erroneous use of the term 'absolute liability'.

[8] S Rosenne, 'Decisions of the International Court of Justice and the New Law of State Responsibility' in Ragazzi, above n 2 at 298.

[9] ibid, at 299 ('At the time of writing, however, there is no certainty that this concept of absolute liability, independent of fault and of damage cause by the act (or omission), will be accepted as today's *lex lata*'). Writing about State responsibility regarding insurrection and civil war, Brownlie, above n 3 at 171, rejected the idea of absolute liability and further contended that such standard finds no grounding in State practice.

[10] On the notion of intent under State responsibility, see J Salmon, 'L'intention en matière de responsabilité internationale' in M Virally (ed), *Le droit international au service de la paix, de la justice et du développement*: *mélanges Michel Virally* (Paris, Pedone, 1991) 413–22.

[11] See, eg: M Shaw, *International Law*, 5th edn (Cambridge, CUP, 2003) 700.

[12] On the situation in Yemen, see SC Res 2014, UN SCOR, 66th Sess, 6634th Mtg, UN Doc S/RES/2014 (2011). For similar reasoning involving Afghanistan and Al Qaeda, see Y Arai-Takahashi, 'Shifting Boundaries of the Right of Self-Defence – Appraising the Impact of the September 11 Attacks on Jus Ad Bellum' (2002) 36 *International Lawyer* 1081, 1096–97.

[13] See, eg: V Pechota, 'The Limits of International Responsibility in the Protection of Foreign Investments' in Ragazzi, above n 2 at 177.

the facts at hand) elements.[14] Reconnecting with previous environmental legal observations, a salient example of 'objective responsibility' is found in Article 51 of the 1973 Treaty between Uruguay and Argentina Concerning the Rio de la Plata and the Corresponding Maritime Boundary.[15] It provides that 'Each Party shall be liable to the other for detriment suffered as a consequence of pollution caused by their operations, or by those of physical or corporate persons domiciled on their soil'.[16] In such instances, no proof of governmental involvement in the polluting activity need be demonstrated, either through an act or omission. This automatic finding of responsibility also simultaneously circumvents the evidentiary impediments often associated with attribution. Similar provisions are found in both the 1967 Outer Space Treaty[17] and the 1979 Moon Treaty,[18] which make State Parties automatically responsible for damage caused by the actions of their nationals in outer space. Borrowing from this reasoning, the Convention on International Liability for Damage Caused by Space Objects[19] also 'codifies a regime of strict liability, stating that "[a] launching State is absolutely liable to pay compensation for damage caused by its space object on the surface of the earth or to aircraft in flight"'.[20] Similarly, influential publicists endorsed theories favouring objective State responsibility starting with Anzilotti's objectivist scholarship,[21] which inspired an impressive academic following.[22] At the outset, a factor limiting this line of argument derives from the

[14] JR Crawford, *International Law Commission's Articles on State Responsibility: Introduction, Text and Commentaries* (Cambridge, CUP, 2002) 81–85; P-M Dupuy, 'State Sponsors of Terrorism: Issues of International Responsibility' in A Bianchi (ed), *Enforcing International Law Norms against Terrorism* (Oxford, Hart Publishing, 2004) 3 at 4; AL Springer, *The International Law of Pollution: Protecting the Global Environment in a World of Sovereign States* (Westport, Quorum Books, 1983) 125–26.

[15] Treaty between Uruguay and Argentina concerning the Rio de la Plata and the Corresponding Maritime Boundary, 19 November 1973 reprinted in (1974) ILM 251 (in force, 12 February 1974).

[16] ibid, at 260.

[17] See Treaty on Principles Governing the Activities of States in the Exploration and Use of Outer Space, including the Moon and Other Celestial Bodies, Annex to UN GA Res 2222 (XXI) of 25 January 1967 reprinted in 18 UST 2410, 610 UNTS 205 (in force, 10 October 1967). For a recent study on Art VI of that convention and State responsibility, see C Schmeichel, *State Responsibility for Non-Governmental Entities in Outer Space* (Saarbrücken, Lambert Academic Publishing, 2010).

[18] See Agreement Governing the Activities of States on the Moon and Other Celestial Bodies, Annex to UN GA Res 34/68 of 5 December 1979 reprinted in (1979) 18 ILM 1434 (in force, 11 July 1984).

[19] Convention on International Liability for Damage Caused by Space Objects, 29 June 1971 reprinted in (1971) 10 ILM 965, Can TS 1975 No 7, 24 UST 2389, TIAS No 7762 (in force, 1 September 1972).

[20] M Bourbonnière, 'National-Security Law in Outer Space: The Interface of Exploration and Security' (2005) 70 *Journal of Air Law and Commerce* 3, 22. For a review of strict liability in international environmental agreements, see, eg: A-C Kiss and DL Shelton, 'Strict Liability in International Environmental Law' in TM Ndiaye and R Wolfrum (eds), *Law of the Sea, Environmental Law and Settlement of Disputes: Liber Amicorum Judge Thomas A. Mensah* (Leiden, Nijhoff, 2007) 1131 at 1135–38.

[21] See, eg: D Anzilotti, 'La Responsabilité internationale des États: à raison des dommages soufferts par des étrangers' (1906) 13 *RGDIP* 5, 5–29.

[22] For a variety of views on objective constructions of State responsibility, see J Basdevant, 'Règles générales du droit de la paix' (1936-IV) 58 *Recueil des Cours* 471, 668 ff; P Guggenheim, *Traité de droit international public: avec mention de la pratique internationale et suisse (vol II)*

idea that all such activity (eg pollution reduction, outer space exploration) is under direct State control/supervision or, at least, received equivalent political treatment at the time those stricter liability standards were conventionally implemented.

Nevertheless, whenever exploring State responsibility for highly hazardous activities, such as terrorism or transboundary pollution, the inherent affinity between strict liability and/or absolute responsibility and the rationale underlying the ILC's *Articles* must be emphasised.[23] Whilst certain scholars call into question the existence of a customary rule or international legal principle enshrining the discipline of strict liability for ultra-hazardous activities,[24] others resolve this discrepancy by inferring that 'there may be a general principle of law that imposes strict liability on a State for abnormally dangerous activity'.[25] Speaking to the *Trail Smelter* and *Corfu Channel* line of cases while using torts-derived language, Higgins echoed some of these views, noting that 'all make clear a duty of care to prevent injury'.[26] She further argued that 'The *standard* of care is still unclear. But, with regard to *some* activities of an inherently hazardous nature, it is increasingly suggested that there is an absolute duty of care, reflected in resultant strict liability'.[27] Although questionable upon closer inspection, Rosenne's conclusions remain illuminating and further reinforce the argument that absolute liability may apply to some wrongful acts: 'Whatever the future of the draft articles, with or without change, there is no doubt that the concept of absolute responsibility, at all events for certain types of unlawful acts, is now implanted in international law'.[28] Given the scope of relevant norms

(Geneva, Georg, 1953–54) 49; H Kelsen, *General Theory of Law and State* (Cambridge, Harvard University Press, 1945) 66 ff, 367; P Reuter, 'Principes de droit international public' (1961-II) 103 *Recueil des Cours* 425, 598.

[23] See, eg: Springer, above n 14 at 133; MJ Matheson, 'The Fifty-Eight Session of the International Law Commission' (2007) 101 *AJIL* 407, 413. See also generally: HH Koh, 'Separating Myth from Reality about Corporate Responsibility Litigation' (2004) 7 *Journal of International Economic Law* 263, 266.

[24] See, eg: VR Hartke, 'The International Fallout from Chernobyl' (1987) 5 *Dickinson Journal of International Law* 319, 335–37. For a sample of divergent and classical views on the application of strict liability regimes to various fields of ultra-hazardous activities, compare: G Handl, 'Liability As an Obligation Established by a Primary Rule of International Law' (1985) 16 *Netherlands Yearbook of International Law* 49, 49–79; G Handl, 'State Responsibility for Accidental Transnational Environmental Damage by Private Persons' (1980) 74 *AJIL* 525; CW Jenks, 'Liability for Ultra-Hazardous Activities in International Law' (1966) 117 *Recueil des Cours* 99; LFE Goldie, 'Liability for Damage and the Progressive Development of International Law' (1965) 14 *ICLQ* 1189.

[25] Z Keyuan, 'Environmental Liability and the Antarctic Treaty System' (1998) 2 *Singapore Journal of International and Comparative Law* 596, 620.

[26] R Higgins, *Problems & Process: International Law and How We Use It* (Oxford, OUP, 1994) 157.

[27] ibid.

[28] Rosenne, above n 8 at 299. Citing T Meron, 'International Law in the Age of Human Rights: General Course on Public International Law' (2003) 301 *Recueil des Cours* 9, 249, he further adds that

> [w]hatever the attitude of Governments – and in the final resort only a widely accepted international convention, State practice, or judicial decisions, can consolidate this new concept of international responsibility – it is certain that this approach will enjoy powerful backing from the most qualified publicists of the various nations (in the words of Article 38(1)(*d*) of the Statute of the International Court).

and the stakes involved, this rationale should presumably become apt with respect to wrongful acts entailing the violation of serious human rights/protection of civilian life obligations, such as those embodied in counterterrorism duties.

However, this is a far cry from actually reading strict liability standards into the ILC's *Articles* – or advancing that this instrument is dispositive on host-State responsibility for failing to thwart private harmful activities – as certain influential scholars have contended after 9/11. Admittedly, imposing strict liability standards vis-à-vis State failures to prevent terrorism extends the legal rationale beyond what is routinely envisaged for that level of engagement on the international scene, particularly for outer space activities, satellite launches, high-risk water dams and nuclear facilities.[29] This legal alignment between highly hazardous fields of activity and stringent liability standards can be best explained by the fact that such operations typically fall under serious and narrow State control. Typically, these activities also significantly benefit host-States, thereby justifying their support and acceptance of the ensuing risk. Upon first glance, such logic cannot be analogised to counterterrorism, as host-States do not derive any tangible benefits from terroristic enterprises (unless they utilise toleration as a foreign policy tool). Nevertheless, compelling policy reasons militate in favour of a responsibility-expanding regime in combating the scourge of terrorism.[30]

Relying upon the non-finalised Draft Articles on their second reading, Professor Franck erroneously inferred that they 'make it clear that a state is responsible for the consequences of permitting its territory to be used to injure another state'.[31] Whilst the notion of 'permitting its territory' could be conceptually dissociated from strict liability logic because giving permission to use a territory arguably entails knowledge of that use by the host-State, Franck further substantiated his claim by invoking Security Council practice. One may ponder whether this practice would presumably also encompass cases of tacit support, whereby States unknowingly allow their territory to be used by terrorists. In particular, Franck opined that paragraph 3 of Council resolution 1368 consecrates a stricter standard of responsibility for terrorism, applicable to 'sponsors of these terrorist attacks' including those 'supporting or harbouring perpetrators'.[32] He ultimately extended his approach to the 9/11 attacks, expounding that the 'Taliban clearly fit that designation'.[33] Whilst Franck's conclusion seems to reflect recent State and institutional practice consecrating the shift to 'indirect responsibility' explored in chapter two, his reliance on the ILC's *Articles* remains somewhat puzzling. Indeed, the *Articles* do not appear to support a legal basis for attribution hinging *solely* on a territorial nexus between

[29] See, eg: M Forteau, 'Space Law' in Crawford et al, above n 2 at 903–14; M Montjoie, 'Nuclear Energy' in ibid, at 915–28.

[30] See, eg: below section IV, especially IV.A).

[31] TM Franck, 'Terrorism and the Right of Self-Defense' (2001) 95 *AJIL* 839, 841.

[32] ibid.

[33] ibid.

a terrorist attack and a host-State, a notion equally mirrored in the law governing recourse to force according to contemporary scholarly accounts.[34] As José Alvarez underlines, endorsing Franck's view could give credence to the notion that the *Articles* actually rely upon a mechanism of strict liability in such scenarios.[35] As Alvarez points out, the ILC narrowly circumscribed, at least in terms of the textual delivery of its *Articles*, the scope of State responsibility for the acts of private persons to specific circumstances, namely where: i) private conduct is directed or controlled by the State; ii) non-State actors exercise elements of governmental authority; or iii) host-States acknowledge or adopt as their own the conduct in question.[36]

This study operates in tandem with the premise that imposing strict liability for failing to prevent terrorism cannot rest on any precise exegesis in the ILC's work and must, therefore, be grounded in customary law or emerge through creative analogies and rapprochements. Certainly, as sometimes advocated in this project, it is possible to reel in the concept of strict liability within the furrow of the ILC's *Articles* when dealing with certain types of primary obligations, a posture that does not stand in contradiction with public international law. In fact, differing legal obligations will entail varying thresholds of responsibility – ranging from due diligence to absolute liability[37] – which will in turn have an impact on the application of secondary rules of State responsibility (at least in terms of how or when, if at all, those norms come into play, depending on whether an actual obligation was breached by reference to the applicable threshold). This argument, however, seems far removed from endorsing Professor Franck's own vision which, if authoritative, would, for all intents and purposes, render this whole exercise purely academic. For reasons discussed above, implementing a model inspired by strict liability under the auspices of the *Articles* might better address the problem of transborder terrorism and help vindicate specific policy objectives in the 'war' on terror, such as prevention. The implementation of strict liability elements under extant State responsibility frameworks is, by no means, accomplished by virtue of the ILC's *Articles*' text alone. Far more rigorous intellectual incursions into disparate facets of international law are required to make the merging of strict liability influences and the ILC's landmark document palatable.

[34] See, eg: J Brunnée, 'The Security Council and Self-Defence: Which Way to Global Security?' in N Blokker and N Schrijver (eds), *The Security Council and the Use of Force: Theory and Reality – A Need for Change?* (Leiden, Nijhoff, 2005) 107 at 123 (opining that the proper framework in tackling global terrorism resides in self-defence and not State responsibility, rejecting the agency paradigm in this setting and expounding that the mere 'harbouring and supporting' of terrorists is insufficient as a basis to invoke self-defence (ie calling for evidence of direct support or tacit approval, at a minimum)); A Nolkaemper, 'Attribution of Forcible Acts to States: Connections between the Law on the Use of Force and the Law of State Responsibility' in ibid at 136.

[35] JE Alvarez, 'Hegemonic International Law Revisited' (2003) 97 *AJIL* 873, 879–80 fn 34.

[36] ibid (essentially paraphrasing ILC Arts 8, 9 and 11).

[37] See, eg: JR Crawford, 'Revising the Draft Articles on State Responsibility' (1999) 10 *EJIL* 435, 438.

A) Striking a Balance: Limiting Governmental Interference in the Private Sphere While Upholding the Sovereign Equality of States

Whilst instilling the right incentives in governmental programmes constitutes a noble objective, the argument developed above is not premised on the promotion of totalitarian States,[38] nor does it strive to implement a system of absolute liability[39] whereby host-States are deprived of the opportunity to exculpate themselves ex post facto. Indeed, eminent publicists convincingly discarded the doctrine of absolute responsibility as a potential policy backbone for the law governing State responsibility.[40] In 1758, drawing from the Grotian assertion that State responsibility for private conduct only flows from State complicity in wrongful acts via the concepts of *patientia* (ie State failures to take necessary steps to thwart wrongful acts despite knowledge of the existence of such acts) or *receptus* (ie the State shelters the wrongdoers after the fact by failing to extradite or punish them),[41] Emerich de Vattel opined that responsibility could only attach to the State if it approved or ratified the act, thereby transforming itself in 'the real author of the affront'.[42] Again echoing the notions of *patientia* and *receptus*, de Vattel further underscored that

> if a sovereign who has the power to see that his subjects act in a just and peaceable manner permits them to injure a foreign nation . . . he does no less a wrong to that nation than if he injured it himself . . . A sovereign who refuses to repair the evil done by one of his subjects, or to punish the criminal or, finally, to deliver him up, makes himself in a way an accessory to the deed, and becomes responsible for it.[43]

[38] Gordon Christenson encapsulates the problem with granting dictatorial control to States over private conduct, an undesirable situation in international relations. See 'Attributing Acts of Omission to the State' (1991) 12 *Michigan Journal of International Law* 312, 368. Nor is the objective to encourage State sponsorship of terrorism through the imposition of multilateral structures. Although not directly on point, consider E Stephenson, 'Does United Nations War Prevention Encourage State-Sponsorship of International Terrorism? An Economic Analysis' (2004) 44 *Virginia Journal of International Law* 1197.

[39] Analysing the possible implementation of a prima facie case of liability under a prospective Convention on Terrorism before 9/11, McCredie highlighted the role of the reviewing court and discarded absolute liability as the preferred mechanism. See JA McCredie, 'The Responsibility of States for Private Acts of International Terrorism' (1985) 1 *Temple International and Comparative Law Journal* 69, 94. Conversely, Bowett had not completely ruled out the possible crafting of a rule of absolute liability in the context of indirect responsibility. See DW Bowett, 'Reprisals Involving Recourse to Armed Force' (1972) 66 *AJIL* 1, 19–20. More radically, see MB Baker, 'Terrorism and the Inherent Right of Self-Defense (A Call to Amend Article 51 of the United Nations Charter)' (1987) 10 *Houston Journal of International Law* 25, 48 ('terrorism may be the functional equivalent of an armed attack for which the perpetrators and their sanctuary states are *absolutely liable*' (emphasis added)).

[40] But see: M García-Mora, *International Responsibility for Hostile Acts of Private Persons against Foreign States* (The Hague, Nijhoff, 1962) 27–30.

[41] H Grotius, JB Scott, (tr), *De Jure Belli Ac Pacis (Vol 2)* (New York, Oceana, 1964) (1646) 523–26.

[42] E de Vattel, CG Fenwick, (tr), *The Law of Nations: or The Principles of Natural Law: Applied to the Conduct and Affairs of Nations and Sovereigns: A Work Tending to Display the True Interests of Powers* (Washington, DC, Carnegie Institution of Washington, 1916) (1758) 72.

[43] ibid, at 71, 75.

Should the duty to prevent terrorism attract the status of an obligation of result, it remains doubtful that its mere existence would dictate specific means to be implemented domestically to attain the prescribed objective, thereby impinging on the quasi-exclusive dominion of nation-States to govern their internal affairs.[44] The ICJ confirmed that obligations of result must be performed 'unconditionally' and that the non-observance of their prescriptions triggers State responsibility. However, the Court added that States bound by obligations of result are free to choose the 'means of implementation', which entails a 'reasonable' grace period to orchestrate constitutional adjustments in order to incorporate the obligations within domestic settings (eg through the adoption of legislation, for instance).[45]

An inherent feature of strict liability resides in shifting the burden of exculpation onto the defendant (ie the wrongful State).[46] Given the brooding private/public sphere dichotomy that underlies counterterrorism efforts and State responsibility for non-State behaviour, any proposed reform of international responsibility must be insulated against 'excessively intrusive or oppressive counterterrorist measures'.[47] Canada, a long-standing champion of human rights and international justice, elected the vehicle of immigration-based security certificates as one mechanism to both neutralise potential national security threats and comply with its international obligation of prevention. Whilst the Supreme Court struck down the security certificate scheme as unconstitutional, this legislative arrangement nonetheless paved the way for questionable human rights practices, sparking considerable controversy in civil society, the general public and academia.[48] We may similarly ponder why any reference to the safeguarding of human rights is absent from resolution 1373 which, in many ways, constitutes the cornerstone of modern counterterrorism policy-making and sets out stringent preventive obligations upon States regarding terrorism.[49] This puzzling (and deliberate?) oversight generated some concern amongst regional organisations, which reaffirmed the importance of upholding human rights and

[44] See, eg: J Combacau, 'Obligations de résultat et obligations de comportement: quelques questions et pas de réponse' in D Bardonnet et al (eds), *Mélanges offerts à Paul Reuter: le droit international: unité et diversité* (Paris, Pedone, 1981) 181 at 198.

[45] *Request for Interpretation of the Judgment of 31 March 2004 in the Case concerning Avena and Other Mexican Nationals (Mexico v United States of America) (Mexico v United States of America)*, Judgment of 19 January, *ICJ Reports* (2009) at 17 para 44.

[46] See, eg: Brownlie, above n 3 at 1.

[47] D Glenn, 'Scholar Would Place Liability on Countries That Harbor Terrorists (Vincent-Joel Proulx of McGill University Faculty of Law's opinion on Pakistan's responsibility in London Terrorist Bombings, 2005) (Interview)' 52 *The Chronicle of Higher Education*, 7 April 2006 at A24. See also: Duffy, above n 6 at 137–38.

[48] See *Charkaoui v Canada (Citizenship and Immigration)* [2007] 1 SCR 350. For commentary on the case and on the broader security certificate scheme, along with its reception in Canadian society, see MT Duffy and R Provost, 'Constitutional Canaries and the Elusive Quest to Legitimize Security Detentions in Canada' (2009) 40 *Case Western Reserve Journal of International Law* 531.

[49] See, eg: Duffy, above n 6 at 138.

humanitarian law in the global counterterrorism struggle.[50] It is no surprise, therefore, that reporting requirements under the Counterterrorism Committee instituted by virtue of resolution 1373 have generated 'predictably opportunistic' documents from 'reliable human rights violators, purportedly justifying old and new repressive national measures'.[51]

This lack of direction prompted some commentators to level charges against the Council to the effect that it foments human rights violations 'by "opening the hunting season on terrorism", including calling for its criminalisation, absent guidelines as to its definition, meaning or scope'.[52] The fact that post-9/11 resolutions have engendered broad-reaching consequences for Member States and individuals, including freezing assets of persons and organisations suspected of involvement in terrorism, signals serious implications for oversight of Council decision-making in the 'war' on terror. Whilst the Council is decidedly not above the law, diverse voices argue that these resolutions might conflict with human rights standards and, in light of rather limited avenues to review these decisions on the international plane, individuals have initiated challenges both at the national and regional levels. Facing a seemingly unchecked international decision-making body, and with a view to limiting governmental interference in private affairs pursuant to State responsibility, inter alia, this legal framework, paired with the emerging practice of individual and/or regional challenges to Council decision-making, raises significant legal questions. Certain scholars query whether States and regional organisations such as the European Union may engage in reviews/challenges/countermeasures against Security Council anti-terrorism resolutions.[53] As discussed above, ECJ jurisprudence seems to resolve this legal conundrum in the affirmative. In *Kadi and Al Barakaat*, the Court invalidated a regulation promulgated by the Council of the European Union targeting specific individuals associated with the Taliban or Al Qaeda, along with their assets, by virtue of UN Security Council resolutions, thereby arrogating power to review and control such functions and resolutions, albeit indirectly.[54]

[50] See, eg: Council of Europe, Guidelines on Human Rights and the Fight against Terrorism, adopted by the Committee of Ministers on 11 July 2002 at the 804th Meeting of the Ministers' Deputies, preamble at para (i), available at www1.umn.edu/humanrts/instree/HR%20and%20the%20fight%20against%20terrorism.pdf; Resolution 1271 (2002) ('Combating Terrorism and Respect for Human Rights'), adopted by the Parliamentary Assembly of the Council of Europe on 24 January 2002, available at http://assembly.coe.int/Main.asp?link=/Documents/AdoptedText/ta02/ERES1271.htm; OSCE Charter on Preventing and Combating Terrorism, 7 December 2002, MC(10).JOUR/2 at para 7, available at www.osce.org/odihr/16609.

[51] Alvarez, above n 35 at 876.

[52] Duffy, above n 6 at 351. See also: ibid, at 359.

[53] See, eg: A Nollkaemper and E de Wet (eds), *Review of the Security Council by Member States* (Antwerp, Intersentia, 2003); A Tzanakopoulos, *Disobeying the Security Council: Countermeasures against Wrongful Sanctions* (Oxford, OUP, 2011); A Reinisch (ed), *Challenging Acts of International Organizations Before National Courts* (Oxford, OUP, 2010).

[54] Joined Cases C-402/05P and C-415/05P *Yassin Abdullah Kadi and Al Barakaat International Foundation v Council and Commission*, European Court of Justice, 3 September 2008, [2008] ECR I-6341, (2008) 47 ILM 923. For a critical comment, see F Francioni, 'The Right of Access to Justice

Whilst this study operates on possible exceptions in the law governing State responsibility, any potential overhaul of liability mechanisms for State inaction or collusion in terrorism should not distance itself significantly from the objective of limiting governmental interventionism in private spheres – paired with upholding human rights – an idea underlying the general rule of non-attribution of private conduct. Indeed, 'The general rule, namely that States are not internationally responsible for the conduct of private persons reflects that States cannot – or should not – control the activities of their citizens'.[55] Should a reform of State responsibility be initiated in the field of counterterrorism, it should probably be accompanied by efforts to 'work in some kind of supervisory mechanism to make sure that constitutional principles and human rights are upheld'.[56] Others address this concern, albeit through vertical integration of international law in domestic courts, observing that 'the long-negotiated rules of state responsibility . . . incorporate some dimension of international due process' and that 'the emphasis of modern state responsibility doctrine on secondary obligations . . . suggests some quasi-procedural mandate'.[57] It becomes clear that the principles underpinning State responsibility for terrorism

> have a direct impact not only on how the interaction between the public and the private sphere is perceived and regulated, but on the kind of public/private relationship the international system seeks to advance. This is because the greater the degree of potential responsibility, the greater the incentive for State interference in the private domain.[58]

Even prior to 9/11 certain scholars attempted to justify the raison d'être of attribution by reference to its – supposedly – corresponding objective of minimising governmental interventionism in private spheres.[59]

Echoing Professor Rosenne's thoughts, certain publicists construe contemporary State responsibility scholarship as crystallising a radical shift and, perhaps, as foreshadowing the implementation of a mechanism of absolute liability based not on assigning unlawful acts to States, but grounded in their failures to act. Jerzy Kranz notes that State responsibility in this setting 'may result not only from controlling irregular units, but also from the lack of sufficient control over them, or failure to act, or negligence, including failure to comply with the

to Challenge the Security Council's Targeted Sanctions: After-Thoughts on Kadi' in U Fastenrath et al (eds), *From Bilateralism to Community Interest: Essays in Honour of Judge Bruno Simma* (Oxford, OUP, 2011) 908–22.

[55] R Wolfrum, 'State Responsibility for Private Actors: An Old Problem of Renewed Relevance' in Ragazzi, above n 2 at 425.

[56] Glenn, above n 47 at A24.

[57] RB Ahdieh, 'Between Dialogue and Decree: International Review of National Courts' (2004) 79 *NYU Law Review* 2029, 2131–32 and authorities cited therein.

[58] Becker, above n 1 at 271.

[59] See, eg: GA Christenson, 'The Doctrine of Attribution in State Responsibility' in RB Lillich (ed), *International Law of State Responsibility for Injuries to Aliens* (Charlottesville, University Press of Virginia, 1983) 320 at 323 (arguing that 'the policy basis for attribution is at the conceptual line preventing the State's entrance into every private sphere under the guise of responsibility').

legally binding resolutions of the Council'. This evolution of the doctrine shifts 'the stress from full control, through relative control, to the duty to maintain due diligence or presumption of absolute responsibility'.[60] If poorly-conceived, this framework is ripe for abuse against weaker States,[61] especially developing countries that may not have the same means as industrialised nations in combating terrorism. Thus, it is vital to distinguish the lack of monetary or personnel resources in combating terrorism from a State's (sometimes voluntary or inadvertent) failure in complying with its due diligence obligations.[62] Consequently, a deficiency in logistical capabilities required to crack down on terrorism is not synonymous with a lack of political will, nor does it necessarily translate into the adoption or endorsement of the terrorists' cause by the State.[63] Hence, failure to fulfil due diligence obligations should not automatically brand a host-State as 'unwilling' to prevent terrorism but rather as 'unable' to achieve such objective.[64] It appears that due diligence, again, acts as a relevant benchmark in gauging State compliance with counterterrorism obligations in this setting: 'Only when the state makes diligent efforts to prevent terrorists from using its territory to plan and prepare for attacks on other states, but is incapable of accomplishing this objective, will it fulfill its international obligation'.[65] Recent episodes involving regional or transnational terrorist groups confirm that a State's inability to contain extremist threats percolating within its territory is not necessarily tantamount to an espousal of the terrorists' cause or ideology. For instance, the Abu Sayyaf terrorist network operating within the Philippines, whose 'stated goal is to promote an independent Islamic state in western Mindanao and the Sulu Archipelago', has consistently eluded effective law enforcement.[66] Similar circumstances surround the activities of the Jemaah Islamiyah organisation, a militant Islamist group carrying out terrorist operations in several south-eastern Asian States whilst furthering its objective of

[60] J Kranz, 'The Use of Armed Force – New Facts and Trends' (2006) 3 *The Polish Quarterly of International Affairs* 68, 80.

[61] On different precedents of abuse against, or undue interference in the internal affairs of, weaker States see generally: C De Visscher, *La responsabilité des États: cours professé à l'Académie de Droit international de La Haye, juillet 1923 (tome 2)* (Lugduni Batavorum, Brill, 1924) 117–18; PC Jessup, *A Modern Law of Nations: An Introduction* (New York, Macmillan, 1948) 95–96.

[62] See J-C Martin, *Les règles internationales relatives à la lutte contre le terrorisme* (Brussels, Bruylant, 2006) 459. In the *Tehran Hostages* Case, the ICJ opined that the shortcomings of the Iranian State were 'due to more than mere negligence or lack of appropriate means'. See *United States Diplomatic and Consular Staff in Tehran* (*United States v Iran*), Judgment of 24 May, *ICJ Reports* (1980) 3 at para 63.

[63] On the question of a host-State's obligations pertaining to counterterrorism capacity-building, see Becker, above n 1 at 144–46.

[64] See, eg: M Lehto, *International Responsibility for Terrorist Acts: A Shift towards More Indirect Forms of Responsibility* (Rovaniemi, Lapland University Press, 2008) 474–75.

[65] J-A Romano, 'Combating Terrorism and Weapons of Mass Destruction: Reviving the Doctrine of a State of Necessity' (1999) 87 *Georgetown Law Journal* 1023, 1034.

[66] US Department of State, 'Country Reports on Terrorism 2004' (April 2005) at 93–94, available at www.state.gov/documents/organization/45313.pdf.

'establish[ing] a pan-Islamic state across much of [Southeast Asia]'.[67] Quite the contrary, 'the governments of states from which terrorists operate may be affirmatively antithetical to, or at least not share, the ideological goals of terrorist groups present in their territory'.[68]

Conversely, indigence and depleted manpower are not, in and of themselves, sufficient bases for exoneration under the framework of State responsibility. This inference seems politically desirable both from *lex lata* and *lex ferenda* perspectives. Consequently, any effective and equitable liability system should ensure that those reasons are accompanied by potential defences – such as civil war on the territory of the concerned State – in order to refute a prima facie presumption of responsibility against a host-State.[69] Granted, the enlargement of the scope of counterterrorism due diligence after 9/11 has undoubtedly enabled numerous rights abuses in various States, and continues to pose a real danger for human rights protection across the globe. Therefore, effective safeguards must be developed to reconcile legally bolstered counterterrorism obligations in the face of enhanced transnational terrorist capacity, on one hand, with the precepts underpinning fundamental human dignity, epitomised by the human rights project, on the other. Equally important is the tension arising between the sovereign equality of States on the international scene and the propensity of powerful States to self-authorise intervention vis-à-vis nations failing to prevent terrorism. The very concept of sovereignty 'as a form of power generated through self-exception' was contemporaneously brandished by a few powerful Western States, notably the US and Great Britain, as a means to justify interventionist stances into the affairs of other States which, incidentally, fostered human rights and humanitarian violations.[70]

The present study and other like-minded, policy-oriented reforms of State responsibility aimed at enhancing the prevention and suppression of terrorism must strike a delicate balance – albeit legally and politically precarious under some lights – between the vital principle of non-intervention and the pressing need to stamp out terrorist networks. Ultimately, endorsing legal standards that indiscriminately subject host-States to highly intrusive consequences flowing from wrongful acts would unequivocally signal a blatant failure in achieving the abovementioned balance. The legal analysis is further compounded by the fact that ensuing interventions may entail some forcible component – particularly under the Responsibility to Protect Doctrine, which has become a multilateral

[67] Council on Foreign Relations, 'Jemaah Islamiyah (a.k.a. Jemaah Islamiah)', 19 June 2009, available at www.cfr.org/indonesia/jemaah-islamiyah-k-jemaah-islamiah/p8948.

[68] AS Weiner, 'The Use of Force and Contemporary Security Threats: Old Medicine for New Ills?' (2006) 59 *Stanford Law Review* 415, 432.

[69] See McCredie, above n 39 at 94.

[70] This language is borrowed from 'Sovereign Self-Exceptionality and International Intervention: Reading Security Council Resolutions as Acts of Declaration', Paper presented at the annual meeting of the ISA's 49th Annual Convention, 'Bridging Multiple Divides', San Francisco, 26 March 2008, available at http://citation.allacademic.com/meta/p_mla_apa_research_citation/2/5/0/9/1/p250911_index.html.

response regime exclusively involving recourse to force – or some other sovereignty-erosive form of extraneous intercession. As a corollary, there is a crucial need, co-extensive with identifying international accountability mechanisms for failing to prevent terrorism, to devise effective safeguards and checks/balances with a view to upholding the sovereign equality and rights of States in the proposed framework. This priority becomes particularly urgent in light of the conceptually fertile interrelationship connecting State responsibility with the all-too-pertinent language shift from a 'right to intervene' to a 'responsibility to protect' that derives from the R2P Doctrine; it should ultimately be harnessed with a view to shedding new light on secondary norms of State responsibility.[71] Moreover, an extra layer of complexity pervades the analysis when those liability mechanisms and, potentially, the ensuing consequences target ineffective or 'failed' States. Such scenarios are considered in the next section in the hopes of developing a theory that is also sensitive to the realities facing the developing world, whilst simultaneously eradicating impunity or the prospect of waging surrogate terrorism through proxies.

B) The Conundrum of Ineffective or 'Failed' States

As seen in chapter one, several factual scenarios involving State failures to prevent terrorism challenge the traditional rules of State responsibility, with sometimes subtle or convoluted questions of State involvement – ranging from tacit acquiescence to direct logistical/financial/military support falling short of the *Nicaragua* standard – further clouding the equation. Yet, a crucial distinction resides in situations involving States capable of thwarting terrorism but reticent to do so owing to lack of political will or regional pressure. Reviving Cassese's pre-9/11 concerns over the 'grey' area of uncertainty permeating possible levels of governmental involvement in terrorism, 'the issue becomes more difficult when a state, which has the ability to control terrorist activity, nonetheless tolerates, and even encourages it'.[72] A case in point is that of Pakistan, whose tribal regions – also contiguous with the Afghan border – serve as refuge for expelled Taliban and Al Qaeda members.[73] Al Qaeda members seeking solace in those areas have also used those contiguous regions as launch pads for terrorist excur-

[71] But see: A Peters, 'The Responsibility to Protect: Spelling Out the Hard legal Consequences for the UN Security Council and Its Members' in Fastenrath et al, above n 54 at 306 (inferring that responses under R2P do not amount to countermeasures but rather to collective security measures).

[72] GM Travalio, 'Terrorism, International Law and the Use of Military Force' (2000) 18 *Wisconsin International Law Journal* 145, 154.

[73] See, eg: Q Jawadullah and PZ Shah, 'Suicide Bomber Attacks Anti-Taliban Meeting in Northwest Pakistan, Killing More than 40', *New York Times*, 11 October 2008 at A10; M Mazzetti et al, 'New Generation of Qaeda Chiefs Is Seen on Rise', *New York Times*, 2 April 2007 at A1. Some allegations also surfaced that there are terrorist training camps on Pakistani soil. See, eg: C Gall and D Rohde, 'Pakistan Lets Taliban Train, Prisoner Says', *New York Times*, 4 August 2004 at A1. See also generally: I Gul, *The Most Dangerous Place: Pakistan's Lawless Frontier* (London, Penguin Books, 2010).

sions into Afghanistan. Furthermore, confusion still surrounds the extent of the involvement of Pakistani intelligence services in sheltering or supporting Osama Bin Laden before his death in 2011; in particular, the ties binding the governing apparatus to both Harakat-ul-Mujahedeen, a group that supported the deceased terrorist in Pakistan, and its leader, Maulana Fazlur Rehman Khalil, remain unclear.[74]

Aside from signalling a 'growing violence stemming from attacks by militants based in Pakistan's unruly tribal areas',[75] this escalating theatre of war lays out a textbook application of complex transborder terrorist insurgency for the purposes of State responsibility, bringing Pakistan's efficacy in containing that threat into sharp relief. Pakistan's inefficiency in combating terrorism is likely at least partially attributable to its lack of political will and not solely to an absence of actual means towards this end. Perhaps swayed by international pressure to step up its counterterrorism efforts, Pakistan started deploying troops in the targeted tribal areas in 2004 to better contain the threat.[76] Similar initiatives have also intensified as a result of renewed pressures by Washington calling for Pakistan to quell the abundance of Taliban and Al Qaeda elements within its borders. These requests undoubtedly stem from some level of reciprocity – perhaps asymmetric – now governing relations between the US and other nations in the pursuit of better counterterrorism norm compliance. Since 9/11, the US has provided colossal amounts of foreign aid to ineffective governments – with over 10 billion dollars going to Pakistan alone – in the hopes of enhancing counterterrorism structures in those States and acquiring more influence in their domestic and foreign policies.[77]

Such behaviour patterns generate the inference that 'The attacks have made the U.S. more dependent on other states for assistance, some form of reciprocity is to be anticipated . . . the U.S. is being more solicitous of Pakistan's request for economic aid than before September 11'.[78] More importantly, it is now foreseeable that Pakistan might become the breeding ground for another large-scale military intervention or, at least, an extension of current efforts in Afghanistan to root out Al Qaeda safe havens and bases of operations. Indeed, American troops have been deployed in the targeted regions in order to mount excursions

[74] See, eg: C Gall et al, 'Seized Cellphone Offers Clues to Bin Laden's Pakistani Links', *New York Times*, 24 June 2011 at A1; DE Sanger, 'U.S. Raises Pressure on Pakistan in Raid's Wake', *New York Times*, 9 May 2011 at A1.

[75] E Schmitt, 'Joint Chiefs Chairman Is Pessimistic on Afghanistan', *New York Times*, 10 October 2008 at A12.

[76] See F Chipaux, 'Le Pakistan a décidé de «nettoyer» les zones tribales des éléments d'Al-Qaida', *Le Monde*, 25 February 2004.

[77] See W Arkin, 'What $10 Billion Has Bought in Pakistan', *Washington Post*, 6 November 2007. See also: C Cohen and D Chollet, 'When $10 Billion Is Not Enough: Rethinking U.S. Strategy toward Pakistan' (Spring 2007) *The Washington Quarterly* 7.

[78] R Keohane, 'The Public Delegitimation of Terrorism and Coalition Politics' in K Booth and T Dunne (eds), *Worlds in Collision: Terror and the Future of Global Order* (Basingtoke, Palgrave, 2002) 141 at 143. See also: DW Larson, 'Exchange and Reciprocity in International Negotiations' (1998) 3 *International Negotiation* 121, 127; DA Baldwin, *Economic Statecraft* (Princeton, Princeton University Press, 1985) 292–94.

against persons linked both with Al Qaeda and the Taliban.[79] Concerns were recently growing that Pakistan was failing to contain the activities of Pakistani Taliban within the tribal region of North Waziristan, as this organisation is believed to have directed and financed Faisal Shahzad in the failed Times Square bomb plot.[80]

Similar eventualities could also result from 'failed State' scenarios – as is certainly the case for Somalia – and, to a lesser extent, from the situations prevalent in Yemen and (arguably) Pakistan.[81] For instance, the Security Council imposed sanctions on Sudan because it harboured terrorists.[82] This possibility signals important implications for the law of State responsibility and certainly raises myriad difficult policy questions when devising an applicable deterrence model. For instance, what if a 'failed' (or inefficient) State is unable to repel terrorist threats percolating within its own borders or, even worse, does not have the capacity to monitor such activity or to even know about such operations? Implicit in this fact is the idea that the host-State has sacrificed a portion of its territorial sovereignty when it lost potential control over terrorist organisations on its territory.[83] Should we expect it to subscribe to alternate 'thwarting scenarios' such as the deployment of troops within its borders, or the implementation of more stringent law enforcement methods? This line of inquiry carries particular implications for Security Council-approved measures against 'failed' States or against nations governed by illegitimate or repressive regimes, which clearly amounts to an ambiguous legal area.[84]

[79] See, eg: J Perlez and PZ Shah, 'Confronting Taliban, Pakistan Finds Itself at War', *New York Times*, 3 October 3 2008 at A1; 'U.S. Airstrike Said to Kill 5 in Pakistan', *New York Times*, 12 October 2008 at A8; 'Pakistani Officials Say U.S. Strikes Kill 12 in Villages', *New York Times*, 4 October 2008 at A8.

[80] See, eg: J Berger, 'Holder Backs a Miranda Limit for Terror Suspects', *New York Times*, 10 May 2010 at A1.

[81] See, eg: O Roy, *Les illusions du 11 septembre: Le débat stratégique face au terrorisme* (Paris, Seuil, 2002) 18. Consequently, the 'war' on terror adversely affects and further impedes democratic institution-building in 'failed' States, such as Somalia. See, eg: K Samuels, 'Constitution-Building during the War on Terror: The Challenge of Somalia' (2008) 40 *NYU Journal of International Law and Politics* 597. See also generally: MB Ndulo and M Grieco (eds), *Failed and Failing States: The Challenges to African Reconstruction* (Newcastle upon Tyne, Cambridge Scholars Publishing, 2010). On Afghanistan's potential status as a 'failed' State, see M Byers, 'Terrorism, the Use of Force, and International Law After 11 September' (2001) 51 *ICLQ* 401, 403; D Thürer, 'The 'Failed State' and International Law' (1999) 81 *International Review of the Red Cross* 731.

[82] SC Res 1054, UN SCOR, 46th Sess, 3660th Mtg, UN Doc S/RES/1054 (1996). On State responsibility in the context of the Sudanese war, see CM Henderson, 'Michael Byers, War Law: International Law and Armed Conflict' (2007) 12 *Journal of Conflict and Security Law* 150, 152–53.

[83] Peter Kovács ponders the implications of such situation, where 'le terrorisme est subi par l'Etat', and identifies the following ramification: 'l'Etat est incapable d'exercer les prérogatives de sa souveraineté territoriale vis-à-vis d'une organisation terroriste ayant son fief sur son sol'. See 'Beaucoup de questions et peu de réponses autour de l'imputabilité d'un acte terroriste à un Etat' (2002) 1 *Journal of European Integration Studies* 20, 23. In such circumstances, Brigitte Stern argues that it would be unfair to attribute terrorist actions to the sanctuary State. See 'La Responsabilité internationale des Etats: Perspectives récentes' in JC Lloréns (ed), *Cursos euromediterráneos bancaja de derecho internacional (Vol VII)* (Valencia, Tirant lo Blanch, 2003) 659 at 688.

[84] See CB Hynes et al, 'National Security' (2007) 41 *International Lawyer* 683, 683–84.

Some authors resolve these questions by arguing that in such circumstances, States are expected to accept extraneous counterterrorism assistance or, perhaps, even to seek out such aid. Failure to accept any such forthcoming help could signal the sanctuary State's unwillingness to comply with its preventive counterterrorism obligations and could be potentially tantamount to the commission of an internationally wrongful act.[85] In fact, the idea of counterterrorism capacity-building lies at the core of the efforts underlying resolution 1373.[86] These problems were further compounded by the recent situation in Iraq, which unquestionably fell under the rubric of 'failed State'.[87] As a result, Iraq now hosted a plethora of terrorist factions and irregular bands, and could plausibly transform into a launching pad for transborder attacks.[88] In sum, 'Violations of human rights today are not always committed by strong dictatorial governments in a police state. They are as likely to be committed by non-state actors in failed states'.[89]

Again, this range of questions brings the tension between upholding State sovereignty and combating terrorism efficiently into sharp focus. It should also be recalled that influential scholar, Hersch Lauterpacht, believed and wrote that the very concept of 'sovereignty' impedes the advancement of the law governing State responsibility.[90] Thus, short-circuiting or trumping the privileges of sovereignty might, in fact, be a solution in cases where host-States are inefficient, or

[85] See, eg: KN Trapp, 'Back to Basics: Necessity, Proportionality, and the Right of Self-Defence against Non-State Terrorist Actors' (2007) 56 *ICLQ* 141, 147 fn 33; Nolkaemper, above n 34 at 161.

[86] N Quénivet, 'You Are the Weakest Link and We Will Help You! The Comprehensive Strategy of the United Nations to Fight Terrorism' (2006) 11 *Journal of Conflict and Security Law* 371, 390–91.

[87] See, eg: AF Perez, 'Legal Frameworks for Economic Transition in Iraq – Occupation Under the Law of War Vs. Global Governance Under the Law of Peace' (2004) 18 *Transnational Lawyer* 53, 60 fn 27; F Rich, 'They'll Break the Bad News on 9/11', *New York Times*, 24 June 24 2007 at WK14.

[88] See, eg: 'War Without End', *New York Times*, 27 May 2007 at 49; JF Burns, 'Iraq to Release Detainees in Bid to Ease Tensions', *New York Times*, 7 June 2006 at A1; M Slackman and S Shane, 'Terrorists Trained by Zarqawi Went Abroad, Jordan Says', *New York Times*, 11 June 2006 at 11. It has also been alleged that Kurdish terrorists are using Iraq as a haven in order to launch excursions against Turkey. See, eg: PW Galbraithm, 'Our Corner of Iraq', *New York Times*, 25 July 2007 at A19. In addition, the occupation of Iraq by coalition forces not only raised the possible question of the international responsibility of the occupant but, alternatively, of the administration established by the occupying power as well. For discussion of these themes, see E Benvenisti, *The International Law of Occupation*, 2nd edn (Princeton, Princeton University Press, 1993) xiii.

[89] DL Shelton, 'International Human Rights Law: Principled, Double, or Absent Standards?' (2007) 25 *Law and Inequality: A Journal of Theory and Practice* 467, 513.

[90] Hersch Lauterpacht believed that 'the traditional respect for State sovereignty refrained the development of the law of international responsibility, particularly regarding the consequences of responsibility'. It followed that

> the traditional theory limited responsibility only to the reparation for damage (material and moral), without it being possible for States, as a result of their sovereignty, to be punished. This vision, however, in exempting the State from the consequences of its own violations of the law, appeared entirely arbitrary, limiting the action of justice at the international level.

See AA Cançado Trindade, 'Complementarity between State Responsibility and Individual Responsibility for Grave Violations of Human Rights: The Crime of State Revisited' in Ragazzi, above n 2 at 261. See also: H Lauterpacht, 'Règles générales du droit de la paix' (1937-IV) 62 *Recueil des Cours* 95, 339, 349–50, 350–52.

when terrorist threats loom large while containment options within targeted territories are depleted. The failed/inefficient State scenario not only directly informs the possible application of attribution standards to challenging factual patterns, but also becomes particularly intractable when contemplated through the lens of the nature of the obligation to prevent terrorism. Indeed, the fact that the scope of this obligation is far from circumscribed engenders additional conceptual and practical uncertainties.[91]

However, the lack of political will does not exclusively foment a State's failure to thwart terrorist threats emanating from its territory. A resounding example is the situation in Chechnya, where terrorist training camps abound despite Russia's ostentatious efforts in combating international terrorism.[92] Similarly, as discussed in chapter two, the 1982 Israel-Lebanon conflict also epitomised a scenario whereby a State had lost control over its territory (the southern portion of Lebanon) from which terrorist organisations were launching excursions.[93] This type of failed/inefficient State paradigm can easily reoccur – as it did in Lebanon in 2006 – as some States currently constitute havens for terrorists looking for potential strongholds where they may conduct operations. Some scholars resolve this dilemma by attenuating responsibility of the (failed/inefficient) local government in favour of a potentially narrower right to recourse to force accruing to the victim-State, so that it may root out terrorist bases of operation within the borders of the sanctuary State.[94] Whilst such construction may appear attractive initially, it also threatens to erode the much-needed equilibrium between devising effective rules of international responsibility in the face of enhanced terrorist capacity and respecting the sovereign equality of States (which inherently entails limiting unchecked interventionism against weaker States). Furthermore, engaging economically weaker States in the elaboration of more efficient State responsibility norms for counterterrorism not only fosters multilateralism and international cooperation, but it will also ensure a greater degree of compliance with the rules being developed. Obviously, this objective remains intimately tied to the goal of protecting developing countries: 'negotiating international rules in multilateral fora gives weaker states greater influence, and this provides them with an incentive to follow the resulting agreements, leads to quasi-voluntary compliance, and thus lowers the costs of

[91] Karl Zemanek summarises these concerns trenchantly in 'Does the Prospect of Incurring Responsibility Improve the Observance of International Law?' in Ragazzi, above n 2 at 131.

[92] See, eg: Martin, above n 62 at 459. See also: CJ Chivers, 'The Chechen's Story: From Unrivaled Guerrilla Leader to the Terror of Russia', *New York Times*, 15 September 2004 at A9.

[93] Martin, above n 62 at 459. For a discussion through the lens of the 2006 Israel-Hezbollah conflict, see Kirchner, above n 3 at 780–82.

[94] See, eg: G Battaglini, 'War against Terrorism *Extra Moenia*, Self-Defence and Responsibility: A Pure Juridical Approach' in Ragazzi, above n 2 at 145 (also citing Y Dinstein, 'The International Legal Response to Terrorism' in R Ago (ed), *International Law at the Time of Its Codification: Essays in Honour of Roberto Ago (Vol II)* (Milan, Giuffrè, 1987) 139 at 146). On self-help vis-à-vis terrorism, see JF Murphy, 'State Self-Help and Problems of Public International Law' in AE Evans and JF Murphy (eds), *Legal Aspects of International Terrorism* (Lexington, Heath, 1978) 553–73.

enforcement (pacification)'.[95] Hence, we must develop safeguards in order to avoid indiscriminate condemnation of host-States, as it is unlikely that the international community will accept a blanket rationale of absolute liability and automatic reprisals against ineffective States in all cases.[96] In fact, forcible reprisals have been expressly excluded from the purview of State responsibility rationale;[97] thus, the only juridically legitimate response to a wrongful act involving force would arguably have to be framed within the furrow of self-defence.

At this juncture, an appropriate dose of political realism seems apposite. The model advocated in this book certainly extends, rather easily from a conceptual standpoint, to straightforward cases of indirect State involvement in terrorism such as those practised in Libya and Syria. However, as the analysis will reiterate later on, harder cases significantly cloud the equation, particularly in light of host-States' capacity, or lack thereof, to meet counterterrorism obligations.[98] A quintessential example of an inefficient State in combating terrorism remains that of Lebanon in 2006, which lost effective control over the southern portion of its territory and, as a result, of Hezbollah factions launching transnational strikes from that region. Whilst considerable bases for engaging accountability might be persuasively established when a State's loss of territorial control enables terrorism, implementing legal consequences flowing from that liability might prove politically impracticable.[99] Indeed, enforcing effective countermeasures against uncooperative States involved in supporting terrorism or carrying out surrogate warfare via proxies (eg Iran, Syria) might prove difficult. Similarly, attempts to seek reparations against ineffective States like Sudan or Somalia – in a truly monetary or restitutive spirit – might be equally improbable. In this light, sceptical outlooks on the potential contributions of State responsibility would call into question the very engagement of its corpus of norms. Under this lens, liability mechanisms can provide little more than some symbolic establishment of the State's wrongdoing without any corresponding coercive sanction.

However, this study contends that this type of reparation – albeit symbolic because it stops at the mechanics of establishing responsibility without registering any tangible restitutive impact (ie in the spirit of 'satisfaction', although perhaps unrequited) – and the effect of such responses should not be dismissed or underemphasised. Granted, whilst the prospect of imposing some forms of

[95] N Krisch, 'International Law in Times of Hegemony: Unequal Power and the Shaping of the International Legal Order' (2005) 16 *EJIL* 369, 373.

[96] See, eg: Byers, above n 81 at 408.

[97] See, eg: Declaration on Principles of International Law Concerning Friendly Relations and Co-operation Among States in Accordance with the Charter of the United Nations, GA Res 2625, UN GAOR, 25th Sess, Supp No 28, UN Doc A/RES/25/2625 (1970) 122 [hereinafter Declaration on Friendly Relations]; E Zoller, *Peacetime Unilateral Remedies: An Analysis of Countermeasures* (Dobbs Ferry, Transnational Publishers, 1984) 38–39.

[98] See also: above ch 1, section IV.D).

[99] See, eg: above ch 3, section III.A); ch 5, sections II.B); IV.C).

diplomatic or official apologies upon those States might be challenging,[100] the establishment of a host-State's responsibility, alone, can nonetheless provide some level of cathartic release from both a legal and political standpoint. It may well be that the ascertainment of a State's commission of a wrongful act – exemplified by its failure to prevent transnational terrorism – suffices as a remedy, much in the same way that a declaratory judgment can provide some degree of closure on contentious issues in domestic judicial settings. Alternatively, this reality does not preclude the opposite scenario, namely where post-wrongful act condemnation acquires traction on the international plane and effectively pressures the wrongful State into redressing the harm, acknowledging its international responsibility or complying with other secondary obligations under State responsibility repertoire. Whilst more controversial, this objective might also be attained via more forceful political means, such as Security Council intercession or ICJ judicially-imposed obligations of reparation or, even more polemically, via coordinated multilateral response regimes involving force under the R2P Doctrine or the scheme of collective self-defence. Consequently, the transfer in onus under the proposed model seeks to partly alleviate some of the problems associated with both host-States' lack of political will and scarcity of means in combating terrorism.

C) Transferring the Onus onto the Host-State

As mentioned previously, a prima facie finding of indirect responsibility would necessarily involve a transfer of the burden of proof onto host-States.[101] Upon first inspection, the premises underlying this proposition might seem to run counter to the ICJ's pronouncements on indirect responsibility. The resolution of hard cases, such as those involving vague State inaction vis-à-vis terrorism, will revolve, to a large extent, around the host-State's exclusive territorial control.[102] This same notion of control, however, might not be sufficient in all cases

[100] However, States having 'caused terrorist attacks' have a corresponding duty to 'publicly acknowledge state responsibility for those attacks, prosecute those responsible, and provide reparations for victims'. See, eg: ES Bates and the IBA Task Force (eds), *Terrorism and International Law: Accountability, Remedies, and Reform – A Report of the IBA Task Force on Terrorism* (Oxford, OUP, 2011) 248.

[101] Conversely, the perpetration of terrorist activities by non-State or private actors does not necessarily or automatically shift the burden of proof onto the claimant (wronged) State. In that regard, Brownlie's remarks, above n 3 at 164–65, are quite instructive.

[102] For hard cases involving State failures to prevent terrorism, see Robert Barnidge's discussion about HLA Hart's description of the tension between the general and the specific, which he then re-designates as the 'plain case' and the 'unenvisaged case'. See RP Barnidge, Jr, *Non-State Actors and Terrorism: Applying the Law of State Responsibility and the Due Diligence Principle* (The Hague, T.M.C. Asser Press, 2008) 140–41. On the original nomenclature, see HLA Hart, *The Concept of Law*, 2nd edn (Oxford, OUP, 1994) 126–29. See also: Barnidge, Jr, above n 102 at 141 fn 17 and accompanying text, inviting the reader to compare his examples of the 'plain case' and the 'unenvisaged case' with the model found in V-J Proulx, 'Babysitting Terrorists: Should States Be Strictly Liable for Failing to Prevent Transborder Attacks?' (2005) 23 *Berkeley Journal of International Law* 615, 662–66.

to persuasively engage a prima facie mechanism of responsibility. Yet, as amply referenced throughout this study, the precedent set forth by the response to 9/11 arguably reversed this line of reasoning, at least in cases of catastrophic terrorism caused by serious violations of an international duty (ie the obligation to prevent terrorism). This stance is further bolstered by myriad Security Council resolutions deploring Afghanistan's regime and calling for it to suppress terrorist activities on its soil, and by that State's egregious disregard for both the Council's exhortations and international law, more generally. In any event, whilst the notion of exclusive territorial control remains inextricably linked to indirect State responsibility for terrorism, it also exerts a direct incidence on, and sometimes complicates pertinent evidentiary concerns. Hence, the role of knowledge – or potential knowledge – in preventing an impugned terrorist attack becomes prevalent in the analysis. Of particular importance are the findings extracted from *Corfu Channel*, which seem apposite here:

> [I]t cannot be concluded from the mere fact of the control exercised by a State over its territory and waters that that State necessarily knew, or ought to have known, of any unlawful act perpetrated therein, nor yet that it necessarily knew, or should have known, the authors. This fact, by itself, and apart from other circumstances, neither involves *prima facie* responsibility nor shifts the burden of proof.
>
> On the other hand, the fact of this exclusive territorial control exercised by a State within its frontiers has a bearing upon the methods of proof available to establish the knowledge of that State as to such events. By reason of this exclusive control, the other State, the victim of a breach of international law, is often unable to furnish direct proof of facts giving rise to responsibility. Such a State should be allowed a more liberal recourse to inferences of fact and circumstantial evidence . . .
>
> The Court must examine therefore whether it has been established by means of indirect evidence that Albania has knowledge of mine-laying in her territorial waters independently of any connivance on her part in this operation. The proof may be drawn from inferences of fact, provided they leave *no room* for reasonable doubt. The elements of fact on which these inferences can be based may differ from those which are relevant to the question of connivance.[103]

Prior to 9/11, some scholars touched upon the possible implementation of a prima facie finding of responsibility in certain cases, which entailed transferring the onus to host-States. These commentators underlined the political and legal consequences of circumventing presumed responsibility in such extreme cases, albeit when dealing with specific types of terrorism: 'With respect to hostage-taking, the State on whose territory it occurs must be presumed responsible and carry the burden of establishing its innocence. Exonerating Lebanon and Iran may lead to dangerous claims of exemption'.[104] Under the proposed model,

[103] *Corfu Channel* Case *(United Kingdom of Great Britain and Northern Ireland v Albania)*, Merits, Judgment of 9 April, *ICJ Reports* (1949) 4 at 18. See also: M Bennouna, 'Réflexions sur la régulation internationale du risque à propos du concept de prévention' in R Hostiou et al (eds), *Terres du droit: Mélanges en l'honneur d'Yves Jégouzo* (Paris, Dalloz, 2009) 371 at 377.

[104] M Flory, 'International Law: An Instrument to Combat Terrorism' in R Higgins and M Flory (eds), *Terrorism and International Law* (London, Routledge, 1997) 30 at 36.

however, the host-State will be able to refute the initial finding of responsibility or, at least, diffuse some of its momentum in the second prong of the two-tiered strict liability-infused approach. In other words, once responsibility has been established and the onus has shifted, the host-State will purport to demonstrate how it exhausted all options offered to it, exercised due care and used all means possible to thwart the terrorist attack.

This will undoubtedly operate by reference to a somewhat objective construction of the notion of due diligence in the second tier of the inquiry, whilst examining State responsibility for failing to prevent terrorism.[105] The very exercise of determining whether the sanctuary State's behaviour can be said to be congruent with the accepted due diligence thresholds does not necessarily entail an entirely subjective component in the application of liability rules. Building on Anzilotti's influential scholarship, one view would rather construe due diligence as a vital and substantive aspect lying at the very core of the obligation of prevention: 'where we are faced with the concept of the State's due diligence in preventing certain acts of private persons, this does not represent a particular subjective element of responsibility, but rather the *very content* of the international duty'.[106] Similarly, other objectivist scholars opine that due diligence should be construed as an 'objective' rule, which serves to complete or enhance the content of certain international obligations.[107] Thus, 'In such cases, the concept of fault is only an ""easy analogy" in order to synthetically express the content of a special State duty to prevent a given event'.[108]

Ultimately, considerations pertaining to the distinction between obligations of means and result,[109] the logistical capacity of the host-State and its loss of territorial control, and so on, should only be invoked in the second tier of the strict liability-infused approach, as an integral part of the defence against the prima facie finding of responsibility. For example, whilst consonant with the proposed model, the repeated strikes carried out since 2004 by the Revolutionary Armed Forces of Colombia (FARC) against Colombian civilians and security forces from Ecuador could be construed as establishing a prima facie case of

[105] For an application of the due diligence standard to counterterrorism for the purposes of the law of State responsibility, see RP Barnidge, Jr, 'States' Due Diligence Obligations With Regard to International Non-State Terrorist Organisations Post-11 September 2001: The Heavy Burden that States Must Bear' (2005) 16 *Irish Studies in International Affairs* 103. See also generally: RP Barnidge, Jr, 'The Due Diligence Principle Under International Law' (2006) 8 *International Community Law Review* 81; H Blomeyer-Bartenstein, 'Due Diligence' in R Bernhardt (ed), *Encyclopedia of Public International Law (Vol 1)* (Amsterdam, North-Holland, 1992) 1110–15.

[106] R Pisillo-Mazzeschi, 'The Due Diligence Rule and the Nature of International Responsibility of States' (1992) 35 *German Yearbook of International Law* 9, reprinted in R Provost (ed), *State Responsibility in International Law* (Aldershot, Ashgate/Dartmouth, 2002) 103.

[107] See, eg: EM Borchard, *The Diplomatic Protection of Citizens Abroad* (New York, Banks Law Publishing, 1915) 213 ff; C Eagleton, *The Responsibility of States in International Law* (New York, NYU Press, 1928) 76–94.

[108] Pisillo-Mazzeschi, above n 106 at 103.

[109] Pursuant to the ILC's *Articles*, assessing the scope of any international obligation will entail the evaluation of several factors, including the conduct/result dichotomy. See Crawford, above n 14 at 125.

responsibility. The fact that those recurrent transborder attacks were not thwarted suggests 'that Ecuador had failed in its due diligence obligation under international law to prevent harm to Colombia, either due to a lack of will or ability to locate and dismantle FARC camps in Ecuadoran territory'; in attempting to cogently refute the presumption of international responsibility weighing against it, Ecuador would be 'required [to] demonstrate effectiveness in counterterrorism'.[110] Before moving on to that analytical step, it is useful to briefly highlight other advantages of the proposed model.

III. OTHER ADVANTAGES OF A STRICT LIABILITY MODEL

The strict liability-inspired approach, coupled with the circumvention of attribution from the equation of State responsibility for terrorism, promotes fairness amongst States and somewhat levels out the disparity in economic and political power.[111] This proposed model would place all host-States on equal footing, at least on a preliminary basis, irrespective of their economic or social status. Moreover, this model would disable the direct responsibility paradigm in most cases, as the new trend towards indirect accountability has become a sort of safety net, save in rare circumstances where aggrieved States can adequately establish direct host-State involvement.

A) Impact on International Relations and Reciprocity

The proposed model also strives to impart legitimacy upon the international legal system[112] while instilling some, albeit modest, level of predictability to the Security Council's decision-making when it applies State responsibility norms. Indeed, the role of the Council in applying the law of State responsibility to State failures to prevent transnational terrorism is rather limited but can nonetheless be an important part of the reparative process. What is more, the Council can sometimes apply its powers in a quasi-judicial fashion.[113] This means that

[110] CM Bailliet, 'The "Unrule" of Law: Unintended Consequences of Applying the Responsibility to Prevent to Counterterrorism, A Case Study of Columbias's Raid in Ecuador' in CM Bailliet (ed), *Security: A Multidisciplinary Normative Approach* (Leiden, Nijhoff, 2009) 175 at 200.

[111] Fairness is undeniably one of the cardinal principles underpinning strict liability in many domestic legal systems. See, eg: JA Henderson, 'Coping with the Time Dimension in Products Liability' (1981) 69 *California Law Review* 919, 931–39. On the moral philosophy underlying certain strict liability regimes, see DG Owen, 'The Moral Foundations of Products Liability Law: Toward First Principles' (1993) 68 *Notre Dame Law Review* 427. On the concept of fairness in international law, see generally: TM Franck, *Fairness in International Law and Institutions* (Oxford, Clarendon Press, 1995).

[112] On the notion of legitimacy in international law, generally, see TM Franck, *The Power of Legitimacy among Nations* (New York, OUP, 1990).

[113] But see: R Higgins, 'The Place of International Law in the Settlement of Disputes by the Security Council' (1970) 64 *AJIL* 1, 17; O Schachter, 'The Quasi-Judicial Role of the Security Council and the General Assembly' (1964) 58 *AJIL* 960, 960–61.

the law of State responsibility provides a legal background or environment against which the Council can make political decisions as to the accountability of host-States in some circumstances. Although different situations warrant different levels of response, Council involvement in the assessment of State responsibility, if applicable, will undoubtedly remain acutely political. It might nonetheless be helpful to define clearer rules or guidelines to govern that eventuality, as the Council might sit as the final arbitrator in implementing State responsibility in some cases and, ultimately, in granting responses involving force against terrorism where justified. Similar reasoning easily extends to the ICJ's decision-making which, under some lights, is perhaps more compatible with the implementation of State responsibility as an alternative to unilateral State action or when one of the permanent five is involved in a dispute under Chapter VI of the UN Charter.

Shifting the onus to the host-State offers several advantages, including an overhaul of the ICJ's fact-finding function in establishing responsibility. As a corollary, such reform would aim to partially counter problematic aspects associated with that Court's practice in this regard.[114] In particular, the Court's process is essentially devoid of any probative fact-finding; it routinely accepts States' factual submissions on faith and ascribes judicial recognition to reports prepared by international organisations or government agencies without independent verification. In attempting to remedy this deficiency, this mechanism shifts the burden squarely onto sanctuary States and aims to effectively streamline the Court's or any other intermediary's or arbitrator's decision-making process when establishing the existence of a breach. Consequently, the decision-maker automatically infers that responsibility flows to the host-State and the focus of the inquiry then turns sharply to the scope and content of that State's actions and diligence in preventing terrorism. Granted, some of the evidentiary problems identified above might still persist under the proposed model. However, there is something rudimentarily equitable in obliging a wrongdoing State to meet the Court's minimal evidentiary threshold (as opposed to the other way around) – ie by demonstrating that it accumulated sufficient due diligence capital to refute the presumption weighing against it – once the claimant has successfully established the defendant's failure to prevent terrorism. In demonstrating that it fulfilled its obligation of prevention, a State might expose itself to alternate peacekeeping arrangements, as opposed to full-scale military invasion, such as the deployment of law enforcement units to capture suspected terrorists.[115] Indeed, vigilant law enforce-

[114] On issues related to the Court's fact-finding activities, see R Teitelbaum, 'Recent Fact-Finding Developments at the International Court of Justice' (2007) 6 *The Law and Practice of International Courts and Tribunals* 119–58.

[115] Several accounts concede that a State allowing its territory to become a launch pad for terrorism may forfeit its right to sovereignty in various contexts and, correspondingly, is entitled to invite outside intervention to neutralise the threat. See Baker, above n 39 at 40; PS Rao, 'International Crimes and State Responsibility' in Ragazzi, above n 2 at 68. See also: M Byers, 'Letting the Exception Prove the Rule' (2003) 17 *Ethics & International Affairs* 9, available at www.carnegiecouncil.org/resources/journal/17_1/roundtable/852.html. It should be reiterated that 'Security

ment will undoubtedly contribute to a productive global counterterrorism campaign.[116] Based on the evidence adduced from the host-State's case, the ICJ or Security Council might consider that a given course of action is disproportionate and therefore gauge the adequate levels of response (even *ex ante* if further terrorist attacks are imminent or expected to emanate from the sanctuary State). When the Council is involved, this determination will be achieved predominantly through a political process that may concomitantly draw on State responsibility repertoire and straddle quasi-judicial analytical terrain. To the extent possible, this type of structure will hopefully strive to eliminate the pursuit of retaliation inspired by retribution alone.

The proposed reform also purports to promote some degree of impartiality in international relations, however modest it may be[117] or, at least, to infuse the principle of reciprocity with some significance as it should constitute a driving force in State responsibility for terrorism. Reciprocity informs much of the logic underlying modern State responsibility, whilst also aiming at stabilising unbalanced or disproportionate power dynamics between States on the international plane.[118] As prefaced in previous chapters, the prospect of maintaining previously established reciprocal relations might act as a significantly more potent deterrent against wrongful acts or, alternatively, as a catalyst in inducing compliance with international obligations. Therefore, reciprocity ensures that States have a vested interest in sustaining the status quo insofar as it amounts to predictable behavioural patterns.[119] Venturing a step further and grounding their arguments in the eventual attainment of full equality between States, some scholars argue that reciprocity becomes systematised. This posture entails

> that reciprocity moves from a bilateral to a systemic level, whereby the state accepts to bear an obligation on the basis of a legitimate expectation that the system will generally ensure the imposition of similar or corresponding obligations on all members of the system.[120]

Council resolutions post September 11, asserted a duty on UN member States to deny safe haven to terrorists and to bring them to justice'. See Duffy, above n 6 at 107.

[116] See, eg: N Kulish and S Mekhennet, 'German Police Arrest 2 Terrorism Suspects on Jet', *New York Times*, 27 September 2008 at A8; H Timmons, 'Police in India Make Several Arrests in String of Bombings', *New York Times*, 15 September 2008 at A10.

[117] A thoughtful account on impartiality in international law is found in SR Ratner, 'Is International Law Impartial?', Unpublished Manuscript, 15 September 2004, available at http://ssrn.com/abstract=643821.

[118] On the role of reciprocity in international relations see generally: RO Keohane, 'Reciprocity in International Relations' (1986) 40 *International Organization* 1; RO Keohane, 'Reciprocity in International Relations' in S Chan and C Moore (eds), *Theories of International Relations (Vol II)* (London, Sage, 2006) 228–53; DW Larson, 'The Psychology of Reciprocity in International Relations' (1988) 4 *Negotiation Journal: On the Process of Dispute Settlement* 281.

[119] See, eg: A Watts, 'The International Rule of Law' (1993) 36 *German Yearbook of International Law* 15 at 41; JS Watson, 'A Realistic Jurisprudence of International Law' (1980) 30 *Year Book of World Affairs* 265, 283. Although not directly on point, consider also D Hume, F Watkins (ed), *Theory of Politics* (London, Nelson, 1951) 119.

[120] R Provost, *International Human Rights and Humanitarian Law* (Cambridge, CUP, 2002) 122. See also: A Paulus, 'Reciprocity Revisited' in U Fastenrath et al, above n 54 at 120–21. However, 'To

Yet, the framework of State responsibility and countermeasures, which is also devoid of vertical enforcement schemes and mechanisms habitually found under domestic law, embodies the disparate nature of international relations. Morgenthau described international politics as a struggle for power[121] and the concept of countermeasure quintessentially illustrates that point. On one hand, countermeasures undoubtedly constitute a forceful – and sometimes fruitful – response to violations of international law.[122] More importantly, countermeasures epitomise the many ways in which public international law attempts to adapt to the anarchical structure of the international community, a reality undoubtedly exacerbated by State-sponsored, State-condoned or State-tolerated transnational terrorism.[123] From a realist standpoint, this idea is not far removed from Kenneth Waltz's Theory of International Politics, which invokes the concept of 'anarchy' as the starting premise in capturing the legal and political zeitgeist of international society.[124] For proponents of this realist canon, the field of international relations strives to uphold the balance of power whilst maintaining its inherent structural independence, a feature ostentatiously absent from domestic politics.[125] For structural realism scholars, therefore, the behaviour of States on the international plane is ultimately informed by their respective foreign policies with the aim of maintaining the aforementioned balance of power, a notion highly compatible with the concept of *reciprocity*. For Waltz and his intellectual progeny, the 'international system functions similarly to the free market system. The tripartite model offered by Waltz – the structure of the

unilaterally submit the fulfilment of existing international obligations to the requirement of reciprocity is illegal and entails international responsibility'. See B Simma, 'Reciprocity' in R Wolfrum (ed), *Max Planck Encyclopedia of Public International Law* (online edn, Oxford, OUP, 2008) para 13, available at www.mpepil.com.

[121] See, eg: H Morgenthau, *Politics among Nations*, 2nd edn (New York, Alfred A Knopf, 1954) 25.

[122] The scheme of countermeasures under existing State responsibility repertoire is enshrined in ILC Arts 49 ff. See 'State Responsibility: Titles and text of the draft articles on Responsibility of States for internationally wrongful acts adopted by the Drafting Committee on second reading', UN Doc A/CN.4/L.602/Rev.1 (2001). The final draft was adopted by the ILC in 2001, with the UN General Assembly taking note of the *Articles* and commending them to States. See 'Report of the International Law Commission on the Work of Its Fifty-Third Session', UN GAOR, 56th Sess, Supp No 10, UN Doc A/56/10 (2001) 41 [hereinafter *ILC Articles on State Responsibility*, *Articles on State Responsibility*, or *Articles*]. Whilst literature dealing with the application of countermeasures to State failures to prevent terrorism is, in many respects, embryonic, analogies can certainly be drawn from the environmental field. See HB Sverrisson, *Countermeasures, the International Legal System, and Environmental Violations: When Two Wrongs Make a Right for the Environment* (Amherst, Cambria Press, 2008).

[123] Dupuy invokes far more cautious language to describe the role of countermeasures in restoring and/or maintaining the public order of the international community, terming it a 'law of coexistence'. See Dupuy, above n 14 at 15.

[124] See, eg: KN Waltz, *Theory of International Politics* (New York, McGraw-Hill, 1979). For a concrete application, see KN Waltz, 'International Politics Is Not Foreign Policy' (1996) 6 *Security Studies* 54–57.

[125] See Waltz, *Theory*, above n 124 at 91. For further exploration of these issues, see, eg: I Motoc, 'Controversial Aspects of Democracy in International Law: The Right to Political Participation in Foreign Affairs' in KK Koufa (ed), *Thesaurus Acroasium Vol 34: State Responsibility and the Individual* (Athens, Sakkoulas, 2006) 275 at 287–88.

international system, the behavior of the States, the systemic result – imposed the hegemony of realism as a theory of international relations'.[126]

As a result, the paramount analytical linchpin of international relations hinges not so much on human nature, or on the makeup of domestic governments, but on careful assessment of the *structure* of the international system.[127] This entails rigorous consideration of various factors governing international affairs and power dynamics prevalent within that very system, as opposed to commissioning meticulous scrutiny of States' potential benevolent cooperative intent. In particular, these observations come to life when contemplated through the prism of the dominant assumptions shared by structural realists. Those postulates may be summarised as follows:

i) Given the absence of any central government on the international scene, the ensuing system can be aptly described as 'anarchic'.
ii) 'States inherently possess some offensive military capability, which gives them the wherewithal to hurt and possibly destroy each other'.
iii) 'States can never be certain about the intentions of other states'.
iv) The 'most basic motive driving states is survival. States want to maintain their sovereignty'.
v) Consequently, a steady dose of strategy is called for under this theoretical canon and States are justified in approaching their survival from that vantage point.[128]

Whilst this study purports to shed more light on how to enhance transnational cooperation on counterterrorism issues, the flipside to the argument also warrants consideration. As structural realism evinces, the anarchical structure of international society potentially erects significant stumbling blocks to the idea of increasing cooperation, as self-serving foreign policies and unilateralism simply cannot be excised altogether from the equation. In fact, such structure rather points in the other direction and compels States to almost jealously guard their fleeting and precarious sovereignty in a setting best described as the political equivalent of the survival of the fittest. Such reality places self-preservation above any form of prospective cooperation aimed at identifying, and moving forwards on, shared understandings and common policies; a sort of cost-benefit rationale then begins to pervade the political thought-process and 'states instead maximize their specific gains relative to other states'.[129] Surely, the international reality is not so bleak and other policy factors may mitigate some of the more inimical aspects of international legal structures towards a more cooperative

[126] Motoc, above n 125 at 287–88.

[127] A-M Slaughter, 'International Law and International Relations Theory: A Prospectus' in E Benvenisti and M Hirsch (eds), *The Impact of International Law on International Cooperation* (Cambridge, CUP, 2006) 16 at 22.

[128] See J Mearsheimer, 'The False Promise of International Institutions' (1999) 19 *International Security* 5, 11–12, 14. See also: J Mearsheimer, *The Tragedy of Great Power Politics* (New York, Norton, 2001) 30–32.

[129] Slaughter, above n 127 at 22. See also: Mearsheimer, 'The False Promise', above n 128 at 14.

transnational legal accountability framework. Yet, concerns formulated by structural realists must nonetheless be internalised in the inquiry and, when striking a balance between enhanced transnational cooperation on counterterrorism and better integration of non-State actors within that project, a policy-oriented reform of State responsibility must always consider potential real-world obstacles driven by asymmetrical power dynamics on the world stage. As a corollary, such reform must also weigh the sovereign equality of States and State rights considerably in the balance.[130]

However, this realist perspective should not be embraced as the sole relevant theoretical line of inquiry into potential contributions of State responsibility in preventing terrorism, whilst still placing particular emphasis on the role of countermeasures within the anarchical structure of international society. Indeed, other theoretical accounts may shed light on this relationship. For instance, institutional neo-liberalism rather characterises 'anarchy' simply as the absence of a common or centralised government, as opposed to the more widespread notions of disarray and chaos.[131] This line of argument becomes particularly interesting when framed within State responsibility's broader normative corpus and is perhaps challenged by the Security Council's heightened role as counterterrorism legislator since 9/11.[132] Nevertheless, designating the international society as an anarchical one also rests at the very core of theses espoused by both neo-realists and institutional neo-liberalists.

For Hedley Bull, the notion of 'anarchy' necessarily carries with it some coextensive rules of peace that despite the anarchical structure of international society, remain indispensable in ensuring the very survival and perennity of that community.[133] Should this school of thought be taken a step further, it could signal that the very idea of return to legality – as embodied in the core mission statement of State responsibility and typically actuated by countermeasures (which, ironically, draw on 'peaceful' methods of dispute resolution/enforcement) – could strive to achieve this broader objective of pacification within a hostile international social structure (here represented by diametrically opposed States at the primary level of counterterrorism obligations, eg Iran versus Israel). Espousing a decidedly different position, constructivists rather explain the notion of 'anarchy' as the outcome of inter-State interaction on the international plane – or as a result of an inter-subjects process – which both converge into a broader social construction.[134] As attractive as these theories may appear,

[130] See, eg: above section II.B).

[131] See, eg: RO Keohane, *International Institutions and State Power: Essays in International Relations Theory* (Boulder, Westview Press, 1989) 1.

[132] See, eg: the discussion of resolution 1373, above ch 4, section V.A).

[133] See H Bull, *The Anarchical Society: A Study of Order in World Politics* (London, Macmillan, 1977) 136–37.

[134] See, eg: A Wendt, 'Anarchy Is What States Make of it: The Social Construction of Power Politics' (1992) 46 *International Organization* 392. See also generally: A Wendt, *Social Theory of International Politics* (Cambridge, CUP, 1999); C Focarelli, *International Law as Social Construct: The Global Struggle for Justice* (Oxford, OUP, 2012); E Adler, *Communitarian International Relations: The Epistemic Foundations of International Relations* (London, Routledge, 2005) 89–115.

much should be said about the importance of 'reciprocity' within the anarchical international society and Waltz's theory remains particularly instructive in this regard.

The case for international compliance and against future deployment of countermeasures under State responsibility is further bolstered by asymmetrical economic *rapports de force* prevalent on the international scene. As Zemanek underscores, reciprocity provides States with 'a shared interest in the maintenance of predictable patterns of conduct' and it follows that

> [a] State which disrupts this web of reciprocal relations by a countermeasure risks to suffer more injury than the target State, unless it is the dominant power in one of the abovementioned asymmetrical relations which, in the world of today, means almost exclusively the United States, with the European Union and China as potential candidates.[135]

Drawing on previous discussion of reciprocity in this field, the most important feature of the proposed reform resides in the need for interaction and multilateralism between States. After all, 'the means necessary to strike back against international terrorism are only partially and imperfectly provided by existing principles of international law . . . further improvement depends on strengthening international collaboration'.[136] Much in the spirit of the *Genocide* Judgment, if all States attempt to prevent terrorism in concert, thereby enhancing State compliance overall, not only do they increase the likelihood of attaining the ultimate result of prevention but they also lower the cost of enforcement, whilst the cost of breach presumably increases as a result. Moreover, obligations enforceable under the law of State responsibility are inextricably intertwined, especially in highly volatile fields such as counterterrorism where prevention is paramount. Therefore, the obligation to prevent terrorism emanating from States' territories remains intimately connected to the duty to extradite or punish terrorists under the rubric of multilateralism: 'Enhanced cooperation for bringing persons to justice and securing reliable evidence is essential if states are to meet their obligations to prevent and punish serious crimes such as those committed on 9/11'.[137]

This line of thinking is inspired by Fuller's seminal work and, more specifically, by his interactional theory of law.[138] As part of his contribution to the field of legal theory, Fuller developed a concept of 'interactional expectancies'[139] in

[135] Zemanek, above n 91 at 129.

[136] Y Daudet, 'International Action against State Terrorism' in Higgins and Flory, above n 104 at 202.

[137] Duffy, above n 6 at 133.

[138] LL Fuller, 'Human Interaction and the Law' (1969) 14 *American Journal of Jurisprudence* 1. For thought-provoking theoretical accounts on interaction and international law, see J Brunnée and SJ Toope, 'International Law and Constructivism: Elements of an Interactional Theory of International Law' (2000) 39 *Columbia Journal of Transnational Law* 19; J Brunnée and SJ Toope, *Legitimacy and Legality in International Law: An Interactional Account* (Cambridge, CUP, 2010).

[139] See Fuller, above n 138 at 7. This idea also aligns with the concept of 'shared understanding', as developed in international relations scholarship. For a detailed discussion of this concept, see

customary law, which may in turn be extended to State responsibility. Borrowing from his reasoning, the idea of excising attribution altogether from State responsibility thus serves the purpose of stabilising interactional expectancies between international actors faced with increasing terrorist threats.[140]

As discussed earlier with reference to the law and economics paradigm and prominent rationalist theories, the proposed reform not only aims at transferring the burden of precaution onto States, but also purports to transfer incentives in combating terrorism to governments[141] and foster enduring multilateral networks.[142] Conversely, as Provost underscores, unilateralism entails very specific implications for the law governing State responsibility: 'The right of states unilaterally to assess a breach by another state and to validate what would otherwise be an illegal act has the potential of significantly destabilizing international relations'.[143] It follows that, under the aegis of State responsibility, countermeasures constitute subjective recourses in that aggrieved States must unilaterally assess the illegality of the initial wrongful act.[144] We must recall that the 'war' on terror is a truly global campaign, an exercise that can only be conducted successfully through multilateral channels.[145] The broader objective of

Brunnée and Toope, 'International Law', above n 138 at 30–33, 35, 49-50, 53, 61, 65–67, 70. For an application of 'shared understanding' to the UN Guiding Principles on Internal Displacement, see H Entwisle, 'Tracing Cascades: The Normative Development of the U.N. Guiding Principles on Internal Displacement' (2005) 19 *Georgetown Immigration Law Journal* 369, 387–88.

[140] For a discussion of this concept, see Fuller, above n 138 at 8–9.

[141] An argument may be advanced that the prospect of incurring liability might prompt States to better thwart terrorism. See, eg: Zemanek, above n 91 at 125–36.

[142] On combating terrorism through multilateral channels, see P Romaniuk, *Multilateral Counter-terrorism: The Global Politics of Cooperation and Contestation* (London, Routledge, 2010); JW Head, 'Essay: What Has Not Changed Since September 11 – The Benefits of Multilateralism' (2002) 12 *Kansas Journal of Law & Public Policy* 1; E Remacle, 'Vers un multilatéralisme en réseau comme instrument de la lutte contre le terrorisme?' in K Bannelier et al (eds), *Le Droit international face au terrorisme: après le 11 septembre 2001* (Paris, Pedone, 2003) 331–44; V Röben, 'The Role of International Conventions and General International Law in the Fight against International Terrorism' in C Walter et al (eds), *Terrorism as a Challenge for National and International Law: Security Versus Liberty?* (Berlin, Springer, 2004) 789–821.

[143] R Provost, 'Introduction' in Provost, above n 106 at xv. Similarly, see Daudet, above n 136 at 202; ME O'Connell, 'Controlling Countermeasures' in Ragazzi, above n 2 at 49–62.

[144] See Martin, above n 62 at 487. See also: *Case concerning the Air Service Agreement of 27 march 1946 between the United States of America and France (United States/France)* (1978) 18 *Reports of International Arbitral Awards* 417 at 483, para 81; D Alland, *Justice Privée et Ordre Juridique International: Étude Théorique des Contre-Mesures en Droit International Public* (Paris, Pedone, 1994) 345; H Labayle, 'Droit international et lutte contre le terrorisme' (1986) 32 *AFDI* 105, 137.

[145] See, eg: SC Res 1989, UN SCOR, 65th Sess, 6557th Mtg, UN Doc S/RES/1989 (2011) ('*Stressing* that terrorism can only be defeated by a sustained and comprehensive approach involving the active participation and collaboration of all States, and international and regional organizations to impede, impair, isolate and incapacitate the terrorist threat'); SJ Toope, 'Powerful but Unpersuasive? The role of the United States in the Evolution of Customary International Law' in M Byers and G Nolte (eds), *United States Hegemony and the Foundations of International Law* (Cambridge, CUP, 2003) 287 at 293–96; JF Lenzner, 'From a Pakistani Stationhouse to the Federal Courthouse: A Confession's Uncertain Journey in the U.S.-Led War on Terror' (2004) 12 *Cardozo Journal of International and Comparative Law* 297, 297–300; McCredie, above n 39 at 73. On a related point, see A Paulus, 'The War against Iraq and the Future of International Law: Hegemony or Pluralism?' (2004) 25 *Michigan Journal of International Law* 691, 721.

combating terrorism through multilateral avenues ineluctably involves the implementation of a 'reciprocity of benefits' between States facing terrorist activity on their territory and potential victim-States: the impetus for compliance with the obligation to forestall terrorism is captured by fear of retaliation or, more importantly, by the possibility that States may not fulfil their international duties.[146]

Furthermore, post-9/11 law governing State responsibility might largely evolve through hostile inter-State relations, a premise highly reconcilable with Fuller's interactional theory. According to his perception of law,

> while enemies may have difficulty in bargaining with words, they can, and often do profitably half-bargain with deeds. Paradoxically the tacit restraints of customary law between enemies are more likely to develop during active warfare than during a hostile stalemate of relations; fighting one another is itself in this sense a 'social' relation since it involves communication.[147]

Endorsing a regime inspired by strict liability – which primarily purports to amplify reciprocal expectations of compliance with counterterrorism duties – should perhaps be largely actuated through positive State actions rather than through rhetorical processes. What is more, this idea is not completely incongruent with the writings of certain eminent constructivists, which collapse both positive State actions and rhetorical commitments under the heading of State practice.[148] This objective, therefore, can be attained through a variety of inter-State actions, including intelligence sharing, transnational cooperation on terrorism policy and law enforcement, extradition of suspected terrorists, subjection of suspected terrorists to international criminal institutions if national prosecutions prove illusory, provision of counterterrorism personnel to inefficient States, etc. Hence, the *sine qua non* application of this theory – and one of the driving forces behind the proposed model – resides in the conveyance of clear messages through reciprocal State actions.[149] At first sight, the proposed two-tiered strict liability mechanism seems to achieve this policy objective as it increases reciprocal and multilateral collaboration, transparency, expectations of compliance, and foments reciprocity of benefits.

Aside from enhancing legitimacy of international efforts to combat terrorism and delineating the ambit of State responsibility, this model would also foster

[146] See Fuller, above n 138 at 32.

[147] ibid, at 31. For a highly reconcilable constructivist take on this idea, albeit through the lens of intervention, see MJ Finnemore, *The Purpose of Intervention: Changing Beliefs about the Use of Force* (Ithaca, Cornell University Press, 2003) 5.

[148] See, eg: F Kratochwil, 'Citizenship: On the Border of Order' in Y Lapid and F Kratochwil (eds), *The Return of Culture and Identity in IR Theory* (Boulder, Lynne Rienner Publishers, 1996) 181 at 190–94; NG Onuf, 'Constructivism: A User's Manual' in V Kubàlkovà et al (eds), *International Relations in a Constructed World* (Armonk, ME Sharpe, 1998) 58 at 59; A Wendt, 'Collective Identity Formation and the International State' (1994) 88 *American Political Science Review* 384, 390.

[149] Fuller, above n 138 at 31 ('Here the prime desideratum is to achieve – through acts, of course, not words – the clear communication of messages of a rather limited and negative import; accordingly there is a heavy concentration on symbolism and ritual').

States' comparative policy-making and collaborative efforts. This policy objective is certainly a running theme throughout rationalist literature.[150] Several other commentators rightly expound that multilateral collaboration should be preferred over unilateral State action in instilling a preventive character to the 'war' on terrorism.[151] Similarly, there appears to be a marked correlation between the circumvention of attribution, the fostering of multilateral cooperation, deriving legitimacy in the international 'war' on terror and promoting fairness amongst nations.[152] States could therefore engage in significant risk control and risk assessment of possible terrorist threats and, one hopes, encourage multilateral exchanges of information and intelligence, along with financial 'red-flagging' of terrorist assets.[153] The overarching objective is to make the global fight against terror a preventive rather than a curative effort; the imposition of strict liability-infused standards for failing to thwart terrorism constitutes a solution of last resort, namely when an excursion could not have been prevented.[154] However, until such attack is carried out, we must contemplate all reasonable steps in between to prevent it. The IACHR spoke to this point in the *Velásquez Rodríguez* Case and aptly encapsulated the tenets of State responsibility:

> The State has a legal duty to take *reasonable steps* to prevent human rights violations and to use the means at its disposal to carry out a serious investigation of violations committed within its jurisdiction, to identify those responsible, to impose the appropriate punishment and to ensure the victim adequate compensation (emphasis added).[155]

[150] See, eg: P-H Verdier, 'Cooperative States: International Relations, State Responsibility and the Problem of Custom' (2002) 42 *Virginia Journal of International Law* 839, 843–44, 846, 849, 852, 853–54; JL Dunoff and JP Trachtman, 'Economic Analysis of International Law' (1999) 24 *Yale Law Journal* 1, 32–33.

[151] See, eg: CC Posteraro, 'Intervention in Iraq: Towards a Doctrine of Anticipatory Counter-Terrorism, Counter-Proliferation Intervention' (2002) 15 *Florida Journal of International Law* 151, 205; D Waxman, 'Terrorism: The War of the Future' (1999) 23 *Fletcher Forum of World Affairs* 201, 205. See also generally: J Quigley, 'The Afghanistan War and Self-Defense' (2003) 37 *Valparaiso University Law Review* 541.

[152] For a thoughtful discussion on the concept of legitimacy in international law, see Franck, above n 112 at 16–17, 19, 24.

[153] Terrorist fundraising – or the lack of control thereof – is another significant dimension of counterterrorism and sometimes a determinant element of indirect State responsibility. On terrorist financing and prevention, see D Cole, 'Terror Financing, Guilt by Association and the Paradigm of Prevention in the "War on Terror"' in A Bianchi and A Keller (ed), *Counterterrorism: Democracy's Challenge* (Oxford, Hart Publishing, 2008) 233–76; W Wechsler, 'Strangling the Hydra: Targeting Al-Qaeda's Finances' in J Hogue and R Gideon (eds), *How Did this Happen? Terrorism and the New War* (New York, Public Affairs, 2001) 129–43; B Zagaris, 'The Merging of the Anti-Money Laundering and Counter-Terrorism Financial Enforcement Regimes After September 11, 2001' (2004) 22 *Berkeley Journal of International Law* 123.

[154] See, eg: MMD Banks, 'Addressing State (Ir-)Responsibility: The Use of Military Force as Self-Defense in International Counter-Terrorism Operations' (2009) 200 *Military Law Review* 54, 57 (observing that 'Various scholars also argue for preventative, rather than curative, measures').

[155] *Velásquez Rodríguez Case*, Inter-Am Ct HR Decisions and Judgments 91 (ser C) No 4 (1988) at para 174.

In addition to sending a message of deterrence to complacent governments, this approach can provide States with a locus to voice, calibrate and test out their counterterrorism policies.

The mechanics of State responsibility must also be accompanied – both preventively and curatively – by a steady dose of diplomacy and international pressure, which may likely translate into a tension between the competing strategies of punishment and deterrence versus containment. Taken in the aggregate context of its tempestuous relationship both with the international community and terrorism, the case of Libya illustrated this trend. In 2003, Muammar el-Qaddafi announced that his nation was phasing out its nuclear and biological/chemical weapons programme, a development that ineluctably drew attention to the recent invasion of Iraq as a possible catalyst. Whilst recognising that this might have been a relevant factor, some commentators rather construe the explanation of the Libyan policy choice as a direct result of a security guarantee given to that State by the US; unlike the situation in Iraq, the objective therefore shifted from regime change to modifying the existing regime's behaviour.[156] More importantly, this development evinced the effectiveness of diplomatic pressure in the context of counterterrorism – particularly as a vehicle to increase the cost of non-compliance with international obligations for the purposes of State responsibility – at least in two ways. On one hand, it offered a *curative* effect in that Libya's decision to bring its conduct closer to conformity with accepted international standards signalled a desire to enhance compliance with primary norms to avoid the application of secondary norms of responsibility. This posture was also motivated by internal political factors within Libya, stemming from the desire to extricate itself from the sanctions regime imposed upon it in light of its ties to terrorism, especially following the *Lockerbie* debacle. This policy shift also generated some cathartic effect for past misdeeds given Libya's ongoing relationship with terrorism, which can be cast at the secondary normative level if one accepts that the application of State responsibility entails the deployment of a web of competing norms, actors and processes. After all, in the Libyan scenario the Security Council dealt with the State responsibility aspects of the dispute whilst the ICJ tackled legal issues pertaining to extradition and, ultimately, political leverage and diplomatic pressure were also applied outside any institutionalised setting. In that case, successful deployment of State responsibility repertoire was contingent on both the involvement of a multiplicity of actors and the superimposition of concurrently applicable legal regimes and political processes. On the other hand, pursuing this new direction produced a *preventive* effect in that this policy choice might actually have prevented or decreased the likelihood of future transnational terrorist strikes originating from Libya, thereby increasing its due diligence capital in the event that it failed to thwart such excursions.

[156] See RS Litwak, 'Containment 2.0', *World Politics Review*, 22 July 2009.

These considerations can also be reconciled with writings emanating from liberal theorists, although some emphatically advocate the implementation of government networks in combating terrorism. Anne-Marie Slaughter points out that

> the United Sates has pushed the even more informal approach of 'coalitions of the willing,' both at the unitary state level of enlisting military allies and at the disaggregated state level of networking to combat terrorist financing, share intelligence on terrorist activity, and cooperate in bringing individual terrorists to justice.[157]

As early as 1975, Jordan Paust emphasised the importance of data and intelligence-sharing in the spirit of transnational cooperation, so as to better advance the global struggle against terrorism.[158] Consequently, 'Promoting actual government networks in all these areas is a far better approach, as it would institutionalize the cooperation that already exists and create a framework for deepening future cooperation in virtually every area of domestic policy'.[159]

The possible formulation of governmental networks would undoubtedly prove indispensable in advancing the 'war' on terror and fulfilling the objectives of State responsibility. The mere fact that concerted and coordinated institutional structures are in place would not only assist States in better complying with their counterterrorism obligations, but might also help better prevent terrorist excursions, thereby curtailing the need to engage State responsibility altogether in preventable cases of terrorism. The idea of networking governments to combat terrorism must also be appreciated against the backdrop of extant State responsibility structures. Whilst the UN General Assembly has now moved towards the idea of enshrining the law of State responsibility in a convention,[160] there is no indication that this agenda constitutes a politically feasible objective. Confronted with the political climate prevalent since 9/11, certain scholars highlight this difficulty whilst reiterating the advantages of favouring transnational and regional cooperation in the hopes of stamping out terrorism in the global campaign against ideological warfare.[161] Not to mention that, whilst

[157] See, eg: A-M Slaughter, *A New World Order* (Princeton, Princeton University Press, 2004) 265.

[158] JJ Paust, 'A Survey of Possible Legal Responses to International Terrorism: Prevention, Punishment, and Cooperative Action' (1975) 5 *Georgia Journal of International and Comparative Law* 431, 448–51. See also: WM Reisman, 'International Legal Responses to International Terrorism' (1999) 22 *Houston Journal of International Law* 3, 15–16.

[159] Slaughter, above n 157 at 265.

[160] See Draft Resolution of 9 November 2007 – Agenda Item 78: Responsibility of States for Internationally Wrongful Acts, United Nations General Assembly, A/C.6/62/L.20, at para 4 (deciding to 'include in the provisional agenda' and to 'further examine, within the framework of a working group of the Sixth Committee, the question of a convention on responsibility of States for internationally wrongful acts or other appropriate action on the basis of the articles'). See also: 'Responsibility of States for Internationally Wrongful Acts, Report of the Sixth Committee', 21 November, UN Doc A/62/446 (2007), at paras 5–7 (confirming that Draft Resolution A/C.6/62/L.20 was adopted by the Sixth Committee without a vote). On the necessity of adopting a convention on State responsibility, see, eg: CP Economidès, 'Le projet de la CDI sur la responsabilité de l'État pour fait internationalement illicite: nécessité d'une convention internationale (2005) 58 *Revue hellénique de droit international* 77.

[161] See, eg: F McWhinney, 'Codifying International Law in Periods of Extreme Ideological and Cultural Conflict: Lessons from the ILC Mandate on State Responsibility' in Koufa, above n 125 at 134.

treaty formulation might generate more dominant and extensive patterns of influence and compliance, as opposed to the more diffused level of authority exerted by the ILC's *Articles* in their current form, the road to adopting a comprehensive convention on State responsibility is fraught with obstacles and political pitfalls.[162] Hence, the challenges associated with the adoption of a convention, coupled with the preferred exercise of transnational or regional counterterrorism cooperation under the existing framework of the *Articles*, align with David Caron's astute 'paradox that [the *Articles*] could have more influence as an ILC text than as a multilateral treaty'.[163]

B) Social Stigma Argument

One final argument must be addressed squarely. Some might surmise that this proposed strict liability-inspired model would unduly impugn the dignity of States that do their best to prevent terrorism, or that put forth earnest efforts in doing so while falling short in producing the expected result. Whilst such States would not be held 'directly' responsible for terrorism, they would nonetheless face the social stigma of having violated international law. However, imposing automatic indirect responsibility for failing to prevent terrorism achieves a certain level of equality between all host-States, at least on a preliminary basis. As a lesser of two evils in a way, in most circumstances this framework would do away with the undesirable prospect of labelling host-States 'directly responsible' or 'complicit' in terrorism, as aggrieved States may opt to proceed under the indirect responsibility paradigm. Conversely, imposing automatic indirect responsibility might cast a socially stigmatic light on host-States. In other words, they might look unfavourably upon the obligation to justify or establish that their conduct was in conformity with their obligation to prevent terrorism, without correspondingly requiring (or by exempting) aggrieved States from establishing attribution of wrongful acts to the relevant host-States.

A similar line of argument runs through other spheres of international law. For instance, we have seen one of its manifestations in the context of the World Trade Organization's treatment of the *Asbestos* Case.[164] In that litigation, France was called upon to justify a decree prohibiting asbestos or asbestos-containing products under Article XX of the General Agreement on Tariffs and Trade. The dispute settlement Panel concluded that although France's ban discriminated against other types of products, that discrimination was justified on the grounds of public health enshrined in Article XX. The Panel Report carried

[162] See generally: JR Crawford and S Olleson, 'The Continuing Debate on a UN Convention on State Responsibility' (2005) 54 *ICLQ* 959.

[163] DD Caron, 'The ILC Articles on State Responsibility: The Paradoxical Relationship Between Form and Authority' (2002) 96 *AJIL* 857, 858.

[164] *European Communities – Measures Affecting Asbestos and Asbestos-Containing Products*, Panel Report (adopted on 5 April 2001) WT/DS135/R and Appellate Body Report (adopted on 5 April 2001) WT/DS135/AB/R.

with it the notion that the banning on the French market of a known carcinogen – whilst discriminatory – could be justified under the structure of GATT. Although France technically 'won' before the Panel, it nonetheless appealed the case to the Appellate Body. The Appellate Body ultimately reversed this reasoning by focusing on the likeness of the products at hand, whilst also discarding the Panel's discrimination rationale. In short, it recognised France's right to afford different treatment to hazardous products without being labelled a violator of the national treatment principle.[165] The Appellate Body seemed somewhat aware of the social stigma or adverse effect involved by steering the same course as the Panel. Put another way, the Appellate Body's decision was driven by its acknowledgement that its potential ruling on a violated international legal obligation carried with it great reputational, dignity and, perhaps, political costs (even if that violation was nullified on technical grounds).[166] Unsurprisingly, the idea that States' reputation on the international scene remains the most significant generator of their compliance with international obligations has attracted the attention of international relations theorists.[167]

This reasoning is also very much alive in the age-old debate over the criminalisation of State responsibility, in that 'the primary justification for State crimes is the moral stigma of criminal conviction'.[168] In stark contrast, the ICJ seems to have eschewed this line of thought in *Corfu Channel*, thereby refusing to condemn the defendant State for a 'grave omission' (which would have also entailed that it had the capability of preventing the wrongful conduct). Rather, the ICJ

> took the easier path of ascertaining a 'knowledge' which really was an instance of collusion. In so doing, the Court avoided to declare that such a wrong had been com-

[165] See, eg: H Horn and JHH Weiler, 'European Communities – Measures Affecting Asbestos and Asbestos-Containing Products' in H Horn and PC Mavroidis (eds), *The WTO Case Law of 2001: The American Law Institute Reporters' Studies* (New York, CUP, 2004) 14 at 38. The rules of State responsibility have also sometimes been extended to the WTO system. See SM Villalpando, 'Attribution of Conduct to the State: How the Rules of State Responsibility May Be Applied Within the WTO Dispute Settlement System' (2002) 5 *Journal of International Economic Law* 393; M Garcia-Rubio, *On the Application of Customary Rules of State Responsibility by the WTO Dispute Settlement Organs* (Geneva, Graduate Institute of International Studies, 2001). Alberto Alvarez-Jimenez rejects the rigid transplantation of the ICJ's perhaps retrogressive interpretation of the rules of State responsibility in the *Genocide Case* to the WTO system. See 'International State Responsibility for Acts of Non-State Actors: The Recent Standards Set by the International Court of Justice in Genocide and Why the WTO Appellate Body Should Not Embrace Them' (2007) 35 *Syracuse Journal of International and Law and Commerce* 1, 15–25.

[166] For a thought-provoking discussion on States' reputational costs under international law, see R Brewster, 'Unpacking the State's Reputation' (2009) 50 *Harvard International Law Journal* 231.

[167] See generally: AT Guzman, *How International Law Works: A Rational Choice Theory* (Oxford, OUP, 2008). Compare with JP Trachman, *The Economic Structure of International Law* (Cambridge, Harvard University Press, 2008). For a critique of Guzman's treatment of the subject, see R Brewster, 'The Limits of Reputation on Compliance', Unpublished Manuscript, Harvard Public Law Paper No 09-37 (1 July 2009), available at http://ssrn.com/abstract=1337826; HG Cohen, 'Can International Law Work? A Constructivist Expansion' (2009) 27 *Berkeley Journal of International Law* 636.

[168] DD Caron, 'State Crimes: Looking at Municipal Experience with Organizational Crime' in Ragazzi, above n 2 at 27.

mitted . . . When they have to condemn a State, international courts prefer to do it at the lowest possible moral cost for the State in question.[169]

In response, it must be recalled that there are no ideal solutions in preventing transnational terrorism; mitigation of the tensions between sovereignty and reputation remains a noble objective in making the world a safer place. Writing about the USS Pueblo case of 1968[170] from the perspective of State responsibility, one commentator pragmatically resolves the aforementioned tension between upholding dignity and combating terrorism efficiently (although such dictum might rather belong to the realm of *lex ferenda*): 'For modern democratic States, what is paramount is to protect their nationals' lives rather than uphold in the abstract the dignity of the State'.[171] The approach advocated in this monograph strives to attain a reasonable ground between the zeal of imposing unreasonable State duties, namely obligations of result, and envisioning a regime too loosely suited for modern ideological warfare, where States can easily elude responsibility. This argument aligns with Brownlie's own remarks on the interplay between responsibility and international organisations, which precludes the possible exoneration of States through subterfuges or alternate legal arrangements: 'A State cannot avoid responsibility by creating an international organization'.[172]

Although the international community should take stock of these concerns, the 'war' on terrorism further complicates the equation: unlike under the WTO system, we are often dealing with human lives and, to the extent possible, with the protection of those lives. From that perspective, it seems desirable and more efficient to slightly sacrifice 'saving face', so to speak, rather than infringe territorial sovereignty and fail in preventing massive deaths and widespread terror. Finally, the social stigma argument can also be interpreted as a positive force, generating realistic incentives and expectations amongst the international community subject, of course, to the further elaboration of the relevant primary legal rules.[173] As seen above, partly through the discussion of the principle of

[169] F Rigaux, 'International Responsibility and the Principle of Causality' in Ragazzi, above n 2 at 91.

[170] For background on the USS Pueblo incident, see, eg: RB Bilder, 'The Role of Apology in International Law and Diplomacy' (2006) 46 *Virginia Journal of International Law* 433, 443; HK Josephs, 'The Remedy of Apology in Comparative and International Law: Self-Healing and Reconciliation' (2004) 18 *Emory International Law Review* 53, 80–81; DP O'Connell, *The Influence of Law on Sea Power* (Manchester, Manchester University Press, 1975) 65.

[171] K Nakatani, 'Diplomacy and State Responsibility' in Ragazzi, above n 2 at 40.

[172] I Brownlie, 'The Responsibility of States for the Acts of International Organizations' in Ragazzi, above n 2 at 361. This reasoning would undoubtedly extend to colluding, terrorism-sponsoring States. See ibid, at 362. See also: S Yee, 'The Responsibility of States Members of an International Organization for its Conduct as a Result of Membership of their Normal Conduct Associated with Membership' in Ragazzi, above n 2 at 448–49; J d'Aspremont, 'Abuse of the Legal Personality of International Organizations and the Responsibility of Member States' (2007) 4 *International Organizations Law Review* 91; F Mégret and F Hoffmann, 'The UN as a Human Rights Violator?: Some Reflections on the United Nations Changing Human Rights Responsibilities' (2003) 25 *Human Rights Quarterly* 314, 318.

[173] Consider J Peirano, 'International Responsibility and Cooperation for Development' in Ragazzi, above n 2 at 193. Finally, an argument may also be advanced that the prospect of incurring liability might prompt States to better thwart terrorism. See, eg: Zemanek, above n 91 at 125–36.

reciprocity, the prospect of States incurring international responsibility for failures to prevent terrorism, or the fear internalised by them that such eventuality might materialise, might enhance their observance of counterterrorism obligations and concomitantly increase the cost of non-compliance with such undertakings (ie bolster the compliance pull of prevention). There is no doubt that prima facie indirect State responsibility responds to similar logic. Publicists have extended this type of reasoning to other facets of the international 'war' on terror, rather equating semantically analogous practices to 'shame sanctions' and a process of international 'shaming'. For instance, writing about detainee abuse at Abu Ghraib prison carried out by American troops, one commentator argues that 'social sanctions like shaming have a powerful role to play in enforcing international law norms' and, as a corollary, 'When properly deployed, shaming activity by the international community can serve to influence the offending state to take corrective action and fill the enforcement gap in international law'.[174] Similar objectives can also be attained through the non-binding 'views' issued by the UN Human Rights Committee.

Conversely, nothing in the foregoing considerations precludes the application of the social stigma rationale to the deployment of secondary rules of responsibility. The above analysis placed significant emphasis on the fact that a mechanism of automatic attribution or a prima facie presumption of indirect responsibility attaching to host-States having failed to prevent terrorism may cast those States in a stigmatic light in the hopes of generating positive incentives. Under this light, the social stigma argument amounts to a *means* to an end: by branding host-States 'internationally responsible', we are compelling them to bring their behaviour within the furrow of their obligations (eg by preventing further attacks, engaging in transnational cooperation, cracking down on terrorist installations/training camps within their borders, freezing terrorist assets, remedying wrongful acts, etc). However, this approach was always contingent on the ability of host-States to refute that presumption pursuant to various factors, which are thoroughly canvassed below under heading IV.B, tending to demonstrate that they fulfilled their obligation of prevention and/or that nothing more could reasonably have been expected of them.

That said, there might be cases where the obligation violated, or the actual international legal breach, is so egregious or straightforward that it will eclipse all further considerations and precipitate the application of the consequences of international responsibility. An obvious case would be a situation where a host-State, upon being found indirectly responsible on a prima facie basis, accepts its responsibility and thereby triggers the application of the remedial provisions of the ILC's *Articles*. Another example would be a scenario whereby the automatic finding of responsibility acts as the remedy, in and of itself, with-

[174] S Gopalan, 'Alternative Sanctions and Social Norms in International Law: The Case of Abu Ghraib' (2007) *Michigan State Law Review* 758, 786, further adding, at 786–87, that 'The [shaming] campaign forced U.S. citizens to come to terms with the fact that their government was acting in violation of internalized international norms (against torture)'.

out any consideration for the various parameters found under the second tier of the proposed framework (below section IV.B). In contrast with the model advocated earlier, these situations signal that the prima facie presumption of responsibility constitutes an *end* in itself and, what is more, *the* end for the purposes of 'closure', albeit an imperfect one, under State responsibility repertoire.

A parallel can be drawn with the ICJ's ruling in the *Genocide Case* in that, if a terrorist attack is actually carried out from a given territory and the host-State fails to thwart it, responsibility can flow to that State (ie trigger the prima facie presumption of responsibility). Under this second conception of prima facie State responsibility, no further analysis is engaged to determine whether the State actually upheld, within reason, the standard of behaviour that could have been reasonably expected from it in the circumstances. In the *Genocide Case*, the Court opined that 'a State can be held responsible for breaching the obligation to prevent genocide only if genocide was actually committed'.[175] However, in such instances all other considerations can be circumvented if the pertinent adjudicating body determines that its declaration that the host-State failed to comply with is obligation of prevention constitutes adequate satisfaction.[176] Whilst perhaps unclear until further developed in practice, such posture seriously threatens to erode and undermine the political equilibrium that a two-tiered model seeks to achieve. Host-States must be given an opportunity to refute the case against them; strict liability logic is solely invoked with a view to generating desirable policy incentives, promoting multilateral cooperation and encouraging diligent State compliance with counterterrorism obligations.

Based on the foregoing and the precedence achieved by indirect responsibility, international law could possibly countenance a regime of strict liability, albeit predicated on the opportunity for host-States to raise defences or justifications vis-à-vis their duty to prevent terrorism. Such approach seems somewhat reminiscent of past doctrines of collective responsibility espoused, inter alia, by William Hall and Clyde Eagleton. For Hall, whilst States could exculpate themselves subsequently by demonstrating their lawful behaviour, the fact remained that '*prima facie* a state is of course responsible for all acts and omissions taking place within its territory'.[177] Echoing a similar viewpoint, Eagleton opined that a State 'should be responsible for the individual's act from the moment of its occurrence', whilst pointing out that local remedies would act as 'a means of discharging this responsibility'.[178] Prior to 9/11, one commentator entertained

[175] *Case Concerning the Application of the Convention on the Prevention and Punishment of the Crime of Genocide (Bosnia and Herzegovina v Serbia and Montenegro)*, Judgment of 26 February, *ICJ Reports* (2007) 43 at para 431.

[176] ibid, at para 463. See also: *Corfu Channel*, above n 103 at 35–36.

[177] WE Hall, *A Treatise on International Law*, 2nd edn (Oxford, Clarendon Press, 1884) 193.

[178] C Eagleton, 'Measure of Damages in International Law' (1929-30) 39 *Yale Law Journal* 52, 56. See also: JA Hessbruegge, 'The Historical Development of the Doctrines of Attribution and Due Diligence in International Law' (2004) 36 *NYU Journal of International Law and Politics* 265, 280–81; R Curtis, 'The Law of Hostile Military Expeditions as Applied by the United States' (1914) 8 *AJIL* 1, 35.

the possibility of establishing a prima facie case of liability for failing to prevent terrorism under the aegis of a prospective Convention on Terrorism. Whilst reserving a role for a reviewing court in assessing State failures of due diligence, he rejected the idea of absolute liability as a potential model and contemplated the possibility for host-States to 'explain their actions' after the fact, on a case-by-case basis. Therefore, host-States would have been allowed to introduce evidence regarding their compliance with counterterrorism obligations. He further identified four 'permissible exceptions for a failure to comply', namely: i) when host-States are faced with civil conflict, thereby impeding their capability to thwart terrorist threats; ii) when host-States demonstrate they acted within the parameters of due diligence to repel the threat but were unable to do so; iii) when host-States demonstrate that they lack the monetary or human resources to adequately contain the threat; and iv) when host-States demonstrate that terrorist attacks were financed/sponsored by other States.[179]

However, an initial caveat sometimes raised in the literature dealing with State responsibility for transboundary environmental harm must be registered. Certain publicists argue that defences available under the logic of indirect responsibility are precisely what impair the advancement of effective preventive environmental obligations, thereby engendering difficulties in applying attribution standards. Moreover, they argue that the very existence of these defences has also motivated States to adopt conduct that would otherwise not be permissible or advisable.[180] Clearly, no such latitude should be afforded in the field of counterterrorism, as the paramount objective often remains to save human lives; no margin for appreciation or derogation can be allotted in such instances, at the risk of people's lives. Put another way, defences available under the second prong of the two-tiered model espoused herein should not create an escape clause for non-compliance. Nevertheless, it is imperative to explore the second tier of the proposed strict liability approach and possible considerations raised by host-States against prima facie presumptions of indirect responsibility formulated against them. As prefaced above, this examination will reinforce the idea that primary counterterrorism obligations remain, to a large extent, intimately connected to secondary rules of State responsibility.

IV. CONTENT OF THE OBLIGATION OF PREVENTION

The book now turns to the analytical task enshrined under the second tier of the proposed model, which rests upon a context-sensitive, policy-informed approach. It is vital to frame the scope of the obligation of prevention, which acts as the analytical cornerstone of the ensuing politico-juridical exploration. In a broader perspective, it is immensely beneficial to address the makeup of

[179] See McCredie, above n 39 at 93–94.
[180] See, eg: Springer, above n 14 at 129.

that obligation both from descriptive and prescriptive standpoints. This task will be better achieved through direct reference to the content of this obligation, as framed in the proposed strict liability model.

As prefaced above, the second tier of the proposed strict liability approach centres on a host-State's attempt to refute or, at least, dissipate the prima facie finding of indirect responsibility weighing against it. Usual considerations surrounding failures to prevent terrorism – be they a host-State's level of knowledge, size of its territory and police/military capacity, nature of the circumstances and history of terrorism within the country, etc – should be invoked throughout this second step. International law could likely countenance a shift in onus flowing from aggrieved nations to sanctuary States: the duty to demonstrate that the latter acted in conformity with their international obligations or that their conduct aligned with international community objectives regarding terrorism should fall squarely on their shoulders. Hence, once the positive act has been carried out, namely when a terrorist strike materialises, responsibility and the burden of justification simultaneously attach to the host-State.[181] That is not to say, however, that no issue of international responsibility arises prior to a State's failure to prevent a transnational terrorist strike (ie counterterrorism obligations are violated as soon as States harbour terrorists on their territory in contravention of international law). Before moving on to the more 'modulatory' policy aspects of the obligation under study, some preliminary remarks are warranted on its very nature.

A) Obligation of Conduct versus Result Dichotomy

Elucidating secondary State responsibility norms in the context of counterterrorism raises the related and difficult question of defining the actual contours and character of relevant obligations, at least at the primary level (if one accepts that secondary norms are automatically triggered once a wrongful act by the State is established). As canvassed above, the exploration of this dimension of counterterrorism is better pursued by reference to the distinction between obligations of means and obligations of result under international legal discourse.[182] Challenges arising from this line of inquiry are particularly acute given the general ambiguity surrounding the status of obligations of prevention, generally, a confusion undoubtedly exacerbated by the delicate and politically sensitive nature of combating terrorism.

[181] The discussion on the role of 'fault' in the context of the ILC's *Articles* should be recalled. In particular, allusion was made to Crawford's response to Gattini, above ch 4 nn 145–48. In his reply, Crawford opened the door to implementing strict liability under the law of State responsibility.

[182] See generally: CP Economides, 'Content of the Obligation: Obligations of Means and Obligations of Result' in Crawford et al, above n 2 at 371–81; P-M Dupuy, 'Le fait générateur de la responsabilité internationale des Etats' (1984-V) 188 *Recueil des Cours* 9, 44, 47–51; GS Goodwin-Gill, 'State Responsibility and the "Good Faith" Obligation in International Law' in M Fitzmaurice and D Sarooshi (eds), *Issues of State Responsibility Before International Judicial Institutions* (Oxford, Hart Publishing, 2004) 75 at 77–80.

Although the distinction between obligations of conduct and result has sometimes proven instrumental under the auspices of the ILC's *Articles*,[183] obligations of prevention 'are usually construed as best efforts obligations, requiring States to take all reasonable or necessary measures to prevent a given event from occurring, but without warranting that the event will not occur'.[184] This presumably operates by reference to the afore-discussed notion of due diligence once the burden of proof has been transferred to the wrongful State, albeit through an objective construction of that concept. Drawing on Anzilotti's seminal work on objective responsibility, any international obligation making States accountable for the acts of private persons must not be construed 'as an "absolute" obligation to prevent or punish harmful activities carried out by private individuals; but as a "relative" obligation to maintain, with regard to such activities, that particular conduct of prevention and punishment which is required by international law'.[185] In broader terms, the distinction between obligations of conduct and result remains somewhat relevant when applying the *Articles* but does not constitute the pivotal focal point: rather, it 'may assist in ascertaining when a breach has occurred'.[186] Conversely, the importance of this distinction cannot be ignored or underemphasised.[187] With respect to judicial enforcement of obligations of result, courts will be more inclined to proceed on a case-by-case basis rather than subsuming all similar obligations under a single legal matrix.[188] Moreover, this distinction has not been engaged as a determinative factor in guiding courts when adjudicating breaches of international obligations.[189] To better frame the discussion to follow, it is nonetheless useful to briefly provide some background on both types of obligation whilst drawing important parallels with international environmental law.

Obligations of conduct/means require or prohibit certain conduct or behaviour by States (eg a treaty obligation stipulating that Member States have to tax polluters at a certain level), whilst obligations of result require States to bring about a certain situation or result. In so doing, States are free to adopt any conduct or use any means at their disposal in attaining the prescribed result (eg Member States have to reduce greenhouse emissions by 30 per cent by a certain date – these States can then use any means to meet their obligation such as taxing polluters, imposing stringent industry standards, imposing fines, implementing restrictive licensing, etc). The ICJ recently interpreted the notion of obligation of result rather liberally, granting, inter alia, a reasonable period of

[183] The transplantation of these civil law concepts into international law has also engendered significant difficulties. See, eg: Crawford, above n 14 at 21.

[184] ibid, at 140.

[185] Pisillo-Mazzeschi, above n 106 at 103.

[186] Crawford, above n 14 at 129. See also: Brownlie, above n 3 at 241.

[187] See, eg: O Schachter, 'The Obligation of the Parties to Give Effect to the Covenant on Civil and Political Rights' (1979) 73 *AJIL* 462, 462 fn 1.

[188] cp, eg: *Colozza and Rubinat v Italy* (1985) Eur Ct HR (ser A) No 89; *Islamic Republic of Iran v United States of America (Cases A15 (IV) and A24)* (1996) 32 Iran-US Claims Tribunal Reports 115.

[189] See Crawford, above n 14 at 130.

time for the implementing State to align its legislative or constitutional structure with the result prescribed by the obligation.[190] At any rate, varying criteria will generally inform the analysis and be invoked to determine a breach of either type of obligation. Under obligations of conduct, the focus of the inquiry hinges on the actual conduct of States whilst under obligations of result, one tends to analyse the actual effects of State action or inaction in the grander scheme of things. However, these criteria are not always mutually exclusive and somewhat merge when it comes to obligations of prevention, a vital observation given that most counterterrorism obligations will be instilled, at least in theory, with a mandatory preventive character. At the primary level, these types of obligations require States to actually forestall the occurrence of a given event or situation. Failing such prevention after the event materialises, or the actual materialisation of the event itself, State responsibility can still arise if State conduct or actions violate the content of the obligation of prevention. For instance, Pakistan violates its international counterterrorism obligations if it harbours Al Qaeda members on its territory, irrespective of whether a terrorist strike is ultimately launched from its soil. If the event does finally materialise, a nexus between the event and the conduct of the alleged wrongful State must be demonstrated. In cases where the event occurs and the State could have prevented it by adopting different conduct or, even when it did not have the ability to thwart a terrorist strike but could have used means to significantly hamper it, the result required by the obligation is not achieved. Thus, the obligation of prevention cannot be construed in absolute terms as such construction would eviscerate it of any real substantive content. One can immediately glean the compatibility of this type of scenario with the notion of due diligence, which was addressed throughout the book and remains the linchpin of many counterterrorism obligations.

Hence, the nature and content of international obligations will have important and direct incidence on the application of the law of State responsibility. The interplay between the very nature of the obligations at play and the conduct or result that is expected of States can also become rather complex. Consequently, the corresponding legal interface of primary/secondary rules that emerges from the foregoing often remains marred by normative discrepancies or vacuums.[191] In this light, it should be reiterated that obligations of prevention are usually equated with best efforts obligations, requiring States to take all reasonable or necessary measures to prevent a given event from occurring without commissioning a specific result (ie the prevention of the given event). The ICJ's judgment in the *Genocide Case* seems to stand for the proposition that the obligation to prevent genocide, whilst not warranting a specific result, nonetheless obligates host-States to put forth their best efforts in attempting to quell genocides. In that case, the FRY authorities should have deployed

[190] *Request for Interpretation in the Avena Case*, above n 45 at 17, para 44.

[191] For a general discussion on the imprecision of the contents of primary obligations of conduct/result across different fields, see Combacau, above n 44 at 185–86.

'the best efforts within their powers to try and prevent the tragic events'.[192] Unsurprisingly, the flipside to this posture is the idea that

> for a State to be held responsible for breaching its obligation of prevention, it does not need to be proven that the State concerned definitely had the power to prevent the genocide; it is sufficient that it had the means to do so and that it manifestly refrained from using them.[193]

Although few efforts have been deployed in actually circumscribing the contents of primary counterterrorism obligations, there might in fact be a legal thrust towards the implementation of obligations of result in the 'war' on terror, at least on a rhetorical level.

In the context of Security Council practice, a popular and recurrent manifestation of this phenomenon is for the Council to impose an obligation to criminalise terrorism – and the corresponding duty to prosecute – without providing an actual definition of 'terrorism'. How do States prosecute or criminalise an undefined activity? This conundrum can be resolved by concluding that a sufficiently diversified group of States share common definitional cardinal points in their respective perceptions of what constitutes 'terrorism', so as to legally circumscribe that term for the purposes of State responsibility. Furthermore, in such instances the Council invariably omits to furnish details as to modes of, and fora for, criminal prosecution. Should national prosecution of terrorist activity prove illusory because of political haggling, jurisdictional issues or other concerns, can we consider referral of the matter to the International Criminal Court sufficient in meeting that State's obligations? In response to this rather broad margin of appreciation of relevant primary norms, States are increasingly criminalising what traditionally constituted mere evidentiary elements in domestic criminal law contexts so as to enhance their due diligence capital in stamping out extremist elements on their soil. As a corollary, we are witnessing a shift towards more indirect modes and forms of accountability both at the domestic and international levels.[194]

Another perhaps more relevant example is the frequent exhortation by the Council for States to refrain from harbouring and supporting terrorists on their respective territories. Again, no operative definition of 'harbouring and supporting' is advanced with a view to prescribing *specific* conduct.[195] This confusion in turn brings about complex additional questions, of which threshold concerns certainly dominate the inquiry. Looking beyond the much-decried provision of political and jurisdictional solace, to the toleration of training camps and other logistical accommodations afforded Al Qaeda by Afghanistan, what other forms of governmental action/inaction will trigger State responsibility for failing to prevent terrorism? If a sanctuary State is oblivious to the concoction

[192] See *Genocide Case*, above n 175 at para 438.
[193] ibid.
[194] See also: above ch 1, section I; ch 4, section II.B).
[195] See Duffy, above n 6 at 57–58.

of terrorist agendas on its territory, is it still 'harbouring' terrorists pursuant to the Council's resolutions? More challengingly, Pakistan and Yemen offer an intractable and hybrid model of compliance and toleration: on one hand, they both serve as key allies to the US in its struggle against terrorism whilst on the other hand, they fail to control portions of their national territory, thereby tolerating extremist elements on their soil (in the Pakistani north-western, semi-autonomous tribal areas or in the Yemeni Abyan, Ma'rib and Shabwa governorates). Further inquiries are potentially endless or, at least, as numerous as possible scenarios and degrees of governmental involvement or inaction vis-à-vis terrorism. This reality is undoubtedly exacerbated by the advent of new weaponry and technology such as the Internet.[196]

Indeed, cyber-terrorism raises particularly intractable challenges for State responsibility, even if accepting that the international struggle against terrorism is governed by straightforward primary obligations.[197] The real difficulty crops up at the secondary level of international breaches, that is to say once the proper invocation of responsibility has been effectuated and an attempt to deploy the mechanics of international liability is engaged. Whilst it is theoretically possible to impute a cyber-attack to a geographically-delimited area, ascertaining authorship of such unlawful conduct is by no means a straightforward task (ie was the conduct carried out by a State, non-State actors, a group, an individual or some mixed configuration of those elements?). Furthermore, the issue of anonymity works in tandem with the speed of online transactions and events in blurring all traces susceptible of leading back to the true culprits.[198] Consequently, 'even discriminate attacks easily become indiscriminate because the Internet is interconnected'.[199] Even the seizure of Internet Protocol addresses can turn out to be a fallacious benchmark, as the web is increasingly utilised as a prised vehicle to pursue subterfuges and engage in unlawful activity through surrogates.[200]

A striking case in point resides in a series of nebulous cyber-attacks carried out against online interests in Estonia in April-May 2007, a succession of events unprecedented in scale.[201] These attacks were likely prompted by Estonia's decision to move a contentious Soviet-era statue to a new location. Over a period of

[196] On the challenges of cyber-terrorism, see, eg: GS McNeal, 'Cyber Embargo: Countering the Internet Jihad' (2007–08) 39 *Case Western Reserve Journal of International Law* 789.

[197] See LCMJ Sklerov, 'Solving the Dilemma of State Responses to Cyberattacks: A Justification for the Use of Active Defenses against States Who Neglect Their Duty to Prevent' (2009) 201 *Military Law Review* 1.

[198] See generally: White House, *The National Strategy to Secure Cyberspace* (February 2003), available at www.us-cert.gov/reading_room/cyberspace_strategy.pdf; S Brenner, 'At Light Speed: Attribution and Response to Cybercrime/Terrorism/Warfare' (2007) 97 *Journal of Criminal Law and Criminology* 379.

[199] SJ Shackelford, 'From Nuclear War to Net War: Analogizing Cyber Attacks in International Law' (2008) 27 *Berkeley Journal of International Law* 191, 199.

[200] See Brenner, above n 198 at 424 (highlighting that a host-State may enlist '"civilian" cyber-criminals and cyberterrorists to conduct their operations from within its borders' in order to conceal the 'purpose and origins of the state sponsored attacks' behind a civilian façade).

[201] For more background on this episode, see M Landler and J Markoff, 'Digital Fears Emerge after Data Siege in Estonia', *New York Times*, 29 May 2007 at A1.

several weeks, unidentified assailants waged an unrelenting onslaught of cyber-strikes against Estonian targets, including: i) immersing parliamentary websites, the President and the Prime Minister with a barrage of junk email messages, thereby causing site crashes; and ii) bringing down several national newspaper websites, thereby provoking high-level consultations on devising strategies to shelter essential services – such as online banking – from further attacks. In responding to this first round of online terrorist strikes, Internet service providers across the globe managed to thwart a majority of the incoming harmful data, thereby reinforcing the argument advanced above that the challenges posed by terrorism must be met with truly international responses whilst transnational cooperation must also be enhanced. Much in the cooperative spirit deriving from the *Genocide Case*, if all States work in concert and take active steps towards repressing and thwarting terrorism on their respective soils, they might increase the likelihood of ultimately bringing about the intended result across the board (ie prevention of transnational terrorism). After what initially appeared to be a diminution in additional prospective cyber-attacks, Estonia proclaimed that the attacks emanated from Russia. This politically driven 'geographical' attribution, for lack of a better term, triggered another wave of online attacks, including: i) 'botnet' attacks resulting in the incapacitation of the online portal of Estonia's largest bank, thereby engendering financial losses exceeding one million dollars; ii) capacity-gauging attacks on networks followed by data flood attacks originating from various sources and saturating the network routers' bandwidth; and iii) a series of smaller-scale cyber-strikes in the following weeks. The principal mode of attack centred on a strategy employing 'distributed denial of service' attacks ('DDOS attacks'), a tactic causing targeted websites to malfunction as a result of continuous bombardment of factice information requests.[202] The final figures are staggering. According to the data collected by Arbor Networks Active Threat Level Analysis System, over 128 distinct DDOS attacks were perpetrated against specific Internet protocols located within Estonia throughout the online conflict; as a result, online traffic expanded from 20,000 packets to more than four million units per second.[203] Ranging between one and ten hours, the strikes emanated from different States including Egypt, Peru and Russia.

Not only does this precedent raise challenging questions regarding the principle of attribution but, even before reaching such analytical stage, it leaves room for doubt as to the characterisation of the cyber-attacks. Some commentators rightly ponder whether these attacks could be potentially construed as: i) cyber-crimes resulting, in part, from Russian Nashi hackers staging a coup; ii) cyber-terrorism carried out by an organisation seeking to further its own political or ideological agenda; or iii) cyber-warfare accompanied by heavy involvement of

[202] See, eg: 'A Cyber Riot: Estonia and Russia', *The Economist*, 12 May 2007 at 55.

[203] See S Kerner, 'Estonia Under Russian Cyber Attack?', *Security*, 18 May 2007 (cited in Shackelford, above n 199 at 203 fn 59).

Russian intelligence operatives.[204] Ultimately, even if those attacks are qualified as emanating from the State directly or, alternatively, as perpetrated by non-State actors, attribution as it currently stands under the ILC's *Articles* remains elusive. Equally challenging is the fact that, similarly to some terrestrial attacks, web-based transnational strikes may span over several States, thereby further compounding the analysis and triggering the potential application of Article 47(1).[205] This transnational complexity significantly affects, perhaps restrictively, the means States may harness with a view to complying with their counterterrorism obligations. Consequently, it is difficult to draw dispositive inferences either way without clearer legal organising principles operating in tandem with a context-sensitive, policy-informed approach as the one proposed below. In this particular instance, there is indication that Russia could have done more to prevent the cyber-attacks and increase its due diligence capital as the nature of the strikes did not, in any way, absolve it from fulfilling its obligation of prevention. Further exacerbating its potential liability were both the fact that the attacks were of a continuing character, thereby requiring Russia to step up efforts to thwart future or imminent strikes or to seek out external assistance in so doing, and concern that the State was intentionally obstructing the criminal investigation because, inter alia, the Russian public hailed the hackers as national heroes.[206] There was undoubtedly a breakdown in cooperation between Russia and Estonia given Russia's conduct, which led to its violation of its obligation of prevention. Indeed, 'States that deny involvement in a cyberattack, but refuse to open their investigative records to the victim-state, cannot expect to be treated as a state living up to its international duties'.[207] Russia's obligation included corollary duties such as the adoption of more stringent criminal legislation, conducting more serious and probing investigations, prosecuting cyber-attackers and, whilst the investigation and prosecution were pending, cooperating with Estonia and other aggrieved States. Within the range of available means in attaining these objectives, Russia could have considered implementing early detection and warning programmes to thwart future cyber-attacks, along with trace programmes to infiltrate virtual intermediaries back to their electronic source and ascertain the identity of the hackers.[208]

For the purposes of the conduct/result dichotomy, the present line of argument, which has been somewhat critical of the Council's lack of direction, does not purport to insinuate that this organ should necessarily have pushed the legal

[204] See, eg: Shackelford, above n 199 at 231; Brenner, above n 198 at 424.

[205] For a discussion of this provision, see below nn 280–88 and accompanying text.

[206] See, eg: D Hollis, 'Why States Need an International Law for Information Operations' (2007) 11 *Lewis & Clark Law Review* 1023, 1026; CJ Levy, 'What's Russian for "Hacker"?', *New York Times*, 21 October 2007 at 41.

[207] Sklerov, above n 197 at 72.

[208] See, eg: R Naraine, 'Chertoff Describes 'Manhattan Project' for Cyber-defenses', *Eweek.com*, 8 April 2008, available at www.eweek.com/c/a/Security/Chertoff-Describes-Manhattan-Project-for-Cyber-Defenses/; DA Wheeler and GN Larsen, 'Techniques for Cyber Attack Attribution', *Institute for Defense Analyses*, October 2003, available at www.dtic.mil/cgi-bin/GetTRDoc?AD=ADA468859&Location=U2&doc=GetTRDoc.pdf.

envelope even further. Indeed, compelling propositions have been put forth that resolution 1373 and its accompanying framework amount to a 'constitutional' revolution. Hence, it is up to international jurisprudence, international practice and legal scholarship to interpret, (de)construct, (re)construct and shape the relevant norms in order to move towards filling this conceptual void. Simply put, a straightforward obligation of prevention exists under international law; the policy thrust of this study rather advocates a renewed emphasis on secondary rules of international responsibility as a way to shed more light on the application of primary rules. The contrary argument must also be weighed in the balance, as further clarification of relevant primary rules could be immensely helpful; additionally, potential implementation of obligations of result in this debate, whilst unlikely and politically impracticable, must nonetheless be considered in light of parallel developments in the field of international environmental law.

Following that logic for a moment, by hypothetically casting overarching counterterrorism obligations of result across the board, the main purpose of the Council would presumably be to disregard any specific means employed by States in fulfilling said obligations. Under this light, the focus of State responsibility mechanisms would be strictly concerned with the actual result, as vague or broad as it may be. In other words, it becomes a way to short-circuit the imposition of policy guidelines – or pre-empts any potential and practical legislating function beyond the promulgation of abstract primary rules – emanating from the Council. However, promulgating broad and far-reaching obligations without defining a more specific range of permissible conduct towards attaining the desired result is dangerous, at least in one obvious way. By completely disregarding the means used to fulfil counterterrorism obligations, the Council actually fails to provide any legislative or normative frameworks through which the legal objective should be perceived or contemplated. In particular, considerable emphasis should be placed on protecting international human rights standards and constitutional safeguards.[209] If no guidance is provided as to what conduct is permissible at a principled level in a highly complex and, in many regards, novel campaign against terrorism, States can become susceptible to overreaction or combating the threat via unlawful means.[210] The flouting of long-established legal standards underpins one of the contemporary criticisms often levelled against US policy in the 'war' on terror since 9/11, for example.[211] Moreover, the realm of State responsibility can

[209] See above section II.A).

[210] Indeed, situations of social or political upheaval may trigger overreactions by executive branches in deploying counter-crisis initiatives. For a thoughtful review of the reasons why executive branches sometimes misgauge the security threat(s) at hand, see O Gross, 'Chaos and Rules: Should Responses to Violent Crises Always Be Constitutional?' (2003) 112 *Yale Law Journal* 1011, 1022–42; JJ Paust, 'Post-9/11 Overreaction and Fallacies Regarding War and Defense, Guantanamo, the Status of Persons, Treatment, Judicial Review of Detention, and Due Process in Military Commissions' (2004) 79 *Notre Dame Law Review* 1335.

[211] See, eg: GP Flechter, 'Black Hole in Guantanamo Bay' (2004) 2 *Journal of International Criminal Justice* 121; HH Koh, 'On American Exceptionalism' (2003) 55 *Stanford Law Review* 1479; D Luban, 'The War on Terrorism and the End of Human Rights' (2002) 22 *Philosophy and Public Policy Quarterly* 9, 9–14; P Sands, *Lawless World: America and the Making and Breaking of*

be conceived as an incubator for the further extension and propagation of the values enshrined in international human rights. As Professor Chinkin points out, the 'assertion of State responsibility for failure to exercise due diligence to prevent, or for acquiescence in, abuses committed by non-State actors, whether they be private individuals, para-military forces, multinational corporations or religious fundamentalists, extends the reach of human rights guarantees'.[212] Similarly, the emergence of a vast multiplicity of non-State terrorist actors – operating nationally, internationally or transnationally – also served as policy impetus for the formulation of the R2P Doctrine.[213]

States that flout international law in combating terrorism are most likely motivated by the blind and egregious pursuit of self-interests or by some politico-ideological inclination, rather than by any ostentatious disdain for the Security Council. Certainly, the lack of respect for the UN's structure of operation – compounded by the existence of what was once perceived as a sole, lonely superpower[214] – remains part of the problem, but it is not entirely symptomatic of recent disregard for international legal norms. However, it is no reason for the Council to fall short in its mandate of clearly reiterating international law and promoting the advancement of peace and security. In its altruistic attempts to set forth guiding principles – such as formulating an obligation to refrain from harbouring or supporting terrorists – the Council might have involuntarily done a disservice to the objectives of international peace and security by essentially giving *carte blanche* to States in meeting counterterrorism obligations. Direct consequences of this oversight are serious human rights violations, as witnessed in certain States, a reality which certainly impairs the prospect of peace and security.

To make this line of argument even more palatable, comparisons must be drawn from the field of international environmental law. As argued amply throughout this book, certain aspects of counterterrorism law closely track similar developments in the field underlying international environmental obligations. At the outset, parallels are striking and equally facilitated by the conceptual affinity shared by international responsibility and international environmental law.[215]

Global Rules (London, Penguin Books, 2005); J Steyn, 'Guantanamo Bay: The Legal Black Hole' (2004) 53 *ICLQ* 1.

[212] C Chinkin, 'Human Rights and the Politics of Representation: Is There a Role for International Law?' in M Byers (ed), *The Role of Law in International Politics: Essays on International Relations and International Law* (Oxford, OUP, 2000) 131 at 145.

[213] International Commission on Intervention and State Sovereignty, *The Responsibility to Protect: Report of the International Commission on Intervention and State Sovereignty* (Ottawa, International Development Research Centre, 2001) 4.

[214] See, eg: Waxman, above n 151 at 205. Even though the US is arguably the world's sole superpower, it still often requires the support of other powerful States in advancing its own agenda. See, eg: SP Huntington, 'The Lonely Superpower' (1999) 78 *Foreign Affairs* 35, 36.

[215] For a general exploration of this last point, see P Okowa, *State Responsibility for Transboundary Air Pollution in International Law* (Oxford, OUP, 2000); H Xue, *Transboundary Damage in International Law* (Cambridge, CUP, 2003).

Both counterterrorism law and international environmental law involve containing serious, sometimes massive or large-scale, and almost always man-made hazardous activities. Not only do these activities bring about grave and immediate damage, but also often engender additional or collateral effects. In both areas, the primary norms, which obviously have an impact on the application of secondary rules of liability, are far from consistent and in many cases fall short in actually prescribing specific conduct. For instance, the Security Council recently promulgated broad-ranging and sweeping principles regarding transnational terrorism without harnessing its prescriptions on more specific expectations of conduct or behaviour accruing to the addressees of its resolutions.[216] Quite the contrary, the Council's resolutions often warrant a specific result without providing adequate grounding as to the rationale or method for doing so, or simply fail to provide elements germane to the fulfilment of obligations promulgated in its resolutions. This reality most likely follows from the inherent limits on the Council's legislative powers.[217]

Whilst the rules of State responsibility governing pollution are far from consistent, some scholars ascertain a noticeable shift towards the acceptance of obligations of result in the environmental field, both under treaty obligations and evolving general principles of law.[218] Invoking a practical example on the inconsistency of liability rules for transnational pollution might be helpful and in turn directly transposable to counterterrorism. In the case of pollution of the sea by ship endangering or damaging a coastal State, relevant treaties provide that it is the ship-owner (often a private person) who is liable towards the coastal State, as well as towards private persons who suffered physically or in their property from the polluting act. In contrast, transboundary harm in State A originating from a private enterprise situated in the land territory of State B entails, as we have seen under certain conditions, the responsibility not of that private enterprise but of State B on whose territory the pollution originated. One can easily glean the inconsistency between different rules involving non-State actors that can perhaps – but flimsily – be explained by the State's exclusive territorial control in the latter scenario from a policy standpoint. Moreover, in international environmental law like in counterterrorism contexts, the contents of primary obligations are not always well-defined; this confusion is further exacerbated by the involvement of non-State actors in polluting activities

[216] See, eg: Duffy, above n 6 at 37–38, 57–58, 70.

[217] On the Security Council's legislative role, see generally: LMH Martínez, 'The Legislative Role of the Security Council in Its Fight against Terrorism: Legal, Political and Practical Limits' (2008) 57 *ICLQ* 333; LD Roberts, 'United Nations Security Council Resolution 687 and Its Aftermath: The Implications for Domestic Authority and the Need for Legitimacy' (1993) 25 *NYU Journal of International Law and Politics* 593, 594. But see: C Dominicé, 'The International Responsibility of the United Nations for Injuries Resulting from Non-Military Enforcement Measures' in Ragazzi, above n 2 at 366–67; M Lehto, 'Terrorism in International Law – an Empty Box or Pandora's Box' in J Petman and J Klabbers (eds), *Nordic Cosmopolitanism: Essays in International Law for Martti Koskenniemi* (Leiden, Nijhoff, 2003) 291 at 306. See also: M Koskenniemi, 'The Police in the Temple: Order, Justice and the UN – A Dialectical View' (1995) 6 *EJIL* 325.

[218] See, eg: Springer, above n 14 at 130.

(we must always bear in mind that a wrongful act must be linked to the official State apparatus for responsibility to attach).[219] When dealing with non-State actors, State compliance with environmental or counterterrorism agreements depends in many cases not simply on State action, but also on the actions of private parties whose failure to reduce their pollution to the levels required by an agreement, or not to carry out transnational terrorism, may cause a State to violate its obligations.

In terms of environmental obligations, a case in point is found in the 1960 Frontier Treaty between the Netherlands and Germany, which provides that parties 'shall neither take *nor tolerate* any measures causing substantial prejudice to the neighbouring State'.[220] Should substantial damage be carried out against one State by the acts of private persons in the other State, the latter could be held responsible for the injury sustained insofar as it tolerated the harmful activity on its soil. Here, as with many restatements of the obligation to prevent terrorism, the international wrong is *toleration*. There is inherent ambiguity in a term like 'tolerate', 'which suggests that a state might be relieved of any responsibility had it made a sincere and determined – but unsuccessful – effort to prevent the polluting activity'.[221] This formulation has been recurrent in Security Council practice, both before and after 9/11, as it often invokes the concepts of 'toleration' and 'support' in tandem.

Another striking example is found in a similar agreement originally struck between Czechoslovakia and Hungary, containing an obligation that might be perceived as straddling both conduct and result terrain. That treaty requires parties to '*take steps to prevent* deliberate damage to the banks of frontier waters'.[222] Again, what is precisely expected of States is not certain: there is decidedly a positive obligation incumbent upon States, anchored in the presence of operative language in the form of 'take steps'. Yet, the notion of 'taking steps' is vague in and of itself, an artificial legal threshold upon first glance; no further guidance is provided as to what types of means or methods are expected or even permissible in meeting the duty. Moreover, the idea of prevention casts another dimension of the specific legal undertaking – possibly that of warranting a specific result, which resides in actually forestalling the given pollution – arguably bringing the specific stipulation within the furrow of obligations of result. However, the invocation of the term 'deliberate' further muddles the content of the obligation since it seemingly imports a degree of intentionality into

[219] As classical author Dionisio Anzilotti proclaimed, 'L'imputabilité, au point de vue du droit international, n'est donc pas autre chose que la conséquence du rapport de causalité qui existe entre un fait contraire au droit des gens et l'activité de l'État dont ce fait émane' ('From the perspective of international law, imputability is nothing but the consequence of the causal nexus between an act contrary to the law of nations and the activity of the State from which such act emanates' (author translation)). See Anzilotti, above n 21 at 291. See also: P-M Dupuy, 'Dionisio Anzilotti and the Law of International Responsibility of States' (1992) 3 *EJIL* 139, 144.

[220] Cited by Springer, above n 14 at 128.

[221] ibid.

[222] ibid.

the equation without correspondingly fixing any modes of threshold. Here, we have the worst of both worlds: vague language regarding potential means to be employed in fulfilling the obligation, along with a prescribed – yet unclear – result which, under ordinary legal construction, would afford the implementing State wide latitude in choosing means to attain the specific result. Therefore, the nature of the obligation, which oscillates somewhere between prevention and result, seems, upon first glance, to make the very mention of 'taking steps' otiose. More broadly, almost all language in such treaty undertakings becomes superfluous since neither dimension of the obligation in question – the actual result and/or identifiable steps in ensuring prevention – can be clearly ascertained nor construed as dispositive in indicating actual behaviour expected from States.

Principle 21 of the Stockholm Declaration similarly holds States responsible for their failure to prevent extra-territorial harm caused by activities under their jurisdiction or control. It provides that

> States have, in accordance with the Charter of the United Nations and the principles of international law, the sovereign right to exploit their own resources pursuant to their own environmental policies, and the responsibility to ensure that activities within their jurisdiction or control do not cause damage to the environment of other States or of areas beyond the limits of national jurisdiction.[223]

However, whilst States agreed on this principle in the abstract, 'it was impossible to reach agreement on the content of that responsibility should harm actually occur'.[224] Again, we have a clear statement of principle without any clarification as to the actual application and content of the rule. This trend pervades much of international environmental law, as unresolved questions still persist on primary rules expressing concepts such as the precautionary principle and sustainable development, for example.[225] This reasoning and the corresponding conceptual incongruities are, of course, integrally transposable to counterterrorism.

Conventional exceptions to this general normative uncertainty exist, thereby suggesting that an inescapable lack of interpretive direction has failed to metastasise to all areas of public international law and, correspondingly, does not pervade nor necessarily govern the entire realm of obligations of prevention. Indeed, certain conventional schemes deliver striking implementation lucidity in carving out obligations for Member States. In particular, Article 2(1) of the International Covenant on Economic, Social and Cultural Rights provides clear guidance on the means to implement the obligations enshrined therein, by direct reference, inter alia, to enabling legislation and international cooperation and

[223] UN Conference on the Human Environment, Stockholm Declaration, 16 June 1972, UN Doc A/CONF.48/14, Principle 21 reprinted in (1972) 11 ILM 1416 at 1420.

[224] Springer, above n 14 at 134.

[225] See, eg: F Roucounas, 'Non-State Actors: Areas of International Responsibility in Need of Further Exploration' in Ragazzi, above n 2 at 401–02.

assistance.[226] What is more, the general comment to this provision offers a high degree of direction – at least in less equivocal terms than usual – on the particulars and modalities of the obligations to be implemented, with both a direct reference to the ILC's treatment of the distinction between obligations of conduct and result, and an interpretive exploration of the notion of 'taking steps'.[227]

Ultimately, the controversy surrounding the distinction between obligations of conduct and result, along with their scope and content, is far from resolved.[228] The ILC simplified 'its classification of wrongful acts without having recourse to the distinction between obligations of conduct, prevention and result, even though the final text, in Article 14(3), still refers to an "international obligation requiring a state to prevent a given event" '.[229] Nevertheless, incorporating this distinction in international law is sound, desirable, and its validity hardly contestable. As a general rule, implementing an overarching, overriding obligation of result in preventing terrorism will not be reasonable, let alone realistic.[230] The dispositive analytical factor will rather lie in the conduct of host-States in addressing the potential threat and in attaining a realistic result in light of the factual circumstances. Consequently, several commentators cast any obligation of prevention as an obligation of means, which inexorably entails a careful analysis of various parameters to gauge whether State conduct matches the content of the duty in a specific instance. The next section delves into this question but a few elements having an impact on determining whether an obligation of prevention is fulfilled can be identified at the outset, namely: the host-State's ability to influence the perpetrators of the wrongful act, the geographical location of the host-State vis-à-vis the location of the actual wrongful act, or

[226] Art 2(1) provides the following:

> Each State Party to the present Covenant undertakes to take steps, individually and through international assistance and co-operation, especially economic and technical, to the maximum of its available resources, with a view to achieving progressively the full realization of the rights recognized in the present Covenant by all appropriate means, including particularly the adoption of legislative measures.

See International Covenant on Economic, Social and Cultural Rights, GA Res 2200A (XXI) of 16 December 1966, 999 UNTS 3 (in force, 3 January 1976).

[227] See OHCHR, CESCR General Comment 3: The Nature of States Parties Obligations (Art. 2, par. 1), UN Doc E/1991/23, available at www.unhchr.ch/tbs/doc.nsf/(Symbol)/94bdbaf59b43a424c1 2563ed0052b664?Opendocument.

[228] Some have taken issue with Ago and Crawford's respective characterisations of obligations to prevent and obligations of result. See, eg: above ch 4 n 244 and accompanying text and compare with Crawford, above n 37 at 440–42. The distinction between obligations of means and obligations of result was also invoked in *Gabčíkovo-Nagymaros Project (Hungary/Slovakia)*, Judgment of 25 September, *ICJ Reports* (1997) 7 at 77, para 135.

[229] P-M Dupuy, 'A General Stocktaking of the Connections Between the Multilateral Dimension of Obligations and Codification of the Law of Responsibility' (2002) 13 *EJIL* 1053, 1059; JR Crawford et al, 'La seconde lecture du projet d'articles sur la responsabilité des Etats de la Commission du droit international' (2000) 104 *RGDIP* 911; JR Crawford et al, 'The ILC's Draft Articles on State Responsibility: Toward Completion of a Second Reading' (2000) 94 *AJIL* 660.

[230] But see: Higgins, above n 26 at 156 (arguing that 'with regard to particular obligations, a standard *higher* than due diligence may be required').

transnational cooperation carried out by the host-State with other States.[231] Indeed, this posture seems to have been endorsed by the ICJ in the *Genocide Case*, albeit in relation to the obligation to prevent genocide.[232]

B) The Obligation of Prevention on a Variable Scale[233]

Most obligations of prevention are highly 'modulatory' and remain shaped and informed by the actual means at the disposal of States called upon to fulfil these legal undertakings, thereby militating in favour of a highly contextualised analysis in post-breach settings. As ICJ Judge Mohamed Bennouna declares, 'la prise en compte des moyens des uns et des autres fait que cette obligation connaît, de par sa nature même, certaines modulations, selon le contexte où elle est censée opérer'.[234] The best way to conceptualise the application of the obligation of prevention in the proposed framework is to visualise a sliding element on a vertical bipolar continuum representing the conduct of the host-State (**see Appendix I**). At one end of the spectrum lies the expected (and specific) result dictated by the obligation to prevent terrorism, namely to thwart attacks completely. At the other extremity of the continuum rests the utmost negligent and careless conduct States can adopt in preventing terrorism, or actual endorsement. All along the way, various degrees of State efficiency in preventing attacks are skewered, increment-by-increment. This scale covers an exhaustive set of possibilities, ranging from near prevention of given attacks to inaction.[235] The sliding element represents the host-State's conduct and is positioned at the angle that best represents that State's action to prevent the given attack, in hindsight. The circumstances of the particular attack will affect the sliding element: should they be favourable to the State, the element will slide up, closer to the expected result. However, if they are construed against the host-State, they will burden the element and bring it down towards negligent or careless conduct.

If a State had the logistical capacity to crack down on terrorist cells that perpetrated an attack but failed to do so (eg by not acting on intelligence reports), the element will descend.[236] In this regard, it is useful to invoke China's proposal

[231] See, eg: Bennouna, above n 103 at 375.

[232] *Genocide Case*, above n 175 at para 430.

[233] Although not directly on point because dealing with the duty to prevent genocide, the ICJ expressed a similar idea, expounding that 'The content of the duty to prevent varies from one instrument to another, according to the wording of the relevant provisions, and depending on the nature of the acts to be prevented'. See ibid, at para 429.

[234] 'The assessment of the varying means at the disposal of States signals that the obligation of prevention is subject, by its very nature, to certain modulations depending on the context in which it operates' (author translation). Bennouna, above n 103 at 379.

[235] Some scholars expressed hints of the idea of a variable State responsibility model, albeit through the lens of armed reprisals. However, much of the pre-9/11 literature hinged on *Nicaragua* and *Tadić*-inspired formulations of control or knowledge. See, eg: Baker, above n 39 at 36–37.

[236] See *Osman v United Kingdom* (1998) 29 Eur HR Rep 245; above ch 1 nn 100–02 and accompanying text; Duffy, above n 6 at 308; McCredie, above n 39 at 86.

at Dumbarton Oaks in 1944 regarding the elements underpinning a definition of 'aggression' contained in the draft Charter articles and later unveiled at the San Francisco conference. For China, that crime was tantamount to the

> [p]rovision of support to armed groups, formed within [a State's] territory, which have invaded the territory of another state; or refusal, notwithstanding the request of the invaded state, to take in its own territory all the measures in its power to deprive such groups of all assistance or protection.[237]

Whilst China's proposal was ultimately discarded, there is every indication that the international community is moving towards a legal standard philosophically adjacent to the one originally espoused by that State. This contention is undoubtedly further substantiated by Council resolutions 1368 and 1373, which ostensibly make 'harbouring and supporting' of terrorists a basis for engaging State responsibility.[238] Governmental inaction when there is clearly capacity to act otherwise also ostensibly extends to State failures in warning potential victim-States of possible terrorist excursions emanating from their territories. Thus, the broader obligation to prevent terrorism is also embedded with a 'duty to warn' component and failure to comply with that portion of the undertaking may also trigger State responsibility.[239] Conversely, whilst a particular State might have garnered sufficient political will and succumbed to diplomatic pressure to exercise jurisdiction over suspected terrorists operating within its borders, locating relevant individuals may prove challenging in some instances.[240]

If the host-State did not manage information flows properly within its own political and intelligence infrastructures, thereby increasing the risk of the given attack, the element will slide downwards. If it could have frozen terrorist assets within its jurisdiction, thereby paralysing the operational autonomy of terrorists, but neglected to do so, the element will slide down the continuum. If the host-State could have acted, based on its knowledge of the impending attack, but failed to do so for reasons of endorsement or promotion of the terrorists' cause, the element will be lowered again.[241] In that regard, the proposed strict liability model has, up to now, addressed many facets of the *Corfu Channel* Case and the potential expansion of the Court's reasoning towards a no-knowledge regime of State responsibility in light of a glaring translation error.[242] Equally

[237] 'Tentative Chinese Proposals for a General International Organization', 23 August 1944 in US State Department, *Foreign Relations of the United States 1944* (Washington, DC, Government Printing Office, 1966) 718 at 725.

[238] See, eg: Franck, above n 31 at 841.

[239] See, eg: TA DiPerna, 'Small Arms and Light Weapons: Complicity "With a View" Toward Extended State Responsibility' (2008) 20 *Florida Journal of International Law* 25, 43. On this topic, see also: A Boivin, 'Complicity and Beyond: International Law and the Transfer of Small Arms and Light Weapons' (2005) 87 *International Review of the Red Cross* 467.

[240] See KW Abbott, 'Economic Sanctions and International Terrorism' (1987) 20 *Vanderbilt Journal of Transnational Law* 289, 298.

[241] This also fits within the logic of the *Tehran Hostages* Case, above ch 2 nn 61–62, 116; ch 4 n 39 and accompanying text. On responsibility by endorsement, see Martin, above n 62 at 461–62.

[242] See the following notes and accompanying text above: ch 1 nn 40–41, 130–34; ch 2 nn 152, 175–76; ch 4 nn 47–48.

important is the issue of constructive knowledge, which becomes paramount in this second tier of the strict liability-infused approach; given the importance of combating transnational terrorism, host-States will no longer be able to hide behind 'wilful blindness' in order to avoid responsibility.[243] An alternate interpretation extracted from *Corfu Channel* is therefore directly transferable to the current framework as the information host-States had, or *ought* to have had, will have a direct incidence on their level of responsibility.

For instance, Afghanistan could not hide behind the fact that it did not specifically know that Al Qaeda was planning the 9/11 attacks on its territory. To the contrary, its knowledge could be constructed or inferred from repeated Security Council exhortations directed against it and urging it to cease harbouring Al Qaeda members, paired with international condemnation of that sanctuary; this tailored Afghanistan's obligation towards an increased duty of vigilance and monitoring of Al Qaeda's activities because of the strong likelihood of transnational, subversive excursions by the group. Much like in *Corfu Channel*, inferences of factual and circumstantial evidence could establish a cognitive nexus – whether real or constructed – between the State and non-State actors in the case of Afghanistan. Discussing the notion of knowledge in *Corfu Channel* regarding the 9/11 attacks, one commentator aptly summarises this line of argument:

> [T]he fact that al Qaeda was operative on its soil does not necessarily presuppose the Taliban's knowledge of the attacks, even drawing on the notion of *culpa*. Yet, it is arguable that without introducing the theory of absolute responsibility, the Taliban's knowledge could be remotely inferred on the basis of the notion of *culpa* in the particular circumstances, where obligations had been imposed on the Taliban by a series of the Security Council resolutions to take steps to prevent and punish international terrorism.[244]

Moreover, if the host-State has knowingly harboured and/or supported members of a terrorist organisation on its territory which overtly perpetrates egregious violations of international law, the element will slide down considerably. This aspect was also canvassed by Bowett prior to 9/11 when assessing the reasonableness of reprisals against a State for terrorism emanating from its territory. Citing Falk, he listed one very important factor amongst several others, ostensibly rooted in the law of indirect responsibility: 'That the appraisal of the retaliatory use of force take account of the *duration and quality of support*, if any, that the target government has *given to terroristic enterprises*' (emphasis added).[245] This would undoubtedly be the case for Afghanistan vis-à-vis the 9/11 attacks, which ignored several pleas by the Security Council demanding it cease

[243] See, eg: Crawford, above n 14 at 82; Martin, above n 62 at 458 fn 37 and accompanying text. For further discussion about the role of knowledge in *Corfu Channel*, see Higgins, above n 26 at 159–60.

[244] Arai-Takahashi, above n 12 at 1096–97.

[245] Bowett, above n 39 at 27.

harbouring Al Qaeda members.[246] Similarly, if a State is in a position to prevent massive human rights abuse or save lives within its territory or extraneously but fails to intervene, its passiveness could engage its international responsibility.[247]

If a State fails to heed the Security Council's instructions regarding the presence of terrorists/organisations on its territory,[248] the element will plummet, irrespective of whether such presence is due to deliberate harbouring by the State apparatus or rather to physical/political loss of control. The 2006 Israel-Hezbollah conflict comes to mind as a poignant account illustrating the potential role that State responsibility could play in such instances. Lebanon's responsibility could plausibly be engaged as a result of it allowing the southern portion of its territory to be used by Hezbollah to perpetrate terrorist attacks against Israel.[249] More importantly, Lebanon's failure to repel the threat within its own territory should be contrasted with past Council pronouncements on the matter urging it to ensure the removal of Hezbollah factions from its soil.[250]

Lack of State control by Lebanon over terrorist factions is by no means a novel phenomenon. As explored above in chapter two, section IV.C)i), the case of the PLO operating on Lebanese territory during the 1982 Israel-Lebanon conflict provides some analogous grounds for analysis. Aside from evoking the image of a 'State within a State', the PLO has had a long-standing history of using Lebanese territory to launch and facilitate excursions into Israel.[251] In more recent years, Hezbollah now seems to carry that torch by making ample use of the same territory to carry out terrorist missions against Israel. Also relevant to the analysis is the fact that in addition to controlling the southern portion of Lebanon, Hezbollah has, for all intents and purposes, also been at times subsumed under the official State apparatus, which might suggest *direct* attribution to Lebanon.[252] Should direct imputation acquire traction in this case, it would convert any ensuing recourse to force into an act of State, as opposed to non-State or private terrorism as this latter activity has been traditionally envisaged pursuant to State responsibility logic.

If the sanctuary State has transferred – either willingly or unwillingly/inadvertently (although only the latter standard would have to be met to fit within

[246] Indeed, commentators highlight the pressing need to outlaw safe havens for terrorism, judging that they 'are at the root of the problem of terrorism'. See Rao, above n 115 at 69.

[247] For an application of this idea, along with a discussion of the government of Afghanistan, see, eg: B Vukas, 'Humanitarian Intervention and International Responsibility' in Ragazzi, above n 2 at 239–40.

[248] See ibid for the case of the government of Afghanistan.

[249] See, eg: Kirchner, above n 3 at 781.

[250] See, eg: SC Res 1559, UN SCOR, 59th Sess, 5028th Mtg, UN Doc S/RES/1559 (2004).

[251] See, eg: D McForan, *The World Held Hostage: The War Waged by International Terrorism* (New York, St Martin's Press, 1987) 46–47; TM Franck, *Recourse to Force: State Action against Threats and Armed Attacks* (Cambridge, CUP, 2002) 57. The image of a 'State acting within a State' has also been brandished when discussing Al Qaeda's operations in relation to the Taliban. See R Gunaratna, *Inside Al Qaeda: Global Network of Terror* (London, Hurst, 2002) 82.

[252] See Kirchner, above n 3 at 780. See also: C Bloom, 'The Classification of Hezbollah in Both International and Non-International Armed Conflicts' (2008) 14 *Annual Survey of International and Comparative Law* 61, 78–82.

the logic of indirect responsibility) – some State functions to private entities such as terrorist organisations, the element will be dragged down.[253] If a terrorist attack is facilitated by the inadvertence or carelessness of the members or representatives of the official State apparatus in the execution of their ordinary functions or operations, the element will also topple down.[254] Drawing on the experience of the ECHR with a view to establishing causation for obligations of prevention, an ex post facto test of foreseeability could be applied and, if the terrorist attack was reasonably foreseeable, the element would correspondingly move downwards (prompted by an inversely proportional correlation between the element and the degree of foreseeability of the attack).[255]

Conversely, if a State does not completely fulfil its obligation or does not attain its potential in preventing the attack because doing so would generate more social unrest and terror,[256] the element will slide up the continuum. In that regard, the case of Pakistan poses particularly intractable challenges regarding its compliance with international counterterrorism obligations. Pakistan has become an important focal point in the global struggle against terrorism, with both Al Qaeda and Taliban members seeking refuge in its north-western, semi-autonomous tribal areas. In 2009, the Pakistani Army signed a truce with the Taliban regarding the Swat District, north of the Pakistani capital, which that State viewed as a method of appeasement because it would 'free up the Pakistani Army, reduce civilian suffering and satisfy popular dissatisfaction with the local judiciary'.[257] However, for the purposes of the proposed responsibility model, it is doubtful that Pakistan's course of action would have in fact increased its due diligence capital and demonstrated that it was actively fulfilling its obligations. Considerable effort, not mere political convenience by relinquishing the coveted tribal areas, in attenuating Pakistan's responsibility – ostensibly by demonstrat-

[253] See generally: C Hoss and P-M Dupuy, 'Trail Smelter and Terrorism: International Mechanisms to Combat Transboundary Harm' in RM Bratspies and RA Miller (eds), *Transboundary Harm in International Law: Lessons from the Trail Smelter Arbitration* (New York, CUP, 2006) 225 at 236. For an application to the 2006 Israel-Hezbollah conflict, see Kirchner, above n 3 at 782 (also citing P Scholl-Latour, *Kampf Dem Terror: Kampf Dem Islam?* (Munich, Ullstein Taschenbuch, 2004) 261, and declaring that 'The terrorist activities of Hezbollah can, furthermore, be attributed to Lebanon due to the fact that state functions have been allowed to fall into the hand of Hezbollah').

[254] For instance, Brownlie underscored that 'general responsibility may be generated by inadvertence in the execution of normal State activity'. Brownlie, above n 3 at 45–46. He alludes to the sequestration of Italian property in Tunisia by France and cites *In re Rizzo and Others* (1955) 22 ILR 317 at 322. See Brownlie, above n 3 at 46 fn 65. In the *Rizzo* Case, the Conciliation Commission found that

> the act contrary to international law is not the measure of sequestration, but an alleged lack of diligence on the part of the French State – or, more precisely, of him who was acting on its behalf – in the execution of the said measure.

See other authorities cited by Brownlie, above n 3 at 46 fn 65.

[255] See B Conforti, 'Exploring the Strasbourg Case-Law: Reflections on State Responsibility for the Breach of Positive Obligations' in Fitzmaurice and Sarooshi, above n 182 at 135.

[256] See, eg: the first 'permissible exception' or defence available under McCredie's model, above n 179 and accompanying text. See also: McCredie, above n 39 at 94.

[257] J Perlez and PZ Shah, 'Truce in Pakistan May Not Mean Peace, Just Leeway for Taliban', *New York Times*, 6 March 2009 at A6.

ing that unmanageable civil conflict or internal/transnational guerrilla warfare would ensue if this truce was not brokered – would have been required to offset the detrimental effects of striking this potentially destabilising agreement.

It later became evident that the truce would probably have the opposite effect to that of appeasing local tensions. Through this arrangement, the Pakistani government may effectively have created terrorist-friendly enclaves or 'mini-states with sanctuaries for Qaeda and Pakistani militants', a possibility further compounded by the fact that Taliban contingents were imposing a particularly harsh brand of Sharia law within the Swat District, crushing any form of dissent, torturing and murdering anti-Taliban militants to secure undisputed control over the region.[258] This reality appeared to be metastasising throughout other regions of Pakistan, notably after the Taliban at one time acquired effective control over the Buner District, 70 miles from Islamabad, thereby exacerbating the difficulty in gauging Pakistan's capability to repress terrorism.[259] Equally difficult tactical choices confront Pakistani authorities in electing the best implementation models for ensuring compliance with counterterrorism obligations. For instance, the wisdom of striking pseudo-law enforcement arrangements or containment missions with *lashkars* – anti-Taliban tribal militias – in Pakistan's Federally Administered Tribal Areas has been called into question.[260] Such agreements could potentially yield immediate pay-offs and modest tactical gains, as long as the mission parameters are highly focused and confined to immediate and localised objectives. Conversely, whilst Washington lobbied for increased collaboration with *lashkars* in combating terrorism in the region, those tribal militias are simply not geared towards conducting large-scale, ongoing military operations. Not to mention that engaging them for the purposes of a long-term campaign against extremist elements within Pakistan's borders might pose significant risks to regional security and, in turn, disrupt the Pashtun tribal hierarchy that enables the attainment of such, albeit limited, *lashkars*-driven tactical victories in the first place.[261]

This whole counterterrorism campaign is an exercise in risk assessment. In any particular case, if the host-State failed to prevent one terrorist attack, it should not exacerbate passions and through an overactive zeal, instigate further terrorism or induce the overthrow of its legitimately elected government.[262] Proportionality and reasonableness should govern this analysis or, at least,

[258] ibid.

[259] See J Perlez, 'Taliban Seize Vital Pakistan Area Closer to the Capital', *New York Times*, 23 April 2009 at A1. These types of situations must be appreciated in the light of the fact that the Security Council remains '*gravely concerned* by the threat of terrorism and the risk that non state actors may acquire, develop, traffic in or use nuclear, chemical, and biological weapons and their means of delivery'. See SC Res 1977, UN SCOR, 66th Sess, 6518th Mtg, UN Doc S/RES/1977 (2011).

[260] See M Kugelman, 'Tread Lightly with Pakistan's Lashkars', *Asia Times*, 16 July 2009, available at http://atimes.com/atimes/South_Asia/KG16Df01.html.

[261] For further elaboration on this line of argument, see ibid.

[262] Bowett, above n 39 at 20, raised this problematic aspect through the lens of reprisals aimed at enticing States to prevent terrorism. Although not directly on point, consider also Battaglini, above n 94 at 145–46; Rao, above n 115 at 183–93.

remain reliable benchmarks in gauging potential responses to terrorist threats. If there is a significant disparity or disproportion between the size of the territory and military capacity of the host-State, as contrasted with the expanse of terrorist activity on its territory, the State's onus will decrease and the element will ascend.[263] If a portion of the State's territory has been taken over whilst the legitimate government does not wield any de facto control over the region in question, although it genuinely desires to do so, the element will rise.[264] If the State is logistically incapable of preventing attacks but considers the panoply of options offered to it, including allowing extraneous forces or law enforcement units onto its territory to neutralise the threat, its burden will be lowered considerably as it will have sacrificed sovereignty in favour of combating terrorism in a bilateral/multilateral setting.[265] When a State relinquishes control over its territory or fails to capture or extradite terrorists operating on its territory, sending external law enforcement units to repel terrorist threats undoubtedly amounts to a proportionate countermeasure under State responsibility.[266] Indeed, counterterrorism capacity-building lies at the very heart of the logic underpinning Security Council resolution 1373 and its accompanying apparatus. Once again, these scenarios are evocative of the tension described earlier between combating terrorism efficiently and upholding State sovereignty. However, this phenomenon of multilateral laissez-faire might also entail that economically weaker States will be called upon to sacrifice their sovereignty more readily in order to repel terrorist threats, a notion that may understandably shock the sensibilities of Third World Approaches to International Law (TWAIL) scholars and sympathisers.[267]

If, even absent actual knowledge about possible terrorist activity, a host-State nonetheless undertakes reasonable and earnest measures to monitor potential terrorist plots or activities within its territory, the element will be pulled up.[268] This policy objective may be pursued through collecting and heeding relevant intelligence, especially when targets of intelligence-gathering are high-profile

[263] On this issue, see ch 2 nn 293–300 and accompanying text.

[264] It is crucial to recall that the Taliban was in fact the de facto government in most of Afghanistan and, at best, provided sanctuary to Al Qaeda. See, eg: GH Aldrich, 'The Taliban, Al Qaeda, and the Determination of Illegal Combatants' (2002) 96 *AJIL* 891, 891, 893; A Cassese, 'Terrorism Is Also Disrupting Some Crucial Legal Categories of International Law' (2001) 12 *EJIL* 993, 999; RA Falk, *The Great Terror War* (New York, Olive Branch Press, 2003) 101. See also: Stern, above n 83 at 688–92.

[265] See Byers, above n 115 under heading 'Exceptional Illegality'. On the virtues of combating terrorism through multilateral channels, see Head, above n 142 at 1–12; FC Pedersen, 'Controlling International Terrorism: An Analysis of Unilateral Force and Proposals for Multilateral Cooperation: Comment' (1976) 8 *Toledo Law Review* 209; Röben, above n 142 at 789–821.

[266] See, eg: Martin, above n 62 at 493.

[267] See, eg: A Anghie, *Imperialism, Sovereignty, and the Making of International Law* (Cambridge, CUP, 2005); A Anghie, *The Third World and International Order: Law, Politics, and Globalization* (Leiden, Nijhoff, 2003); M Mutua, 'What Is TWAIL?' (2000) 94 *ASIL Proceedings* 31; DP Fidler, 'Revolt against or From Within the West? TWAIL, the Developing World, and the Future Direction of International Law' (2003) 2 *Chinese Journal of International Law* 29.

[268] See, eg: Duffy, above n 6 at 57. See also: Stern, above n 83 at 691 (applying similar reasoning to Afghanistan in relation to 9/11).

and vocal proponents of terrorist methods. Whilst we must strike a sensible balance between civil liberties protection and combating terrorism efficiently – most importantly by limiting governmental interference in the private sphere[269] – egregious cases of terrorism-friendly rhetoric and activity fail to attract the same level of governmental restraint. Thus, an individual or group that openly endorses the agenda of renowned terrorist organisations and actively participates in recruiting similarly inclined individuals for their local chapters loses the benefits of privacy/anonymity and, by the same token, becomes a red flag for the purposes of devising intelligence programmes. A salient case in point is that of Belgium regarding the activities of Malika El Aroud, the widow of one of two men who assassinated Ahmed Shah Massoud, the anti-Taliban resistance leader, in Afghanistan two days before 9/11 following a direct order from Osama bin Laden.[270] Ms El Aroud has since remarried and established herself as a leading Internet 'jihadist' in Europe and openly promotes Al Qaeda's agenda, grants interviews to CNN and other high-profile news outlets, actively recruits potential candidates for the organisation and encourages its audience to take up arms against the West.[271] One of her key target demographics is women, whom she openly urges to join the ranks of terrorist organisations. In 2007, confronted with accusations of supporting radical Islamic organisations via websites, Switzerland's Federal Criminal Court found El Aroud guilty of aiding and abetting her Tunisian husband, Moez Garsalloui, in his support of criminal organisations and incitement of violence, imposing a six-month suspended sentence. By monitoring El Aroud's activities and placing her at the centre of its counterterrorism intelligence-gathering, which it is actively doing, Belgium will ensure that it considerably increases its due diligence capital in the second tier of the proposed strict liability model and alleviates the scope of its potential responsibility (provided it acts upon intelligence gathered if reasonable to do so).

If the host-State's conduct in response to, or prevention of, the terrorist act can be qualified as diligent[272] whilst the level of diligence exerted should be, to the extent possible, inversely proportionate with the level of risk *known by the host-*

[269] See, eg: the discussion above in section II.A).

[270] For a detailed account of the assassins' trajectory and the role played by their respective wives in the assassination, supplemented by El Aroud's testimonials, see M-R Armesto, *Son mari a tué Massoud* (Paris, Balland, 2002). For more background on Ms El Aroud, see E Sciolino and S Mekhennet, 'Belgian Woman Wages War for Al Qaeda on the Web: Belgian's Online Jihad Reflects Rise of Female Extremists', *International Herald Tribune*, 27 May 2008; E Sciolino and S Mekhennet, 'Al Qaeda Warrior Uses Internet to Rally Women', *The New York Times*, 28 May 2008.

[271] See, eg: P Cruickshank, 'Suicide Bomber's Widow Soldiers On: Wife of Assassin Professes Undying Affection for Bin Laden', *CNN World*, 24 August 2006, available at http://edition.cnn.com/2006/WORLD/asiapcf/08/15/elaroud/index.html. El Aroud was also arrested by Belgian authorities in 2008 under suspicions of entertaining links with terrorism. See S Erlanger, 'Terror Arrests Ahead of E.U. Summit', *New York Times*, 12 December 2008 at A18. On the similar cases of Colleen LaRose, aka 'JihadJane', and Jamie Paulin-Ramirez, see D Webber, 'Can We Find and Stop the "Jihad Janes"?' (2001) 19 *Cardozo Journal of International and Comparative Law* 91.

[272] See, eg: the second 'permissible exception' or defence under McCredie's model, above n 179 and accompanying text. See also: McCredie, above n 39 at 94.

State at the time of the attack,[273] the element will move upwards. A perhaps extreme example of a due diligence failure may be gleaned from the alleged killing by Israel of 22 Palestinian police officers manning West Bank checkpoints. Whilst Israel's posture was undoubtedly grounded in the idea of reprisal, the killings were apparently also predicated on the failure of Palestinian police officers to prevent the transit of terrorists who killed six Israeli soldiers earlier the same year.[274] This reinforces the idea that due diligence remains paramount when exploring State responsibility for failing to prevent terrorism, as amply referenced throughout this study.[275] Some scholars construed Afghanistan's obligation before 9/11 as embodying due diligence standards exceeding what would ordinarily reign as the prevalent international legal template (ie *une obligation de vigilance doublement renforcée*).[276] Whilst counterterrorism obligations decidedly embody due diligence standards, it must be reiterated that under this scheme 'it is the omission on the part of the state, not the injurious acts by the private actor, which constitutes the internationally wrongful act for which the state may be responsible'.[277]

This rationale presumably applies to States adopting measures aimed at cracking down on terrorism within their own borders following a strike emanating from their territory; this reactive but simultaneously pre-emptive (under certain lights) posture would undoubtedly help alleviate that State's responsibility in the event that subsequent attacks were carried out. An illustration of this mitigating factor can be extracted from Pakistan's toleration of – and potential involvement with – certain extremist elements on its territory having participated in the Mumbai attacks in India. Following the excursions, Pakistan attempted to thwart future attacks or, at least, neutralise potential threats having, inter alia: raided the properties of suspected terrorists, arrested 20 members of terrorist groups, including Lashkar-e-Taiba, the group suspected of having coordinated and carried out the Mumbai attacks, and arrested Zaki-ur-rehman Lakhvi, described as the mastermind behind those strikes.[278] Barring any addi-

[273] See, eg: SE Smith, 'International Law: Blaming Big Brother: Holding States Accountable for the Devastation of Terrorism' (2003) 56 *Oklahoma Law Review* 735, 754 ('modern States therefore only become accountable for failing to act when a terrorist threat is known to them').

[274] See, eg: J Bennett, 'Israel Steps up Counterstrikes; 22 Palestinians Slain', *New York Times*, 21 February 2002 at A1.

[275] This idea also pervades the field of international environmental law – which has been invoked comparatively throughout the present study – with some scholars calling for the analytical juxtaposition of State responsibility and due diligence standards in this setting. See, eg: AE Boyle, 'State Responsibility and International Liability for Injurious Consequences of Acts Not Prohibited by International Law: A Necessary Distinction?' (1990) 39 *ICLQ* 1, 22–23.

[276] On Afghanistan's violation of its obligation, see Stern, above n 83 at 688–92.

[277] Duffy, above n 6 at 57. There is no universally accepted definition of 'due diligence'. As one author suggests, a due diligence obligation 'consists [in taking] the reasonable measures of prevention that a well-administered government could be expected to exercise under similar circumstances'. See D Shelton, 'Private Violence, Public Wrongs, and the Responsibility of States' (1989–90) 13 *Fordham International Law Journal* 1, 21–22. See also: Pisillo-Mazzeschi, above n 106; P-M Dupuy, 'Due Diligence in the International Law of State Responsibility' in J-M Bischoff (ed), *Legal Aspects of Transfrontier Pollution* (Paris, OECD, 1977) 369.

[278] See, eg: J Perlez, 'Pakistan Moves to Curb Group Linked to Attacks', *New York Times*, 10 December 2008 at A6.

tional damaging factor burdening Pakistan's obligation of prevention, its diligent efforts to stamp out the roots of terrorism within its own borders would militate in favour of propelling the element upwards in the proposed model, at least upon first glance. However, Pakistan's responsibility vis-à-vis the Mumbai attacks is particularly thorny, predominantly because the extent of the involvement of the State apparatus in that transborder excursion has not been clearly ascertained. Indeed, several extremist groups within that State 'have functioned as an arm of Pakistan's military and intelligence services for two decades'.[279] In the event that a clear nexus can be established between the State and terrorists, such a relationship would undoubtedly burden the element on the abovementioned continuum and militate in favour of expanding Pakistan's responsibility (likely in the direction of direct attribution). Conversely, this reality would wield little incidence on the determination of State responsibility for future attacks if it can be demonstrated that Pakistan has undertaken serious and good faith efforts to eradicate terrorism on its territory and severed ties with those extremist elements operating within its borders (ie that whatever rogue factions/entities involved in future attacks cannot be construed as binding the Pakistani State pursuant to the direct responsibility paradigm discussed in chapter two).

If the host-State amounts to a link in a chain of sanctuary States in which the terrorist attack has been planned and executed, its responsibility will be commensurate with its level of accommodation/support in relation to other links in the chain;[280] the upward movement of the element will remain inversely proportionate with the proximity between the State's conduct and the crystallising moment of the attack within the chain. This type of situation challenges the very core and rationale of the ILC's *Articles*, engendering a plethora of secondary questions.[281] We might think of States that are used as frequent launch pads for attacks or even territories that constitute 'havens' for terrorists. What should be the applicable legal regime in those instances? What kind of normative frameworks should govern a series of preparatory terrorist activities spanning over more than one State and ultimately culminating in either terrestrial or cyber-attacks? How do we define the crystallising moment? Do we hold the State from which the attack is launched as the ultimate responsible? Or do we expect every involved government to fulfil an obligation of conduct or result in preventing terrorist operations from reaching the next step of the plan? Is every link of the chain or thread of a given terrorist attack only significant in the overall picture, or can it be thwarted independently? There seems to be support for assessing each participating State's responsibility independently pursuant to ILC Article 47(1), a proposition having received jurisprudential support. In the *Phosphate Lands in Nauru* Case, the ICJ found that Australia's responsibility

[279] ibid.

[280] Consider SN Schiedeman, 'Standards of Proof in Forcible Responses to Terrorism' (2000) 50 *Syracuse Law Review* 249, 261; Smith, above n 273 at 746.

[281] See, eg: C Dominicé, 'Attribution of Conduct to Multiple States and the Implication of a State in the Act of Another State' in Crawford et al, above n 2 at 281–89; A Orakhelashvili, 'Division of Reparation between Responsible Entities' in ibid, at 647–65.

could be assessed individually, even though both New Zealand and the UK also administered Nauru while it was a trust territory.[282] Similarly, when addressing Albania's responsibility in *Corfu Channel*, the Court was not swayed by the fact that another actor – likely a State – had carried out the contentious mine-laying.[283] But how, exactly, this rule – now codified at Article 47(1)[284] – would be brought to bear in cases of passive support of terrorism, as was the case in Afghanistan for example, remains to be seen.

Brigitte Stern aptly frames the relevant scheme of inquiry along the following lines: 'La question insoluble est de déterminer jusqu'à quel point l'Etat afghan aurait pu prévenir les attentats du 11 septembre et jusqu'à quel point les personnes responsables des attentats se trouvaient bien avant les attentats sur le territoire afghan'.[285] The salience of the Hamburg cell in the planning and perpetration of the 9/11 attacks must also be recalled, as it likely played a determinant role.[286] This type of scenario also brings about serious evidentiary impediments regarding the application of Article 47(1), as already noted in the field of environmental protection.[287] Given that gradual and cumulative pollution arises from multi-State sources following the contamination of natural elements (eg international rivers, sea, atmosphere) by land-based elements, and 'As the contribution of every single source of pollution is extremely difficult to assess, it would be inequitable to require that the injured party prove a causal nexus between a specific activity undertaken and the ensuing damage'.[288] Whilst

[282] See *Case Concerning Certain Phosphate Lands in Nauru (Nauru v Australia), Preliminary Objections*, Judgment of 26 June, *ICJ Reports* (1992) 240 at 258–59. See also generally: JE Noyes and BD Smith, 'State Responsibility and the Principle of Joint and Several Liability' (1988) 13 *Yale Journal of international Law* 225; A Nollkaemper, 'Issues of Shared Responsibility before the International Court of Justice' in E Rieter and H de Waele (eds), *Evolving Principles of International Law* (Leiden, Nijhoff, 2012) 199–237.

[283] See *Corfu Channel*, above n 103 at 18.

[284] This provision states that 'where several States are responsible for the same internationally wrongful act, the responsibility of each State may be invoked in relation to that act'. See *ILC Articles*, above n 122.

[285] 'The unanswerable question is to determine to what extent the Afghan State could have prevented the 9/11 attacks and the extent to which individuals responsible for those excursions were located on Afghan territory before those attacks were perpetrated' (author translation). Stern, above n 83 at 691.

[286] ibid, at fn 66. For a similar line of inquiry with regard to use of force principles, see Duffy, above n 6 at 191–92. The Hamburg cell was composed of Mohammed Atta, Ramzi bin al-Shibh, Marwan al-Shehhi and Ziad Jarrah. This determinant cell carried out its preparatory operations unimpeded because of Germany's 'lax security environment'. See The 9/11 Commission Report: Final Report of the National Commission on Terrorist Attacks Upon the United States (New York, W.W. Norton, 2004) 160–68, 366; M Sageman, *Understanding Terror Networks* (Philadelphia, University of Pennsylvania, 2004) 103–07.

[287] Legal standards of causation are exceedingly difficult to apply in such circumstances. See, eg: Okowa, above n 215 at 182–87. On the difficulty of applying causation-inspired standards in the work of the Iran-US Claims Tribunal, see JS Borek, 'Other State Responsibility Issues' in RB Lillich and DB Magraw (eds), *The Iran-United States Claims Tribunal: Its Contribution to the Law of State Responsibility* (Irvington-on-Hudson, Transnational Publishers, 1998) 303 at 316–23.

[288] T Scovazzi, 'Some Remarks on International Responsibility in the Field of Environmental Protection' in Ragazzi, above n 2 at 217–18. This phenomenon also appears to fly in the face of the reasoning extracted from *Corfu Channel*. See, eg: Smith, above n 273 at 754.

fact-intensive and similar to assessing the emission of transboundary toxic pollutants, identifying every relevant source of planning and execution of a terrorist attack might prove challenging or even improbable in some cases.

In analysing the host-State's conduct ex post facto, and given the specific circumstances of the case, if one cannot reasonably fathom an ounce more of effort within the State's contemplation as contrasted with what it actually did, the element will slide up.[289] This is consistent with the logic of the *Colozza* decision referenced above.[290] In that case, a person had been convicted *in absentia*, without having received notice of the trial. After being sentenced to six years in prison, the individual was unable to challenge the conviction. Centring his claim on Article 6(1) of the European Convention before the ECHR, which provides that 'In the determination of his civil rights and obligations or of any criminal charge against him, everyone is entitled to a fair and public hearing within a reasonable time by an independent and impartial tribunal established by the law', the individual opined that there had not been a fair hearing. Ultimately,

> [t]he Court thus considered that article 6(1) imposed an obligation of result. But, in order to decide whether there had been a breach of the Convention in the circumstances of the case, it did not simply compare the result required (the opportunity for a trial in the accused's presence) with the result practically achieved (the lack of that opportunity in the particular case). *Rather it examined what more Italy could have done to make the applicant's right 'effective'* (emphasis added).[291]

For instance, when a State genuinely and earnestly sets out to root out terrorist networks within its borders but nonetheless fails to prevent an attack, its responsibility would undoubtedly be mitigated to some extent.[292] Finally, although this scenario should not be invoked as a defence in and of itself without being accompanied by other mitigating factors, if the host-State lacks the financial wherewithal and/or human resources to adequately contain the threat,[293] the element will move up.

Now visualise a second sliding element mounted on another vertical bipolar continuum representing the obligation of prevention, placed in a parallel and proximate position to the first bipolar continuum (**see Appendix II**). At the top of this continuum, facing the expected (and specific) result pole on the other spectrum, one can find *jus cogens* obligations. Should the obligation to prevent terrorism be framed alongside the prohibition enshrined in Article 2(4) of the UN Charter and retain *jus cogens* status, it might arguably sit at the summit of that spectrum. Indeed, international law generally recognises the *jus cogens*

[289] But see: García-Mora, above n 40 at 30.

[290] Above n 188.

[291] Crawford, above n 14 at 129.

[292] In such scenario, the host-State would presumably remain sheltered against self-defence. See, eg: TD Gill, 'The Eleventh of September and the Right of Self-Defense' in WP Heere (ed), *Terrorism and the Military: International Legal Implications* (The Hague, TMC Asser Press, 2003) 23 at 29.

[293] See, eg: the third 'permissible exception' or defence under McCredie's model, above n 179 and accompanying text. See also: McCredie, above n 39 at 94.

character of the prohibition on recourse to force, as formulated in that provision. Citing the ILC's commentary on Article 50 of the Draft Articles on the Law of Treaties, the ICJ spoke to this point in the *Nicaragua* decision: 'the law of the Charter concerning the prohibition of the use of force in itself constitutes a conspicuous example of a rule in international law having the character of *jus cogens*'.[294] This statement also received wide support in legal scholarship.[295] Hence, the rule developed by the ILC and subsequently endorsed by the ICJ would seem to put the whole debate surrounding direct responsibility to rest. If a host-State directly participates in a forcible terrorist attack, it will evidently not fulfil its *jus cogens* obligation regarding the Article 2(4) prohibition. As discussed above, *jus cogens* obligations might arguably – and certainly not without controversy – attract a stricter regime of State responsibility. If such categorisation were ultimately retained, the host-State's international responsibility would thus be easily established in such instances.

At the other end of the second continuum rests the minimal standard of conduct prescribed by international law, this time sitting across from the utmost negligent and careless conduct pole. Similarly to the other continuum, various degrees of international obligations are scattered between both poles, ranging from obligations to endeavour to obligations *erga omnes*.[296] The gap between obligations of conduct and result, albeit a sliding concept as well, is dissimulated somewhere in the continuum of international obligations. On the second continuum, the element represents the formal characterisation by the international community of the specific obligation under study.

Consider that both elements are connected by an elastic band and that the ideal objective is to maintain the elastic in a horizontal position or the elements aligned (**see Appendix III**). As soon as a slight incline is felt in either continuum, the elastic will stretch, thereby creating a gap between the elements. For host-States to demonstrate that they used all necessary and reasonable means in preventing terrorism, there should be as small a gap as possible between the expected obligation and the conduct in question. Should such a cavity widen significantly, it will undoubtedly inform the responsibility analysis: the host-State's liability should be proportional to that gap (**see example in Appendix IV**).

[294] *Military and Paramilitary Activities in and against Nicaragua* (*Nicaragua v United States of America*), Merits, Judgment of 27 June, *ICJ Reports* (1986) 14 at 110, para 190.

[295] See, eg: JR Crawford, *The Creation of States in International Law* (Oxford, Clarendon Press, 1979) 106; A Verdross, '*Jus Dispositivum* and *Jus Cogens* in International Law' (1966) 60 *AJIL* 55; M Virally, 'Réflexions sur le "*Jus Cogens*"' (1966) 12 *AFDI* 5, 28.

[296] 'Whilst obligations of result necessarily entail that a successful result must be achieved, obligations of means only entail that States deploy best efforts . . . the failure of which . . . is never in and of itself a cause for responsibility' (author translation). See Combacau, above n 44 at 196 (noting that 'tandis que les obligations de résultat sont des obligations de réussir, les obligations de moyens ne sont que des *obligations de s'efforcer* . . . et l'échec . . . n'est jamais à lui seul une cause de responsabilité' (emphasis added)). For Robert Kolb, obligations to endeavour should be assessed in relation to international law's principle of 'good faith'. See 'The Exercise of Criminal Jurisdiction over International Terrorists' in Bianchi, above n 14 at 257.

In theory, the distinction between obligations of conduct and result will slide along the second continuum and adapt to the circumstances of the case, namely the conduct of the host-State represented by the position of the element on the first continuum. Reasonableness will exert an influence in guiding the elements as to what constitutes an acceptable threshold for the host-State. Should the circumstances indicate that more could reasonably have been done by that State, the element will ineluctably fall lower on the first continuum, in which case the gap between elements will widen and, as a result, the elastic will elongate.

To complicate the equation, the formal characterisation of the obligation to prevent terrorism by the international community will also interact with the elements. Should this obligation be characterised as *erga omnes*, it will correspondingly attract a stricter regime of responsibility. A case in point can be contemplated through the lens of the 2006 Israel-Hezbollah conflict, which evinced that every State is under an obligation *erga omnes* to combat terrorism; therefore, allowing its territory to be used for the purposes of transboundary terrorism amounts to a violation of a primary norm by the State.[297] Consequently, under the proposed model there will be a significant upward movement of the second element, along with the gap between obligations of conduct and result; should the actual conduct of the host-State on the first continuum fall below what is required by the scheme of the obligation *erga omnes*, this will engender a considerable gap between the elements.

The most visible upward thrust might arguably result from the characterisation of the obligation of prevention as a *jus cogens* engagement.[298] Some authors have flirted with the idea of characterising State support of terrorism – and the corresponding failure to prevent transborder terrorism – as a *jus cogens* violation.[299] Other accounts put forth more categorical proposals not directly applicable to State failures, suggesting that 'It is widely accepted that there is at least a presumption that most acts of terrorism, if not all of them, amount to breaches of peremptory norms, as they violate basic principles of human rights

[297] See, eg: Kirchner, above n 3 at 781.

[298] Similarly to obligations *erga omnes*, *jus cogens* obligations might also attract a stricter State responsibility regime. See, eg: Crawford, above n 14 at 132. However, it is sometimes asserted that *jus cogens* rules are, in fact, narrower than obligations *erga omnes*. See, eg: RSJ Macdonald, 'Fundamental Norms in Contemporary International Law' (1987) 25 *Canadian Yearbook of International Law* 138; T Meron, *Human Rights Law-Making in the United Nations* (Oxford, Clarendon Press, 1986) 187. Other scholars expound that *jus cogens* and *erga omnes* rules are essentially equivalent, albeit both dealing with different facets of the same norms. See, eg: M Byers, 'The Relationship Between *Jus Cogens* and *Erga Omnes* Rules' (1997) 66 *Nordic Journal of International Law* 211, 230 (citing B Simma, 'Bilateralism and Community Interests in the Law of State Responsibility' in Y Dinstein and M Tabory (eds), *International Law at a Time of Perplexity: Essays in Honour of Shabtai Rosenne* (Dordrecht, Nijhoff, 1989) 821 at 825).

[299] See, eg: Dupuy, above n 14 at 12. But see: ibid, at 12 fn 29. Martin, above n 62 at 463–64, also explores the possibility of characterising the obligation of prevention as a *jus cogens* duty. But see: ibid, at 491 ('l'interdiction de soutenir le terrorisme ne relève certainement pas du droit impératif ou *jus cogens*'). For a recent exploration of State accountability for violations of *jus cogens* norms, see L Yarwood, *State Accountability under International Law: Holding States Accountable for a Breach of Jus Cogens Norms* (London, Routledge, 2011) (albeit advocating a broader conception of State accountability, extending beyond State responsibility repertoire).

and/or humanitarian law'.[300] This conclusion will inexorably turn on the further development of a legal duty to prevent terrorism – whether through a more confined or regional radius of operation and compliance, or through a generalised and universally accepted rule – as mirrored by customary law.[301] The higher the obligation to prevent, the more onerous the burden of refuting indirect responsibility will be on the host-State. Irrespective of where the elements ultimately fall, there will often be a constant sliding gap not only between the characterisation of the obligation[302] and the actual conduct of the State, but also between the obligation of conduct/result dichotomy and all other inter-polar degrees on both continuums (see **Appendix V**).

Whilst largely fact-driven, these dimensions of State responsibility require further elaboration by the international community, without succumbing to idiosyncrasy. These cases are governed by factual considerations and should be guided by overarching principles of reasonableness and proportionality.[303] However, to require that all obligations of prevention be categorised under a single legal matrix is unrealistic. One inference becomes self-apparent: regardless of the approach ultimately espoused by the international community and the resistance exhibited by scholars to discussing standard of care issues under the rubric of State responsibility,[304] this area of indirect responsibility should be governed by a variable threshold model or, at least, would benefit from some level of case-by-case adjustment or adaptation characterised by a context-sensitive and policy-informed approach. To impose an obligation of result to prevent terrorism in all cases would prove unreasonable and inefficient. However, this does not preclude the application of an obligation of result when the facts of the case warrant it, such as when the host-State holds all the information and means to prevent a given attack but decides not to thwart the excursion. In such exceptional cases, namely where the misalignment between both continuums is so astronomical and the regime governing responsibility akin to a bright-line rule, breaches of international obligations are easily cognisable. In such scenario, there is no question that the breach of an obligation of means could also be ascertained. Finally, the international community must redefine some primary international legal rules after all, but not in the fashion proposed by those scholars who resist the engagement of secondary norms in so doing, as the principal counterterrorism obligation is arguably clear: a State has an affirmative duty to forestall transborder excursions emanating from its territory

[300] Dupuy, above n 14 at 15 (citing Art 33 of Geneva Convention IV, along with provisions of the Statute of the International Criminal Tribunal for Rwanda and of the Rome Statute).

[301] See Byers, above n 298 at 228 ('The principal source of *jus cogens* rules may thus be identified as the process of customary international law').

[302] On the relationship between *erga omnes* and *jus cogens* rules, see generally: ibid, at 230–38.

[303] Whilst framing his observations in the context of the 1986 US-led campaign in Libya, Baker, above n 39 at 47, warned about the inherent dangers in attempting to mount a military response against terrorism, a caveat that is rightly concerned with potential (and disproportionate) harm to civilians. For more background on the Libya incident, see D Turndorf, 'The U.S. Raid on Libya: A Forceful Response to Terrorism' (1988) 14 *Brooklyn Journal of International Law* 187.

[304] See, eg: Higgins, above n 26 at 157.

and injurious to other States.[305] However, defining the contours of that norm, namely whether it should impose a specific result or belong to the realm of *jus cogens*, and so on, could send the international community back to the drawing board for quite some time. In aiming to shed greater clarity on this debate, the present chapter has attempted to partly facilitate this endeavour through a critical appraisal of State responsibility rules.

Considerable efforts have been deployed above to underscore the potential contributions of State responsibility in suppressing and preventing transnational terrorism whilst highlighting the shortcomings of that normative scheme in the very same debate. However, even when accepting that State responsibility can play a role in neutralising asymmetrical power dynamics and enhancing transnational cooperation on counterterrorism issues, the application of secondary rules of responsibility engenders logistical, conceptual and political impediments during the post-breach appraisal.[306] The legal confusion is particularly acute with respect to devising legal consequences following a State's failure to prevent terrorism.

C) Legal Consequences of an Internationally Wrongful Act

Ample reference has been made throughout this book to the application of secondary norms of responsibility once a State's obligation of prevention has been violated. The legal consequences of internationally wrongful acts are also expressly enshrined in the ILC's codified rules of State responsibility. A particularly intractable dimension of this normative scheme lies in the idea of compensation or restitution for failure to fulfil this duty of prevention. An obvious difficulty inexorably crops up at the outset: how do we put a dollar figure on the deleterious repercussions of terrorist attacks? Granted, the focal point of this study predominantly gravitated towards the protection of civilian life and attempted to tease out the theoretical and rationalist implications of attempting to quantify the loss of human life and collateral damage stemming from terrorism. However, the aim of this line of argument was not, by any means, to delegitimise the economic loss and property damage that can accrue from terrorist activity. As 9/11 has shown, private transnational subversion can engender deleterious economic repercussions, both in terms of property damage and more

[305] This obligation was also recognised prior to 9/11. See Baker, above n 39 at 40.

[306] Conversely, the fact that parties to an international dispute sidestep a judicial and/or arbitral avenue in resolving the situation does not signify that the substance of the disagreement fails to hinge on State responsibility considerations. See, eg: *Reparation for Injuries Suffered in the Service of the United Nations,* Advisory Opinion of 11 April, *ICJ Reports* (1949) 174 at 177–78. As a corollary, mediation and diplomacy can lead to the peaceful settlement of such disagreements in the same manner that judicial settlement of disputes seeks to achieve. See, eg: *Free Zones of Upper Savoy and the District of Gex Case*, 1929 PCIJ (ser A) No 22 (19 August) at 13 (equating the judicial settlement of disputes with 'an alternative to the direct and friendly settlement of such disputes between the Parties').

intangible financial consequences.[307] Some terrorist attacks – for instance, those perpetrated in cyberspace – can sometimes solely engender financial losses without any corresponding physical harm to individuals. As explored above, such was the case following a series of nebulous cyber-attacks launched primarily from Russia and targeting online interests in Estonia in April-May 2007. As a result of one wave of attacks specifically targeting Estonia's largest bank, losses exceeding one million dollars were incurred in a single day.[308]

The confusion surrounding the computation of actual damages for the failure to prevent terrorism is mirrored in the formulation ultimately espoused in ILC Article 36(2), which provides that 'compensation shall cover any financially assessable damage'.[309] The *Chorzów Factory* Case injected into the fold the notion that some correlation between the State's wrongdoing and the harm suffered by the victim can animate the compensation calculus. On this front, the PCIJ proclaimed that 'The damage suffered by an individual is never therefore identical in kind with that which will be suffered by a State; *it can only afford a convenient scale for the calculation of the reparation due to the State*' (emphasis added).[310] Whilst this correlation could potentially be cast as the imposition of punitive damages in international law, this idea has acquired little traction in the literature.[311] Rather, leading publicists resign themselves to the idea that putting a dollar figure on governmental wrongdoing is an inherently 'flexible' and somewhat 'arbitrary' exercise, and that different degrees of governmental omissions or wrongdoing respectively command different levels of compensation.[312] Institutionalised precedents of the application of State responsibility, especially the practice of the US and Mexico Mixed Claims Commission, further support the arbitrary nature of the post-breach calculation of reparation. In that context, one commentator remarked that 'The Commission's theory is useful, however, because it is analytically correct and because it recognizes various degrees of governmental delinquency . . . The difficulty will always remain of measuring or computing such degrees of delinquency . . . That must, in any event, be arbitrary'.[313] Moreover, the compensatory uncertainty and speculative character of determining reparation are further exacerbated when terrorist

[307] See, eg: A Rose and SB Blomberg (eds), 'The Economic Impacts of the September 11, 2001, Terrorist Attacks' (2009) 15 *Peace Economics, Peace Science and Public Policy*, available at www.bepress.com/peps/vol15/iss2/.

[308] For background on this episode, see Landler and Markoff, above n 201 at A1.

[309] *Articles*, above n 122. On the speculative and theoretical character of determining compensation/restitution damages following terrorist strikes, see above ch 4, section V.C).

[310] *Case Concerning the Factory at Chorzów (Germany v Poland) (Claim for Indemnity, Merits)* 1928 PCIJ (ser A) No 17 (13 September) at 28.

[311] See, eg: S Wittich, 'Awe of the Gods and Fear of the Priests: Punitive Damages and the Law of State Responsibility' (1998) 3 *Austrian Review of International and European Law* 101; S Wittich, 'Punitive Damages' in Crawford et al, above n 2 at 667–75; C Gray, *Judicial Remedies in International Law* (Oxford, OUP, 1987) 28. But see: Eagleton, above n 178 at 61–62.

[312] See Becker, above n 1 at 22.

[313] E Borchard, 'Important Decisions of the Mixed Claims Commission United States and Mexico' (1927) 21 *AJIL* 516, 518.

strikes are planned or executed over the territories of multiple States, thereby engaging the Article 47(1) considerations discussed earlier.[314]

From a practical standpoint and invoking the 9/11 attacks as an example, let us assume that Afghanistan's responsibility is engaged for failing to prevent those excursions. Reparation under the ILC's *Articles* becomes seemingly difficult when dealing with such a politically charged situation. Would Afghanistan be responsible for shouldering the millions of dollars in damages resulting from the 9/11 terrorist strikes? Upon first glance, it might seem far-fetched to think so. However, an interesting parallel can be drawn with the Security Council's treatment of Iraq's international responsibility in the context of its invasion of Kuwait. Following that initial wrongful act, the Council imposed a broad-ranging obligation of reparation upon Iraq, proclaiming that it '*is liable under international law* for any direct loss, damage, including environmental damage and the depletion of natural resources, or injury to foreign Governments, nationals and corporations, as a result of Iraq's unlawful invasion and occupation of Kuwait' (emphasis added).[315] More controversially, the Council established a Commission and a compensation fund aiming to indemnify victims of the conflict.[316] It thus instituted a mechanism seeking to redress massive international law violations and, in so doing, transacted colossal compensatory amounts. Whilst the implementation of that Commission was highly controversial,[317] it is not inconceivable that similar mechanisms could be developed in the future and applied to failures to prevent large-scale transnational terrorism. The Iraq-Kuwait scenario certainly provides a strong precedent – coupled with relevant conceptual tools – that may be harnessed with a view to diversifying reparative options under secondary liability norms, even if only to apply them on a more modest scale. There is no reason to exclude, as a matter of course, analogous logic or the deployment of similar legal responses from the treatment of breaches of the obligation to prevent terrorism.

While on the topic of deploying diversified secondary norms, it is useful to recall the tension that pervaded much of the discussion regarding the relationship between international law and domestic counterterrorism. When devising a workable scheme of State responsibility, competing interests will inexorably

314 For a discussion of the impact of this provision, see above nn 280–88 and accompanying text.

315 SC Res 687, UN SCOR, 46th Sess, 2981st Mtg, UN Doc S/RES/687 (1991) at para 16.

316 ibid, at paras 18–19.

317 Certain scholars opined that the Security Council overstepped the bounds of its powers in instituting the Commission and compensation fund. See, eg: B Graefrath, 'International Crimes and Collective Security' in K Wellens (ed), *International Law: Theory and Practice: Essays in Honour of Eric Suy* (The Hague, Nijhoff, 1998) 237 at 244–45. For more background and divergent views on the efficiency of the UN Compensation Commission for Iraq, see, eg: DJ Bederman, 'The United Nations Compensation Commission and the Tradition of International Claims Settlement' (1994) 27 *NYU Journal of International Law & Politics* 1, 33–34; GA Christenson, 'State Responsibility and the UN Compensation Commission: Compensating Victims of Crimes of State' in RB Lillich (ed), *The United Nations Compensation Commission* (Irvington, Transnational, 1995) 311 at 348–58; G Cottereau, 'De la responsabilité de l'Irak selon la résolution 687 du Conseil de sécurité' (1991) 37 *AFDI* 105; A Kolliopoulos, *La Commission d'indemnisation des Nations Unies et le droit de la responsabilité internationale* (Paris, LGDJ, 2001) 232–33.

come into conflict; such is the case of sovereignty and combating terrorism efficiently, a tension that proved recurrent throughout the present study. Exemplified, inter alia, by the 1982 Israel-Lebanon conflict, the quintessential scenario was depicted in rather straightforward terms. All agree that Lebanon, for instance, has an obligation to prevent terrorist excursions emanating from its territory. However, what if it is unable to completely repel or contain the threat? What if it has relinquished control over the southern portion of its territory, in which terrorist bases are located and operating? What if we are seeking ways to contain subsequent terrorist attacks originating from its territory after Lebanon has violated its primary obligation to prevent an initial terrorist strike (thereby triggering both the application of the general set of secondary rules and, more specifically, the provisions of ILC Article 14(3) given Lebanon's continuing violation)?[318] Should we expect it to allow extraneous forces or law enforcement units on its territory to repel the threats, thereby infringing State sovereignty in favour of combating terrorism more efficiently?[319]

A range of possible solutions to these questions has been advanced, depending on the interlocutor and the school of thought underpinning the argument. As a general rule, many seem to agree that sacrificing sovereignty in favour of combating terrorism should have some kind of mitigating or attenuating effect on State responsibility, a reality directly embedded in the factual/policy tier of the proposed model advocated above.[320] Interestingly, some commentators frame the issue as one of capacity-building. For instance, Tal Becker's causation-based treatment of State responsibility for terrorism essentially equates liability with capacity.[321] His proposed regime contemplates a State's responsibility for failing to prevent terrorism as inversely proportionate to the capacity that it had or ought to have ensured in conducting its counterterrorism operations. Similar views were echoed by others, with some authors even advocating that States are under a duty of counterterrorism capacity-building that includes a requirement to seek external assistance should they become unable to adequately pursue counterterrorism operations within their own borders. Failure to do so, in their view, could signal a State's failure to meet its obligations and, correspondingly, point to the commission of an internationally wrongful act.[322] Recent Security Council practice and the creation of its Counter-Terrorism Committee substantiate this proposition, especially when contemplated through the prescriptions enshrined in resolution 1373 and the ensuing requirements of counterterrorism capacity-building.[323]

When grappling with these difficult policy questions, the choice will often oscillate between sacrificing sovereignty and upholding a rigid and State-centric

[318] This dimension of State responsibility was explored above in ch 4, section III.A).

[319] This line of argument was thoroughly canvassed above in ch 2, section IV.C)i) especially nn 293–300 and accompanying text.

[320] See above sections IV.A); B).

[321] For more sustained discussion on his approach, see above ch 3, section II.

[322] See, eg: Trapp, above n 85 at 147 fn 33; Nolkaemper, above n 34 at 161.

[323] See Quénivet, above n 86 at 390–91.

conception of international law, perhaps at the detriment of more effective counterterrorism structures. According to one reading of competing legal regimes that may be juxtaposed with the present inquiry, such as the Responsibility to Protect Doctrine, a sounder counterterrorism policy might be achieved by resolving the above tension in favour of sacrificing sovereignty (especially if Lebanon, for example, cannot efficiently thwart terrorism emanating from its territory).[324]

Following Pakistan's provision of sanctuary to terrorists that carried out the Mumbai excursions, similar arguments were canvassed in the political mainstream. Particularly radical proponents of the idea of circumventing sovereignty in favour of combating terrorism advocated the deployment of invasive legal responses vis-à-vis Pakistan's failures to prevent terrorism, loosely grounding their proposals in general international law and in the R2P Doctrine.[325] Implicit in their argument was the notion that sovereign rights are by no means absolute and need to be deserved in this day and age. Equally vocal – and symptomatic of the neo-conservative canon of foreign policy thought that dominates this line of argument – is Robert Kagan's solution when addressing Pakistan's involvement in, and failure to prevent, the Mumbai terrorist attacks. His proposal strikes at the very core of what was surveyed above and illustrates the complexities and potential political pitfalls in devising unconventional secondary obligations under State responsibility repertoire. Following the Mumbai attacks, he framed his solution as follows:

> Rather than simply begging the Indians to show restraint, a better option could be to internationalize the response. Have the international community declare that parts of Pakistan have become ungovernable and a menace to international security. Establish an international force to work with the Pakistanis to root out terrorist camps in Kashmir as well as in the tribal areas. This would have the advantage of preventing a direct military confrontation between India and Pakistan. It might also save face for the Pakistani government, since the international community would be helping the central government reestablish its authority in areas where it has lost it. But whether or not Islamabad is happy, don't the international community and the United States, at the end of the day, have some obligation to demonstrate to the Indian people that we take attacks on them as seriously as we take attacks on ourselves?
>
> Would such an action violate Pakistan's sovereignty? Yes, but nations should not be able to claim sovereign rights when they cannot control territory from which terrorist attacks are launched. If there is such a thing as a 'responsibility to protect,' which justifies international intervention to prevent humanitarian catastrophe either caused

[324] See the remarks above in ch 2, section IV.C)i) especially nn 293–300 and accompanying text. For a similar discussion in the context of 'failed' States, see above section II.B).

[325] For critical appraisals of the R2P Doctrine, see C Focarelli, 'The Responsibility to Protect Doctrine and Humanitarian Intervention: Too Many Ambiguities for a Working Doctrine' (2008) 13 *Journal of Conflict and Security Law* 191; P Hilpold, 'From Humanitarian Intervention to Responsibility to Protect: Making Utopia True?' in Fastenrath et al, above n 54 at 462–76; C Stahn, 'Responsibility to Protect: Political Rhetoric or Emerging Legal Norm?' (2007) 101 *AJIL* 99. For a Canadian perspective on the matter, see J Brunnée, 'International Law and Collective Concerns: Reflections on the Responsibility to Protect' in Ndiaye and Wolfrum, above n 20 at 35–51.

> or allowed by a nation's government, there must also be a responsibility to protect one's neighbors from attacks from one's own territory, even when the attacks are carried out by 'non-state actors.'
>
> In Pakistan's case, the continuing complicity of the military and intelligence services with terrorist groups pretty much shreds any claim to sovereign protection.[326]

Whilst there are undoubtedly myriad philosophical, logistical and political problems associated with this course of action,[327] Kagan's proposed model nonetheless foreshadows the intellectual pay-offs of entertaining a dialogue outside of the existing State responsibility boxes (ie by identifying secondary obligations extending beyond purely monetary indemnification or symbolic reparation, so as to shift the focus on preventing future terrorist attacks).[328] As advanced under the second tier of the strict liability-infused mechanism, in demonstrating that it fulfilled its obligation of prevention, a State might expose itself to alternate counterterrorism arrangements as opposed to full-scale military invasion, such as the deployment of law enforcement units to capture suspected terrorists.[329] Other similar arrangements could also contribute to increasing a host-State's due diligence capital in refuting a presumption of indirect responsibility directed against it.

V. CONCLUSION: A PARTIAL POLITICO-LEGAL SOLUTION LYING AT THE HEART OF INTERNATIONAL LAW

As demonstrated above, State responsibility is not always a politically relevant or viable option. Its application has been completely eschewed in massive cases of transnational pollution where it could have been instrumental in devising partial compensatory or symbolic resolutions. When State responsibility is set in motion, however, it is nonetheless not always governed by clear precedents or uniformly applied principles, as the specific facts of each case inform the deployment of restitutive justice mechanisms. Even a cursory review of contemporary incidents involving transnational terrorism or public international law reveals both the absence of uniform and consistent application of State responsibility

[326] R Kagan, 'The Sovereignty Dodge: What Pakistan Won't Do, the World Should', *Washington Post*, 2 December 2008, available at www.washingtonpost.com/wp-dyn/content/article/2008/12/01/AR2008120102438_pf.html.

[327] For a searing critique of Kagan's position, see DL Davis, 'America the Arbiter? Hubris Has No Place in Foreign Relations', *Washington Times*, 12 December 2008 at A23.

[328] See generally: B Simma, 'Peace through Law: The Role of the ILC' in G Nolte (ed), *Peace through International Law: The Role of the International Law Commission* (Dordrecht, Springer, 2009) 189 at 189–90. That said, compensation and restitution still play a central role in normalising international relations between sovereign States. See, eg: D Butt, *Rectifying International Injustice: Principles of Compensation and Restitution between Nations* (Oxford, OUP, 2009). For a critique of the broader concept of reparation, see C D'Orsi, 'L'obligation de réparation dans le Projet d'articles sur la responsabilité de l'État: Une analyse critique' (2005) 58 *Revue hellénique de droit international* 115.

[329] See Baker, above n 39 at 40. See also: Byers, above n 115.

principles, along with a highly varied and diversified record of terrorist strikes. The very fact that many terrorist activities can be distinguished in scope, method and execution obfuscates the prospect of developing specific rules of State responsibility or, more generally, of public international law, even if those new principles are tentatively framed within the furrow of a *lex specialis* dealing with transnational terrorism. Hence, the exercise of generalising terrorism is anything but a straightforward one, thereby militating in favour of the adoption of flexible and context-sensitive international legal rules.

It is with striking this normative equilibrium in mind that the present study has operated, especially in the policy reform advocated in this chapter. However, further defining primary counterterrorism rules might prove challenging and ultimately lead to a deadlock. Undoubtedly, this confusion is further exacerbated by the lack of a universally agreed-upon definition of 'terrorism', thereby making the elucidation of primary obligations on an undefined term that much more convoluted. What is more, the ICJ arguably perpetuated this apparent definitional and legal opacity in cases where it could have provided some guidance on the concept of 'terrorism', most notably in *Nicaragua*, *Tehran Hostages* and the *Armed Activities Case*. This precedential dearth is sometimes accompanied by a similar reluctance to advance the law governing State responsibility within that forum, although the ICJ's posture could conversely be construed as one of tactical judicial restraint. For instance, the Court's perhaps uncritical reading of ILC Article 8 in the *Genocide Case* has been interpreted by some as paving the way for State practice to fill the void and, perhaps, to marshal in new tests of attribution.[330]

Conversely, a contrary argument can certainly be advanced that primary counterterrorism norms are sufficiently defined – whether 'terrorism' is construed as a term of pure political convenience or deemed to have acquired sufficient legal status – to commission specific behaviour under international law. The premise that may be extracted from this conclusion is relatively straightforward: States have a positive duty to prevent terrorist attacks emanating from their territory. How this obligation is to be fulfilled remains largely fact-driven and generates controversy, obviously depending on the interlocutor assessing both its normative strength and compliance pull. As such, the present study attempted – particularly in this chapter – to bypass the sometimes-futile debates over the content of primary counterterrorism obligations so as to give credence to the notion that the obligation of prevention is now firmly implemented in international law. The more relevant exercise is rather establishing how the obligation is breached and ascertaining the repercussions flowing from that violation, the latter proposition having underpinned the central argument above. Therein undoubtedly lays the crux of the analytical challenge in this field. As Roberto Ago famously declared, 'It is one thing to define a rule and the

[330] See, eg: M Milanović, 'State Responsibility for Acts of Non-State Actors: A Comment on Griebel and Pluecken' (2009) 22 *Leiden Journal of International Law* 307, 321.

content of the obligation it imposes, and another to determine whether that obligation has been violated and what should be the consequences'.[331] The present study elected to shed some light on this issue by contemplating the obligation of prevention on a variable scale and by placing significant analytical emphasis on the mechanics and policy implications of secondary norms of responsibility. Put another way, the policy objectives driving the proposed reform centre on instilling some enforceability into the obligation of prevention, promoting incentives for compliance with counterterrorism obligations and compelling both multilateralism and transnational cooperation.

As the present study has demonstrated, no one dominant model of privately inflicted transnational violence may be identified, thereby militating in favour of acute contextual sensitivity in applying secondary rules of responsibility. However, even if a highly contextualised approach is ultimately endorsed, the actual mechanics of State responsibility are further compounded by the fact that the application of that normative scheme often remains contingent on States' unilateral determination of unlawful conduct, a process marred by auto-qualification and self-judging.[332] In order to partly counteract this unilateral dimension, proposals may be advanced towards institutionalising the implementation of State responsibility for failing to prevent terrorism, most notably through the Security Council. Alternatively, scholars advocated the implementation of a third-party objective institution in the hopes of somewhat allaying disproportionately political or vindictive self-help initiatives, a school of thought within which Kelsen's own vision featured prominently.[333]

Whether seen through the possible institutionalisation of the implementation of international responsibility via the Security Council, or contemplated through the lens of instituting a third-party institution mandated with overseeing the application of liability mechanisms, it will be impossible to entirely dissociate political considerations from the application of State responsibility. Even when analogising the 'war' on terror to other transnational legal phenomena, such as global warming and precautionary approaches, State responsibility is often synonymous with an uneven mix of normative and political, depending on the facts of each case and internationally wrongful acts (and gravity, intensity, etc) to which it is applied. It would also be naïve to attempt excising the process of self-judging altogether from the equation. The seizure of a third-party objective institution would necessarily entail self-judging of internation-

[331] 'Report of the International Law Commission on the Work of Its Twenty-second Session' (1970) 2 *Yearbook of the International Law Commission* 217, UN Doc A/8010/Rev.1 at 306, para 66(c).

[332] See, eg: DW Bowett, 'Contemporary Developments in Legal Techniques in the Settlement of Disputes' (1983-II) 180 *Recueil des Cours* 169, 213 (opining that 'resort to self-help is less objectionable when used in order to execute a judgment of the [ICJ] (or, indeed, any competent arbitral tribunal) than when used by a State on its own subjective view of its rights').

[333] See H Kelsen, *The Legal Process and International Order* (London, London, Constable & Co, 1935) 18; H Lauterpacht, *The Function of Law in the International Community* (Oxford, Clarendon Press, 1933) 424. On this issue, O'Connell's remarks, above n 143 at 53 seem apposite.

ally wrongful acts by at least one party at the pre-adjudicative stage, which may or may not be reinforced or exacerbated by international public perception. Similarly, if two States agreed to submit a dispute involving a failure to prevent terrorism to the ICJ, the very *compromis* by which the judicial apparatus is triggered would be premised on one State's self-judging of the harm it sustained. Granted, the whole purpose of institutional objective adjudication is to provide some authoritative judicial pronouncement on the dispute in question but this exercise may nonetheless fail to dissipate the political dimensions present in States' unilateral self-judging of unlawful acts. Ultimately, the institutionalised decisional outcome may actually be less one-sided, which is probably a step in the right direction in some cases. Therefore, the concern does not lie with completely reducing self-judging nor does it lie with necessarily decreasing the political undertones pervading this international legal field. Rather, the objective is to reduce unilateralism so as to increase the chances of combating transnational terrorism effectively and cooperatively, whilst enhancing multilateralism and generating desirable governmental incentives in compelling compliance with international legal undertakings. To that end, this chapter attempted to demonstrate that the law of State responsibility can offer a partial politico-legal solution to this issue in some instances.

As forewarned by Roberto Ago, the existence of primary counterterrorism obligations may be relatively uncontroversial. Indeed, few would challenge the idea that States have a duty to prevent terrorism emanating from their territory when formulated in the abstract. The true legal challenge, therefore, rather crops up at the stage of ascertaining a breach of that obligation and, most importantly, when devising potential legal consequences to redress the internationally wrongful act. It is precisely the prospect of legal and political consequences that infuses State responsibility with some modicum of bindingness and in turn promotes compliance with international law at the pre-breach stage.[334] Absent a third-party arbitrator or decision-maker pronouncing on a dispute, and remaining firmly within the furrow of a self-adjudicative paradigm, a State's unilateral determination of a wrongful act perpetrated by another rings pretty hollow politically unless that State wields significant influence on the world stage or, perhaps, when the underlying facts are particularly sympathetic to it so as to elicit international support. In many cases, however, it is likely that aggrieved States will need to generate a constituency of conscience and garner international support to bolster their invocation of remedial mechanisms under international law, especially in the field of counterterrorism. But even when this threshold is met, the range of available reparation schemes lends to State responsibility a particularly rarefied quality.

[334] This line of argument should be contrasted, and ultimately nuanced, in light of earlier discussion dealing with State responsibility's and, more generally, international justice's potential for devising symbolic reparations and resolutions. See, eg: above n 99; ch 3 nn 88–98 and accompanying text. On State responsibility's ability to generate incentives for governments to comply with international obligations before any violation of the law is registered, see Zemanek, above n 91 at 125–34.

As noted, traditional assessment of compensatory damages in the face of deleterious transnational activity – be it terrorism or pollution – can hardly escape some sense that it remains a speculative endeavour in many instances. Whilst devising international liability mechanisms for failing to prevent terrorism might be politically desirable, perhaps even objectively founded in some regards, actually deploying those regimes in the face of transnational subversion might prove subjectively unenforceable. For instance, whilst the responsibility of a host-State may be ascertained by virtue of the model proposed above, implementing the consequences of that determination might prove politically or logistically improbable. One would be hard-pressed to expect compensation or restitution from uncooperative States involved in supporting terrorism or waging surrogate warfare through proxies, such as Syria or Iran.[335] Expectations of reparation should be equally quelled vis-à-vis attempts to obtain redress from weak or ineffective States, such as Sudan or Somalia.[336] In such cases, can it be said that the true benefits of State responsibility might have met their match, as one can only hope for some symbolic acknowledgement of the host-State's wrongful conduct without any effective, corresponding sanction? In such scenarios, the remedy of satisfaction – embodied, inter alia, in the expression of diplomatic and official apology – can play some cathartic role but fail to register any restitutive impact.[337] Moreover, the declaration of a host-State's violation of international law can sometimes suffice in providing some level of reparation – albeit symbolic – much in the spirit of some non-judicial equivalent of a declaratory judgment. Even when transposed to international judicial settings, this eventuality can ring true.[338] Indeed, it animated part of the ICJ's reasoning in the *Genocide Case*. After holding that Serbia could not be held to the principle of *restitutio in integrum* in the particular circumstances because of the absence of a nexus connecting its failure to prevent genocide with the events perpetrated at Srebrenica, the Court nonetheless opined that the applicant was entitled to reparation in the form of satisfaction. As per the applicant's own suggestion,

[335] Even prior to 9/11, Iran's support of terrorism had been widely reported, coupled with deep cynicism regarding the prospect of entertaining a politically viable dialogue with that State in the hopes of reducing such sponsorship. See, eg: RS Litwak, *Rogue States and U.S. Foreign Policy* (Washington, DC, Woodrow Wilson Center Press, 2000) 4, 161, 174, 186–88.

[336] The Al Qaeda-inspired Islamist group Harakat al-Shabaab al-Mujahideen exerts quasi-exclusive control over large swathes of central-southern Somalia, where it imposes a particularly harsh brand of Sharia law and intends on overthrowing the government of Somalia. See, eg: P Bergen et al, 'Assessing the Jihadist Terrorist Threat to America and American Interests' (2011) 34 *Studies in Conflict & Terrorism* 65, 73; JM Isanga, 'Countering Persistent Contemporary Sea Piracy: Expanding Jurisdictional Regimes' (2010) 59 *American University Law Review* 1267, 1277 fn 64; M Ibrahim and J Gettleman, 'Bomb Kills Dozens in Somalia's Capital and Signals Return of Militant Group', *New York Times*, 5 October 2011 at A10. The Security Council also condemned terrorist attacks perpetrated by Al Shabaab as threats to the international community. See, eg: SC Res 1910, UN SCOR, 64th Sess, 6266th Mtg, UN Doc S/RES/1910 (2010); SC Res 1964, UN SCOR, 65th Sess, 6461st Mtg, UN Doc S/RES 1964 (2010); SC Res 2010, UN SCOR, 66th Sess, 6626th Mtg, UN Doc S/RES/2010 (2011).

[337] See generally: E Wyler and A Papaux, 'Satisfaction' in Crawford et al, above n 2 at 623–37.

[338] See, eg: *Corfu Channel*, above n 103 at 35–36; *Genocide Case*, above n 175 at 234–36.

the Court acknowledged that such reparation could take on the form of a declaration in its judgment that Serbia had failed to comply with its obligation of prevention.[339] Ultimately, these symbolic modes of redress should not detract from the primary objective: developing context-sensitive, policy-oriented liability models suited for the disparate and self-adjudicative nature of State responsibility and international relations.

[339] ibid. See also: *Case Concerning Pulp Mills on the River Uruguay (Argentina v Uruguay)*, Judgment of 20 April, *ICJ* (2010), available at www.icj-cij.org/docket/files/135/15877.pdf at paras 269, 273, 282 and authorities cited therein; *Certain Questions of Mutual Assistance in Criminal Matters (Djibouti v France)*, Judgment of 4 June, *ICJ Reports* (2008) 177 at 245, para 204.

Conclusion to Part II

THE WORLD IS now faced with new threats, coupled with the need to rethink international legal mechanisms. 9/11 is certainly one of the most pivotal moments in recent memory regarding international law. It changed the way States protect their borders, the immigration flows in most Western countries,[1] the way States conceive terrorism and counterterrorism, etc. The importance of the response to 9/11 should not be underemphasised, as it marked a clear departure from prior practice in several international legal areas, State responsibility being central in that development. Not only did the response to 9/11 considerably challenge the application of *jus ad bellum*, it also initiated an important shift in the law governing State responsibility. With the advent of important milestones in that field, such as the *Corfu Channel* Judgment and the ILC's *Articles*, the transition from a model of attribution and direct responsibility to an indirect responsibility paradigm seems natural and logical. Also considering the Security Council's resolve to eradicate terrorism, the move toward a mechanism inspired by strict liability does not seem improbable, provided it is endowed with significant safeguards for host-States. The objective underlying this project has been to instil life and rigour into a truly global counterterrorism campaign.

The strict liability-infused model embodies great potential for change, progress and efficiency on the international plane. Not only does it promote fairness amongst States but it also provides governments with the right incentives: combating terrorism can only be successfully accomplished on a multilateral level, through the mutual exchange of information and policies. The pursuit of egregious and blind self-interests will adversely affect the efficacy of international responsibility regimes in promoting compliance. Whilst certain archetypal social elements such as crime and violence will never be completely obliterated, the objective remains to design a scheme of State responsibility that is the most conducive to international peace and security.[2]

[1] On the immigration debate following 9/11, see, eg: L Lebowitz and I Podheiser, 'A Summary of the Changes in Immigration Policies and Practices after the Terrorist Attacks of September 11, 2001: The USA Patriot Act and Other Measures' (2002) 63 *University of Pittsburgh Law Review* 873; KC Tumlin, 'Suspect First: How Terrorism Policy Is Reshaping Immigration Policy' (2004) 92 *California Law Review* 1173.

[2] See J Kraska, 'Torts and Terror: Rethinking Deterrence Models and Catastrophic Terrorist Attack' (2007) 22 *American University International Law Review* 361, 383, fn 89 ('Concepts in civil

Conversely, this model also poses problems and is potentially ripe for abuse by economically stronger States. Efficient State responsibility mechanisms can be encapsulated in one word: compromise. This notion has pervaded the discussion above. Situations like the 1982 Israel-Lebanon conflict illustrate the inherent political tensions in establishing the parameters of indirect responsibility. Throughout most episodes of transborder aggression, the principle of sovereignty/territorial integrity is challenged by the crucial and often time-sensitive need to prevent terrorist attacks. If members of the international community hope to empower the global counterterrorism campaign, they will have to relinquish or, at least, concede some aspects of the fundamental values underpinning the Westphalian system of nation-States. In many cases, the choice will ultimately land somewhere between sacrificing sovereignty or reputation/dignity. To make inroads into the latter concept would seem less offensive in a world where most States are omnipotent within their own national boundaries. As illustrated above, the central problem lies in the fact that States might be called upon to answer for acts that fall outside of their immediate control and ensure compliance with international standards that are largely dependent on the behaviour and compliance of non-State actors with those norms. This is what prompted Pierre-Marie Dupuy to identify two possible avenues to promote compliance in those scenarios, especially in areas most in need of observance by non-State actors such as international human rights, humanitarian law and terrorism. Dupuy therefore concluded that enforcement of State responsibility can be achieved either by i) expanding the scope of subjects under international law, thereby extending international responsibility schemes directly to non-State actors; or ii) widening or loosening attribution rules in order to engage State responsibility flowing from the conduct of non-State actors.[3] The present account has amply grounded its central argument within the furrow of this second proposal.

The international community is seriously concerned with preventing attacks and deterring terrorist organisations. To forestall the proliferation of terrorist activity through the channel of host-States can be a judicious strategy, if well orchestrated. However, logistical considerations abound and we must take stock of the realities facing developing countries and ineffective States. For example, to require a small country like Lebanon to effectively thwart PLO terrorists whilst it has already surrendered a considerable region of its territory is probably unrealistic. Similarly, it is fair to ponder whether the oft-discussed due diligence standard is actually objective and equitable. As underscored throughout

law may be particularly useful in designing effective responses to terrorism', and supporting the proposition that 'the strict liability model of state responsibility promotes "international peace and security"').

[3] See, eg: P-M Dupuy, 'Quarante ans de codification du droit de la responsabilité internationale des États: un bilan' (2003) 107 *RGDIP* 305, 318; P-M Dupuy, 'State Sponsors of Terrorism: Issues of International Responsibility' in A Bianchi (ed), *Enforcing International Law Norms against Terrorism* (Oxford, Hart Publishing, 2004) 3 at 7.

this volume, a sensible reform of State responsibility in counterterrorism contexts should seek innovative ways to address the challenges engendered by the North/South divide.[4] Developing countries undoubtedly have fewer resources at their disposal in combating transnational terrorism. As a corollary, any potential overhaul of State responsibility cannot steer clear of the question whether the due diligence standard should operate on a variable scale, in that it should be lowered in inversed proportion to the actual means possessed by States in preventing terrorism. Prior to the adoption of the finalised ILC *Articles*, Rosalyn Higgins declared that

> a poor state with limited resources would have a low due diligence standard to meet, in seeking to control private behaviour that harms others . . . in the *Montijo Case*, before the US-Columbia Claims Tribunal, the Tribunal found a failure of due diligence to prevent injury to aliens, notwithstanding the problems the state had in exercising this standard of care.[5]

Nevertheless, questions of State responsibility crop up in that context and become particularly relevant in modern reality, exemplified by the aftermath of the 2006 Israel-Hezbollah conflict. In the years following that conflict, tensions were once again mounting between Lebanon, Israel and Syrian/Iranian-backed Hezbollah factions.[6] In light of such realities, this study advocated the circumvention of attribution altogether in the context of counterterrorism. An alternate but similar solution to this problem from the standpoint of semantics was also envisaged through a mechanism of 'automatic attribution'. Thus, instead of short-circuiting the mechanics of attribution once a terrorist strike is launched, the ILC's *Articles* could rather operate on the premise that this act is *automatically* attributed to the sanctuary State so as to better facilitate the implementation of the prima facie finding of indirect responsibility. The impugned State could then proceed to refute the claim of responsibility pending against it, pursuant to the parameters discussed earlier. Indeed, it is fair to query whether a host-State's failure to prevent a terrorist strike emanating from its territory triggers its responsibility via the application of automatic attribution.[7] Some scholars have touched upon this idea after 9/11, albeit using different jargon. For instance, highlighting the lack of nuance or distinction underlying the American posture vis-à-vis terrorists and their sanctuary States, Ben Saul

[4] See generally: AA Fatouros, 'International Law and the Third World' (1964) 50 *Virginia Law Review* 783; RA Falk et al (eds), *International Law and the Third World: Reshaping Justice* (London, Routledge-Cavendish, 2008).

[5] R Higgins, *Problems & Process: International Law and How We Use It* (Oxford, OUP, 1994) 156 (footnotes omitted).

[6] See, eg: N Bakri, 'Backers of Hezbollah and Government Clash As Strike Disrupts Lebanon', *New York Times*, 8 May 2008 at A6; N Bakri and G Bowley, 'Confrontation in Lebanon Appears to Escalate', *New York Times*, 8 May 2008 at A6; RF Worth and N Bakri, 'Hezbollah Threatens Attacks on Israeli Targets', *New York Times*, 15 February 2008 at A6.

[7] See, eg: A Cassese, *International Criminal Law* (Oxford, OUP, 2001) 390–91.

queries whether the mere toleration or harbouring of terrorists on its territory is sufficient to trigger a State's *direct* responsibility.[8] He concludes that

> [i]t is too soon to judge the customary force of this view, but it exerts pressure to modify customary rules of State responsibility on attribution, by holding States directly responsible for private acts even if a State does not 'effectively control' (or exercise 'overall control' over) the private actor.[9]

The concept of automatic attribution not only offers an interesting policy option for counterterrorism by shifting incentives onto governments to monitor terrorist activity within their borders more effectively, but it also remains intimately intertwined with other important milestones in the law of indirect responsibility. The aforementioned *Corfu Channel* decision and resolution 1373 certainly come to mind and, in many ways, underpin both the modern shift to indirect State responsibility and the possible revision of attribution standards. As one commentator notes, the symbiotic relationship between these highly relevant precedents and the concept of automatic attribution comes into sharp focus when contemplated through the lens of Lebanon's potential State responsibility in the 2006 Israel-Hezbollah conflict: 'This is not a secondary aspect of attribution; the duty to deny safe havens for terrorists on one's territory is a primary obligation. Pursuant to this analysis, Lebanon has violated international law by harboring Hezbollah terrorists'.[10]

When applying the above principles to the 9/11 context, a few conclusions become apparent. By failing to prevent the 9/11 attacks, Afghanistan violated its obligation to prevent terrorism. This conclusion is further corroborated by the stringent prescriptions enshrined in resolution 1373. Moreover, this violation, which is undoubtedly tantamount to a threat to international peace and security, can be subsumed under the furrow of Chapter VII of the UN Charter.[11] In fact, certain publicists construe the 9/11 precedents as 'falling under the newly enlarged definition of "a threat to international peace and security"'.[12] Consequently, this characterisation carries with it significant implications. First and foremost, this construction implies that counterterrorism obligations can fit within the ambit of Security Council powers and potentially engage the Council's review or action on questions of State responsibility in certain

[8] See D Jinks, 'State Responsibility for the Acts of Private Armed Groups' (2003) 4 *Chicago Journal of International Law* 83; R Wedgwood, 'The Fall of Saddam Hussein: Security Council Mandates and Preemptive Self-Defence' (2003) 97 *AJIL* 576, 583; G Travalio and J Altenburg, 'Terrorism, State Responsibility, and the Use of Military Force' (2003) 4 *Chicago Journal of International Law* 97, 100–10; A Cassese, 'Terrorism Is Also Disrupting Some Crucial Legal Categories of International Law' (2001) 12 *EJIL* 993, 998–99.

[9] B Saul, *Defining Terrorism in International Law* (Oxford, OUP, 2006) 197 (footnotes omitted).

[10] S Kirchner, 'Third Party Liability for Hezbollah Attacks against Israel' (2006) 7 *German Law Journal* 777, 781–82.

[11] See, eg: Dupuy, 'State Sponsors', above n 3 at 7–8.

[12] See P-M Dupuy, 'The Law after the Destruction of the Towers' (2001) *EJIL Discussion Forum*, cited in P Kovács, 'Beaucoup de questions et peu de réponses: autour de l'imputabilité d'un acte terroriste à un État' (2001) 17 *Anuario de derecho internacional* 39, 47–48, fn 15.

circumstances. Second, and more controversially, this legal interpretation also signals that an internationally responsible host-State like Afghanistan could arguably be targeted in self-defence following a terrorist attack.[13] However, to the extent possible, the deployment of these legal devices should preferably be achieved under the auspices of the Security Council. This line of reasoning certainly subscribes to the discipline embodied in resolution 1373.[14]

However, the legal response to 9/11 should always be appreciated with some degree of caution, as it aimed at redressing a particularly singular and unprecedented set of events. However, the pre-9/11 record does not invariably support a right to invoke self-defence following the finding that a State harboured and supported terrorist factions launching transnational strikes from its territory. By way of example, in 1985 Israel proceeded to aerial assaults on PLO headquarters in the Tunisian suburb of Hammam-Plage following transborder excursions by that terrorist group. In substantiating its recourse to force, Israel relied upon the now-prevalent State responsibility-derived notion that Tunisia had harboured terrorists who subsequently attacked Israel.[15] Ultimately, the Security Council discarded that basis for invoking self-defence and adopted a rather disapprobative stance vis-à-vis Israel's intervention.[16] Whether such scenario would now qualify as a predicate for triggering a right to adopt a forcible response by aggrieved States – under the new paradigm ostensibly crystallised by the response to 9/11 – is a matter to be determined through future international practice and remains largely governed by the facts arising in every single instance. What is important to retain for present purposes is that such scenarios are consistently contemplated through a State responsibility prism, with some authors querying 'Why was responsibility not attributed to Tunisia in 1985 but was presumed to be attributed to the Taliban in 2001?'[17]

In short, the 'harbouring and supporting' principle has essentially taken over as the analytical linchpin of modern State responsibility vis-à-vis terrorism.[18] Some scholars identify a tendency that may broaden the scope of international responsibility 'allant jusqu'à l'attribution des actes accomplis par les organisations terroristes aux Etats qui les soutiennent d'une façon ou d'une autre, en les

[13] But see: PN Okowa, 'II. Case Concerning Armed Activities on the Territory of the Congo (Democratic Republic of the Congo v. Uganda)' (2006) 55 *ICLQ* 742, 748. However, lawful recourse to self-defence should be distinguished from the practice of 'defensive armed reprisal', which is unlawful and thus excluded from the purview of the ILC's *Articles*. On this last point, see Y Dinstein, *War, Aggression and Self-Defence*, 4th edn (Cambridge, CUP, 2005) 222; D Brown, 'Use of Force against Terrorism after September 11th: State Responsibility, Self-Defense and Other Responses' (2003) 11 *Cardozo Journal of International and Comparative Law* 1, 35; JN Kendall, 'Israeli Counter-Terrorism: "Targeted Killings" Under International Law' (2002) 80 *North Carolina Law Review* 1069, 1082.

[14] See Dupuy, 'State Sponsors', above n 3 at 7–8.

[15] See UN Doc S/PV.2615 (4 October 1985) at 86–87.

[16] See, eg: A Conte, *Security in the 21st Century* (Aldershot, Ashgate, 2005) 66–69.

[17] M Williamson, 'Security in the 21st Century' (2006) 11 *Journal of Conflict & Security Law* 293, 296.

[18] Consider SR Ratner, '*Jus ad Bellum* and *Jus in Bello* after September 11' (2002) 96 *AJIL* 905, 914.

abritant sur leur territoire ou en les aidant de quelque manière que ce soit'.[19] Based on the new paradigm, therefore, host-States can be found responsible as would be the babysitter who fails to prevent the children under his or her guard from burning down the neighbour's house.[20] By way of example, the framework laid out in the *Civil Code of Québec* provides an instructive illustration of this mechanism by stipulating that

> [a] person having parental authority is liable to reparation for injury caused to another by the act or fault of the minor under his authority, unless he proves that he himself did not commit any fault with regard to the custody, supervision or education of the minor.[21]

Vehement propositions advocating the maintenance of classical attribution principles seem somewhat distant and the question of *direct* State involvement does not hold the relevance it once did. However, this new paradigm of indirect responsibility carries with it new and sometimes nebulous legal challenges such as the necessary elucidation of the difference between obligations of conduct and result, further defining the nature of the obligation of prevention, identifying the applicable legal standard to ineffective States in combating terrorism etc. Given the current legal climate and lack of consensus on these issues, it is difficult to clearly and uniformly establish a legal regime governing these politically volatile situations. Nevertheless, it is imperative to devise general rules and parameters applicable to all normative breaches and, more importantly, to failures of due diligence leading to transnational terrorism. Such objective was attempted above, through the possible implementation of a two-tiered strict liability-inspired system of indirect responsibility for terrorism. Yet, much still

[19] MG Kohen, 'Les controverses sur la question du "terrorisme d'état"' in K Bannelier et al (eds), *Le Droit international face au terrorisme: après le 11 septembre 2001* (Paris, Pedone, 2003) 83 at 89. But see: B Stern, 'La Responsabilité internationale des Etats: Perspectives récentes' in JC LLoréns (ed), *Cursos euromediterráneos bancaja de derecho internacional (Vol VII)* (Valencia, Tirant lo Blanch, 2003) 659 at 687 (arguing that this approach is predicated on too much of a tenuous institutional link to warrant the imputation of the 9/11 attacks to Afghanistan).

[20] This analogy is inspired by the general remarks in V-J Proulx, 'Babysitting Terrorists: Should States Be Strictly Liable for Failing to Prevent Transborder Attacks?' (2005) 23 *Berkeley Journal of International Law* 615.

[21] *Civil Code of Québec*, RSQ c 64, art 1459(1). See also: ibid, art 1460, which provides that

> [a] person who, without having parental authority, is entrusted, by delegation or otherwise, with the custody, supervision or education of a minor is liable, in the same manner as the person having parental authority, to reparation for injury caused by the act or fault of the minor . . . Where he is acting gratuitously or for reward, however, he is not liable unless it is proved that he has committed a fault.

Although not directly on point, the American experience also provides a microcosmic sampling of this practice. Following the implementation of a one-strike policy for termination of tenancy due to drug or criminal-related activities in the context of federally-assisted housing leases, American courts sometimes impose a strict liability standard vis-à-vis childcare providers. See, eg: *Syracuse Housing Authority v Boule* (1996) 172 Misc.2d 254 (Syracuse City Ct) (ruling that no valid cause for termination of tenancy can be confirmed where a tenant has no knowledge of, or did not consent to, and could not foresee the illegal act perpetrated by her babysitter), affirmed 177 Misc.2d 400 (Onondaga County Ct 1998), reviewed, 265 A.D.2d 832 (4th Dept 1999) (applying a strict liability standard).

needs to be done and written to advance both the intellectual discourse and potential deterrence models in a fruitful fashion. In the meantime, we can only hope that our extant scheme of State responsibility, paired with vigilant law enforcement, will be able to contain the most serious threats.

Concluding Observations

THE CURRENT POLITICO-LEGAL zeitgeist raises significant challenges to the task of devising effective legal responses to transnational terrorism. Whilst the political evolution of modern terrorism might have crystallised in the 70s and 80s, the threats now posed by private transnational violence have taken on a form of their own which, ironically, is polymorphic in scale and makeup but unequivocally dangerous for the international order. The terrorism of past decades relied heavily on State support, favouring a model of execution predominantly actuated through transborder aggressions or escalating guerrilla warfare within regional or bilateral armed conflicts. It is no surprise, therefore, that international law was somewhat resistant to harbour State accountability mechanisms for purely private conduct.

When traced back through time, the law governing State responsibility remained painstakingly dependent both on State-centrism and a bilateral typology of wrongful acts. As seen in Part I, a stringent and dominant model of agency gradually developed to regulate State responsibility for transnational violence, whilst also bearing the influence of other competing theories such as the 'separate delict' doctrine and the notion of 'collective guilt'.[1] Whilst some construed the application of attribution principles in such settings as regulating the behaviour of non-State actors, to cast such legal scheme as State responsibility *for* private conduct might be a misnomer. The whole purpose of agency – consecrated by *Nicaragua* and ILC Article 8 – was precisely to connect the conduct of seemingly non-State actors to the formal State apparatus via customary law-inspired normative operations involving attribution logic and inconsistently applied causal and fault-driven considerations. However, the overarching social objective underpinning such standards could certainly not be construed as targeting purely private unlawful conduct, as it eschewed more subtle cases of indirect State involvement translating into tacit acquiescence or passive toleration of terrorists on national territory. Short of egregious and active/direct support by a subsidising government, establishing State responsibility for failing to prevent terrorism appeared impossible and remained narrowly intertwined with the

[1] See generally: T Becker, *Terrorism and the State: Rethinking the Rules of State Responsibility* (Oxford, Hart Publishing, 2006). On doctrinal formulations of State responsibility more broadly, see M Koskenniemi, 'Doctrines of State Responsibility' in JR Crawford et al (eds), *The Law of International Responsibility* (Oxford, OUP, 2010) 45–51.

onerous legal demonstration of a relationship of principal and agent connecting non-State actors and their originating State. This standard engendered considerable evidentiary impediments, thereby arguably promoting an attitude of laissez-faire since States could become complacent given the unlikely prospect of being branded internationally responsible.

However, today we live in a post-agency world and the threats posed on a global scale unquestionably compound the international liability of sanctuary States. Whilst difficult to precisely pin down a prevalent terroristic model, that practice takes on various manifestations and bolsters the assertion that a wilfully blind or overly tolerant host-State not only fails to meet its due diligence obligations, but might also benefit politically from the use of its territory for terrorist operations (ie by doing indirectly what it cannot do directly). As seen on 9/11, the most noxious type of terrorism has far-reaching effects and can engender deleterious consequences across borders and cultures. Regardless of structural components characterising specific terrorist organisations, the overall threat is becoming increasingly transnational. We are now witnessing the proliferation of criminal 'networks', with many terrorists operating with a wide degree of autonomy and exploiting ungoverned spaces or host-States with weak counterterrorism structures (eg Western Sahara, Lebanon, Yemen) and, to a lesser extent, stronger States more suited for the clandestine cellular structure of some organisations (eg Britain, Canada).[2] Some terrorist networks have the capacity to wield State-like power and influence, thereby both challenging international legal rules and exerting force on a level once falling under the exclusive dominion of sovereign States. This reality is further exacerbated by new technologies (eg Internet) and by new weaponry (eg biological/nuclear weapons), which may considerably affect potential deterrence models rooted in international responsibility mechanisms.[3]

Contrary to terrorism of past decades and given enhanced transnational capacity, networks like Al Qaeda and Lashkar-e-Taiba can self-finance in a sometimes untraceable manner – through such means as the *hawala* underground banking system and charitable subterfuges[4] – and self-direct without much State input, if any at all. Organisations like Hezbollah conceal some of

[2] On the cellular structure of Al Qaeda, see R Gunaratna, *Inside Al Qaeda: Global Network of Terror* (London, Hurst, 2002).

[3] See, eg: B Kellman, 'State Responsibility for Preventing Bioterrorism' (2002) 36 *The International Lawyer* 29. On the relationship between State responsibility and nuclear counter proliferation in the Iranian context, see NJ Calamita, 'Sanctions, Countermeasures, and the Iranian Nuclear Issue' (2009) 42 *Vanderbilt Journal of Transnational Law* 1393. For a pre-9/11 account, see P Rubenstein, 'State Responsibility for Failure to Control the Export of Weapons of Mass Destruction' (1993) 23 *California Western International Law Journal* 319. On the nuclear issue and Iran, see generally: Y Ronen, *The Iran Nuclear Issue* (Oxford, Hart Publishing, 2010).

[4] An inherent characteristic of the *hawala* underground banking system lies in the fact that it makes some transactions virtually untraceable or imperceptible to allies in the global struggle against terrorism. See generally: W Wechsler, 'Strangling the Hydra: Targeting Al-Qaeda's Finances' in J Hogue and R Gideon (eds), *How Did this Happen? Terrorism and the New War* (New York, Public Affairs, 2001) 129–43.

their operations behind a veil of political legitimacy whilst seeking solace for their armed wing on a territory where there is no strict control over terrorists. As seen in Part I, terrorist organisations often rely on their host-States' passive toleration or acquiescence to operate; absent the prospect of covertly waging surrogate warfare through proxies, the extent of those States' support is of a logistical nature, at best. Yet, it is patently unjust to allow States to evade international responsibility by hiding behind perhaps outdated legal standards that obfuscate the connection between private terrorism and the means that such States could have harnessed to prevent avoidable excursions. The legal focus has considerably shifted from questions of State complicity or condonation of non-State terrorism to the imposition of primary obligations to act and intervene.[5] This evolution supports enhancing States' counterterrorism obligations and, once those obligations are violated, endorsing a responsibility-expansive application of the ensuing legal consequences. Indeed, contemporary Security Council and State practice appear to corroborate this legal inclination.

The analytical crux, which was formerly so dependent on notions of control by the State over, and interdependence with, the principal misfeasors for the purposes of triggering responsibility has morphed into the acknowledgement that the *failure to control* irregular units may also engage international liability. Part I identified – both descriptively and prescriptively – a paradigm shift towards more indirect modes of State accountability, a development also occurring in areas related to individual international responsibility mechanisms and international criminal regimes.[6] These changes are also mirrored in municipal legal orders as States increasingly criminalise behaviour that, formerly, only amounted to evidentiary elements, thereby increasing their due diligence capital in complying with counterterrorism obligations. These domestic legal commitments also signal that the prospect of incurring international responsibility may incentivise governments to divert public funds, law enforcement and policy infrastructures with a view to enhancing compliance with international law. Consequently, this book argued that whilst immensely instructive, the *Nicaragua* legacy also presents considerable shortcomings, one key example being that its reasoning can exacerbate the confusion engendered by merging State responsibility and use of force repertoire. The purpose was not to completely disavow that jurisprudential current but simply to recognise that an equally – if not more – relevant strand of cases could animate the intellectual discourse and foment new deterrence models based on State responsibility. Indeed, it was argued that *Corfu Channel* convincingly grounds a primary obligation for States to prevent terrorism emanating from their territory.

With the shift towards indirect responsibility in mind, the inquiry raised and analysed two considerable challenges in Part II: the establishment of State

[5] For a recent account on 'complicity' under the law of State responsibility, see HP Aust, *Complicity and the Law of State Responsibility* (Cambridge, CUP, 2011).

[6] See generally: M Lehto, *Indirect Responsibility for Terrorist Acts: Redefinition of the Concept of Terrorism beyond Violent Acts* (Leiden, Nijhoff, 2010).

responsibility and the ensuing enforcement gap, along with a policy-driven reform of secondary rules of responsibility. The *ILC Articles on State Responsibility* ultimately relegated to inter-State devices the tasks of ascertaining international law violations and applying corresponding legal consequences to those breaches. This codification choice necessarily entails a process of self-judging and autoqualification by aggrieved States, along with the idiosyncratic application of secondary norms within the loosely coordinated context of disparate – and often asymmetric – diplomatic relations. This does not mean that the intercession of international organisations could not play some role or that those bodies did not contribute to the further development of State responsibility. Indeed, an in-depth study exploring alternate routes to the vision enshrined in the ILC's text and exploring the possible institutionalisation of the implementation of State responsibility would be welcome to address the enforcement gap and the structural inequities that may ensue from unilateral implementation.

Any study addressing State responsibility must also come to grips with the dominant model of implementation espoused by the ILC, namely through inter-State mechanisms. Bearing in mind the objectives of better integrating non-State actors under international law and enhancing compliance with counterterrorism obligations, a policy-oriented reform of secondary norms of responsibility was set out in Part II, favouring a critical appraisal of attribution principles under the ILC's *Articles*. In light of the new legal focus on States' failures to prevent terrorism and control the activities of non-State actors, particular resistance was also exhibited regarding the notion of 'control' as enshrined in the *Articles*. Contemporary discussion regarding attribution of questionably private acts to States has been framed predominantly within the furrow of ILC Article 8, including in the *Genocide Case*. In response, this study advanced a series of arguments ranging from policy considerations to hermeneutics, to rationalism, to structural realism, to legal pragmatism, to legal pluralism, in order to identify more viable bases for attribution under State responsibility and fully implement Security Council counterterrorism resolutions.[7] One potential legal avenue promoted within this framework hinges on international responsibility for failing to prevent terrorism by sole reference to ILC Article 12, which is persuasively mirrored in the reasoning underpinning both *Corfu Channel* and *Tehran Hostages*.

More importantly, an international responsibility model for failing to prevent terrorism drawing heavily on domestic law analogies, rationalist legal theory and recent policy thrusts favouring more stringent counterterrorism State obligations was expressly put forth in Part II. It argued for the establishment of a prima facie finding of indirect State responsibility whenever States fail to

[7] Presumably, other commentators also call for a context-sensitive construction of ILC Art 8, which could increase government accountability for the noxious actions of non-State actors. See, eg: A Randelzhofer, 'Article 51' in B Simma et al (eds), *The Charter of the United Nations: A Commentary*, 2nd edn (Oxford, OUP, 2002) 788 at 801–02 fn 32.

prevent transnational terrorism emanating from their territory. Replacing the mechanism of attribution, this normative operation – which could plausibly be analogised to a version of automatic imputation – then shifts the onus of refuting the presumption of indirect responsibility squarely upon host-States. Whilst considerably informed by domestic manifestations of tort law, other municipal legal analogies and international environmental law, this model is strongly influenced by strict liability undertones without embodying the full range of that legal standard as it has become to be understood, at least in domestic settings.[8] The crux of its policy reform is characterised by a 'rebuttable presumption of responsibility followed by a shift in the burden of proof'[9] which, inter alia, purports to allay some concerns associated with fact-finding performed by international institutions along with other evidentiary hurdles plaguing the law of State responsibility.

The present study attempted to tease out the theoretical and practical implications of further delineating secondary rules of State responsibility, while also identifying potential challenges for future scholarly investigations of the topic. Whatever model of State responsibility is ultimately endorsed by the international community, sensible consideration should be accorded to whether a responsibility-expansive regime can be equally applied to both weaker and powerful States. A shared understanding that compliance with counterterrorism obligations is politically desirable, coupled with the prospect of incurring international responsibility for failures in prevention, might induce governments to engage in a delicate assessment of whether they should divert their resources and policy infrastructures to combat transnational terrorism. However, in contrast with other hazardous fields of activity such as nuclear energy and outer space exploration, terrorism fails to generate immediately tangible benefits for host-States. Therefore, policy enticements favouring enhanced counterterrorism initiatives will have to be furnished to those States that frequently harbour extremist elements. Indeed, the risk assessment and risk management dimensions of counterterrorism bring the tension between allocating (sometimes scarce) resources and political will into sharp relief.

Ultimately, we are working from the premise that the progressive evolution of international law, paired with the prospect of incurring liability for failing to bring conduct within the parameters of such framework, can induce States to modify their behaviour and inform their internal policy choices. In all modesty, this task can be something of an uphill political climb when attempting to cast terrorism within the same category as ultra-hazardous fields of activity, such as

[8] For an analysis of this position as expressed in a previous account, see RL Johnstone, 'Unlikely Bedfellows: Feminist Theory and the War on Terror' (2009) 9 *Chicago-Kent Journal of International and Comparative Law* 1, 28 (2009) (highlighting that this model 'prescriptively argues that the rules of attribution should be circumvented altogether in favor of a form of "strict liability" for terrorism', but adding that the reform 'mitigates this slightly by introducing a possible defense for states whose territory is used by terrorists to prepare attacks, allowing them to exclude their liability should they successfully demonstrate that they have exercised due diligence to prevent the attacks').

[9] ibid.

nuclear programmes or outer space exploration. For instance, the development of nuclear energy falls within narrow State supervision given that considerable benefits may be derived from controlling such sector, thereby prompting States to readily accept the application of more exacting liability standards in the event of behavioural slippages arising in the context of those operations. Granted, such symmetry is not directly mirrored in the present context as exploiting terrorism simply does not yield the same kind of strategic and tangible gains that other activities imply. Conversely, it was argued on numerous grounds that States do have a shared interest in better controlling terrorism taking root on their territory and may derive more intangible gains when engaging in enhanced counterterrorism operations (ie by both accruing reputational goodwill internationally and increasing their due diligence capital for the purposes of attenuating international responsibility). However, additional policy and legal 'sales pitches' must be envisaged to convince States like Iran, North Korea or Pakistan, for example, that bolstering their respective counterterrorism infrastructures may prove comparably advantageous – perhaps even from the perspective of strategic international posturing – when contemplated alongside developing enriched uranium or other nuclear programmes. This study has attempted to partly fill this enforcement void through an analysis of the concepts of reciprocity (both bilateral and systematised), reputational costs, rationalist choice theory and a pronounced emphasis on both multilateralism and transnational cooperation on counterterrorism.

Equally challenging is the imposition of secondary obligations flowing from internationally wrongful acts once the mechanics establishing State responsibility have been engaged. Aside from the speculative exercise of putting a dollar figure on damage caused by transnational terrorism, failures to prevent such harm also raise the controversial possibility of invoking forcible responses. In that regard, scholarly and policy discussions are often articulated from two conceptual vantage points: i) by reference to ILC Article 8; and ii) by equating the emergence of the 'harbouring and supporting' of terrorists by sanctuary States with a potential new rule. However, both frames of reference have begun to merge into a single, consolidated approach with the proviso that Article 8 would have to be tempered whilst the 'harbouring' or 'toleration' of terrorists might now constitute stand-alone attribution criteria within State responsibility repertoire. Such evolution would require wide acceptance of a 'presumption of conformity between attribution in the law of self-defence and in the law of State responsibility', a threshold easily traversed according to some.[10]

This shift in the law would concomitantly entail that attribution under State responsibility has been informed and transformed by parallel developments in the law governing recourse to force, a self-contained regime. This premise

[10] A Nolkaemper, 'Attribution of Forcible Acts to States: Connections between the Law on the Use of Force and the Law of State Responsibility' in N Blokker and N Schrijver (eds), *The Security Council and the Use of Force: Theory and Reality – A Need for Change?* (Leiden, Nijhoff, 2005) 133 at 158.

prompts any interlocutor concerned with the progressive development of international law to ponder whether such modulated standard would remain confined to the application of State responsibility *for the unlawful use of force* – be it through equating State failures to prevent terrorism with Article 2(4) violations or through more direct State participation in wrongful acts – or whether it would wield transformative influence over the full gamut of secondary norms. Decidedly, little grounding can be invoked to substantiate this latter position. It is doubtful that a State that simply 'harbours' or 'tolerates' individuals carrying out transnational credit fraud from its territory or engendering transboundary pollution actually opens itself up to a forcible response for the mere reason that this novel attribution threshold has been observed. Conversely, should self-defence repertoire wield such commanding and pervasive influence over international accountability mechanisms – a proposition itself ripe for profound disagreements – such impact would arguably remain limited to the former scenario above. In such settings, the invocation of self-defence vis-à-vis State failures to prevent terrorism (ie by harbouring or tolerating terrorists) would constitute a *lex specialis* within the law of State responsibility.[11] Future explorations of the topic will also have to bear in mind that the paradigm shift towards more indirect modes of accountability is actually mirrored in international jurisprudence – perhaps best embodied by *Corfu Channel* – and that any corresponding relaxation of attribution principles should invariably be balanced out by a policy-driven, context-sensitive approach such as the one advocated in Part II.

This is undoubtedly the recurrent mantra that should be extracted from the above exercise: only a fair and balanced approach can guide a fruitful legal analysis and concurrently take into account the competing stakes involved in incentivising governments towards better patterns of compliance with counterterrorism duties. Indeed, counterterrorism is not a zero-sum game; a delicate balance between various competing interests must be struck whilst attempting to better integrate various stakeholders under relevant frameworks, amongst which non-State actors feature prominently from the standpoint of both international justice and legal pluralism.

Scholarly and rhetorical reactions to 9/11 provide an apt concluding case in point. In the last decade, several interlocutors have uncritically proclaimed that *9/11 changed everything*. Whilst this study and other similar works have drawn – rather liberally – from that precedent, it is also vital to balance out that

[11] ILC Art 55 provides that these 'articles do not apply where and to the extent that the conditions for the existence of an internationally wrongful act or the content or implementation of the international responsibility of a State are governed by special rules of international law'. See 'State Responsibility: Titles and text of the draft articles on Responsibility of States for internationally wrongful acts adopted by the Drafting Committee on second reading', UN Doc A/CN.4/L.602/Rev.1 (2001). The final draft was adopted by the ILC in 2001, with the UN General Assembly taking note of the *Articles* and commending them to States. See 'Report of the International Law Commission on the Work of Its Fifty-Third Session', UN GAOR, 56th Sess, Supp No 10, UN Doc A/56/10 (2001) 41.

viewpoint by entertaining the notion that the response to 9/11 did not necessarily consecrate a novel and binding rule. After all, this response constituted an exceptional response to exceptional circumstances. Whether a new *lex specialis* has been entrenched within State responsibility remains up for debate and could require supplementary State and institutional practice. More importantly, a lucid construction of the law governing State responsibility signifies that we cannot deal in absolutes –we must inexorably take the political with the legal and attempt to make sense of it all with a view to enhancing both prevention and cooperation. Ironically, these concluding observations align somewhat with a rationalist critique of what is perceived as legally idealistic – or politically myopic – accounts exploring this subject-matter. It cautions that such endeavours should avoid promoting a deterrence model that

> largely ignores the most likely scenario: that nations that approved of or acquiesced in the U.S. invasion of Afghanistan did so for geopolitical reasons and did not believe that they thereby committed themselves to a general legal norm that permits any nation attacked by foreign terrorists – India, Israel, Russia, Iraq – to invade a country that harbored them.[12]

Granted, political pragmatism is called for at every step of the analysis but the impact of such developments on international law should not be disregarded altogether. Whilst it is impossible to precisely assess the incidence of a legal norm in shaping State behaviour or in generating predictable conduct, neither supporters nor detractors 'recognize that *multiple factors almost always affect the decisions of policymakers*. In very few situations, probably, is international law wholly determinative of what a state does; but in very few situations, probably, is international law wholly irrelevant'.[13] Hence, again the picture that emerges is one of balance: context is vital and cannot be dissociated from both legal and politico-social realities. Thus, more equitable and effective narratives on State responsibility for failures to prevent terrorism can only result from an inclusive process – supplemented by ongoing policy dialogue at domestic, international and transnational levels – that gives due regard to some practicable middle ground between legal and political dimensions of international relations. And, at the end of the day, is this not what international law should truly be about?

[12] EA Posner, 'Terrorism and the State: Rethinking the Rules of State Responsibility' (2006) 121 *Political Science Quarterly* 505, 506 (reviewing Tal Becker's book on the subject of State responsibility and terrorism). See also: RS Litwak, 'Containment 2.0', *World Politics Review*, 22 July 2009 (essentially arguing that 9/11 did not drastically change the nature of international relations).

[13] MJ Glennon, 'Does International Law Matter?' (2004) 98 *ASIL Proceedings* 315, 315. On the imprecision of predicting the impact of international legal norms on the outcome of situations, see ibid, at 316. But for a contrary view, see TM Franck, 'The Power of Legitimacy and the Legitimacy of Power: International Law in an Age of Power Disequilibrium' (2006) 100 *AJIL* 88 (2006).

Appendix I

CONDUCT OF THE HOST-STATE

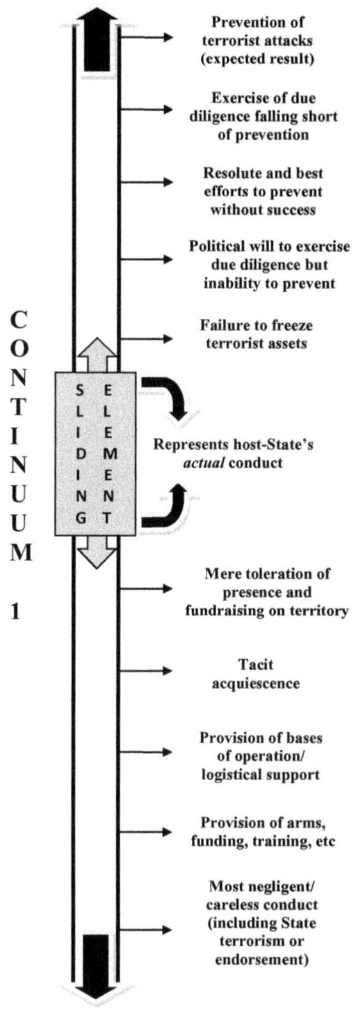

Appendix II

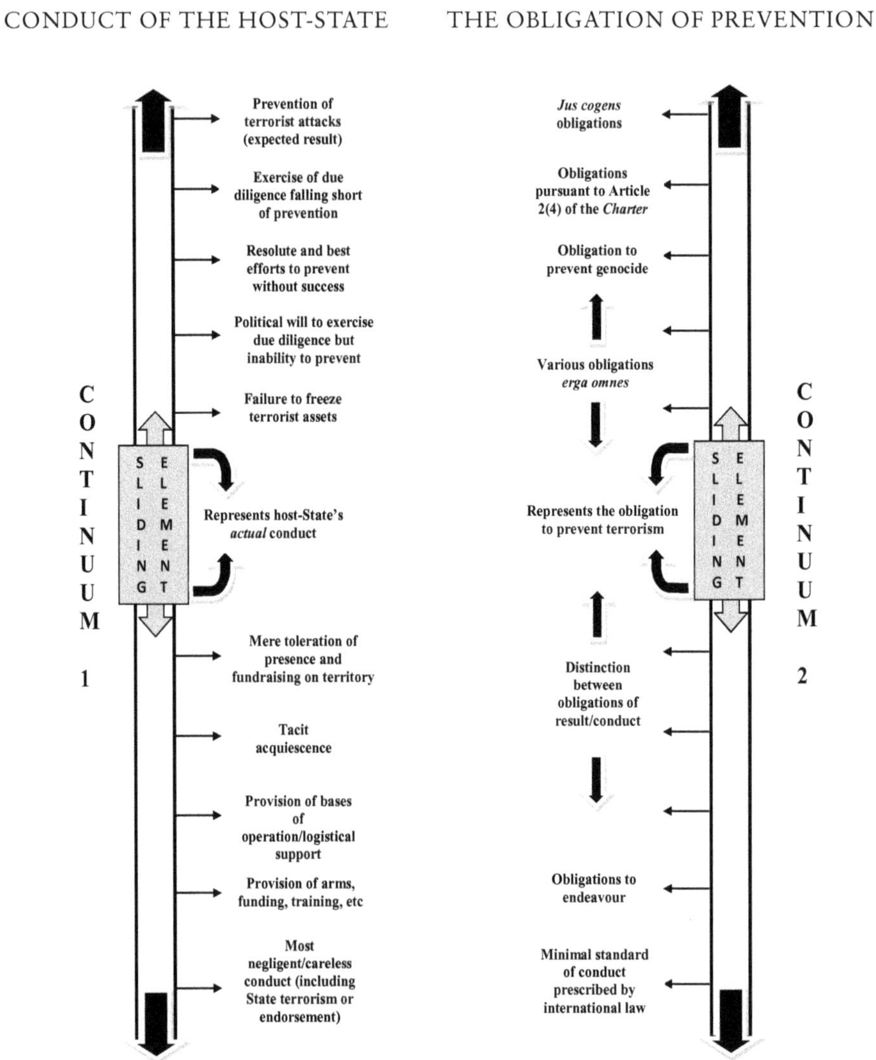
CONDUCT OF THE HOST-STATE
THE OBLIGATION OF PREVENTION
Prevention of terrorist attacks (expected result)
Exercise of due diligence falling short of prevention
Resolute and best efforts to prevent without success
Political will to exercise due diligence but inability to prevent
Failure to freeze terrorist assets
SLIDING ELEMENT
Represents host-State's *actual* conduct
Mere toleration of presence and fundraising on territory
Tacit acquiescence
Provision of bases of operation/logistical support
Provision of arms, funding, training, etc
Most negligent/careless conduct (including State terrorism or endorsement)
CONTINUUM 1
Jus cogens obligations
Obligations pursuant to Article 2(4) of the *Charter*
Obligation to prevent genocide
Various obligations *erga omnes*
SLIDING ELEMENT
Represents the obligation to prevent terrorism
Distinction between obligations of result/conduct
Obligations to endeavour
Minimal standard of conduct prescribed by international law
CONTINUUM 2

Appendix III

CONDUCT OF THE HOST-STATE THE OBLIGATION OF PREVENTION

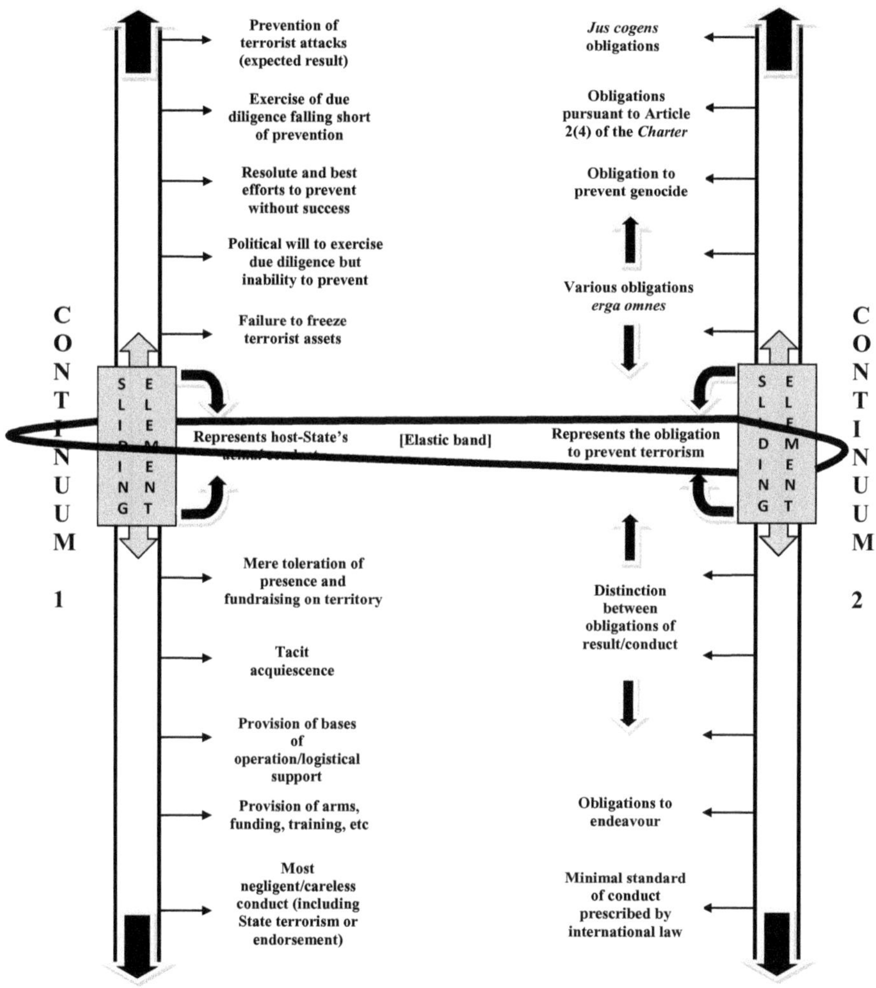

Appendix IV

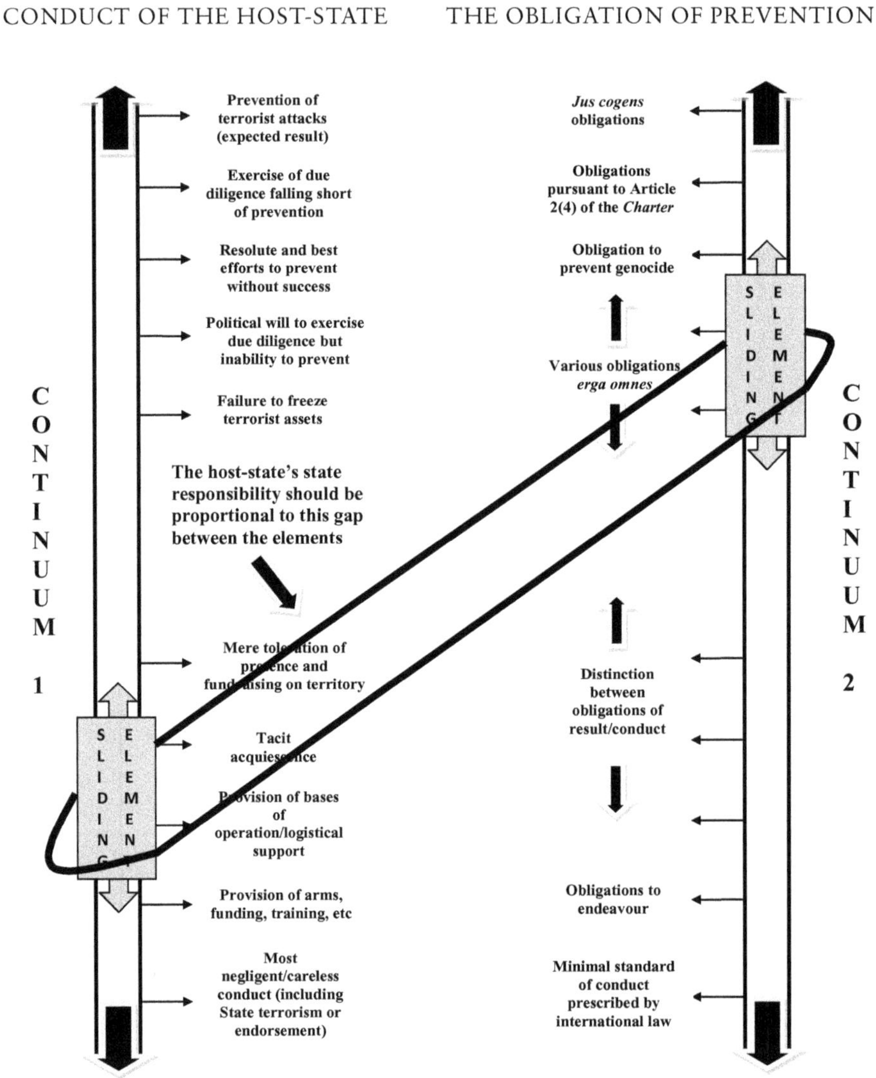

CONDUCT OF THE HOST-STATE
THE OBLIGATION OF PREVENTION
Prevention of terrorist attacks (expected result)
Exercise of due diligence falling short of prevention
Resolute and best efforts to prevent without success
Political will to exercise due diligence but inability to prevent
Failure to freeze terrorist assets
The host-state's state responsibility should be proportional to this gap between the elements
Mere toleration of presence and fund-raising on territory
Tacit acquiescence
Provision of bases of operation/logistical support
Provision of arms, funding, training, etc
Most negligent/careless conduct (including State terrorism or endorsement)
CONTINUUM 1
SLIDING ELEMENT
Jus cogens obligations
Obligations pursuant to Article 2(4) of the Charter
Obligation to prevent genocide
Various obligations erga omnes
Distinction between obligations of result/conduct
Obligations to endeavour
Minimal standard of conduct prescribed by international law
CONTINUUM 2
SLIDING ELEMENT

Appendix V

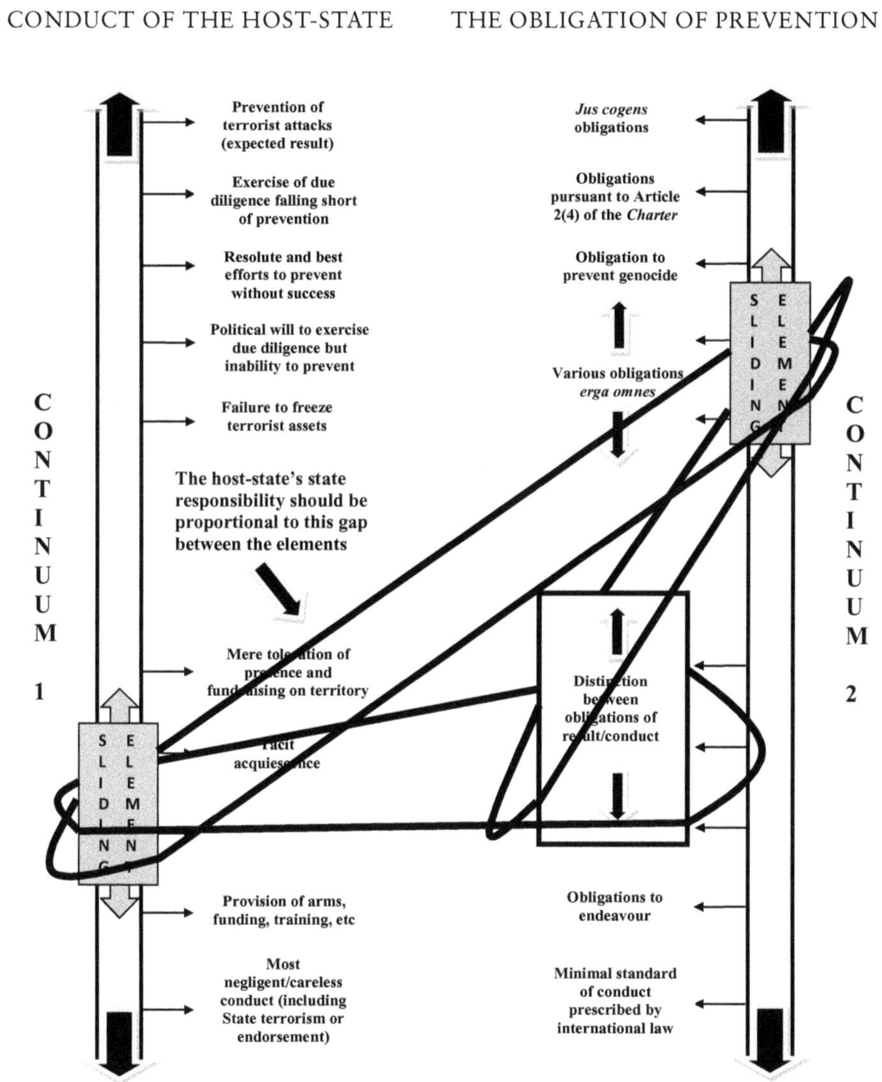
CONDUCT OF THE HOST-STATE
THE OBLIGATION OF PREVENTION
Prevention of terrorist attacks (expected result)
Exercise of due diligence falling short of prevention
Resolute and best efforts to prevent without success
Political will to exercise due diligence but inability to prevent
Failure to freeze terrorist assets
The host-state's state responsibility should be proportional to this gap between the elements
Provision of arms, funding, training, etc
Most negligent/careless conduct (including State terrorism or endorsement)
CONTINUUM 1
SLIDING ELEMENT
Jus cogens obligations
Obligations pursuant to Article 2(4) of the *Charter*
Obligation to prevent genocide
Various obligations *erga omnes*
Obligations to endeavour
Minimal standard of conduct prescribed by international law
CONTINUUM 2
SLIDING ELEMENT

Index

www.ingramcontent.com/pod-product-compliance
Ingram Content Group UK Ltd.
Pitfield, Milton Keynes, MK11 3LW, UK
UKHW020233290926
15470UKWH00002B/523

9 781849 462853